W9-BVW-513

WALLACE STEVENS

WALLACE STEVENS

The Early Years
1879–1923

JOAN
RICHARDSON

BEECH TREE BOOKS
WILLIAM MORROW
New York

Copyright © 1986 by Joan Richardson

Grateful acknowledgment is made to Alfred A. Knopf, Inc., for permission to reprint previously published material from: *The Collected Poems of Wallace Stevens*, copyright 1954 by Wallace Stevens; *Opus Posthumous: Poems, Plays, Prose* by Wallace Stevens, edited by Samuel French Morse, copyright © 1954 by Elsie Stevens and Wallace Stevens; *The Necessary Angel* by Wallace Stevens, copyright 1951 by Wallace Stevens; *Letters of Wallace Stevens*, selected and edited by Holly Stevens, copyright © 1966 by Holly Stevens; *Souvenirs and Prophecies: The Young Wallace Stevens* by Holly Stevens, copyright © 1966, 1976 by Holly Stevens.

Grateful acknowledgment is also made to The Huntington Library, San Marino, California, for permission to reproduce previously unpublished material and photographs (previously published and unpublished) from The Wallace Stevens Collection, and to the University of Chicago Library for permission to quote from a previously unpublished letter from The Harriet Monroe Poetry Collection.

Part of Chapter 6 appeared in *Raritan: A Quarterly Review*, Volume IV, Number 3, Winter 1985.

All rights reserved. No part of this book may be reproduced or utilized in any form or by any means, electronic or mechanical, including photocopying, recording or by any information storage and retrieval system, without permission in writing from the Publisher. Inquiries should be addressed to Permissions Department, Beech Tree Books, William Morrow and Company, Inc., 105 Madison Ave., New York, N.Y. 10016.

Library of Congress Cataloging-in-Publication Data

Richardson, Joan, 1946–
  Wallace Stevens: the early years, 1879–1923.

  (Beech tree books)
  Includes bibliographical references and index.
  1. Stevens, Wallace, 1879–1955—Biography. 2. Poets,
American—20th century—Biography. I. Title.
PS3537.T4753Z758   1986   811'.52   [B]   86-5393
ISBN 0-688-05401-3

Printed in the United States of America

First Edition

1 2 3 4 5 6 7 8 9 10

BOOK DESIGN BY ELLEN LO GIUDICE

BĪB

The word "book" is said to derive from *boka*, or beech.
The beech tree has been the patron tree of writers since ancient times and
represents the flowering of literature and knowledge.

To the memory of my parents
and of my grandmother,
who first taught me
about memory

A Note on Texts, Abbreviations, and Other
Technical Details

This note precedes the Introduction since there, as well as in my text, I have quoted from primary Stevens sources. These are: *The Collected Poems of Wallace Stevens* (New York: Alfred A. Knopf, 1955), abbreviated parenthetically in the text as *CP; Opus Posthumous: Poems, Plays, Prose by Wallace Stevens*, ed. Samuel French Morse (New York: Alfred A. Knopf, 1957), abbreviated *OP; The Necessary Angel: Essays on Reality and The Imagination* (New York: Vintage, 1951), abbreviated *NA; The Letters of Wallace Stevens*, ed. Holly Stevens (New York: Alfred A. Knopf, 1966), abbreviated *L; Souvenirs and Prophecies: The Young Wallace Stevens*, ed. Holly Stevens (New York: Alfred A. Knopf, 1977), abbreviated *SP; The Palm at the End of the Mind: Selected Poems and a Play*, ed. Holly Stevens (New York: Vintage, 1972), abbreviated *Palm;* and unpublished manuscripts and letters from the Wallace Stevens Collection at the Huntington Library, abbreviated WAS plus the catalog number and date, the latter sometimes indicated in the text. In one instance I have noted Robert Buttel's *Wallace Stevens: The Making of Harmonium* (Princeton, N.J.: Princeton University Press, 1967) as a primary source since that is the only published locus of an early version of a poem that I quote. In addition, I have quoted from or referred to material from Wallace Stevens's library; the greater part of what remains is at the Huntington Library and a small part at the University of Massachusetts/Amherst Library in its Special Collections and Rare Books division. These indications as to location are made parenthetically within the text but without abbreviation. I have also made use of, though not in all cases directly referred to, material that belongs to the Department of Special Collections, University of Chicago Library; the Collection of American Literature, the Beinecke Rare Book and Manuscript Library, Yale University; the Baker Library at Dartmouth College; and from publications of the Hartford Insurance Group. Volumes mentioned by Stevens but not part of his library I have read at the New York Public Library when I have not been able to acquire copies of my own.

In quoting from primary sources, I have generally given the volume and page numbers for lines or sections from poems whenever they appear, even when they appear more than once. Contrarily, for portions of essays I have indicated the volume and page references only the first time I have quoted or

7

referred to them. Readers are advised that page numbers are the same for both the hardcover and paperback editions of *The Collected Poems* and *The Necessary Angel*, but in the case of *Opus Posthumous* different after page 235 because of the deletion of "On Poetic Truth," mistakenly included in earlier hardcover editions as being by Stevens (actually, Stevens copied this essay into one of his notebooks; it was written by H. D. Lewis, a British aesthetician).

In terms of material taken from *Letters* and *Souvenirs and Prophecies* two curiosities must be noted to avoid any possible confusion for the readers. First, often early letters and journal entries appear in both volumes. When the passage as I have quoted it does appear in both volumes, I have given both volumes and appropriate page numbers for each. When, on the other hand, a passage as I have quoted it appears in its more complete version in one or the other of the volumes, I have indicated only that one as the source. Similarly, when a passage I have used appears partially in *Letters* or *Souvenirs and Prophecies* and I have added material from unpublished manuscripts, I have indicated *Letters* or *Souvenirs and Prophecies* and the Huntington Library's WAS catalog number and date (whenever necessary) within the parentheses or brackets following the citation. Secondly, in *Letters* Stevens's habit of using plus signs in the place of ampersands to indicate "and" has been preserved, while in *Souvenirs and Prophecies* the plus signs were printed as ampersands. If the passage I have quoted appears in both *Letters* and *Souvenirs and Prophecies*, I have retained the plus sign as well, while in the cases where the passage appears only in *Souvenirs and Prophecies* I too have used the ampersand. Finally, regarding all quotations, both from Stevens and others, what appear to be irregularities of punctuation—such as the poet's habit of using two instead of three dots for ellipses—and capitalization in light of today's conventions have been preserved without *sic* indications; *sic* has been used, however, after spelling irregularities to protect the printer and final proofreader from unnecessary accusations of carelessness.

I have not included a bibliography since it alone would constitute a small volume. All works cited or referred to have been documented fully either in the text or in the notes.

Acknowledgments

Among the host of scholars and critics who have over the years enriched our understanding of Stevens, those without whom this study would not have been possible, but whom it is impossible for reasons of space to list fully here, I would like to acknowledge by name some of those who were prominent in my consciousness as I contemplated the lines of Stevens's thought and feeling around which I composed this biography. I shall then go on to thank those individuals and institutions whose direct help made this work a reality.

First and foremost I want to express my appreciation to Holly Stevens for her long devotion to the monumental task of making it concretely possible for me and others to know anything more about her father than what lies folded into the lines of his poems. Her editions of his letters and early journals, together with her insightful comments, illuminate his life and work with the light of firsthand perception. In addition, her transfer of unpublished and otherwise unavailable personal material to the Huntington Library in San Marino, California, has made it possible for me and others attempting to understand her father's "studious ghost" to do so without the necessity of intruding on her privacy, though she has always been most gracious in the instances when this could not be avoided.

Secondly, I would like to thank Samuel French Morse for his work in putting together the volume of *Opus Posthumous* with its informative introduction, and also for his pioneering biographical study, *Wallace Stevens: Poetry as Life* (1970), one of the first steps toward a portrait of the poet's life. I would like next to acknowledge in a listing that does not begin to do justice to the depth and breadth they added to my vision of Stevens the many poets, editors, scholars, and critics whom I mentioned in opening. This I shall do alphabetically since they do not exist in order of importance in my mind; some of those not included here will be thanked more specifically a bit farther on: James Baird, Michel Benamou, Charles Berger, Marius Bewley, R. P. Blackmur, Richard Allen Blessing, Harold Bloom, Louise Bogan, Marie Borroff, Cleanth Brooks, Ashley Brown, Merle E. Brown, Gerald Bruns, Kenneth Burke, Robert Buttel, Eleanor Cook, J. V. Cunningham, Guy Davenport, Donald Davie, R. H. Deutsch, Frank Doggett, Richard Eberhart, J. M. Edelstein, Doris Eder, Richard Ellmann, William Empson, John Enck, Sidney

9

Feshbach, Northrop Frye, Daniel Fuchs, Robert Haller, Bernard Heringman, Randall Jarrell, Frank Kermode, Edward Kessler, Alfred Kreymborg, David LaGuardia, George S. Lensing, Frank Lentricchia, A. Walton Litz, Louis Martz, Francis O. Matthiessen, Diane Middlebrook, J. Hillis Miller, Harriet Monroe, Marianne Moore, Adalaide Kirby Morris, Eugene Paul Nassar, Howard Nemerov, William Van O'Connor, Robert Pack, Roy Harvey Pearce, Sister M. Bernetta Quinn, John Crowe Ransom, Joseph Riddel, Delmore Schwartz, John Serio, Hi Simons, Newton Phelps Stallknecht, Herbert Stern, Ronald Sukenick, William York Tindall, Louis Untermeyer, Carl Van Vechten, Helen Vendler, Jean Wahl, Thomas F. Walsh, Henry W. Wells, William Carlos Williams, Edmund Wilson, Yvor Winters, Leonora Woodman, Morton Dauwen Zabel.

Each of these individuals in different ways helped me read Stevens more deeply, sometimes because they elucidated a way of seeing his work that I had not thought of or because they clarified a perception that was hazy in my mind, and sometimes, as in the case of Yvor Winters, because an opposing view was presented that forced me to articulate more carefully what I saw. In some cases their contributions represent major long-term efforts, while in others—the poets Marianne Moore, Randall Jarrell, Delmore Schwartz, and William Carlos Williams, for example—just a few pages of their special imaginative insights were sufficient to prompt serious reflection on my part. Then others, like J. M. Edelstein, William Ingoldsby, and Thomas Walsh, provided scholarly machinery that saved me and others years of work. Editors like Ashley Brown and Robert Haller, R. H. Deutsch and, more recently, John Serio—the last two heading the *Wallace Stevens Journal*—selected and published important articles. Still others, like Robert Buttel, Harold Bloom, A. Walton Litz, and Helen Vendler, offered in their research and in their readings of Stevens accesses to the poet that have become the foundation for later readings. To all of them and to the others whom I have not named but appreciate as well, I am heavily indebted.

I would like next to thank a few whom I have come to know since undertaking the project for a biography and with whom, in addition to learning from their scholarly efforts, I have been able to exchange ideas over lunches, dinners, and cups of coffee and tea. The first two among these are Peter Brazeau and Milton Bates, both of whom have also recently published books that are the results of their biographical researches. As in the cases of J. M. Edelstein, Wiiliam Ingoldsby, and Thomas Walsh, Milton Bates, long before the appearance of his *Wallace Stevens: A Mythology of Self* (1985), contributed an enormous part to the scholarly apparatus in the form of checklists of the Huntington Library's holdings in the Stevens material; my work would have been enormously more difficult and drawn out were it not for his diligent efforts. Similarly, Peter Brazeau, before the publication of his oral biography, *Parts of a World: Wallace Stevens Remembered* (1984), contributed a checklist of the Stevens holdings at the University of Massachusetts Library at Amherst. More, both Peter Brazeau in Hartford and Milton Bates at the Huntington spent hours driving to Stevens's sites or walking in gardens and talking with me about our subject. Whatever I had not learned from them through their articles and, later, their books, I did in these conversations.

Also at the Huntington I was fortunate to come to know and exchange ideas with Glen MacLeod, with whom I giggled at many lunches over some of the details of Stevens's connection to the Arensberg circle. Marjorie Perloff, too, I met over one of the tables in the Huntington's Rare Book Room. We later came to discuss many aspects of Stevens's work and his relationship to other literary figures during lunches at the Huntington and in her home, where I was most graciously invited. Lisa Steinman I met in that same Rare Book Room as well, as we patiently waited for each other to get through with volumes from Stevens's library that we had both called. Through her I came to ponder the poet's curious apparent absence of interest in the technological progress of his time. She is at present completing a study on the major twentieth-century American poets' relationships to science and technology. And one more Stevens scholar whom I did not meet at the Huntington but here in New York and with whom I share a very special interest in Stevens is Barbara Fisher. Through her work on the erotic element in his poetry, understood with keen philosophical acumen, and on echoing in Stevens from earlier poets, I have learned a great deal.

Finally, I want to thank those who have most directly made this work a reality. Very much first among these is John Hollander who, since my years as a graduate student and as director of my dissertation on Stevens until the last few months when he read through the accumulating chapters of this biography, has guided me through all the stages of coming to understand Stevens. His perspicacious eye and bristling ear have helped me enlarge, correct, pare, and generally sharpen my perceptions and find a measured tone in which to voice them. His encouragement gave me, more than anything else did, the confidence and fortitude necessary to tackle what I have. To him I express my deepest gratitude.

I would also like to express my appreciation and thanks to Charles Molesworth, who read and commented on a considerable portion of this first volume. His masterful critical sense made me attentive to the inextricable link between my own form and its content down to even the smallest details of tense choices and patterning of imagery. I would, in addition, like to thank Denis Donoghue, Lillian Feder, Alfred Kazin, and Bradford Morrow for reading various sections and offering their very different and special perspectives, from all of which I profited greatly, as I did from their encouragement as well. I want, too, to extend my appreciation to the History of Psychiatry Section at the Payne-Whitney Clinic of the New York Hospital and Cornell Medical Center—especially to Dr. Lawrence Friedman and Dr. Eric Carlson, who invited me first to join their bimonthly seminars and then to give a paper on my work in progress. The questions and comments that followed my presentation were most useful in honing my approach and in giving me additional intellectual support.

I owe debts of gratitude of different kinds to Allen Mandelbaum and Irving Howe, on the one hand, and to Richard Poirier and R. H. Deutsch on the other. Professors Mandelbaum and Howe, long ago as readers of my dissertation, provided either in written responses or in the form of observations during my doctoral defense, important insights that modified my views of Stevens. Richard Poirier and R. H. Deutsch, as editors of journals where either preliminary or actual sections of the biography appeared, provided the absolutely indispensable judgment concerning readers' responses and aspects of my style that I hope I have learned to integrate.

I want to extend warm thanks to a few of my contemporaries who read portions along the way as well, or helped me with technical details, and to one close to me who in his own way also made this work possible. In the first category, I am indebted to Anne Dobbs, Thomas Fink, Neil Rossman, and Charles Whitney. In the second, long-standing appreciation goes to Roberto Picciotto, with whom I learned to consider, as I still do, the fourteenth way of looking at a blackbird.

Finally, I am indebted to John Brockman, my epistemologist-agent with whom fifteen years ago I developed a friendship built around conversations about Wallace Stevens. It was because of his prodding that I took the chance of writing a proposal for the book about Stevens that I had wanted for so long to do. I want also to thank him and Katinka Matson for reading through the complete typescript and expressing their perceptions with such enthusiasm. And for Jim Landis, my editor, I have not only heartfelt appreciation for his delicate and trusting sense in dealing with me as a writer, and for his vigorous expressions of support, but full admiration for his acuity in seizing on precisely the points in my text where I had misgivings and in giving me the suggestions necessary to take care of them.

In closing I would like to express my gratitude to the individuals at libraries and foundations who helped make this biography possible. First, to James Thorpe, Martin Ridge, Virginia Renner, Dan Woodward, Tom Lange, Sarah Hodson, Mary Alice Schucart, and Mary Ellen Wright at the Huntington Library I offer many thanks. I would also like to thank the Huntington for the Research Award that allowed me to begin work on the unpublished Stevens material and the Stevens library. Thanks, too, to John D. Kendall and Royann Hanson of the Special Collections and Rare Books section of the University of Massachusetts Library at Amherst, and the librarians and staffs at the Beinecke Rare Book and Manuscript Library at Yale, the University of Chicago Library, the Baker Library at Dartmouth College, the New York Public Library, and the Wadsworth Atheneum in Hartford.

I would also like to thank Herbert J. Schoen and the others at the Hartford Insurance Group who made time to share their memories of Stevens with me and who escorted me through the various rooms where Stevens spent so many of his days. I want to thank Mr. and Mrs. William Bissell of Hartford as well for their time in relating their recollections of Stevens to me during an extended telephoned interview. And a special thanks goes to Dr. Norman

Winston of Reading, Pennsylvania, who took time away from the medical practice he conducts at 323 North Fifth Street to escort me through the house where Stevens grew up.

Over the years of doing my research and writing I have been supported by fellowships and awards from the Andrew Mellon Foundation, the Research Foundation and the Professional Staff Congress of the City University of New York, and a Senior Fellowship from the National Endowment for the Humanities. My sincere thanks go to these institutions for the assistance and encouragement that were indispensable in allowing the successful completion of my project.

If in these pages I have inadvertently omitted acknowledgment of someone, I apologize.

CONTENTS

INTRODUCTION

In one of the first letters to his future wife Wallace Stevens wrote, "It seems insincere, like playing a part, to be one person on paper and another in reality. But I know that it is only because I command myself there" (L 80). The biographer faced with this observation and, as the greatest part of her evidence, thousands of letters and hundreds of early journal entries cannot help but feel caught in the maze of the Cretan paradox: "All Cretans are liars," announced the Cretan. This, like all paradoxes, brings us to the end of language's possibility of revealing reality—and the biographer begins her task, to uncover through and with language whatever lies beyond and behind it. Language is then—to borrow a metaphor from a classical Zen text—like the finger pointing at the moon.

The question of why Stevens considered there to be a distinction between the self he commanded "on paper" and the self he presented "in reality" is the central intrigue of this biography. What were the combined circumstances that produced in the poet what his father once called his "power for painting pictures in words" (L 14), his ability to unravel the most tangled truth in masterfully reasoned argument, his skill as the verbal sleight-of-hand man who could simultaneously conceal and reveal what lay beneath the surface of things as they are—all "on paper," without his being able to feel that he commanded himself "in reality." Why would a man in his seventies, having won full recognition of his stature as a major figure both in the world of letters and in the business world, where he was considered the dean of surety claims in the country, be afraid that he would be laughed at by an audience assembled to honor him with an award for his poetry, or be afraid, too, that he might lose his job as vice-president of the insurance company where he had been employed for almost forty years were he not to be at his desk every day? Why did the man who devoted himself to learning and passing on in his poems how to live and what to do in a world just beginning to come to terms with what J. Hillis Miller has called the "disappearance of God" regard himself as having an "invalid personality" (CP 368)? Why did the poet who gave such pleasure with his words feel like "A most inappropriate man/In a most unpropitious place" (CP 120)?

WALLACE STEVENS

Stevens's life spanned one of the periods of greatest change in history. He was raised in a place where a man truly was part of the "intelligence of his soil" (CP 27), soil that either he or his father before him worked with his hands and smelled in his spirit, at a time when time itself was measured by the rhythms of day and night. He came of age without the least suspicion that every notion he had believed to be fixed as securely as the stars that filled the lucid blue nights of his childhood was to fall into nothingness or explode into a multitude of particles too small to be seen. The years of Stevens's childhood were the last years of America's innocence, years that still seemed to offer some possibility of fulfilling the promise contained in the idea of the New World. When Stevens later in his life looked back to the surroundings of his past, he remembered them as belonging to a pastoral idyll filled with "Greek days." While his memorializing was no doubt colored by the same rosy glow radiating from most evocations of lost paradises, and while the terms comparing his birthplace to a kind of Arcadian classical ideal belonged to the Victorian vocabulary that was the first language of the cultured during the second half of the nineteenth century, Stevens did not mythologically distort what he remembered. Even today the farmland and countryside around Reading, Pennsylvania, seem to have been omitted from the category of modern times. Cows lie in unfenced meadows beneath willow trees; well-ordered fields crowded with blackbirds pattern hills with their geometry still proportioned to human scale; a room in a family-run hotel costs twelve dollars a night.

But it was during Stevens's youth that the combined impacts of industrialization and urbanization made it quite difficult to remain part of the intelligence of one's soil. The path to the future led to the large cities, while machinery gradually chewed away the tie binding man to land. By the time Stevens at twenty-one came to New York to try his hand at journalism, the intermittent sizzling of electric street-car cables and the regular roar of elevated trains darkening the streets as they passed had almost completely hushed the clop-clop of horses pulling the various conveyances people had devised over hundreds of generations to get them and their burdens from one place to another. Within a few years hardly any of the city dwellers would remember the stench of manure-filled streets or the comfort of hearing the animals neigh through the night. In the city senses learned to sleep. Everything was slowly swallowed in the constant drone of power. It began to be difficult to know what was real. "On a few words of what is real in the world/I nourish myself" (CP 308), Stevens wrote years later.

If this quick transition into the clatter of modern city life was unsettling to the spirit, how much more disruptive was the change in inner landscape that followed Darwin's uncovering evidence for our "base" animal natures. It almost seems that the speedy acceleration allowed by the major scientific and technological developments following the Industrial Revolution were meant to whisk people as far as they possibly could get from acknowledging their brutish sources. Believing as true what Darwin theorized was especially troubling because accepting our ancestors to be "hairy quadrupeds, primarily arboreal in

18

their habits" instead of Adam and Eve also meant accepting that there was no possibility of heavenly reunion with the Creator and the spirits of loved ones already dead. And if there was no heaven, there was also no hell. Who and what in this new world would ensure that, at least in the end, justice would be served? How could evil be dealt with? These were among the questions Stevens had had to face during his tender years at Harvard, even before his rude awakening to the brash harshness of New York. Then, within the next five years there were Freud and Einstein to consider—the world Wallace Stevens had been raised to inhabit no longer existed. How could one bred to be certain of his place, as well as the place of every other creature and thing in the great chain of being, not feel uncertain of self in the century when everything became uncertain, even certain principles? And so, Stevens, like Einstein who shared precisely the poet's years and who, like him too, observed himself as part of nature, came to measure the "velocities of change" (*CP* 414), the only constant in the spinning and hissing of the present.

But it would take him more than half his life to come to easy acceptance of this. From Heraclitus through Zen Buddhism Stevens wandered, and— preserving the Protestant habit of introspection, which persisted while its supernatural justification evaporated[1]—he recorded what he found along the way, first in regular journal entries, later in poems. In the process he fashioned a new self "on paper," one who was in command and who could teach how to live, what to do.

This biography will respect the sense of the man Stevens shaped himself to be, but will do so without the idealizing reverence given a hero. I believe it is important to honor the choices that individuals have made for themselves. Stevens called poetry "a health" (*OP* 176) and chose to express through it the "impossible possible philosophers' man" (*CP* 250), a self abstracted from himself and from the possibilities inherent in all beings in their relationships to the other elements of nature. This projection was an act of love. As George Santayana, one of the important figures in Stevens's young life, observed, what we love in people is much more their possibility than their actuality. Following this, Stevens's monumental attempt to discover the full range of possibilities in his relation to the world—a relation he defined as the function of poetry to express—could be seen, in part, as his attempt to love himself within the broader project of coming to know himself that tied him to the philosophic tradition passed down from the Greeks. To love himself would mend the narcissistic tear that had rent Western consciousness almost beyond repair after the excesses of the romantic period.

Insofar as it was necessary to discuss what are generally regarded as weaknesses of character, offensive habits or behavior, and intimate details in order to make clear what kinds of difficulties Stevens faced in making the choices he did, I have. But I have not dwelt on them, nor have I described more than representative examples. On the other hand, I have not simply sung the praises of Stevens as major-man. This would be to miss the point entirely, especially since for Stevens the notion of the individual as hero was an outworn

19

one. The hero that emerges from his work is nature itself or, rather, consciousness as it understands itself to be part of nature. In this sense the biography, in tracing the development of Stevens's consciousness, is as much a
biography of America from 1879 to 1955 as it is of the poet who was so
integrally bound to his time and place. This broadened perspective is in keeping with Stevens's desire to create a mythology of our region at a moment in
history when none of the myths on which human beings had sustained themselves over hundreds of generations could support belief any longer. As Stevens expressed late in his life, the greatest problem of his age was what
William James had called the "will to believe." It was not just for poetic
effect that Stevens memorialized familiar elements of America's landscape and
human creation—like Augustus Saint-Gaudens's statue of General Sherman,
which graces Manhattan's Grand Army Plaza. A coherent mythology begins
with nature and ends in monuments, and it is the development of consciousness that moves us from the cold facts of stone and metal to vibrant
shapes that prompt imaginings.

In following the evolution of Stevens's consciousness I have concentrated
on both the rational and irrational elements. Stevens would not have become
the successful lawyer he did, nor would he have been able to set down the
subtle arguments folded into his poems like those unheard melodies sweeter
still that jazz musicians hear in their mind's ear as they play the riffs around
them, had he not honed the tool of reason to murderous possibilities. In this,
too, he was very much a child of America, constitutionally established as a
place of pure reason. But he was also a child of his time, a time that Freud
made frighteningly attentive to the unconscious. Stevens was equally concerned with marshaling the force of what he called "this potent subject," the
"irrational element" (OP 229), and using it, too, to disclose the nature of
things as they are. "They will get it straight one day at the Sorbonne," he
wrote as he brought his "Notes Toward a Supreme Fiction" to a close:

> We shall return at twilight from the lecture
> Pleased that the irrational is rational,
>
> Until flicked by feeling, in a gildered street,
> I call you by name, my green, my fluent mundo.
> You will have stopped revolving except in crystal.
>   (CP 406–7).

In that poem, as though parodying Kant's *Prolegomena to Any Future Metaphysics*, the poet completed the task begun years before by his poetic mock-
hero Crispin in "The Comedian as the Letter C" who "wrote *his* prolegomena"
(italics mine; CP 37) before coming to terms with the inextricable connection
between thinking and feeling. Unlike Kant, or any philosopher, the poet
could state categorical imperatives with impunity. He could simply set down
as truth that "Sight/Is a museum of things seen" (CP 274) and feel, in doing
so, that he was the creator of his own universe—at least small comfort for one

who had lost the possibility of believing in the Creator of the universe. The work the poet cut out for himself was to fabricate "the fiction that results from feeling" (*CP* 406), feeling this loss as well as everything else that belongs to the human comedy.

To construct a convincing fiction requires reason. Stevens's commitment to the use of reason belonged to the dominant tradition of the West, which had begun with the pre-Socratics and Plato and was passed down through time in different thinkers in different countries—a line that, in terms of the intellectual currents charging the air of the generation that produced the poet, was particularized in Charles Sanders Peirce. For Peirce, reason was a power of transforming things. In Stevens's words, it was the force that allows us to "look [not] *at* facts, but *through* them" (*L* 32). Though Stevens did not claim familiarity with the work of Peirce, he was nonetheless heir to the same strains of thought that engendered in the philosopher a desire to justify God's ways to man by bridging the gap made by Darwin between the scientific outlook on the place of human beings in the world and the threatened religious view. In pursuing the origin and course of human development, the central question to emerge for the seriously inquiring thinkers, philosophers, and poets was and is whether the habit of dividing the mind, or consciousness, from the rest of the world really reflects a genuine division in nature and not just an accident of convention or intellectual history.[2] This question naturally became more urgent after Darwin, for if what is known as mind reflects a division in nature, the possibility of arguing for some kind of special creation remains; if not, then where can or should the line be drawn that separates the human from what is not? Stevens attempted in his reading, his thinking, his musing, and his writing to push toward the border of answering this question. His involvement with the idea of a supreme fiction linked him in a chain of others who around the turn of the century were pursuing the efficacy of fictions to offer the mind new possibilities of conceiving its place in the world. These others included William James and Hans Vaihinger,[3] and in the realm of pure poetry, Stéphane Mallarmé.

As a lawyer well versed in the vocabulary and method of constructing fictions following logic's intricate steps, Stevens also came to understand reason's limits. Though its systematic use through history enabled human beings to understand and manipulate nature more and more effectively, Stevens realized that there is always a point at which any reasoned fiction turns on itself to become self-reflexive and paradoxical. In the language currently used to describe this situation, this would be called turbulence in a domain—a point at which consciousness, like an electron itself, jumps or shifts from the path it has been following to another. For the poet keenly attentive to consciousness, this movement was detectable as the tension between first person and third person perspectives that he translated into the counterpoint of voices—his inflection and the innuendos of his personae. It was also detectable in the juxtaposition of discursive language and nonsense syllables, in the interplay between the reasoned progress of words making up seemingly logical statements and the metaphorical leaps between some of the words in those statements, and in those leaps between statements and stanzas, and between entire poems and their titles. In recording this movement, Stevens mirrored the process of his mind and revealed his implicit trust that in doing so he was also revealing his "bond to all that dust" (CP 15), the normally imperceptible dance of nature at levels beyond those apprehensible by the senses alone.

It was not for nothing that the poet was fascinated by Max Planck's formulation of quantum theory. Stevens finally satisfied what he called in an early letter his "instinct of faith" (L 86) by yielding to his irrational element, granting it as much possibility in disclosing the nature of things as he did to the rational working of thought. In allowing himself to be stirred by what he called the "pathos" of everything (L 53)—the unreasoned sympathy or feeling for what was around him, which he translated into the rhythms and sounds of his words—the poet tried to understand the rational animal he was. If his lines were longer in the poems he wrote in summer than in late fall, it was because his breaths were longer as he walked to and from the office composing his lines: This reflected his actual relationship with the weather of his region—part of the mythology he was creating. If during the wars that he saw as "periodical failure[s] of politics" (OP 164) the sounds of his words were violent and strained, it was because he felt it was necessary to meet the very violence of things as they were. If his thoughts stopped cold at the recollection of the woman he loved as she used to be, was it because reason was inadequate to understand what had happened or because the pathos of what had happened would bathe him in tears? Stevens called poetry "a cure of the mind" (OP 176), and its therapeutic potential resided in his being able to recognize in the rhythms, sounds, and shapes of his lines the feelings that attended perception—"There is a sense in sounds beyond their meaning" (CP 352)—and in his having the possibility of examining, in the mirror of his mind that his words were, the occasions that prompted leaps and turns, his tropes, from one thing to another.

As he had learned with Plato from Socrates, the unexamined life was not worth living. In following the dance of Stevens's consciousness around the facts of his life, we come to understand what he meant when he wrote that "Life is a composite of the propositions about it" (OP 171). By extending the various propositions about life through the fiction-making of his poetic process, Stevens could consider and choose propositions that would foster what he called the "highest pursuit . . . the pursuit of happiness on earth" (OP 157). Seeing himself reflected in his words and through them seeing and hearing in his imagination the propositions both prompting and contained in them, Stevens came up against the same difficulty all of us face in the attempt to know ourselves—closing our ears to voices from the past and present that threaten what we want or think we want until a moment when we feel capable of battling them in imagined dialogues. Accompanying Stevens as he came to know himself, we will hear many familiar voices from the chorus of history's "studious ghosts" (CP 14) with whom we continue to try to discover how to live, what to do. Curiously, had Stevens's sense of self not been precarious—had he felt himself to be "in reality" what he was "on paper"—he would not have been as susceptible as he was to these other voices. It was his ability to feel the pathos of everything that made him a poet. His being was constantly changing like the world around him.

The voices Stevens engaged came from both his particular experiences in his time and place—the voice of Victorian morality and that of the "good Puritan," for example, as well as those he heard at Harvard exploring themselves and the world as it had become—and from his extraordinary breadth of reading. In composing this biography I have refrained from dealing extensively with some of the figures whose voices I think were strongest for Stevens—Plato, Spenser, Goethe, Emerson—though I have indicated, except in the case of Spenser, the nature of the poet's involvement with them. To present an in-depth analysis of Stevens's dialogue with any one of these figures would itself be a healthy volume. Indeed, a great deal of scholarly work has already been done on the poet's tie to Plato, whom, I believe, Stevens reread at different points throughout his life, but no book-length study has appeared. Similarly, many critics have dealt with Stevens and Emerson, though Spenser and Goethe have not yet received sufficient attention. In my text I have not directly indicated the significance of Stevens's careful reading and annotating of Spenser's *Faerie Queene* (his two-volume edition is at the Huntington Library), preferring to let allusiveness speak alone in this instance through the terms of reference Stevens chose to use in defining his early relationship to himself as a poet and to Elsie Moll, his future wife. Then, too, the nature of what Stevens seemed to be attentive to in Spenser was somewhat different from his focus with the other figures. Here it was, I think, primarily the sound of words and a certain formal manner that excited his interest, while in the others it was primarily the content of the words that moved him.

It is at the same time fitting, in terms of how this biography attempts to mirror the consciousness of its subject, that the major voices—Dante and Whitman also whispered to him their "heavenly labials" (*CP* 7)—remain as stage whispers, so to speak, since it was with these voices of those he considered "man-poets" (*L* 26) that Stevens had to contend most forcefully in order to speak himself. As will become apparent in the pages to follow, Stevens was consistently reticent to admit what Harold Bloom has called the "anxiety of influence." A good part of his deceptiveness "on paper" was to deny that he read other poets at all. This is understandable, since the greater receptivity of the greater poets to the pathetic force of everything around them makes them particularly permeable to the power of others' ideas and feelings, and so, uncertain as to what can properly be understood as their own. In Stevens's case it almost seems that the more meaningful the dialogue he had with a certain figure, the more circumspect he was about uttering that figure's "divine" name. The evidence for the importance of what was silently discussed, however, appears in the magical ciphers of the lines he shaped into poems.

I have refrained as well from detailing—for the same reasons—the many strong echoes in Stevens's work of Eastern texts and the fainter notes from Heraclitus and the other pre-Socratics, though I have indicated what I feel to be the importance of these strains. There is much work to be done in these areas, and, again, some scholars have recently begun to examine them. In connection to Heraclitus, in this note, it is sufficient to mention only the philosopher's countless images of change; a perusal of Charles Kahn's edition of the fragments—*The Art and Thought of Heraclitus* (London and New York: Cambridge University Press, 1979)—will, I think, offer much food for thought to future Stevens scholars. In connection to the Eastern texts, my perception is that it was the literature of Zen Buddhism that most enticed Stevens though no titles of the classical Zen collections remain in Stevens's library, if he had, in fact, once acquired them—and he did not name any of these works in the papers that are part of the Huntington Library holdings. Nonetheless, beyond the parallels that are described later in this text there are many, many other striking resemblances between concepts expressed throughout the *Mumonkan* and *Hekiganroku* and concepts that were clearly operative for Stevens. I offer one such observation here to illustrate my point. One of the lessons of the Sixth Patriarch involved settling a dispute between two monks who were arguing about the movement of a temple flag. One said the flag moved, the other that the wind moved. The Sixth Patriarch said, "It is not the wind that moves, it is not the flag that moves; it is your mind that moves."[4] The same experiential phenomenon was explored by Stevens in his "Thirteen Ways of Looking at a Blackbird," its penultimate section anchoring the various excursions of awareness with:

> The river is moving.
> The blackbird must be flying.
> (*CP* 94).

In addition, the programmatic formal elements of the Zen canon, including the purpose of using nonsense syllables to mimic the insufficiency of reason to deal fully with reality and the use of obvious paralogisms in the koans to prompt enlightenment, are echoed in Stevens's use of nonsense syllables and in his repeated counterpointing of titles and poems. The design behind these devices in the koans was to provoke the sublime laughter that accompanies insight. The Zen collections were conceived as a series of cosmic jokes[5] meant to unsettle the initiate from the complacent illusion of certainty. Stevens's early stated motto for himself, "Angelic hilarity with monastic simplicity" (*L* 101), and his covert project to rival the *Divine Comedy* with his own new "vulgate of experience" (*CP* 465) partook of the same spirit.

I have also not developed the full significance of the movies on Stevens's style though from the fact that he loved films, especially foreign films, this seems to me to be another area full of possibility for exploration. The evolution of cinematic technique from a series of still shots with titles to the complex interweaving of time sequences in a fluid unfolding could not have escaped mental comment by Stevens, though there is very little direct evidence of his interest. But, again, his silence on the subject is not an indication that it was not important to him.

One last thing I have not mentioned, again, for lack of evidence, is the intriguing fact that the Hartford Insurance Company employed another individual besides the poet who was equally fascinated with language—Benjamin Lee Whorf, who worked as an engineer at the home office for the Hartford Fire Insurance section from 1919 until his death in 1941. If, in fact, Stevens never came to know this man so deeply immersed in the "idea map" of language as a "fact of nature,"[6] who in his study of linguistic relativity suggested that "all one's life one has been tricked, all unaware, by the structure of language into a certain way of perceiving reality, with the implication that awareness of this trickery will enable one to see with fresh insight,"[7] it seems itself a perverse trick of fate that he did not. "Language is the best show man puts on," observed Whorf,[8] and few knew this better than Stevens. What delightful lunches the two men might have had—or perhaps did have.

In reading through, over the past fifteen years, the material Stevens referred to in his journals and letters and what remains of his library, I have found that the poet held imaginary dialogues not only with the "man-poets" but also with a host of less celebrated individuals who considerably affected his thought and action. These figures have not, in general, been dealt with in the great body of secondary literature on Stevens. While I have not expanded on Stevens's ties to the major voices mentioned above for the reasons given, and while I have not gone on at length concerning the affinities between Stevens and other strong figures like Santayana, Nietzsche, Whitman, and the symbolist poets—because these ties have been uncovered and developed more than adequately by others—I have been careful to reproduce these other voices in their dialogues with the poet. My intention is to complete a portrait of Stevens without, wherever possible, going into details that have been well drawn before. And too, unlike the voices of the great "man-poets," which he seemed to have to quiet in his mind in order to hear himself, these others belonged to what for him was a minor chorus so he did not fear their rhythms would override his own. More, for the man who did not have the kind of life where regular conversations with friends and acquaintances could offer him the stimulation he needed, these silent discussions contributed that part to his everyday experience. They came, he learned from them, and they left. Consequently, I have been able to deal with each of them in a few pages. This would have been impossible in the cases of the larger presences with whose shades Stevens spoke intermittently throughout his life. In all instances I have tried to be attentive to the integrity and dignity of the majestically modulated voice of Stevens himself—striking his "hullabaloo among the spheres" (*CP* 59).

This last observation brings me to discuss how I hear my own voice as Stevens's biographer. I have already explained the reasons for some of the broader choices I have made in dealing with the material at hand. I would like now to describe the involvement with Stevens's work that brought me to want to do a biography, before going on to point out the problems that it raised. In the process I shall also indicate the reasons for the stylistic and technical choices that also had to be made, in the hope that the readers will feel themselves more comfortable in the "fluent mundo" of words that Stevens created and subsequently called forth from me and so many others.

It was out of pure frustration almost twenty years ago that I became fascinated with the idea of the man who wrote poems that kept calling me back to read them again and again though I could not understand them. I was in college, majoring in philosophy, writing term papers on such topics as "Is Metaphysics Nonsense?" and "A View of the World Without Verbs," and doing well in understanding the issues and threading out my arguments. I had never had difficulties in understanding before; I could perceive through mathematical equations the abstract structures that don't exist. Yet there I was—stymied by Stevens. Years passed. I read and reread his poems. I enrolled in a Ph.D. program in comparative literature and concentrated in linguistics and literary theory with my interest focused on metaphor—its history, its operation, its difference in ordinary versus poetic language, how it discloses the world. I was still rereading Stevens and trying to understand. Then in 1970 I acquired Holly Stevens's edition of her father's letters. Glimmers of recognition, if not understanding, began. Certain words and phrases that I knew from poems appeared in letters; there was, at least, a connection between the beautifully shimmering arrangements of sentences shaped into poems and a life. Following the finger pointing at the moon, I nosed through each of the references Stevens made in his journals and letters—additional glimmers. At the same time, I read through the already substantial secondary material on his work. By 1977 I completed my dissertation: one half a discussion of earlier critics' readings of Stevens, the other half my readings, tying some of the major poems to his life—my breaking away from the New Critical tradition.

Along the way and later, additional material accumulated. Listings of the titles remaining in Stevens's library kept me reading well into the time pages of sketches for the biography began littering my desk like the leaves the poet conjured in "Sunday Morning" (CP 69). Pointings from the poems continue to keep me playing the game with Stevens's mind that began so many years ago. His observation that "Poetry is the scholar's art" (OP 167) has certainly been proven true for me since I have understood both how Stevens made his own scholarship his art and I have been made a scholar in the deepest sense as well. His work, an epic for the age of disbelief, memorialized in the subtle suggestions contained in its lines whatever the poet felt should be preserved from both the Western and Eastern traditions. His heroes were not warriors but those who had, like him, spent their lives contemplating how to attune themselves to, and voice their parts in, the harmony of nature.

As I reread Stevens and read those with whom he held his imaginary dialogues, I gradually found myself becoming increasingly attentive to the quiverings of my own nature in response to the world around me. More and more often as I walked, various lines from Stevens's poems came to accompany my rhythm. I began to see again with an ignorant eye, the eye of a child. Reflecting on what was going on, I came to realize that what Stevens had managed to do was to preserve throughout his life the freshness of vision that belongs to the child while monumentally increasing the terms of reference that he had available to describe that vision. It was precisely because he valued this constant newness of perception above anything else that he remained until his death uncertain of the self he presented "in reality." Had he at any point integrated himself into a particular role fully enough so that he would not have to feel unsure of how to act or of how he was being seen, had he, in other words, taken on as second nature, as most of us do, the being quietly assigned by time, place, and circumstances, he would have lost—again, as most of us do in the process of becoming completely socialized—his childlike imagination. And it was this, after all, that made him a master of metaphor, one of those Aristotle named as the "best" because they can restore that pristine vision to us, remind us platonically of the past. It was as though Stevens intuitively knew that he could protect this vision only by never becoming complacent in a fixed sense of self, that he could keep this sense alive only by acting *as if* he were one thing or another. "There is a perfect rout of characters in every man," he wrote in one of his early journal entries or letters. Putting on his various masks, fulfilling the role of the money-making lawyer and knowing all the time that he was acting, playing, kept his eye responsive to the trembling present. "The final belief is to believe in a fiction, which you know to be a fiction, there being nothing else. The exquisite truth is to know that it is a fiction and that you believe in it willingly" (*OP* 163).

Discovering these things slowly, I imagined the life of the man who restored my ability to see this way. Of course, at first it was an idealized life I conjured for this figure who at different stages took on for me roles of father, teacher, lover. Later, my fiction shifted abruptly as I carefully read through his published letters and saw him as a victim of others, of circumstances; he became my other self. Then, still later, he became victimizer, cold and uncaring of the feelings of those around him, attentive only to what could not speak. Gradually, as though working through what in psychoanalytic terms are called transference and countertransference and reading through the vast quantity of unpublished material, my vision became adjusted to what I hope now is seeing things as they were—insofar as that is possible for any of us. Still, it is my vision, though after having been immersed in Stevens's "fluent mundo" for so long I have questioned whether I could or can properly call my consciousness my own.

In writing the pages that follow, sentences as they came often brought as part of them phrases from Stevens. At the risk of falling into what Helen Vendler has recently observed to be a fault of critics of poetry,[9] that is, consciously or unconsciously imitating the styles of their subjects—a kind of second-level inversion of the pathetic fallacy—I initially attempted during my first revision to purge my prose of these traces. But they continued to find their way through the neural passageways that guided the fingers leading my pen across first draft pages. After a while I let these echoes have their way and stopped removing them as I revised. I wanted to see what kind of pattern, if any, would emerge, and I wanted to stop doing violence to my consciousness which, I had come to realize, had simply learned to speak Stevens, as it were. Since I envisioned my own text as having a reciprocal relation to Stevens and his work, I recognized that it was fitting that I allowed expression to something I had discovered through him, my own Kantian faith that the patterns emerging from consciousness uncensored reveal connections to things as they are in a way that mimics the object or subject—in this sense the two merge into one—of attention at deep structural levels. This is, I think, a version of what is today called intersubjectivity, though it can only be recognized as such if, first, the abstract object/subject of attention is granted imaginatively the same presence as a concrete, responding interlocutor and, secondly, if one is patient enough to refrain from immediately revising to allow the pattern growing out of one's response to the object/subject of attention to show itself.

The result, as Charles Molesworth described it, I think accurately and beautifully, is fugal. Certain phrases appear again and again, sometimes the same, sometimes changed, bringing with them evocations of major themes in Stevens's experience. While most come from his own vocabulary, one or two like "a place on the front bench" and "power of painting pictures in words" come from his father's, as expressed in letters to his son. Among those properly belonging to Stevens, "up and down between two elements," "first, foremost law," "man number one," "need of some imperishable bliss," "that monster, the body," "man-poets," "how to live, what to do," "studious ghosts," "bring a world quite round," "bond to all that dust," "things as they are," "fluent mundo," and "nothing that is not there and the nothing that is" establish the pattern of thematic recall and variation. There are also phrases borrowed from Stevens that appear only once as part of a description of a landscape familiar to him or of a particularly moving experience. This is the case in the opening paragraph of the biography, for example. In all instances of using Stevens's words to express a sense of things, I feel that his "noble accents/And lucid, inescapable rhythms" (*CP* 94) are far superior to any that I might have invented to communicate the tremulous brilliance of his intricate mind in its engagement with the world.

Deciding whether to interrupt the fluidity of sentences as they came—as I heard them—with quotation marks in order to indicate the phrases belonging to Stevens was quite difficult. On the one hand I wanted to let them rest comfortably as parts of the sentences, but then felt uneasy about seeming to claim as mine, for those not well versed in Stevens's poetry, his images. On the other hand I was hesitant about possibly annoying readers with not only quotation marks but the parenthetical indications of sources that became necessary once the decision was made not to let the phrases stand as they were. I finally made a choice knowing that in writing this biography I was addressing both general readers and Stevens specialists, and hoping that the initial impatience of the latter in being pointed to where they are able to go by heart would be more than made up for by making it possible for the former to become familiar with the precise poetic and experiential contexts from which particular phrases were taken. With this same idea in mind, in the cases of repeated phrases, I gradually let quotation marks and page indications drop as I felt the newer readers would also become fluent in speaking Stevens. My expectation was that these phrases would slowly integrate themselves into the readers' vocabularies as they indeed became integrated into the vocabulary of Stevens. On the few occasions when passages or words appear in my text with quotation marks but without page indications it means that the original source has either been referred to just before the quoted material or will be just after. And specifically in the cases of poems named and quoted from, the page numbers are given repeatedly to save readers the effort of looking up the appropriate locations after the first reference, should they want to see the entire poem once again in light of the different way it is being considered in my text. In the instances where I have simply mentioned titles in passing and where reading the poem will not illuminate my meaning, I have not given page numbers; conversely, in cases where just titles are given and there is a page number as well, I am suggesting that reading or rereading the poem might be useful in view of the discussion being presented.

In addition, I have played on the sense of another major word in the poet's vocabulary, "comedian." While when it is used with a capital and quotation marks it refers in some way to the figure of "The Comedian" from "The Comedian as the Letter C," when it is used with a capital and no quotation marks it indicates Stevens in the role he aspired to fulfill as major poet, and when it is used simply with a lowercase *c* and no quotation marks it describes Stevens in an everyday guise, playing with "reality." I have myself played with these variations in order to establish both the central significance of Stevens's epic desire to rival Dante's *Divine Comedy* in being the new vulgate of experience for his time and place and the importance of his coming to practice in his own life after the crisis of his middle age the attitude of a comedian, giving as much pleasure as he could through subtle games and pranks, most often through words. This second aspect became vitally important to Stevens, who in 1909 transcribed in his journal and communicated in a letter to his future wife an observation of Charles Lamb's that he had found in Kakuzo Okakura's *Book of Tea,* "The best thing by far is to do good by stealth and have it discovered by chance."

While I did not consciously intend a musical structure for this biography—my only organizing principle as I began was an outline for thirteen chapters or "ways" of looking at Stevens, a form I have maintained, the first volume's eight chapters covering Stevens's early years from 1879 to 1923 and the second's five chapters to cover the remaining years until his death—it became apparent to me at a certain point that since I was attempting, at least on one level, to reflect the process of Stevens's mind, a musical structure was unavoidable. One of the most striking features to emerge from following the threads of Stevens's experience was the rhythmic repetition of motifs both in his work—where it would be expected as part of the conscious shaping of his art—and, extraordinarily, in his life. In tracing his movement through his days, weeks, months, and years, I found myself caught in a kind of cyclic, spiraling pattern where images, phrases, expressions of feeling and thought recurred, all with their own periodicity syncopating one another with the actual breath and step of the poet's dance with time. More, with each circling back on the spiral the repeated image, feeling, thought, phrase was broadened both by the poet's increased experience and the memory, sometimes vague, sometimes sharp, that he had seen, felt, or thought this before.

I am not certain as to how conscious Stevens was of the way he precisely exemplified, by recording in his journals, letters, and poems notations of his own movement, the ideas of Henri Bergson concerning the dual nature of our perception of time. While Bergson did not invent these ways of experiencing, in naming and describing the difference between time as conventionally known—*le temps*—and time as the idiosyncratic inner awareness of extension belonging to each individual—*la durée*—he made those who became familiar with this distinction attentive to the counterpoint of these two elements in themselves. At what point Stevens became aware of his own up and down between these two elements is, in the end, not that important. But what is, is that this central notion for the century played its central part in his apprehension of his relation to the world.

Again, just as I did not consciously intend a musical structure, I did not plan even to attempt mimicking in the biography's form the tension between the two senses of Bergsonian time. Yet as the chapters unfolded in terms of the significance of certain years or spans of years for Stevens, it became apparent to me that I was, once more, in following the poet's perception and ordering it against the external unfolding of events in "real" time, moving in both senses of time. The result is the contracting-expanding pattern of the chapters where, for example, as many pages (themselves time markers) are devoted to one year, 1900, as to another period of seven years. Within this frame readers will get a deeper sense of Stevens's experience of his internal time if they carefully read through the passages from the poet's journals and letters giving themselves time to consider the points the poet must have stopped to muse about before going on in his writing. Knowing that it often took Stevens six to seven hours to compose a four- to five-page letter provides a prompt to do this. Similarly, it is, I think, especially important not to skip over the longer passages quoted since they directly communicate in the very "duration" of their breath and attention an awareness of internal time—something that is being threatened more every day in the century that prides itself on offering as many distractions as possible to fill whatever few moments of "free" time remain in our well-ordered lives. Reading through these letters and journal entries, then, will slow readers down and allow them to feel Stevens's time.

Finally, as the poet himself moved more deeply into the century with its constantly accelerating pace, more and more external time was covered in more or less the same number of pages until, that is, the last few years of the poet's life when he began to separate himself from the external world where he had for so many years participated fully and made himself a success. With this gentle withdrawal there was a slowing down back into the tempo of time past, a natural completion of the music of his life.

Of course, readers will not be able to experience the wholeness of this movement until after the second volume of the biography has appeared. But even this interruption, this long rest, is imitative of the poet's life. From his initial experiences in the world through his bursting fully clad from the head of his time onto the stage of modernism, there was not a moment for stopping. By 1923 when Stevens in middle age marked his progress with the publication of *Harmonium,* his first volume, a deep breath was overdue. Much had happened, almost too much. The world he had known as a young man no longer existed; in the post–World War I years disillusion was—to paraphrase him (*CP* 468)—the only illusion left to strip away. Naturally, his relation to the world changed as he, too, said good-bye to his own youth and faced the moment of awareness that marks the transition into what he called the "faith of forty" (*CP* 16)—that from this point on all choices, both those made in the past and those still to be made, have binding consequences. At the same time, this change of life seemingly contradicted his other experiences of the same moment. At forty-four he was apparently just beginning, having only now presented his premier volume and being about to become a father for the first time. The confusion of preparation, expectation, and reality required silence to consider—"Whereof one knows not, thereof one cannot speak." Coming to this point with Stevens and stopping with him to rest—which he did for six years after the appearance of *Harmonium*— will help readers appreciate more fully, even though their rest will be for no more than a year (until the appearance of the second completing volume of this biography), how devastatingly difficult a moment in cultural history the post–World War I period was and how equally difficult a moment in personal history the period of coming to middle age. Feeling these things will, in turn, explain more adequately the difference between *Harmonium* and all of Stevens's later volumes. The movement from the sleek, sophisticated city poems of that first book to the meditative *Ideas of Order* and later poems had all to do with the resolution of the crisis of these changes of life. It was during his years of silence that Stevens in life began to complete the task he had imagined for his incomplete poetic hero Crispin—the letter *C* as an unfinished *O,* symbol of wholeness, wonderfully mimicking the incompletion he sailed "over-*seas*" to complete, in the process of "over-*seeing*" himself and his past.

Between the thing as idea and
The idea as thing. She is half who made her.
This is the final Projection, C.

(CP 295)

During this period of quiet Stevens began to bring the idea he had in mind of himself into being. He had succeeded in driving "away/The shadow of his fellows from the skies" (CP 37) of his mind; he had strengthened and sharpened his voice to proclaim himself amid and above them, and so could now listen to his own voice and follow its directions for how to live, what to do. When he began to speak again his voice would sound quite different.

This difference together with the breaking up of the biography into two volumes made the use of the repeated phrases almost a necessary formal element. A work dealing at all imitatively with the life and work of a major figure who himself had epic aspirations naturally becomes lengthy and requires tag phrases that work like Homeric epithets to recall to the audience's attention the aureole of past meanings that illuminate new contexts.

In closing this prologue to what was possible for me in composing this story of a life around the feelings and thoughts of a man who lived in the mind not to escape from reality but to increase his sense of it, I shall quote once more, I think appropriately, from his own "Prologues to What Is Possible" and hope that readers will find, after going through the pages to follow, at least a slight answer to the question phrased in the lines:

What self, for example, did he contain that had not yet been
    loosed,
Snarling in him for discovery as his attentions spread,
As if all his hereditary lights were suddenly increased
By an access of color, a new and unobserved, slight dithering,
The smallest lamp, which added its puissant flick, to which he
    gave
A name and privilege over the ordinary of his commonplace—

A flick which added to what was real and its vocabulary,
The way some first thing coming into Northern trees
Adds to them the whole vocabulary of the South,
The way the earliest single light in the evening sky, in spring,
Creates a fresh universe out of nothingness by adding itself,
The way a look or a touch reveals its unexpected magnitudes.

(CP 516–17)

I
THE MAKING OF
A GOOD PURITAN
1879–1897

EVERY MAN'S BIOGRAPHY IS TO
BE UNDERSTOOD IN RELATION TO
HIS FATHER.

—LIONEL TRILLING,
Introduction to
The Portable Matthew Arnold

I mean to think well of everyone in my family and if there are any of them that were not as fortunate as the others or, say, as they might have been, I mean to forget that. When I think of my father's pride and of all the anxiety that he must have felt, and then look at this last picture of him in which he seems so completely defeated, the feeling isn't anything that I want to renew. I very much prefer to look at him and think of him in his prime. The truth is that I rather think that, seeing him as a whole, I understand him better perhaps than he understood himself, and that I can really look into his heart in which he must have concealed so many things. I say this because he was one of the most uncommunicative of men.

—From a letter of WALLACE
STEVENS to his niece,
November 2, 1943, *Letters* (p. 458)

Wallace Stevens's mother bore him at home in the bed where she would die. Home was Reading, Pennsylvania, an industrious, newly industrialized city of the nineteenth century's last quarter; the house, at 323 North Fifth Street, still stands. October 2, 1879, Stevens's birth date, fell during a drought (*SP* 7) in the already dun-colored mountainous region. Out of this "gray, particular" (*CP* 528) landscape, the child grew into a young man, surrounded by the stone and rock he later transformed and used as the skeleton of his poetry. This was the "basic slate" (*CP* 15) detectable through even the rosiest tints of description.

In that October there was also a yellow fever epidemic, but neither this nor the drought seems to have affected the bustling prosperity of the city, and neither seems to have touched the Stevens family, though the young parents—both about thirty-one—must have been somewhat concerned for their newborn Wallace and their then almost two-year-old first son, Garrett, Jr. Garrett, Sr., who had arrived in Reading about eight years earlier to read law and apprentice himself in a law office, had by this time established himself as a practicing attorney. His wife, Margaretha Catharine Zeller (known as Kate), had been born and raised in Reading. She had supported herself as a local schoolteacher before her marriage. Because of her father's death when she was between thirteen and fourteen (*L* 416), she had been forced, while still quite young, to think of economic independence. She began working as soon as she could, and after her mother's death, when Kate was about twenty-four, she was completely on her own until her marriage to Garrett Stevens four years later.

The couple had a great deal in common, both with each other and with the place of which they were a part. They naturally worked together to pass on to their children values derived from their upbringing and from their individual experience—values that were, to the largest degree, consistent with the Puritan work ethic, focused, as it was and is, on the virtues of industry, sobriety, and thrift.[1] Both Garrett and Kate had come from large families branching from the original stock of Pennsylvania Dutch and German settlers, whose strong religious attachments as well as practical traits still dominated the lives of their descendants. And both, for individual reasons, had at fairly young ages left the security of the family to make their ways alone. But they took with them the almost inescapable, implicit faith in the tradition that had shaped them, a tradition equally responsible for the tremendous growth and the concomitant ills of America. The child who grew into the poetic insurance executive experienced this split as the everyday climate of his parents' world. Later he expressed it in a profoundly moving yet, at the same time, recalcitrant way in his writing.

Garrett Stevens had been raised on a farm in Feasterville, a town in Bucks County, Pennsylvania. He was one of six children (five boys and one girl) of Elizabeth Barcalow Stevens (1811–1900) and Benjamin Stevens (1808–1894) (L 4). Benjamin was also the son of a farmer and during his lifetime, besides managing the farm, actively involved himself in political issues; after the Civil War, for example, he was treasurer of the Society for the Prosecution of Horse Thieves (SP 5). He also participated in the religious life of the community. As his grandson later noted, he was "a pillar in the Dutch Reformed Church" and "for a large part of his life . . . associated with the Feasterville Sabbath School" (SP 5). Living as one who belonged in both a religious and a historical community was very much in keeping with his place in a line whose earliest-known member in Bucks County, Abraham Stevens, had married his bride, Blandina Janse van Woggelum, in the First Presbyterian Church in Philadelphia in 1732, the "year," as Wallace Stevens later commented, "in which Washington was born" (L 672). Throughout the generations after and, as indicated above, including Stevens's grandfather Benjamin, the Stevens family remained strongly connected to the Dutch Reformed Church in Bucks County (L 405).

Of the family history of Benjamin's wife, Elizabeth Barcalow, less is known (though Stevens tried, over a period of years—from about 1942 through 1946—to trace her branch, as well as others of his family tree; with others he was far more successful). Originally the family name was Buckalew and so, presumably, also Dutch. This family was tied to a Benham line, the first member of which had, like the Stevenses, "come over very early" (L 694). These Benhams were among a group of New England settlers (Dorchester, Massachusetts) who eventually moved to New Jersey to found the town of Shrewsbury (L 694).

Garrett and Kate Stevens had five children: Garrett, Jr., who was nick-named Buck, Wallace, John, who followed Wallace after a little more than a year, and then, after long breaks of five and nine years,[2] two daughters, Elizabeth and Mary Katharine, known in the family simply as Katharine. Wallace, together with his brothers, sisters, and cousins used to spend time on the farm in Feasterville.[3] They fished in the same creek, the Perkiomen, where Garrett, Sr., had fished for bass as a boy, and they played in the same fields, perhaps searching for arrowheads and other artifacts of the Indians who had inhabited this and other parts of western Pennsylvania well into the nineteenth century (*SP* 5). These visits to his grandparents and the farm, that Stevens later looked back to "the way American literature used to look back to English literature" (*L* 732), continued until he was fifteen, when his grandfather died at the age of eighty-six.

After this, he continued to visit his grandmother, Elizabeth, who, after her husband's death, moved to Ivyland, Pennsylvania, to live with one of her daughters. Stevens "was very proud" of his grandmother, as he stated in a journal entry upon hearing of her death in 1900 (*SP* 70). At this point he had already been away from home for almost three years, having begun Harvard in the fall of 1897. He was quite saddened by the loss, even though she was eighty-nine at the time. He had cared enough for her that as a young man on his own he had not only sent her greetings and gifts on holidays and birthdays but also occasionally made special side trips to visit her on his way between Cambridge and Reading.

Looking at parts of a letter he wrote to his mother from Ivyland, where he spent the summer of 1896, gives both a sense of the woman whose loss he mourned and a glimpse into the household of his aunt Maria Stevens Bennet, Garrett's sister. This household, in a country-cousin way, reflected the same spirit as Wallace's city household in Reading. This is evident in the young man's attention to some of the volumes that helped make up the "furnishings." Also evident in the letter are a meticulous yet expansive descriptiveness and a playfully ironic style that Stevens later developed into the characteristic tones of *Harmonium,* his first volume. Here is the letter:

July 31, 1896

Cuff-Notes.
I have seen the grave of Franklin,
And his good-wife Deborah
I was but six-feet away from him
All the potentates of Europe could get no nearer.
Conclusion: I am as happy as a king.

The piping of flamboyant flutes, the wriggling of shrieking fifes with rasping dagger-voices, the sighing of bass-viols, drums that beat and rattle, the crescendo of cracked trombones—harmonized, that is Innes band [a local band]. Red geraniums, sweet-lyssoms, low, heavy water-lilies and poultry—that is Ivyland. A shade tree, meagre grass, a peaky, waxen house, a zither, several books of poetry, a pleasant room—mine—that is our house. An antique bureau, daguerreotypes of some ancient people, a shoe case, a wash-stand, an ill-fed carpet, a featherbed reaching to my girth, with linen trap-pings, that is my room by day. Gloomy cadaverous shadows, a ha' moon, astride a crowing cock on a gilded weather-vane, a chair which when I attempt to sit upon it moans itself to sleep, a clock—oh that clock—it is a vigilant sentinel of the hours but its alarms are premature and unnerving, every quarter of an hour or so the trembling creature springs with a whirr into its covert among the depths of the springs—that is my room by night.

A Puritan who revels in catechisms and creeds, a hand-to-mouth man, earnest, determined, discreet—Uncle Isaac [Isaac Bennet, married to Maria]. A self-sacrificing, whole-souled woman who says not much but too well—that is Aunt Mariah [the same Maria]. . . .

Gil Blas by Le Sage presented to Emma [the daughter of Maria and Isaac; at the time of this letter, about thirty years old] by her Uncle Garrett Ste-vens [Stevens's father] Xmas 1879, Old Fashioned Roses, Green Fields and Running brooks both by James Whitcomb Riley, Les Miserables by Hugo, Lucille, Symonds "Southern Europe ["], Emerson—these the pith of furnish-ings within excepting a photograph taken in Juneau, Alaska—poor bleak Juneau—it holds a firm of American photographers and lawyers—two evils [a naïvely ironic comment on his later life]—Juneau, Juneau, Amen. A dame upon a bed of auld-farrant marigolds and not a tombstone, as lissome though not as fickle as a maiden of 60 seasons, one whose head is rather dusky but whose face is most expressive, though wrinkled, and whose face would not be wrinkled who has so long bided her time in the bed of the world, a black house-bonnet which sets out an intellectual profile, a careful studied voice, a gait, which totters, that is gran'mother Stevens. . . .

I have exhausted my present resources and must retreat to the horizon of indigence and conjure again an indifferent Muse. Adios!—Papa's "quid" just arrived—most fortunate—many thanks, leave Ivyland at once.

Forever with supernal affection, thy rosy-lipped arch-angelic jeune

WALLACE STEVENS (L 9–10)

This sensitively drawn portrait of a good Puritan family, complete with its eldest member in her "black bonnet," calls attention to the homely, almost religious climate of the Pennsylvania Dutch community that bred Stevens's parents and, to an extent, Stevens himself. For him this background was modified by the changes brought with advancing industrialization and by a different kind of education, but its hold on him never loosened.

This tradition had a tremendously pervasive and lasting influence on those raised in it since it preserved the virtues of industry, sobriety, and thrift, while encouraging a strong sense of individualism. This was and is the underlying motive accounting for the success of the Puritan work ethic. In implicitly generating the struggle for the economic survival of the fittest, this code ensured the growth and development of the still-burgeoning country. Stevens's father, Garrett, provides an excellent example of how this system operated at a time when the young nation was undergoing the changes brought both by the Industrial Revolution and by the influence of Darwinism, with its concomitant questioning of traditional beliefs. Together with these changes came a tentative new faith in science and an attempt to sustain the old morality—previously guarded in a secure religious foundation—with a more enlightened, secularized cultural outlook.[4] But even if there was no mention of God by those participating in and so creating this new tradition, the values and ideals cherished by those who had originally come to found the New Jerusalem were still to be venerated and passed on.

Having grown up in the kind of puritanical atmosphere maintained by his sister, as described above by the sixteen-year-old Wallace, and having an obviously well-developed sense of the individualism nurtured in that atmosphere, Garrett chose early, at fifteen, to leave farm life behind. After finishing his primary and whatever was required of secondary education in Bucks County at the time, he left Feasterville and continued to educate himself to be a teacher. Clearly very motivated and quite intelligent, he was "appointed to his first place when only 17 years of age" (*SP* 6). Then "after three years' experience [he] decided to take up the legal profession" (*SP* 6). It was at this point, in 1870, that Garrett went to Reading. He studied and apprenticed himself as a clerk "in the law office of John S. Richards and was admitted to practice in the Berks [County] courts on August 12, 1872" (*SP* 6). As Wallace Stevens's daughter, Holly Stevens, points out, in noting her grandfather's self-reliance and discipline, the preparation for passing the bar examinations at the time were quite rigorous, requiring, in addition to the expected reading in law and history, the ability "to translate at sight both Latin and Greek" (*SP* 6). And, as she goes on to indicate, "classical languages were not taught in country schools at that time," so he must have either taught himself or had a private tutor. She speculates that it might have been through this tutor, if there was one, that Garrett met his future wife. In any case, it was sometime after beginning his apprenticeship at the law office and before being admitted to the bar that he met Kate, as evidenced by a volume of *The Poetical Works of Alexander Pope* that he presented to her, inscribed with his "Compliments" at Christmas 1871 (*SP* 6).

By this time, shortly before her mother's death in 1872 and already nine years after her father's death, Kate was earning her own income and helping support her mother's household, where some of her seven siblings, too young to work, were still living. A very handsome young woman with both strength and softness suggested in and around her eyes and mouth, Kate, herself obviously quite independent, must have found the young law clerk, who had himself been a schoolteacher, very sympathetic. Equally sensitive to poetry and to making something of himself, he no doubt impressed her as someone to whom she could entrust her spirit as well as her physical well-being. And, as someone having a similar family background as she, Kate could be fairly certain of their fundamental agreement on questions concerning the rearing of whatever children they might have. She could also feel comfortable about maintaining her ties to the religion in which she had been raised, still being a member of the First Presbyterian Church in Reading. Her instincts proved right since she not only remained an active church member throughout her life but also involved her children in the church and fostered a religious consciousness at home. Wallace, for example, was an attendant at Sunday services. He later recalled his mother sitting at their piano, playing and singing hymns on Sundays. He also remembered her reading to him and the other children from the Bible every night (L 173).

With her own sense of self-sufficiency, Kate, in turn, must have been attractive to Garrett, the self-made young man. In addition, descended, as she was on one side, from the same Pennsylvania Dutch stock of farmers as he, she moved as freely among the farmers' wives who sold their produce in Reading as in the bustling life of the city where she worked educating the young. Stevens remembered his mother going to market and talking to these simple women in a kind of rude farmers' German; they commented about the weather and haggled over prices (L 417).

Though feeling a kinship with these rural inhabitants, however, both she and Garrett were—as Stevens noted fairly late in his life, apropos of one of his genealogical searches—already somewhat distanced from the primal communion with the soil of their peasant ancestors. Garrett's family, in spite of their roots in the Pennsylvania farmers' community, gave the impression of being English and had connections with the first Dutch community of settlers in Brooklyn, New York (L 405). To Stevens this seemed to suggest a kind of aristocracy of first settler spirit, which was properly evidenced, in fact, by his grandfather's political involvement.

His mother's family, in turn, having already made the move to an urban environment, had become "bourgeois," as their house, which Stevens later described as such, reflected (L 4). Kate's father had left farming to establish himself as a shoemaker in Reading (someone who *made*, not just repaired shoes as Stevens later noted [L 3–4]). In keeping with the life of a family of a good burgher, it would have been natural for Kate to have had music instruction[5] and training in the manners of a city girl. In her own household she would also provide a bourgeois education for her children. Young Wallace, together with his younger brother, attended first a private kindergarten run by "a French lady" (SP 9); the curriculum included French and German. Following this, they went on to one of the best parochial schools in town, the school attached to St. John's Evangelical Lutheran Church (SP 9).

Kate's tie to a French-German past was more than sentimental. From the information Stevens later uncovered, it appears that the Zeller family descended from one Jacques Selliers, who, with his wife, Clothilde de Reni,[6] left the town of Deux Pontes somewhere near the French-Swiss border to go to England with two of their children, Jean and Jean Henri. In London, just before this Huguenot family was to set out for the New World, Jacques died; Clothilde and her two sons arrived then in 1709 and, after a stop in New York, went to New Paltz and from there, led by Conrad Weiser, to the Lebanon Valley around 1723 (*L* 466). Somewhere along the line the son who was the progenitor of Stevens's mother's family married a Dutch woman. It seems that John Zeller, Kate's father, descended from this parentage; in any case, John was connected to one George Zeller, who, in 1772, was among those who dedicated the Trinity Tulpehocken Church (near Myerstown, Pennsylvania). Its keystone bears the inscription "WER GOTT BERTRAUT HAT WOL ERBAUT (Who trusts in God has built well). G.Z. 1772," which Stevens later had copied and used for bookplates (*L* 541).

John Zeller, Kate's father, was, like his forebears, moved by religious motives. His involvement was both serious and subtle enough to prompt him either to change from one form of Protestantism to another or to rejoin the church after a period of agnosticism. Whichever the case, in 1843 he joined the First Presbyterian Church "by a profession of faith" (*L* 448).[7]

Though Wallace Stevens did not know either of his maternal grandparents, he sensed their spirits from the dour portraits of them that hung in his boyhood house (*L* 399). Moreover, the depth of their attachment to their tradition was passed on to him by his parents. Their daily contact with the life of the community in Reading—at the time still largely German-speaking (*SP* 9)—made this spiritual tie to a cultural and religious past concrete. This was true not only of Kate, who had grown up there, but also of Garrett, who, beyond the immediate involvements connected with his work as a lawyer, became active in local journalism and politics, even coming close to being nominated for the legislature. Garrett had obviously won a place of respect in Reading; by the time of Wallace's birth the warm popularity he enjoyed contributed to his being able to support his family well above the average standard (*SP* 6).

As a young man Wallace felt the family tie to a European past strongly enough so that in a series of letters to Elsie Viola Kachel Moll, his future wife, written in 1909, he identified himself with the simple German peasant stock he had seen depicted in a group of canvases at the Metropolitan Museum of Art in New York:

[January 10, 1909] Sunday Morning
. . . The Germans have sense enough to paint what they like. . . . How many senses the picture touched! I am German to the uttermost. All the exiled ancestors crowded up to my eyes to look at the *Vaterland*—to see those goslings in the water by the fence, the man and woman and baby trudging home through the rainy twilight, the meadows with the meadow

41

trees, the oddities of undeveloped imagination, the infinite humble things. . . .— One would like to understand the Germans. They seem like a nation of peasants. All their qualities seem to be primarily, essentially, peasant qualities. They are as much what they are as the Japanese are; but it is hard to see it distinctly. . . . (L 117–18)

[January 13, 1909] Wednesday Evening
. . . —I hope you were not giving me a beating with your "Dear Germany." I said I was German to the uttermost. Look at my letter, please.— And I am glad.—Peasants are glorious. Think. Who inhabited Arcady? Who inhabited Sicily?—You see the oration I might make.—I do not mean your staring, open-mouthed, poor devils. The cottage has been the youthful ideal of all men. I suppose that by peasant one means cottagers of one kind or another, people who dwell—

> When morn is all aglimmer
> And noon a purple glow
> And evening, full of the linnet's wings. (L 119–20)

And then, a week or so later, in the same vein but prompted by something he had read about contemporary German art, he made his sense of kinship with the Germans even more explicit:

[January 24, 1909] Sunday Evening
. . . You know I am still hammering at them, trying to get the feel of them. Here is a classification of them by [Johann Ludwig] Tieck: "the warlike and pious Bavarians (we have got so many Bavarians at home)—the gentle, thoughtful and imaginative Swabians—the sprightly, gay Franconians—the upright Hessians, the handsome Thuringians—the Low Germans, resembling in true-heartedness the Dutch, in strength and skill the English." The Low Germans, too, are very common at home. True-heartedness surely describes them. I love them, my dear. You must not think that I do nothing but poke fun at them—in spite of Theresa Powdermaker or Antoinette Himmelberger [two inhabitants of Reading].—I feel my kinship, my race. To study them is to realize one's own identity. It is subtly fascinating.—In *Scribner's*, there is a picture of an iron foundry. The mass of machinery, the hot iron, the grimy workmen—I looked at them for a long time, they were so familiar.—There was also a picture of two old women sitting in a field, tending geese. The hard faces full of suffering endured revived the old puzzle: what do old people think?—Only the moderns reflect much on old age. The Greeks shuddered at it. In that respect I am Greek. To live while one is strong—that is enough, I think. No race has ever occupied itself with the realities of life more than the Germans.—I should rather spend a year in Germany than in any other part of Europe, provided, of course, I had facilities for getting into the life and thought of the day— and wandering through villages and smaller towns—. . . (L 127)

By the time he wrote these letters at nearly thirty, other factors—besides remembering his mother's speaking German, the Germanness of Reading, the Lutheran-Calvinist tenets of his religious training, and his own private tutoring in German—had gone into the making of this sense of kinship, of race. Among these other elements was what he had read, especially what he had read of Johann Wolfgang von Goethe's work and life. This interest was additionally bound in an emotional tie to his friend Edwin Stanton ("Livy") Livingood, who, like Stevens, was a Reading native who attended Harvard. Livingood was a Goethe specialist, and Stevens often went to him with questions about Goethe's life and philosophy. Though this later intellectual contribution to Stevens's development will be dealt with more fully later on, it is noted here both because it illustrates how a childhood influence can mature to draw into itself larger themes as an individual grows and moves through life and because it is part of what is one of the single most important elements of Stevens's soil, *reading.*

John Donne playfully yet seriously accounted for his attention to off rhymes like "there-appear" or "meat-get" by saying that as he had suffered throughout his life with the terrible rhyme of his own name, "John-Donne," he could not help picking out those sounds from the names of the things around him.[8] In the same way, the written form of Reading named not only Stevens's home but also the activity that in the most profound sense shaped him. It was natural that reading would play a leading role in the household of two ex-schoolteachers especially because they both had depended so much on independent reading to establish themselves in their professions. Books were like additional family members. As Stevens later recalled, what most characterized the home life of his family was that each member would be "in a different part of the house reading" (*SP* 4) and that it was usual for his father on Sunday afternoons to retire to "the library"—". . . no real institution . . . just a room with some books where you could go and be quiet"—and consume a 500- to 600-page novel (*SP* 8).

There were advantages to this devotion to silent conversation with the spirits of others—the fluent ease Stevens developed in integrating even the most complex philosophical and scientific ideas into his poetry, for example. But there were also disadvantages. Imaginatively discussing subtle perceptions and reactions with physically absent authors too easily took the place of communicating equally subtle feelings and perceptions about the everyday world with those present. Late in his life Stevens was quite open in describing this climate, which he attributed largely to his father's inability to express feelings and needs:

> He wasn't a man given to pushing his way. He needed what all of us need, and what most of us don't get: that is to say, discreet affection. So much depends on ourselves in that respect. I think that he loved to be at the house with us, but he was incapable of lifting a hand to attract any of us, so that, while we loved him as it was natural to do, we also were afraid of him, at

least to the extent of holding off. The result was that he lived alone. The greater part of his life was spent at his office; he wanted quiet and, in that quiet, to create a life of his own. (*L* 454)

Unfortunately, Stevens was never able to escape his father's shade, so that, as Holly Stevens relates, when she was growing up, her father's involvement with books at home was the same as his father's had been (*SP* 4). This was broken only by musical interludes of listening either to recordings or to the New York Philharmonic on weekend radio programs—new ways of spiritually sharing with those absent offered by the technological advances of the twentieth century.

Stevens was aware that the consequences of this way of being were not entirely beneficial. Early in his mature life he noted, in a letter to Elsie Moll sometime during the period of their courtship, that he felt more comfortable, more himself "on paper," declaring himself through silent black ciphers rather than in direct utterance (*L* 80). But he did not or could not work through this perception sufficiently to enable him to change the habits he had learned in his parents' household. The impression of his father as someone reserved, uncomfortable with, and even frowning on shows of affection or emotion was the same impression Stevens was to leave behind. Late in his life, looking back at himself, he sadly noted in "Adagia" (his collection of aphorisms) that "Life is an affair of people not of places. But for me life is an affair of places and that is the trouble" (*OP* 158), especially since the places were largely only imagined.

Though a certain kind of psychological interpreter might hypothesize some kind of trauma in the early lives of either Stevens or his father to account for their extreme reticence to reveal or "to indulge"—as Stevens often put it—feeling, it is more likely that this attitude and the behavior stemming from it were simply aspects of the deep Puritan strain running through the Stevens and Zeller families, a strain that was sustained by the Victorian manners adopted in America during the second half of the nineteenth century. Still unconsciously attempting to prove to their fathers across the ocean that indeed˙ they had founded the New Jerusalem, inheritors of the Puritan tradition were quick to adopt any way of being that would deny animality and sensuous appetites in order to maintain their saintly image—as false as it had been from the very beginning.

Quite contrary to this image—spread abroad from the time of their first arrival—was the brutal reality of the Puritans' lives, which more often than not required them not only to act on feelings but also to recognize their bodily needs as primary, as they lied, cheated, robbed and even killed simply in order to survive in "the wild, the ruinous waste" (*CP* 24) that America was.[9] This serious split between the intended mission and the made reality produced, in turn, an equally serious split between the rhetoric of the accounts of their experience in the New World sent back to the judging fathers left behind in the Old and the truth of that experience.[10] From here began that wished-for projection of promise fulfilled and the requisite self-satisfaction in being "American." Once one arrived here, the myth of finding the promised land had to be believed in if faith in the tradition and the idea of self forged from that tradition were to be maintained.

Stevens's father's generation was probably the last that could avoid looking at this situation squarely. The promise offered by what Stevens later called "the westwardness of everything" (*CP* 455) still hung unpicked in that "heavenly, orchard air" (*CP* 14). And the impact of Charles Darwin's finding our ancestor to be a "hairy quadruped furnished with a tail and pointed ears, probably arboreal in his habits,"[11] had not yet been fully felt. Garrett Stevens, however, reading all the time and subscribing to *Popular Science Monthly*, could not but be affected by the impending changes suggested by the currents of his time. In fact, in this magazine during the year before Wallace's birth appeared a series of six articles by Charles Sanders Peirce that seem to have influenced Garrett's thought. In these pieces Peirce laid out the bases and method of his idiosyncratically American philosophy, which attempted to bridge the gap between the morality of the now-threatened traditional religious doctrines and the new scientific outlook. As part of his practice of "pragmaticism"—so named to distinguish it from William James's "pragmatism," Peirce's original coinage borrowed and used by James—Peirce offered new scientific terms, which he believed were central to founding a new American philosophy. These terms named vague, religious feelings and ideas as well as technical concepts. His doctrine of agapism (evolutionary love) incorporated the notions of tychism (chance) and syncretism (continuity) on which his philosophy was based.[12]

In a letter Garrett later wrote to Wallace just after he had begun his studies at Harvard, he presented for his son's consideration a way of perceiving that outlined the method Peirce had discussed. Comparing an excerpt of this letter with a brief description of Peirce's ideas clearly illustrates this. Dated November 14, 1897, the excerpt follows:

DEAR WALLACE,

. . . I am still concerned about your progress in your study and on that score you seem a trifle reticent—I should like to know whether you feel that you are really improving your power to reach proper conclusions, and educating yourself in discerning that after all the positive knowledge the best have is mighty little. You have discovered I suppose, that the sun is not a ball of fire sending light and Heat—like a stove—but that radiation and reflection is [*sic*] the mystery—and that the higher up we get—and nearer to the sun the colder it gets—and a few old things like that—but you are taught and directed in your studies in a way that you must acknowledge widens your range of vision and upsets your previous notions—teaches you to think—compels you reason—and provides you with positive facts by which you know a conclusion is correct. When this comes to you—you will first begin to absorb and philosophize—and but for eccentricities in your genius you may be fitted for a Chair—Do not be contented with a smattering of all things—be strong in something.

Yours as ever
GARRETT
(L 16)

Remarkable here is the closeness of Garrett's layman's description of the function and power of reason to Peirce's, outlined by John E. Smith, who notes Peirce's particular contribution in the following:

> The chief value of Peirce's insistence that we pay attention to genuine doubt and to the actual conflict of ideas within the individual consciousness lies in its forcing us to consider the role of thought in living experience. In its critical or reflective form, thought comes into play in response to certain demands of life and its success or failure comes to be estimated in terms of human needs. Were habitual action always effective in every way and were the circumstances of life such that they never contradicted our ideas or thwarted our plans, inquiry would probably never take place. For under such ideal conditions doubt would not exist and there would be no goad to inquiry. But as it happens in actual experience, our ideas are contradicted and our purposes often come to naught; many of our beliefs are false and our plans misguided. If this is so and if our rational faculty is called into play on those occasions when old beliefs and habits let us down, our reason must have practical business in our life. Instead of a power which is exhausted in the contemplation of things, it is a means of transforming them. [13]

In Garrett's letter the order in which he presented "his" ideas follows that of Peirce. In the example using the sun—most interesting in light of his son's preoccupation with the images of the sun and the cold north in his poetry—Garrett illustrated Peirce's stress on the importance of doubt and of having our habitual notions upset. And in noting that reason provides the "positive facts" by which a correct conclusion is known, Garrett focused on using reason as an empirical tool having practical value. This aspect is the keystone of Peirce's thought, in which it is "the *empirical method* which gives the answer." [14] The last sentence above, describing Peirce's understanding of reason, could just as easily describe how Stevens later used reason in his poetry: "Instead of a power which is exhausted in the contemplation of things, it is a means of transforming them."

Whether or not Garrett internalized these ideas from reading Peirce, they were representative of the pragmatic spirit of his age. In this atmosphere young Wallace grew up. Charged both with the rigorous religious tradition that had led his forebears to see themselves as the elect on whose survival the founding of the New Jerusalem depended and with the new scientific theory of the biological survival of the fittest, the "arch-angelic jeune" competed

46

strongly, first within his immediate family with his brothers and later with his peers, always urged on by his father "to use tooth and nail" and "to make something of [him]self"—perhaps even "a President" (*SP* 17). This same, though possibly largely unconscious, competitiveness also contributed to Stevens's reaching the heights where his private "pantheon" of "man-poets"— Homer, John Milton, William Shakespeare, John Keats, Robert Browning, Alfred Lord Tennyson, Dante Alighieri (*L* 26)—sat smiling.

?●

Largely because of the difference in age between Wallace, his brothers and their sisters, Wallace was closest to Garrett, Jr., and John. From what Holly Stevens records, it appears that her father and his brothers were typical boys. She relates the following incidents, one of which provided a memory that contributed to one of the enticingly obscure poems of *Harmonium.*

The first adventure she notes took place at Grandfather Benjamin's farm in Feasterville, where on discovering "an old musket in the attic [Wallace and his brothers] paraded around with it recklessly, much to the dismay of their grandmother and a visiting cousin" (*SP* 8–9). Then there was, again from Holly, another "story about the Stevens boys [which] relates that when a steeple was being erected on a nearby church, they used to climb up and hide in the scaffolding. They would sit there, chewing tobacco, and at an opportune moment, often when a prominent citizen was passing below, would expectorate. According to the story they were never caught. And, like all boys, they stole fruit from a neighbor's tree; when discovered, they called out as they ran away, 'God helps those who help themselves!'" (*SP* 9).

The last prank Holly reports involves Wallace—or, as he was known, Pat—alone. "When a streetlight on North Fifth Street shone in a neighbor's window, who then painted it green to reduce the glare, Pat would steal out at night, shinny up the pole, and scrape the paint off, thus awakening the neighbor who would paint it again the next day" (*SP* 9). Later in his life, when he was in his mid-thirties, Stevens titled a playful but cryptic poem, "Disillusionment of Ten O'Clock":

> The houses are haunted
> By white night-gowns.
> None are green,
>
> . . . .
> None of them are strange,
>
> . . . .
> People are not going
> To dream of baboons and periwinkles.
> (*CP* 66)

Here the poet combined a recollection of his early childhood power to disturb people's soothing, green-lit dreams by making them flit around in white nightgowns, drawing shades and shaking fists, with a later image of ladies in nightgowns moving around their rooms at night while he observed them from his window across a New York brownstone courtyard (L 68). These memories fused with his night thoughts into a poem that would equally disturb other people's dreams. Seeing this transformation gives a sense of Stevens's ability to translate his juvenile joy into the mature "pleasure" he felt had to be an integral part of poetry that could be a "Supreme Fiction," poetry that could be believed in willingly and so help people live their lives.

This idea of poetry as a force that could help people live their lives, a central notion for Stevens, also had its roots in the intellectual soil of his boyhood, soil well cultivated by his father. One of Garrett's first gifts to his future wife, it will be remembered, was a volume of poetry (Alexander Pope's); among the books that the young Wallace noticed as part of the "furnishings" of his aunt's house was another volume presented by Garrett to his then-adolescent niece—this was a romance, a "fiction," *Gil Blas*. In addition to these evidences of his father's interest in what Stevens later called the poetical was another volume, his "father's copy of Burns' poems" (L 102), which the poet never left behind as he moved from one place to another as a young man. More, Garrett himself wrote poetry, though he was of too "practical" a nature—as his son described—to allow himself to regard it as more than an "afflatus" (L 23), since writing poetry was not the kind of work that was in keeping with the Puritan ethic.

Desiring that each of his sons would do well, "just a little slicker" than the "other fellow" (L 24), Garrett tried assiduously to deflate Wallace's literary ambitions. He was slightly more willing, however, to accept journalism as a career since it was a field in which one could earn a living while making a name for oneself. But he was ambivalent enough to reveal his implicit trust in the power of poetry, of "romance," to his son. This is obvious in the contrasting suggestions made in some of the letters he wrote to Wallace at Cambridge—in one written on September 27, 1897, for example, only a few weeks after Wallace had left Reading for Harvard for the first time. Just after a curiously prophetic remark apropos of imagining Wallace in his new environment, Garrett went on to modify his sense of what was "practical" for his son:

> And midst these environments I am content you shall dwell. You will see about Cambridge some nook perhaps seen by the eyes of those to whose greatness the world yielded niggardly homage then and who moved on to describe some other cloister in the words that never die. And who knows but bringing to its description your power of painting pictures in words you make it famous—and some Yankee old maid will say—it was here that Stevens stood and saw the road to distinction.
>
> A little romance is essential to ecstasy. We are all selfish—Self Denial doesn't seem to be a good thing excepting in others—the world holds an unoccupied niche only for those who climb up—work and study, study and work—are worth a decade of dreams—and romantic notions—but I do not

believe in being so thoroughly practical that what is beautiful, what is artistic—what is delicate or what is grand—must always be deferred to what is useful. And there is no better exercise than an effort to do our best to appreciate and describe to others the beauties of those things which are denied to the vision of the absent. . . .

Point in all this screed—Paint truth but not always in drab clothes. Catch the reflected sun-rays, get pleasurable emotions—instead of stings and tears. (L 14–15)

But by spring of 1899, when it had become clear that Wallace had taken this early urging to paint pictures in words seriously, there came a letter severely checking the young poet's impulses. There was also a suggestion that Wallace himself was developing a kind of ambivalence about the "afflatus" since, as his father indicated, he was now addressing poems he wrote only to his mother—not to Garrett or to both of them, as he had done in the past. The passage quoted here, from the letter dated February 9, 1899, follows Garrett's mentioning that business had not been going well and that he was in debt—a situation which may have contributed to his renewed stress on the practical: "I shall be glad to hear from you—I am convinced from the Poetry (?) you write your Mother that the afflatus is not serious—and does not interfere with some real hard work" (L 23). And in a letter written a few months later (May 21, 1899)—which is remarkable in illustrating Garrett's own delight in words and wordplay—came another admonition, following some rather ironically faint praise for Wallace's having been elected to the Signet Club at Harvard:

DEAR WALLACE

Just what the election to the *Signet signi*fies I have no *sign*. It is *signi*ficant that your letter is a *sign*al to *sign* another check that you may *sigh* no more. I suppose you thus win the privilege to wear a seal ring or a badge with the picture of a *Cygn*et on it—to distinguish you from commoner geese, or it may be you can con*sign* all studies de*sign*ed to cause re*sign*ation, to some as-*sign*ed port where they will trouble you no more.

You will know more about it when you have ridden the goat of initiation, and kneaded the dough enclosed.

Keep hammering at your real work however my boy—for a fellow never knows what's in store—and time mis-spent now counts heavily. (L 26)

What had happened to effect Garrett's unequivocal dissuasion of his son's interest in poetry isn't known. Perhaps it was a result of his personal, negative judgment of Wallace's early poems. Perhaps it was the change for the worse in his and in the general economic situation that made him increasingly attentive to the harsher realities of life and eventually brought him to a nervous collapse. Or perhaps it was an inadmissible jealousy of his son's realizing a possibility that he had never fully allowed himself, coupled with a natural and quite common desire to make his sons in his own image—as, in fact, he succeeded in doing, at least on the surface, for all three became, like him, practicing lawyers. And Wallace, also like him, continued writing poetry "on the side," though that side grew to be at least half his being, even if it was hidden like the dark side of the moon he was so drawn to imagining.

In addition to the very strong influence exerted on him by his father, there were other personal promptings as well as a number of accidental factors that were important elements of Stevens's soil. From his mother he felt he had gotten "imagination" (*SP* 8). He remembered being lulled by the melody and rhythm of her voice into a half-dream state as she read from the Bible to him and his siblings every evening. Later, as a law student in New York, he found himself lingering in the public library on weekday evenings, "brushing up" on the Bible stories he had completed as a child with his slumbering images. He remembered that as she sat at the piano on Sundays, playing accompaniments to the hymns she sang with ease, she looked into an unseeable distance with an abstracted, faraway look in her eyes. Years later, his poetical counterpart, Peter Quince, sitting at his clavier, similarly moved from his playing into an imagined biblical world where Susanna bathed, watched by the "elders" (see *CP* 89).

Wallace also learned from Kate certain "indulgent" habits that stayed with him throughout his life. Like his mother, who, when he was very young, used to go periodically from Reading to New York to shop (*L* 126), Stevens made fairly regular day trips to New York from Hartford, Connecticut, where he eventually settled. Besides the expected visits to bookstores like Scribner's on Fifth Avenue or to the Gramophone Shop for new and rare recordings,[15] he visited Dean's bakery to buy peach pies and plum cakes. He stopped in as well at an exclusive vintner's to buy a rare Meursault or other wines he had read of or tasted. Then, returning to Hartford, where he occasionally made a meal only of one of the desserts he had bought, he re-created his childhood delight in eating the sweets his mother had brought him from New York. This taste for the "good things in life" was obviously not part of the Puritan aspect of his mother's background, though it did belong to the desire to escape provincialism belonging to the upwardly mobile "bourgeois" experience of a family, like hers, that had already made the move from the farm to the city. These values were reinforced in Stevens's personal experience by his father's desire to have his children have a better education and so a broader horizon than he had had. For Stevens this meant the years spent at Harvard. There he was exposed to new, refined pleasures both through contact with individuals of a certain class and through reading more and more European and English literature—especially of the late eighteenth and nineteenth centuries, with its evocations of salons and drawing rooms and the manners appropriate to them.

Stepping out of one of the imagined rooms and into the living room at North Fifth Street was one of Wallace's uncles, James Van Sant Stevens. This older brother of Garrett's was a bachelor whom Stevens fondly remembered speaking French, smoking big cigars, and being very free with the money in his pockets (*L* 126). Unlike his sister—Stevens's Aunt Mariah—he had obviously cut his ties to the family's puritanical past. An art dealer or agent of some kind (*L* 126), with cosmopolitan ways, this uncle seems to have played a leading part in Stevens's interior life. His shade appears in more than one poem, in "Le Monocle de *Mon Oncle*" (italics mine; *CP* 13) and as the evoked addressee of "The Emperor of Ice-Cream" ("Call the roller of big cigars . . ." [*CP* 64]), for example, though both these personae reverberated with others' voices as well. It is also not unlikely that Stevens's fascination with French— originally inspired, perhaps, because of his early tutelage (as Holly Stevens observes [*SP* 9])—was tied up with this figure, just as it is quite likely that his youthful desires both to go to Paris after college (which his father strongly advised him against) and to remain a bachelor himself represented an identification with this uncle. This identification seems to have remained with Stevens throughout his life, showing itself in his later interest in collecting art and contributing to his perception of French and English as a single language (*OP* 178). The admired individual who spoke both French and English presented them to the child as a unity, a function of his own singularity. Stevens's fastidious attention to his dress and habits also seemed to mimic the image of his dandylike uncle.

In the same letter in which Stevens described this uncle and other pleasurable childhood memories is the brief account of the death of his aunt Emmy Schmucker, who had been a repository of stories about Wallace's "rowdy" behavior as a boy. Stevens's recollection of her, coming after the evocation of so many experiences that represented "indulgences" of one kind or another, gives the letter the peculiar effect of a homily. He recorded how Aunt Emmy—very unpuritanically—adored eating and that the occasion of her final illness and death had been the unrestrained consumption of some of her best-loved delicacies. On her deathbed she asked to see Wallace, who had always been one of her favorites. He came, she kissed him, he her, and then said, "Good-bye." Probably Stevens's first direct experience of the death of an adult (two, possibly three children borne by Kate died as infants during Stevens's boyhood; see Note 2 to this chapter), it must have left a deep and lasting impression. This memory seems to have associated itself with the later experiences of his grandmother's and mother's deaths; combined with the images of his cigar-smoking uncle, these residues seem to have produced a kind of prototype for the curious contradictions suggested in "The Emperor of Ice-Cream"—a poem in which the consequences of overindulging in pleasures like ice cream are drummed home by the rhythm of lines describing the death of an old woman:

> Call the roller of big cigars,
> The muscular one, and bid him whip
> In kitchen cups concupiscent curds.
> Let the wenches dawdle in such dress
> As they are used to wear, and let the boys

Bring flowers in last month's newspapers.
Let be be finale of seem.
The only emperor is the emperor of ice-cream.

Take from the dresser of deal
Lacking the three glass knobs, that sheet
On which she embroidered fantails once
And spread it so as to cover her face.
If her horny feet protrude, they come
To show how cold she is, and dumb.
Let the lamp affix its beam.
The only emperor is the emperor of ice-cream.

(*CP* 64)

Stevens, in his thirties when he wrote this poem, had not yet eluded his Puritan conscience.

Perhaps most important as Stevens approached maturity were the evolving relationship between him and his brothers and the effect that the closeness of this relationship had on his feelings for young women. As a result of the age difference separating him from his sisters and of his having attended boys' schools, Stevens often felt uncomfortable with girls. At fifteen, away on summer holiday, he clothed this disquietude in a descriptive attack in a letter to his mother: "—I hate *ladies* (such as are here) [.] [They] are all agreeable enough but familiarity breeds contempt—poor deluded females—they are contemptible without familiarity" (*L* 5). Only after a few weeks, however, familiarity proved not to have bred contempt but to have gotten him into "the very best graces with the girls" (*L* 7). Later in his life, recalling experiences at high school (where the girls were segregated from the boys), he wrote: "I . . . never knew any of the girls belonging to the class [his year]. Well, perhaps I did; but they do not come back to me now" (*L* 126). At Harvard—another all-male institution—this ambivalence about the opposite sex was mirrored in certain curious, though charmingly poignant, incidents involving his relationships, or absence of relationships, with different women. (These will be discussed in the next chapter.)

But even before becoming aware of his discomfort with females, Stevens had begun to experience another kind of ambivalence as he approached adolescence. Being between his brothers in age gave him the feeling of moving "up and down between two elements" (*CP* 35). This sense later set the tone and theme of much of his poetry. It was as though being in the middle became a feeling Stevens could never entirely escape, even though he went well beyond it in reality, eventually surpassing both his brothers in school, in professional life, and, ultimately, in leaving his name behind in history. In connection with this, Wallace was the only one of his parents' children not named for a family member; he was named for a politician of the time, Wallace DeLaMater (*SP* 7). It was almost as though the drive to make his place in the world came from a desire to establish his nominal legitimacy in and for his family, though his motivation to succeed actually derived from a combination of many factors, among them the family's inherited Puritan attitude and his father's particular urgings, described earlier. In addition, his place between his brothers accentuated natural competitiveness and made the pervasive survival of the fittest spirit part of Wallace's immediate experience. Reinforcing it even more were one or two "accidental" situations involved with his getting ahead in school.

The first was an unusual change of schools for Wallace while he was still attending primary school. For one full academic year he was sent away to a parochial school attached to St. Paul's Lutheran Church in the Williamsburg section of Brooklyn, a church where his uncle was pastor (*SP* 9–10). The circumstances of this year away from home remain vague. Whether his brothers were also sent away, whether it was because he had had, just before that time, a fall from his velocipede that had injured his back and forced him to miss school (*L* 126) and so was sent away to catch up—these details are not known. Whatever the case, however, this early dislocation had to have left its mark on the boy.

The second "accident" occurred after Wallace's first year at Reading Boys' School, where he was enrolled in September 1892. As Holly Stevens notes, Wallace's average at the end of that year was 5.88 (out of a possible 10), but the minimum average required to pass into the next year was 6.50 (*SP* 10). Whatever the reasons for his being left back—whether it was at this time rather than earlier that Wallace had his cycling accident and so had to remain out of school; whether it was because he had been ill too long with malaria; or whether it was because he hadn't, as he later noted in a letter to a friend, studied enough because of "too many nights out" (*SP* 10)—the result was that the following year, 1893–94, he found himself in the same class with his younger brother, John.

The curriculum at Reading Boys' School was classical and demanding; it included Latin, Greek, English classics, analytical grammar and composition, physical geography, and the history of Greece as well as algebra and arithmetic.[16] And now, competing with John so as not to lose face, Stevens applied himself to his studies quite diligently. This application was to have far-reaching effects beyond the immediately desired one of getting ahead of his brother. After this year Wallace made the honor roll in two of his courses, the history of Greece and physical geography (*SP* 10)—both areas where his imagination resided for years afterward. During the next year, 1894–95, Wallace's class rating was 8.37, John running close behind with 7.93. Only one student had a higher rating; by the end of the year that student had made the honor roll without either Wallace or John as companions. Wallace, however, had compensated by broadening himself by working on the editorial staff of the first newspaper ever issued at the school, *Dots and Dashes* (begun by his older brother Garrett's class). At the end of this year Garrett—who had also not made the honor roll, but was his class's president—was graduated to go on in the fall to Yale (where he would last only four months; he later continued at a less prestigious school). Holly Stevens notes that after Garrett's leaving for college the competition between Wallace and John grew even more intense (*SP* 12).

During that third year together, 1895–96, perhaps because of too much "lampoon[ing] [of] Dido's tear-stained adventures in the caves, [too many] enigmatic couplets to gazelles" (*SP* 11), and too little completed homework, Wallace lost his edge over John. "At the end of the second term, in March, John had been ranked second in the class and Pat [Wallace] third" (*SP* 11). Nonetheless, they both were obviously doing well; "only the ubiquitous Erle Meredith, who always came in first, was ahead of them" (*SP* 11). At this point, not to be daunted, Wallace entered and won a competition sponsored by a local newspaper, the *Reading Eagle,* for the best essay written under supervision on a particular subject given at the time of the writing (*SP* 11). The prizes were two books, which Stevens never discarded, and a nascent confidence in his rhetorical skills, gleaned from the Greek and Roman authors he had studied. These skills would sustain him both in the near future and throughout his life.

A few months later, during his last year, in December 1896, on the occasion of "Alumni Night" at his school, Wallace again exercised his rhetorical gift. This time he delivered an oration and once again competed for a prize.[17] The topic he chose (over "My Hero") was "The Greatest Need of the Age." Echoing his father's self-made man morality and the language and cadence of his mother's Bible reading, the young man elaborated on opportunity's being the "greatest need"; he did very well. The judges unanimously awarded him the prize—a medal—and the boys in the audience applauded and cheered him loudly, as they would only a favorite (*SP* 12; *Reading Eagle,* December 23, 1896, p. 5). Six months later, at his graduation, Wallace delivered another oration, this one entitled "The Thessalians." Once more the newspaper report reinforced the praise he received stating that "he spoke as though he were a veteran speaker," that his sentiments were "patriotic," and that he was "rewarded with loud acclamation" (*SP* 12; *Reading Eagle,* June 24, 1897).

Woven into these speeches were ideas and sentiments that the young Stevens had internalized from those who had most influenced him at school as well as at home. At school it was Martin E. Scheibner (affectionately referred to by Stevens and the other students as "Skib"), the principal who guided the boys as well as his faculty with his vision of imbuing all aspects of life with the spirit of the classics while preserving a tone of levity and playfulness. Holly Stevens records this recollection of the widow of Stevens's friend, Edwin ("Ned") de Turck Bechtel:

> Whenever Ned met Wallace Stevens, the poet, who had been a class ahead of him, they told uproarious tales of Skib's treatment of stupid pupils. . . . [Skib was a] teacher of Greek, Latin and Moral Philosophy. Ned wrote of him: "He was an imaginative, well-educated Russian nobleman, who had

fled because of some political offense against the Czarist regime. He cajoled us into translating Homer and Virgil at sight, and in his enthusiasm introduced us to other classic authors." (*SP* 11)

Holly Stevens also notes that in the memorial note on her father in the *Century Association Yearbook* for 1956, Scheibner is mentioned as having "had a lasting influence on Stevens" (*SP* 11). This influence strengthened that of Stevens's father in reflecting at least one very important aspect of the spirit of the age. This enlightened late-Victorian spirit looked back to the classical world in order to retrieve what Matthew Arnold called the "Hellenic" sense that the Renaissance had attempted to resurrect but that had been superseded by the puritanical "Hebraic" sense focused on "doing" to prove oneself to be one of the "elect." The "Hellenic" sense was directed rather to contemplation, "to see[ing] things as they really are."[18] Stevens sympathized with the "Hellenic" spirit. Later, for example, in his "Adagia," he wrote that Greek mythology was the best of all mythologies. But he had taken on as well the "Hebraic" desire "to do" from his Protestant forebears. His response to the "Hellenic" aspect also echoed his father's interest in the developments of his time. Assuredly Garrett had heard or read of Arnold's American lectures. These the English man of letters delivered as he traveled along the East Coast in 1883 and 1884, when Wallace was still a young boy.

In contrast with the more popular millennial desire for renewed vigilance and faith displayed in performing acts that would prove one's purity, Arnold suggested a return to what was considered a pagan attitude by the inheritors of the Puritan tradition. One raised as Stevens had been—within this tradition but with the modifications resulting from his father's more enlightened attitude as well as by the classical education received at Reading Boys' School—would be sensitive to the tension between the two elements: the one carefully cultivated in the soil where he had grown up and the other quietly speaking through those like Arnold.

Though this tension was not yet strongly felt in the seventeen-year-old young man, its seeds had been planted. Within a year of his leaving home and going to Harvard—with the changes brought by the emotional distance from his "good Puritan" background and the additional complications of spirit coming from more reading and exposure to other well-developed minds— Stevens had already begun the internal voyage of discovery that he later evoked with ironic, if not emotional, distance in "The Comedian as the Letter C" (*CP* 27). In 1909, writing to his future wife shortly before their marriage—when he tried to expose as much of himself "on paper" as he could, before having to in his person—Stevens noted the change in his life that Harvard brought: "My first year away from home, at Cambridge, made an enormous difference in everything" (*L* 126). The boy who had been one of the "rowdies" in Reading, playing poker and football, "hop[ping] coal trains to ride up the Lebanon Valley—[and] steal[ing] pumpkins and so on—with a really tough crowd," (*L* 125) now, as a "special student," joined the intellectually "tough crowd" at Harvard. The boy who had worn "patent leather pumps with silver buckles on 'em" to go to Sunday school and "listen to old Mrs. Keeley [weep] with joy over every pap in the Bible," the boy who had sat "back of the organ and watch[ed] the pump-handle go up and down" (*L* 125) now spent Sundays listening to instructors and friends express their thoughts about Goethe, the English poets, philosophy as religion or sat in his room strumming his guitar. The tanned boy who had swum for hours before lying to rest and muse "on the stone walls of the canal" (*L* 125) while looking up at the sky now walked the streets and squares of Cambridge for hours, musing on "art for art's sake" and the compatibility of "Poetry and Manhood" (*L* 24 and 26). The young man who had taken all the prizes for his rhetorical skills was going to Harvard "to be a writer" (*L* 13). The "whimsical, unpredictable young enthusiast" (*SP* 11) of Reading Boys' School was on his way to becoming the "Comedian."

II
THE HARVARD MAN
1897–1900

To make reason and the will
of God prevail!

—Bishop [Thomas] Wilson, [Sr.],
quoted by Matthew Arnold
in *Culture and Anarchy*

To me, the accumulation of lives at a university has seemed to be a subject that might disclose something extraordinary. What is the residual effect of the years we spend at a university, the years of imaginative life, if ever in our lives there are such years, on the social form of our own future and on the social form of the world of which we are part, when compared with the effects of our later economic and political years?

—From "Imagination as Value,"
The Necessary Angel (p. 146)

In September 1897 Stevens began Harvard as a "special student." This meant that although he formally belonged to the class of 1901, he was graduated after three years and while in attendance chose his courses freely. He qualified for this status both academically and financially. His father had three sons in college; the economic burden was relieved by Wallace's attending for three instead of four years. Again, set somehow apart—distinguished now by his promised abilities but also by a leaner purse than that of some of his patrician peers—the young Stevens maintained the diligent, competitive habits he had learned to cultivate during his three years at high school in class with his brother John. By the end of John's first year at the University of Pennsylvania, he edgily expressed jealous resentment about his lesser college choice and Wallace's more successful performance (*SP* 13). At the end of his first year Wallace had done well in all his courses: A's in English rhetoric and composition, the history and development of English literature in outline, and French prose and composition; B's in constitutional government, leading principles of constitutional law (selected cases, English and American), and medieval and modern European history; and a B − in German grammar, composition, and translation and reading at sight, selections in prose and poetry (*L* 23).

Reflected in this "free" choice of courses were both the wishes of the young man who wanted to be a writer and the wishes of the young man's father, who was sending him to Harvard "to make something" of himself. Over the next three years these two strains intensified those already sounded during his childhood and early youth. The feeling he had had of being between his brothers translated into a more general sense. He expressed it as moving between "imagination" and "reality." This eventually became the poet's central theme. Its first notes were struck as the young man began questioning himself and searching out the parts of his nature. He believed he had gotten his "imagination" from his mother and his "practical" sense of reality

59

from his father (*SP* 8), who "always seem[ed] to have reason on his side, confound him!" (*L* 53).

At college, "imagination" announced itself in his enrolling in language and literature courses and in transmuting what he learned into poems he wrote and sent home to his mother. His "reality principle," on the other hand, expressed itself in his taking courses in constitutional government and law, for which his father gave him unqualified praise, while he half joked about its being good preparation for one who "one day [was] to be President" (*SP* 17). By the end of this first year at Harvard Stevens had made his first attempt to resolve these two strains into one theme by planning a career in journalism. In that way he could combine his "power for painting pictures in words" with the practical "first, foremost law" (*CP* 17) of making a living.

In the interim, his movement up and down between the two elements continued, though the young man found an "anchorage of thought" (*L* 27) in the various contacts he made and in the books he read. These resting places provided Stevens with the implicit approval he needed to begin seriously "in-dulging"—as he put it on more than one occasion—his "need for poetry." These influences supplanted his father's guiding role and so allowed the young man to take the first major step in "bring[ing the] world quite round" (*CP* 165) that occasioned his later remark that the years in Cambridge had "made an enormous difference in everything." Stevens developed for Harvard and what it meant (*L* 44) a deep devotion that lasted until he died. What Harvard meant during the last years of the nineteenth century was best represented by the pursuits of the people there. While parts of the country were still being wrested from the Indians[1] and parts of the planet remained unexplored, those whom the young Stevens followed were preoccupied with less "practical" matters.

George Santayana was pursuing truth through the caverns of poetry and religion, while William James was attempting to separate the darkness of mysticism and religion from the light of everyday experience with his "prag-matic" way. Charles Eliot Norton was giving courses on Dante, while Plato's shade spoke again at the meetings of the Jowett Club.[2] A brisk walk away was Ernest Fenollosa's collection, which had spurred America's interest in the Ori-ent; before Stevens left Cambridge, Fenollosa (who had lived in Boston, mak-ing notes, lecturing, and cataloging from 1886 to 1892) returned to America from the East and made this interest even stronger with his series of lectures on the collection and on Chinese and Japanese art in general.[3]

For Stevens and his generation, these figures were like waves of influence that broke into the more visible foam of everyday conversations with contem-poraries and instructors. Thus "what Harvard meant" was not confined to formal lectures. Intellectual exchange permeated even the homeliest activities. Because of this, associations developed between ideas and commonplaces. Thinking about the most exalted realms became fixed in lasting memories of lived experience. For example, although Stevens never had a formal course with Santayana, a close friend of his was one of the philosopher's students.

One day, when Stevens was packing up to leave Cambridge, this friend spent the time with him reading class notes from Santayana's course in aesthetics that year (*SP* 71). Through this and other contacts (Pierre LaRose, for instance, one of Stevens's first-year instructors, faculty advisor to the Signet Club [of which Stevens later became a member], and a close friend of Santayana's [*SP* 17]), Stevens came to be on familiar, even intimate terms with Santayana. He often visited him in his rooms, where they discussed poetry and the function of religious belief. Eventually they exchanged sonnets on the subject.[4] Similarly, though Stevens did not attend Charles Eliot Norton's classes on Dante, Russell Loines, another friend and housemate, did. Together on long walks, they spoke about poetry, about the Middle Ages, about Dante—the "Comedian." And so, though Stevens did not participate in Norton's class, he read *La Vita Nuova* and *Divine Comedy* on his own with ease.

There was also a network of contacts which centered in the Misses Parsons' boardinghouse at 54 Garden Street, where Stevens (who had not "made it" into any of the social clubs) spent his three years in Cambridge. These contacts were not just literary. Besides Loines, who, though "very much of a poet" when Stevens knew him,[5] later went to law school and became a lawyer, prefiguring the path Stevens himself would take (ironically, he moved into Loines's attic room after he left), there were two classmates of Stevens's. One was Arthur Pope, "who later became chairman of the art department at Harvard and director of the Fogg Museum,"[6] and the other was "Harold Hastings Flower who [also] became a lawyer" (*SP* 13). In addition, there were various other undergraduates as well as graduate students and some young instructors (*SP* 13). The community was a close one, and out of it grew relationships that Stevens maintained throughout his life. Beyond the intellectual companionship and stimulation, the young poet also received emotional support for his imagination's indulgences. This is apparent in one of Arthur Pope's reminiscences of Stevens, recorded by Holly Stevens: "I recall especially his bursting out of his room to recite a new combination of words or a new metaphor that he had just invented, and to show his delight which was most infectious" (*SP* 15). It was, in part, because of this receptivity to his poetic activities and the encouragement he got from Loines (*SP* 16 and 163) and others that Stevens felt confident enough to begin sending out some of his early work for publication.

As though announcing himself as a poet to those back home, he sent one of these early poems to a magazine, *The Red and Black,* "established the previous autumn at Reading Boys' High School" (*SP* 16). As Holly Stevens notes, the January 1898 issue led off with "Autumn," Stevens's first-known published piece (*SP* 16):

> Long lines of coral light
> And evening star,
> One shade that leads the night
> On from afar.

And I keep, sorrowing,
This sunless zone,
Waiting and resting here,
In calm above.[7]

Just as Stevens was revealing his preoccupations to his new crowd, so they were sharing their interests with him. Arthur Pope's involvement with art stimulated Stevens's own. Together they no doubt commented on pieces Fenollosa had gathered for the Oriental Collection at the Boston Museum of Fine Arts. This interest also provided subjects for conversation with Witter Bynner and Arthur Davison Ficke, who were also at Harvard at the time and both deeply immersed in discovering as much as they could about the art and literature of China and Japan. Pursuing his interest, eventually Bynner made two extended visits to the Orient: to Japan and China in 1917, and to China for almost a year in 1921.[8] Later he collaborated on translations of the work of Lao-tzu and of a major Chinese anthology, published under the title of *The Jade Mountain* (*A Chinese Anthology, Being Three Hundred Poems of the T'ang Dynasty, 618-906* [1929]). This edition, with its introduction by Bynner and his Chinese co-worker, had a remarkably profound effect on Stevens. But this would not become fully apparent until nearly the end of his life with the publication of his *Collected Poems*.

The enthusiasm about the Orient at Harvard during this period was prompted by both political and cultural developments. There were the regular reports of the situation that culminated in the Boxer Rebellion. And there was the scholarly interest in F. Max Müller's translations of Sanskrit texts and editions of Japanese Buddhist works. Stevens later referred to Müller as the foremost Orientalist of the day (L 381) and indicated that he had shared the interest in his work. As a student of Friedrich Schelling and Arthur Schopenhauer and translator of Immanuel Kant, Müller applied what he had learned from them—especially what he had absorbed about the root meanings of words—to his philological investigations of Sanskrit and Pali. As a result, in his speculative writing, in his *Science of Thought*, for example, he postulated a purely linguistic basis for any future philosophy. He grounded this on his scientific findings concerning the origins of language as well as on the historical evidence of the early Greek philosophers, who, in their study of Logos made no separation between language and thought.[9] Stevens, in the same letter in which he mentioned Müller—written during a period when he was again actively engaged in studying the Orient (late thirties and early forties)— commented that "in those days [he] read everything [he] could get [his] hands on." It is most likely, then, that it was through Müller's work that Stevens was introduced to Oriental religion and philosophy, to the *Sacred Books of the East,* and even, perhaps, to Schopenhauer, whom he read later, in 1905, though Santayana, or his own curiosity, could just as easily have led him there. These combined influences eventually prompted Stevens to translate into his mature work the basic tenet expressed by Müller as his epigraph to

Science of Thought: "No Reason without Language, No Language without Reason." While integrating this, however, Stevens preserved the knowledge gleaned through Kant and Hegel about the limitation of reason and language in apprehending reality as later expressed in different ways by both James and Santayana. Accepting this limitation and still believing language to be the only possible access to truth ultimately produced in Stevens the desire to make poetry that would be both religious—in fostering the acceptance of limitation—and philosophical—in expressing whatever could be known of truth. This desire began to take distinct shape during this period at Cambridge when he read Matthew Arnold. From him Stevens learned to consider the Hellenic ideal of contemplation to be as important as the puritanically Hebraic "doing" that his father stressed the more Wallace indulged "the pleasures of merely circulating" (*CP* 149) in his mind.

The university and the surrounding atmosphere, with its collection of faculty and students, functioned as a surrogate parent for the young Stevens. This enlightened parent permitted him to "find himself" by rebelling, at least to a certain degree, against the overly practical voice of his real father. That this displacement occurred raises some subtle and interesting points about the place of the university, particularly the oldest university in America, in the life of the community. Garrett Stevens could be quite happy that Wallace was at Harvard. The university would expose the young man to the best possible range of "liberal" ideas, from which he could choose those that would enable him to live his life well. But either it would also ensure that these ideas remained in the realm of theory—if they were *too* liberal—or it would direct them to their practical application in a career in business, law, medicine, or an equally staid and serious profession.

Stevens sensed both these seemingly contradictory aspects while he was still at Harvard. In connection with an observation about a college friend, Stevens noted in his journal: ". . . Harvard feeds subjectivity, encourages an all consuming flame + that, in my mind, is an evil in so impersonal a world. Personality must be kept secret before the world. Between lovers and the like personality is well-enough; so with poets + old men etc. + conquerors + lambs etc.; but for young men etc. it is most decidedly a well-enough to be left alone" (*L* 44). However, in another note, made in the margin of a copy of Samuel Johnson's *Rambler,* next to the July 9, 1751, entry (*SP* 41), he commented: "The Harvard system keeps one closer to the aims of life and therefore to life itself. But in many other cases this is probably true. When one accomplishes a set task or finishes a prescribed course of studies the feeling is natural that one has finished the only worthy task and the one accepted course of studies. Freedom of choice gives liberality to learning." [10]

Apropos of the delicate line drawn by Harvard, it is curious that though in the second passage Stevens began with a clear and definite statement concerning the efficacy of the Harvard system, he closed with what is, in the context established by the first three sentences, a seemingly ambiguous coda. It was as though he had astutely sensed the alternatingly liberating and constraining key to Harvard's success. Here, too, he found new aspects to add to his "two elements."

During his first year of adjustment to the movement up and down between the two, the young man could not have had enough distance to observe what he later would. He simply participated and enjoyed things as they were. His reality was for the most part quite pleasant. There were weekend nights of drinking beer and singing in friends' rooms (SP 14). There were the Misses Parsons, who gave social parties for their young men and who cared for Stevens particularly (L 16; SP 16). There was also a sense of independence and well-being that even made him want to remain in Cambridge over his first Christmas holiday there, despite parental pleadings that he come home (SP 15). These he perhaps should have heeded, however, since, as it turned out, he became extremely depressed and didn't even go, as he had intended, to Charles Eliot Norton's gathering for students who remained on campus during the break (L 575). Stevens was just eighteen, alone, and experiencing, maybe for the first time, the peculiar sadness that Christmas brought him, when, as he put it years later, "an every-day sorrow became unbearable" (L 703). When he finally did go home to Reading the following summer, the younger family members teased him about his "Harvard airs" and the accent he affected (SP 16).

ᏋᎦ

In Harvard's new reality the promptings of Stevens's imagination never stopped. The most insistent of these came from those who expressed the spirit of the age in a language the young man could easily understand, a language concerned as much with saying things well as with saying them at all. Though by no means a major figure at Harvard, Barrett Wendell was a gifted instructor whose love of his subject and of his students brought ideas to life. He inspired the young poet and planted seeds that grew throughout his life, coming to full flower nearly fifty years later in Stevens's most explicit poetic prescription, "Notes Toward a Supreme Fiction." Wendell taught both the history and development of English literature in outline and English composition. As Holly Stevens notes (L 25; SP 17), it is likely that her father had Wendell as an instructor in one of these two courses (L 23); this is further attested to by the fact that Wendell later provided Stevens with a letter of introduction to present to a New York City editor. In any case, Stevens carefully read Wendell's edition, *English Composition: Eight Lectures Given at the Lowell Institute, 1890*. He not only commented in his journal on Wendell's point of view as a rhetorician, adding his own substantial qualification,[11] but also adopted from Wendell's chapter on "Elegance"[12] and from his closing "Summary" the tripartite scheme for achieving the "elegance" of a "great work" and used it as the basis for the three sections of "Notes." He also internalized certain key phrases and ideas Wendell described as essential to writing, the "first object" of which is—again, particularly startling in connection with "Notes"—"to give pleasure."[13]

Wendell defined *elegance* as an attempt at perfection of style and gave as a prime example—in keeping with a post-romantic, symbolist sensibility—art that comes closest to the condition of music. In making his point, he cited lines from Alexander Pope's *Essay on Criticism* ("Music resembles Poetry"), from James Lowell ("Set it to music; give it a tune"), and, as the best instance, the "Music-drama of Wagner": "There is no single example of this more notable . . . most characteristic of this last half of the nineteenth century." Richard Wagner's greatness, he wrote, lay in the fact that he tried "to express in music, too, the thought and emotion for which poetry alone is an inadequate vehicle" and that he brought "other fine arts to his aid" as well: "architecture . . . painting in scenery, costumes and groupings of heroic figures . . . even sculpture, as when . . . Parsifal stands motionless as any figure cut from marble."[14] Even more important, Wendell noted something beyond all this: "Yet when all was done by this man, who seems to me the greatest of modern artists; when at this point where each art by itself had done its utmost, a fresh art came to do more still—*the final reality* (the real thought and emotion which all this marvellous thing would express) is as far away as ever"[15] (italics mine). Wendell went on, giving Shakespeare as another example, like Wagner, of the artist who, "do what he may [has] his ideal always beyond him. . . . [T]here can never be any moment of accomplishment when he may not eagerly hope to do better and better still."[16]

What is important here is not so much a matter of influence as a matter of seeing how certain things Stevens read and heard fed his spirit the way food and drink feed the body. Just as some elements interact with others, while yet others simply pass through the system, what Stevens read or was exposed to acted in the same way on his spirit. Some of Wendell's ideas catalyzed others already waiting, and some became the bases that would be acted on by later ideas, while others simply passed through Stevens's consciousness. Stevens wrote in response to reading Wendell's "Principles," as he called them: "What does not have a kinship, a sympathy, a relation, an inspiration and an indissolubility with our lives ought not, and under healthy conditions could not have a place in them" (*L* 25).

Wendell's stress on the significance of the musical quality contributed to Stevens's appreciation of Stéphane Mallarmé's and Arthur Rimbaud's symbolist poetry. What he learned eventually went into making *Harmonium*.[17] Wendell's praise of Wagner's skill in borrowing from all the fine arts the better to express his thought and feeling, Stevens incorporated in his own synesthetic approach, where the techniques of painting and musical composition were used to intensify a poem's intended effect. It was reflected, too, in poems in which pieces of imagined sculpture ("The great statue of General Du Puy" [*CP* 391] or the statue as varying symbol in "Owl's Clover" [*OP* 43-71]) appeared to have more reality than people and things in the actual world. Stevens employed these devices to illustrate how poetry makes the imagination as real as, or even more real than, reality itself.[18]

More, the notion of great art as an "attempt," as something never complete in itself, became Stevens's dominant theme in his later work and in his theory of poetry—as in "Notes *Toward* [italics mine] a Supreme Fiction." It is the same notion, too, that Wendell must have expressed to the students in his composition class when they attempted in their "essays" to catch and fix the feelings and ideas flitting about like butterflies in their minds. The suggestion of this never-to-be-reached "final reality" became Stevens's "final slate" (*CP* 96), the "final *elegance*" (italics mine; *CP* 389), the "final change" (*CP* 455), the "final filament" (*CP* 396), the "poem that never reaches words" (*CP* 396). In addition, this idea of always striving struck a responsive chord in the young man whose father's "get more than ahead" promptings never failed to punctuate his letters: "Do not be contented with a smattering of all things—be strong in something" (*L* 16); ". . . you will be like I was myself at 16—bound to 'paddle your own canoe'" (*L* 18); "The Crack-a-Jack is the fellow who is always ready in any emergency, and meanwhile fills his pockets with more stones + his head with more wisdom" (*L* 20); "Stick to it my boy—I know you can do whatever any other fellow did and perhaps—who knows—just a little slicker" (*L* 24). With the guidance offered by Wendell and others like him, Stevens eventually transformed these "dry catarrhs" of his Calvinist background into the music of his imagination's "guitars" (*CP* 10–11).

Perhaps the most significant lesson Stevens translated for his own use was the distinction Wendell made between the "written words which stand for the thought and feeling that were in the writer's mind . . . [and] the thought and feeling which they incarnate."[19] About forty years later, in a lecture Stevens delivered at Harvard ("The Irrational Element in Poetry"), he pointed out and elaborated on the same contrast,[20] naming the two aspects the "poetry of the subject" and the "true subject" (*OP* 221). This division between a poem's "surface" and what he poetically called its deeper "fluent mundo" (*CP* 407) became the single most important stylistic feature of Stevens's life and work. It allowed him to hide beneath a "piano-polished" surface (*CP* 100) thoughts and feelings that would have been considered indecorous or, at least, inappropriate to one raised as a "good Puritan." This split also reflected the American dissociation of sensibility that began with the first Puritans giving the rhetorical lie to the truth of their experience. This dissociation continued to be expressed in the nineteenth-century works of Edgar Allan Poe and Nathaniel Hawthorne that Stevens read while still a boy (*L* 125). The lesson he learned from these was that actions resulting from true thoughts and feelings were punished by the spiritual rhetoric of an overbearing sense of sin and guilt.

Stevens adapted a subtle ramification of this split into another key distinction: that between "inflections" and "innuendoes" (*CP* 93). This idea began to percolate in the young man's mind as Wendell pointed out the differences between "denotation and connotation." According to Wendell, it was the fine tuning of these two aspects of language that made for elegance. As he noted by taking *elegance* back to its Latin roots, *ex-lego* means "to pick out, to choose from among the great mass of things, the one thing that shall best serve our purpose." Moreover, "no expression can be so perfect that a better cannot be imagined. . . . The better we can make our words and compositions denote and connote in other human minds the meaning they denote and connote in ours, the greater charm style will have. . . ." Further, when successfully managed, style, "the expression of thoughts and feelings in written words [will] affect readers in three distinct ways": intellectually, emotionally, and aesthetically.[21] Stevens later prescribed these as the necessary elements of his "Supreme Fiction" (*CP* 380-408): "It Must Be Abstract" (to affect readers intellectually); "It Must Change" (to affect them emotionally); and "It Must Give Pleasure" (to affect them aesthetically).

The "anchorage of thought" Wendell offered Stevens was more secure than those offered by literary influences because Wendell was not one of those "man-poets" Stevens revered[22] but shied away from imitating. As Stevens noted later in his "Adagia," "When the mind is like a hall in which thought is like a voice speaking, the voice is always that of someone else" (*OP* 168). Wendell simply functioned like a lens, enabling Stevens to see more clearly the ideas he could translate into the reality of his poems. He could practice Wendell's lessons without being afraid that his attempt would be found wanting and without being afraid that the voice of one of the "man-poets" would hush his own.

Lastly, the attitude underlying Wendell's lessons about writing—that is, presenting for the world's inspection only thoughts and feelings dressed decorously in "elegance"—was most congenial to the young man reared in America's late-Victorian atmosphere. This attitude affected Stevens's personal life as much as it did his art.

By the middle of his second year at Harvard (1898–99) certain aspects of this attitude had made themselves apparent in the habits he kept. The first was keeping a journal, something Wendell suggested cultivating as he stressed the importance of noting one's perceptions both about the present and about the great writers of the past. From Stevens's journal entries emerges a portrait of the artist as an extremely self-conscious young man. As he became more introspective, he became increasingly concerned about the image he saw reflected on paper. He reread and excised earlier entries or commented on them, assuming various poses and imitating others' styles. This searching after an image to present in words echoed his taking on in his person the manner of the "Harvard man." Once he had begun shaping this new self, he worked to maintain it, even testing how effective it was in doubling as reality. Once, for example, after leaving Harvard and setting out on his own in New York, when asked where he was from, he answered, "from Massachusetts" (*SP* 76).[23]

Whether or not he ever took off his mask during his first summer back home, he did try out for the role of journalist. He worked, it seems, for the *Reading Times* (*L* 20). The correspondence between Wallace and his father shortly before the summer reveals signs of insecurity in the young man. These notes of reticence make his taking on "airs" understandable. With his mask, he at least appeared mature and independent. A letter Garrett wrote at the beginning of May 1898 (*L* 19) indicates that Wallace had asked his father to find him a summer job, something that would "aid muscular development[,] mental diversion and keep down expenses." Garrett suggested something in journalism: "If your aim is still journalism—a summer job on a Boston or N.Y. large Daily in almost any capacity—would be of greatest value as a stimulus or to cure you." About ten days later another letter from Garrett showed that the young man did not see himself as capable of tackling the "big city scene": "So your modesty is shocked at the idea of getting on a big Daily in N.Y. or Boston—I don't know why—I believe you have the stuff in you— and gall is nowadays appreciated and well paid for—You're getting to be a man now. Take an inventory of your capacities" (L 19). As it turned out, a week or so before Stevens returned to Reading, his father had not yet found him a job but promised to "find something to assist in keeping afloat" (SP 18) once he arrived. That something was probably the job on the *Reading Times* procured through its editor, Thomas C. Zimmerman, a close friend of Garrett's *and* a poet (L 20; SP 18).

Wallace's contact with Zimmerman evidently offered him encouragement in cultivating his poetic sensibility. When he returned to Harvard that fall, he applied himself even more assiduously to purely literary activities. He was helped by what he was learning from Wendell. The courses he took during this year and his performance in them reflect the fact that his tendency toward a life of letters was becoming serious and that the role of imagination was exerting its influence most strongly. In English composition he received an A; in two half-year courses in English literature ranging from the death of John Dryden (1700) to the publication of William Wordsworth's *Lyrical Ballads* (1798), a B the first term and an A the second (one of these was taught by Charles Townsend Copeland, who later became a friend of Stevens); in a French course in prose and poetry, covering Corneille, Racine, Molière, Beaumarchais, Hugo, Musset, Balzac, and composition, a B; in a German course on Goethe and his time given in German, a B+. But in European history from the middle of the eighteenth century, and in the outline of economics he received Cs, "the lowest grade [given] at Harvard" (L 23; SP 25). The grade in economics must have displeased his father most. He, after all, had developed an intuitive sense of economics well enough to have acquired and run "a bicycle factory and a steel plant" (L 3) at one time, beyond his practice as an attorney.

The energy that might have gone into Stevens's applying himself to these more practical lessons in reality he was devoting to writing. Over that year he published a number of poems and stories.

In the December 12, 1898, issue of the *Harvard Advocate* (Vol. LXVI, p. 78) appeared "Vita Mea," a poem "written November 28" (L 21):

> With fear I trembled in the House of Life,
> Hast'ning from door to door, from room to room,
> Seeking a way from that impenetrable gloom
> Against whose walls my strength lay weak from strife,

All dark! All dark! And what sweet wind was rife
With earth, or sea, or star, or new sun's bloom,
Lay sick and dead within that place of doom,
Where I went raving like the winter's wife.

"In vain, in vain," with bitter lips I cried;
"In vain, in vain," along the hall-ways died
And sank in silences away. Oppressed
I wept. Lo! through those tears the window-bars
Shone bright, where Faith and Hope like long-sought stars
First gleamed upon that prison of unrest.

(SP 23)

Unlike "Autumn," his first published poem (written during the previous year, before he had begun to be serious about being a poet and before he had begun paying close attention to and imitating styles of other poets), the diction and setting of this poem belong less to Stevens's sensibility than to that of the Victorian, pre-Raphaelite poets like Dante Gabriel Rossetti, whose "House of Life" metaphor here controlled the young poet's thoughts and feelings. Reacting badly to this poem himself late in his life in 1950, Stevens commented to Donald Hall (then president of the *Harvard Advocate*) that "Vita Mea seems a particularly horrid mess" (*L* 684). Yet even in this conscious imitation something marking Stevens's genius was apparent in the image of "the winter's wife."

The difference between the two poems and what they reveal becomes even clearer by comparing "Autumn" to the drawing of doves done by Pablo Picasso when he was nine. When his father, himself a painter, saw it, he reputedly put away his own brushes, having recognized in the untrained, spontaneous grace of his son's drawing an expression he had long been trying to achieve. It was this natural style that later emerged as Picasso's genius, perceptible through the styles of the masters he imitated in polishing his skills. In "Autumn" Stevens's developing style suggests itself in the "Long lines of coral light" and in "This sunless zone" as clearly as Picasso's lines pointed out his gift to his father. Both Picasso and Stevens, at relatively parallel points in their careers—at the stage when they were beginning to practice skills (for Stevens, around 1899; for Picasso, between 1897 and 1900)—chose to imitate not great masters but figures belonging to the generation just preceding theirs, figures whose reputations had been established, though without the triumphant accolade of centuries. Picasso imitated Henri Toulouse-Lautrec at one point; Stevens, Rossetti. Following such men seems to have allowed these strong young artists the freedom to express their individual talent, something they felt imitating a great master might inhibit. In addition, modifying the styles of those closer to them in time enabled the younger artists to perfect and then go beyond the particular idiom of the time, an idiom that was the language of their fathers.

Over his second year at Harvard Stevens tried his hand at many styles. He even experimented with a different genre, the short story. But before this and "Vita Mea," another, shorter poem appeared in the *Harvard Advocate* (November 28, 1898). In this, "Who Lies Dead?," Stevens's peculiarity is marked by the curious use of a light lyric quatrain for a subject that reflects the rather morose sensibility of the young poet:

> Who lies dead in the sea,
>   All water 'tween him and the stars,
> The keels of a myriad ships above,
>   The sheets on a myriad spars?
>
> Who lies dead in the world,
>   All heavy of heart and hand,
> The blaze of a myriad arms in sight,
>   The sweep of a myriad band?
>
> (SP 22)

In itself the despairing note of this and the other early work is not remarkable. A young poet reared by the romantic sensibility would be expected to mourn his own lost or never-to-be-gained paradise and his separation from indifferent nature. What is surprising, however, is the sharp contrast between the tone of these early pieces and the characteristic ironic tone of *Harmonium*. Though fifteen years intervened, this alone cannot account for such a difference.

It could be argued that Stevens's tone and sensibility were affected and that by the time of writing the poems of *Harmonium* he had abandoned the tragic mask for his authentic comic one, but this would be to mistake, in our reading *Harmonium,* the "poetry of the subject" for the "true" one. This is something Stevens thought likely to happen, as he later expressed in "The Irrational Element in Poetry." While the "poetry" of *Harmonium*'s "subject" provides its comic aspect, that aspect hides a still melancholy, almost tragic "true subject" in the same way that Stevens's pose as a "Harvard man" hid the insecure youth. In the fifteen years between his first published work and his first volume, Stevens perfected the image he wanted to project. Carefully heeding Wendell's lessons, he decorously covered his "thoughts and feelings" in a most elegant style. The more indecorous the "thought or feeling" might be judged to be, the more he polished its surface with "pistache" (his wonderful pun on "pastiche") and "droll" (*CP* 102) to distract attention from his inner world.

What made this inner world painful is apparent in the work and journal entries of these early years. The comedian's costume he later donned was still in the making. One of the short stories[24] published during this period, "A Day in February," is openly autobiographical (*SP* 26) and reveals at least two aspects of the young man's dissatisfaction and uneasiness with his life at Cambridge.

First, his having moved away from the close contact with nature he had at home was problematic: "When he first came to college, he had been tall and fresh, but, as he piled up theme upon theme and thesis upon thesis, a slight bend became noticeable in his shoulders, and he felt empty and unambitious; for the few steps that carried him every day to two or three recitations were not to be compared with the walks he had taken at home, alone on the roads, free and high spirited" (*SP* 26). In further developing the theme of the split between abstract learning and nature, Stevens went on to describe how the wind that had been so sweet was now "frightened [and] driven . . . away" by "economic calculations and mathematical designs that made him remember it was still winter." Here he expressed his aversion to the practical discipline urged by his father. He also established the association between cold reason and winter that later played such an important part in his poetry. Stevens's hostility to reason at this point issued in his character's uneasiness. This represented, in part, Stevens's quiet rebellion against the man who "always [had] reason on his side." At the end of the story the young man resolves to "be less Faust than Pan," thereby asserting his independence. But this desire, in the academic situation in which he finds himself, makes him even more of an outsider. As a result, the youth's despair deepens. Unspoken in and through this turmoil of the story was an absence in the real life of its author. What was missing was the most necessary inhabitant of Pan's world: a female to be wooed and won by his panegyric.

Not that there had been any female company back home. Wallace's all-male society at Harvard had merely supplanted the boys' crowd in Reading. The kind of social segregation that was very much in keeping with late-Victorian morality merely reinforced the young man's reticence and added to the dissatisfaction he expressed. He could neither become Pan nor bargain like Faust for the promised beauty of Marguerite. For the time his only longings were for the fulfillment of imagination's offerings, not reality's. And it was perhaps because he had made a trip back home (Christmas 1898) to "reality" and attempted to renew his contact with nature that his sense of the incompleteness of his own nature was sharpened.

Having begun to keep a journal that fall, he took it home with him. From the entries it is clear that he was looking at the world through the lens Wendell and others at Harvard had provided. He was also polishing the lens, following Wendell's advice to practice and perfect his descriptions of perceptions while adding his observations about great masters.

During this Christmas holiday the young man retraced his steps to the rocks where he used to lie looking at the sky when he was a boy. But now he saw the world around differently. Looking at the familiar valley, seeing "the sun go down behind a veil of grime" became "terrifying . . . from an allegorical point of view" (*L* 22; *SP* 24). He no longer walked freely, perceiving things as they were. No longer one with the world around him, no longer part of his native soil, he now felt like the "jar . . . upon [the] hill" (*CP* 76), an observing eye, the subject around which the whole "slovenly wilderness . . .

sprawled . . . no longer wild" (*CP* 76). "Reality" was now caught and tamed in allegories and anecdotes.

Following his solitary afternoon pilgrimage, Stevens, that evening, together with "Livy" (Edwin Stanton Livingood)—his friend and neighbor from Reading who was also a Harvard contact—met with some other friends. In addition to his interest in Goethe, Livingood was a devoted student of philosophy. Stevens valued his times with him. This evening the group discussed "Livingood's theory that a man who writes poetry, in many cases will be found to be a poor singer . . . in short that any emotion expressed in one form of art tends to exclude the possibility of its expression through any others" (*SP* 25). Cambridge had "made an enormous difference in everything." Discussions about art took the place of conversations about life itself that less sophisticated young men would have had. Just as over the term before Stevens had read Edward FitzGerald's and Benjamin Jowett's letters (*L* 20) and now continued with Livingood and his knowledge of Goethe to get at a sense of their work through an understanding of their lives, he, in a curious reversal, projected himself through the lens of his learning. He was attempting to get at and see his own life through art. Faust was tempting him in reality as well as in imagination.

There was a consolation that came with this painstaking self-consciousness. It was Stevens's unspoken trust—or great desire—that at some point the image he was projecting would be seen by others as well. Because he saw "how clearly [the letters of FitzGerald and Jowett] illustrate the man" (*L* 20) and imagined the "great pleasure to generations who became more and more intimately acquainted with [Goethe's] work to become more and more deeply interested in the human being" (*L* 22), he, in leaving behind a record, was trying to make himself, like Goethe, whom he so greatly admired, "A nucleus for his productions, unlike Shakespere [*sic*] . . . a nonentity about which cluster a great many supreme plays and poems" (*L* 22 and *SP* 26).

Early in his career Stevens recognized his need to show himself as a man, not merely as a "non-entity" who left only work. This might seem the biographer's wished-for situation since the reciprocal reading of life through work and work through life was part of the intention of the subject, rather than just a later applied interpretive device. There are, however, many difficulties about this since a subject as self-conscious of purpose, who was also, as Stevens was, ambivalent about revealing or "indulging personality," is going to have become expert at hiding, even in what appear to be the most spontaneous revelations.

Stevens began hiding early. He erased, crossed out, commented, and tore entire pages from his journals as he periodically reread them. Completed poems as well as personal reflections shaped into finished sketches disappeared this way.[25] Other entries, like the account of that Christmas holiday walk around Reading (December 27, 1898), were later "worked over" or "revised" (*SP* 24). In his first journal the entries that seem not to have suffered are

impersonal observations about writers and art or terse, epigrammatic procla-
mations about poetry and life: "Verse is not poetry: it is the vehicle to poetry"
(*SP* 25); "Poetry is Man"; "Labor conquers everything except itself" (*SP* 26).
Between these the young poet destroyed lines where he might have revealed
the stories illuminating these "morals."

Stevens had an almost obsessive concern with image. Though he inscribed
his journal with an epigraph from Jowett suggesting that in the pages to
follow he would describe himself and things as they were ("If I live I ought to
speak my mind"), he seems to have quickly understood how difficult this was
for him. This is apparent in a subtle self-admonition to be direct and open
where he got caught in a tangle of circular reasoning: ". . . as long as I feel
that I am really sincere just so long I shall dare to be candid with myself" (*L*
21; *SP* 23). Though this makes no real sense, the unconscious stress of repeating the defining and contradicting predicates revealed the young man's ambivalence about showing himself. Together with the tremendous pressure to
bare what was beneath the surface—"to be candid"—was an equally strong
desire to remain hidden. As a result, though the grammatical form of his
statement—"as long as . . . then . . ."—indicated that he was moving beneath his surface, being "sincere," in actuality he only played on the surface of
the statement's form, moving nowhere, like Narcissus transfixed by his own
image.

Precisely why Stevens was so preoccupied with image is impossible to
know. But we can guess reasons from recognizing the tendency in ourselves
and from being familiar with Stevens's personal history, especially with the
situations where his "fitting in" and earning approval were so important.
These guesses become better educated when set against the broader background of the late nineteenth and early twentieth centuries. Romantic self-
consciousness fed what Christopher Lasch has recently named, for our century,
the "Culture of Narcissism." This is a particularly apt epithet for the situation
in America with its residues of the Puritans' careful attention to presenting a
perfect image of themselves and their mission to their spiritual fathers back in
the Old World. Focus on image and extreme self-consciousness are connected
with insecurity.

In historical terms, the insecurity of the nineteenth century was largely
the result of the gradual breakdown of the social and moral orders evident in
the political and philosophical changes at the end of the eighteenth century.
The insecurity was reinforced through the nineteenth century's uncovering of
man's "base" nature. This was described objectively by Darwin. But it was
experienced subjectively, as industrialization relegated human beings to inhu-
man extensions of machinery. In America the general sense of insecurity was
even more deeply ingrained by the threat the Civil War posed to national
identity. On the purely economic level, insecurity grew out of the widening
rift between the satisfactions promised by the nation's ideals and the actual
dissatisfactions of those caught in the machinery of advancing industrialization. The renewed stress on the work ethic by the end of the nineteenth

century ensured, at too great an expense to the life and liberty of the many, the pursuit of happiness of seemingly fewer and fewer.

Against this setting it is not surprising that Stevens noticed how, in spite of the apparently "impractical" concerns of those whom he followed, "Harvard [fed] subjectivity." But he too began drinking from its spring, though he had strong misgivings about doing so. It was natural that Harvard shared the spirit of the age and place of which it was a part. Cultivating "personality" meant preparing strong individuals who would find places on America's "front bench," as Garrett Stevens urged his son to do (L 20). By expressing their "individualism," young men would contribute to the common good. And just as Harvard reflected the time and place in general ways, so Stevens reflected them in his particularity. Thus isolated, the negative aspects implicit in the ideals showed themselves as well.

The indulgence of personality fostered by the Cambridge atmosphere provided a healthy corrective to Stevens's "good Puritan" training. This in part allowed the poet and his poetry to emerge. But it also prompted guilt. This showed itself in Stevens's alternating perceptions of himself as recorded in his journals. These mirrored a conflict between self-indulgence and restraint. Some of these journal entries as well as some of the sonnets written during this middle year, when Santayana's influence was beginning to have its effect, were quite explicit in connecting the young man's uneasiness with a loss of faith: "I wish that groves still *were* sacred—or, at least, that something was: that there was still something free from doubt, that day unto day still uttered speech, and night unto night still showed wisdom. I grow tired of the want of faith—the instinct of faith. Self-consciousness convinces me of something, but whether it be something Past, Present or Future I do not know. What a bore to have to think these things over, like a German student, or a French poet, or an English socialist! It would be much *nicer* to have things definite—both human and divine. One wants to be decent and to know the reason why. I think I'd enjoy being an executioner or a Russian policeman . . ." (L 86–87); "The feeling of piety is very dear to me" (L 32). Years later he was still preoccupied with this. Writing in 1943 to Gilbert Montague, who had been at Harvard with him, apropos of "Notes Toward a Supreme Fiction," Stevens specified the underlying idea of that poem as "what in your day, and mine, in Cambridge was called the will to believe" (L 443). It was not only in Cambridge in 1899 that the "will to believe" was the central problem. Though there William James and George Santayana were trying to "put Humpty-Dumpty back together again" after Schopenhauer, Darwin, and Nietzsche had toppled him, outside the walls of the academy the "will" became a fervent wish as the nineteenth century's close opened the last of the millennium, and faith in science had not yet replaced faith in God.

Stevens was not approaching the edge of the abyss alone, but because of his religious training, facing it was difficult. For him the abyss was not an abstraction. Loss of belief meant not only loss of a figured ideal and set of guiding principles but loss of an identity that had been carefully and subtly

74

shaped by years of "hankering for hymns" (*CP* 59); years of Sunday school and services; years of his mother's bedtime Bible stories; years of constant reminders, in the persons of those "good Puritans" he saw around him, of the rewards of faith.

In connection with familial influence, it is interesting to speculate about whether the effects of this training would have been as strong had Stevens's father been open in speaking with his children and expressing to them, at earlier stages, the skepticism acquired from his reading and experience that he later voiced in letters he wrote to his son at Cambridge. A good example of how he tried to teach his son, then, to question appearances was the lesson about the sun not being "a ball of fire sending light and Heat" quoted earlier (see p. 45). Stevens clearly never forgot this; the sun became the most constant presence in his poetry. Similarly, the method of reasoning Garrett outlined in the same letter would have gone a long way in loosening the insidious hold that the Calvinist tradition had bred into Stevens had it been presented in warm discussions that were as regular a part of everyday life as Kate's hymn singing. But like others who had been swayed by holy rhythms and had heeded their Sunday school lessons, Stevens learned from an early age to believe himself one of the elect. As a result, part of what Harvard meant was the beginning of an extreme moral and personal crisis.

For Stevens the lessons in reasoning came too late to mediate the effects of religious training. Consequently, he lived in tension, feeling the vestiges of his faith being attacked by the scientific, questioning attitude now suggested by his father and fostered by the academic environment. Though exerting their powerful influence, however, the religious residues were not overt in Stevens. This was as much in keeping with the nature of Presbyterianism as it was in keeping with Stevens's nature, in which the aspects touching deep feelings were always hidden beneath a smooth "piano-polished" surface.

Presbyterianism was particularly effective as a religion and especially well suited to the most industrious of New World settlers because it translated even the most paradoxical of Calvinist tenets into practical applications that simultaneously ensured the prosperity of the community and the salvation of souls. The nub of this ingenious device is the doctrine of predestination and grace. The effectiveness of its application, in turn, depends on a groundwork of belief secured by the proper education of children.

Unlike Catholic and Lutheran interpretations, which hold that grace is something to be earned by good works, Calvinist doctrine maintains that grace is something given by God to his elect. These individuals are able to perform good works because they already have the gift of grace. Doing good works, then, identifies them as chosen. Calvinism became the spiritual genius of capitalist societies since its prime virtues—industry, sobriety, and thrift— "produce" the most good. More particularly, Presbyterianism has the additional advantage of further translating these virtues into even the most intimate and homely activities, which then become, if practiced with the common good in mind, "high-toned" (*CP* 59) and worthy of respect.

The key to all this begins to be turned early in the individual's life, when before reaching the age of reason, a child is taught that certain things and activities are good, and others bad. The next turn comes when, for example, in Sunday school the child learns that practicing what is good means that he has the gift of grace and is, therefore, one of the elect, predestined to enter God's kingdom—unless, of course, through his own perversion of free will, he chooses to do "bad" instead of "good." The lock is now secure.

But most children, and Wallace Stevens was no exception, do not take Sunday school lessons seriously enough to prevent them from playing nasty pranks and being even more than occasionally "bad." This, too, however, is taken into account by the tradition: Children are not fully formed. They play; they are not accountable until they are adults—eighteen, ready to be on their own. Suddenly—though until then probably indifferent to whether they "believe"—the associations to what is good or bad that were established in childhood begin to play themselves out. Most often this happens without certain consciousness of the germs of the original associations. The result—especially for one like Stevens, whose ties to the tradition were reinforced by so many aspects of ritual—is that in young adulthood that individual, even if he professes to atheism, cannot escape at least minor anxiety whenever engaged in activities or ways of being not connected with what was learned to be good throughout childhood. In other words, not to be somehow industrious, not to be temperate still mean, to the prerational consciousness—now traveling on its own as a "conscience"—that the individual has freely chosen to fall from grace and deserves to be damned. Nonetheless, occasional lapses are expected and can be forgiven. The state of grace can be regained by the resolution to stop what is "bad." This desire, coupled with prayer, "bring[s the] world quite round" once more.

It isn't surprising, then, that during his time at Harvard (as evidenced in his journals) and continuing into the period he lived on his own in New York as a young lawyer, when he expressed his uneasy thoughts and troubled feelings in letters to Elsie Moll, all episodes of self-indulgence or of enjoying something simply for pleasure's sake were immediately followed by periods of self-criticism, when he repeatedly resolved to refrain from his bad habits in the future.

It also isn't surprising to see what kinds of activities Stevens considered indulgences. Expectedly, excessive eating, drinking, or smoking of "big cigars" fell into this category. Any gratification of the senses beyond simple hygienic needs was self-indulgent. Stevens's inability to keep himself in check eventually led him, while still a young man, to refer to his body as "that monster" (L 176), the part he could not control. The practical effects of this attitude were obvious in certain episodes of his life at Harvard and continued to be evident in his later life. Then they colored not only his relationship to himself but his relationship to Elsie Moll.

Less obvious, but even more apparent in the choices he eventually made concerning his work, were the associations established between what was and was not *spiritually* self-indulgent. Here the line was tenuous. He could see his talent for "painting pictures in words" as a manifestation of the gift of grace if he transformed it so as to contribute to the common good or if he could see it as a form of prayer to honor or express the sacred. In this way his particular gift could help ensure the spiritual progress of the individual within the community. But it would certainly *not* be evidence of the gift of grace if its only purpose were personal self-expression, especially not the kind of sentimental outpouring that led to ennui. This led at worst to total immobility and at best to maudlin self-pity for having lost the way back to paradise. Since the romantic period it was this second aspect that most strongly characterized the image of the poet. By the end of the nineteenth century it deteriorated into Baudelairean caricatures of dandies and aesthetes. In "Puritan" America this image became associated with Oscar Wilde and Old World decadence—at least until Walt Whitman's song of himself and his "body electric" sounded out the tendencies to decadence in our own native soil.

In light of this, Stevens's early criticism of his writing of verses as "positively lady-like" and "absurd" (*L* 180) and his youthful commitment to transform his gift into the practical end of journalism are quite understandable. After he had unsuccessfully tried his hand at reporting during his first year on his own in New York, this attitude contributed to his yielding to his father's advice that he go to law school rather than to Paris or, for that matter, anywhere else in the world (*L* 52).

ॐ

But while Stevens was still in Cambridge, however, which seemed to him "not really [to be] a part of the United States" (*L* 813), the pressures of reality in whatever form—whether his father's austere urgings or the proddings of his own Puritan conscience—did not have full effect. As long as Stevens remained in this special atmosphere, he could afford to indulge in the pleasures of his imagination. He did not yet have to consider "what avails" (*L* 34). And he continued to receive recognition and approval for his literary pursuits. So he was able to wage a fair battle against the forces in himself that nonetheless periodically enjoined him to fast after his feasting.

In a series of sonnets Stevens wrote over two months during the second semester of his second year (February 22 to April 14, 1899, *SP* 29–35), he attempted to meet the demands of reality and imagination at the same time. He used these expressions of his spirit to satisfy the practical requirement for a "long theme" in the remaining half of his composition course (*SP* 29). There is nothing remarkable in this sequence of about fifteen poems. The young poet was still imitating others' styles, now notably Shelley and Keats.[26] But again certain images and perceptions burst out to show his genius, and the sadness that characterized his earlier poems was in these too.

A good example is the first sonnet. Five months after its writing it was published in the *Harvard Advocate* under the pseudonym of John Morris 2nd, one of many names Stevens used over the next year and a half. Whitmanian images[27] of sea and sky appear coupled with feelings of inadequacy and despair. These same kinds of linking later marked his mature style in poems purified of the voices of other poets. In "The Doctor of Geneva," for instance, there is a similar experience described, but it is so particularized that the original, sentimental perception is almost completely obscured beneath the ironically imagined reality of the "doctor." The difference between the two poems illustrates how in the twenty-two years separating their composition Stevens found his own voice. He abandoned the youthfully adopted pose of the melancholy romantic and accepted his Puritan identity. This he projected through the mask of the "doctor." Here are the poems:

I strode along my beaches like a sea,
The sand before me stretching firm and fair;
No inland darkness cast its shadow there
And my long step was gloriously free.
The careless wind was happy company
That hurried past and did not question where;
Yet as I moved I felt a deep despair
And wonder of the thoughts that came to me.

For to my face the deep wind brought the scent
Of flowers I could not see upon the strand;
And in the sky a silent cloud was blent
With dreams of my soul's stillness; and the sand,
That had been naught to me, now trembled far
In mystery beneath the evening star.

(SP 29)

THE DOCTOR OF GENEVA
The doctor of Geneva stamped the sand
That lay impounding the Pacific swell,
Patted his stove-pipe hat and tugged his shawl.

Lacustrine man had never been assailed
By such long-rolling opulent cataracts,
Unless Racine or Bossuet held the like.

He did not quail. A man so used to plumb
The multifarious heavens felt no awe
Before these visible, voluble delugings,

Which yet found means to set his simmering mind
Spinning and hissing with oracular
Notations of the wild, the ruinous waste,

Until the steeples of his city clanked and sprang
In an unburgherly apocalypse.
The doctor used his handkerchief and sighed.

(CP 24)

It was perhaps because he recognized, even at nineteen, that his romantic image was false that he chose to sign the first poem with his particularly finicky pseudonym. Apropos of this and his other work of the period, he wrote Donald Hall in 1950 that "Some of one's early things give one the creeps" (*L* 667; *SP* 35). Through the rest of the sonnets, too, the sentimental strain sounds loudly, coloring with rosy overtones even naïve perceptions about nature, humanity, and himself that he had recorded spontaneously in his journal. Thus, from a description of what he had seen on one of his walks back home in December—

> The edge of the woods . . . was very tangled with long, green, thorny tendrils of wild-roses. The ground at the foot of the hill was marshy in spots, elsewhere the leaves were mottled and laid by the weight of a snow which had melted. Clusters of green fern spread here and there. . . . At the top of the hill I sat down on a pile of rocks with my back to the city and my face towards a deep, rough valley in the East. The city was smoky and noisy but the country depths were prodigiously still except for a shout now and then from some children in the woods. . . . I forget what I was thinking of—except that I wondered why people took books into the woods to read in summertime when there was so much else to be read there that one could not find in books. I was struck by the curious effect of the sunlight . . . (*L* 22; *SP* 24)

—emerged the artificially weakened perception of the sixth sonnet:

> If we are leaves that fall upon the ground
> To lose our greenness in the quiet dust
> Of forest depths; if we are flowers that must
> Lie torn and creased upon a bitter mound
> No touch of sweetness in our ruins found;
> If we are weeds whom no one wise can trust
> To live an hour before we feel the gust
> Of Death, and by our side its last keen sound
>
> Then let a tremor through our briefness run,
> Wrapping it in with mad, sweet sorcery
> Of love; for in the fern I saw the sun
> Take fire against the dew; the lily white
> Was soft and deep at morn; the rosary
> Streamed forth a wild perfume into the light.
>   (*SP* 31)

Again, sentimentally describing his tenuous situation at Harvard—for a while yet enjoying the respite from having to pay attention to the "real hard work" (*L* 23) of making a way for himself—in the second stanza of the fifth sonnet he clothed the stings of a Puritan conscience in the sweetness of a borrowed style:

> Upon this wide and star-kissed plain, my life
> Is soon to feel the stir and heat of strife.
> Let me look on then for a moment here
> Before the morn wakes up my lust for wrong,
> Let me look on a moment without fear
> With eyes undimmed and youth both pure and strong.
>
> *(SP 31)*

And in yet another, he so hid his desire for love behind a Tennysonian imitation that the point of the poem—love in books can never take the place of the real experience of it—was contradicted by its very expression:

> The soul of happy youth is never lost
> In fancy on a page; nor does he dream
> With pitiful eyes on tender leaves that turn
> With mournful history of beings crossed
> In their desires; nor is he rudely tossed
> By energy of tears for the warm beam
> Of endless love that doth already seem
> All cold and dead with Time's destroying frost.
>
> For his own love is better than the tale
> Of other love gone by; and he doth feel
> As fair as Launcelot in rustling mail,
> Hard-driven flowers bright against his steel,
> Passing through gloomy forests without fear
> To keep sweet tryst with still-eyed Guenevere.
>
> *(SP 32)*

The young Stevens was never satisfied with this sonnet. Even after at least two revisions (*SP* 32) he did not attempt to have it published. Though he rejected the vitiation of love into sentiment, as expressed in the poem, the same distancing artificiality reappeared later but, sadly, in connection with his actual, not literary, experience. In many of the letters he wrote to Elsie Moll, as will be noted, he employed the same elevation of feeling and of her reality. He transported them into a "Faery" world (*L* 116) where Elsie was the "princess" and he the adoring "juggler-clown" who entertained her with songs. This kind of etherealization of emotion and physical desire—very much in keeping with the late-Victorian tenor of the period and with the poet's Puritanism—made his coming to terms with the reality of marriage something quite difficult. It also prompted, at the midpoint of his life, his rejection of all that had gone into his creating an imagined paradisal world where ripe fruit never fell.

But at nineteen, as though unconsciously aware of the consequences of this impending crisis and aware, too, that facing the actual is the primary aspect of maturity, he already feared the passing of youth. This he expressed in another of the unpublished sonnets, as he voiced it again many times in his later letters to Elsie:

> Yet mystery is better than the light
> That comes up briefly in the gloom, and goes
> Before it well defines the things it shows,
> Leaving it doubly darkened; and the sight
> That seeks to pierce a never-ending flight
> Of dim and idle visions had best close
> Its many lids; the heavy-petalled rose
> Lies still and perfect in the depth of night.
>
> So youth is better than weak, wrinkled age
> Looking with patience on a single beam
> Of fancied morn; and no disturbing gleam
> Most futile and most sinister in birth
> Mars the high pleasure of youth's pilgrimage
> Passing with ardor through the happy earth.
>
> (*SP* 33)

Stevens was closely following Barrett Wendell's advice to be decorous. In one of the sonnets he even paraphrased his teacher's central lesson:

> My song, thou art unjewelled and uncouth.
> I adorn thee like the month of May,
> With loveliness and fervor; and thy way
> Shall be a spiritual reach for Truth.
>
> (*SP* 34)

Here he was striving so hard "to sing what none/[Had] sung" that he destroyed, at least for a while, the seeds of his own style. Yet in other attempts he relaxed somewhat, and the seeds began to grow. The image of himself as a "youth . . ./A tall, fair figure in the sullen plain" (Sonnet XIII, *SP* 34) burgeoned into the central metaphor of the "jar in Tennessee" (*CP* 76). The vision of "cities on uncertain hills" (from the last sonnet of the sequence [*SP* 35]) far surpassed the image borrowed from Edward FitzGerald's *Rubáiyát of Omar Khayyam* and forecast the most successful of Stevens's later evocations of landscape. And from the same poem, the description of a robin singing "to allay/Her wild desire" perfectly symbolized his understanding of how poetry

81

functioned for him. Indeed, he later expressed this same perception explicitly, calling poetry a "health," a "completion of life" (*OP* 162 and 176) since it was in imagination, rather than in reality, that he fulfilled his desires.

Stevens at nineteen was mourning the passing of youth because he was not able to satisfy his natural yearnings with any kind of ease. Constantly aware of the pressure to succeed, he not only applied himself energetically to his studies but involved himself in additional commitments that would, beyond their immediate reward of recognition, pay off in his projected future. By the second semester of his middle year he had been appointed to the staff of the *Harvard Advocate* (*SP* 37), which then became an outlet for some of the sonnets and stories he wrote. By April of the same term he had been elected a member of the Signet Society (*SP* 40). Understandably, considering his diligence, throughout this entire period there was no mention of young women in or around Cambridge.

A curious combination of later reminiscences—his own and others'—and instances of the present described in his journal, but away from Cambridge, suggest that it was not his industriousness alone that prevented Stevens from experiencing the pleasures of companionship with the "fair sex."

His natural reticence, coupled with his never having been at ease in the society of females his age while he was growing up, made it difficult for him to approach a particular young woman to whom he was strongly attracted. He believed her to be beyond his reach. Though in the eyes of others he seemed to have the same qualities he admired in her, he was not sure enough of himself to risk a rejection. To others Stevens appeared "a large, handsome, healthy, robust, amiable person, with light curly hair and the most friendly of smiles and dispositions." At the same time he was also perceived as "modest, simple . . . almost diffident" (*SP* 37). It was clearly because of these last three qualities that this most desirable young man never spoke to Sybil Gage, the young woman in question. While they both lived in Cambridge, and his route home took him past her door almost every day, he never dared approach her. Ironically, they did find themselves brought together a few years later, when Stevens was already apprenticed as a law clerk. Almost fifty years after this meeting he remembered it as he recorded in a letter to Richard Eberhart, apropos of the two poets' having been together in Cambridge. In his description he displayed a curious forgetfulness:

> After leaving you, I walked through Hilliard Street, the name of which seemed to be familiar, until it came out on Cambridge Common by Radcliffe. At the point where it comes out Radcliffe is on the left. At the right there is an old dwelling where one of the most attractive girls in Cambridge used to live: Sybil Gage. If your wife is a native of Cambridge, she may have heard of Sybil Gage, although I am speaking of a time long before your wife was born. Her father was a friend of W. G. Peckham, a New York lawyer in whose office I used to work at one time, and the two of them, and some others, were, I believe, the founders of the Harvard Advo-

cate. But my principal interest in Mr. Gage, who was dead when I lived in Cambridge, was the fact that he was the founder of Sybil. A few years after I had left Cambridge I was a guest at Peckham's place in the Adirondacks and who should turn up but this angel; so that instead of being a street that I had never heard of Hilliard Street turns out to be a street that I passed every day. (*L* 700; *SP* 102)

As Holly Stevens notes, after their meeting at the Peckhams', some kind of relationship was established, but "what was between them" is not known. They did become close enough to discuss their interests. At the time she was an "enthusiast" about the educational theories of Friedrich Froebel and Johann Pestalozzi and had obviously told Stevens about them. He was, according to her, "a bit skeptical about the two" and wrote her the following poem, tinged with the ironic tone and the belief in the power of imagination that characterized his later work:

TO MISS GAGE

Froebel be hanged! And Pestalozzi—pooh!
No weazened Pedagogy can aspire
To thrill these thousands—through and through—
Or touch their thin souls with immortal fire.

Only in such as you the spirit gleams
With the rich beauty that compassions give:
Children no science—but a world of dreams
Where fearful futures of the Real live.

—WS
(*SP* 103)

It is revealing that the relationship did not go further, particularly in light of Stevens's still remembering her as an "angel" so many years later. Perhaps he remembered her this way because she belonged only to the world of his imagination as an interior paramour. Considering that she was described in her maturity as a "gracious, highly intelligent woman, much interested in literature . . . [and] especially fond of poetry" (*SP* 102), it seems unfortunate that their early contact did not develop into something more lasting. This seems all the more so since Elsie Moll was content to play the role of muse only as long as the poems Stevens wrote remained part of the "Faery" world she inhabited with him in imagination. She gave up her role as soon as this imagined world began to become part of reality. After years of encouraging the young man who had been introduced to her as "a poet," after years of reading and writing poems to each other, at precisely the point when Stevens's identity as "a poet" began to be recognized in the real world, with the publication of his first mature poems, Elsie became enraged. She resented his sharing what she thought belonged only to her and began objecting to his indulging in poetry at all.

The details of this later relationship, certainly the single most important one of Stevens's life—at least until the birth of his daughter—will be dealt with further on. But in this context it is necessary to consider what prevented Stevens from deepening his acquaintance with Sybil Gage and what prompted him to pursue one with Elsie Moll. Unlike Miss Gage—her sensibility educated at Radcliffe as Stevens's at Harvard—Elsie Moll, at the time Stevens met her, had never been exposed to anything more than Reading. Because of her family's financial situation, she had not even been able to complete more than about a year of secondary education.

What led Stevens to fall in love with this young woman—besides her remarkable beauty (she later became the model for the Liberty head dime and the walking Liberty half dollar)—is suggested in his journal entries beginning at the end of his second year away, when he went back home to the familiar countryside around Reading. This long stay through the rich green Pennsylvania season was as truly different from his last at Christmas as summer from winter. The fullness of "summer-seeming" (*CP* 99) made it unnecessary for the young poet to dress reality in imagination's colors as he had done in winter, when he clothed the stark, cold landscape in allegory and anecdote. His imagination now worked to complete himself. It was as if with nature's showing all that is only promised through other seasons, the young man, who felt part of that nature, could begin to show himself. And in keeping with all the season meant, this was the only period, from the time he began Harvard until he met Elsie Moll five years later, that he mentioned young women at all. Both the reasons for his ease with some kinds of young women and his discomfort with others are apparent in these brief descriptions, in which he alternately revealed and hid himself behind certain roles.

Back in the reality of his soil, he felt "[f]reedom, beauty [and a] sense of power etc. press [him] from all sides" (*L* 30; *SP* 48). His pleasure was in noticing and recording "quick, unexpected, commonplace, specific things," like seeing "a big pure drop of rain slip from leaf to leaf of a clematis vine" (*L* 29; *SP* 45). Here he could get "below the delightful enough exterior into the constantly surprising interior" of things (*L* 30; *SP* 48), so that he felt "completely satisfied that behind every physical fact there is a divine force." He looked not "*at* facts, but *through* them" (*L* 32; *SP* 54) and realized "how different literary emotions were from natural feelings" (*L* 27; *SP* 42). Here he felt safe. He could temporarily "change [his] intellectual vestment" (*SP* 59) and at the same time be recognized as young "Mr. Stevens"—the one who went to Harvard—by the sisters of his old acquaintances. But to Sybil Gage, he feared, he would have been just one more undergraduate admirer.

During this summer the dryness of his school-year journal entries concerning the "worthlessness" of "art for art's sake" (*L* 26; *SP* 40), "Poetry & Manhood" or "The Scope of College Stories" was replaced by his savoring "the real thing [in] green fields, woods" (*L* 27; *SP* 41), the twang of the local farmers' dialect, the joy of fishing and watching herons, finding fox holes, killing a rattlesnake. Dressed in the "overalls" he had exchanged for his "intellectual vestment," he was "making hay," as he put it (*SP* 43–44). Back for three months in this environment, which seemed to him to belong to a "golden age" (*SP* 59) full of "Greek day[s]" (*L* 29; *SP* 46), he came into his own. He found himself "more truly and more strange" (*CP* 65). It was not that he abandoned the role of "dull scholar" (*CP* 16) and simply relaxed into acting the country boy. No. In this natural atmosphere, unmediated by art and intellect, it was as if he were seeing his own projection reflected clearly for the first time. "There is one advantage in being here. Instead of the bad photographs of Tintoret [*sic*] and Reynolds or the reproductions of Hermes and Venus you have the real thing" (*L* 27; *SP* 41). Away from the "literary life" (*L* 52) of Harvard, without its confirmation of his *role* as poet, he found he was actually a "poet in more than mute feeling" (*L* 25; *SP* 39). This made him grateful for the investment he had made at school polishing his skills: "It was a monstrous pleasure to be able to be specific" and record the commonplace (*L* 29; *SP* 45).

For the first—and perhaps the last—time he felt like what he later named as an ideal: "The Figure of the Youth as Virile Poet" (*NA* 37). He was enjoying both the fullness of his body and his mind. He began to strike a balance between his two elements. Rather than create other "Faery" worlds, his imagination seeded the reality of the soil of which he was a part and from which he continued to draw nourishment. Strewn throughout the accounts of his walks, his observing rabbits and crows, his lying on his back and watching the sky change from sun to moon colors were the perceptions about life and art that he had learned to articulate at Harvard. But now, rather than being scattered, blown here and there by the wind of intellectual discussions in dusty attic rooms, these ideas found a place to root in the ready ground of a nature that he had always known but that he seemed to see for the first time. Interspersed with his lyrical and minutely concrete descriptions in his journal that summer are accounts of his meetings and outings with friends. Livingood, like him, was home from Cambridge. The rest either had gone away to other schools and were also now home for the summer or had never left.

Sometimes with individuals and sometimes with groups Stevens discussed what he had learned and what he was curious about. He debated Christopher Shearer, a painter who believed that "the ideal was superior to fact since it was man creating & adding something to nature. He [Shearer] held however that facts were best since they were infinite while the ideal was rare" (*SP* 45). The young poet went on in his journal to muse on Shearer's point of view. He concluded that Shearer seemed "unaware of anything divine, anything spiritual in either nature or himself."

With Livingood, now finished with his year of graduate work at Harvard (1898–99) and returned to Reading, he shared his feeling for Goethe and for poetry in general. They also spoke about "the law," which his friend was then being urged to take up and practice. About Livingood's reaction Stevens perceptively noted that he began "to yield to the expectations of the community, desiring more or less to be well-thought of, quenching his independence" (*SP* 50). Stevens seemed to sense his own proclivity in his friend. After one discussion about the English poets and their habits of study Stevens, elaborating on what he now began to recognize as his own habits and need, observed that,

> they used study as a contrast to poetry [Livingood had held that they acquired their learning simply as part of their trade]. The mind cannot always live in a "divine ether." The lark cannot always sing at heaven's gate. There must exist a place to spring from—a refuge from the heights, an anchorage of thought. Study gives this anchorage: study ties you down; and it is the occasional willful release from this voluntary bond that gives the soul its occasional overpowering sense of lyric freedom and effort. Study is the resting place—poetry the adventure. (*L* 27; *SP* 41)

On another occasion, with Shearer and Levi Mengel, also a native of Reading, Stevens attentively gathered "natural facts" as he followed the two, madly running and naming butterflies they tried to net. Stevens's short journal description revealed his spontaneous pleasure in having been with these two. He tinged his account with the playful irony that later colored his characterizations of personae he created in his poems: "As we walked along Mengel would suddenly cry out, 'Oh! There goes a liptides Ursula' (or something of the sort), making a wild lunge in the air with his net, while Shearer at the very moment, with a senile shriek, would fly down the road after an 'argymous Cybele'" (*SP* 49). Long before translating this kind of perception into poetry, Stevens used this entry in another way. The following October he published a short story entitled "Pursuit" in the *Harvard Advocate*. It was based strongly on his experience of that day (*SP* 49).

And over these very important three months there were, notably, his first recorded regular contacts with young women. There were the three Wily sisters, Kate, Rose, and Sally, daughters of John Wily who owned the house where he was staying. There was the sister of one of his male acquaintances, who, though she "welcomed [him] in an extremely formal way" one morning when he was looking for her brother, asked him, although it was only 9:00 A.M., to stay for dinner. This young woman Stevens found a "dry sort of person . . . [a]n empty husk . . .—but interesting none the less—" (*SP* 51). There was Miss Benz, whom he met one day when she accompanied him, Livingood, and other friends on a fishing trip. Stevens immediately began to reeducate her. Having found her to be taken with the "latest," he asked her on the trip to "distinguish between what she loved and what she merely liked." He followed it up by lending her a book of essays on aesthetics that focused on the relationship of man to the world around him. (This was George Edward Woodberry's *Heart of Man*, which had just been published [*SP* 47]). It seems to have been this young lady who prompted the following poem:

IMITATION OF SIDNEY
TO STELLA (MISS B.?)

Unnumbered thoughts my brain a captive holds:
The thought of splendid pastures by the sea
Whereon brave knights enact their chivalrie
For ladies soft applause; the thought of cold,[28]
Cold steps to towers dim that do enfold
Sweet maidens in their forceless chastitie;
Of snowy skies above a Northern lea
In their bright shining tenderly unrolled;

Of roses peeping dimly from the green;
Of shady nooks, all thick with dull festoon
To hide the love of lovers faintly seen
By little birds upon a pleasant tree;
Of meadows looking meekly to the moon—
Yet these do all take flight at thought of thee.

(*L* 31; *SP* 50)

In this undistinguished "imitation" Stevens was again romantically sentimental in expressing the "thoughts and feelings" he had for this young
woman, toward whom he had taken on the role of preceptor. This same pattern emerged later in his relationship to Elsie Moll. Because she had a great
deal to learn from him, she played Heloise to his Abelard with ease, thus
fostering, as did Miss Benz, Stevens's tendency to hide behind the masks he
picked up from what he read.

But in contrast with the role he played with Miss Benz was the way he felt
and acted with the Wily girls. He never referred to any of them as "Miss."
They were "Kate," "Sally," and "Rose." Perhaps because he had known them
before or perhaps because their family situation did not permit them to have
an attachment to what was "latest" like Miss Benz, Stevens reacted to them
familiarly, almost as if they were parts of the landscape. The Wilys, at this
time fairly destitute and renting rooms to supplement John Wily's various
enterprises (*SP* 42), had also been, like the Stevenses, one of the first settling
families, having had land ceded to them by William Penn. Though they had
lost the place they once held in the community, the traditions of their family
history were kept alive and respected. As Stevens put it, they were "attempting to maintain . . . a decent dignity" (*SP* 52). Kate, Rose, and Sally showed
Stevens aspects of themselves that were tied to their past and their place—ties
the young poet shared. With these young women, he became the student. It
was as though in responding to them as part of his soil, he returned to the
protection of his mother earth's spirit.

Sitting in the "piano room," he listened to Sally "play a few pieces which
she admired: 'The Shepherd Boy,' by Wilson, Gottschalk's 'Last Hope,'

'Heart's Desire' by somebody or other & Beethoven's 'Sylphs'" (*SP* 42). He found them "very pleasant." Out on walks during the evenings of long summer light, she named each of the flowers[29] and weeds. On his return to his room the "inquisitorial botanist/And general lexicographer of mute/And maidenly greenhorns" (*CP* 28) recorded in his journal what he had learned (*L* 28; *SP* 44–45). With Rose, he glimpsed more details of their family history and so better understood the "pain" of their present. "Rose strikes the real note of despair, particularly in handing me the poems of John Wily, 1719 etc.—as though she, the last of her family, were saying 'You see what we once were—well I and Kate & the rest are all that are left'" (*SP* 52). On the way to visit the Wilys' original family property with her and Kate, riding through the lush countryside that "confounded" him with so "much natural splendor," Stevens felt not only the pull on the horses' reins that he had to control but the strain in his being as well.

Sensing his kinship with these young women, he, on the one hand, imagined himself in their situation:

> If my own family were to end—that is if I came from a long & powerful family [which he would later discover to be the case, perhaps prompted by an unconscious wish]—if it were about to topple over—what a splendid place for ruins to be found in! Under a tangle of roses to find a musty bookcase! The roots of an oak grasping the ivory keys of a piano! A dead wall glistening with dew! *Morituri* to *Salutamus*! (Look up phrase) We who are about to die salute you! (*SP* 52)

On the other hand, because he did identify with the young women, certain feelings were raised that he did not want to face. When this happened, he found devices to block his feelings. The passage above is a good example of this. Immediately upon feeling the unexpected tug of unwanted emotion—here accompanying the thought of both his personal and familial extinction—he began first to qualify: "—if it were. . . ." Next, he repeated, paraphrasing himself in a euphemism: "to topple over" replaced "to end." Then, having reined in his feelings, he relaxed into the pace of familiar sentiment which he gradually increased with each exclamation until he was finally completely separated from his original feeling in the attempt to remember a Latin quotation. The pattern established here—of feeling; qualification; repetition in some kind of trope, which then replaced the feeling and became the basis for other tropes—is one that was repeated throughout Stevens's life. It remained one of the clearest marks of his style.

Stevens realized, even in the process of distancing himself from his feelings, that he was distanced. As soon as he began to sense Rose Wily's despair, instead of allowing himself to continue feeling, he directed his attention to the external world, just as he did for the rest of his life: "There is too confounded much splendor here . . . to allow one to feel deeply the human destitution" (*SP* 52). But in his very denial there was the implicit acknowledgment of what he did not want to face. Even more explicit is the following excerpt from his journal. He connected his present way of being with an earlier period in his life. He then compared himself with Livingood and found himself wanting:

> Somehow what I do seems to increase in its artificiality. Those cynical years when I was about twelve subdued natural and easy flow of feelings. I still scoff too much, analyze too much and see, perhaps, too many sides of a thing—but not always the true sides. For instance I have been here at Wily's almost a month, yet never noticed the pathos of their condition. The memory of one day's visit [Livingood had come the short distance from Reading to spend a day with Stevens a short time before] brought tears to Livingood's eyes. I am too cold for that. (*SP* 50)

Much later in his life, when he no longer attempted to weigh himself on an imagined scale, this kind of judgment was replaced by a simple categorical statement: "Sentimentality is a failure of feeling" (*OP* 162). But before he reached the point at which this kind of acceptance was possible, the only areas where Stevens seemed to be able to express feeling and at the same time avoid sentiment were in his relationships to nature and to his imagination. He observed these with meticulous attention to detail and without borrowed attitudes. Within a few days of his noting the pathos of the Wilys' situation and his apparent coldness in response to it, for example, he recorded the following:

> Just as I was writing the last [a cataloging description of the scene around him] two yellow jackets began to play around my ankle. Wishing to get rid of them I jumped from my chair and ran about 20 steps, accidentally crushing one of them under my foot. As I turned to see what had become of them I saw the uninjured one struggle with his wounded fellow and lift it heavily in the air, flying to a place of safety in a tree. (*SP* 54)

Here, without the self-consciousness evident when he considered himself in relationship to other people, and without the fear of displaying his emotions, he touched simply and directly a chord of real feeling in describing the behavior of the insects. He did this naïvely, effortlessly. First, he chose the verb "to play" to name the indeterminate activity of the yellow jackets. Secondly, he contrasted himself as an awkward giant somehow unfit in a natural environment where creatures "play." He felt himself to be a monster who "crush[ed]," though "accidentally," one of the bees as a consequence of his being out of place. Thirdly, he used "struggle," "fellow," "heavily," "place of safety," implicitly attributing to animal behavior the qualities of human experience. Personifying a situation involving nonhuman creatures was not threatening. Feelings could be evoked and revealed since there was no possibility of their being judged inappropriate, cold, or wanting. In the world of nature Stevens found a refuge for his spirit. Throughout his life it was to remain, like the imaginary world he created, a place where he could respond. There he could show aspects of himself that he never risked exposing in the real world of people and of places.

In the world of his imagination walked the "figure of the youth as virile poet," shaped from his native soil and given breath by the spirits of those he read. They had found some way to truth. Just as his response to nature was direct and reflected his genuine feeling, so his response to what he read, recorded in his journals and letters, shows him to have been able to see "through" the "physical facts" of words on a page to the "divine force behind them." He took on the knowledge of himself as the power who could detect this force. In his imaginary world, fed by his contact with nature, he was able to feel the sense of might and supremacy that he could not in the real world. But in this "fluent mundo," he was "sovereign *ghost*" (*CP* 27; italics mine), his powers invisible except to those who could recognize in him the "divine force" he could see in others.

That summer Stevens completed the reality of his walks through familiar hills and his talks with friends with perceptions from what he read. This included Robert Louis Stevenson's "Providence and the Guitar," Thomas De Quincey's "Essays on the Poets," and John Keats's *Endymion.* Having exchanged the "dusty road" of Cambridge for a "path through green and happy fields" (*SP* 59), feeling his own nature in nature, Stevens became more sensitive to what was not genuine in what he read, to what did not "have a kinship, a sympathy, a relation, an inspiration and an indissolubility" with life. While he appreciated the care with which "Stevenson's story" was written, he noticed, too, "how artificial" it was; its main character was "entirely literary, partly illustrating the difference between literary creation and natural men" (*L* 27; *SP* 41–42). In contrast, De Quincey's essays, particularly that on Oliver Goldsmith—reflective, as all of De Quincey's observations, of his own idiosyncratic nature as much as of his subject's—Stevens found "remarkably well-done . . . one of the best things [he had] ever seen on any poet (or prose-writer either for that)" (*L* 29; *SP* 48). Hearing the tones of a strong voice reinforced his desire to write poems (*SP* 45). And sensitized now both to nature and artifice, the young poet read *Endymion,* not as he would have at Harvard a few months earlier, as a student of literature, but naïvely, allowing himself to be suspended in its illusory world. He was affected by it as though it were real. Its poetic elements and his actual ones became curiously intermingled:

The moon was very fine. Coming over the field toward the bridge I turned to see it hanging in the dark east. I felt a thrill at the mystery of the thing and perhaps a little touch of fear. When home I began the third canto of "Endymion" which opens with O moon! and Cynthia! and that sort of thing. It was intoxicating. After glancing at the stars and that queen again from the garden I went to bed at ten. The room was quite dark except for the window and its curtains which formed a big, silvery, uncertain square at my bed's foot. (*L* 29; *SP* 46–47)

What Stevens described here was a version of the experience Ralph Waldo Emerson laid out most clearly in *Nature*.[30] Perhaps somewhere deep in his being Stevens remembered these words[31] as he looked at the night sky overlaid with Keats's lines:

Philosophically considered, the universe is composed of Nature and the Soul. Strictly speaking, therefore, all that is separate from us, all which Philosophy distinguishes as the NOT ME, that is both nature and art, all other men and my own body, must be ranked under this name, NATURE. In enumerating the values of nature and casting up their sum, I shall use the word in both senses—in its common and in its philosophical import. . . . *Nature,* in the common sense, refers to essences unchanged by man; space, the air, the river, the leaf. *Art* is applied to the mixture of his will with the same things, as in a house, a canal, a statue, a picture. But his operations taken together are so insignificant, a little chipping, baking, patching, and washing, that in an impression so grand as that of the world on the human mind, they do not vary the result.

The young man was involved in the "transcendental," feeling his "bond to all that dust" (*CP* 15)—the bright motes of heaven and the palpable soil of his native countryside.

૨૦

When Stevens returned to Harvard a few weeks later for his last year, many of the experiences of this summer became transformed into poems and stories. These appeared in the *Advocate* as well as in the *Harvard Monthly.* "The memory of those months which surpass[ed] any other" was fixed in these pieces. Stevens had learned that it was only out of direct contact with reality that his imagination could find the "bright threads" (*SP* 48) to weave into fictions in which he and others could "believe . . . willingly" (*OP* 163). Besides the obvious reminders of the summer's reality (the dialect of John Wily was used in one of the sketches in "Four Characters" [*SP* 42–43], and, as noted earlier, the chasing butterflies episode in "Pursuit"), there were also the more subtle carryovers from the changes in his internal life. New and marked notes of irony and unexpectedness appeared. There was also an edge of pessimism, somewhat like Thomas Hardy's, in response to the gradual disappearance of the natural world before the harsher reality of advancing industrialization and city life. This was evident in "The Minstrel":

> The streets lead out into a mist
>   Of daisies and of daffodils—
> A world of green and amethyst,
>   Of seas and of uplifted hills.

There bird-songs are not lost in eaves,
  Nor beaten down by cart and car,
But drifting sweetly through the leaves,
  They die upon the fields afar.

Nor is the wind a broken thing
  That faints within hot prison cells,
But rises on a silver wing
  From out among the heather bells.

(SP 63)

These figures, in addition to his use of certain images that reappeared often in later poems,[32] indicate that during this period Stevens had begun to speak in his own voice.

In "The Revelation," which appeared in a November 1899 issue of the *Advocate,* Stevens used irony to characterize his concern with image and its relation to his contacts with a particular young woman. It is, as Holly Stevens notes, an "eerie story of a young man who takes a photograph of his sweetheart to be framed; after it is done and he opens the package, he finds a picture of himself" (SP 60). It was as though Stevens had understood that in his Pygmalion-like role with Miss Benz what he was attracted to was the possibility of seeing himself reflected in her taking on more and more of what he taught.

In another piece, "Outside the Hospital" (published under the pseudonym of R. Jerries in the *Advocate* the following March), Stevens coupled another memory of that summer (". . . I lay in a field near the Hospital and watched the wind in the goldenrod and wild-asters—letting it do my thinking for me" [SP 58]) with the romantic Tennysonian mode he was so fond of imitating. But now there was an ironic twist. What would have appeared a year earlier as a direct utterance of despair was transformed into a maudlin way of looking at the world, expressed in a most unexpected pairing of elements. This kind of linking escapes the label of what would later be called surrealist because the situation described is still attached to what is human.[33] Stevens turned reality just slightly to see it in a different light. This developed into another of the characteristic features of his mature style.

OUTSIDE THE HOSPITAL

See the blind and lame at play,
  There on the summer lawn—
She with her graceless eyes of clay,
  Quick as a frightened fawn,
Running and tripping into his way
  Whose legs are gone.

How shall she 'scape him, where shall she fly,
  She who never sees?

Now he is near her, now she is by—
Into his arms she flees.
Hear her gay laughter, hear her light cry
Among the trees.

"Princess, my captive." "Master, my king."
"Here is a garland bright."
"Red roses, I wonder, red with the Spring,
Red with a reddish light?"
"Red roses, my princess, I ran to bring,
And be your knight."

(SP 58)

The transition from the derivative apprentice with flashes of genius to the young master was not that sudden. Among the pieces that appeared that fall and winter were some that showed none of the idiosyncrasies of the poet's nascent style. A sonnet, "To The Morn," echoed, as Holly Stevens points out, "Keats and Santayana" (SP 60) more than it voiced Stevens. Another, "Song"—

Ah yes! beyond these barren walls
Two hearts shall in a garden meet.
And while the latest robin calls,
Her lips to his shall be made sweet.

And out above these gloomy tow'rs,
The full moon tenderly shall rise
To cast its light upon the flow'rs,
And find him looking in her eyes.

(SP 61)

—is so undistinguished that it seems to have no author at all. Perhaps some of the unevenness was due to the pressure of deadlines, which as president of the *Advocate* in his last term Stevens had to meet. Perhaps this also accounts for the pseudonyms he used.[34] He had to fill each issue and didn't want it to be "Wallace Stevens" from cover to cover. In any case, by the end of his time at Harvard, there had come about a number of changes that were first hinted at by the distinction in tone marking some of the earlier pieces that year.

One of the subtlest yet profoundest developments involved Stevens's rejecting—for a while at least—the traditional religious attitudes that had shaped him. In their place, tempering his romantic sensibility with the new "scientific" awareness of man's place in evolutionary terms, came a kind of secularized or purified—"puritanical" perhaps—pantheism. After his "golden" summer in the hills of Pennsylvania, though convinced that "behind every physical fact there is a divine force," Stevens gradually moved farther away from the stringency of the idea of a god to be worshiped in chapels and cathedrals and closer to a version of paganism celebrating not only sun, sea, and wind but the body as well.

This transition showed itself in various ways. It is clear in the attitude he expressed in the journal entry of August 1 of that previous summer, just as the change began to occur. It was evident in some of the poems written over that year, which culminated in two mocking pieces composed at its end. And it announced itself as well in the *one* journal entry from his last term at Harvard that recorded his feelings about leaving Cambridge for good.

In the August 1, 1899, entry, after a number of derivative romantic "Thought for Sonnets" ("Frost in a meadow. Is there no bird to sing despite this? No song of Love to outquench the thought of Death?") and after noting his absence of feeling for Kate Wily and her family, Stevens went on to describe something he did feel. He then made a peculiar wish for a twenty-year-old young man:

> The feeling of piety is very dear to me. I would sacrifice a great deal to be a Saint Augustine but modernity is so Chicagoan, so plain, so unmeditative. I thoroughly believe that at this very moment I get none of my chief pleasures except from what is unsullied. The love of beauty excludes evil. A moral life is simply a pure conscience: a physical, mental and ethical source of pleasure. At the same time it is an inhuman life to lead. It is a form of narrowness so far as companionship is concerned. One *must* make concessions to others; but there is never a necessity for smutching inner purity. The only practical life of the world, as a man of the world, not as a University Professor, a Retired Farmer or Citizen, a Philanthropist, a Preacher, a Poet or the like, but as a bustling merchant, a money-making lawyer, a soldier, a politician is to be if unavoidable a pseudo-villain in the drama, a decent person in private life. We *must* come down, we *must* use tooth and nail, it is the law of nature: "the survival of the fittest"; providing we maintain at the same time self-respect, integrity and fairness. I believe, as unhesitatingly as I believe anything, in the efficacy and necessity of fact meeting fact—with a background of the ideal. (*L* 32; *SP* 53–54)

This entry is extraordinary not only because it reflects the saintly aspirations of the young man who had not even begun to experience the fleshy realities that Augustine converted into his halo but also because it presents for the first time the list of elements that went into making the conflicts he was beginning to face. Against these he underlined three "musts" that he later translated into the softened lessons of "Notes Toward a Supreme Fiction." The love of beauty had excluded evil.

By the following April a poem, "The Beggar," appeared as one of his "Street Songs" (*SP* 62). Here not only was there no evidence of "a feeling of piety," but a cathedral was described bitterly as merely "a place to beg." By the end of the school year he admonished himself for having "smutch[ed] inner purity" by having derived his "chief pleasures" not from saintly contemplation but from having gotten "drunk about every other night" and, toward the end of the last term, having done "nothing but loaf" (*L* 33; *SP* 70). The poems of this period reflect his complete turnaround. They are almost wholly ironic and disrespectfully parodic of the same traditional forms he had for years been dutifully imitating. A good example is "The Ballade of the Pink Parasol," written under the pseudonym of Carrol More. It displays, as Holly Stevens notes, the "wit and talent" that came "to fruition" in the poems of *Harmonium* (*SP* 67) when the disillusionment that had begun during this last year was complete:

> I pray thee where is the old-time wig,
>   And where is the lofty hat?
> Where is the maid on the road in her gig,
>   And where is the fire-side cat?
>   Never was sight more fair than that,
> Outshining, outreaching them all,
>   There in the night where lovers sat—
> But where is the pink parasol?
>
> Where in the park is the dark spadille
>   With scent of lavender sweet,
> That never was held in the mad quadrille,
>   And where are the slippered feet?
> Ah! we'd have given a pound to meet
>   The card that wrought our fall
> The card that none other of all could beat—
>   But where is the pink parasol?
>
> Where is the roll of the old calash,
>   And the jog of the light sedan?
> Whence Chloe's diamond brooch would flash
>   And conquer poor peeping man.
> Answer me, where is the painted fan
>   And the candles bright on the wall;
> Where is the coat of yellow and tan—
>   But where is the pink parasol?
>
> Prince, these baubles are far away,
>   In the ruin of palace and hall,
> Made dark by the shadow of yesterday—
>   But where is the pink parasol?
>   (*SP* 66–67)

What occasioned this change of temperament that made the diligent, pious young man act in ways that would "make widows wince" (*CP* 59) was indicated in the journal entry of June 2, 1900, written "at the end of [his] college life." Brief but important accounts of two deaths informed his sense of the "end." He mentioned these just after noting that he had been "too lazy to make a start" of keeping his "diary" for the year and that he would "be rather glad to forget many things that [had] happened." Easing himself into recording what he most wanted to forget, he first chided himself for the behavior that was his way of dealing with the feelings he wanted to repress. But he also wanted to forget the behavior because it represented the feelings and because it was a way of acting that was uncharacteristic of the image he had worked so hard to make: "Nine months have been wasted. In the autumn I got drunk almost every other night—and later, from March until May, and a good bit of May, I did nothing but loaf. . . ." Immediately following came the "all-speaking" (CP 14) facts:

> Grandmother Stevens, my father's mother, died in September—that made a deep impression on me because I was very proud of her. I stopped over at Ivyland on my way back to Cambridge and got a last glimpse of her. She looked very much as I had always known her. There was nothing unnatural in the little white parlor where she lay. Her face was calm and beautiful. Then at the Easter vacation I had a second though less personal loss. Kate Wily died of pneumonia. I don't know just how I felt about it. When I had come back to college I found the rose she had stuck in my hat still there. I did not dare to visit or to write to her sisters. (SP 70)

The impact of these deaths on the young man who had never learned to deal with his emotions is felt more keenly in this recollection of laziness and inability than it would be in an account of how he openly grieved—had he been able to—precisely because the terseness and ellipticality of the description reflect the impossibility of expression he experienced. These qualities, together with his deflecting attention away from the events occasioning feeling—the way he did here by focusing on the *dissolute* habits he took on to *dissolve* the pain before being able to look at the events prompting it—became more prominent in Stevens as he grew into full maturity. Indeed, they became the primary features of his work and life. The real man, the feeling subject, existed more in absence, in the world completed by imagination, than in presence. He is found in the spaces between words, between sentences, between titles and poems, rather than in the words, sentences, or poems. He lived more in the moments of composing while walking than he did in the office he left from or went to, where he was the polished executive, or in his home, where he moved through others' imagined worlds.

The events of Stevens's last year at Harvard inscribed this pattern of absence indelibly. In sharp contrast with the sense of himself he had had at the end of the previous summer, when in the fullness of his being he had become certain that he *was* a poet "in more than mute feeling," this nine-month period was marked only by "mute feeling." His journal keeping ceased. The mocking, ironic tone of his poems muted the notes of pain. His coarse "bar-room" behavior masked the feelings of the tender young man who had just a few months earlier mourned the impending death of a yellow jacket. Though during that summer it was already apparent that it was hard for him to face the idea of death—how he responded to thinking of his and his family's end after visiting the ruins of the Wilys' old home—his grandmother's death accentuated that difficulty and set up a pattern of dealing with it that gave shape both to the internal structure of individual poems and to the larger form of what he later intended as "The Whole of Harmonium."[35]

At this point nine months had passed between an event that profoundly affected him and his reborn possibility of speaking about what he felt. Between the time of the painful event and that expression, the cry that it occasioned was silenced deep in a pool of desired forgetfulness. This was a period of inertia, a small death in itself. There were other, longer times like this in Stevens's life—one lasted six years—as well as brief, gasping moments between poems. In all instances it was in that submerged place, the silent space between two elements, where the real, feeling man was to be found, using his handkerchief and sighing. When a poem like "The Emperor of Ice-Cream" appeared thirty-odd years after the poet's first experience of death (his aunt when he was a boy), twenty-odd after his grandmother's and Kate Wily's deaths, and about ten after his parents' deaths, the distraction offered by its brilliantly "gaudy"[36] surface had grown in proportion to how deep the pain of the occasions had been and how long that pain had been submerged, gathering associations it presented to cover feeling.

In the same way that the surface of his poems belied the reality of his feelings so did his behavior. During that last year at Cambridge, unable either to express what he felt or to console himself with a myth of "imperishable bliss" (*CP* 68) for those he loved who had died, he hid his tenderness behind "bawdy" behavior that was the equivalent of the "gaudy" aspect of his poems. He no longer felt whole as he had that "last summer" because he had blocked his grief about his grandmother's death and, later, Kate Wily's—about which he did not even let himself "know how [he] felt"; he could not dare to see or to write to her sisters. He again took on the protective coloration he was used to wear. He lived up to the expected images others provided: He was the college "rowdy" (*L* 126) or the young man who would "make something of himself" to feel secure in his father's approval, if in nothing else.

The difference between how he had felt the previous summer and how he felt on the eve of leaving Harvard was expressed clearly in the rest of the entry for June 2. Picking up immediately after noting his inability to face Kate Wily's sisters after her death at Easter (which probably occasioned the absolute immobility from March until May, as opposed to the "getting drunk almost every other night" that followed his grandmother's death in September), he went on:

Today has been stifling. I have been working in the College library in preparation for the final examinations. The same birds are back in the garden—

97

the same flowers; but somehow I do not have the affection for them that I used to have. To be sure they still delight me—but the delight is not the enchanting kind that I experienced last summer. I am conscious that when I leave Cambridge I shall leave all the surroundings that I have ever lived in—Reading, Berkeley, the mountains—and perhaps the clouds. I am going to New York, I think, to try my hand at journalism. If that does not pan out well, I am resolved to knock about the country—the world. Of course I am perfectly willing to do this—anxious, in fact. It seems to me to be the only way, directed as I am more or less strongly by the hopes and desires of my parents and myself, of realizing to the last degree any of the ambitions I have formed. I should be content to dream along to the end of my life—and opposing moralists be hanged. At the same time I should be quite content to work and be practical—but I hate the conflict whether it "avails" or not. I want my powers to be put to their fullest use—to be exhausted when I am done with them. On the other hand I do not want to have to make a petty struggle for existence—physical or literary. I must try not to be a dilettante—half dream, half deed. I must be all dream or all deed. But enough of myself—even though this is my own diary of which I am the house, the inhabitant, the lock, and the key. (L 33–34; SP 70–71)

In contrast with the stated intention of following a career in journalism—the "practical" literary life suggested by his father—in an unguarded response to a question put to him "just before he left Cambridge" by Charles Townsend Copeland (by now his friend "Copey"), to whom he had gone to say good-bye, Stevens said he was going to be "a poet." Copey reacted with "Jesus Christ!" (SP 68). It is impossible to know what went into that exclamation. But it might have had something to do with Copeland's perception of Stevens when they found themselves together on another occasion. This was recalled by Witter Bynner, who confusedly attributed to this "rowdy" incident the reason for his friend's leaving Harvard after three instead of four years (an amusing bit of distorted memory in itself):

It would seem to me interesting to preserve a brief account of the reason for Pete's [Stevens's college nickname; a subtle shift from the "Pat" of his childhood] leaving Harvard. In the square at the time was a restaurant called Ramsden's or colloquially "Rammy's" where not only undergraduates but a few of the faculty would eat midnight buckwheat cakes. The favorite waitress there was a witty Irish-woman who seemed to me in those days almost elderly—her face wrinkled always with smiles and her spirit and repartee highly appreciated by customers. One night Pete had come in from Boston fairly lit and, announcing jovially that he was going to rape Maggie [Bynner later recalled that the correct name was "Kitty"], vaulted the counter, landing so heavily behind it that both of them fell to the floor. When she screamed with enjoyably dramatic terror, a member of the English Department who was present left his buckwheats and severely interfered. From him came a deplorable report to the college authorities which led to Stevens's expulsion, which I think happened a year before his graduation.

It was after this episode that Stevens, in saying good-by to Copey announced his intent of being a poet. I do not think this occasion has been as yet recorded by a witness but I happened to be there and think what happened was an interesting and pertinent exploit. None of us who were there were given any chance to testify in his behalf but I am sure that what we might have had to say would not have borne weight against the word of a faculty member. Maggie, I am certain, bore no untoward testimony. Pete was one of her great favorites and I wish I could remember some of their banter. (*SP* 67–68)

Most surprising here is the image of the young man seen up until now being hesitant with Sybil Gage, to whom he was attracted; being instructive to those like Miss Benz, by whom he was not quite so threatened; being fraternal with the Wily sisters, for whom he cared, now being opening sexual in a rough, even if playful, way, on one of those nights when he had gotten quite drunk. There was nothing to risk with Maggie-Kitty. She obviously cared for him, and being of a different class and older—old enough to be his mother—he would not have to worry about measuring up to an image she had of him. He could get affectionate, implicitly motherly approval from her no matter what he did. Nonetheless, it was because of the strength of the feelings revealed by this kind of exuberance that the young man could not approve of himself. He was, after all, the son of a high-toned old Christian woman, and it was her approval he sought when he verbally chastised himself in his journal for his overindulgent behavior. Still, the desires of "that monster, the body," were there. Finding a woman who would satisfy "that monster" and at the same time provide the spiritual sustenance his upbringing made him crave would not be easy. In view of the additional difficulty he had in showing himself as he was, the conclusion he would come to just a short time after leaving Harvard once he was on his own in New York—that he would never marry—was to be expected.

The uncertainty of self that made it nearly impossible for him to show himself without a mask or without being drunk quickened the movement up and down between two elements as the last year at Harvard drew to a close. As he observed, he was about to leave behind everything he had ever known. The feeling of ending had been sharpened by death. One night he was drunk; the next, sober and self-recriminating. One day he was going to be a journalist and "make something of himself"—"all deed"—and the next he was going to be a poet—"all dream." At the beginning of the year he would have "sacrifice[d] a great deal to be a Saint Augustine," and at the end "he was going to rape Maggie." Things did not remain as they were long enough for him to see anything at all.

The intellectual problem of the age, the loss of faith he mourned, came to have deeper reverberations as he prepared to go out and "knock about the country—the world." The country had just begun knocking about the world itself, having extended its imperialistic arm all the way to the Philippines the year before[37] under the guise of establishing the faith that was being lost. The Puritans' lie was still at work. As President William McKinley announced America's intention to "educate the Filipinos, and uplift and Christianize them,"[38] the young Stevens was just beginning to feel how downtrodden his spirit had been by his own Christian education. Though this was not yet explicit, the doubting attitude that later emerged aimed directly at Christianity in the aggressive sarcasm pointed at the "high-toned old christian woman" (CP 59) or in the gentler irony of "Sunday Morning" (CP 66) now showed itself in his shifting feelings about himself and in his implicit unwillingness to maintain with any consistency the image of the "good Puritan" he had been prepared to take on. Preserving any image in a world presenting a false one was not something an intelligent, sensitive young man would want to do.

Perhaps it would have been easier for Stevens to recognize why he was shifting up and down so abruptly and to reject the role that had been written for him if he had felt more secure as a boy in the family drama. But as it was—with parents who were physically and emotionally undemonstrative and from his being the only child without a family name to having been sick and then having to compete with his younger brother, John—being secure in anything except the movement up and down was impossible.

Even the series of names he chose as pseudonyms pointed to what the young man had not gotten during childhood and adolescence but still wanted. "John" is the first name of two of these: "John Morris 2nd" and "John Fiske Towne."[39] The jealousy of an older for a younger sibling—especially of the same sex, who intrudes into his once-favored position—was exacerbated in Stevens's case by the circumstance of finding himself left back in the same class with this threatening creature. What could be more expected than the wish to destroy him, consume him, become him? Wallace took over John's name; he became him at least on paper. More, in "John Morris 2nd"—his first pseudonym, it appears—he incorporated not only the identity of his younger brother but also that of his older brother, Garrett Stevens, Jr. Unlike Wallace, whose name belonged to someone he did not know who could not be imitated within the family, Garrett (who, in addition, came to be known as big, rough "Buck"), was fixed securely in identification with the father from whom they all wanted approval. "Pat" naturally would have wanted to be in his position as well. Interestingly, too, "Morris" is a more definitely shaped form, in sound, of the liquid "Wallace"—the W and l's rolling away, stopped by their inverse complements, the sustaining M and hard r's. It was as though by renaming himself with this version of his name, the young poet had imaginatively remade himself both in the image of the son who was the "spitting image" of his father—and whom "Pat" must have felt their father favored because of this—and in the image of John, who, as the baby (at least until

"Pat" was seven, when their first sister was born), he must have seen as Kate's favorite.

Another name he used, "R. Jerries" (repeating again the double *r*'s of Garrett's name), is intriguing in its semianonymity. This suggested the uncertainty of the young man's identity in another way, while a fourth, "Kenneth Malone," announced itself as boisterously as "Pete" leaping over the bar at Rammy's to rape Maggie-Kitty. It is easy to imagine reading a local news report of "Kenneth Malone" doing just that. Burly coarseness was an aspect with which Stevens was uncomfortable. Being giantlike as he was—Alfred Kreymborg[40] and others remembered feeling dwarfed by his bulk—was something that contributed a real, physical sense to Stevens's uncertainty about fitting in. This was clear in the incident where he described himself as a clumsy giant after injuring the yellow jacket, as it was in his referring to his body as "that monster." While his size had been valued when he played football at Reading Boys' School, it no doubt made him feel ungainly at tea-party gatherings with young women in Cambridge parlors, when he sat on chairs supported by lady-like legs and sipped from cups through the delicate, ear-shaped handles of which his fingers awkwardly fitted.

Finally, another pseudonym, "Carrol More," which he used to sign his first, bitter ironic pieces during the spring of 1900, pointed to what he wanted for himself: "more." The double *r*'s of "Carrol" reappeared as reminders that it was Garrett with whom he wanted to identify, in the hope that he might in this way win "more" approval from him. Accordingly, though wanting to indulge the "imagination" he had inherited from his mother, he followed his father's voice of "reason" and tried to "make something of himself." Harvard had done its job.

III

NEW YORK

1900

For he cares not to seem the
bravest but to be,
Harvesting thus the furrow of his
mind.

—Aeschylus, *Seven Against Thebes* (Philip Vellacott, translator)

> . . . this electric town which I adore.

—Journal entry, March 11, 1901,
Letters (p. 52); *Souvenirs and Prophecies* (p. 100)

Poised between the slow step of the nineteenth century and the dash of the twentieth, Stevens arrived from Cambridge on Thursday, June 14, 1900, to seek his fortune in New York. The city moved as uncertainly as he. The young man walked through dimly lit nights and blazoned days. He followed shadowy streets crowded with clattering horse-drawn cabs, clanking elevated trains, and electric cable cars. He was at first dismayed. He saw it with a mind of simpler ways, educated by Pennsylvania's broad views and Cambridge's subtle arguments. He found the city wanting, the coarse, "money-making" pace of its life incompatible with his fine-tuned spirit:

> All New York, as I have seen it, is for sale—and I think the parts I have seen are the parts that make New York what it is. It is dominated by necessity. Everything has its price—from Vice to Virtue. I do not like it and unless I get some position that is unusually attractive I shall not stay. What is there to keep me, for example, in a place where all Beauty is on exhibition, all Power a tool of Selfishness, and all Generosity a source of Vanity? New York is a field of tireless and antagonistic interests—undoubtedly fascinating but horribly unreal. Everybody is looking at everybody else—a foolish crowd walking on mirrors. (*L* 38; *SP* 72–73)

But he did stay. He found his position—with the *New York Tribune,* one of the two newspapers (the other was the *Post*) that he did not judge to be "rank" (*SP* 74)—and within a few months he was completing New York in his imagination as he had himself and other places he loved. By the following March New York had become that "electric town which [he] adore[d]." He no longer noticed the familiar leftovers of the nineteenth century—the horses, the mud roads above Ninetieth Street. These were things he had always seen.

Equipped with letters of introduction supplied by the Harvard old boys' network, Stevens began a bustling city life. After checking in at the Astor House, a fashionable residence hotel across from St. Paul's Church on lower Broadway, where he was to spend his first night, he walked the short distance to 29 Park Row, crossing in front of the magnificent Victorian post office. Once there, at the offices of the *New York Commercial Advertiser,* he "presented a letter from Copeland [Copey, who only a few weeks before had "severely interfered" between him and Kitty behind the bar at Rammy's] to Carl Hovey who introduced him to [Lincoln] Steffens a Californian, the city editor" (*L* 37; *SP* 71). After leaving, he industriously went on to the offices of the *Evening Sun,* a few doors away. Then, after that, off to dinner with Rodman Gilder, another Harvard contact (class of 1899), who was working for the *Sun* (*L* 37) and who had provided his lead there. After this dinner with Gilder and his "Aunt Julia"—"a witty, old lady of some avoir-dupois and watery eyes who was disappointed because the sherbet was pineapple instead of orange" (*L* 37; *SP* 72), he was off on another quick trip, this time uptown to the East River (Carl Schurz) Park in Yorkville, where he covered a band concert for a sample piece for the *Advertiser.* In the middle of the German-speaking neighborhood, Stevens felt both familiar and strange, trying to see with the eyes of an outsider how the people with whom he felt "such a kinship" passed their time on a near-summer evening in the new Babylon, far from the soil where neither their virtues nor their vices bore capitals.

Returning that night to his room, he looked out. On one side St. Paul's steeple interrupted the sky with its path to heaven. On the other, the rounded cupola and concave mansards of the post office hinted at the city's ties to Paris and a European past. Mimicking the underlying religious spirit of the work ethic, the highest towers of government office buildings and banks looked like church steeples and belfries. Like him, the city had been raised with the image of a "good Puritan" in mind. Like him, too, the city's sensibility had been educated with a Victorian longing for fanciful neo-Renaissance shapes. The mid-nineteenth century's finicky façades looked back at him decorously. Here, too, he would go up and down between two elements.

The next day he entered a different kind of American scene. Though the Astor House was an appropriate address for a young gentleman visiting New York from Cambridge, it was not the place for a young man trying to make it on his own, for a while at least still living on money advanced by his father. The move was abrupt. From one night with a window on the gracious past Stevens found himself in a tenement neighborhood. The boardinghouse where he stayed was run by two maiden Frenchwomen. Had he heeded the advice given in *Appleton's* guide to New York[1] about the kinds of inhabitants likely to be in such residences, where one didn't need a letter of reference to get a house key, he might have made a different choice. But he didn't, and in his journal that same evening he recorded his first impressions of the two "ladies" and of the adventures of his second day with a naïve ambivalence that reflected his uncertainty about the place. Though in some ways it seemed "hard and cruel and lifeless," he wanted, half-ironically, to make it his "Paradise," his "Elysium of Elysiums"—strange echoes of the Puritans' plight:

> This morning I called to see Charles Scribner who was not at his office, and Arthur Goodrich of the Macmillan Company with whom I am to take lunch.
> Goodrich took me to lunch at the Players Club—an interesting place where we saw celebrities. We sat on the verandah. Nearby was Reid the artist—I think it is Reid although now I see the word in black and white it

may be Read. The walls of the house are covered with memories of the stage and actors. It is a near approach to Bohemia.

I called at Scribner's again and found Charles Scribner in his offices. He is a plain man with a keen face. He was pleasant to me and put my name down. Speaking of pleasantness, I must give the preference to Goodrich who although a stranger treated me like an old friend.

The house where I am living in is a boarding-house kept by two unmarried French women. The elder, about thirty years of age, has a bosom a foot and a half thick. No wonder the French are amorous with such accommodation for lovers. The younger, about twenty-eight years of age, is of more moderate proportions. She had dark rings under her eyes. I have just slaughtered two bugs on a wall of my room. They were lice! Dinner next—wherever I can find it—with an aimless evening to follow.

Took dinner in a little restaurant—poached eggs, coffee and three crusts of bread—a week ago my belly was swagging with strawberries. Bought a couple of newspapers from a little fellow with blue eyes who was selling *Journals* & *Worlds* & who had to ransack the neighborhood for the ones I wanted. As I came back to my room the steps of the street for squares were covered with boarders etc. leaning on railings and picking their teeth. The end of the street was ablaze with a cloud of dust lit by the sun. All around me were tall office buildings closed up for the night. The curtains were drawn and the faces of the buildings looked hard and cruel and lifeless. This street of mine is a wonderful thing. Just now the voices of children manage to come through my window from out of it, over the roofs and through the walls. . . .

The carpet on the floor of my room is gray set off with pink roses. In the bath room is a rug with the figure of a peacock woven in it—blue and scarlet, and black, and green, and gold. And on the paper on my wall are designs of fleur-de-lis and forget-me-not. Flowers and birds enough of rag and paper—but no more. In this Eden, made spicey with the smoke of my pipe which hangs heavy in the ceiling, in this Paradise ringing with the bells of streetcars and the bustle of fellow boarders heard through the thin partitions, in this Elysium of Elysiums I now shall lay me down.

I shall say my prayers up the chimney. That is their only chance of getting above the housetops.

I have just looked out of the window to see whether there were any stray tramps on the roof. I' Faith, there were stars in heaven. (*L* 37–39; *SP* 72–73)[2]

On the third day he rose again to make his way, but alone, unlike the previous two days, when his Harvard contacts had properly introduced him to some of the more pleasant aspects of a gentleman's life in the city. Without the distraction offered by others and prompted by a letter from his father that he found waiting for him that morning at the Astor House—where he had stopped to collect mail—Stevens felt pangs of doubt. In the journal entry of that evening he uncovered the roots of his uneasiness. He counterpointed what he projected his father's imagining of him to be—"a sad-eyed, half-starved individual"—against his own: to be one of the "gentlemen" working at the *Post:*

June 16

This morning I called at the Astor House for my mail and found a letter from my father. He called me a "brave fellow" for coming here. Great Scott! The streets are full of "brave fellows." He probably imagines me a sad-eyed, half-starved individual wandering about in search of Employment. As a matter of fact I went to bed at half-past nine last night, woke at six this morning, dozed until eight, took a cold bath, and went downstairs for breakfast. Then I made my call at the Astor House and later at the office of the *Evening Post.* The *Post* is run in an ideal manner—nine to three, and everybody a gentleman! I shall write some special articles—That is necessary before any engagement is made. (*SP* 73)

Moving between these two images, unable to reconcile them, he felt raw. There was not even lunch or dinner with someone that day so that he would have had to present at least an image of himself. Alone and afraid, the young man found himself wandering around what was to become one of his favorite locales, along West Street and the wharves poking into the North (Hudson) River:

I went down to the wharves along the North R. On one I found a rather pleasant, fat, red-faced, middle-sized old man surrounded by a half-dozen little Terrier dogs and a Newfoundland. I played with the dogs a quarter of an hour or more. Continued mousing about the wharves [revealingly, he took on the characteristic of a terrier himself] and saw hucksters, draymen and the like eating green beans and canned fruit for their luncheons. I found a ring of foreigners in a park "shooting craps." They were having an exciting but good-natured time—making and losing ten-cent fortunes. I struck up Canal Street and saw an Italian family making its living. The husband was bent over an ice-cream freezer on the pavement—it was an invention of his own. It did not make my mouth water. In the doorway was his wife stitching at some piece of cloth. By her side was a little girl playing with a doll— an invention like the ice-cream freezer, but much dirtier. I stopped to eat a dozen clams for ten cents and got about half-way through the dozen. (*SP* 73–74)

Among the foreigners, visibly more displaced than he but nonetheless having a good time and making their living, Stevens sensed his isolation even more sharply. He transferred the poignancy of what he felt onto what he saw around him. In the juxtaposition of the Italian making ice cream in an "invention of his own" and his wife "stitching at some piece of cloth," an instant of experience was frozen into an image that later melted and mixed with others in *his* own invention to emerge remade, "whipped" into the "concupiscent curds" of "The Emperor of Ice-Cream" (see pp. 51–52). The main actions of its two stanzas echo those recorded by the twenty-year-old who looked at the world colored by his pain. His old life was dead, and he could not believe in his own promise of paradise. The unconscious rhapsodist deep inside him was embroidering fantails of associations on the cloth of his life.

When he came back to his room, the lamp affixed its beam to illuminate the darkness of his spirit:

> I spent the afternoon in my room, having a rather sad time with my thoughts. Have been wondering whether I am going into the right thing after all. Is literature really a profession? Can you single it out, or must you let it decide in you for itself? I have determined upon one thing, and that is not to *try* to suit anybody except myself. If I fail then I shall have failed through myself and not through the imitation of what such and such a paper wants. . . . (*L* 39; *SP* 74)

That night he went out again. He walked to Washington Square to let his spirit mingle with what he saw around him to dissipate his sadness and isolation. In the journal entry written the following Sunday morning, the holy hush of ancient sacrifice announced by the church bells' ringing was transformed into a personal resurrection while the young poet, remembering the evening before, lifted his spirit as he noted what he had lifted his eyes to see: "on top of the bus . . . a group of girls in neat Spring jackets and bonnets covered with cherries and roses." His mood lightened, he "experiment[ed]" on "special articles" for the *Post*. Again projecting his change of feeling outside, he named New York the "most egotistical place in the world" (*SP* 74), as though the city wanted the job of a "gentleman" at the *Post*.

By afternoon, feeling well-pleased, he rewarded himself with what turned out to be "Trop de Cuisine Bourgeoise" ("too much home cooking") (*SP* 75) and ended up spending the rest of the day in bed. This was at least symbolic punishment for having indulged both his imagination and "that monster, the body" on his first Sunday alone in New York—when his mother would have had him praying.

The next morning, recovered, after dropping his articles at the *Post,* he headed southwest to the Battery, where he ambled, watched, and collected material for another story ("A Battery Naples"), which he wrote up that same afternoon (*SP* 75). Following the steeple of Trinity Church as his guide up and down through the busy, twisting downtown streets, he stopped in on passing it. As though struck by what he had not done the day before, he noticed people praying. Later he remarked in his journal that it was a "really impressive sight" (*SP* 75)—the very first of the sights he had seen in New York during the last four days that earned this stressed adjective.

The next occasion on which he was equally impressed was his visit to

Columbia's Low Library two days later. It was a welcome moment. He had been running up and downtown, making calls, following up on contacts, dining with Russell Loines at the Harvard Club. Or he had been waiting in his room for hours that seemed days for a message to arrive telling him that he had been hired. During these endless periods he "read Wordsworth and Thackeray . . . smoked several disagreeable pipes" (*SP* 75), rewrote stories he had written a few days earlier, and recorded impressions in his journal. There he noted the details of the library's "grandeur." This came immediately after his commenting about the impressiveness of the people praying in Trinity Church. This juxtaposition pointed ahead to another poem, "A High-Toned Old Christian Woman" (*CP* 59), in the same way that the Italian ice-cream maker and his wife stitching became incorporated in the paired images of "The Emperor" and the dead woman who "embroidered fantails once." This time the suppressed cries of the poem's occasion were the feelings surrounding his mother, the high-toned old Christian woman, and the way he was replacing her "hankering for hymns" with the "hullabaloo" of words he wrote and words that filled the library. Here follow excerpts from the journal entry and from the poem:

> Also went out to Columbia College at Morningside Heights—a delightful place. The Seth Low library has a great deal of grandeur to it—its approach consists of terraces of granite stairs rising to a domical building with a porch of lofty columns. There are roses and evergreens planted here and there on adjacent terraces. Their scent filled the hot, motionless air that hung about the structure. Inside is a huge dome supported by encircling galleries and alcoves. From these, I could hear the song-sparrows singing in the foliage without. (*SP* 75)

> A HIGH-TONED OLD CHRISTIAN WOMAN
> . . . But take
> The opposing law and make a peristyle,
> And from the peristyle project a masque
> Beyond the planets. Thus, our bawdiness,
> Unpurged by epitaph, indulged at last,
> Is equally converted into palms,
> Squiggling like saxophones. And palm for palm,
> Madame, we are where we began. Allow,
> Therefore, that in the planetary scene
> Your disaffected flagellants, well-stuffed,
> Smacking their muzzy bellies in parade,
> Proud of such novelties of the sublime,
> Such tink and tank and tunk-a-tunk-tunk,
> May, merely may, madame, whip from themselves
> A jovial hullabaloo among the spheres.
>
> ·

In addition to seeing again how a painful or problematic situation of his youth became the core of a poem made complex with later associations, these instances of sequences in the journal reappearing in poems illustrate how the older poet used his journals. Just as he quarried them during this period for the material of the early poems and stories, later in his life he went over them again and again. In this process he re-created past experiences, which he could then transcend by shaping the feelings attached to them into poems. As a twenty-year-old young man Stevens avoided the conflict between what he had taken on of his mother's expectations and his own need to write poetry that could replace religion, thus ignoring the strictures of the religion in which she had educated him. Hiding from the conflict, he simply got sick after following his own bent. But about twenty years later, with a great deal more self-knowledge and the ability to "whip" his feelings into the shape of a poem, he wrote what, on one level, was the apology to his mother that he could not make when he was twenty. At the same time it was an *apologia pro vita sua,* an apology to/for himself, a justification for his writing poetry.

Considering what this process involves makes it clear why Stevens called poetry "a health," a "completion of life." In verbally reconstructing events, he voiced feelings he could not express at the time the events occurred. "A poem is the cry of its occasion" (*CP* 473). The process of going back over the past, looking at it again and again, finding words to embody buried feelings was not different from what Sigmund Freud intended as the purpose of his "talking cure." Stevens did not name Freud "one of the great figures in the world" (*OP* 218) lightly. He called Freud's "eye" the "microscope of potency" (*CP* 367). He came to understand that it was only by being able to express feelings that he could become free of them, at least to the extent of controlling and shaping them, rather than being controlled and shaped by them. In venting feelings to and about the "high-toned old Christian woman," the poet simultaneously explained himself and created a fiction that, in existing on its own, was an indication of a measure of freedom. He was no longer constrained by the training that would not have allowed him to mock it openly, as he did in the lines of the poem.

Understanding this process does not mean that for Stevens this or any other poem had only one "analytic" purpose or that for any poem there was only one occasion. "A High-Toned Old Christian Woman" was addressed to many things. It was about Elsie, about the part of his own nature that was like a high-toned old Christian woman, about any high-toned old Christian woman, as much as it was addressed to and about the high-toned old Christian woman who was his mother.[3] More, this or any poem is always also about the pleasures of merely circulating through words, about the joy of indulging in the sounds and shapes of language with all its power of suggestion, allusion, and association. But not to see the connection Stevens's poems have to the real "facts"[4] of his life is to miss what gave them their "potency," what made them part of the *res* and not about it.

Though at this point Stevens had not felt the impact Freud's ideas were to make in the century just beginning, he had just come from Harvard, where William James had, as the content of the course Santayana took with him while still an undergraduate, read "from the manuscript, chapter by chapter, his new *Principles of Psychology*."[5] Stevens did not escape the force of James's stress on "understanding" the "facts" of the normal by studying the abnormal.[6] It had been passed on to Santayana and to the others who came into contact with him in classrooms and crossing the Harvard Yard. James left hanging in the air his suggestion that it was in the "recesses of feeling, the darker, blinder strata of character . . . [where] we catch real fact in the making."[7] Those who breathed it in could not avoid having it affect their sensibilities and having it contribute, as it did in Stevens's case, to the self-consciousness left over from the romantics.

In the last ten years of the century not only had James's *Principles* been published, but so had Henri Bergson's work on consciousness, on memory, and—importantly for Stevens, who used it later—on laughter.[8] F. H. Bradley's *Appearance and Reality,* naming what became one of Stevens's major themes, also appeared (1893). This work, too, derived from the attempt to rationalize and analyze what could not be seen except in dreams and imagination. Freud approached the problem individually, as in *The Interpretation of Dreams* (the English edition came out in 1900). James G. Frazer considered the same issue culturally (the first volume of *The Golden Bough* was published in 1890; subsequent volumes followed until 1915). These pioneering works were quickly followed both by more specialized explorations of the "unseen"— Havelock Ellis began his *Studies in the Psychology of Sex* in 1897—and by broader explorations, such as Wilhelm Wundt's *Comparative Psychology,* published in 1900, which already attempted to provide an overview and safe categorization of the new discipline. The thrust of all this work was to destroy the Victorian habit of mind. When Victoria, who had given her name to the last reign of appearances, died in 1901, she was no longer dressed in what she was used to wear but wrapped in the same sheet on which the age symbolized in her had been examined "like a patient etherized upon a table."[9] If her horny feet protruded, they only showed how cold she was, and dumb.

Just as in the seventeenth century Galileo's invention of the telescope catalyzed the change in world view that had begun with Nicolaus Copernicus's turning things around, a similar revolution was completing its turn around the year 1900, with Wilhelm Röntgen's discovery of X rays five years earlier now allowing things unseen before to be seen. The broader suggestion prompted by this discovery was that all appearances would ultimately disclose their hidden realities: "Let the lamp affix its beam. . . ./Let be be finale of seem" (*CP* 64).

The age that had first spoken of the "spirit of the age"—a concept born out of the Victorians' desire to imitate other ages frozen and gilded in their imaginations (the Renaissance, classical Greece)[10]—was breathing its last. As it did, it was as though the moist impression left on the mirror held up to verify that, indeed, the body still had a bit of life had become miraculously fixed, as on an X-ray plate. It remained as physical evidence to be examined. The spirit, psyche, soul, never before captured, was now being looked at through Freud's microscope.

を

At the same time as the twenty-year-old young man explored the dark city at night, passing concert saloons that lined streets around the Bowery, hearing the regular honky-tonk of the "Harlem Rag" or the newest success, the "Maple Leaf Rag," [11] on "badly thumped pianos," [12] the scientists of the spirit, preceding him by a generation, explored the darkness of human motivations and experience with a renewed faith in reason. After Darwin's discoveries this new faith attempted to replace faith in God as the ensurer of continued progress toward truth. As Stevens roamed away from everything he had ever known, alone, without a job, feeling like one of the itinerant piano players who found their sustenance working in the disreputable establishments he passed, he responded to the irregular syncopated rhythms of the new ragtime music. Hidden beneath the quick, playful tempos were experiences of dislocation and of continued desire for faith. Stevens could hear the sad strains of a gay waltz adapted and transformed in the rags. [13] Like the black musicians roaming "free" up from the South, he had moved away from his familiar soil. Just as they reproduced in beats mimicking the quickening pace of city life the deeper movements of ring shouts they had sung in their churches back home [14]—movements of songs that proclaimed their faith—he, too, changed what he was experiencing of the newborn century into poems that re-created his yearning for his native place and the faith that was lost.

Years later, in the thirties and forties, when critics were again registering the complaint that Stevens's poetry, though beautifully impressionistic, showed no moral concern, no contact with the pressing social and political realities of his time, [15] among the poems published in the volumes that appeared during those decades (*Ideas of Order* in 1936 and *Transport to Summer* in 1947) were two that reflected an intimate awareness of the difficulties of being an American in an age of transition. Both these poems voiced feelings that began at this moment of Stevens's great transition from the relative security of life as a youth, still not pressed by necessity, to life as an adult, aware of responsibility for both present and future in making every choice. Stevens opened the twentieth century, the "Age of Anxiety," approaching in his twenty-first year that same "age" himself. The anxiety continued and deepened. Eventually, in 1935, Stevens interwove aspects of his experience of dislocation and disbelief with that of ". . . these sudden mobs of men,//These sudden clouds of faces and arms"—like those he first saw thumping pianos in New York's saloons. He felt in himself and in them "An immense suppression, freed," and described their "voices crying without knowing for what,//Except to be happy, without knowing how,/Imposing forms they [could] not describe,/Requiring order beyond their speech" (*CP* 122).

And after another eight years—World War II already having erupted—in

"No Possum, No Sop, No Taters" (*CP* 293) the connections between his early days in New York, his later realizations, and the reality of others torn from their roots[16] were again carried in the strain of a musical metaphor that evoked ragtime and what it represented. "Possum and Taters" was a 1900 rag. It described "a Negro feast, without a hint of big city life."[17] Its "easy going"[18] syncopated phrases celebrated an integral part of the life being left behind. In Stevens's poem the irregular rhythm was preserved. With an opening line that could have come from a black song, it memorialized the absence of "the old sun" and the loss of belief in God, who, symbolized by the sun, had maintained the "old" hierarchical order. The addition of "Sop" and then its negation, together with "Possum" and "Taters," reinforced the sense of loss. With the death of God, His "eyesight falling to earth," even imagination was lost. There was not nothing, no, no, never nothing . . . no possum, no sop, no taters.

❦

After he had spent almost a week in New York Stevens's uneasiness had not ceased. He consoled himself with imaginings of being back in the security of home (*SP* 75). But he also soothed himself with some of the pleasures the present had to offer. In the journal entry of June 25, just after voicing his intention to return to Reading if things did not improve, he recorded how he prodigally indulged himself rather than remain in his room, alternately brooding and bolstering his spirit with wished-for palliatives: "Have just been to a barber's shop where they put four different kinds of oil on my face—not to mention a dab of vaseline in my hair and a spray of violet water up my nostrils. I feel like an 'embalmèd sweet'" (*SP* 75). But the voice of reality that had until this point been exerted by his father whispered to him as his own. So, for lunch, to economize, he "bought a box of strawberries and ate them in [his] room." By the time he entered the morning's luxurious experience in his journal, guilt and morbidity had set in, so he compared himself to an "embalmèd sweet."

This connection was secretly stretched over the years to reappear subtly shaped when the poet himself became "a shearsman of sorts" and composed "The Man with the Blue Guitar" (*CP* 165) in 1936 and 1937. In this poem the persona of the barber-shearsman was linked, through a historical tie, to that of a surgeon. Through a homonymic pun on the etymologies of "barber" (κομμωτής) and "comedian" (κωμῳδός) this figure was tied to the persona of the juggler-entertainer-comedian as well.[19] In the poem the "shearsman" plays the unheard melody *sweeter* still than what he is asked to play. This he does in the process of dissecting his already "embalmèd" brain: "To lay his brain upon the board/And pick the acrid colors out" (*CP* 166). Again, an experience of youth became metamorphosed over a period of time—here over thirty-five years—into a mature and powerful poem. The sensibility being groomed in the barber's chair, feeling the strain between indulgence and threatened punishment, finally took control, in the later poem, of the feelings

114

only implicit in the journal entry and openly named his conflict as "a duet/With the undertaker" (*CP* 177).

What Stevens was experiencing personally in 1900, the culture was experiencing as well. Matthew Arnold had already named the danger threatening the established order: anarchy. Stevens had read his theoretical exposition of the problem in *Culture and Anarchy,* as well as Ivan Turgenev's realistic description (*L* 509–10), unfolding it as part of the problem between fathers and sons, something with which he could immediately sympathize. The culture attempted to preserve things as they were, embalmed as the ideal to be sought. But this attempt was no longer sufficient insurance against the combined forces of dissolution that attacked, like "jades affecting the sequestered bride" (*CP* 34), what had been. The desire to maintain the old order was so strong that nearly half a century later, when Stevens wrote "The Man with the Blue Guitar," he could characterize his imagined audience as still calling for a song of "things as they are," echoing Arnold's lesson:

For as there is a curiosity about intellectual matters which is futile, and merely a disease, so there is certainly a curiosity,—a desire after the things of the mind simply for their own sakes and for the pleasure of seeing them as they are,—which is, in an intelligent being, natural and laudable. Nay, the very desire to see things as they are implies a balance and regulation of mind which is not often attained without fruitful effort, and which is the very opposite of the blind and diseased impulse of mind which is what we mean to blame when we blame curiosity. Montesquieu says: "The first motive which ought to impel us to study is the desire to augment the excellence of our nature, and to render an intelligent being yet more intelligent." This is the true ground to assign for the genuine scientific passion, however manifested, and for culture, viewed simply as a fruit of this passion; and it is a worthy ground, even though we let the term *curiosity* stand to describe it.[20]

Stevens's preoccupation with death—which he had begun to make explicit just before he left Cambridge (in many of the stories and poems he had written over his last year there, death or disappearance is a repeated motif[21])—reflected itself both in his personal experiences around this time, as he recorded them in his journal, and in the general tenor of what was being voiced by those who were the literary arbiters of the period. Edmund Clarence Stedman, whose *Victorian Anthology* Stevens spent many hours perusing during these first months in New York, "spoke of the hour in which his *An* [*sic*] *American Anthology* appeared [1900] as a 'twilight interval.'"[22] And as a later critic of Stevens noted in this context, "Poetry seemed less and less significant in a world of science, industrialism and middle-class culture."[23] This situation contributed to Stevens's wavering about pursuing the purely literary life of a poet and following, instead, the more practical way of journalism urged by his father. It could also in part account for the attention Stevens gave to writing stories during his last year at Harvard and now, as he tried to peddle his talent for "painting pictures in words" to big-city editors. If in the world of poetry in America in 1900 even the "sweeping innovations of Whitman and the incisive wit and haunting suggestiveness of Emily Dickinson were largely ignored,"[24] how could he hope to be recognized?

Against this shifting background and still without a job—though a visit on the previous Wednesday, June 20, to an editor at *Munsey's* had given him a bit of hope that he would "get something after all" (*SP* 75)—Stevens sought some fixed point. He attempted to recapture a moment of his past only to find that, too, tinged by death, the death of his "rose-colored" memory and a reminder of the death of an uncle, Henry Strodach, the Lutheran pastor with whom he had lived and whose church school he had attended for a year as a boy. The entry recording this visit to Brooklyn on the morning of June 22 is especially interesting because of two instances of seeming pretense and because, as Holly Stevens notes (*SP* 76), the remembrance suggests a connection with a later poem, "Piano Practice at the Academy of the Holy Angels" (*OP* 21).[25] One of the pretenses was his describing himself as being from Massachusetts, noted earlier in relation to the masks he had begun to wear at Harvard:

> Yesterday I went over to Brooklyn to see the parochial school I attended when I visited my uncle Henry Strodach many years ago. My memory of it had gone through the customary rose-color process. It is unnecessary to say that the real was not the ideal. I found the place [St. Paul's Lutheran Church, at the corner of South Fifth and Rodney streets], but hardly recognized it. The front of the church was covered with ivy—ineffectually. I went to the yard of the old school and found a little girl playing in it. She called to her mother who took me about the building. I asked her what had become of Strodach. She told me the whole sad story—though she said his death had taken place in Albany instead of Reading. [Strodach had committed suicide; he was the husband of Stevens's mother's sister.] I told her I was from Massachusetts etc. She introduced me to her husband, Hugo; and the two of them chattered away. . . .
>
> . . . the girls of the school once cornered me and tried to borrow a pocket-knife—a ruse to find out whether I had one. They presented one to me shortly afterward on my birthday—one which went the way of all my knives. As I was leaving I caught a glimpse of the iron steps in the yard leading up to the door through which I had thrown kisses to the knife-presenting misses the day I took my leave. I wonder where they all are now. I have forgotten their names and even their faces though if I had kept my early letters I should find several from them with old little designs thereon which I remember their writing to me after I had returned home. The old organ I used to drum upon was gone; and in its place was a piano wrapped in a dusty linen cover. (*SP* 76)

The second pretense involved his having asked about his uncle, it seems, disingenuously since he did know that the death had occurred in Reading, not in Albany. This inconsistency also puts into question whether Stevens knew it had been a suicide but did not indicate it, the suicide of a religious man having particularly strong and pointed implications. Strodach was the brother-in-law of Kate, the high-toned old Christian woman who had read Stevens bedtime stories from the Bible and who, until she died, "always maintained an active interest in the Bible and found there the solace she desired" (*L* 173). If one bears this in mind—and that she had entrusted her son to the care of this man and her sister for a year—it is not farfetched to suggest that Stevens's "ruses" were in response to having known of this suicide. He used "ruse" to describe the trick the girls had played on him. His uncle's death, which had to have taken place at a time before this visit—perhaps even before Stevens had left for Cambridge—in a town as small as Reading was not something that would have gone unnoticed. Stevens's knowledge of it could easily have fed into his cry for something sacred in which to believe. Moreover, it could help explain the habit of posturing he had begun while at Harvard.

The young man who had already intellectually explored the question of faith and the relationships of poetry, religion, and manhood would not have to move far to reach deep skepticism about Christianity if it could not sustain even one of its propounders. This also would prompt profound doubt about the identity that had been shaped by this morality. Without the core of being so carefully nurtured by his years of religious training at the hands of his mother, his uncle for that year, the parochial elementary school he attended, Sunday school classes, singing in the choir, his years as an altar boy, who was he but a young man made out of words, words that were feints, "ruses," tricks of a sleight-of-hand man? What counted was mythology of self. There was nothing left of him except in faint, memorial gesturings. He could not have done otherwise. Without a firm knowledge of who he was, who he had been bred to be—part of the intelligence of his soil, part of the old order that was dying—all he could do was "pose" (*SP* 90).

Stevens returned from his visit to Brooklyn in late afternoon. After his ride on the elevated railway over the still newly famed East River Bridge (later named Brooklyn) or on the Williamsburg ferry—which, besides being closer to the neighborhood he had visited, was three cents cheaper than the elevated's five-cent fare[26]—he made his way uptown. He moved from the polyglot chatter of the shorefront to the stately area of better restaurants, hotels—the Fifth Avenue, the Victoria—and shops of "masculine character."[27] Their patrons filled Madison Square, where he stopped and "sat in the garden, watching the fountain, and reading newspapers" (*SP* 76). At the edge of the square he could see the monument to General William Jenkins Worth. Around him nurses, shaped into hourglasses by their high-necked, bustled dresses, pushed prams and tended children. Others, like him, sat, read, and looked around.

At one edge of the park was the Dewey Arch, recently constructed (1898–99) to commemorate the admiral's victory over the Spanish fleet at Manila Bay. Imitating the Roman arches of Titus and Vespasian and aligned with the Washington Arch, it converted the "lower stretch of Fifth Avenue into a 'triumphal' thoroughfare,"[28] evoking an attachment to the glories of a European past rather than the present reality of America's imperialist expansionism. At another edge was the Jerome Mansion, where "Winston Churchill's mother lived as a girl,"[29] and across from that was the extraordinarily fanciful Madison Square Garden. This structure (the second Garden constructed around 1890 at a cost then of $3 million) imitated the Moorish Giralda Tower in Seville. A baroquely fashioned roof colonnade, open cupolas, and an arcade at street level all finished in buff brick and terra-cotta tiles gave both the building and the surrounding area a hint of exoticism. And topping the tower of this "largest building in America devoted entirely to amusements," was Augustus Saint-Gaudens's figure of Diana, arching forward, delicately balanced on one foot (she now stands in the Philadelphia Museum). Ironically, she stretched in very un-Victorian nakedness, her original drapery having been stripped away in a thunderstorm. Only five days later, atop the *World* building, stretching himself to see the city from its best viewing place, Stevens was the victim of a similar storm. "A stroke of lightning" from a suddenly breaking summer storm hit a flagstaff on a nearby building and knocked him down (*SP* 78). He scrambled up and got to the street, but he had been stripped bare as well. He had, it seems, received a sign.

But before the sign came and he got his job at the *Tribune,* there were still a few more days of despondency and nights of fitful reading and edgy writing. The evening after his excursion to Brooklyn and his afternoon at Madison Square, he alternately read "more newspapers"—trying to get a sense of what he should be writing—and reread some of his favorite pieces. One of the writers he turned to was Robert Louis Stevenson. Moving up and down between straining to find an appropriate style to imitate if he wanted to get a newspaper job and comforting himself with the familiarity of some of his best-loved writing, like *The Silverado Squatters* (he also read "Letter to a Young Gentleman Who Proposes to Embrace the Career of Art" and "A Christmas Sermon"), Stevens found himself writing a poem, "A Window in the Slums." It borrowed its diction from the echoes of Stevenson's quatrains he heard intoning in his prose and, as Holly Stevens points out (*SP* 77), from another poem, William Ernest Henley's "Margaritae Sorori, I.M.,"[30] which was quoted by Stevenson in his "Christmas Sermon." Couched in a rocking rhythm was Stevens's perception of the strangeness of his new life in New York. This sense was artificially blended with the London of Henley's poem. It focused ambiguously around "late birds" with Stevens's Keatsian feeling of belatedness in relation to writing poetry at all:

> I think I hear beyond the walls
> > The sound of late birds singing.
> Ah! what a sadness those dim calls
> > To city streets are bringing.

But who will from my window lean
    May hear, neath cloud belated,
Voices far sadder intervene
    Sweet songs with longing weighted—

Gay children in their fancied towers
    Of London, singing light
Gainst heavier bars, more gay than in their flowers
    The birds of the upclosing night

And after stars their places fill
    And no bird greets the skies;
The voices of the children still
    Up to my window rise.

                                  (*SP* 77)

The prison image ("Gainst heavier bars") evoking "Vita Mea" written at Harvard (see p. 69) reappeared here. But there was something more. The kind of reversal suggested by "upclosing night" for nightfall was repeated later in "Le Monocle de Mon Oncle," in which "A deep up-pouring from some saltier well/. . . bursts its watery syllable" (*CP* 13). The hourglass marking the century was being turned.

Stevens was extremely sensitive to this reversal and to the turning shapes it occasioned. His sense was sharpened by his sympathy for Stevenson—a sympathy that lasted his lifetime and affected more than his poetic sensibility. During the years of his letter-writing courtship of Elsie Moll he recommended, as part of the "required readings" with which he attempted to educate her, *A Child's Garden of Verses* and *Virginibus Puerisque*. And much later, swinging their child high in the air of Elizabeth Park in Hartford, he recited lines to which I, too (as Holly Stevens remembers she was[31]), was swung:

How do you like to go up in a swing,
    Up in the air so blue?
Oh, I do think it the pleasantest thing
    Ever a child can do!

Up in the air and over the wall,
    Till I can see so wide,
Rivers and trees and cattle and all
    Over the countryside—

Till I look down on the garden green
    Down on the roof so brown—
Up in the air I go flying again,
    Up in the air and down![32]

The aspect that touched his mind now had to do with Stevenson's attention to the meeting of old and new on American soil. In *The Silverado Squatters* especially, he elaborated on the passing of the old in the industrialized life of the expanding continent. Stevens's sympathy for Stevenson's interest in the evanescent was born out of a combination of things, not the least of which seems to have been an unconscious identification with this marvelous shaper of fictions who traveled and visited places in reality the way Stevens eventually did only in imagination. *The Silverado Squatters* provided one of the concrete bases for this identification. In describing a meeting with one of the rather raw characters Stevenson encountered in his travels in northern California's mountain foothills, he was addressed as "Mr. Stevens."[33]

Deeper than this nominal coincidence there were other reasons for the spiritual closeness Stevens felt to this storyteller. Stevenson, too, had been shaped by Presbyterianism and was painfully aware, as he expressed fictively in *Dr. Jekyll and Mr. Hyde,* of the ravaging effects of this constraining morality on personality.[34] In *The Silverado Squatters,* where he recorded his actual stay in Silverado and Calistoga, California—two deserted mining towns on the slopes of Mount Saint Helena—he described, in the straightforward manner of travel accounts appearing in the late-nineteenth-century issues of the *Century Magazine* (in which it was first published in November 1883) how unfit the European was to the wild and ruinous waste of the Pacific shores of the American frontier: "It is difficult for a European to imagine Calistoga. The whole place is so new, and of such an Occidental pattern."[35]

It was years later when Stevens wrote "The Doctor of Geneva." In it he seemed to compound the suggestions played on by the naming of "Dr. Jekyll" and "Mr. Hyde" with Stevenson's naïve yet sophisticated perception about the differences between the European and American experiences. "Jekyll" is an English equivalent of the German "Jaeckel," one of the diminutive forms for "John" (as well as for "James" or "Jacob"). "Hyde," by an obvious homonymic pun, represents the nature repressed by the doctor's "rational" religion. In Stevenson's story what was repressed emerges under the pressure of animal needs. In Stevens's poem the doctor is, on one level, the embodiment of Dr. John Calvin of Geneva, reduced by his confrontation with natural forces to the emotional state of a little boy, "Jaeckel," left crying at its close. The "lacustrine man" used to calm mountain lakes reaches America's western shore wholly unprepared for what he sees and feels. He is overwhelmed by the experience and by the duplicitous inaccuracy of language that had prepared him to see the "Pacific" as peaceful as the European lakes and seas he was used to. Instead, there are "visible, voluble delugings." The only reaction possible is for him to cry, to revert to a state without language at all. He, who had been responsible for the Geneva Bible—on which so much of what the experience of those coming to the American shores had been based—finds himself a most inappropriate man in a most unpropitious place.

Stevens characterized the unsuitability of the doctor to the American landscape in two ways. First, he inserted vagrant lines of French meter, the alexandrine, to describe what the doctor sees when he looks at what most overwhelms him. Secondly, he referred to Jean Racine and Jacques Bossuet— particularly rational and measured writers—to whom the doctor implicitly looks for words to help him define his experience. The rhythms of their seventeenth-century lines were, of course, unsuitable to the abundance of the American vistas. Similarly, Stevenson, in his piece, repeatedly referred to European masters for terms to describe what he saw and the people he met (a "tutti" of stars above the mountain or, of a Chinese desperado at a bar, ". . . while he drained his cocktail, Holbein's Death was at his elbow"[36]). And at one point, waiting to leave for another town, he commented, with the same kind of consciousness belonging to "The Doctor of Geneva": "The bulk of the time I spent in repeating as much French poetry as I could remember." After quoting some of the lines recited, he continued:

> The redbreasts and the brooks of Europe [subjects of the lines] in that dry and songless land; brave old names and wars, strong cities, cymbals and bright armor [other images from the poems], in that nook of the mountain, sacred only to the Indian and bear! This is the strangest thing in all man's travelling, that he should carry about with him incongruous memories. There is no foreign land; it is the traveller only that is foreign, and now and again, by a flash of recollection, lights up the contrasts of the earth.[37]

The traveling doctor of Geneva, too, was foreign and unfit for the American soil. When he became overwhelmed and embarrassed, Stevens helped him "hide" his emotion. Though he tugged his shawl and stamped the sand, he denied that he "quailed." In *The Silverado Squatters,* Stevenson described himself as "quailing" at a particular encounter.[38] At the moment Stevens's doctor sighs and takes out his handkerchief the poem closes. But the issue was not closed for the poet. Unfortunately, those raised with a Presbyterian morality hid not just those emotions evoked by external nature:

> And thus it is that what I feel
> Here in this room, desiring you,
>
> Thinking of your blue shadowed silk,
> Is music.
>
> (CP 90)

The poet as "Peter Quince" felt "music" instead of the impulse to act on his desire to satisfy "that monster, the body." This was something Dr. Jekyll could do only as Mr. Hyde.

Something else that contributed to Stevens's feeling himself a spiritual son of Stevenson involved the Scotsman's sense of isolation. Because of his insular nationality and his tuberculosis, he felt different from others. In his American heir this sense resulted from the combined accidents of his past: being the only child without a family name;[39] having been ill as well, and removed, for a while, from the constellation of home; being a special student at Harvard. Stevenson remarked on this aspect of himself by generalizing his situation to include that of all Scotsmen and likening it to that of the Jews. He concluded: "It is at least a curious thing . . . that the races which wander widest, Jews and Scots, should be the most clannish in the world."[40] The immediate consequences of this feeling for Stevenson were that when he met a countryman while on his travels, he sought out his company and delighted in sharing inflections and memories of mists. There were subtler resonances, however, that were more interesting, especially in connection with certain images he created that later appeared in Stevens's work.

The Silverado Squatters opens with an image that repeated and expanded an experience of isolation from Stevenson's childhood which he transformed poetically in "The Land of Counterpane." There, the child

> . . . was the giant great and still
> That sits upon the pillow-hill,
> And sees before him dale and plain[41]. . . .

"The scene of [*The Silverado Squatters*] is on a high mountain."[42] From this vantage point the mature Stevenson surveyed all around him, landscape and people, with the same compensating sense of power that the confined child exhibited when surveying his imagined "planted cities" and "leaden soldiers" on the bedclothes. With this sense of power, the real landscape and people were changed into scenery and characters highlighting and supporting the action of the hero—himself—as he mused about America, Europe, nature, and time. As the observer and discloser of what he saw, Stevenson felt himself "the abstract countryman" who, as he noted, was "perfect."[43] Again and again throughout the account Stevenson improvised on this theme, pointing out the differences between the appearance of things seen from his abstract distance and the way they really were when he approached them and saw them closely. A few years later, when Stevens was reading Lafcadio Hearn's descriptions of Mount Fuji—whose ethereal blue-misted presence in the distance showed itself in reality to be black, molten ash incapable of sustaining any life or even the footsteps of those who tried to climb to its summit[44]—Stevenson's understanding of the beautifying power of the abstract would strike him again. Slowly, with time and distance, Stevens's notion of the abstract—so central to his mature work—was becoming defined.

"Anecdote of the Jar," widely anthologized as characteristic of Stevens's most typically obscure and cerebral style, has as its controlling image the "jar" that, in one sense, Stevens felt himself to be in nature (the "giant" injuring the yellow jacket, see p. 89) and in his own nature, exiled as he was from the possibility of expressing emotions directly. "I placed a jar . . ./. . . upon a hill./ It made the slovenly wilderness/Surround that hill.// . . . It took dominion everywhere" (*CP* 76). The power of the "jar," like that of Stevenson's child "upon the pillow-hill" is that of the abstract: "The wilderness rose up to it,/ And sprawled around, no longer wild," even though the jar is, like all abstractions, "gray and bare."

Many other seeds from *The Silverado Squatters* found fertile soil in Stevens's imagination. Stevenson drew a parallel between Scots and Jews, which he expanded in describing how the periodically itinerant "Kelmars," loading their horse-drawn "waggon" and selling kettles from outpost to outpost in the nearly deserted region, were devoted to nothing so much as "pleasure" and to being "free from care." This Stevenson named the "root of their philosophy."[45] Later in his life Stevens observed, somewhat longingly, his own admiration for the Jews, given as they were to "feasting" rather than "fasting" (*L* 348). This perception also contributed to the figures of the dark and rose rabbis in "Le Monocle de Mon Oncle" and the unmodified simpler rabbis of "The Auroras of Autumn" and other poems.

Other traces of Stevenson, again in connection with "Le Monocle," have to do with that elusive phenomenon John Hollander has so aptly named "echo"[46]—a suggestive repetition in a later writer of the cadence, alliteration, phrase or clause configuration, rhyme scheme, meter, or the like of an earlier writer's line or lines. Echo is particularly enticing because a reader's hearing it does not mean that the writer using it himself or herself consciously heard it. Much of what has meaning to us when we read becomes part of our own internal rhythms, sustaining or constraining our breaths and words, so that as we speak or write we often imitate unknowingly. This was true for Stevens as well. When, for example, he evoked in "Le Monocle" the sound of a "frog" that "Boomed from his very belly odious chords" (*CP* 17), he was not necessarily hearing Stevenson's frogs that "all about . . . sang their ungainly chorus," though his sensibility had been formed, as is the case for all of us, by the voices that had sung his "favorite pieces," making his mind a region full of intonings.

Another instance of echo from *The Silverado Squatters* was less precisely linked but operated more broadly, its resonance broken into different frequencies. Describing the sound of an unidentifiable bird, Stevenson wrote: "*It did not* hold the attention, *nor* interrupt the thread of meditation *like* a blackbird or a nightingale"[47] (italics mine). The first reminding note comes from the structure of this sentence which seems to have been condensed in "Anecdote of the Jar," in which, as already pointed out, Stevens, like the child watching the play he makes himself on the counterpane, observed "the weather of his stage, himself" (*CP* 170). He ended his description with:

> It *did not* give of bird *or* bush
> *Like* nothing else in Tennessee.
> (*CP* 76; italics mine)

A deeper reverberation comes from this same sentence's content. Stevenson's distinguishing the cries of blackbirds and nightingales as capable of holding attention and interrupting threads of thought lends an additional and important layer of meaning to Stevens's use of the blackbird as a controlling figure in "Thirteen Ways of Looking at a Blackbird" (*CP* 92). There its presence stopped his thought, interrupted reason's power over the irrational.

Still another echo comes from an observation Stevenson made about impressions of a heavy sea fog in the valley he saw below him from his place on the mountain. This long, lyrical passage has strong similarities to Stevens's "Sea Surface Full of Clouds" (*CP* 98). More, at one point Stevenson interrupted his description with a perception about the activity of the imagination that could apply just as directly to Stevens:

> The imagination loves to trifle with what is not. Had this been indeed the deluge [the fog he observed], I should have felt more strongly, but the emotion would have been similar in kind. I played with the idea, as the child flees in delighted terror from the creations of his fancy. The look of the thing helped me. And when at last I began to flee up the mountain, it was indeed partly to escape from the raw air that kept me coughing, but it was also part in play. . . .[48]

Stevenson continued improvising on the underlying theme of metamorphosis, beautifully noting that if the fog had been water surging in the valley, "with what a plunge of reverberating thunder would it have rolled upon its course, disembowelling mountains and deracinating pines! And yet water it was, and sea-water at that—true Pacific billows, only somewhat rarefied, rolling in mid-air among the hill tops."[49]

In "The Man with the Blue Guitar" Stevens noted this same property in relation to the weather of his region, where snow replaces fog:

> It is the sea that whitens the roof.
> The sea drifts through the winter air.
>
> It is the sea that the north wind makes.
> The sea is in the falling snow.

This section continues, closing with Stevens's perception of himself and a poetic explanation for his similar metamorphoses:

> The demon that cannot be himself,
> That tours to shift the shifting scene.
> (*CP* 179–80)

There are many more instances of Stevens's echoing themes from *The Silverado Squatters*. Stevenson saw the landscape around him as "green green's apogee." He also suggested "bucks clattering." He, too, identified himself as a pagan, but not, as Stevens would, echoing Milton as well, though in a "varnished car" (*CP* 170).[50] In Silverado, Stevenson lived "on the dump," as Stevens later did; there was a palm outside his door to which he repeatedly referred. And Stevenson seems to have prefigured Stevens's later musings around the theme of "the rock," as he carefully described the change within the belly of a tree in a petrified forest from wood to stone.

There were, in addition, instances from Stevenson's other writings. In "On Style in Literature,"[51] he made a distinction between the surface appearance of artistic creations and their deeper springs of meaning that could easily have contributed another feature to what Stevens later elaborated about the difference between the "true subject" and the "poetry of the subject" in "The Irrational Element in Poetry." This passage from Stevenson seems to make the theme of Stevens's essay more explicit:

> There is nothing more disenchanting to man than to be shown the springs and mechanism of any art. All our arts and occupations lie wholly on the surface; it is on the surface that we perceive their beauty, fitness, and significance; and to pry below is to be appalled by their emptiness and shocked by the coarseness of the strings and pulleys. In a similar way, psychology itself, when pushed to any nicety, discovers an abhorrent baldness, but rather from the fault of our analysis than from any poverty native to the mind. And perhaps in aesthetics the reason is the same: those disclosures which seem fatal to the dignity of art, seem so perhaps only in the proportion of our ignorance; and those conscious and unconscious artifices which it seems unworthy of the serious artist to employ, were yet, if we had the power to trace them to their springs, indications of a delicacy of the sense finer than we conceive, and hints of ancient harmonies in nature. This ignorance at least is largely irremediable. We shall never learn the affinities of beauty, for they lie too deep in nature and too far back in the mysterious history of man.[52]

Going on, Stevenson quoted lines from Samuel Butler's *Hudibras* that also informed an important motif for Stevens. The title of "The Sense of the Sleight-of-Hand Man" (*CP* 222) seems to point back to these lines from Butler:

> still the less they understand
> The more they admire the sleight-of-hand.

Stevens exhibited the same kind of receptivity to Stevenson's work as he did to the lessons of Barrett Wendell and other secondary figures. What was it about these figures that allowed Stevens to be so open to their ideas?

❧

It is impossible to pinpoint what it was about Wendell or about Rossetti and Stevenson and the many like them that prompted Stevens to hear their voices as his own. There is no one reason, and the reasons vary for each of these echoes. In the case of Wendell, it could have been a winning personality or the force with which, as a teacher of rhetoric, he drove home theoretical points to his students. In the case of Stevenson, it could have been the leftover affection of a young person for a weaver of tales that suspended disbelief without that suspension's having to be willed. But what is most interesting and offers material for speculation is that unlike his reaction to those who fitted his category of "man-poets," whose lines he was conscious of hearing in his head and whom he intentionally parodied, Stevens, who wrote that he avoided reading others' poetry because he did not want it to influence his own, was not resistant to fainter echoes from the minor chorus of secondary figures. In connection with this it should be recalled that both Whitman and Dickinson were largely ignored by Stevens's generation.[53]

The reasons do not have to be looked for very far, though, besides the obvious ones that will be indicated here, all of which have their roots in Stevens's personal, historical, and cultural soil, there might be others unseen, deeper still, that have yet to be uncovered. To begin with the cultural situation, it need only be noted that all ages look back to a golden age that seems to threaten but that actually explains the futility of present action and the impossibility of attaining perfection. As W. Jackson Bate points out in his biography of John Keats, this sense was particularly heightened for the romantic poets and especially epitomized in Keats, who had a painfully keen "sense by contrast [with the work of the past] of how little he himself [had] to offer."

> This is the fearful legacy that the great writers of the eighteenth century had seen coming to themselves and, even more, to their successors. The burdens of government, as Pliny said, become more oppressive to princes when their predecessors are great. . . . [T]his large, often paralyzing embarrassment . . . accompanied the rise of romanticism . . . intimidated the Victorian poet, and . . . was to threaten the vitality and range of poetry even more in the twentieth century. The embarrassment is that the rich accumulation of past poetry, as the eighteenth century had seen so realistically, can curse as well as bless. . . .
>
> Whether we want it or not, the massive legacy of past literature is ours. We cannot give it away. Moreover, it increases with each generation. Inevitably, we must work from it, and often by means of it. But even if we resist paralysis and do try to work from and by means of it, the question at once arises, does the habitual (and almost sole) nourishment of the imagination by the great literature of the past lead to the creation of more poetry of equal value?[54]

This question was even more pressing for Stevens than it was for Keats. It accounts, in part, for his eventually dismissing the possibility of being in both dream and deed, complete, a poet, and choosing instead a life that concretized the fear he expressed early on of being "half-dream, half-deed . . . a dilettante." He could not have known at the time he made the choice that he was to transcend the fear by transforming it into the kind of poetry that would place him among those who made up his imagined pantheon.

Compounding this cultural burden and giving it reality in the perception of the young man still unsure about committing himself to the "literary life" was the untimely end of one of America's young but already established writers, Stephen Crane. Stevens was present at Crane's funeral in New York on June 28, 1900, more than two weeks after his death in Germany on June 5.[55] His experience of it—a very poorly attended ceremony in a tawdry situation ("The church is a small one and was about a third full. Most of the people were of the lower classes and had dropped in apparently to pass the time" [*L* 41; *SP* 78–79])—confirmed his own Keatsian sense of belatedness:

> There was a sprinkling of men and women who looked literary, but they were a wretched rag, tag and bob-tail. I recognized John Kendrick Bangs [a noted parodist of the day]. The whole thing was frightful. The prayers were perfunctory, the choir worse than perfunctory. . . .—[O]n the line of premature death—he [the pastor] dragged in Shelley; and speaking of the dead man's later work, he referred to Hawthorne. Finally came the judgment day—all this with most delicate, sweet and bursal gestures—when the earth and the sea shall give up their dead. A few of the figures to appear that day flashed through my head—and poor Crane looked ridiculous among them. But he lived a brave, aspiring, hard-working life. Certainly he deserved something better than this absolutely commonplace, bare, silly service I have just come from. As the hearse rattled up the street over the cobbles, in the stifling heat of the sun, with not a single person paying the least attention to it and with only four or five carriages behind it at a distance I realized much that I had doubtingly suspected before—There are few hero-worshippers.
> Therefore, few heroes. (*L* 41; *SP* 78–79)

Circumstances seemed to be conspiring with the pervasive cultural situation to counter the young poet's incipient heroic aspirations. Had there not been a lag between Crane's death on the other side of the Atlantic and his memorial service in New York, perhaps Stevens would have witnessed bravura adequate to him. But as it was, even though he would, within the next day or two, get his job on the *Tribune* and, just after, be offered another on the *Post,* the writing he did for the paper, which was good enough to secure him better than average earnings over the next year, was not satisfactory to him. Perhaps he thought that journalistic prose was simply not his métier. But it is more likely that the death of Crane had made a subtle yet deep impression. Really a contemporary, only eight years older than Stevens, he was successful in the same profession. But he died entirely without the accolade Stevens imagined proper to him. This must have provoked serious questioning and self-doubt about the way he had chosen to "make something" of himself.

This questioning lasted throughout the period of his working on the *Tribune.* It prompted various attempts to succeed in some way at one thing.

But in the end it was again the reality of his father's voice that determined the direction Stevens's life took. During this time of wavering the shade of Crane lived in Stevens's imagination. After his second-rate funeral Crane's voice joined the chorus of those Stevens could listen to without being overwhelmed, as he was by his father's.

On the stage of his inner life major figures stood in the place of Garrett, Sr. When Stevens wrote as the virile poet he wanted to become, he symbolically acted out what he could not toward his father. He made it seem that he ignored what they wrote. Yet at the same time he exhibited mastery over them by parodying their forms with his own strong verbal and metrical attacks. He mocked them in magnificent measure. This aspect showed itself most directly in the poet's most clearly autobiographical piece, "The Comedian as the Letter C."

Stevens listened to minor figures because they did not threaten him. With them he imaginatively competed and won, as he had not always been able to do with his brothers. Like John Keats in relation to Leigh Hunt,[56] he could do everything they did but better. Because they were largely unrecognized, Stevens could learn from them without its being apparent. And from living figures like instructors—who were minor in being mediators, presenting ideas of great figures to the ephebes, followers who one day might themselves become teachers—the young man got the approval for his poetic explorations that he did not get from his father. Besides Barrett Wendell, Santayana, still a young instructor, given more to poetry than to philosophy at the time Stevens knew him, had taken on this role.[57]

Having left Cambridge's world of the spirit behind for the relentless contact he desired with the starker, barer world of New York, Stevens held an imaginary dialogue with the ghost of Crane, the virile youth of hard city streets and prose. Just as his silent conversations with Stevenson had sharpened his sense of how imagination functions to compensate for feelings of isolation and difference, his implicit sympathy for Crane directed his attention to the facts of his surroundings and to arranging his life so that he could, emulating his "antihero," devote himself wholly to writing. In the journal entries of this period, when he was supporting himself, as Crane had for a while, as a journalist, there are perceptions that could have been drawn directly from Crane's prose pieces about life in late-nineteenth-century New York: ". . . last night I saw from an elevated train a group of girls [the spiritual sisters of Crane's Maggie] making flowers in a dirty factory near Bleecker-st." (L 53; SP 101).

Stevens used this image to illustrate the change that had come over him, pursuing the "literary life" in the city he had begun to "adore." He had become a native of its brutal reality. Gone were the softer sentiments he recalled from the pastoral world of the previous summer. As he noted, the "pathos" of such a sight then "would have bathed [him] in tears" (L 53; SP 101). He felt this was a sign of stronger character and continued the entry with one of the clearest statements of his desire to devote himself entirely to writing, as Crane had done and as Stevenson had done: "I recently wrote to father suggesting that I should resign from the *Tribune* and spend my time in writing. This morning I heard from him and, of course, found my suggestion torn to pieces. If only I had enough money to support myself I am afraid some of his tearing would be in vain. But he always seems to have reason on his side, confound him."

But it took him a long time to express this. The entry is dated March 12, 1901, after nine months of moving up and down between hidden imaginings and the pressures of everyday reality.

٭

Now it was still July 1900, a few days after Crane's funeral. On July 4 Stevens made a journal entry that, had he been at all certain of his direction, could have shown him celebrating his independence together with the nation's. Instead, he was floundering, looking for a "sort of buoy" to steady himself. He found it in the recollection of the spiritual fathers who had shaped him at Harvard. He was moving up and down between a romantic evocation of the natural world associated with the "country about Reading" and the hellish reality of "infernal, money-getting" New York, suffused in his mind with "sulphurous air." In place of a sense of self-sufficiency and self-reliance in relationship to his father, he felt inadequate and dependent. He wrote that he had not "yet" asked him for money, as though expecting that he should certainly have to at some point:

Fourth of July! but a commonplace one for me. I have been working on the New York *Tribune* almost a week. The *Tribune* had no sooner taken me than the *Evening Post* sent me a telegram offering me a position. I was forced to decline it of course. I loaf about the office a great deal waiting for something to happen, and that is not especially profitable since I am paid according to the space I fill. Today I did not write single line. But I planned much, read much and thought much. A city is a splendid place for thinking. I have a sonnet in my head the last line of which is—

And hear the bells of Trinity at night—

bells which start ringing in my remotest fancies. In coming down to brick and stone I must be careful to remember the things worth remembering. I am going to get a set of [Jowett's—as Milton Bates has noted, Holly Stevens mistook her father's handwriting in reading this as "Lowell's"] *Plato* as soon as I can afford it and use that as a sort of buoy. I still think New York a wretched place—with its infernal money-getting. Towards evening it rained and the showers washed the roofs and walls so that the city looked like a workingman who had just bathed. After dinner—shredded wheat, milk, batter cakes, chocolate—I went to the office, then to Palisades (115th St. Harlem) and saw the sunset. I could not get rid of the lines—

"outwinged in flight
The pleasant region of the things I love" [from Santayana (*SP* 79)]

The region was before me. . . . (*SP* 79)

At any rate I have regained my good spirits. I have not changed my address but expect to go over to West 9th St. within a few days.

Perish all sonnets! I have been working until 4 in the morning recently & have had plenty of time, therefore, to look over Stedman's "Victorian Anthology." There's precious little in the sonnet line there that's worth a laurel leaf. Sonnets have their place, without mentioning names; but they can also be found tremendously out of place: in real life where things are quick, unaccountable, responsive.

The other morning as I came home I walked up to Washington Square to take a look at the trees. The birds were just beginning to cheep & there was a little warm wind stirring among the leaves. I was surprised to find the large number of people who were sleeping on the grass and on the benches. One or two of them with collars turned up and hands in their pockets shuffled off through the sulphurous air like crows in rainy weather. The rest lay about in various states of collapse. There must have been a good many aching bones when the sun rose. The light was thin and bluishly misty; by the time I was in my room it had become more intense & was like a veil of thin gold.

I still patronize restaurants though I have been sick of them for a long time.

A month has passed since I have been in N. York & I have not yet written father for money. I am beginning to save already—perhaps a bad week will come and consume what I have laid up—still I have saved & the sense of miserliness in me is tickled.

Whatever else I may be doing I never fail to think of the country about Reading. During August I hope to run over & see all the roads and hills again. Besides, they do not seem real to me unless I am there. I can hardly believe that Wily's garden, for example, is as fine a thing as it was last summer. I am going up there, however, some day & shall see for myself. I miss my diary of last year, which is still in Cambridge. If it was here I could live over a few days at least. Now my flowers are all in milliner's windows & in tin cans on fifth-story fire-escapes. (*L* 41–42; *SP* 79–80)

Stevens could not leave behind attachments to his now-idealized past. Had he been able to live wholly in the pressing present of New York without fear that he, too, might become one of the "large number of people . . . sleeping on the grass and on benches," he could have become free of the hidden dependence on his father and on the romantic dream of his past. Instead, as suggested by the discontinuities of the entry, the kind of life his father was coming to represent for him preserved and ensured a way of being that was closer to Stevens's pastoral imagining of natural order. The shuffling tin-can reality of the life he was facing on his own had nothing to do with this golden age. It is not surprising, in light of this, that a few months later when he felt himself—following Crane's example—inured to the industrialized suffering of the metropolis, he felt mature and independent as well. It is also not surprising that this sense could not sustain itself, based as it was on his having put on another mask. He had not been raised as Crane had been. The "brick and stone" he was used to were not the tenement buildings on New York's Avenue A (now, ironically, Sutton Place). Crane was used to the cries from the derelict brick and stone buildings on Blackwell's Island, where those fortunate enough not to sleep on grass and benches were housed.[58] The brick and stone of Reading were of a different kind. They belonged to stolid burghers' houses, like Stevens's, and to the fields and locks of the surrounding countryside. It was there the young poet had spent countless hours lying on his back looking at the sky or, on his belly, had watched water swirling in currents beneath him.

As he was trying to harden his surface to survive and succeed in the city's "impersonality," a quality he eventually found congenial to his spirit,[59] in the deepest recesses of his being he heard the dying strains of the Victorian's music. Though he seemed to disparage the tone of what he read in Stedman's anthology, calling it unsuitable for the "quick" responsiveness of "real life," the lines he spoke to himself made a lasting impression, not solely on the poetry he later wrote. In the attitudes these lines embodied, Stevens found reconfirmation of his ties to Victorian ways of being and seeing the world. Stedman's canonization of Tennyson, Algernon Swinburne, and Browning[60] was not ignored by Stevens. Moreover, in this anthology he first came across the work of Bliss Carman, a Canadian poet living in the United States. He became another of the minor figures Stevens followed, later recommending Carman's volumes to Elsie Moll and borrowing from them some of the characters and images he used in writing his own verses to her. At this moment, however, what touched him most was the Victorians' tendency to "idyllize" the past and nature in the manner of medieval romances. Rather than perceive New York as it was, then, and attempt to describe it in its own terms, Stevens found himself in the midst of brick and stone lamenting that the moon was not "the one [he] called 'that queen' last year" (*L* 43; *SP* 80) and commenting that New York lacked the "distinct, defined" quality of permanence or "locality" that belonged to medieval cathedral towns or to those American cities like Cambridge, Massachusetts, that imitated European models.

The city he saw as always "disintegrating, dislocating" mimicked too well what he sensed and feared but didn't want to face in himself. To block these feelings, he fell back into sentimental imaginings of a golden past and comforted himself by writing about places where he felt at home in his lofty aspirations: "I have been wondering today [Sunday, July 22] why I write so much about skies, etc. I suppose it is because—Why does a mountaineer write about his Alps: or an astrologer about his magic?" (*L* 43; *SP* 81). He also soothed himself with homely wishes that poignantly remind us of how young he was, how lonely and unsure:

July 26
This has been a busy + therefore a profitable week. To-night I received no assignment + so I am in my room. I almost said at home—God forbid! The proverbial apron-strings have a devil of a firm hold on me + as a result I am unhappy at such a distance from the apron. I wish a thousand times a day that I had a wife—which I shall never have, and more's the pity for I am certainly a domestic creature, par excellence. It is brutal to myself to live alone. . . . I don't know—sometime I may marry after all. Of course I am too young now etc. as people go—but I begin to feel the vacuum that wives fill. This will probably make poor reading to a future bachelor. Wife's an old word—which does not express what I mean—rather a delightful companion who would make a fuss over me. (L 43; SP 81–82)

Stevens's fantasized self-aggrandizement—being native to the sky—and his desire to have someone "make a fuss" over him reveal how profoundly insecure and unprepared he was to make a life on his own in a place that could not offer him the least tenderness. New York was in 1900 (and perhaps still is) the harshest city in America. But his father's earlier goad that he had the "stuff" to make it "on a big Daily in N.Y." (L 19) still taunted him to prove his mettle, and so he went on. Had Garrett been more measured, less demanding that his sons meet the standards he had once set for himself, or had the tenor of the household he established been different, allowing open expression of fears, hopes, desires, he probably would not have advised his son the way he did. But as it was, the sensitive and shy, though highly competent, young man found himself on the threshold of life unable to imagine ever feeling again the comforts of the hearth.

This need was accentuated by the unnaturalness of his days, organized around his erratic schedule at the *Tribune*. Often beginning work after dinner and "hanging around" the half-deserted office until 4:00 A.M. waiting for a story to happen were not conducive to establishing relationships or to feeling part of a regular pace of life. With night becoming his day, and at least part of the day, his night, he moved even more uncertainly up and down between reality and imagination. He spent his free hours alone, reading, writing, and being in contact with whatever of nature he could find in parks and across the river on the Palisades. He became more isolated. Though he occasionally found himself in conversation with someone who happened to be sitting at one of the Village bars or restaurants he frequented, his reticence precluded his approaching someone to whom he had not been formally introduced or his getting far beyond what he named in the following entry his initial "suspicion" of strangers:

Pleasant little saloon at corner of 6th Ave. & 11th St. Went there last night
for a beer and found a corking cat that curled up in my lap. A fellow of
about 30 came in and saw me. He came up, sat down, chatted & drank &
was genial until 12 o'clock. I was suspicious of him—something had happened to him—but he was agreeable & I accepted him with no other introduction than Life's. He'd been around the Horn & was full of stories which
he told unusually well, having once been a newspaper man in San Francisco.
We—he rather—talked about shark's teeth, shark's timidity, the Magellan
cloud (of stars), flying fish & their flight & sailors [*sic*] methods of catching
them by means of a lighted sail at night etc. etc., calms, characters—he
thought himself an awful ass—which he was not etc. He rolls his own
cigarettes—thin, sweet-smelling wisps—& lives under the roof above a taxi-
dermist's on 6th Ave. (*SP* 85)

Instead of the kind of Jamesian social flitting he could have participated
in—he did have Cambridge contacts and certainly could have moved in their
circle had he wanted to—his flitting was in imagination. His only real interlocutor was the echo of his own voice responding to what he read, did, and
saw. His childhood habits had not changed. Reading, having silent dialogues
with dead and absent writers took the place of actual exchanges with friends
who might have shared his perceptions or stimulated him with different ones.
He walked for miles through city streets to reach a spot in a park from where
he could watch the sun set behind a hill rather than between darkening buildings. This was not as satisfying as walking through the Pennsylvania countryside, but it served the same purpose. He at least felt at home beneath
the sky.

He wanted more than anything to feel the self-sufficiency his father
seemed to exemplify and certainly praised, as here in another of his letters to
his son:

Our young folks would of course all prefer to be born like English noblemen
with Entailed estates, income guaranteed, and in choosing a profession they
would simply say—"How shall I amuse myself"—but young America understands that the question is—"*Starting with nothing, how shall I sustain
myself and perhaps a wife and family—and send my boys to College and live* comfortably in my old age." Young fellows must all come to that question for
unless they inherit money, marry money, find money, steal money or somebody presents it to them, they must earn it and earning it save it up for the
time of need. How best can he earn a sufficiency! What talent does he
possess which carefully nurtured will produce something which people want
and therefore will pay for. This is the whole problem! and to Know Thyself!
(*SP* 71)

Stevens maintained Garrett's habit of mind and chided himself for not meeting its standard: "Self-dependence is the greatest thing in the world for a

young man + Savage [a Harvard alumnus who had recently died, about whom Stevens had just read an article] knew it. I cannot talk about the subject, however, because I know too little about it. But for one thing, Savage went into the shoe business + still kept an eye on sunsets + red-winged blackbirds—the summum bonum" (*L* 44; *SP* 82–83).

Stevens had taken on the "all-American" set of values that ensured the economic "survival of the fittest." With this and without regular contact with those who *had* chosen the "literary life" he secretly desired, Stevens became an introspective exile, lecturing to himself alone. Had he sought out those who inhabited the "Bohemia" he had glimpsed on first arriving in New York, when he had lunched at the Players Club and been impressed with seeing "celebrities" and artists, he might have begun to emulate a different kind of model or found approval from a different source, as he had found at Harvard. But because he was alone, without this kind of support, it was natural that he turned again to his father, the emotional complement to the intellectual "buoy" offered by Plato and the others he read. Unfortunately for Stevens this created a psychologically untenable situation since no matter what he did, he never got a secure and realistic sense of himself from Garrett. In this way the father continued to be largely responsible for the son's unsatisfiable need. The man who fancied himself a "Sphinx" (*SP* 5) posed a question, which the young man, who did not believe it possible for himself or any other to be a hero in the belated age in which he lived, would not even attempt to answer. The Sphinx went on blocking the way into Stevens's fated kingdom until he slowly began finding the answer to what it meant to be a "man" himself. This, of course, required the death of the Sphinx.

ॐ

Stevens had relocated to his small apartment at 37 West Ninth Street, in the heart of New York's Bohemia. But since he did not participate in its life, the move represented yet another phase of creating a mythology of self, rather than an attempt to respond to the essential question about whether the life he had chosen pleased him. This he could have done only if he were free of the need for his father's approval, able to establish his own standards against which to measure himself. In place of recognizing his desire for Garrett's emotional support was the fear that he would have to ask again for monetary support, even though his average earnings were more than adequate for him to begin saving. Ironically, the $20 to $25 a week he made on filling space in the paper with his stories, according to the standard of the time—with rent taking about a quarter of his monthly income, a healthy dinner at a fashionable "chop-house"[61] costing roughly forty cents, and rides on streetcars and subways ranging between two and five cents—meant that he was quite successful, in his father's terms. This presented a sharp contrast with the failure Stevens felt himself in his own terms years later, when, after finally declaring himself a poet with the publication of *Harmonium,* he received only $6.40 for the first year's royalties, in 1923 much less than a third of the weekly wage he earned at twenty-one. (This cold fact contributed to the six-year silence that then followed, when he devoted himself instead to "other things" belonging to the "fell clutch of circumstances" [*L* 141], things he had learned to value from Garrett.)

Stevens revealed how greatly he measured himself in terms of these values in opening weekly journal entries with statements of how much he had earned: "Made $21.65 this week" (*L* 43; *SP* 82); "Made $24.50 last week" (*SP* 85); and after having been perhaps a bit too successful over his first three months for the newspaper's economic good, "I start today [October 18] on a salary of $15.00 a week. This is considerably less than I have been earning on space—but I suppose I can get along. I have been promised an immediate raise if I do good work" (*SP* 87). His financial statements were like assertions of self-worth. They took precedence over perceptions of both external reality and inner states or musings about what he read. But this "money-making" set of values could not give him a true sense of worth because it did not satisfy primary needs. This is clearly illustrated by the opening of his entry of August 3: "Today I had a fascinating time. I received no assignments + from the point-of-view of money-making the day was a failure; from that of enjoying myself, 'a grand success'" (*L* 44–45; *SP* 83). He continued with a description of what constituted this "grand success." He detailed his pleasures and the imaginings they prompted in an almost aleatory, lyrical form, pleasurable in itself. This prefigured the lapidary manner of associating characteristics found in his later poems, especially in *Harmonium.*

In the morning I read poetry & inwardly told the rest of the world to go to the devil (where I wish a good many of them really might go & stay). In the afternoon I wandered about—saw the Tombs, with Howe & Hummel's law offices right across the street; rode on the tail end of a dray till my rear was full of splinters and my entrails had changed places; and poked in and out among the wharves. I found a charming sailing vessel—the "Elvira" of "Lisboa"—a Portuguese ship. She was a dandy—an old-timer. Her hull was painted pink & blue and black; I forget how many masts she had; but there was a jungle of ropes overhead, in which were several sailors hanging like monkeys. The officers [*sic*] quarters were forward. The men were cooped up in the stern—a half-circle of filthy berths—excuse me! One fellow—the real thing—was dressed in pajamas of an explosive and screaming character. He said he talked a little English—but American was different. By the way, I had to ask a deck-hand where the quarters of the men were & not knowing the word for quarters I used "chambres"—"Où sont les chambres des matelots?" ["Where are the rooms of the sailors?" following English syntax] which is execrable French—("Les chambres—où etc.?" ["The rooms where . . ."—the same question phrased in French syntax]). The fellow snickered. The "chambres," or rather this single "chambre" was more like a salle à manger, à dormir, à baigner, à fumer, et à jouer les cartes ["a dining room, a bedroom, a bathroom, a smoking room, a room to play cards,"] etc. It was an extraordinarily fine mise en scène ["stage setting"] for a "wee bit tale." I'm a wild polyglot tonight & no wonder! On deck were a number of chickens—several fighting cocks with which the sailors probably passed the evenings of unspeakable voyages. There was also a coop of pigeons—one a big beast that glistened as it strutted in the sun. If ever a ship opened up a new world to me that one did. She sails for Freemantle, South Australia, in about a week, to be gone for four months.

I also saw a fleet of canal-boats—a wilderness of domesticity. They lay like villagers and greenhorns in the water—the tide bounced them about like huge, clumsy logs. I could not help being a bit contemptuous. A dead cat lay under the rudder of one. Nearby was a little butterfly hunting sustenance. Silly jumble!

In the evening I went to the "Syrie Restaurant" on top of the Tract Society Building: 23rd floor. My first—or practically my first sunset of the summer. Everything deliciously pure & calm. Over Brooklyn was a low, dark ridge like a mountain with deep crimson peaks—or like a wall over which one looked into the rose-gardens of Paradise. There were no other clouds visible. Looking toward the West I could see the river—like a shattered crystal. The sun simply went down—no colors—no delays—a simple progress. But the air was incomparably clear & revealing.

I begin to like New York & do like it hard. Reading seems childish & weak—but I like it, too—Boetia [sic] is Boetia especially when one is born in it. My liking for N.Y. & for R. are, however, quite different. I might spin any number of balanced sentences etc. around the difference—which amounts to this   that I saw Reading first.

I left Wily's today a year ago.

Among the poems I read this morning were thirty sonnets by David Gray, a young Scotchman who died of consumption December 3, 1861. The poems were called "In the Shadows" & were in the Bibelot. David Gray must have been a brave fellow, both rugged & melancholy. There are some things in these sonnets which almost bring tears to one's eyes—David Gray is in them. He's a new acquaintance & although probably a solitary person makes one love him & regret him. His verses occasionally have much beauty—though never any great degree of force—other than pathetic. (L 44–46 and SP 83–84)

Though the tone here was punctuated by notes of melancholy (his feeling for the "pathetic" force of Gray's sonnets, for example) and violence (his feeling "contemptuous" and imagining the sun reflected on the river's surface as a "shattered crystal"), a strong sense of happiness comes through the entry. This was significant for a number of reasons. First, the experiences were wholly solitary. While he spoke to a sailor, he did so as an observer who would have spoken in the same way to the ship itself could it have responded. He addressed the sailor as an object about which he was curious. He referred to Gray as a "new acquaintance," but it only went to confirm that indeed, dead writers did replace living beings as companions. Secondly, the experiences had nothing to do with integrating the pressures of reality into his world. They were entirely escapist. Thirdly, the way the experiences were recounted bespoke an indulgence of his peculiar narcissism which involved his either taking on different roles or identifying with others. He reveled in his ability to use French, even if somewhat incorrectly, and commented joyfully on being a "wild polyglot," having interpolated a phrase he could have found either in Gray, the Scotchman he was reading at the moment, or in Stevenson, for both of whom he felt great sympathy.

This entry is remarkable because it reflects one of the privileged moments when Stevens's world arranged itself into a poem. This accounts for the happiness perceived through it. As such it represents in raw form the sense of himself that later appeared through his poems, though in them the linear, sequencing connections that mimic the movement through real time are absent, as are any explicit descriptions or revelations of self.

In his making a poem, for example, Stevens's choice or creation of a particular persona replaced the openly misanthropic statement found in the opening here: "I . . . inwardly told the rest of the world to go to the devil (where I wish a good many of them really might go & stay)." (This statement was made even stronger by the addition within the parentheses, given to ensure that the wish be taken seriously and not be misunderstood as simply a figure of speech.) The depiction of a character like the high-toned old Christian woman, toward whom the poet had hateful feelings, could be read, in part, as expressing his mood, as it was directly stated here. Moreover, the process of associations, prompted by and alternating with perceptions of external reality, commented on here as being a "Silly jumble," represents in cruder form the movement between imagination and reality marking Stevens's mature style and accounting, in large measure, for the opacity of surface that is both its difficulty and its success. This perfectly mirrors the poet's moving about in the world and in his consciousness like a force of the weather—that is, appearing to be unpredictable, yet exhibiting a greater order or consciousness of the movement of time, as revealed here in the various reminders of its passage. (These will be noted in the following paragraphs.) This culminates in the closing paragraph, which, in specifying which poems he read in the morning, took him as it would take his future readers, whom he implicitly addressed, back to the time of the opening sentence.

That this entry should so directly prefigure devices found in Stevens's later poetry is not as surprising as it might at first seem. The actual occasion described here—of the pleasures of merely circulating, walking through a city, noticing the similarities and differences in it to itself on other days and to other cities and places as well—is the same kind of occasion on which he later composed the greater number of his poems. Walking back and forth from his home to his office and, in rarer instances, walking through different cities, he noted what he saw outside and in his imagination on pieces of paper he carried in his pockets. He sometimes completed whole poems this way. He sometimes completed them at the office, where he often tested out the effect of a word on an employee as he did on his housemates when he lived in Cambridge.[62] Or he completed them at home at night in the silence of his rooms.

Writing poetry was a "health" for the older man in the same way that keeping a journal was for the young one. The therapeutic value was in his expressing feelings and in reflecting on and ordering the experience of a day or group of days. What was different now was the nature of the experience. As Stevens grew older and the facts of his life became complicated with the facts of another's very close to him as well as with facts of the everyday world, it became increasingly difficult for him to express at all openly the feelings occasioned by these facts. It was not accidental that the habit of keeping a journal was replaced by the habit of recording fragments of experience on bits of paper. Bits of paper do not invite linear, discursive revelation as do blank pages of a journal. Nonetheless, the images recorded in a poem and in the tone established by taking on a particular mask preserved the elements of experience, especially to the one who reread—"One does not write for any reader except one" (OP 165)—as Stevens reread his journals and, later, his poems. Shaped into lines and stanzas were the facts, feelings, and memories necessary to make sense of the present, the melting moment—the "Nothing that is not there and the nothing that is" (CP 10).

The first external observation recorded in this August 3 journal entry reflected the ironic underside of Stevens's vision. Out of reality's constant flux it selected an object that revealed the preoccupations of his spirit: "the Tombs." Its morbid name and what it was pointed back to the prison and death images of his last year at Harvard. And "right across the street" he noticed something that reminded him of the "imprisoning" wishes his father had for him: "Howe & Hummel's law offices." ("I had a good long talk with the old man in which he did most of the talking. One's ideas don't get much of a chance under such conditions. . . . We talked about the law which he has been urging me to take up. I hesitated—" [L 52; SP 100]). Countering this, the archetypal object of a young man's fancy appeared: a ship on which he could escape and find a "new world" and self. Within this wish he became a man of many tropes, a "wild polyglot" able to get by in any port, a sailor dreaming of red weather off jungled shores where monkeys hung and screamed. When he spoke, he showed himself more truly and more strange. He shaped syllables not in "execrable French" at all but echoing lines he had learned long ago: "Où sont les. . . ."

The contrast between the young man who would take the desired voyage and the one who would follow in his father's footsteps was sharpened as Stevens's negative capability attached itself to the canal-boats he described as a "wilderness of domesticity." For these he felt contempt. Only a few days before he had referred to himself as a "domestic creature par excellence." His hidden self-hatred was connected to feelings of inadequacy. These derived from his not believing that he could ever measure up to his father's standard of self-sufficiency and that he would always need the security of being tied to the "apron-strings" of the domestic scene. At the same time he doubted that he would ever earn enough to support the wife and children who would be its necessary actors. Caught in this paradoxical situation, "imprisoned" by expectations that did not correspond to his own deepest needs, he naturally wanted to escape. But the covert wishes suggested by seeing the *Elvira* temporarily freed him from his metaphorical prison.

Seeing how these connections operated helps explain a curious aspect of "Vita Mea" written years before (see pp. 68–69). This in turn illuminates what is being expressed here. The "I" there wanted to escape from the house of life, which appeared to him as a prison. More than an exercise in rephrasing a romantic death wish, Stevens voiced there the feelings prompted by his hesitant contemplation of a future life that would fulfill not his need to circulate dreamily in a literary "mundo" but the "money-making" need and "Presidential" ambitions extolled by his father.

Echoing through the bars of prison associations now was the voice of François Villon, the model of the poet as prisoner. Whispering *"Où sont les . . . ,"* his shade provided an unconscious shelter for the young man. Putting on the vagabond-poet's mask, Stevens could satisfy many aspects of himself at once. Sympathizing and identifying with the feelings of a prisoner, he could at the same time transcend these feelings by fancying himself as Villon, an irreverent adventurer. And elaborating the details of the adventures, he could become the successful wooer of damsels heightened by eternal bloom in his imagination. This projected image was certainly preferable to being the "villager or greenhorn" he feared he was. This image of himself he finally attempted to escape years later as the "Comedian," the "general lexicographer of mute/And maidenly greenhorns" (*CP* 28), who made the voyage the young man wished to make now.

As in the "Wily girls" entry considered earlier, in which, when moved too close to painful feelings by their situation, he distracted himself by directing his attention to seemingly trivial aspects of nature, here he distracted himself again. As soon as he began to recognize his feelings, he attempted first to contain them by finding a name for them: He was "contemptuous." But rather than reflect his uneasy state, the term cloaked in conceptual generality a complex of feelings: self-contempt; uncertainty; self-hatred; hatred of his father and the values he represented; insecurity; fear; need. To distance himself further from exploring why he was contemptuous, he looked around. A "dead cat," associated with his sense of being buried in a "tomb," was under the controlling "rudder" of the canal-boat, the "wilderness of domesticity." And a little butterfly he revealingly imagined to be "hunting sustenance," like him. These served his purpose of taking attention away from what he was feeling. But his selection of these objects of attention from the great disorder of reality around him revealed his feelings in spite of his distractions. His "Silly jumble!" comment then put a full stop to this disturbing sequence in the same way as the Latin exclamation in the Wily entry (see p. 88).

The reality of New York was, of course, more varied than the countryside about Reading. It offered more distractions and provided a rich network of associative nodes to which feelings could surreptitiously attach themselves. An evening in Berkeley, or any of the other small towns near Reading where he had stayed and wandered, did not have a very different sense of reality from an afternoon. But New York's countless neighborhoods with their distinctive styles and sounds gave Stevens an endless possibility of excursions into fantastic worlds. Here the unity of experience did not come from the permanence of unchanging landscape, as it did in the country. It had to be created by the power of his imagination which found the nodes to which to fix associations.

Stevens's visit to the Syrie Restaurant, for example, was connected in an associative pattern with his having seen the Tombs that morning. Their Egyptian Revival style, together with the Oriental suggestion of the restaurant's name, figured to point his imagination to the East. He envisioned "Paradise" filled with "rose-gardens" beyond the wall of clouds over Brooklyn. On his mental route he stopped somewhere in the lost paradise of his childhood, where the mountains held him securely and reminded him of "Rose" Wily. Then, as though breaking through the paradisal wishes, the "shattered crystal" image brought the poet back to seeing things as they were in the "clear and revealing" air. By the next paragraph he was already moving West. "Boetia" replaced Egypt. Symbolically it was Reading, his native soil that he would always love, even if loving it and following what he was taught there would lead him into the "wilderness of domesticity" he both desired and feared. Liking New York "hard" expressed, together with how he had just described one of its aspects—a "shattered crystal"—his equivocation. While New York offered him the possibility of participating in the "literary life," doing this would mean "breaking" completely from his father and how he had been raised. The now idealized, crystallized relationship to the past would be "shattered." At the same time, because of his insecurity, taking the risk of following the "literary life" under the "hard" pressure of New York would mean "shattering" the romanticized image of himself as poet.

With the next sentence, "I left Wily's today a year ago," Stevens brought his "world quite round" to close the yearly cycle that had begun when he left behind all the things he had ever known. It was as though in this entry he were commemorating the completion of his first revolution, his moving away from what he had loved. The superconsciousness of time, of moving like the planet of which he was a part not only provided a sense of unity to his experience but expressed—again, in a naïve way—the sense of himself as one of the

necessary elements of nature, a force of the weather, that figured so promi-
nently in his later poetry. This sense, to some degree inherited from the
romantic sensibility, belonged to his need to feel himself as belonging to some
kind of familiar constellation. He had left his immediate family. He feared he
would never have a wife who would make a fuss over him. So he imaginatively
projected himself among the spheres of heaven. It was no wonder he wrote "so
much of skies." Confirming his planetary consciousness of the passing of time,
he noted that it was "today" that he left Wily's "a year ago." His marking of
the year's coming around was not of the date, as commonly observed, but the
day of the week. Though he had left Wily's on August 5, he marked the
year's end now on August 3—from the Friday it had been in 1899 until
the Friday in 1900 (because it was a leap year, there was a two-day difference
in the dates). His internal calendar, though not as precise as the Gregorian
numbered version, observed the regularity of names that are the reminders of
the movements of planets and moons in and out of days and nights.

After this large compassing of his sense of being in time came the final
paragraph of the entry. In it he returned to the present and the precise moment—"this morning"—when he began his real and imaginary excursions.
Within this classical unity of time, place, and action, he voyaged as far as a
fantasized *Elvira* could have taken him: from visions of a biblical paradise,
through a return to the paradise of his past, to completing the adventure of
the last year, to his present meanderings through the streets of New York on a
particular day.

Informing this paragraph and, through it, the entire entry, was his reference to the poems of David Gray, whose volume *In the Shadows* he had found
in his room. As Holly Stevens notes, these poems "made a great impression"
on her father, so much so that he quoted from one of them in a letter he wrote
eleven years later to Elsie Moll. Either he had memorized the lines, or he had
kept the book from the Italian's bookcase (*SP* 84).

Though it might at first seem curious that Stevens marked the date of
Gray's death, it was pertinent. It revealed that Stevens knew that the volume
had been written during the period when Gray knew he was dying. This
information came from a preface describing Gray's short, painful life.[63] These
biographical details struck responsive chords in Stevens, as did the poems.
Stevens seems to have identified strongly with this "rugged and melancholy"
young poet. Dying at twenty-four, Gray felt himself a victim of his own
indulgence in having yielded to the muse rather than having followed the
straighter path on which his father had set him. Stevens expressed his sense of
kinship with Gray by referring to him in his journal entry as a "brave fellow,"
the very same epithet he recorded his own father's having applied to him in
the first letter he received from him in New York (see p. 108).

On his own for the first time, Stevens was feeling the pressure of reality.
Remembering his father's many admonitions, it is not difficult to imagine
what Stevens felt on reading these lines from Gray:

O Many a time with Ovid have I borne
My father's vain, yet well-meant reprimand
To leave the sweet-aired, clover-purpled land
Of rhyme—

. . . .
To batten on the bare Theologies!

. . . .
I clung to thee, heart-soothing Poesy!
Now on sick-bed racked with arrowy pain
I lift white hands of gratitude, and cry,
Spirit of God in Milton! Was it well?[64]

Though Garrett Stevens did not, as did Gray's father, direct his son to follow "bare Theologies" and become a minister, his advice to Wallace to "make something of himself" served the same purpose. Like Stevens, Gray had ignored the voice of his Calvinist conscience and had turned away from the "dogmas of faith" to pursue the "beauty of Greek mythology"[65] and the spirit of romantic poets like Keats, whom he emulated.[66]

In the above poem and throughout the sonnet sequence making up *In the Shadows,* Gray expressed the feeling that his death was fit punishment for this indulgence. Stevens, having experienced his own loss of faith, must have trembled as he read these lines:

I tremble from the edge of life, to dare
The dark and fatal leap, having no faith.[67]

It was only a little more than a month since he had been touched by Crane's death. Reading Gray emotionally corroborated his intellectual perception of the futility of attempting to scale the heights of an imagined Olympus to become one among the pantheon of "man-poets." ("There are no hero-worshippers. Therefore, no heroes.")

Like Stevens, Gray was a "solitary person." Stevens responded to his loneliness and "pathetic" force without fear that he was indulging in self-pity. More, the tears almost brought to his eyes by feeling the presence of Gray *in* the poems went a long way in eventually persuading him not to take the risks Gray did. And there was another aspect of personality that Gray had in common with Stevens, an extreme alternation between expressions of grandiosity and self-doubt.[68] After seeing its effect on Gray, Stevens consciously tried to extirpate it—at least in the professional choice he made—so as not to suffer as did his "new acquaintance." The movement up and down between opposite poles of feeling and experience has been noted repeatedly in our following Stevens's development. He attempted, with all the force of his will, to escape its unbalancing effect by choosing to be "all deed" and becoming an industrious "money-making lawyer," but he also learned how distinct a shade the fluttering of his spirit made in evading his will.

In light of this, it is not surprising that intermittently throughout his later career, as he yielded to his muse in moments stolen from his business days, images or patterns of rhyme or rhythm from Gray appeared. Poised on the edge of his own experience, Stevens made Gray's "edge of life" metaphor his own. Its echoes intone in Stevens's "edge of sleep" (*CP* 386), "edge of afternoon" (*CP* 482), and "edge of night" (*CP* 495; *NA* 114)—ironically, borrowed to name one of television's first "soaps." Gray's "choral/auroral" pairing from the second sonnet of *In the Shadows:*

> Chant on funereal theme, but with a choral
> Hymn, O ye mourners! hail immortal youth auroral![69]

reemerged in an appropriately reversed form in these lines from the closing stanza of "Peter Quince at the Clavier":

> So maidens die, to the auroral
> Celebration of a maiden's choral.
> (*CP* 92)

Similarly, the movement mimicking death in "Sunday Morning" of the "wide water" and "ambiguous undulations" of Stevens's "pigeons" as they "At evening . . ./. . . sink,/Downward to darkness, on extended wings" (*CP* 70) whispered cadences of Gray's lines contrasting the ongoing movement of time with his toward death:

> . . . the time shall glide
> On smoothly, as a river floweth by
> Or as on stately pinion, through the gray
> Evening, the culver cuts his liquid way.[70]

In "Sunday Morning," too, the image of death as the "mother of beauty," alone responsible for pleasure, "Within whose burning bosom we devise/Our earthly mothers waiting, sleeplessly" (*CP* 69), evoked Gray's more literal utterance:

> In dying mother, I can find no pleasure
> Except in being near thee without measure.[71]

Yet another strong expression of Gray's feeling as he died,

> No more, no more the spring shall make
> A resurrection . . .[72]

lent at least one chord to Stevens's early-voiced farewell to life in "Le Monocle de Mon Oncle": "No spring can follow past meridian" (*CP* 13).

Again, it is important to remember that this line, as, indeed, any of the lines resonating with others' words or images, is not to be seen as evidence of direct influence or of Stevens's conscious borrowing. This can be easily understood by noting that just as the above line echoes Gray, so the three lines immediately preceding it in "Le Monocle"—

> I am a man of fortune greeting heirs;
> For it has come that thus I greet the spring.
> These choirs of welcome choir for me farewell.
>
> (*CP* 13)

—reverberate with the following lines from a Chinese poem of Ou Yang Hsiu, which Stevens could have read at any time from his first contact with Witter Bynner and other Orientalists at Harvard until the moment of actually composing "Le Monocle":

> Under the full
> Moon of April young men welcome
> The Spring with wine and love. But
> Me, once more greeting the Spring,
> My head is white. . . .[73]

It is also important to see how the fluttering of Stevens's shades of feeling were stilled in the lapidary settings of his poems. Stevens was a man made out of words. Though this is true for all human beings, only very few are conscious that this is so and, at the same time, strongly ambivalent, as Stevens was, about this consciousness. Stevens desired a more relentless contact with the world. He wanted to meet it directly as "that monster, the body," yet he feared this rawness. Up-pouring syllables spoken by others who had shaped him, who had affected him like a sequestered bride with their words, was a way of getting rid of them—the unwanted feelings and false selves, the images he had taken on to protect his nakedness.

Gray described the effect of a Calvinist conscience on a spirit drawn to pantheism and the models of a pagan past that celebrated life in nature. He saw his death as a just "end of false ambitions, sullen doom/Of [his] brave hopes, Promethean desires."[74] At twenty-one Stevens was not able to escape the hushed whispering of his own conscience and turned away from Gray's threatening example. But by his mid-thirties, when he wrote "Le Monocle de Mon Oncle" and the other poems of *Harmonium*—like "The Snow Man" and "A High-Toned Old Christian Woman"—that in various ways expressed his later realization of the damage done by his religious and cultural upbringing, he was ready to exorcise with his "opposing law" the fearful voice of Gray, together with all the others who had helped build his haunted heaven.

Stevens's reaction to Gray was extreme. Immediately after feeling so much for this "new acquaintance," there was a marked change in tone in Stevens's journal and, as reflected through it, in his life. He turned his back on any hint of the pathetic force he felt in Gray that he had until then expressed himself as well.

In sharp contrast with the unconscious care reflected in the lyrical unity of the journal entry that began and ended with Gray was the following, just one line: "I have settled down & am going to be 'as lazy as I dare'" (*SP* 84). For Stevens, being lazy meant not being idle but following whims. This "seize the day" attitude was triggered by his imagined confrontation with his own death, experienced through his identification with Gray. "Being lazy" this way lasted until the end of the year. Three weeks after his excursion around Gray, Stevens openly expressed this change in a rather disconnected entry that also shows him to have been preoccupied still with the *Elvira:*

> The "Elvira" was formerly called the "Argonaut"—an English ship. She had not been to New York since '79 or '89 or some such date. '79 was the year in which I was born.
>
> These last two weeks I have been working until 4 in the morning & am naturally tired of it all & impatient to be up and doing something that has some flash to it.
>
> Hang it—a fellow must live with the world—& for it and in it. (*SP* 85)

Unlike the imaginative, introspective illumination around the facts recorded in the August 3 entry, here Stevens presented the facts alone. The professional style of note taking and reporting had affected the way he reported on himself. Most of the entries from this point until the end of the year were similarly telegraphic, reflecting Stevens's shift in attention to the surface of things instead of to the deeper recesses of his spirit. Years later Stevens wrote that "A change of style is a change of subject" (*OP* 171). Here the change indicated by his directive to "live with the world—& for it and in it" was connected to a sense of rebirth, of renewal; he mentioned that '79 was the year of his birth. In the three weeks between the two entries he had been voyaging, finding out about the *Elvira* and about himself.

Before the end of the month, with this new outlook, Stevens visited Reading. An incomplete entry from this brief stay revealed how little of the old self remained: "Along the road apples were beginning to look red & indeed everything was there as usual—excepting myself" (*SP* 85). He stopped and saw the same friends he had spent so much time with summers before. Unlike himself, Levi Mengel and Christopher Shearer were "settled," "in their cottages," and "happy, comfortable, content" (*SP* 86). The summer before, he had exulted in being one with his native soil. After this visit he returned to New York certain that he would "never . . . settle down in Reading" (*SP* 96). The "golden" world of "Greek days" had come to appear the "acme of dullness" (*L* 52; *SP* 100).

Within the next four months Stevens became a native of New York. His starker, barer self in this starker, barer world began to see with an ignorant eye. "An eye of land, of simple salad-beds,/Of honest quilts," (*CP* 27) the eye of Stevens now hung on city scenes instead of apples and beheld them with the joy previously reserved for his pastoral idyll. Instead of bilious comments about the coarseness of New York's money getting or its bleak impersonality, there were lyrical descriptions untinged by the implicit judgments that had colored his earlier perceptions. Those judgments belonged to the outsider, the pilgrim coming to the new Babylon. But now, for a while at least, nothing of his old self remained. The shift is evident in this excerpt: "Yesterday I saw a case of the delirium tremens at the foot of W. 10th St. (North River). A tall, husky Irishman struggled and squirmed—a snake himself. In spite of the horrible sight & example, a bystander picked up & emptied the drunkard's bottle" (*SP* 85).

Though he noted that it was a "horrible sight," he drew a comparison, "a snake himself," instead of, as would have been the case a few months before, being blocked from a poetic association by directing attention to *other* things around. He now looked squarely at the painful object and was able to embellish it. His first revolution against the constraining forces of his past was complete. He marked the day of his freedom with the imaginary voyage he recorded in the journal entry framed by Gray's presence. After this he took on the qualities belonging to the place of which he was now a part.

Besides being able to observe and record what he saw around him without judgment, he began to enjoy what the city had to offer. He went to the theater, to concerts. He liked "doing the art galleries and exhibitions" (*SP* 88) and stopping in bars. The entries of the next four months were filled with descriptions like the following:

Sept. 10—4 A.M.
Have just returned from work. A most lovely night—The morning star—
    How keen, how bright, how free from all despair—*So,* I have gone to seed. The city deliciously still. A few magic stars dropping through the sky—which startle and dazzle one. Amazing freshness & purity in the air. (*SP* 86)

Or this, about a month later:

I have been walking in the Park of late in the mornings. The weather has been cool and clear and bright. The leaves begin to fall thickly & the wind is becoming audible. Somehow the Park is exquisitely musical—perhaps it is the music just "dying" from the harp of the muse under the head of Beethoven—near the terraces. The statue of Burns is unspeakably rotten. (*SP* 87)

Though the tone of these excerpts sounded the change in Stevens's attitude toward New York, which reflected the change in himself, there was the curious italicization of the "So" preceding his comment that he had "gone to seed." A short time later he italicized again: "I have been earning good wages of late—16.75, 26.50, 22.30 etc.—that's nothing *now*" (*SP* 86). This followed his perceptions about a production of *Henry V* starring Richard Mansfield that he had just seen. For Stevens, "going to seed" meant enjoying himself, indulging his whims, participating in his new world enthusiastically, without hints of melancholy, pathos, or nostalgia. His momentary lapses into minor stresses on certain words were reminders that his old spirit had not entirely vanished. Nevertheless, Stevens energetically pursued this quickening of life for a while and profited from temporarily abandoning his bookish habits in the solitude of his rooms for habits more appropriate to a virile youth of twenty-one.

He was helped into this change of habit by the kind of work he was asked to do for the *Tribune*. For the period of the political campaigns of 1900 he had to cover countless speeches, follow various candidates on their routes through the city (*SP* 88–89). And though he had not intended to vote during the election, between October 5, when he recorded his nonintention in his journal, and election day, he changed his mind and went home to vote "the Democratic ticket—Bryan" (*SP* 89). Perhaps listening to William Jennings Bryan's impassioned words—striking out against privilege, calling for an early end to imperialism and the free coinage of silver, which would benefit farmers and workers rather than an elite minority—made the young man realize that words could shape a real, future world, not only imagined or remembered worlds. In any case, something happened, and Stevens exercised his right to the franchise, for which he was eligible this year for the first time.

There were many other things that also could have contributed to his acting on his now publicly recognized political maturity. October 5 was only three days after his twenty-first birthday. The feeling of having reached adulthood had not yet impressed itself. In fact, on the same day he recorded that he was planning to return to Reading again for a few days because he wanted to see, among others, his father to speak to him about a position on the *Times* there. Though he had already begun to like life in New York, until the end of the year he considered going back to Reading and getting a job on the newspaper run by Thomas Zimmerman, Garrett's close friend. It was partly because he had come to a decision about this that Stevens had started to articulate his positive, unqualified feelings about New York. This naturally coincided with leaving behind the old self that would have fitted in with a life in Reading.

It is not known exactly when the possibility of work on the *Times* presented itself or whether it was Garrett's idea or Stevens's. But it seems that the issue came up on his previous visit to Reading at the end of August. This was just a few weeks after the entry in which he expressed that he had begun

147

to like New York "hard" but that he liked Reading, too, and that even though it seemed "childish and weak," he "could spin any number of balanced sentences"—as balanced as he was between liking the two—"around the differences" that made him like both. By just after the new year, however, Stevens stopped moving up and down between the two. The scales tipped, and he left what was "childish and weak" behind.

But on October 5 he felt neither his personal nor his political adulthood, although things began to change on his two-day stay at home. In the journal entry recording this visit, written after he returned to New York, there was no mention of what transpired between him and his father. In contrast, he was specific about what went on with the other two he had gone to see, Ed Livingood and Frank Mohr, a naval officer just "fresh from the Philippines" (*SP* 86) and a trip around the world (*SP* 87).

A little more than a year before, Stevens had also stopped to see Livingood. In the office where he practiced law, between moments of looking out the window, his friend imagined the scenes of Goethe's life. Stevens then observed to himself that Livingood had failed to take the risks necessary to fulfill the imaginings he had for himself. He chose, instead, to meet the expectations others had of him and to remain secure in the bosom of his hometown and those expectations. Now Stevens saw him as "still a sickly Hamlet" (*SP* 87), unable to choose between being and not being what he wished he could become. He spent a great deal of time with Livingood during those two days. On both Wednesday night and Thursday afternoon they walked the familiar fields and country roads, stopping "at every tavern." Livingood, at least, as Stevens noted, got very drunk, and both of them held "dialogues with the moon," apostrophizing it. They had "good fun" asking bartenders about "Mike Angelo, Butch Petrarch, Sammy Dante." They asked one about "whether he had heard that John Keats had been run over by a trolley at Stony Creek in the morning." He responded that "he had not—he did not know Keats—but . . . he had heard of the family." On this Stevens remarked in his journal, "Spirit of Adonais!" and followed it with an appropriately Keatsian observation: "How much more vigorous was the *thought* of the old fellows than is that of any modern man" (*L* 46; *SP* 87).

The irreverent poking at masters that Stevens enjoyed harmlessly with "Livy" later became incorporated into his style. This youthful pranking was itself a maturer version of the jokes he had played with his brothers or alone, scraping the paint off the streetlight to annoy his neighbor. As the range of his experience spiraled, these playful attempts to test his powers and see their effects touched greater and greater objects on the peripheries of the invisible circles his movements made. Like a cub who first practices its instinctual skills pouncing on and biting the others in its litter in preparation for the time when it will have to hunt and kill to sustain itself, Stevens first practiced on neighbors and bartenders the skills he would need to scent out the words and ideas of those who could nourish him. He then would kill them with his own. These skills would be most effective if unseen, if they seemed playful. Being the cleverly pranking child rather than the delinquent, being a comedian rather than a committed crusader in verse, allowed him to make his kill without serious consequences. Once he was secure, well fed, smacking his muzzy belly in parade, the threatening figures dead, the need to hunt disappeared. The poetic pranks and parodies of *Harmonium* were exchanged for *Ideas of Order.*

One of the nourishing/threatening figures, one of the "man-poets" he heard now moving greatly through his mind's jungle, was John Milton. In the same way that John Keats was deeply affected by Charles Cowden Clarke's reading to him aloud from Chapman's *Odyssey,*[75] Livingood's reading *Paradise Lost* aloud, as Stevens "sat in a shaft of sunlight" during a long morning in his office on this visit, had as profound, if not as immediate, an effect. In the "four or five hours that followed" Clarke's reading, Keats composed "On First Looking into Chapman's Homer," the extraordinary sonnet marking this occasion.[76] Within the accelerated pace of his life Keats at twenty-one was already an "actively writing poet,"[77] while Stevens, whose lifetime spanned almost three times Keats's years, was still struggling to announce, if only to himself, that he was a poet. Nonetheless, Livingood's voicing of Milton's words describing Satan and his heroic plight—in spite of Stevens's comment that "The sun was better than the poetry, but both were heavenly things" (*L* 46; *SP* 87)—deeply moved him, so deeply that he did not want to acknowledge the words' full impact.

His poetic response to Milton came years later. It was most evident in "Le Monocle de Mon Oncle"[78] and was as direct and as strong as Keats's to Homer. But now the contrast Satan and his noble, if doomed, intent—"Better to rule in hell than serve in heaven"—offered to Livingood himself (who served others' expectations without ever having attempted his own noble aims) and to the ghost of Gray (who in the end repented his not having served his father's wishes) provided Stevens with a very different kind of model from that he had ever before had. The satanic suggestions of wholly becoming what he wished to be tempted Stevens enough so that three months later he decided not to settle in Reading and also promised himself to go to England, Paris, or, at least, Arizona and Mexico the following summer. Sadly, however, his newly found sense of independence did not withstand Garrett's continued reasoned attempts to "[hold him] in check" (*L* 49). By the time the summer actually came Stevens's intentions had collapsed. He was persuaded, instead, to go to law school.

The other prompting of his desire to "be off somewhere" (*SP* 90; *L* 48) came from the contact he had with Frank Mohr, a "first class fellow" in Stevens's mind (*SP* 87). Mohr was full of tales of adventure and enticing descriptions of people and places he had seen on his trip around the world. Stevens was as enthralled by these tales as he was by the "great variety of Oriental odds and ends" Mohr had brought home from his travels. Besides the time they spent together in Reading, there was an extended period later in the month when Mohr went to visit his friend in New York. There they shared experiences, wishes, and dreams at closer quarters. Mohr's views about the American presence in the Philippines seems to have added the necessary element of reality to what Stevens had heard idealistically thundered in Bryan's speeches (on one day he had "heard him make 4 speeches in 3 hours" [*SP* 88]). By election day Stevens cast his vote against imperialism. In the month between October 5 and November 6, after covering the campaign and exchanging ideas with Mohr, Stevens came of age.

Reflecting this change is a sonnet written about the middle of this period:

> Build up the walls about me; close each door;
> And fasten all the windows with your bars;
> Still shall I walk abroad on Heaven's floor
> And be companion to the singing stars.
>
> Whether your prison be of greatest height
> Or gloomier depth: it matters not. Though blind
> I still shall look upon the burning light,
> And see the flowers dancing in the wind.
>
> Your walls will disappear; your doors will swing
> Even as I command them. I shall fare
> Either up hill or down, and I shall be
> Beside the happy lark when he takes wing,
> Striking sweet music from the empty air,
> And pass immortal mornings by the sea.
>
> (*SP* 88–89)

Though the prison metaphor still controlled this poem, it no longer controlled him. Stevens was now ready, like Endymion, the poetic hero about whom he had read the previous summer, to "burst its bars." He expressed his new sense of self in the conviction that he would transcend all bars to becoming what he wanted to be and doing what he wanted to do. But two contradictory comments followed the poem, which he crossed out in his journal: "Sorry I wrote it. Sorry I crossed it out" (*SP* 89). His ambivalent reactions foretold that the change was only temporary. He was merely covering the old, unsettling up and down. But for a while at least the change carried his spirit up "Beside the happy lark," and he felt the world to be a hospitable place. He enjoyed the "Clattering trucks and drays, tinkling and bouncing horse-cars, hundreds of flags at mast-heads, glimpses of water between piers, ticket-brokers & restaurant piled on restaurant" (*SP* 88) along West Street.

Again projecting himself onto what he saw outside, toward the end of this period, he found W. Bourke Cockran, one of the politicians campaigning right before the election, "the most fluent, the most lofty and potent and admirable speaker even if it was true that he was "bribed" (*SP* 89). He seemed to perceive in this speaker what he knew in himself. Even if there was something uncertain, something to be hidden, it was possible to create out of words alone "Striking sweet music from the empty air," an image of "magnetic beauty" (*SP* 89).

Stevens now recognized that words could transform reality rather than simply complete it with imaginative embellishments or allow escape from it into "Faery" worlds. This discovery was new and was connected to another event, which he also described in the entry of October 5—the date when he began the rite of passage into his manhood. He had just seen, as noted above, *Henry V*, a play built around the multileveled ambiguities of language. Here "words" were as powerful and sharp as "swords" in winning wars and women and as deceptive as Harry in Erpingham's cloak, not showing but hiding himself and reality. From this—and from the puns of the Chorus on "gilt" and "guilt" to the Hostess's misunderstanding of "incarnate" as "carnation" to the French princess's confused shame in pronouncing *"De foot et de coun"* and Pistol's mistaking the French soldier's "Seigneur Dieu" for "Signieur Dew"— Stevens learned a great deal. What he learned showed itself years later, when he wrote "The Comedian as the Letter C" and some of the other poems subsequently collected in *Harmonium,* in which he played himself on the difference between his "true subject"—hiding like Harry in Erpingham's cloak—and the "poetry of the subject"—the surfaces of words projecting, like Cockran's "profound convictions (*SP* 89)," a masque beyond the planets. At that point, looking back on his career and tracing it poetically in "The Comedian," Stevens pointed directly back to this moment. Crispin's voyage was a cipher for the passage he began now. The battle on St. Crispin's Day commemorated in *Henry V* became the battle the poet waged with the "sovereign ghosts" that inhabited him, the images made out of words that he had to destroy with *hiswords*. Now, at twenty-one, Stevens felt his first inkling of his ties to Harry in his cloak and to Cockran in his words, covering their true selves.

Between this moment of hidden illumination and the end of the year the young man-about-town was touched by two other plays and some of the music he heard in concert.[79] His senses fully open to what was around him, he remarked on the beauty of some aspect of the audience—their hands seeming "to simmer" in applause from where he sat watching above (*SP* 91)—even if the music did not wholly please him. His perceptions revealed an eye familiar with painting. While this one evoked Edgar Degas's rendering of the audience's reacting to a performance of *Robert le Diable,* another of the young poet's comments synesthetically connected a piece of music to a painting by Antoine Watteau. His absorption of what later critics saw as the influence of the impressionists[80] and Nicolas Poussin had begun to show itself. What he had learned to be attentive to at Harvard, talking to Arthur Pope about painting, was beginning to declare itself as an important element of his life. In a few years, this interest put him in contact once again with Walter Arensberg, another of his contemporaries at Harvard, in whose studio on West Sixty-seventh Street in New York he not only saw some of the "newest" work from the Continent—pieces by Georges Braque, Pablo Picasso, Francis Picabia— but also met, among others, Marcel Duchamp, whose irreverent stabs at tradition Stevens understood and enjoyed.

The other plays he saw shared a feature that sharpened his sensitivity to the difference between things as they seemed and things as they were. In both Edmond Rostand's *L'Aiglon,* which he saw twice (though with different lead players in two of the first American productions[81]), and *Hamlet,* it was a woman who acted the leading male role: Maude Adams first ("There's something about Maude Adams that wrings a fellow's heart") as Napoleon's son, the Duke of Reichstadt, then Sarah Bernhardt, who also starred as Hamlet. In response to these occasions, Stevens departed from the staccato tone he had recently taken on in his journal and returned to the lyrical mode of the Gray entry. In these, as in that, the presence evoked by the work informed the passages and established a unifying key. Controlled by that key's holding a part of his consciousness in the way a prelude holds and holds, Stevens played the notes of his scale, rising and falling between the heights of his wishes and the rock of necessity. As in the Gray entry, in these there were perceptions that he developed in later poems.

Informing his wishes and what he noted in the passage below was the theme of *L'Aiglon,* which focuses on the sense of belatedness felt by the Duke, who can never match his father's glory. His only recourse is to participate in the myth of that glory by imaginatively reconstructing it. In this he is helped by the reminiscences of an old soldier of his father's imperial army, who— significantly for Stevens—has been disguised but reveals his true identity in this retelling. The play functioned to reinforce Stevens's Keatsian sense of belatedness and of being haunted, at the same time, by the myth his own father had woven. As a result, after seeing it, he returned to considering the brutal reality of having to make money and wished to be "the proprietor of a patent medicine store" instead of the bearer of the laurel crown. Yet in this movement up and down he discovered elements he shaped into later poems. The "wind-machine" here contributed an idea for the "machine of ocean" in "Sea Surface Full of Clouds" (*CP* 98). The "stars . . . clear . . . and geometrical" shone again at Tallapoosa: "The lines are straight and swift between the stars" (*CP* 71). His "blinking" at reality became the widow's winking in "A High-Toned Old Christian Woman" (*CP* 59). And the "idea of life in the abstract" certainly, as Holly Stevens points out (*SP* 91), occasioned "some reflection."

> Last night I saw Maude Adams as the Duke of Reichstadt in Rostand's *L'Aiglon.* The scene on the field of Wagram was too thrilling to thrill—the accusing voices in the wind (*id est*—wind-machine) must have had a fine effect on serious minds—they made me laugh. But it was all vastly entertaining as everything of the sort is bound to be in New York. There's something about Maude Adams that wrings a fellow's heart. Perhaps it is the pathos she inspires one to feel.

My desire to be off somewhere still exists, though no longer so exactingly. Summer is gone & the city is decidedly cozy and smart. Still I could enjoy mornings in Florida and afternoons and long nights in California—breathing fresh air and living at leisure—away from the endless chain to which I am fastened like a link—at constant strain. But Florida and California are limited regions & and so my desire is limited. The calling is remote—there is not a voice in every bit of green or open space. May will be maddening when it comes. I keep asking myself—Is it possible that I am here? And what a silly & utterly trivial question it is. I hope to get to Paris next summer—and mean to if I have the money. Saving it will be difficult—with all the concerts and exhibitions, and plays we are to have—not to mention the butcher, baker and candle-stick maker. But to fly! *Gli uccelli hanno le ali* ["Birds have wings"]—that's what they're [from this point the rest of the entry has been crossed out but is still legible] not here. Whenever I think of these things I can see, & do see, a bird somewhere in a mass of flowers and leaves, perched on a spray in dazzling light, and pouring out arpeggios of enchanting sound.

My work on the *Tribune* is as dull as dull can be. I'm too lazy to attempt anything outside—& the fact that I work two days a week—Wednesday & Thursday—in Brooklyn spoils whatever laziness hasn't made on her own. Brooklyn is *the* most hideous—

The moon has not been bad of late. The stars are clear and golden and geometrical and whatever else they try to be. I rather like that idea of geometrical—it's so confoundedly new!

Sometimes I wish I wore no crown—that I trod on something thicker than air—that there were no robins, or peach dumplings, or violets in my world—that I was the proprietor of a patent medicine store—or manufactured pants for the trade—and that my name was Asa Snuff. But alas! the tormenting harmonies sweep around my hat, my bosom swells with "agonies and exultations"—and I pose.

I was speaking to a Tammany Hall man tonight. He had a remarkably comprehensive view of things—I remember his saying—

"Well, we are all human beings. Money is our object. Hence—"

Politics, I suppose.

After all, blink at it all we will, look at it from every point of view, coddle, coax, apologize, squirm or what one pleases we cannot deny that on the whole "money is our object." We all get down to that sooner or later. I won't cross this out either.

I heard another man today say—

"I've seen enough of life."

This idea of life in the abstract is a curious one & deserves some reflection. (*SP* 89–90)

Within the month he saw the play again, this time with Bernhardt (on December 7). Then, before seeing her in *Hamlet* on the twenty-eighth, he made two short trips, one on his day off to Boston and Cambridge and another on Christmas Day to Reading. Rostand's words marched in their regular rhythm and rhyme in his memory, vaguely reminding him of his place among "les petits, les obscurs, les sans-grades" ("the little ones, the obscure ones, without rank").[82] He felt female-like himself in his father's shadow; the irony was suggested by Maude Adams and Sarah Bernhardt playing the Duke. In Cambridge he looked for something familiar, a sense of the past to hold on to. But he found it "did not seem what it used to be" (*SP* 92). Stripped of the habits once appropriate here, he was left with only "animal spirits." He indulged them by seeing a couple of old acquaintances and downing a couple of bottles of "St. Estephe [*sic* accent]" before taking the midnight train back to New York. In the morning light he saw it "filled with veils of sweet vermeil" (*SP* 92).

The next day trip—back home for only a few hours—brought his "animal spirits" up against Garrett once more: "Talked with father—who's kept busy holding me in check. I've been wanting to go to Arizona or Mexico but do not have any good reason for doing so. I am likely to remain here until Spring, at least. Europe is still on the other side of the ocean" (*L* 49; *SP* 94).

Returning to New York, Stevens reexperienced his uncertainty. Straining against the parental expectations he had already made his own, though unhappily, he lost himself in the "intricate metamorphosis" of Bernhardt's "*D'être ou ne pas d'être, c'est là la question . . .*" ("To be or not to be, that is the question . . ."). Though the critics "jumped on her" (*SP* 92), the basses of his being throbbed in recognition of her "conception of the character"—a female conception. The effect was so intense that more than forty years later Stevens could still precisely describe the details of the performance. This he did in the essay entitled—ironically in this light—"The Figure of the Youth as Virile Poet."[83] The focus of his preoccupation with her when he himself was a youth was the difference between her character changes and the constancy of her appearance: "In this scene her character changed instantly—although her appearance remained pretty much the same as ever" (*SP* 92). This duality he ascribed to the "intense *abstraction* of Hamlet's character" (italics mine) that Bernhardt had been able to suggest. He was also struck and pleased by Hamlet's "cunning" and by his "ruse" as she communicated them. Following the play with text in hand (*SP* 93), Stevens seems to have been unconsciously rehearsing his own cunning in later life when he presented the "ruse" of his constant, staid appearance to the world while wrestling beneath its surface with his own "mad" thoughts and imaginings.

Closing the chapter he began poised between the past and the future, Stevens posed the question that remained to be answered by the figure of the poet as virile youth. His last entry for 1900, written as the noise of the New Year's celebrations outside reached a crescendo stifling even the possibility of the prayer he wanted to utter, was grounded in his attachment to his old self: "But time's scythe is not a magic wand and though the century changes, I still remain W.S. + can say *adieu*! to no part of me" (*L* 49; *SP* 94–95). But he would "pose" to cover his parts. Being a poet for him meant striking a pose. At Harvard it had shown itself in his "taking on airs" and in his pseudonyms. Now it meant devising subtler disguises. The problem he faced being a poet was tied to what remained in him of the century. While God might "rest her [the century's] bones," as he wished in his journal, her spirit in him wouldn't die. Though he proposed the ideal of the youth as virile poet, his mind simmered and hissed with unnerving whispers. He felt it was from his mother that he had gotten imagination. The virile youths, like Keats and Gray, who had tried to find bravura adequate to the great hymn of nature, had died as youths. Whitman, who sang the song of his body electric, was not only not recognized but not a "*man*-poet." He tried to escape the web these associations wove, but the Victorian habit of mind was part of who he was as much as was Garrett's practical "reason." It was a few years later when Stevens would say to himself that this writing of verses was "absurd" and "positively lady-like." But to be "man number one" . . .

IV
THE OPPOSING LAW
1901–1904

. . . THESE INDEED SEEM,
FOR THEY ARE ACTIONS THAT A MAN MIGHT PLAY:
BUT I HAVE THAT WITHIN WHICH PASSETH SHOW;
THESE ARE BUT THE TRAPPINGS AND THE SUITS OF
WOE.

—WILLIAM SHAKESPEARE,
Hamlet

> But what a terrible avenger the Law is.
>
> —Journal entry, January 31, 1901,
> *Souvenirs and Prophecies* (p. 97)

To find a way of becoming "man number one" (*CP* 166) in America during the first years of an uncertain century was not easy. Gone was the queen whose standard had been the last chivalric code. Friedrich Nietzsche, unsuccessful in living through the superman morality he had proposed after the death of God, had already come to his insane end. Closer, an anarchist's assassination of President McKinley suggested that the dissatisfaction with the old order was not confined to the old world. The age of imperialism, with its implicit justification in the theories of social Darwinism,[1] continued. But there were other evidences—besides the violent end of the president who had been elected to ensure that the old order might maintain its hold—that the myth of progress was beginning to wear thin, and that the nineteenth century's renewed faith in science was shaken.

The young man sensitive to himself and the world around him felt the anxiety of the age as the century became more self-conscious and, at the same time, more deceptive in its rationalizations. The conflict finally broke out in the explosion of World War I. The eight-year period beginning in 1901 when Stevens shaped himself into a man was the last bridge spanning the abyss between the nineteenth and the twentieth centuries. The next two chapters will follow Stevens as he crossed it. He reached its swaying center in 1904, when he met Elsie Moll and stopped to survey himself, the world he was leaving, and the one he was about to enter.

The tenor of this period was epitomized by Theodore Roosevelt. The aristocratic "Rough Rider" was America's version of the courteous cavalier. He translated the military heroism of the conqueror of San Juan Hill into the various dialects he needed to become head of New York City's police board, assistant secretary of the navy, governor of New York, vice president, and finally—if accidentally at first—president. After receiving his summons while on a gentlemanly hunting expedition, to accede after McKinley's assassination, he perfected his speech and found the most appropriate slogan for the age: "Walk softly and carry a big stick." Under the guise of his warm and friendly manner which promised enlightened leadership and the spread of "civilization," he continued American imperial expansion. At the same time, at home, he cracked down on trusts and monopolies with expert muckraking techniques. He solidified America's foothold in the Pacific, South Pacific, and Caribbean by appointing governors in Guam, Puerto Rico, and Cuba. And after making the Panamanians' revolution against Colombia possible, he took over the Panama Canal enterprise.[2] All the while people were buying the newly designed "teddy bears" to charm their children.[3] With his well-polished manner and old family background, Roosevelt soothed Americans into believing that they had taken on the banner until recently waved by Victoria.

With major cities swelling with immigrants, "native" Americans wanted to identify with an imagined ideal of gentility. The scion of Sagamore Hill, cultured, energetically given to the pursuits of the more adventurous type of English gentleman—hunting, exploring, writing (finding time for all these activities even during his various terms of office)[4]—fathered the image America wanted to have of itself. Besides the tie to a European past suggested in his bearing and habits, he exhibited frontier "manliness." Having compensated for the delicate health of his childhood with his later hardy habits, and having spent time in the Dakotas and elsewhere in the West with "rough and ready" guides who could read only the language of nature, Roosevelt spoke to the "little men" he seemed to defend against the encroachments of "big business" in words they could understand. He had "made himself" as well. He was a model of the spirit of individualism. The Rough Riders were a volunteer group he organized and led. After being out of office for a term when William Howard Taft had been elected—largely because of Roosevelt's designation and support—he organized the Progressive ("Bull Moose") party and ran again in an attempt to win the presidency back from Taft, who had alienated the liberals of the Republican party.[5]

For his term of office, at least, Americans could imagine themselves leading the way to civilization. Though the century symbolically turned around the Eiffel Tower erected for the Universal Exhibition of 1889 in Paris, and though it was in Germany that Max Planck in 1900 formulated the quantum theory, marking the first stage of the illness that finally brought about the death of the materialist world view by 1926,[6] it was in America that Reginald A. Fessenden, also in 1900, five years after Guglielmo Marconi's invention of radio telegraphy, transmitted human speech by way of radio waves. America sensed the greatest need of the age. Exhibiting the keen instinct of the upholders of the work ethic for the economic survival of the fittest, both American science and politics focused on communication. In the same way that the radio meant that Americans could eventually broadcast their way of life to places most of them would never visit, and hear of what went on—often in languages they couldn't understand—Roosevelt established America's role as communicator in international relations. Skilled in negotiating from his early training as a lawyer, he applied what he had learned to beginning what came to be known as U.S. dollar diplomacy. In 1905 he took over the Dominican Republic's debt to European bondholders by appointing an American receiver of customs, thus effectively reinforcing control and police power in the Caribbean.[7] This exercise of power had begun earlier with his intervention in the Venezuela claims dispute and in the matter of the Panama Canal. Ranging farther, Roosevelt mediated to end the Russo-Japanese War (the peace conference met at the Portsmouth Navy Yard in 1905). He also supported the Hague Tribunal and vigorously helped bring about the Algeciras Conference of 1906, which gave France and Spain control of Morocco. In the same year he was awarded the Nobel Peace Prize. The next year, cleverly negotiating at home as well, he extended government control over "big business" by tacitly approving United States Steel's absorption of the Tennessee Coal and Iron Company during the financial crisis of 1907. He also diverted attention away from this—the new century's first sign of the intrinsic weakness of the capitalist system—by sending the navy on its first world cruise, symbolically asserting America's power to keep "peace." During the same year, in extension of frontier power, Oklahoma was admitted as the forty-sixth state to the Union.[8]

While operating as effectively as he did in foreign issues, Roosevelt, because of his education and his cultural interests, raised the tone of American life and made the public conscious of preserving and extending its national character abroad. At the same time he stressed the importance of conserving natural resources and of taking pride in the soil. Both the rhetoric and the actions of the administration were directed toward creating a sense of America's "native" power and right in dealing with all aspects of reality, from the natural world to the most abstract exercise of authority in the world of international politics.

In view of what he accomplished and the image he projected, it is not insignificant that Roosevelt, too, was a graduate of Harvard. It is impossible to know to what extent, if at all, Stevens identified with Roosevelt. But it is worthwhile to consider how he might have found in Roosevelt an image on which he could model himself, an image that in some way justified the choices he was about to make for his life. Stevens was just coming into maturity and was clearly ambivalent about his relationship to his father. This was especially true during this period when Garrett suffered a nervous breakdown (around 1901) that was in part his response to the pressure of the time's economic crises.[9] Stevens had also left behind the figures in Cambridge who had served as parental substitutes. In the absence of other models Roosevelt could easily have taken the place of Garrett. In him, Stevens could recognize the rightness of his father's direction that he take up the law and become a man who could find a place "on the front bench" and perhaps even become a "President" someday himself. Besides also being of Dutch heritage, Roosevelt had studied and practiced law, become president, and still found time for—if not the "summum bonum" of "red-winged blackbirds"—the adventures of hunting big game and writing books.[10]

One of the important events punctuating Stevens's eight-year period of exploration and settling, when he tried to make something of himself, again following his father's advice, as a law student, clerk, and practicing lawyer, was a hunting trip, on which he learned practically what it meant to be "rough and ready." In 1903 he accompanied W. C. Peckham, his employer at the time, to British Columbia, where he spent four weeks feeling more like a "man" than he ever had before. This was one of the most significant experiences of his life. He carefully described each of its details in his journal. His impressions of what he saw, felt, and did were so strong that they were among the things he spoke of most in the weeks before he died (*SP* 117). This adventure—his last vacation before being admitted to the bar in spring of 1904—marked the end of his time of youthful balancing. After this all choices had binding consequences. Though his account of this trip will be dealt with later, it is mentioned here in order to give a sense of the associations and experiences contributing to Stevens's sense of himself as a man. Hunting and being "self-sufficient" before nature—in an Emersonian way[11]—were major aspects of the life of the president as well as of the lives of a certain class of "gentlemen" of that time and later. This was the class to which Peckham belonged. This is important to keep in mind while we attempt to reconstruct the possible determinants of Stevens's choices.

This feature also helps explain, at least partially, Stevens's later expressed personal hostility to Ernest Hemingway,[12] who, unlike him, integrated this aspect—the constant proving of his manhood against nature—in the hunting and fishing adventures that were essential parts of his life. We can only smile sadly at the unconscionable treachery of fate that left Stevens on his deathbed longingly re-creating the scene where his manhood was proven against nature, while a few years later the one who seemed to fulfill the fantasy of the "all-American male" and who was *also* a writer blew his brains out with one of his hunting guns. The mythology of our region makes it very hard for the figure of the poet as virile youth to escape being only a "figure" and to come into real manhood.

In light of what is being suggested about Stevens's sense of himself and his attempt at becoming "man number one," it is worth remarking that during this period he physically experimented with his image. At various times he sported a full beard or a mustache (which he grew again about fourteen years later and kept for a few years, when it was not as much in fashion as it was during the first decade of the century). It is almost as difficult to conjure a picture of Stevens with a "heavy"[13] beard as it is to conjure him smiling. Almost all the published photographs, including those remaining from his childhood and youth, show him with variations of the pensive expression familiar from the dust jackets of *The Collected Poems* and *Opus Posthumous*. The exceptions where he is smiling are shocking because the image of a man at ease is not one easily associated with the man hidden in his gray business suit, writing the cold lines characteristic of the poetry after *Harmonium*. But the exercise of imagining him with a beard provides one of the mental pictures necessary to ground a significant aspect of Stevens's personality. He first let his beard grow on the hunting trip to British Columbia where it easily became associated with his sense of being a man. This lends an essential element of reality to the mask of Crispin, the "Comedian as the Letter C." On his voyage he had to have grown a beard. Stevens described him as "farouche and droll." Certainly his own beard added a "farouche" quality to the "droll" part of

Stevens as "Comedian" himself that seems to have disappeared after *Harmonium.* This part continued to exist, however, though only in certain circumstances and always hidden from "a certain pair of blue eyes"—the eyes, as he later described them, of Elsie Moll.

⁊❧

The role of the comedian began to take on reality as Stevens gradually abandoned that of journalist during the first six months of 1901. This shift was marked by periods of great despair that bordered, at least on one occasion, as recorded by William Carlos Williams, on thoughts of suicide.[14] It is not clear how, as Williams also noted, Stevens came to feel a failure as a reporter, especially since his earnings just a few months earlier indicated the opposite. It seems that it was not against an external standard that Stevens didn't measure up, but, to judge from his responses to what he was being sent out to cover, that it was a failure of nerve. Facing the hard facts of the cruder aspects of city life made him feel less than a man. A "man"—like Stephen Crane, the "hero"—could have met these facts without being moved to tears by the pathos of them.

Stevens had tried to temper his sensitive spirit. He commended himself on being able to see a Crane-like sight without being "bathed in tears." But more often he had to hide his softness from himself by recoiling from what he saw. He responded to the Bosscheiter murder case (four men murdered young Jennifer Bosscheiter) in Patterson, New Jersey during January 1901, for example, by turning away. Rather than recount the facts coolly, objectively, in the manner of a good reporter, Stevens in his journal commented:

> The imagination cannot project itself forward as far as to conceive the future lives of these men. But what a terrible avenger the Law is. It seems as though the sense of Justice which dictated such sentences was not human. The mere length of time is a ghastly thing to contemplate. Jonah must have written the Law, where it is so terrible as this. A Judge ought to tremble when he executes it. (*SP* 97)

His imagination had begun to complete the reality of these four men, though he denied its power to do so. He contradicted his experience because it was not his imagination that could not conceive of this possibility. Another part, not equipped to accept his projection, backed away and stopped imagination cold. The report of the sentencing in the *Tribune,* which appeared the day before the above entry, closed with an observation betraying the writer's inability to remain detached, in keeping with the paper's "non-yellow" tone. After the description of the important facts—one of which was how the judge's voice trembled as he spoke the sentence—came this revealing detail: "Mrs. Bosscheiter [the murdered girl's mother] sat at the end of a seat, and her skirts were brushed by the four men as they were led in and out of the courtroom." Holly Stevens notes that it is uncertain whether her father wrote this piece (*SP* 97). If it was not Stevens who revealed himself in this sentence, it was probably reading this poetical perception that prompted his inability to imagine the fates of these men. In connection with this, it is not accidental that with one or two exceptions, it was not "real life," but the life of nature or the associations of his imagination to the facts of life, that became the subject of Stevens's poems. It was also not accidental, in light of what he wrote at twenty-one about the terrible avenging power of the law, that later, as a lawyer, he devoted himself to dealing with bonds' claims rather than with the concerns of individuals.

In remembering Stevens after his death, Witter Bynner noted that though he was unsure of what had motivated the poet to work as a reporter—whether it was connected to his literary ambition or whether it was for financial reasons—"it was a very good offset to the fastidious instruction" they had received at Cambridge (*SP* 96). While meeting the baser realities of life on the streets of New York might have balanced the sheltered, aristocratic gentility of the Cambridge campus, for Stevens the corrective had a harsh cathartic effect that seems to have left him rather shaky. He faced his weakness with more than a little pain. He reacted by shielding himself, transforming his youthful proclivity for parody into its more hardened form of irony. Together with this internal shift, he began playing the comedian. This tempered the slashing of his irony. The posture also concealed his deeper sense of not having measured up to the image of a man. As a comedian he was in control.

This change was evident both in his beginning to become a different kind of writer (in late February he wrote a play, a "romantic comedy") and in the new attitude he developed by the middle of March toward another of the horrors he was sent to cover as a reporter. His account of this assignment in his journal was the last entry for 1901. From this point until the summer of 1902 he seems to have kept no record. Perhaps meeting this fact brought his career as a journalist to its end: "I've just come from seeing a two-headed Hebrew child—Horrible sight. The first head is all right—the 2nd protrudes from it—there is, of course, only one face. The mother looks dreadfully. She told me that the doctor had told her that an operation would be necessary. She asked him if the child would be alive after the operation. He said it would not. If that is not murder, what is?" (*SP* 101–02).

Coupled with his only comments—"Horrible sight" and "If that is not murder, what is?"—the terseness of the description pointed out the irony of the situation. The pain prompted by the "sight" and situation turned into ironic distance. Later, painful occasions generated the same kind of response:

> "There is not nothing, no, no, never nothing,
> Like the clashed edges of two words that kill."
> And so I mocked her in magnificent measure.
> Or was it that I mocked myself alone?
>
> (*CP* 13)

Between the Bosscheiter case and seeing the monstrous child, Stevens began moving away from looking at the world's cold facts. He not only did this in imagination and attitude but began escaping in reality as well. He went to the theater more. He saw plays featuring his favorite female leads two and three times. In spite of his father's periodic advice to the contrary, he continued planning to go abroad. Just after the Bosscheiter case he noted his intention quite firmly: "I have determined to go to England this summer, if nothing unexpected happens. I already have the price of passage one way—and a little more" (SP 97). A few days after this entry, on the occasion of his father's being in New York for the day, Stevens seems to have escaped—perhaps for the first time—the force of Garrett's personality. The description of their encounter and his reaction to it revealed in its ellipticality his new cool attitude, the same one that appeared in his comments about the two-headed child:

> February 6
> Father was in town two days ago. I took luncheon with him at the Astor House—baked shad, asparagus, etc. We remarked that we looked well.
> It is cold as the deuce this morning. No doubt of the season & midsummer is damned far off.
> By the way, I have moved to No. 124 East 24th St. Am in a hall bedroom, as they say, and rather like it. (SP 97)

Lunching with Garrett at the staid Astor House, where he had spent his first night in New York, made Stevens quietly conscious of beginning to act in his own play. He commented on the food as part of the stage setting. The brevity and coolness of his recording what passed between them—only that they "looked well"—belied its import. He had taken on the role of his father's equal. His use of the first-person plural pronoun implied both this and the identification that allowed him to feel the maturity he had to feel if he was to make his own choices for the future—something he had "determined" to do just seven days earlier.

Following this, his telegraphic report on the weather contained two mild expletives—a most unusual feature of his journal-keeping style. Playing his part seems to have enabled Stevens to use roughened, "manly" forms of expression. The forms themselves, translated into his feelings about the weather, belonged more properly to his feeling about the man who had kept himself "busy holding [him] in check."

Stevens closed with an aside, "By the way. . . ." The offhand manner coupled with the almost direct statement of his feelings—"I *rather* like it" (italics mine)—also belied its significance. Stevens's move to East Twenty-fourth Street took him away from "Bohemia," away from the garrets and studios of Greenwich Village to an area closer to the stylish neighborhood surrounding Madison Square. This went with his subtle role change. But it

165

was also another escape: out of the world of struggling immigrants and artists into a world of "romantic comedy," where his view of reality was filled not by Italian ice-cream makers and six-story tenement buildings but by fashionable ladies and nurses pushing prams while their gentlemen sat around the fountain in the square enjoying occasional cigars away from carefully decorated drawing rooms.

Mimicking this change in setting, the play Stevens wrote only two weeks later—after being inspired by having seen Ethel Barrymore in Clyde Fitch's *Captain Jinks of the Horse Marines*—was a "drawing room comedy" the characters of which could have been among those who moved around Madison Square. Though the piece was never completed, Stevens's outline (*L* 51–52; *SP* 98–99) detailed the contours of his imagined figure of the poet. These became more precisely defined as he translated play into reality by actively taking on the role of poet later on. Stevens borrowed largely from the stock of comic devices learned from Shakespeare, William Congreve, Richard Sheridan, as well as from the play he had just seen, for his romance, which involved the exchanged affections of one brother and sister for another brother and sister. One scene turned around mistaken identity, recalling *Twelfth Night* with its Olivia—the name becoming the title of Stevens's play. Though the outline exhibited no strong originality or genius for the theater, the characterization of the figures revealed central aspects of both Stevens's personal and cultural vision.

The action centered on the romantic entanglements of a rather Jamesian pair of Americans—Olivia Rainbow and her brother, Harry—with an aristocratic French pair—the Duke of Bellemer and his sister, the countess, whom Olivia and Harry visit at the château of the duke, a friend of Harry's. Before the situation resolved in Olivia's re-pairing with the duke and Harry's with the countess, a number of minor incidents focused on Olivia's flightiness and flirtation with three seemingly unnecessary characters. Each of them fell in love with her at first sight. She then tested her three suitors in a reversed parody of the Judgment of Paris. One of these three was a poet—the one wholly unsuccessful figure in the play. He was made "ridiculous" by Olivia: He could not pass her test of knocking a flower off her shoulder. He was pitied by the countess. But though she "adored" him, she ended by accepting Harry. Curiously, the poet was the only character who was physically described and who had non-romantic, non-comic reactions attributed to him: "He [was] tall, dignified, [wore] a frock coat"; at being made fun of by Olivia, he showed "consternation"; and at the end of Act II he entered—for no apparent reason, in terms of furthering the action—and simply "poetize[d.]"

Beyond the projection illustrated by this characterization of the poet, in his depiction of Olivia, Stevens disclosed other aspects of himself as well as certain feelings about the nature of women. Though it was appropriate to the heroine of a turn-of-the-century piece that she be fickle and sometimes cruel in her light treatment of those taken by her charms, it was unusual and revealing of Stevens's perception that she be entirely unimpressed by the poet, the most developed of the characters. After belittling him gratuitously, she chose the attractions of the duke in a typically American fairy-tale response. In doing this, she also parodied the behavior of Olivia in *Twelfth Night*, who rejected the duke. At the same time Stevens's Olivia had gone to France to find her fate, as the real young poet had wanted to the previous summer. But once there, she was blind to the only one who revealed anything approaching genuine engagement with reality. The poet could not knock the flower from her shoulder precisely because he was the only one who felt her beauty deeply enough to have it affect the spirit he would need to compete. He recognized her because she was like him. But unlike her, the real poet felt he could not even attract one doting female. Four years later he was still in this unhappy state, as he lamented to himself in his journal: "Here am I, a descendant of the Dutch, at the age of twenty-five, without a cent to my name, in a huge town, knowing half-a-dozen men + no women" (*L* 69).

Within months after sketching out *Olivia,* Stevens gave in to his father's advice. He did not go abroad but remained in New York "to make something of himself." His planned play contained the hidden realizations that led him finally to agree that Garrett did indeed have "reason on his side." In *Olivia,* Stevens outlined the promptings of what were to be his own actions over the next few years as much as he outlined the action of the play. There was a play within the play in which he was the actor who learned the lines written by himself, a being already acting on the stage of a world he did not make, taking cues from an unseen director.

The most striking feature of the play within Stevens was the subtlest aspect of the play he imagined: the relationship of the poet to reality, specifically the place of the poet in American society. At this point in his development Stevens questioned the possibility of his becoming a poet and being recognized if he remained in America. This was revealed in the play by the interaction of Olivia and the poet and in the character of Olivia herself, who gave up her Americanness by going to Europe and choosing the duke. She aspired to belong to an order that was already dying. The situation was problematic. On the one hand, there was "the poet" in *Olivia,* a Frenchman, accepted and recognized as such by his society, unlike the poet in turn-of-the-century America. On the other hand, there were Olivia and Harry. Like the characters in a novel by Henry James, they left the American scene and went back to the Old World in search of "real" culture and refinement. But once there, Olivia revealed the naïvely coarse spirit of still young America. She was unable to recognize the poet and the sincerity of his feelings. She opted for the duke's display—for form alone (since it was clear from Stevens's outline that the duke did not love her).

Between the lines—or, rather, between the acts—of this "comedy" Stevens uncovered the contradictions and concomitant ambivalence he felt about his sense of himself as a poet and as an American at this turning point in his career. This uneasiness reinforced his general insecurity. Now, at the moment he began life on his own, the contradictions and ambivalence he felt were exaggerated while they at the same time became the most characteristic features of the age. As Jackson Lears abundantly shows in *No Place of Grace,* the movement up and down between two elements belonged not only to Stevens as the "Comedian" he hoped to be. There was almost no aspect of American life between 1880 and 1920 that was not suffering from this *"dis*ease."[15] By 1914 the movement quickened to the shattering moment that left the world and all its actors in fragments.

Already feeling the longer, gentler oscillations for a while and in some sense anticipating their consequences, at least personally, Stevens attempted, in choosing to remain in America, to stop the movement, ease the tensions. He wanted to become something more than the "dilettante," "half-dream, half-deed" he feared he would become if he yielded, like so many of the generation that had educated him at Harvard, to the search for stillness somewhere away from the gray particular landscape in which he had been reared. Stevens knew of too many in Cambridge who had gone to Europe or the Orient looking for an alternative to becoming just more parts in the machine of spiritual and material progress that America wanted to believe itself. They had ended as dilettantes at best. Many could not even muster enough energy or focus enough attention to appreciate anything at all. They sank into depressions or developed neurasthenic symptoms that made them, at least in some way, centers of their experience. The most successful of them were like Charles Eliot Norton, who managed to come to a stoical acceptance of things as they were only in old age—when Stevens knew him. But this was after a lifetime of ups and downs, in and out of depressive conflicts with himself and others, in and out of America, traveling far in time and distance in an attempt to find something that would suffice.[16]

This need was a response to what Lears has called the "crisis of cultural authority," which America experienced most acutely during the first years of the century, though the steps leading to it began twenty to thirty years earlier, as the impact of Darwinism and industrialization gradually penetrated more and more aspects of life.[17] The crisis was felt most keenly by those who, because of the nature of their professional preoccupations, were deeply aware of the implications and consequences of continued belief in the myth of progress. Not surprisingly, these were privileged individuals centered on Boston and Cambridge. Because of either class affiliation or personal interest in areas concerned primarily with the spirit—art or aesthetics—these were the first to sense themselves becoming the "superfluous men"[18] of America. Most were teachers at Harvard, like Charles Eliot Norton, Barrett Wendell, Pierre LaRose, from all of whom Stevens had learned.

But the age demanded more than the solutions offered by these men, who attempted to correct the ills they experienced and the greater ills they foresaw by recoiling from the present time and place and looking instead to the preindustrial past or to the East for different ways of being. This was the impetus behind Norton's focus on Dante, or Henry Adams's on the Middle Ages, or Fenollosa's on China and Japan. They picked up and theoretically expanded what John Ruskin and William Morris had seen and expressed about the personal, identifying value to be derived from an individual's involvement with a piece of work made before or without the innovations that began in the Renaissance. During the last quarter of the nineteenth century the Harvard intellectuals tried to translate the American understanding of individualism into areas that could once again provide the satisfactions experienced by the medieval artisan, but not by the Renaissance craftsman and certainly not by the industrial or bureaucratic man of their century.

What these seekers soon discovered was that this return was not possible without a return as well to some kind of faith in an order that would ensure that each individual's personal, idiosyncratic expression represented more than his or her own personal idiosyncrasies. What was created had to have some place or purpose in a larger order, even if the order was not immediately recognizable. While the rest of the culture was trying to maintain faith in the myth of continuing spiritual and material progress, these members of the elite class were beginning to experience the nightmarish underside of the American dream. They realized that the myth of progress was nothing more than a convenient adaptation and coupling of the theory of evolution with a secularized version of the Protestant ethic. This pairing guaranteed ongoing industrial production and the imperial expansion that made the material and spiritual "goods" of America available to more and more inside and outside its borders. But the myth had no bottom, no sustaining purpose. Some of those who already had the goods, but who still found themselves wanting, tried to find another faith.

The faiths these "enlightened" rebels turned to were based not on masculine, driving forces but on female, accepting qualities. Henry Adams consoled himself and others with imaginings of the all-comforting Virgin of the Middle Ages, a version of the eternal female well suited, in her permanent unavailability, to the Victorian vision. He found her far more attractive than the impersonal goddesses or the intangible heaven of the Orient, though he had sought solace in them as well. Others of his generation, however, like William Sturgis Bigelow, George Cabot Lodge, Percival Lowell,[19] did find— at least for a time—in Oriental mysticism the required faith in something larger than themselves. Buddhism, especially in some of its forms, offered a particularly workable alternative to those who had lost faith. It did not posit or necessitate belief in any unseen heaven. Transcendence came immediately, if at all, in the present relinquishing of the individualism that was understood to be at the core of the problem.

Unfortunately, those who had been shaped by the opposing Western laws, by the values of individualism, could not sustain their newly adopted faiths without breaking. The record of depressions, neurasthenic symptoms, and collapses suffered by these pioneers of the spirit is staggering.[20] Of the important figures of the age who were involved in this collective crisis of conscience, it seems that none escaped at least one of these indications of disease. And later their heirs, moving deeper into the darkness of the century, fell as well while trying in their own ways to find resting places for their uneasy souls. T. S. Eliot and Ezra Pound were perhaps the most striking examples. Both searched in other cultures for the answers they couldn't find in their own; we recall the Sanskrit invocations of *The Waste Land* and Pound's fascination with the troubadours before he reached Cathay. And both, during or after their explorations, attempted to stop their movements up and down, back and forth, by attaching themselves to some firm foundation. Eliot fixed himself to Anglo-Catholicism; Pound, to fascism.[21] Significantly, neither of them returned from their journeys to settle finally in America. Of those who did return, most, in the end, also reattached themselves to a firm foundation, tying up once again to the rock of Puritan values from which they had originally set out. This was the case for Percival Lowell, Charles Eliot Norton, G. Stanley Hall (who arranged Freud's visit to America in 1909), and Van Wyck Brooks,[22] all of whom had searched abroad and followed different ways, though not without suffering the pains and conflicts occasioned by their separation.

But what of those like Stevens, who never left?

Exposed to those at Harvard who attempted to abandon the masculine ideals of the American way, Stevens observed that yielding to the lures of feminine virtues was putting oneself in danger of breaking. Nevertheless, he could not ignore the possibilities these alternatives presented to his spirit. Incorporating them in some way meant broadening his perception, seeing the world from an entirely opposite point of view, experiencing doubly. For him, who had begun early in life feeling the strain between reality and imagination, these other ways of being—offered with the authority of those he most respected at Harvard—had to be taken seriously. At the same time, not belonging to the same class as these men, and so unable to fall back on familial care and financial support if the attempt to live through another way failed, he knew he could not afford to break down or lose himself in a host of neurasthenic symptoms, especially since his father had suffered a nervous collapse himself, though for externally different reasons. Stevens's solution was to live what became, in effect, a double life.

While in imagination Stevens followed his masters, explored the places they had actually visited, and indulged the female aspect of his spirit in writing "lady-like" verses, in reality he adapted himself to what seemed to be the greatest need of the age. Until 1914, at least, this meant resolving the ambivalence and contradictoriness of the crisis of cultural authority by acting as though there were no crisis. This demanded cultivating the qualities embodied by Theodore Roosevelt: gentility, endurance, discipline, dedication to the native soil and ethic, and, perhaps most important, living as though one believed in the myth of progress. Here was an American heroic ideal that could serve in place of the idea of God and provide the authority that faith in

His existence had until recently furnished. Against this background, in autumn of 1901, Stevens chose to try his strength at becoming "man number one" by following the model wished for by the age and cultivating the necessary habits. Rather than attempt to resolve the ambivalence as others before him had tried and failed, he accepted it. He lived his life moving up and down between two elements. Instead of pursuing the "literary life" and becoming a journalist who wove his gift for "painting pictures in words" into the material of his survival, he put on the lawyer's dress by day, while at night and on weekends, sweatered and moccasined in his easy chair, he imagined himself wearing the poet's crown. With this solution he stopped wishing, as he had only a year earlier, that he "wore no crown" since he did not have to depend any longer on others' seeing it in order to win his bread. The "posing" he understood to be an essential aspect of his being he put to real use, acting the role of the gentleman-lawyer.

Stevens's sense of how much reality pressed was based on more than intuition or deductions arrived at from knowing what had happened to his forerunners in the Harvard circle. Just before finally abandoning the hope of following a writer's career and just before abandoning his journal for what would be more than a year, he made two entries that reflect that his fears were confirmed by facts: He could not expect to live on the wage he might earn in the publishing business, and his father would not begin to think of supporting him if he were to spend his time writing. (Garrett was at this point experiencing the worst of the financial strain that was to lead to his breakdown.)

March 11, 1901

   The streets are blue with mist this morning.

   Went home last Thursday for a few hours—first time since Xmas. . . . I had a good long talk with the old man in which he did most of the talking. One's ideas don't get much of a chance under such conditions. However he's a wise man. We talked about the law which he has been urging me to take up. I hesitated—because this literary life, as it is called, is the one I always had as an ideal & I am not quite ready to give it up because it has not been all I wanted it to be. The other day, after returning to New York, I called on John Phillips of McClure, Phillips and [I] had a talk about the publishing business. P. is philosophical and serious & yet, I think a person of no imagination—or little. He told me that the business was chiefly clerical— unpleasant fact—& that I could hardly expect to live on my wages—etc. etc. I was considerably jarred by the time he got through. The mirage I had fancied disappeared in the desert—where I invariably land. However, I've made a market for Mss—if it's at all worth while!

   I've been giving "Olivia" a rest for a short time—so as to be able to inspect it as it should be inspected, before I start it.

The mist outside has grown visibly thicker since I wrote the above. The season is changing. (SP 100–01)

Indeed, the season had changed.[23] The hope Stevens once had of making the "literary life" the one that could support him had to be given up. From now on unity would be expressed only in and through words, as it was here. His opening and closing observations about the weather held together the wandering passages about life. In this focus on the moving yet constant forces of nature, Stevens prefigured his own most moving and constant metaphor. The light and dark, wind and stillness of his mind changed and held together what he observed around him and transformed it, through his days, into the body of poems that became his "completion of life."

The next day Stevens noted his intended resignation: "I recently wrote to father suggesting that I should resign from the Tribune + spend my time in writing. This morning I heard from him +, of course, found my suggestion torn to pieces. If I only had enough money to support myself I am afraid some of his tearing would be in vain. But he seems always to have reason on his side, confound him" (L 53; SP 101). Ironically, Garrett would not have "reason on his side" much longer. But this Stevens could not have known.

æ

By the time Stevens took up his journal again during the summer of 1902, he had completed his first year at the New York Law School. He had also established a more than professional relationship with W. C. Peckham, the man for whom he worked as a clerk that summer and then again after completing his second year of study. In June 1902, while visiting Peckham's Adirondack vacation home, he was formally introduced to Sybil Gage, the beauty of Cambridge for whom he had silently longed as an undergraduate. As noted earlier, this relationship did not develop, though his imaginings of her seem to have preoccupied him throughout his life. At this point he wrote her a poem. Years later he considered naming his daughter Sybil.[24] Still later, in 1950, he described his infatuation with her to Richard Eberhart. And the year before he died, her name figured homonymically in "The Sail of Ulysses" (OP 99), one of his most complex poems about desire. Beyond his trembling in response to women he felt to be out of his reach, his more general feelings of uncertainty about his own development and his place in the world naturally prevented him from seriously pursuing Miss Gage more assiduously that summer. He had first to establish himself, at least in his own mind, before he could offer himself to any woman.

Setting out to do this, Stevens spent the next two and a half years working diligently at his studies and at his clerkship in Peckham's office. The only interruptions were weekly long walks in the country, occasional overindulgent nights out with old and new acquaintances, sporadic visits back home to Reading, certain weekends in the mountains with the Peckhams, and the noted trip to British Columbia in the late summer of 1903, again at the invitation of Peckham. Though there were a few indications in the journals of this period of occasions of self-doubt or depression, they were mild. The decision to follow his father's advice seemed, for the time being, to be the right one. Having made it, Stevens began to move in a regular rhythm, doing what was necessary during the days of the week and yielding to his pleasure during the nights and weekends.

As would be expected, his depressions came at moments when he realized the implicit consequences of his choices. Just before returning to school for the fall term of 1902, he expressed his sad frustration at his sense of "imprisonment" in a life that answered the demands of necessity rather than pleasure.

Saturday, August 9, 1902
Oh, Mon Dieu, how my spirits sink when I am alone here in my room! Tired of everything that is old, too poor to pay for what's new—tired of reading, tired of tobacco, tired of walking about town; and longing to have friends with me, or to be somewhere with them: nauseated by this terrible imprisonment. Yes: I might put a light face on it and say it is merely a depression rising from lack of exercise, but from my present point of view I see nothing but years of lack of exercise before me. And then this terrible self-contemplation! Tomorrow if the sun shines I shall go wayfaring all day long. I *must* find a home in the country—a place to *live* in, not only to *be* in. (L 58; SP 103)

And just before taking the bar exam at the end of the following spring, he wrote: "I'm sure of my law degree. One week more and the drowning out process begins. It feels like entering the hospital for an operation. Nevertheless, I'm not so gloomy as I might be" (L 63; SP 114).

These two entries were the strongest and almost sole expressions of his discontent during his time as a law student and apprentice. He felt he was finally making something of himself even if it was not what he ideally wanted. His commitment permitted him even fairly regular lapses into self-indulgent habits without the severe recriminations with which he used to chastise himself for the same things while at Harvard and during his first year in New York—before he had made this *reason*able choice. It was as though he felt he had won his father's approval and could indulge freely once again—as he had done when he was a boy—in imagination, the part he shared with his mother. It was like a return to the security of childhood, the fulfillment of a wish made then.

His journal entries now were focused almost wholly on the half of his life spent walking and thinking during nights and weekends. There was hardly a mention of what filled his days. This pattern was mirrored later in his poetry, in which it is nearly impossible to detect, through its lines, any of the daily activities of the Hartford insurance man. The poems reflect the unseen side of the public man's life. The regularity of his habits as recorded in the journal also reflected a return to another established pattern learned in childhood. Then his days were filled with doing what was required: going to school; studying; chores. Afterward he played. On weekends he went into the country, walked in the woods, lay on the rocks and looked at the sky, and on Sunday, following his mother's guiding hand, he went to church, served as an altar boy, sang in the choir. Now his days were filled with law school, the clerkship. After doing what was required, he did as he liked; on weekends he went once more into the country, lay on rocks and looked at the sky. But there was a subtle change. Sundays in church were replaced by Sundays in nature. Communion with trees, birds, wind, and trembling shadows took the place of the communion of the faithful. He recorded his "observance" regularly in his journal and drew parallels between the two kinds of experience:

Sunday, August 10, 1902

I've had a handsome day of it and am contented again. Left the house after breakfast and went by ferry and trolley to Hackensack over in Jersey. From H. I walked 5½ miles on the Spring Valley road, then 4 miles to Ridgewood, then another mile to Hokokus [*sic;* Hoboken in *L*] and back towards town 7 miles more to Paterson: 17½ in all, a good day's jaunt at this time of the year. Came from Paterson to Hoboken by trolley and then home. In the early part of the day I saw some very respectable country which, as usual, set me contemplating. I love to walk along with a slight wind playing in the trees about me and think over a thousand and one odds and ends. Last night I spent an hour in the dark transept of St. Patrick's Cathedral where I go now and then in my more lonely moods. An old argument with me is that the true religious force in the world is not the church but the world itself: the mysterious callings of Nature and our responses. What incessant murmurs fill that ever-laboring, tireless church! But today in my walk I thought that after all there is no conflict of forces but rather a contrast. In the cathedral I felt one presence; on the highway I felt another. Two different deities presented themselves; and though I have only cloudy visions of either, yet I now feel the distinction between them. The priest in me worshipped one God at one shrine; the poet another God at another shrine. The priest worshipped Mercy and Love, the poet Beauty and Might. In the shadows of the church I could hear the prayers of men and women; in the shadows of the trees nothing mingled with Divinity. As I sat dreaming with the Congregation, I felt how the glittering altar worked on my senses stimulating and consoling them; and as I went tramping through the fields and woods I beheld every leaf and blade of grass revealing or rather betokening the Invisible. (*L* 58–59; *SP* 104)

This habit of Sunday walks continued over the next few years. After beginning his relationship with Elsie Moll, Stevens recorded his observance in Sunday letters to her. He was translating the function of the poet in nature into the function of priest. Doing this was in keeping with the secularizing spirit of the age.[25] If there were to be religion at all, it would be pantheism. His attention to the details of distances covered suggests that he saw his involvement with nature to be like a religious discipline. But there was another aspect as well.

He recorded only the day before that he had been depressed, in part because of lack of activity. His commitment to vigorous walking, to exercise, belonged to the period's stress on "strenuosity." This became a prominent feature of daily life, especially for those who had, like Stevens, moved to an urban environment around the turn of the century.[26] Popular magazines like *Scribner's, Atlantic Monthly,* and *Harper's,* all of which Stevens read more than occasionally, ran regular articles devoted to the ills of urbanization and the need to counteract its effects by careful attention to regular exercise. The deleterious effects of inactivity ranged from simple atrophying of the muscles—which went together with a sedentary office life—to the more frightening range of neurasthenic symptoms resulting from the various pressures of city life. Constant noise from crowds, horses, cable cars, trains filled days and nights. One had to be "on time," something that had only just recently begun to have meaning in America.[27] Everyone felt isolated and anonymous on the busy streets and avenues. And there was the unspoken but pervasive fear of the many strangers who were all around in and out of the city.[28]

Stevens's walks took him away from all this. When he was in the pure air of the countryside, purged of the city's poisons, his ideas began to crystallize. As Holly Stevens points out, the perceptions he recorded in his journal during this period prefigured the major preoccupations of his mature work. Certain lines and images are linked directly to sentences he wrote now in 1902. The strongest of these grew out of moments of extreme intimacy with himself, when he recognized and accepted significant aspects of his being. On these sallies into the gold and crimson forms of nature, Stevens crossed bridges between his past and present. They offered him at least temporary resting places from which he could survey himself and what he saw around him.

This is apparent in the entry of Sunday, August 17. He first described a long Saturday walk and an overnight stay in a small New Jersey town where he read Francis Bacon's essay "On Friendship" at the local library before retiring. He then went on to detail observations from Sunday's walk. At one point he naïvely used a form of expression that he seems to have self-consciously registered as being something he would later develop into a controlling metaphor:

> *Up—and down* [italics mine] to breakfast at eight with glorious weather awaiting me. Astonished by the magnificent view from the village street— and by the price of breakfast (which I hastened to forget). Turned out of my way to climb a hill called the *Torn,* though an ancient Irish farmer told me he had so much as heard it called the Rattlesnake—geography is in a feeble condition up that way. Well, I was immensely pleased by the views from the top of this hill, whence I could look all about the Northern region of the

state. By all odds, one of the most beautiful scenes within a Christian distance of New York. Lay down on a rock and took a sunbath for a half-hour. . . . (*SP* 105–06)

Here the poet strikingly re-created past experience. He surveyed the landscape from the hilltop in the same way that he used to from the Tower atop Mount Penn in Reading. This, in turn, was linked to his internalizations of R. L. Stevenson's perceptions from hilltops that Stevens remembered from *The Silverado Squatters* as well as from "The Land of Counterpane." This current experience was another of the bridges that led to his imagination's Tennessee and "Anecdote of the Jar." In the same way, his sunbathing on a rock recalled the countless childhood sunbaths on rocks around Reading and forecast his own gradual poetic metamorphosis into "thinking stone" and finally to "The Rock" of his last years, when he became one with the planet of which he was a part.

Moving up and down across these bridges, Stevens found himself. In the same entry he noted two of the more unpleasant aspects of his personality. Though in his youth these qualities might have seemed neutral or even positive, in later life they became rather obsessive and isolating habits. His comment on the price of breakfast, which he wanted to forget, was connected to the necessary frugality he had to exercise as a student-clerk. But it also reflected something deeper and more generalized, something he had had an inkling of the previous year, when apropos of his having begun to save money while working as a reporter, he expressed his delight in having the miser in him tickled. This trait developed into such an overconcern with security that it interfered with his human relationships—most significantly with the most important, that with Elsie Moll. During the years of their courtship he would not consider marriage until he was absolutely certain of his ability to support her and a household permanently. This led to uncertainties and periods of unhappiness for Elsie, who felt herself moving past the age when she should have been married. Even more painful for her, after their marriage, was her husband's reluctance to have a child, again until he was sure of earning more than a sufficient amount to enable them to live well.[29] Though this concern was in some sense real, it was greatly exaggerated and in that exaggeration suggested itself as a symptom of much more serious doubts about security of a different kind. In his most successful years as a prosperous executive, when it was certainly no longer necessary for him to worry about money, this habit turned on itself to become a group of eccentricities mocked by others. It showed itself as one of those compulsions which people use to order their lives but which have a greater function in blocking alternative ways of being that demand the openness and self-questioning the obsessive habits themselves preclude.

Stevens finally settled in one of the most exclusive yet conservatively understated neighborhoods of Hartford. His house, which few of his friends or associates visited, was filled with exquisite objects, beautiful Orientals, and paintings he had collected (though he was careful to bargain for them whenever he could). On his walks to the office he was occasionally picked up by the wife of another executive of the Hartford Accident and Indemnity Company as she drove her husband to work. Periodically, on days when Mr. Stevens was carrying a paper bag and she stopped to offer him a ride, he asked her to take him farther downtown to the Hartford Electric Company. There he got out and dropped off his paper bag, full of used light bulbs. For each of these he received a few cents' reduction on his bill for the following month.[30] More than just an amusing anecdote giving a glimpse into Stevens's very hidden private life, this detail reveals that the retentive, puritanical aspects of his character never disappeared. Even though, at the same time, he indulged his extravagant tastes and was generously charitable with family and friends in need, there was always something he did to show that he kept himself in check.

At this point, besides the miserliness he observed in himself, another negative trait he exhibited also reflected his introversion. This was noted earlier as well in connection with his reluctance to open to strangers he met when he first lived alone in New York. Now, on his Sunday walk, interrupting his feeling of exuberant oneness with the landscape where he completely relaxed—falling asleep for a while "on a cool hilltop"—he heard a sound that troubled him: "While dozing I heard and recognized a dozen wood sounds and was undisturbed; once, however, I heard the crackle that a man makes in moving and was on the alert at once. Why? What is the reason for this instinctive guard against our own kind? Weiss nicht [I don't know]." Lapsing into the artifice of German (the language he perhaps associated with his frugal habits, inherited from his ancestors' stress on thrift), Stevens distracted himself from contemplating further on the sources of his "instinctive guard against [his] own kind." He then went on to indulge a particularly strong misanthropic feeling; this was an indirect complement to his mistrust and fear:

> Took trolley at Paterson (Haledon) and rode to Passaic. I detest the inhabitants of this neighborhood, who are still savages, so took the train at Passaic for Jersey City. Scarcely seated when one of the above-mentioned inhabitants came along, placed a little girl beside me, who was all elbows, and then sank down herself. Three in one seat! My God, I took flight. Crossing the meadows, the rushes were green and the sky pink. City overhung with smoke, which the moon struggled to silver. (*SP* 106)

If this were an isolated instance of intolerance, it would be unimportant, but it was not. He described similar unpleasant encounters with usually anonymous individuals in his later journals. And in his dealings with many employees at the Hartford—as recalled by some of them—the same attitude emerged. This feature of Stevens's personality was beginning to harden into a permanent contour already at twenty-two. Though a result of his own tenderness—in the deepest sense attached to an overweening fear of judgment by others—the consequences were rather harsh and difficult on others not sensitive enough to see beneath his aloof and severe manner. They didn't know of his youthful uncertainties between his brothers or about how concerned he had been about measuring up in his father's eyes. Still less could they imagine that he had felt like an oafish farmer among his patrician classmates at Harvard. It was with an understanding of the defensive transformation of his weaknesses and fears into offensive "poses" that Stevens wrote in a letter to Elsie a few years later that he could show his real self only on paper, not in direct contact with her or anyone else.

But had he been gregarious, he would not have spent so many of the weekends of his youth alone, communing with nature and opening the sources of thought that flowered into the beauty of his poems. There is, nonetheless, a sad irony in imagining Stevens on his August weekend jaunt, when he was to have met a friend who never showed up, reading that Saturday evening Bacon's essay "On Friendship." It was as though he attempted to discover what friendship meant "on paper" rather than through examining his own experience. No doubt he was disturbed that his friend had disappointed him, yet he failed to use his journal to express his feelings. He focused instead on the natural world, as he had at nineteen in reaction to the "pathos" of the Wilys' situation. The ghost of Bacon was his silent interlocutor, just as in childhood the writers and characters of the books he read replaced direct contact with those around him. In Bacon's essay, as in so many of the things Stevens read that acted as hidden determinants of his behavior, he found perceptions about the solitary individual that conditioned those he later recorded in the same journal entry. And an aspect of these perceptions offered him a way of considering himself that alleviated the pain of his isolation.

"On Friendship" opens with an anonymous quotation: "Whosoever is delighted in solitude is either a wild beast or a god." To that Bacon added:

> For it is most true that a natural and secret hatred and aversation towards society, in any man, hath somewhat of the savage beast; but it is most untrue that it should have any character at all of the divine nature; except it proceed, not out of a pleasure in solitude, but out of a love and desire to sequester a man's self for a higher conversation . . . as Epimenides the Candian, Numa the Roman, Empedocles the Sicilian, and Apollonius of Tyre; and truly and really in divers of the ancient hermits and holy fathers of the church.[31]

Bacon's suggestion about a "natural and secret hatred and aversation towards society" could easily and subtly have combined with Stevens's understandably hostile feelings about the friend who disappointed him to produce his misanthropic outburst at the end of the entry. But more important, the alternative of the holy hermit Bacon offered to being considered a savage beast—if one suffered in solitude in order to commune with the divine—was one that

Stevens used to comfort himself. Later, in journal entries, letters, and poems Stevens described himself as the hermit-monk who performed his service in enforced solitude. This mask was most appropriate for one increasingly concerned, as he was, with making poetry a form of "higher conversation" for the century that could no longer pray to an empty heaven.

The suggestions prompted by this essay worked in the underworld of Stevens's mind. Within the next few months "solitude," as both word and idea, became prominent in his journal entries. It coupled with the image of the hermit to transform the woods where he walked into his "temple" (*SP* 109, 111), where he felt "angels all about" (*SP* 113). It was as though he imagined himself St. Francis in Jan Van Eyck's Renaissance depiction. Using this subtle fiction as a backdrop against which he played out the intricacies of his spiritual life over the next few years, Stevens was also able to neutralize things that otherwise could have hurt him. Covertly cultivating this idea of himself as a holy hermit who chose solitude because only alone could he have the "higher conversation" he sought, he could, for example, a few months later view the company of a friend as an interference, something that held him up from taking his sacred walk (*SP* 111). With this attitude he would never again feel that he had been "stood up" by someone with whom he had expected to share his perceptions. The outlines of his double life were beginning to become well defined.

The fiction of the holy hermit allowed Stevens to protect his sensitive parts beneath the cloak of solitude necessary for "higher conversation." In his equally necessary mingling with others in the real world of business and law, these parts unseen, he assumed the requisite social role, mimicking his surroundings and company with consummate skill, acting parts learned in books. But as this split became more accentuated, it became more difficult for Stevens to make the transitions smoothly. To ease the role changes, he slowly leaned, more and more, on America's most common social prop, alcohol. Much later in his life the difference in his behavior with and without alcohol was so great that it seemed he could hardly speak at all comfortably unless he had had his martini; at the Canoe Club in Hartford, where he lunched frequently, the waitress knew that Mr. Stevens's "martini" meant a pitcher.[32] As though sensing now, in his early twenties that this was a potentially serious problem, he periodically "swore off spirits," even though he was not yet, as he put it, "boozing" (*SP* 112).

In his "higher conversations," the subjects he began exploring were those that occupied him over a lifetime. They emerged from his direct observation of himself and his reactions to the world around him. This interaction he later named the "true subject" of his poetry. His notion of the "abstract," for example—central to understanding both the scope of his poetic intention and the idea of the abstract in painting, to which his own interpretation was tied—grew around the kind of perception found in the journal entry of Sunday, August 24, 1902: "I am not at home by the sea; my fancy is not at all marine, so to speak; when I sit on the shore and listen to the waves they only suggest wind in the trees. A single *coup d'oeil* [glance] is enough to see all, as a rule. The sea is loveliest far in the *abstract when the imagination can feed upon the idea of it* [italics mine]. The thing itself is dirty, wobbly and wet" (*L* 59; *SP* 107). Though he had already in R. L. Stevenson come across the idea of the "abstract"—as seeing something from a perfecting real or imaginative distance—now it was no longer just an intellectual apprehension but a concrete aspect of his sensory experience. And it was tied to a deepening understanding of himself, as here, where he did not feel at home by the sea. This particular understanding developed to inform the motto of "The Comedian"—"His soil is man's intelligence"—and the description of "The Snow Man"—"nothing himself" but part of the "Nothing that is not there and the nothing that is."

In naming these and other preoccupations over the closing months of 1902, Stevens also began articulating a personal system of order, of belief, against other systems he knew of or had learned about. One of the clearest early statements of this kind came in the first days of September, just after the long Labor Day weekend, when he had a Monday of dreaming in the sand at Manhattan Beach to add to his usual Sunday communion. He seemed more than usually lucid about his internal state, which he revealingly attributed to his having refrained from overly indulging one of his pleasures:

> I have smoked only two cigars this week and my mind is like a drop of dew as a result. Today while thinking over organic laws etc. the idea of the German "Organismus" ["Organism"] crept into my thoughts—and as I was lunching on Frankfurters and sauerkraut, I felt quite the philosopher. Wonderfully scientific + clear idea—this *organismus* one. Yes: and if I were a materialist I might value it. But only last night I was lamenting that the fairies were things of the past. The organismus is truck—give me the fairies, the Cloud-Gatherer, the Prince of Peace, the Mirror of Virtue—and a pleasant road to think of them on, and a starry night to be with them. (*L* 60; *SP* 108–09)

This succinct profession of belief was itself an abstract of the most formative aspects of his experience: his youthful desire, inherited from his mother, for an object of faith; his conversations with Ed Livingood about Goethe and the idea of *Organismus;* his exposure at Harvard to the antimaterialist reactions of William James, Charles Eliot Norton, George Santayana, Barrett Wendell, and Pierre LaRose. (These last two were closely involved with Henry Adams, who, though he had not yet written *Mont-Saint-Michel and Chartres* or *The Education,* had explored with his friends the ideas that found full expression in these works.) Stevens was reacting in a personal way against the materialist view and its formal phrasing in naturalism. He had just attempted that seemingly realistic mode in emulating the manner of Stephen Crane, reporter par excellence of an evolutionarily conceived social order. But the role did not suit him. Now that he no longer had to consider selling himself in the literary marketplace dominated by writers like Crane, Frank Norris, and Hamlin Garland,[33] Stevens could afford to give up imitating successful models and begin formulating his own "system," however idiosyncratic or out of date it might have seemed.

He was haunted by images from a lost hierarchical order with quasi-religious or mythological overtones: the "Prince of Peace," the "Cloud-Gatherer." Instead of lamenting the loss of such figures and searching for a past world where they lived, as Henry Adams had done, Stevens superimposed these presences on the world he actually inhabited. He described an old acquaintance from around Reading, whom he saw on a brief visit back home in October, in terms borrowed from mystical visions of wooded temples where saints communed with angels: "I visited Kuechler on his hill-top and found him still and pale—his beautiful beard spread over his bosom, the gleam of an invisible sword darting about him" (*SP* 110). Years later, as he clarified the details of his masque beyond the planets, he went over these early journal entries and culled images of the beings who inhabited his heaven. In "Anecdote of the Prince of Peacocks," written sometime in 1922 or 1923, Stevens reworked, in both its final version and in an unpublished manuscript version, these and other perceptions of the period. The following preliminary draft depicts a character seemingly borrowed from old Kuechler, while the Prince of Peacocks incorporates the wished-for aspect of the Prince of Peace:

> In the land of the peacocks, the prince thereof,
> Grown weary of romantics, walked alone,
> In the first of evening, pondering.
>
> "The deuce," he cried.
>
> And by him, in the bushes, he espied
> A white philosopher.
> The white one sighed—
>
> He seemed to seek replies,
> From nothingness, to all his sighs.
>
> "My sighs are pulses in a dreamer's death!"
> Exclaimed the white one, smothering his lips.
>
> The Prince's frisson reached his fingers' tips.
> (WAS 4107; also reproduced in Buttel,
> *The Making of Harmonium,* pp. 192–93)

The revised, published version, even more complex in its suggestions, significantly showed the "white philosopher" changed into "red Berserk," while the seeming dream landscape was transformed into reality with images and perceptions drawn from the 1902 walks:

In the moonlight
I met Berserk,
In the moonlight
On the bushy plain.
Oh, sharp he was
As the sleepless!

And, "Why are you red
In this milky blue?"
I said.
"Why sun-colored,
As if awake
In the midst of sleep?"

"You that wander,"
So he said,
"On the bushy plain,
Forget so soon.
But I set my traps
In the midst of dreams."

I knew from this
That the blue ground
Was full of blocks
And blocking steel.
I knew the dread
Of the bushy plain,
And the beauty
Of the moonlight
Falling there,
Falling
As sleep falls
In the innocent air.

(*CP* 57–58)

The "red," "blue," and the "sun-colored" figure of the poem came out of the remembered landscape seen from an abstract distance, as recorded in his journal. It was a temple inhabited by mythological presences: "The blue sky stretch[ed] vastly to the low horizon. . . . I lay under a group of dark cedars near that strange wind-sown cactus with its red blossom. The sun glittered among the boughs" (*L* 59; *SP* 106).

More specifically, in connection with the moon and the "blocking steel"— the steel that appears so strangely as the traps of Berserk—there was this description of a Sunday walk between Englewood and Tenafly in another of the journal entries just around the time of the one describing Kuechler: "Overhead the moon shone from a strange azure of its own creating. Spirits seemed everywhere—stalking in the infernal forest. The wet sides of leaves glittered like plates of steel. . . . But pooh! I discovered egg-shells! Sure signs of a man + his wife + a child or two, loafing in my temple" (*L* 60–61; *SP* 110–11).

The association to "steel" in the journal and in the poem, together with the intrusion of Stevens's misanthropic reaction to the presence of real yet imagined beings suggest important preoccupations. "Steel" was more than a pictorial figure of Stevens's perceptual landscape. Advancing industrialization had been particularized for Stevens by steel manufacturing. It marred his external view of cities seen in the distance from the woodland hilltops he walked; Reading and New York were often described as shrouded in smoke and in terms evocative of visions of hell. But more, his internal vision of reality was also affected by "steel." His father had become involved in a steel plant, thus joining, in yet another way, America's promise of progress to those enterprising enough to sense its growing needs. Stevens had recently made the decision to follow his father's advice and pursue a career that would prepare him to take up similar opportunities in his own future. But his poetic sensibility was snared by the traps set in the dream of progress by his years at Harvard with men of similar spirit and more experience. Stevens's choice of "steel" as a metaphor pointed to the threat actually and symbolically represented to a life of contemplation and communion with nature, the life he had only on weekends.

In his journal entry this intimation was followed by his imagining not one intruder but a family of trespassers into his temple. His vehemence suggested his unspoken feelings. He resented the external change to his world brought by industrial urbanization. More and more people profaned his "temple." He also feared the imminent changes to his internal life as he prepared for a career that would secure not only his survival but that of a wife and family as well. Though two years earlier he had realized he was a "domestic creature par excellence," the reality of a family also presented itself as one of the traps set in the midst of dreams since considering its needs would always have to take precedence over simply indulging imagination and following his poetic bent.

In his whispered violence toward an imagined family here, and beneath the idiosyncratic leaves/steel comparison in "Anecdote of the Prince of Peacocks" were the implications of the life he had chosen. He had taken the first step toward becoming "man number one." He wanted a "seat on the front bench." The rest of the action followed of itself. The actor played out his part.

A wife and family were necessary characters in this play. Sybil Gage was beyond even his imagination's reach. In New York he moved only outside the drawing-room circles, and proper young women did not wander the streets as he did. But on the occasions when he visited Reading, he began "calling on" certain young ladies there. One of the first accounts of the early, awkward steps of his courtship dance appeared in a journal entry from which, just after the opening description, two pages are missing: "Called on Miss Lewis and found her to be without manners: that is without any more than I have myself. I have . . ." (*SP* 110). It is impossible to know whether Stevens himself excised what followed because it revealed him as also being without manners or whether Elsie later did the cutting. As Holly Stevens notes, after her father's death her mother destroyed and edited out a great deal of material from her husband's letters and journals. What was said here perhaps implied certain comparisons with herself that she found disturbing. Or she might simply have been troubled by the thought that her husband had even considered another before her. Or she could have felt that how he had shown himself here was inappropriate to how she felt he should be remembered. In any case, Stevens expressed something that either he or Elsie, or both, did not want exposed. It is possible that it had to do with his feelings about women since in an entry a week later he was preoccupied with one of the differences between the sexes:

> An unattractive woman can draw almost any man to her by discreet flattery; but when a man flatters a woman the woman doesn't feel any the kindlier toward the man but takes his praise as quite true and winds up by cutting him—as not quite good enough for so fair a creature. Flattery mollifies a man, elevates a woman. Voilà!
>
> Yet a man can be flattered against his better sense. He may know he's rotten, and yet be persuaded that nothing is sweeter than he is. (L 61; SP 110)

Stevens voiced his uncertainty and reticence with women in the form of a cultural truism that nonetheless expressed his fear: that he would be *cut*. This later became a major motif in his poetry. It came out most explicitly in the "So may the relation of each man be cut" of "The Comedian," in the "two words that kill" of "Le Monocle," and in the barber-shearsman figure of "The Man with the Blue Guitar." But its implicit associations colored every instance of his own *cutting* of other poets he parodied in his irreverent lines.

ॐ

By the end of 1902 Stevens had become fairly comfortable moving between imagination and reality and had found internal and external models that suggested how he should act in each of these worlds. The holy hermit communed with angels in the woods, and the young lawyer, well established as protégé to his employer, learned about more than law on his weekend visits with Peckham and his family. He learned how to live and what to do to succeed in a world different from the provincial world of Reading. Though he never lost his taste for German sausages, frankfurters, and sauerkraut,[34] with the Peckhams he also tasted the delights of fine French wines and delicacies that came with living in late-Victorian imitation of the dying style of the European *belle époque*. Though at Harvard there had been occasional intrusions of St. Estèphe into beer-drinking evenings, now there was a settled and congenial environment, complete with country house and horses, where the young man got used to the appurtenances of the good life. Its attractiveness quickly obscured that of struggling alone in the attics of the "literary life."

His education in these gentlemanly ways explains some of the subtle changes in his attitude toward himself and the outside world as well as some of the preoccupations with having a "sufficient" income. These changes and concerns began to show themselves in his journal entries over the next year. This set of values belonged to the "good life," and it expressed, in the most concise terms, excellence of all kinds—spiritual and material. The first indications that Stevens was joining this order showed themselves in his last journal entry for 1902:

> What I have resolved to do next year so far as possible is this: to drink water + to abstain from wet-goods—not that I booze but that I love temperance + that the smallest liqueur is intemperant. . . . And in the second place, to smoke wisely. And in the third place, to write something every night—be it no more than a line to sing to or a page to read—there's gold there for the digging: *j'en suis sur* [I am sure of it]. And lastly, not to go to bed before twelve candles of day gutter in their sockets + the breeze of morning blows; for sleep only means red-cheeks and red-cheeks are not the fit adornments of Caesar. (*L* 62; *SP* 112)

Beyond his expressed "love of temperance"—itself an indication of cultivating the philosophically ideal "middle way," to which he was conveniently predisposed by his Presbyterian training—Stevens's incorporation of the possibility of achieving excellence himself was reflected in his certainty that "there [was] gold there for the digging" and in the playful comparison of himself to Caesar. Informed by later experiences, he eventually deflated this figure to an "Emperor of Ice-Cream." But now, before the tests of the real world, he indulged imagination freely, though half-humorously, and planned to discipline himself to reach his end. The edge of a comic tone heard here was a significant feature that was repeated later whenever Stevens dealt with his heroic aspirations. Because he was aware of his uncertainties and unsure of his place in the world he wanted to inhabit, taking on the role of comic actor protected him from tragically failing to meet his desires. The artificiality of this pose, however, was belied by the seriousness of his commitment to the discipline necessary to attain his goal.

But just after committing himself to this discipline, he seems to have failed to maintain it. Though he had resolved to write something every night, three months passed before he wrote in his journal again. The lapse coincided with "two months of rainy Sundays." During this time Stevens became, as he put it, "quite topsy-turvy" (*SP* 113). Embedded in this seemingly innocuous fact about the weather is an extraordinary perception about the sensibility of the poet that reveals a way of truth concerning more than Stevens.

In our scientifically analytic century the poet's sympathy with nature, expressed in personifications of sky, clouds, rocks, trees, has continued to be regarded as an exercise of the pathetic fallacy, which describes the tendency of poets and painters to credit nature with the feelings of human beings. Considering fallacies of any kind in reacting to poetry—when we remember Odysseus' encounter with the shades in Hades or Kubla Khan in Xanadu— might at first seem strange. But in both Homer's and Coleridge's worlds, truth still seemed to be ensured by the existence of another order of being that informed the apparent order of ours. By the end of the nineteenth century, however, John Ruskin condemned Samuel Taylor Coleridge's "pathetic fallacy" precisely because it suggested the existence of a transcendent order when science had already called this other order into question. In the absence of a religious mythology coherent with the facts of a deterministically understood universe, poetry was looked at in light of how truly its words advanced knowledge. By 1926 Bertrand Russell was calling for poems that expressed "justified true belief" about the place of human beings in the natural order. On the basis of this kind of demand Friedrich Schiller's earlier important distinction between naïve and sentimental poetry was applied. Homer's anthropomorphizing of natural forms and functions was accepted as a "justifiable" expression of a simple, prescientific view of the world. But the romantics' rehabitation with human spirits of what had come to be known as an indifferent universe, unguided by an anthropomorphic God, had to be regarded as sentimental and counter to "justified true belief" in "things as they are"—a phrase that appeared more and more in the writings of the late nineteenth and early twentieth centuries.[35]

Stevens was strongly attached to a prematerialist view of the world and, like the romantics, wanted to repeople a heaven of some kind. At the same time his response to the natural world revealed that his experience of it was not at all sentimental. In fact, when deprived of his excursions into the countryside, as for this short period at the beginning of 1903, he lost contact with his own spirit. It was precisely his sympathy with nature, as it was coming to be understood in his time, that allowed him to see and understand himself and what it meant to be a human being. What he expressed in his poetry over the years of his career reflected, in a brilliant transformational application of the pathetic fallacy itself,[36] scientifically true facts of this experience. As his consciousness of the world changed through the first half of the century, his perception of time and space in the poems changed. Because it consistently employed the pathetic fallacy, this record pointed to the inadequacy of purely analytic judgments concerning what could or could not be admitted as leading to "justified true belief." This ultimately went to prove Stevens's later assertion, carefully developed from what he had first learned from Wordsworth and Arnold, that poetry was better than philosophy in revealing truth about experience.[37] Specifically, poetry was better because it expressed—primarily in its manipulation of the pathetic fallacy and the movement of rhythms accompanying it—the oneness of the percipient with the world, indifferent, cold, yet beautiful as the poems themselves.

Stevens's perception of what he was to do came not out of a simple, intellectually derived apprehension but out of feeling himself, as at this moment, "quite topsy-turvy" when separated from nature. In light of his real pain and confusion in the face of leaving behind, with the new century, a way of life that was inextricably tied to nature, it is extremely ironic that he came to be thought of as a totally cerebral poet, unfeeling, unconcerned with morality.[38] In reality Stevens's primary preoccupation was with how to live, what to do, in a time when all aspects of experience began moving him—as they move us at greater and greater speed—toward greater and greater separation from our source, so that we feel, as he expressed poetically, that it was a myth we were ever born, that earthly mothers suckled us.

At twenty-two Stevens was already paying careful attention to what was being taught about how to live and what to do by those professionally committed to morality. Taking what he heard seriously heavily counterbalanced his desire for the materially good life that so attracted him. In his first journal entry for 1903 he commented on a sermon given by Dr. Morgan Dix, who preached:

> . . . an exceptionally beautiful sermon on the powers and principalities of heaven. It was old-fashioned—no boasting or bragging of new thought, but a lament that in this world the good are polluted and the pure, ruined. Angels have visited the earth and there are angels all about us now—and roaring lions. There was not one single blessed word of cant or conventionality—rather it was Dr. Primrose's good heart flowing in Oliver Goldsmith's words. I feel quite simplified and content. (SP 112–13)

The Reverend Dr. Dix's sympathies echoed the antimodernist cries of the Harvard circle, which railed against "the whole machinery which builds up cold, heartless, highly conceited, voluptuous lovers of themselves, despisers of the brethren, doubters of God." At the same time he attacked with old Puritan vehemence "overindulgence" and "selfish luxury."[39] As Jackson Lears points out, by the late nineteenth and early twentieth centuries "this was standard language for backcountry fundamentalists but not for the shepherds of fashionable urban flocks."[40]

About ten days later Stevens went to hear a professional moralist of another kind, a practitioner of the law, as he was soon to become himself:

> Heard Chief Justice Alton B. Parker in Earl Hall, Columbia University, on his court, the Court of Appeals, this afternoon. Remarks chiefly historical and anecdotal. Parker very handsome, very strong, very much of a man. Impressed me as a man of great morality & of lofty determination & kindness of heart. Is in his prime. He was wonderfully encouraging and cheering and agreeable. Something of the country-boy about him—it struck me. He has lived away from cynics & dreamers. He seemed to think that the chief function of the court of appeals is to expand the law. (SP 113)

In Parker Stevens found someone who incorporated "country-boy" virtues which he felt he had as well and of which Dix would approve. He also noted

Parker's physical appearance in the same way as his moral excellence. He seemed to see in him the exemplary man he wanted to become.

The juxtaposition of these two impressions suggests the kind of balancing Stevens had managed in order to satisfy the contradictory elements of his nature and his choice. These terms should be understood in a reciprocal rather than a causal relation. On the one hand, he felt "simplified and content" in following and contemplating Dix's purifying sentiments. On the other hand, he felt compelled to succeed. But he was able to evade this rather brutish want to become the best by imaginatively rationalizing it into the desire to become someone like Parker, one of the men on the front bench, who also had all the material benefits attached to that position.

What Stevens aspired to now was connected to the practical concerns and cultural attitudes of his family, which had been put into sharp relief by his exposure to the materially good life of his Harvard acquaintances and W. C. Peckham and his family. In the following excerpt from his journal he clearly expressed the tensions between his reality and his imaginings:[41]

> . . . on a salary in some law office and to work as hard as I can work until I get enough business of my own to hang out a shingle. The mere prospect of having to support myself on a very slender purse has brought to my mind rather vivid views of the actual facts of existence in the world. There are astonishingly few people who live in anything like comfort; and there are thousands who live on the verge of starvation. The old Biblical injunctions to make the earth fertile and to earn one's bread in the sweat of one's brow are one's first instructions. True, it [is] not necessary to start from the soil; but starting with nothing whatever—to make a fortune—is not wholly inspiring after a fellow has spent more or less time lolling about. It is decidedly wrong to start there with one's tastes fully developed + to have to forego all satisfaction of them for a vague number of years. This is quite different from beginning as other men do. It is more like being up already + working down to a certain point. Another phase of the thing is that when one has lived for twenty-five years with every reasonable wish granted + among the highest associations—starting at the bottom suddenly reveals millions of fellow-men struggling at the same point—of whom one previously had only an extremely vague conception. There was a time when I walked downtown in the morning almost oblivious of the thousands and thousands of people I passed; now I look at them with extraordinary interest as companions in the same fight that I am about to join. At first, I was overwhelmed. . . . (L 63; SP 114)

Hidden here, though not very well, was strong resentment, probably directed toward his father, for having been educated among a certain class but without the financial backing that allowed his fellows to indulge their tastes and whims freely. Unlike him, they did not have to pay attention to "that first, foremost law," which here sounded thunderously, proclaiming his ties to his Bible-reading Pennsylvania Dutch past. Its echoing notes later lent a particularly unexpected tone to the eleventh stanza of "Le Monocle de Mon Oncle," written in 1918, after nine years of marriage and many more of struggling to get ahead:

> If sex were all, then every trembling hand
> Could make us squeak, like dolls, the wished-for
>   words.
> But note the unconscionable treachery of fate,
> That makes us weep, laugh, grunt and groan, and
>   shout
> Doleful heroics, pinching gestures forth
> From madness or delight, without regard
> To that first, foremost law. Anguishing hour!
> Last night, we sat beside a pool of pink,
> Clippered with lilies scudding the bright chromes,
> Keen to the point of starlight, while a frog
> Boomed from his very belly odious chords.
>
> (*CP* 17)

For Stevens, sex, or any simple feeling, could never be all. The peculiar treachery resulting from the combination of his personal circumstances with his education at Harvard at a time when the best in Roosevelt's America sought the best in everything produced in Stevens "a *taste for style* in everything, a taste for the brilliant, the graceful, and that common-place, the beautiful." He continued this observation about himself with the following judgment. Considering his love of beautiful "whimsicalities," it curiously contradicted the image he wanted to cultivate of himself: "Moral qualities are masculine; whimsicalities are feminine. This seems hardly just but I think it is exact" (*SP* 114). Though Stevens rarely, if ever, deprived himself of his "whimsicalities" (later these included glazed fruit shipped from Florida or California in the middle of winter, vintage wines, exquisite lamps, rugs, paintings, books with precious bindings), there was an inner resistance to these indulgences. This attitude was very much in keeping with the aspect of the spirit of the age expressed by Morgan Dix, whose words struck Stevens's deepest Pennsylvania Dutch "country-boy" chords.

It was no wonder that as a young man Stevens could never keep his resolves or stop making them; that he alternated between enjoying the gracious aspects of not simply the "good" but the "best" life; that he even purified himself with fasting and sitz baths (*L* 73), as recommended by some of the more rabid, clean-living moralists of the day.[42] The last journal entry, just before he left for the British Columbia hunting trip a little more than a month after receiving his law degree, revealed these two strains. In the last paragraph

Stevens gave a wonderfully accurate sense of a fashionable evening at Mouquin's (a New York equivalent of Maxim's in Paris) through the eyes of a
young man jaded by his guilt at being part of the scene at all:

> July 26 [Sunday]
>
> Another day at Manhattan [Beach]. Water warm, air cold. Saw a "pretty
> pair of legs," as George Moore would say. But mostly my face was buried in
> the sand & my thoughts were busy making wise saws such as, A cynic is the
> name the torpid give a wise man, Abstractions bear only a spirit aloft, and
> so on. Felt rather domesticated and friendly to people. Came home for tea &
> after a Bock Panatela crawled up to bed, where I was soon rescuing a drown-
> ing beauty etc. Alas! I couldn't fall asleep. And so when the clock struck ten
> I jumped out of bed—and now, damme, I'll read till my eyelids drop of
> their own weight.
>
> I've just been reading my journal. A month or two ago I was looking
> forward to a cigarless, punchless weary life. En effet [In effect], since then I
> have smoked Villar y Villar & Cazadores, dined at Mouquin's on French
> artichokes and new corn, etc. with a flood of drinks from crème de cassis
> melée, through Burgundy, Chablis etc. to sloe gin with Mexican cigars &
> French cigaroots. I have lunched daily on—Heaven's [sic] knows what not (I
> recall a delicious calf's heart cooked whole & served with peas—pig that I
> am) & on Tuesday, I start for British Columbia to camp and hunt until
> September in the Canadian Rockies, Quem Deus vult [The first three words of
> "Quem deus vult perdere prius dementat"—"Whom a god would destroy he
> first drives mad."—]
>
> This Mexican cigar life has its drawbacks. The faces one sees through its
> smoke are not the faces of St. Paul or St. Francis or of Mary or Ruth. At this
> table sits a Saturday night fop, at that is an unaccountable fellow with a
> pampered looking belly, at another is a charming looking girl in tremendous
> spirits smiling & chattering, at another is a coarse animal & its mate. One
> talks. It is gossip. Then it is Durham Cathedral. Then it is Bar-le-duc jelly
> and Gervais cheese. Then it is gossip again. The orchestra comes in &
> plays—How deathly tired one is by midnight! (SP 115–16)

Stevens was surprisingly open here. His tone was almost carefree, beginning with his oblique—through Moore's words—observation of a "pretty pair
of legs," through his startling comment that he felt "domesticated and
friendly to people," to his naïvely telling account of his fantasy while lying in
bed and not admonishing himself for not having kept his resolves. He revealed
himself tenderly, his face buried in the sand (something he commented on
doing almost whenever he had been to the beach), surrounded by people in
colorfully striped bathing costumes. His ease was a response to a number of
things. He had just completed law school and was about to leave on a long
holiday. He was also among people, both on the beach and at Mouquin's. But
there was also a hint of decadence. The evocation of the saints and biblical

women, even in their absence from the real scene, was a clue to the sense of his having "fallen," which was subtly suggested. On his solitary walks in the woods, meeting only saints and angels in his imagination, he felt both insufficient before them and exalted by their presence. But among people the tension between these contradictory feelings disappeared. There was no need to measure himself, although he implicitly did anyway and sensed himself superior and bored—"How deathly tired one is by midnight!" Having fallen from the place of "higher conversation," he felt disdain.

۶◆

In sharp contrast with the sophisticated, droll tone of these city scenes was the direct, childlike excitement characteristic of the entries describing his trip to British Columbia. This and his meeting Elsie Moll the following summer were the most important experiences of this four-year period, and they became shaping forces for the rest of his life. It is easy to understand how and why this would have been so in relation to the woman with whom he spent his life. But it might not at first be clear how this six-week excursion could also have had such a profound effect. In the simplest terms it was because, as in his relationship with Elsie, though obviously in a different way, he knew himself to be a man. He had no doubt, either in standing erect before nature or in being the mate and support of Elsie, that he was fulfilling a male role, though in other subtler aspects of his experience, including the writing of poetry, he did question whether he was really manly.

On this respite from the artificially real world of the city Stevens participated fully in the undeniably real world of nature. High in the mountains, where one hunted for food, there were no useless, empty forms. These days provided him with some of his most constant and burdened images. All were connected with his idea of what it meant to be a man and served to define him as a poet. It was, perhaps, because of his prolonged contact with nature on this trip that Stevens was able to become a powerful poet. The impact of many of his most successful later repeated images derived from the reality of what he saw, heard, and felt then.

On his arrival two impressions struck him. He reacted first to the "rock character of mountains above the timber line" and to the way their mass appeared in the distance. Secondly, so many of the things he now actually saw were things that had had only imaginative value before. They were things he had read about or learned of in school: "I have seen cowboys; I have seen prairie dogs; hundreds of wild ducks, Indians in camp, with smoke coming through their discolored tent-tops; I have seen mountains swimming in the clouds and basking in snow; and cascades and gulches . . ." (*L* 64; *SP* 118). Over the weeks he transformed these storybook images into the basic vocabulary of his mature style. At the same time, in the company of the roughest of guides and of his employer, he showed himself as he was. While one of the guides cleaned a trout, he read Ovid's *Art of Love*. Being accepted in this way—as he was helped to do by Peckham, who invited his young clerk to try out all the possibilities offered by the gentlemanly life—was extremely significant. In his journal Stevens recorded his feelings about being accepted by the guides, Hosea Locke and Tommy, who taught him how to shoot and hunt. He also noted how happy he was about Peckham's acceptance of him and his difference from him and the others.

One of the first idiosyncratically strong images that went through many permutations over the weeks of his stay in the mountains and later, over the years of his poetry-writing career, was this one: "There are three fires burning now. One, the moon, *lights mountainous camels moving, without bells, to the wide North*" (*L* 65; *SP* 119 [italics mine]). The next entry followed the camels that "turned to purple clouds" (*L* 65; *SP* 119). Almost two weeks later the camels became associated with real horses and mules of the camp, which *did* have bells; in the "twilight" their "clink clink . . . [made him] drowsy" (*SP* 122). These images combined with the descriptions of the "Vermilion Pass faintly blue and white like a gate into the Sun" (*SP* 119) to give weight to one of the most suggestive images of "Le Monocle de Mon Oncle":

> The mules that angels ride come slowly down
> The blazing passes, from beyond the sun.
> Descensions of their tinkling bells arrive.[43]
>
> (*CP* 15)

On a more protracted scale, the evocation of camels moving was also tied to Stevens's later repeated imagery of palms and oases, which were associated with finding a place of ultimate religious peace: "the palm at the end of the mind" or the dream landscape of "Sunday Morning."

It is impossible to know by what process of association young Stevens's view of northern clouds and mountains suggested beasts of the desert, but the adventure of merely speculating is too tempting to resist. The surprising conjunction seems to be linked to Stevens's general tendency to move between opposite poles in his nature and more precisely to the accident of his reading Ovid's *Art of Love* with its strong evocations of the spirit of the South and its opening reminders of "chanting Hosannas" and the landscapes of Caesar. Even more particularly, the blending of the tall spruces of the North and the swaying palms of the South could easily have been prompted by one of Heinrich Heine's poems, which Stevens heard read aloud one night by Peckham:

> A spruce is standing lonely
> In the north on a barren height.
> It drowses; ice and snowflakes
> Wrap it in a blanket of white.
>
> It dreams about a palm tree
> In a distant, eastern land
> That languishes lonely and silent
> Upon the scorching sand.[44]

PHOTOGRAPH BY SYLVIA SALMI, COURTESY OF THE HUNTINGTON LIBRARY

It was the custom
For his rage against chaos
To abate on the way to church,
In regulations of his spirit.

"WINTER BELLS"

Interior of the North and Southampton Reformed Church at Churchville in Bucks County. The Stevens family was associated with this church for over two hundred years. Benjamin Stevens and his wife, Elizabeth, and her parents, Garrett Barcalow and his wife, Eleanor Hogeland, are buried in the cemetery here. Benjamin Stevens, grandfather of Wallace, had the gold-headed cane presented to his grandfather, also Benjamin, after he gave up his work of forty years in the Sunday school here.

THE HUNTINGTON LIBRARY

. . . It is the grandfather he liked,
With an understanding compounded by death

And the associations beyond death, even if only
Time.

"THE LACK OF REPOSE"

Benjamin Stevens, the poet's grandfather, owner of the farm in Feasterville, Pa., where Stevens and his siblings spent time as children. Note the farmer's gnarled hands.

THE HUNTINGTON LIBRARY

Politic man ordained
Imagination as the fateful sin.
Grandmother and her basketful of pears
Must be the crux for our compendia.

"ACADEMIC DISCOURSE AT HAVANA"

Elizabeth Stevens, wife of Benjamin, of whom Stevens was "very proud"

THE HUNTINGTON LIBRARY

"I very much prefer to look at him and think of him in his prime. The truth is that I rather think that, seeing him as a whole, I understand him better perhaps than he understood himself, and that I can really look into his heart in which he must have concealed so many things" (*Letters*, p. 458).

Garrett Barcalow Stevens, the poet's father

THE HUNTINGTON LIBRARY

". . . with everything she wore . . . so fresh and clean, and she herself so vigorous and alive" (*Letters*, p. 172).

Margaretha Catharine Zeller Stevens, the poet's mother

THE HUNTINGTON LIBRARY

"She said that she had had her 'boys' and asked, 'Do you remember how you used to troop through the house?'" Wallace Stevens recalling his mother on her deathbed (*Letters*, p. 174).

The Stevens boys: Wallace, Garrett Barcalow, Jr., John Bergen

THE HUNTINGTON LIBRARY

These are the heroic children whom time breeds
Against the first idea—to lash the lion,
Caparison elephants, teach bears to juggle.

"NOTES TOWARD A SUPREME FICTION"

The Stevens children: Elizabeth, Garrett Barcalow, Jr., Mary Katharine, Wallace, John Bergen

THE HUNTINGTON LIBRARY

"A Puritan who revels in catechisms and creeds, a hand-to-mouth man, earnest, determined, discreet—Uncle Isaac" (*Letters,* p. 9).

Isaac Bennet, husband of Stevens's father's sister, Maria, with whom young Wallace spent part of the summer of 1896 in Ivyland, Pa.

THE HUNTINGTON LIBRARY

"A self-sacrificing whole-souled, woman who says not much but too well—that is Aunt Mariah" (*Letters,* p. 9).

The same Maria, sister of Garrett, Sr., and married to Isaac Bennet. This portrait shows her as a younger woman than Stevens would have known her that summer of 1896.

THE HUNTINGTON LIBRARY

"Sometimes an uncle from Saint Paul visited us. He could talk French and had big dollars in his pockets, some of which went into mine" (*Letters,* p. 126).

James Van Sant Stevens, brother of Garrett, Sr., the bachelor uncle involved in some way with art, whom the poet probably had in mind as one of the models for the elusive persona of "Le Monocle de Mon Oncle"

THE HUNTINGTON LIBRARY.

THE HUNTINGTON LIBRARY

Two pages from letters the young Stevens wrote to his mother, the first from the summer of 1895 and the second from the summer of 1896. Note the difference in handwriting and especially in the signatures.

THE NEW-YORK HISTORICAL SOCIETY

"I came to New York yesterday. Stopped at the Astor House" (*Letters*, p. 37).

This panoramic view (c. 1895) shows St. Paul's, Vesey Street, Astor House, Broadway, and the Post Office as Stevens would have seen them in 1900 when he arrived in New York to make his way.

THE NEW-YORK HISTORICAL SOCIETY

A slash of angular blacks
Like a fractured edifice
That was buttressed by blue slants

"THE PUBLIC SQUARE"

The Sixth Avenue El, Sixth Avenue from Eighteenth Street looking north, in 1899 (when this stereograph was taken) and 1900 one of the main shopping districts of the city

NEW YORK HISTORICAL SOCIETY

Building and dream are one.

There is a total building and there is
A total dream. There are words of this,
Words, in a storm, that beat around the shapes.

"SKETCH OF THE ULTIMATE POLITICIAN"

Madison Square Garden and the Jerome Mansion (to the right) seen from
Madison Square as Stevens knew them. Note Augustus Saint-Gaudens's statue
of Diana atop the tower. It was this statue that in a storm was stripped bare of
her drapery—"I am the woman stripped more nakedly/ Than nakedness,
standing before an inflexible Order . . ." ("Notes Toward a Supreme Fiction").

THE NEW-YORK HISTORICAL SOCIETY

DANCE OF THE MACABRE MICE

In the land of turkeys in turkey weather
At the base of the statue, we go round and round.
What a beautiful history, beautiful surprise!
Monsieur is on horseback. The horse is covered with mice.

This dance has no name. It is a hungry dance.
We dance it out to the tip of Monsieur's sword,
Reading the lordly language of the inscription,
Which is like zithers and tambourines combined:

The Founder of the State. Whoever founded
A state that was free, in the dead of winter, from mice?
What a beautiful tableau tinted and towering,
The arm of bronze outstretched against all evil!

Broadway and Twenty-third Street at the Fifth Avenue intersection as it was in 1900. Note the fashionable Fifth Avenue Hotel and the newly constructed Dewey Arch and imagine the sound of the cable cars, "like zithers and tambourines combined."

THE NEW-YORK HISTORICAL SOCIETY

"I begin to like New York + do like it hard" (Letters, p. 45).

Fifth Avenue north from Fifty-first Street as seen from the roof of Saint Patrick's Cathedral. Central Park is in the center distance. Though this photograph was taken around 1883 or 1884, not much had changed by 1900, when the poet would have first seen this neighborhood.

THE NEW-YORK HISTORICAL SOCIETY

"New York is so big that a battle might go on at one end, and poets meditate sonnets at another" (*Letters,* p. 47).

Broadway at Seventy-third Street as it was on September 1, 1900, when this photo was taken. The scaffolding on the left covers the Ansonia Apartment House, then under construction.

THE NEW-YORK HISTORICAL SOCIETY

We live in a camp . . . Stanzas of final peace
Lie in the heart's residuum . . . Amen.

"EXTRACTS FROM ADDRESSES TO THE ACADEMY OF FINE IDEAS"

Fifth Avenue around Ninety-third Street as it was in the 1890s and early 1900s. The buildings are squatters' shacks.

STATE OF NEW YORK :
COUNTY OF NEW YORK : ss:-

W.G.PECKHAM being duly sworn says: I am a
counsellor-at-law of the Supreme Court of the State of
New York. Wallace Stevens has actually served a clerkship
in my office at Trinity Building,No. 111 Broadway, Borough
of Manhattan,New York City, and later at No. 54 William
Street of the same, under the rules of the Court of Appeals
for the admission of attorneys and counsellors-at-law,
after the age of eighteen years, and for a period of upwards
of twelve months, in addition to the time,which I am informed and believe, that said Stevens has spent in the
Law School. This period is made up as follows: Said
Stevens came to my office prior to June 23rd,1902, but
commenced his clerkship on June 23rd,1902 by filing his
certificate, as I am informed and believe. Ever since
then said Stevens has been a clerk in my office, and was
continuously, except a vacation of about two weeks in 1902
and about four weeks in 1903. Said Stevens is now in said
actual service, and has been so since about June 9,1902,
except the vacations as above, and said Stevens has not
taken more than two months' vacation in any one year of
said clerkship.

Sworn to before me this :
11th day of May,1904 :

W. G. Peckham

J. A. Slury
Notary Public, Westchester Co.
Cert. Filed in NY Co.

State for a period not exceeding three months, beginning on
June 23rd, 1902, and continuing to September 23rd, 1902;
that after his graduation from said school on June 10th,
1903, he resumed his clerkship and actually served said
clerkship thereafter to date, with the exception of the
period from July 29, 1903, to September 17, 1903, making
a total period of clerkship actually served of twelve months
and upwards; that during the service of his clerkship
no vacation was actually taken by him exceeding two (2)
months in any one year, as will more fully appear from the
certified copy of the certificate of W.G. Peckham, in whose
office said clerkship was commenced, as filed in the office
of the Clerk of the Court of Appeals, hereto annexed and
marked "C", and from the affidavit of W.G. Peckham, with
whom said clerkship was served, showing the actual service
of such clerkship, the continuance and end thereof, and
that not more than two months vacation was actually taken
in any one year, hereto annexed and marked "D".

Sixth: That he has had the following periods of
vacation, to wit, the periods beginning on June 12th, 1902
and ending on June 23rd, 1902; beginning on September 23,
1902 and ending on October 1st, 1902; beginning on June
5th, 1903 and ending on June 10th, 1903; beginning on
July 29th, 1903 and ending on September 17th, 1903; as
more fully appears in Paragraph Fourth and Fifth herein
and the papers hereto annexed marked "B, C, and D".

Sworn to before me this
11 day of May, 1904

Wallace Stevens

Otto J. Kest
Notary Public Kings Co.
Cert of Cert. Filed in NY Co.

-3-

THE HUNTINGTON LIBRARY

The affidavit of W. G. Peckham and the last page of Wallace Stevens's affidavit, both dated May 11, 1904, marking his admission to the New York
Bar. Note well the similarity of the signatures of the two men.

THE HUNTINGTON LIBRARY

"The farm was fat and the land in which it lay
Seemed in the morning like a holiday."

"From the Packet of Anacharsis"

The countryside around Reading where Stevens roamed himself and with Elsie Moll, his future wife. The photograph, commissioned by Stevens from Sylvia Salmi, shows the area as it was in 1943, but, as he commented in a letter to a friend, it looked the same then as it had when he was a young man—and as it still does today.

THE HUNTINGTON LIBRARY

THE HUNTINGTON LIBRARY

"I've been shovelling snow and it made my arms so tired that now my hand shakes as I write. It has been snowing all day—confound it! This morning I thought I should have to stay indoors all day and so, after breakfast, I put on my loafing outfit and began to read a volume of new poems that I bought yesterday. But shortly after ten o'clock there was a lull and I started out. Good Lord, how I needed it! My blood leaped. I wanted to wash my face in the snow—to hold it there. I *did* let the wind blow through my hair. Then I ran a long way and towards noon, when it had started to snow again, I was on the Bronx River, or, rather, along it. It was enchanting there" (*Letters,* p. 95).

". . . sometimes I get glimpses of Washington Bridge and its neighborhood, and I think it is all very impressive and Roman and wonderful, in its way" (*Letters,* p. 94).

The house on Sedgwick Avenue in Fordham Heights where Stevens was taking meals when he lived next door (see arrow on upper left of card) in 1907. A few days earlier he wrote the letter quoted from above telling of his shoveling the snow that is still on the ground in this photo.

THE HUNTINGTON LIBRARY

The first page of "A Winter Night" letter referred to in Chapter VI. Note the passage about "gold medal boys."

There was an additional association to another line of Heine's that could have played its part. This one came from one of the German poet's prose pieces that Stevens remembered either from his years in college or from his own reading: "A tree will shade my grave. I would have liked a palm tree, but it will not grow in the North."[45]

Stevens's experience in the vivid landscape, this brilliant meeting with reality, continued to combine with visions engendered by what he read or heard read to him. He reveled in the sounds the thunder made during an approaching storm. He hunted deer and lion at dizzying heights in spite of his vertigo. Being "a man subject to being dizzy" (*L* 70; *SP* 131), he "aimed [at a mountain goat] but was afraid to shoot off [his] gun, since [he] had all [he] could do to keep [his] balance" (*SP* 124). He shivered with wet and cold during a snowstorm (*SP* 123). These things filled his days, and at night, in addition to Ovid, he read Jacques Bossuet's *Lettres Spirituelles* (the title Stevens apparently had, probably containing Bossuet's *Lettres Pastorales*). Another strange-seeming choice in this setting, it provided an even denser web of associative complexity for his poetic preoccupations. Years later, the "doctor of Geneva," meeting the Pacific for the first time, as Stevens was meeting it and the high mountains rising from it, recalled Bossuet and presented himself in the French master's prosaically adapted alexandrine rhythms.

Imagination and reality were keenly sharpened for Stevens during these weeks. Perceptions from each overlapped and reflected his heightened double vision. His descriptions fused: "The peaks to the South shelve off into the heavens. Snow and cloud become confused. And the blue distances merge mountain and sky into one" (*SP* 121). This kind of conflation was also suggested by Heine's characterization of nature: "Like a good poet, nature does not like abrupt transitions. The clouds, as bizarre as they sometimes appeared to be shaped, have a white or at least a soft tint that corresponds harmoniously with the blue sky and the green earth, so that all the colors of the region melt into one another like gentle music, and every view of nature has the effect of quieting pain and calming the spirit."[46]

Some of the other things Stevens read were closer to the adventure he was experiencing: R. L. Stevenson's *Kidnapped* and *King Solomon's Mines;* tales by Heinrich Zschokke. Within the young poet's escape from the mechanical quotidian of city life were these further escapes into the fantastic and exotic. The hidden realities suggested by these fictions made Stevens even more aware of what hid beneath the surface of the reality he inhabited moment by moment. The careful depictions from the strange worlds of Stevenson and Zschokke were balanced by the equally meticulous descriptions of the poet's inner world revealed to him night after night as Peckham read more from Heine. Each installment brought out ancient aspects that touched Stevens's new mind. In addition to various specific images and perceptions that struck their notes deep in Stevens's being, there was Heine's mordant irony, directed at reason and rationalists, religion and social codes. His irony was worn lightly, voiced in almost nursery-rhyme cadences. Using simple meters to communicate profound, and often disturbing, observations linked Heine to Goethe, whose doggerel throughout *Faust* belies the high seriousness of the true subject while ensuring the accessibility of the text. (*Faust* was so accessible, in fact, that ·during the nineteenth century a good number of educated German youths prided themselves on having committed to memory both Parts One and Two in their entirety.)

Stevens learned from Goethe and Heine to use forms that were as easily assimilable as theirs, not to call direct attention to himself and his "true subject" by using innovative forms. The reason lying behind this choice is well expressed in the following short poem of Heine's. Stevens seems to have taken its "message" deeply to heart. He certainly found in its lines images he used and expanded.

THE MESSAGE
German singers! sing and praise
German freedom—till your song
Takes possession of our souls,
And inspires us to goals,
As the noble Marseillaise.

No more Werthers need be heard—
We have cooed and wooed too long—
Be your people's guide and rock—
Tell them that the hour has struck;
Speak the sword, the dagger word!

Do not be the tender flute,
The idyllic soul. Be strong.
Be the trumpet of the land!
Be the cannon—take your stand—
Shatter, thunder, blare, uproot!

Shatter, thunder, night and day—
Till you've righted every wrong!
Sing to waken, to incite!
—But be careful that you write
In the vaguest sort of way. . . .[47]

Stevens never forgot the central images here: the poet as his "people's guide and rock" with his "dagger word," his "sword." His own use of "rock" as a controlling metaphor carried the same connotations Heine, like Matthew Arnold, also suggested: Poetry would replace religion as the people's "rock," their spiritual "guide." Stevens enriched the symbol over the years with the full range of his experience until it resonated with associations ranging from the broad American cultural scene, with its foundation at Plymouth Rock, to his personal memories of rocky landscapes he loved: the countryside around

Reading; the Canadian Rockies, where he became a man; eventually, the rock of Earth itself. In the same way he developed the image of words as swords into one of his most powerful symbols. Its most specific expression came in "Le Monocle": "There is not nothing, no, no, never nothing,/Like the clashed edges of two words that kill" (*CP* 13). But the general suggestion of words as lethal instruments played in each instance when, with his own words, images, and rhythms, Stevens cut away at those of the "studious ghosts" (*CP* 14) that had shaped him.

Especially important to bear in mind in noting these uses and applications is how carefully Stevens heeded his German master's lesson about writing "in the vaguest sort of way." These parallels to Heine, or those to other writers and thinkers Stevens incorporated, are of the vaguest sort, just as his general use of the pentameter line evokes the vaguest kind of emotional response. Goethe and Heine phrased their lines in simple and familiar rhythms because they wanted their poems to be recited and internalized without thought, without difficulty. Unstopped by conscious attention to complex forms, audiences would take in their words like water. These poets were, in effect, doing precisely what Plato implicitly warned against when he banished poets from the ideal republic. It is the same thing all good advertisers do today: enchanting through rhythm and rhyme, lulling reason to sleep to set traps of suggested meanings in the midst of dreams.

Stevens learned this lesson well because he knew that his intended "true subject" was as revolutionary in his time and place as Heine's or William Blake's, for that matter, in theirs, though his "poetry of the subject" communicated his message "in the vaguest sort of way." The nature of this "true subject" will show itself gradually as we go through the pages of Stevens's life.

Now the young traveler still moved among the snowy mountains. By the time he crossed the continent again and arrived home in New York, he was happy to be charged once more by this "electric town." Another benefit of the trip was that it had made him realize its enticements anew: "Lying in one's tent, looking out at the sky, one's thoughts revert to New York: to the trains stopping at the L [*sic*] stations, to the sinuous females, to the male rubbish, to the clerks and stenographers and conductors and Jews, to my friend the footman in front of Wanamakers, to Miss Dunning's steak, to Siegel and his cigars" (*SP* 120). By the last week of the trip, in fact, he had found himself often bored by camp life: "Camp-life is infinitely dull—we are all busy with some small thing or other merely to occupy our time—all of us have taken a turn at chopping wood. Hosey has been singing 'We're only waiting here below'; Tommy is half-dead with tooth-ache (teeth-ache, says Hosey) & I am just a wee, wee, bored" (*SP* 126).

After he had been back in New York just more than a month, the residues of this realization combined with fragmentary memories of hearing some of Heine's lines on "Marie Antoinette," which describe how the moonlight caught glimpses of the queen's headless ghost being served by the flitting headless ghosts of her handmaidens. These evocations colored his experience:

October 20

It is a pleasant enough life that I lead. After the day's work I climb up these stairs into the distant company of strange yet friendly windows burning over the roofs. I read a few hours, catch glimpses of my neighbors in their nightgowns, watch their lights disappear and then am swallowed up in the huge velvet October night. (L 67–68; SP 127)

Years later two poems echoed this same perception. He opened one, from about 1915, "Disillusionment of Ten O'Clock," with "The houses are haunted/By white night-gowns" (CP 66). In the other, "The Ordinary Women," from about 1922, the house became a palace, like the one Marie Antoinette and her maids inhabit in Heine's poem:

> Then from their poverty they rose,
> From dry catarrhs, and to guitars
> They flitted
> Through the palace walls.
>
> (CP 10)

The October 20 entry quoted above continued to present, in a raw state, a number of the major themes that Stevens developed in his mature work. At the same time it pointed to some of the sources of his thought and feeling. The later incorporation of Heine's image in his poem, for example, recalled his hunting trip in the mountains covered with snow, as much as it did Heine's own account of his journey in the Harz Mountains, which he described as being "in their white nightgowns."[48] In the following passage from the October 20 entry, the words and phrases that prefigure later themes or point back to other sources are italicized and annotated:

On Sunday I stretched my cramped legs—doing my twenty-five miles with immense good cheer. Fetched home a peck of apples in my green bag. The wind pounded through the trees all the day long. At twilight I picked my way to the edge of the Palisades + stretched out on my belly on one of the dizzy bosses. Overhead in the *clair de crépuscule* [twilight] *lay a bright star* ["In the high west there burns a furious star" (CP 14)]. I've grown such a hearty Puritan + revel in such coarse good health that I felt scarcely the slightest twinge of sentiment. But tonight I've been polite to a friend—have guzzled *vin ordinaire* + puffed a Villar y Villar and opened my dusty tobacco-jar—and my nerves, as a consequence, are a bit uneasy, so that the thought of that soft star comes on me most benignly. Tomorrow, however, I shall reassume the scrutiny of *things as they are* ["'Things as they are/Are changed upon the blue guitar'" (CP 165)]. [Henry] Fielding, in *Amelia*, rightly observes that our wants are largely those of education and habit, not of nature. My *poverty* ["Then from their poverty they rose . . ." (CP 10)] keeps me down to the natural ones; and it is astonishing how the tongue loses a taste for tobacco; how the paunch accommodates itself to the lack of fire-water. Indeed, sound shoes, a pair of breeches, a clean shirt and coat, with an occasional stout meal, sees one along quite well enough. Only at the same time, one must have ambition and energy or one grows melancholy. Ambition and energy keep a man young. Oh treasure! Philosophy, non-resistance, "sweetness and light" [Matthew Arnold] leave a man pitiably crippled and aged, though pure withal. (*L* 67–68; *SP* 127–28)

This kind of exercise can be done fruitfully with a great number of Stevens's journal entries and letters. Knowing that he went back and reread his journals and his letters to Elsie again and again makes the later reappearance of themes in his poems less surprising. It also points out that Stevens treated not only his poems but his actual experience musically. It was as though he saw the passing years as measures in which he could sound again the notes of earlier time. He later translated this symphonic sense of reality into the project for "The Whole of Harmonium: The Grand Poem." Much more than a structural device, intellectually expanding on a Mallarméan/symbolist model of *le grand Oeuvre* (the Great Work), this project was *properly* a "projection" of Stevens's emotional and physical apprehension of himself and the world, something "organic" in *its* most literal sense as well.

Stevens's innate sense of musically repeating and varying the aspects of his experience reflected itself both on the large scale of years that separated the different stages of his life and on the smaller scale of his movement through each of his weeks, months, and years. Looked at from the outside and from a distance, the abstract shape of this movement is like the elliptical path of a planet as it turns around its sun. Though it is impossible to know whether Stevens had this awareness at this point in his life, he certainly had it in his maturity. He imagined his "meridian" in "Le Monocle" and was quite explicit in describing himself as a "planet" in one of his last poems (*CP* 532). The cyclical repetitions of experience established order for him in the same way as his weekly Sunday walks. If he was not aware at twenty-two of the larger pattern, his instinct seemed to direct him to do things he had done before and then to compare his newest reactions to those he had had earlier.

Such was the case in his again taking up the rhythm of city life after he had returned with fresh eyes from the purifying excursion in British Columbia. As he had during his first year in New York, he now began once more going to concerts and plays, dining out, occasionally seeing old acquaintances. And with this return to indulging in pleasures not attached to the solitary pleasures of nature came a return as well of periodic depressions.

February 7 [Sunday]

These last two months have been utterly useless to me. Pleasant enough by day but horrible to see in retrospect. What a duffer I am! I live as much without energy as if I were an old man with a bank account. I don't even dare to make new resolutions—they are so damned disappointing. I have my golden haze——+ that's all. That's all that's worth while, too; but, odds boddikins, I have my way to make——+ disdain a good many ways of making it, at that. My pleasures seem illegitimate because they are pleasures. Here am I, a descendant of the Dutch, at the age of twenty-five [he was really still twenty-four], without a cent to my name, in a huge town, knowing half a dozen men + no women. God bless us, what a lark! (*L* 68–69; *SP* 128)

February 14. Sunday
    Whatever I was going to write when I turned to this page has escaped me. I'm in the Black Hole again, without knowing any of my neighbors. The very animal in me cries out for lair. I want to see somebody, hear somebody speak to me, look at somebody, speak to somebody in turn. I want companions. I want more than my work, than the nods of acquaintances, than this little room. I do *not* want dreams—my castles, my haunts, my *nuits blanches* [white nights], my companies of good friends. Yet I dare not say what I do want. It is such a simple thing. I'm like that fool poet in *Candida*. Horrors! (*L* 69; *SP* 128)

More obviously repetitive was his going to see a new production of *Hamlet*. His description of his response counterpointed the way he had reacted to Bernhardt's portrayal just over three years before:

March 7, 1904
    Another Hamlet—Forbes Robertson's. By no means, an old story. The tendency seems to be to thicken the clouds about this character—but they were all blown away. There was very little shadow, no melancholy; rather delay than resolution. I don't know that it pleased me. Robertson raises no stage illusion; he is incorrigibly sane, cold, indeed almost familiar and commonplace. But I believe he was a man. . . . The whole thoroughly English and unemotional. (*SP* 129)

The oblique comment "But I believe he was a man" was as ambiguously revealing of Stevens's uncertain sense of manhood as the variations of his behavior and moods again became over the next few months. As he approached the end of his clerkship and his admission to the bar, he was moving closer to becoming "man number one." And as he approached, he felt the encroachment of his old doubts and fears about the path he was on.
    The doubts and fears expressed themselves in returned eruptions of his misanthropic spirit and in quicker alternations between different kinds of behavior. He went to more plays and concerts and spent more evenings out drinking with friends. Although the almost nightly entries of the second week in March showed him to be seemingly enjoying himself, by the end of the same week his enjoyment and appreciation were judged to be vain and wasteful:

Walking is my only refuge from tobacco + food; so today I put on an old suit of clothes + covered about twenty miles or more—to Palisades and back. Felt horrible when I started: heavy, plethoric, not an idea in my head + accusing myself for having let the past week go by so vainly. I must instantly become a harder taskmaster to myself. This is all simple enough when one is free on a good road but somehow it becomes next to impossible in town. . . . It enrages me to see my sleek figure + fat face and to think how I have lost ambition + energy. I haven't a spark of any kind left in me—no will,—nothing. And the worst of it is that if I make any new resolutions, I do it with my tongue in my cheek. Well, while I was thinking pleasant things like this, I saw two bluebirds, gathered some willow catkins, munched birch buds and otherwise noted the advent of Spring. A most beautiful day in the woods, but there was no spirit in me to feel any elation. The sky was silver, the trees were touched with blue shadows, the melting snow gleamed on the emerging rocks. Yet feeling that I had done no good, of late, I felt quite as though I carried the burden of some undefined sin— and that feeling deadened me to all others. I bought a cake at Fort Lee + ate it contritely, thought twenty devils were at each of my ears suggesting methods of spending the evening more politely; I enjoyed the cake at all events. (*L* 69–70; *SP* 129–30)

But the next week he indulged his pleasures again, his "will" obviously not strong enough to keep him from adding to the "burden of [his] undefined sin."

By the end of the month the tension between his behavior and attitude was breaking in waves of vituperation. These were disclosingly directed toward a "neighboring Jew" and "fat Greek" at a concert of Tchaikovsky (Sixth Symphony) and Anton Rubinstein (Melody in F), given in the "reeking basement of Cooper Union" (*SP* 130–31). It was as though the pitching movements up and down between his moods had so increased in tempo that there could be no rest, no pause between indulgence and punishment. Rather than go to the concert and focus on the music alone, which he had found "profound + ravishing," and then two or three days later express his negativity, as he had done in the past, he revealed the storminess of his spirit all at once in his condescendingly sneering at others who were enjoying themselves. He particularly singled out those southern Oriental types who were given more to "feasting" than "fasting." Once again, as in his attitude toward women, Stevens was expressing his defensiveness in a cultural cliché of the period.

As cities overflowed with European immigrants, those concerned with preserving a "pure" American strain—individuals spanning the range from Whitman to Roosevelt—warned against the effects of foreign influence on national character.[49] Whether the influence came from "dandified, aristocratic fops" or from the lower-class "unleashed rabble," who too often threatened the established order with radicalism and anarchy, the danger prophesied was either the "race suicide" of an overcivilized bourgeoisie or revolutionary over-throw.[50] While pogroms had begun in Russia, and less extreme examples of social violence erupted in various parts of Europe, McKinley's ghost flitted through the pages of popular magazines and newspapers, whispering to readers that they beware of foreign devils. However, there were also a few voices calling out a very different prophecy, voices that to someone like Stevens, already committed to the American way of life, were perhaps even more effective in preserving "race" and the status quo. Many critics of the overcivilized, repressive, and increasingly pressured way of city life advised Americans to learn from these other types, "Oriental people, the inhabitants of the tropics, and the colored people generally," how to "cultivate relaxation and repose."[51] But someone as highly attuned to succeed as Stevens was would find in these models particular targets for his inability to accept what came to them naturally. Rather than follow their example to find spiritual and physical ease, Stevens took on the more vigorous habits of exercise and clean living advocated by those who used their president as model.

Stevens was speeding up in his race to make a high-ranking place for himself. It was as though he had become caught up in the country's obsession with record making. Just after the Wright brothers completed their first flight in 1903 and America was crossed coast to coast by car in only sixty-five days, Stevens increased the mileage and pace of his Sunday walks. By late spring of 1904 he commended himself on having covered forty-two miles on one excursion from 4:00 A.M. until 6:00 P.M., "without stopping longer than a minute or two at a time" (L 71; SP 132). This renewed commitment to healthy, good living sharpened after his last contact with his soft-living enemies at the concert. It was put into even greater relief by his noticing how sickly people had looked during the first weeks of that spring, after months of their terrible overindulgence:

> April 4, 1904
>
> Extraordinarily brilliant day. A day for violet and vermilion, for yellow and white—and everything of silk. *Au contraire* people looked like the very devil. Men who'd been taking a drop of the Astor House Monongahela now and then through the winter, or else had been calling in at Proctor's for an olive or a fishball before starting up town, looked like blotchy, bloodless, yes, and bloated—toads; and many a good honest woman had a snout like a swine. And this on a day when the rainbows danced in the basin in Union Square! Spring is something of a Circe, after all. It takes a lot of good blood to show on a day like this. . . . Personally, I felt quite up to the mark. . . .
> (L 70; SP 131)

The young man's need to exclude himself from this group—his self-admonition now wholly projected onto them—was so strong that at one point, in a letter to Witter Bynner, just before he was to take his bar examinations, he presented an image of himself that absolutely contradicted what he had elsewhere described as his experience. In that letter, which seems to have been a response to an invitation of Bynner's for a night out, Stevens wrote:

DEAR HAL [Bynner's college nickname]:

Last week my insides were in great disorder—I was, indeed, sick with a sickness. But by dint of going to bed at eight + of much Sitzbathing, + dieting + lithia-ing [presumably, drinking lithia water, lithium carbonate or chloride] + porous plastering, I am knocking about again. My bar exams are on June 7 + until then I intend to apply myself most conscientiously to grinding. Therefore our congeniality must ex necessitate [of necessity] be a thing apart from "drink" (as you call it—hideously). In fact, I detest rum, + never intended that, if we were to see much of one another, there should be so much liquor spilled. It is a tiresome thing. My idea of life is a fine evening, and orchestra + a crowd at a distance, a medium dinner, a glass of something cool + at the same time wholesome, + a soft, full Panatela. If that is congenial to you, we can surely arrange it after June 7—unless I flunk. In the meantime we must be without much ceremony, although eager enough. (L 73; SP 135–36)

What is strange here is not that Stevens followed the self-helpers' clean-living regimen—understandable in light of his preparing to take his exams and having overindulged the last time they were together—but the false image he presented of himself, of what he did and didn't like, and of what constituted his "idea of life." Like the other "abstractions" he had made for himself to follow, this image was a borrowed *idea*l. And the model now was W. C. Peckham. It was his "idea of life," suitable for a proper and prosperous gentleman, peacefully enjoying the middle way like "a medium dinner" that Stevens adopted. Unfortunately, this "idea" had nothing to do with how Stevens actually enjoyed himself with Bynner and other friends.

Though their evenings together during this period might have begun with their sipping St. Estèphe as Stevens read entries from his journal about his walks along the Hudson that Bynner especially liked to hear, by the time they parted Stevens had not failed to show himself again as the "wild youth" Bynner remembered from Cambridge, Stevens's now heavily bearded face animated with more that poetic high spirits.[52] Perhaps in his letter, "on paper," Stevens wanted to correct the impression he made on the younger man, his protégé on the *Advocate,* whom he found "An inexplicable fellow—[with] the manners of a girl, the divination, flattery + sympathy of a woman, the morbidness + reverie of a poet, the fire + ingenuousness of a young man . . ." (L 71; SP 132). If others provided models for him, he, too, could provide a model for others, especially for one who, like him, wanted to be a poet and suffered the same kind of impressionability Stevens knew in himself. His last comments in the journal entry quoted above suggest this sense, which could have come only from his own experience: "He has gathered his own impressions + odd ones they are. Has he passed safely through the sentimental, sketchy stage?" Over the years some of Bynner's odd impressions developed into his serious involvement with Oriental poetry and ways of thought—as noted earlier, something that was to be significant for Stevens.

If Stevens at this point was concerned with providing an example for Bynner, he seemed to have no such preoccupation in relation to two other contacts of the time, Charles Dana and someone referred to only as Zubetkin, with both of whom he also shared his high spirits. Indeed, his behavior with them, as described in his journal, ran so counter to the image of himself that he painted for Bynner that it is hard to believe that within so short a period— knowing what he had done and what he recorded—he could have presented that other idealized portrait at all. Perhaps Zubetkin was one of those corrupting Europeans, and it was his influence that swayed Stevens to get "so drunk" one night with him that they did "a very improper thing." This was touchingly adolescent, but the Victorian attitude Stevens assumed toward it, before noting that it was only having their photographs taken, suggests that even though he realized its charming triviality, he felt a deeper sense of impropriety that went together with this repeated instance of prodigality. Again, however, his momentary regrets did not prevent him from continuing his bawdy adventures.

The journal account of two days spent with Charles Dana revealed him once more being the wild youth:

May 23. Monday

Charles Dana & I took the Patten Line "up the picturesque Shrewsbury" last Saturday afternoon & stayed in the neighborhood until last evening. From Pleasure Bay we took the trolley to Asbury. Strange country—filled with the crudest display of architecture in the world, I should think, and, at this season of the year, quite deserted. We found a saloon in a cellar within a very short time & then wandered to the beach where we joshed two servants for an hour or more. The night was too lovely to waste in bed, so after filling the ladies with soda, we returned to the boardwalk. At the end of it we crawled under a pier & thus reached Bradley Beach. There the sea beat at our feet & the Milky Way etc. etc. etc. The sand sparkled electrically near the surf under our shoes as we gathered wood. We soon had a fire & circle of light & for a while we ate corned beef from a can & drank whiskey from a bottle. When the fire fell in, we lay on our backs & watched the stars, Charles sporting chestnuts. Ere long the sun rose like the side of a house & we dozed off—. . . . (SP 135)

The difference between what and how he described what they did and saw and what he did and saw when he went on his solitary excursions predisposes us to be perversely grateful that he did not share more of his experiences with friends. Once more, as in childhood and youth, with company Stevens found himself able to "josh" strangers, to be bold and carefree, as he could never be when alone. Since it was out of his solitary, ambling musings—whether on long afternoons in the country or, later, on shorter walks to and from the office—that his poems sprang, it is difficult to lament with him that his life was an affair of places, not of people, and that that was the trouble. But in spite of his words and his sense of himself, an affair with one who was to become the most significant person in his life was about to begin. This affair became his life and so seemed to prove his statement untrue.

V
IT WILL EXCEED
ALL FAERY
1904–1907

AND AH FOR A MAN TO ARISE IN ME,
THAT THE MAN I AM MAY CEASE TO BE!

—ALFRED, Lord TENNYSON, *Maud*

Whenever the desire becomes so strong as to make one unreasonable, I find it a great help to inquire about the price of
eggs and pine-apples and coal.

—From a letter to ELSIE MOLL,
April 9, 1907 (WAS 1789)

How did the young lawyer feel that deep green June night, back home in
Reading, on being introduced to the most beautiful girl in town as a "very
fine poet" from New York (*SP* 138)? No doubt her blue eyes pierced him as
the light playing on her golden hair created a mystic aureole around her head.
She was as lovely as, perhaps more lovely than Sybil Gage. Her natural reticence touched his own. And she was simple, unthreateningly untutored in the
ways of the world or of books. To her he could present the figure of the poet as
virile youth without fear that she would find him wanting. Beneath his polished surface, he could feel secure in the knowledge that just having been
admitted to the bar, he had established himself on the road that would ensure
a comfortable future. Possibilities of all kinds opened themselves. He knew he
could follow his father's example: settle in Reading and practice law. He could
return to New York and make his way there. He could begin to imagine a life
with wife and family to satisfy the needs of the "domestic creature" he felt
himself to be. She smiled. They spoke. Within a few weeks he was deeply in
love, dreaming during the hours when they were not together of "that warm
mouth . . . that ravishing hand . . . and that golden head trying to hide in
[his] waistcoat somewhere; and those blue eyes looking at [him] sweetly
though without intent" (*L* 78; *SP* 138). Over the next four years that golden
head and those blue eyes became the center of his experience.

What was it about Elsie Viola Kachel that allowed Stevens to overcome
his shyness and open himself to the possibilities that began to offer themselves? Of course, it wasn't only Elsie. At this moment he was at the center of
his own stage. His sense of accomplishment as a lawyer had not yet been
tested by the real challenges of the professional world. More, he was back
home in the summer landscape where he felt happiest, where imagination and
reality came together most completely. Here and now he met this angel, still
untasted in her heavenly orchard air. She quickly became for him a damsel
heightened by eternal bloom. Though she carried herself stiffly, "very stiff,
straight and stiff . . . like a gendarme almost" (*SP* 138), she yielded easily in
his arms. Though she had not even finished the first year of high school, she
was curious about books and poetry and responded eagerly to her new lover's
instruction. Though demure, she was also enticing. She offered him, in the

contradictions apparent between her surface and her deeper self, a perfect mirror in which to see his own. And even more, to this young woman who knew of the world beyond Reading only in her imaginings, Stevens could present himself as the sophisticated yet gentle man of the world he so much wanted to be, and she would have no real standard against which to measure him.

Probably all occasions of falling in love involve mutual idealizations, but for each instance the contours of the other conjured in the minds of the lovers differ. There are expectations made as much from prior experience as from what each has wished for. Because there are so many determinants, it is impossible ever to know completely what one individual sees in another. Most often the individuals themselves are not aware of what moves them. They feel lost in love, pierced by an invisible arrow from Cupid's quiver, magically smitten by a pair of blue eyes.

But a poet who allows the imagination free rein to express itself in associations of words and images uncovers sources of dreams and desires and makes those attentive to his words sensitive to these promptings in him, themselves, and others. In Stevens's case the record of associations left both in his poems and in the letters he wrote to Elsie, in spite of the heavy editing, provide more than enough details to complete a portrait of the woman he imagined or wanted her to be. In Elsie's case, on the other hand, since her letters are not available, a certain amount of intuitive reconstruction is necessary to complete her imagined portrait of the man she would marry.

The exquisite young girl Stevens met that June night of summer-seeming had just turned eighteen. What were her dreams as she approached womanhood in the place she had never left at a time when becoming a woman did not mean becoming an autonomous being? Had she read of the woman in New York who, just that year, had been arrested for smoking a cigarette in public?[1] If so, did she gleefully but silently identify with her, or did she condemn her as improper indeed? We cannot know. But we do know this. Within a few weeks of their meeting Elsie went out with her beau unchaperoned and unsafely unaccompanied by a group of other acquaintances, as would have been proper for an unbetrothed girl of her time. And she had yielded, even then, at least her "sweet, warm mouth." It doesn't seem that her modesty was offended by his repeated approaches during those long midsummer days and nights. What did she see and wish for that allowed her to give herself to him?

At first his size must have both startled and impressed her, the top of her head barely reaching the edge of his collar. The man she would marry would have to protect her. Her father never had. Perhaps he would have, had he lived to see her tenderness grow together with her being. But he had died before she even knew his name shaped on her lips. If there was a memory of his face, his voice, it stirred in time before words could come to take his place. He died almost as she was born, before a number could mark the passage through her first senses of the seasons' change. But, then, perhaps he hadn't wanted her at all and had died because he couldn't face the change her life would bring to his. Not even a trace of his memory could protect her then. And this was more than likely, or so it seemed. He had waited until only a few months before she was born to marry her mother. But at least she must have come from deepest feelings, not out of some fair arrangement or mere acceptance. And he must have looked at her mother the way this young poet looked at her, beckoning but knowing, wanting and cajoling. He obviously desired her yet was gentle. The feelings she most yearned to know could, it seemed, come to be. She had never felt her worth, except as someone to help her mother support the household she had set up with the man who took her father's place when she was eight. This man, Lehman Wilkes Moll, had never even adopted her to give her his name legally; she added it herself, probably after too many questions in school about why her name was different from her family's had made her more than a little uneasy. Suddenly now being seen as a radiant princess, and praised in words she might never have otherwise heard, made her more than compliant.

Meeting someone from New York, too, made a difference. She was not so much attracted by the magical evocations of that electric city brought by the stranger, though these had their fascinations, as by the simple fact that he was introduced to her as being from New York. To him she could appear without the train of associations she trailed behind her in Reading. For one night, at least, she could be Cinderella: forget the aspersions on her legitimacy cast at her from the time she was born; forget that she lived on the wrong side of the tracks, where the nice girls of town didn't even venture (*SP* 138); forget that the next day would find her advertising and selling sheet music as she performed at the piano of the department store downtown. And his voice—it was "a voice on tiptoe at dawn."[2] Though from his size she might have, as others had, "expect[ed] him to roar. . . , when he [spoke] . . . the gravest, softest, most subtly modulated voice"[3] shaped itself around the most carefully mannered speech. Why should she be afraid?

And if she allowed herself to dream of what might come beyond that first night, what did she conceive? His manner obviously came from good breeding and ease. He must be fairly well-off. She had had to leave school and work because her mother and Mr. Moll could not even afford the eyeglasses she needed to see the blackboard (*SP* 138). Thus it would come as no surprise if she dreamed of a life free from cares like this. It wasn't just material concern. Who would blame her for wanting to see? If she gave herself so quickly without regard to the fast and formal law about how young women should comport themselves, weren't there more than enough good reasons?

And he, what did he see and feel? A young woman, unmarked and innocent yet unguarded enough to show him what no others had—unless it was behind the bar at Rammy's or on a silent beach because the girls he met there would never see him again and he was always "half-lit." The Wily girls, of course, and Miss Benz had shown themselves to him, but in the dresses they were used to wear, of almost familial familiarity, on the one hand, or of properly social reserve, on the other. But this was something else. There was in Elsie a want he detected for something she felt he could give. Had he ever felt this before: that someone would see in him possibility fulfilled? Hadn't he always been wanting on the scales he imagined himself being weighed? More, she emerged from a night belonging to his pastoral dream, the green and "fluent mundo" of summer around Reading. They sat beside a pool of pink, watching the lilies scud the bright chromes, while a frog boomed from its very belly odious chords they laughed at then. In the still, mother grass where they lay in the pale nights, seeing the crickets come out, he helped her discover herself and her bond to them and all that dust. "When you were Eve . . ." (CP 14).

Perhaps the only thing he could have found to mark her imperfection that night were her earlobes, fleshy and large, indelicately attached to the skin of her cheek, but he probably didn't notice them, or if he did, he made them, too, into part of the imperfect that was their paradise. With Elsie the world began to turn into an enchanted imaginary garden, a long and tranquil poem, as the journal entries and letter excerpts marking the beginning of the courtship reveal. When he returned to New York during the second week in August to set up his first practice in partnership with Lyman Ward the next month, Stevens felt cast out from his paradise. He expressed this as nostalgia for the very place he had been so happy to leave behind as the "acme of boredom" the year before:

August 18

Tonight, I am still faintly homesick—remembering home & thinking of it, as if it were—Dash the hurdy-gurdies. At least half-a-dozen have rattled up the street—they distract me utterly. Yet I was just recalling Lou Heizmann's pianola. And for recollection's sake let me take note of sleeping on the steps at O'Reilly's Gap, of that quiet *sentier* [path] through the woods on the nearest ridge, of H's piazza & Bull Durham cigarettes. (SP 139)

In spite of the hurdy-gurdies, which later played their part in contributing another element to the complex of associations around the metaphor of the "harmonium,"[4] Stevens went on to recollect a number of important details. Unfortunately, it seems that those which touched on Elsie and on his budding relationship with her were cut. But enough hints remain to give a good sense of the young lover's state of mind:

. . . cloud in the East, of Mrs. Wily's showing me her books, of that idle drive [illegible word—"single"?] Lance, of that ossified morning at the Tower,—[about five words have been crossed out heavily here and are illegible] of the bitterness of Greater Reading cigars—the ragginess rather—, of [illegible name, beginning with S] & Nolans & John Kutz at the Club (damn 'em), of Elsie & I taking a peep into Christ Cathedral, of the odor of sachet she exhaled, of the spirituality she suggested [two words have been crossed out here and are illegible]. Is there nothing else? I want every little thing—there's that bug-killing performance with Katharine Loose who is to spend the winter in Florence. I see Bob Hoff paying Nine ($9.00) Dollars— it *was* mine—as pew rent to a white-haired man in a cool cellar-ish room at Trinity. S'help me, I almost forgot reading Heine with Miss [illegible name, beginning with *B*] at the home of the author of "Olla Podrida." She wrote to me saying that she liked those Hebrew songs when played on my bassoon. With what amused disgust I used to read the *Times,* sitting at breakfast in my pyjamas! Then I must think occasionally of the cherries I ate, of the strawberries, of the little cobs of sweet corn, of the first sweet apples—

> Par derrier chez mon père,
> Vole, mon coeur—vole!
> Par derrier chez mon père
> Li-ya-t-un pommier doux.*

of the cantaloupes & sweet potatoes & that one massive huckleberry pud-ding—and the ice-cream. Also, of the cigars I smoked late at night on the steps & in my room, & of memorizing several hundred lines of Maud & of the incomparable regularity of life. Alas! I have reserved nothing by way of climax (unless it be the red moon casting its light. . . .

[The following page has been excised; the next continues seemingly un-interrupted ". . . on Levi Mengel's cigars."] Well, these things are all mere marionettes for my fancy at most. They need no climax where they play. I have built them here & now a little stage set round with tapers. Let them drop in & out as they will. (*SP* 139–40)

A number of things here are shadowy. Was the mention of "that ossified morning at the Tower" a poetic rendering of an especially still summer morn-ing crystallized in limpid air? Or, was this Stevens's euphemistic way of re-cording being still very drunk early one morning? Were the illegible words a comment on that, or did they refer to Elsie? In connection with being in Christ Cathedral with Elsie, whose smell and spirituality replaced the incensed service, what two words were crossed out? Why did he, through Bob Hoff, pay nine dollars as "pew rent" to the old verger? Perhaps it wasn't only in Madame Bovary's France that lovers met in cathedrals. And what about Kath-arine Loose and Miss B.? Were they friends with whom he and Elsie spent

---

* "Behind my father's house
Fly, my heart—fly!
Behind my father's house
There is a sweet apple tree."

Holly Stevens mistakenly transcribed "Par" as "Pas" in deciphering her father's often inscrutable hand-writing.

time together, or was Stevens also considering other young ladies that summer? Most of the friends of his age had already married or left Reading by this time, and he began moving with a younger crowd (L 77). These two women probably belonged, then, together with Elsie, Bob Hoff, John Kutz, and the others mentioned, to the same circle. With them Stevens was entertaining. He sedately read Heine. With these juniors he seemed to be playing the role Peckham played with him. In a more boisterous mood he accompanied Hebrew songs on "his bassoon." Was it with the help of spirits that sometimes left him "ossified" that he showed himself this way? Were the high spirits of the group cheering him enough? Or was it Elsie's attention that enabled him to be so gay? He overcame his reticence with himself and even with his hard-earned cash, though the capitalized first letter of the amount spent for him by his friend indicate that the miser in him was still alive and prickled.

Stevens was experiencing a change of heart. The ditty he remembered in French reflected this as playfully as his behavior. He was no longer following his father, no longer "behind his house." Not in his father's house would he find what tempted him, so he would steal what he wanted and fly. This trivial trope revealed a way of truth. And the truth showed itself in another way as well. The young lover had memorized "several hundred lines of Maud." In rehearsing Maud's many and various verse forms, mouthing Tennyson's images, Stevens found new and different possibilities of expressing and describing himself. It was not that he found Maud's subject of frustrated love against a background of feuding and civil war close to his own experience, but there were, nonetheless, certain images congenial to his spirit and certain parallels of occasion that allowed him to associate himself with Maud's poet-speaker and Elsie with Maud. This fusing process began unconsciously during this summer as the poet laureate's rhymes and rhythms fixed themselves in Stevens's memory. It completed itself almost fifteen years later after particular aspects of Stevens's experience and perception had overlapped some of those expressed in Maud. At that later point the abstraction of forms reemerged blooded with meaning and offered itself to be reshaped by Stevens's personal vision.

As Stevens memorized the lines of Maud, he recognized the changing feelings and moods that prompted Tennyson's choice of meters and sounds. Though the poetry of the English master's subject allegorized those feelings into a tale of a distant time and place (where the death of the poet-speaker's father, as a result of a feud between his family and another, interferes with his love for Maud, who belongs to the other family), the poem's true subject involved primary situations that Stevens also knew. These were: a father's death—for him, at this point, symbolized by his leaving Reading; his deep-felt and loyal tie to his father nonetheless, in having become, like him, a lawyer; his seeing Elsie, as Tennyson's hero sees Maud, as a link to the soil from which he had sprung, to a past that could be retrieved only through her.

Each of these themes played on his spirit, touching feelings he expressed later in images that echoed what he silently intoned now. By the time Stevens wrote "Le Monocle de Mon Oncle," these themes resounded with the knowledge he had gained of himself, of Elsie, and of the other spiritual fathers besides Tennyson, whose works had shaped him and whom he wished to kill, mocking them and himself in magnificent measure.

Maud's controlling metaphor, repeated in variations throughout the poem, is the speaker's having had to turn his heart to stone (". . . make my heart as a millstone, set my face as a flint," [Part I, VIII]) in order to achieve, against the circumstances opposing his love, a "passionless peace" (Part I, IV, ix) that was a "bury[ing]" (Part I, I, xix) of himself in himself. In "Le Monocle" the metaphor Stevens uses to anchor the excursions through memory that make up the poem's twelve stanzas is the "wish that [he] might be a thinking stone" (*CP* 13). More, like Elsie, Maud has "a cold and clear cut face . . ./Perfectly beautiful" (Part I, II) which Tennyson first describes in a stanza of eleven lines, like "Le Monocle"'s, and in the following stanza which begins:

> Cold and clear cut face, why come you so cruelly meek,
> Breaking a slumber. . . .
>
> (Part I, III)

Stevens's love for Elsie, after nine years of marriage, was opposed by their own circumstances, which he could not have foreseen during this first summer. In "Le Monocle" he recalled this time as a dream. In the poem her image disturbed his attempt at imitating the "old Chinese/. . . tittivating by their mountain pools" (*CP* 14), his attempt at the equally "passionless peace" of "a philosopher's life in the quiet woodland ways" (*Maud,* Part I, III, ix). He addressed his figurative Elsie in the poem in the same way that Tennyson's poet-speaker addressed his female:

> Why, without pity on these studious ghosts,
> Do you come dripping in your hair from sleep?
> (*CP* 14)

At twenty-four Stevens's heart had been stolen by Elsie. He was, as he expressed indirectly through the French ditty in his journal, like Tennyson's hero, "heart-free" (Part I, II). But after years of disillusionment that made the satisfaction of his love impossible—as the familiar feuding made it impossible for Tennyson's hero with Maud—Stevens voiced his wish to be a "thinking stone." The impossibility was expressed in Tennyson's poem by a "wintry wind" (Part I, III). The slow dissolution of Stevens's and Elsie's love was similarly washed away by even stronger "rotting winter rains" (*CP* 16). The lines memorized at twenty-four emerged years later in their half-remembered meanings to help Stevens unburden himself. While now he repeated:

213

Oh, what shall I be at fifty
Should Nature keep me alive,
If I find the world so bitter
When I am but twenty-five?

. . . .

If Maud were all that she seem'd,
And her smile were all that I dream'd
Then the world were not so bitter
(Part I, VI, v)

at almost forty, he comforted himself about the differences between his and Elsie's seeming and being with these lines of his own:

If men at forty will be painting lakes
The ephemeral blues must merge for them in one.
(CP 15)

The most direct connection between *Maud* and "Le Monocle" is the impelling motive for the series of various distractions and meditations that make up both poems. Tennyson's soliloquizing speaker bursts out with "Scorn'd, to be scorn'd by one that I scorn" (Part I, XIII, i), expressed about Maud's brother, the figure keeping him from his love. Similar words escape the prison of Stevens's teeth, directed at both himself and the woman who kept themselves and each other from being able to express their love:

And so I mocked her in magnificent measure
Or was it that I mocked myself alone?
(CP 13)

The echoes of Tennyson's *Maud* haunted Stevens that summer of 1904 as well. Just after he had memorized hundreds of its lines, images cradled in the enchanting rhythms he felt deep within him appeared in his journal (in the August 18 entry quoted above) and shortly after in letters he wrote to Elsie. His recollected descriptions of himself, of Elsie, and of the others he named as "mere marionettes," who "need[ed] no climax where they play[ed]" on the "little stage set round with tapers,"[5] evoked Tennyson's "puppets, Man in his pride, and Beauty fair in her flower" (Part I, IV, v). These "puppets . . . whisper, and hint, and chuckle, and grin" (Part I, IV, v) in abrupt movements. These were played out again in the "dolls" of "Le Monocle" who "weep, laugh, grunt and groan, and/shout" in response to the "unconscionable treachery of fate" and "that first, foremost law."[6]

Tennyson's "puppets" are "fools," transformed by nature's indifference and human pride. His hero is reminded of this state of nature by a "raven" that

. . . ever croaks, at his side,
Keep watch and ward, keep watch and ward,
Or thou wilt prove their tool.
Yea, too, myself from myself I guard,
For often a man's own angry pride
Is cap and bells for a fool.

(Part I, VI, vii)

Within months of committing these lines to memory, Stevens put on "cap and bells" himself in his letters to Elsie, transforming the hermit he had been in solitude into a jongleur-fool entertaining her as his Virgin, the "damsel heightened by eternal bloom" (*CP* 15).[7]

Tennyson's rhythms, like those of others that moved Stevens when he read them, were the undertones that unified his outwardly changing experience. What he took in helped him lead his life. Back in New York, waiting for letters from Elsie, exasperated that she did not write as much or as often as he, he noted his dependence on literary masters:

Nov. 7

Last week was the first since Elsie and I began writing to one another that I have not had a letter from her. Everything hangs in suspense as a result. I say to myself that I am sure to hear from her in the morning and I convince myself that if I do not I shall feel abominably cut up [again, the metaphor of being "cut"]; and no doubt I shall. I think I shall have to use the tactics approved of by the novelists—feigning indifference and the like. (*L* 79; *SP* 143)

As his sense of everyday reality wavered more uncertainly, according to the responses and reassurances he awaited from Elsie, he became more dependent on the echoes of those from whom he had learned. Although he now had a constant companion—Arthur Clous, an old acquaintance from Harvard, who had moved in with him around the middle of September—he saw him as able to "dispose of only one idea at a time" (*SP* 142) and so incapable of being the confidant of his doubts and fears. These he reserved to share only with his studious ghosts. Stevens and Clous went walking through Central Park and other parts of the city together. They visited exhibitions of watercolors and oils at the National Academy of Design and at galleries. And Clous was an ever-present witness to Stevens's "strange, insane kind of life" of working "savagely" yet being "so desperately poor at times as not to be able to buy sufficient food—and sometimes not any" (*SP* 142). His partnership with Lyman Ward was not successful and was soon to fail. But it wasn't to Clous that Stevens turned for comfort. He looked instead to Horace, Shakespeare, Tennyson, and other "man-poets." Just as in childhood, when "everyone [was] in different parts of the house reading," communing with the silent ciphers of

215

invisible authors instead of with one another, Stevens in young adulthood kept the words describing his feelings only for those he couldn't see. As his friend walked beside him, they spoke about the news and weather or the delicate tints of a painting they had seen. It was as though they had stepped out of the pages of a novel by Henry James.

But something had changed. One of Stevens's absent interlocutors now was Elsie. In his letters to her he expressed what he could not in her presence, though he wanted to. Just before going back to Reading for Thanksgiving, he wrote that he hoped that once he was there, his "real feelings [would] explode all fake ones" (L 79; SP 143). After noting to himself that he would learn to feign indifference to her from the novelists, he observed that their "letters seem[ed] to have wrought changes" and that when they met again, "It [would] be like two new persons facing one another." He followed this, most uncertainly, with "Will it be *two* happy ones?" (L 79; SP 143).

The answer, as in so many of the instances involving what actually went on between them, has been lost, the secrets of their relation cut by either his or Elsie's scissors. Here two pages were excised. After, we have Stevens's comments about how things "in other respects" (L 79; SP 143)—apparently other than with Elsie—seemed. Both his family and the countryside again seemed "insuperably dull." This perhaps reflected his own dull mood on not finding "*two* happy" persons. To soothe himself, he called on the ghost of Horace. He recalled and quoted from one of his most nostalgic odes (Book III, xiii) to express his own feelings about his home and soil:

Yet Reading is my "fons Bandusiae, splendidior vitro"*
and while I muddy it yet I bring my lamb duly

Child of the race that butt & rear
Not less, alas! his life-blood clear
Shall tinge thy cold wave crystalline
O babbling Spring! (SP 143)

A few years later, in 1907, apropos of voicing strong feelings about painful and important human situations and citing Catullus' lines on the death of his brother, Stevens noted in his journal that "Most men, who can, quote Latin in such cases." Such cases for the poet were those when he was in, as he put it, "an incomparable state of mind" (L 104). Stevens used the shaped, timed words of others to relieve him of the burden of his own feelings. The more removed the words were from his present experience—the ideal being words from a classical text quoted in the original—the more distance he could place between himself and the feeling. He had discovered this device while still an adolescent, confronting the "pathos" of the Wilys' situation. Now he used it consistently.

* "Fount Bandusia, brighter than glass"—this fountain may have been on Horace's Sabine farm, or near his birthplace, Venusia.

In spite of his spontaneous troping—turning to another's words or to some adjacent object on which to fix attention instead of confronting and expressing feeling directly—feeling nonetheless showed itself in the way the distraction was recorded. Stevens's doing this paralleled the Hebrews' not being able to utter the name of God or Moses' not being able to face the burning bush. As though himself the figure with which he closed "Sunday Morning," Stevens circled downward to darkness through rings of memory and other experience before being able to ascend toward the light of self-acceptance and knowledge of self. The implicit irony is that once feelings have been faced and expressed directly, words become unnecessary. The individual is alone, no longer distracting himself with words that allow others to know him and, through him, themselves. Truth, like light, is silent.

A strange observation, perhaps, for a biographer.

But—or, perhaps, thus—to return to our subject, the planet on the table. Turning to Horace, Stevens found a group of images that, conjoined, were as oxymoronic as any he later projected. They expressed his contradictory feelings about home and Reading. Stevens returned to Reading, in reality and memory, as Horace's young lamb, just budding horns, "foretokening love and strife," but about to be sacrificed, its potential thus frustrated, vain. Though Reading was the place from which he sprang, the ever-cool grotto that remained, like Horace's spring, unspoiled in memory, the changes Stevens had wrought in himself could not be recognized there. At home the image of the man he had become was sacrificed to the one known by those he had left behind, though not to Elsie, the one person who belonged to the source and who did not have the older image against which the present one threatened to shatter.

The importance of the state of mind Stevens described through this reference to Horace (the "state of mind" rather than the reference being the thing of significance, as Stevens noted in the same journal entry, where he specified the kind of occasion that prompted resorting to Latin [*L* 104]) was established by his transformation of the poem's controlling image, *splendidior vitro*. Horace's brilliantly well-chosen term of comparison does not carry its weight when improperly translated, as it often is, as "crystal." It means, simply, "brighter glass," a mirror. In this "mirror"—home, the source—Stevens, like Horace, saw himself reflected in the eyes of those he saw on visits who reminded him of who he was and what he had done. This "glass" means also a "lens," a device through which to see the rest of the world. For Stevens this association lent its weight to his "jar in Tennessee," his "monocle," and to the spy-eyeglass that his hero Crispin used on his voyage out of goblinry in "The Comedian as the Letter C." Behind or, rather, with all these later images was Reading, reading its meaning into the clickering syllables through which we see and hear the poet's source.

Stevens carried Horace's lines with him. Just over nine months later he made his first visit to Tennessee and saw it through the lens the Roman poet had provided. During the months before this trip a number of external changes in his life served as counterpoints to the more gradually developing movements of his spirit. By the time he actually found himself "Going South . . . approaching Tennessee" (L 83; SP 150) on August 10, he had already prepared himself to meet that "green, hilly, sunny-cloudy place" in imaginings that had begun months before. But during these months there had either been silence or cursory, epigrammatic journal entries. On January 20 he noted only that "A journal's a bore at times" (SP 144). On March 5 "Work, concerts, letters from Elsie, books, jaunts around town—these are what I seem to live for. I feel that Spring is in the ground, seething. But there is still plenty of snow and ice and I continue to wear a sweater (& sometimes) mocassins in bed" (SP 144). But April 10 brought a marked difference. The young poet showed a renewed, though blocked, interest in self-examination, which he recorded in a most cryptic manner:

> I fear the habit of journalizing has left me. Still one doesn't care to write a story all of one thing and my own history nowadays would make a monotonous Odyssey at best. Yet how irresistably one changes—in details. Tonight, there was a long twilight and after dinner I took a stroll as I am wont to do in summer-time. I could not realize that it was I that was walking there. The boy self wears as many different costumes as an actor and only midway in the opening act is quite unrecognizable. Now and then something happens to me, some old habit comes up, some mood, some scene (both of the sun, and of the moon) returns, and I return with it. But more often my days are mere blots on the calendar. There is nothing new in the Spring for me, or so it seems; and yet my spirits are high enough: I do not write this in melancholy. I feel a nervous desire for work. That is all that is left. Long ago, I gave up trying to make friends here, or trying really to enjoy myself. C'est impossible. I dream more or less—often of Elsie. [Here seven words have been crossed out and are illegible.] But I actually plan more—making one day fit another and keeping ends together. I feel a little inclined toward deviltry now and then, but *only* a little. I have money in pocket but not in bank + pay most of my bills promptly & all of them eventually. Still my hands are empty— + that much idolized source of pathetic martyrdom, *mon pauvre coeur* [my poor heart]! How scandalous it is not to regret "the silver seas!" I thought yesterday that four and twenty blue-birds baked in a pie might make me a modest breakfast—because one must have blue-birds one way or another (even if one only says silly + affected things about them). Sometimes, just before I go to sleep, I fancy myself on a green mountain— Southward, I think. It's simply green, the grass,—no trees, just an enormous, continental ridge. And I have windows there—(John Bland + I drink lager + porter at the Old Grape Vine for three hours here—no more of the green mountain tonight). (L 81; SP 144–145)

The closing fantasy here was another part of the raw material of "Anecdote of the Jar." The identity Stevens projected was connected to Horace's symbolic glass-lens through the "windows" in the entry. Though the "habit of jour-nalizing" had been partially replaced by the habit of writing letters to Elsie, there was more than this to his lapse. As he observed, at this point he felt his life to be a "monotonous Odyssey at best." But he immediately followed this with a contradiction, noting, though in a general and metaphorical way, his realization of how much he had changed "in details." Implicit here was his extreme unwillingness to reveal those details, even to himself. This showed itself, too, in his distancing use of the impersonal third-person "one" and in the opacity and vagueness of the comparison of himself to an actor—his first direct naming of the persona that developed into the comedian he became. Most unclear was how Stevens perceived the "I [who] was walking there." Was it the boy as himself or the actor or both simultaneously? Equally signifi-cant was the setting up of the scenes of sun and moon that became the back-drops of so many later poems. The changes in reality brought with their lights and darknesses were like changes in costume for the boy-I-actor.

Stevens did not develop the suggestions of his comparison. Again he turned his attention to the external world. But he nonetheless revealed him-self. He noted his inability to make friends and tipped his hand about the pain and uncertainty this prompted by slipping into a French exclamation, as he used more measured Latin verse on even more painful occasions. He fol-lowed this immediately by mentioning his dreams of Elsie and disclosed how easily she was becoming overvalued in his spirit's economy. In the absence of friends he felt her interest and love to be the gold of his kingdom. Appropri-ately, in the next sentence he outlined the "plan" he would have to continue following if he were going to have her by his side, making "a fuss over him." Until then he would go on, condemned to the "martyrdom" of his isolation, expressing paltry versions of his feelings in French exclamations—"mon pauvre coeur!"

The movement from this phrase to the end of the entry traces a significant pattern of Stevens's consciousness. Again he used another's verse form, this time a nursery rhyme remembered from childhood, to contain and convey his feeling. He changed "blackbirds" to "blue-birds," as though not wanting to deal with the innuendos the former provoked, something he grappled with only years later, when he wrote about them in thirteen unpropitious ways. This association back to a time of childhood wishing eased his present way so that he could finally soothe himself with the marvelous fantasy that was the prototype not only for "Anecdote of the Jar" but for the process of writing poetry. The peace and power expressed through the fantasy were the imag-inative counterweights balancing the nervousness and inability he experienced in reality, as he recorded earlier in the entry. Later the poems he composed during solitary nights in his room counterbalanced the weight of his days in the same way. Even more particular, apropos of this last transition to being atop a green mountain, was a subtle gliding through the Mother Goose rhyme to another Stevens remembered, Stevenson's "Land of Counterpane," with its little, sick hero fantasizing himself "atop a hill." The hidden suggestion *jar*red Stevens into his own imagining of himself atop his hill.

This musing conditioned the young poet for what Tennessee was to mean. In a later letter he expressed to Elsie that he had "always been of two minds about" Tennessee (*SP* 151). The association established here between the blue-blackbirds and his green mountaintop fantasy was the raw material for the image of the three blackbirds in a tree that was a metaphor for his mind. Tennessee was linked to this metaphor. The doubling of all but its initial letters was the verbal equivalent of a mirror. In this place about which he was of two minds his own doubling was reflected. Its evocations embodied the feeling of his constant up and down between reality and imagination, between being boy and actor. The jar as lens, Tennessee as mirror together radiated and expanded all the shimmerings of Horace's *splendidior vitro* in ways that would make not only widows but Horace himself wince at the power of the hand that struck such a hullabaloo of reverberations from such trivial chords—something an Augustan poet could never have done.

Even before seeing Tennessee, Stevens tried to make his wish to be atop a green mountain a reality. He felt he had to "find a place in the country." So, near the middle of May 1905, he left his friend Clous behind and moved out of the city to East Orange, New Jersey. This came just after the Easter holiday he had spent in Reading, where he experienced once again the joy of being in the countryside. Now, with Elsie, it was like being "in the seventh heaven" (*SP* 146). Returning to New York after this was difficult, as he wrote a week later:

> April 30
>
> I am in an odd state of mind today. It is Sunday. I feel a loathing (large + vague!), for things as they are; and this is a result of a pretty thorough disillusionment. Yet this is an ordinary mood with me in town in the Spring time. I say to myself that there is nothing good in the world except physical well-being. All the rest is philosophical compromise. Last Sunday, at home, I took communion. It was from the worn, the sentimental, the diseased, the priggish and the ignorant that "Gloria in excelsis!" came. Love is consolation, Nature is consolation, Friendship, Work, Phantasy are all consolation. (*L* 82; *SP* 146)

About this and the other April entries Holly Stevens notes that they contain "premonitions of 'Sunday Morning' . . . not written until ten years later" (*SP* 146). The connection prefiguring this poetic elaboration is the glaring contradiction between action and feeling that is the entry's core: "Last Sunday, at home, I took communion. It was from the worn, the sentimental, the diseased, the priggish and the ignorant that 'Gloria in excelsis!' came." Again faced with an incomparable state of mind, Stevens deflected his attention onto something external. Here it was New York, the city's spring, that was blamed for his "loathing." Had he instead probed his feeling, he would have precipitated the crisis of faith born during his years at Harvard. But this he could not afford just now as he was trying to present for Elsie's examination an image of someone whole. Nonetheless, he could not help sensing the discrepancy between his need to do this (and so accept things as they were) and how he felt about these things—the conventions maintained to preserve a semblance of order in a world disillusioned by Darwin and Nietzsche. The impulse to take communion on that Easter Sunday came from the part of him that still yearned to return to his source, the part trained to believe. This part had been taught that when one felt doubt or uncertainty, the proper response, instead of questioning and probing the doubt, was to reaffirm faith and resurrect the spirit through this reaffirmation. But in so doing, Stevens was in yet another way, like Horace's lamb, returning to his source to be sacrificed, giving up the part that had developed reason's budding horns and had gathered facts of experience. Accordingly, after participating in the communion, symbolizing sacrifice, he felt "worn . . . sentimental . . . diseased . . . priggish and . . . ignorant."

Because he refused to question his disillusionment and loathing, he could not resolve—or, rather, dissolve—his negative feelings. He retreated instead into escapist wishes:

If I were to have my will I should live with many spirits, wandering by

> caverns measureless to man,
> Down to a sunless sea.

I should live with Mary Stuart, Marie Antoinette, George Sand, Carlyle, Sappho, Lincoln, Plato, Hawthorne, Goethe and the like. I am too languid even to name them. (*L* 82; *SP* 146)

Interestingly, in the wished-for consolation four female figures appeared (though two of them carried more than a suggestion of masculinity with their names). But much as and as hard as he tried, he could not still his "tempest of discontent" (*SP* 146). It continued intensely for more than two weeks, though he deployed all his usual defenses, beginning that first evening after the fateful Easter communion, by memorizing Shakespeare's Sixty-sixth Sonnet ("Tired with all these, for restful death I cry"), wishing "it had been a thousand times as long and a thousand times as bitter." But nothing helped. Again, another poet's lines provided a model for his experience. After railing against all "things as they are" in a brilliantly repetitive and contradictory sequence of lines—which precisely reinforced the aspects of Stevens's feelings—Shakespeare closed his poem with:

> Tired with all these, from these would I be gone,
> Save that, to die, I leave my love alone.

Expectedly, a few weeks after memorizing this sonnet and moving out of the city but still not content, Stevens consoled himself by noting that in spite of everything he was "Still deeply in love" (*SP* 147). More and more Stevens was making Elsie his reason for being. The occasion on which this was most clearly articulated was that same Easter Sunday morning when he acutely experienced, without facing it, his loss of the religious reason for being with which he had been raised. On that very Sunday Elsie became for him "une vraie princesse lointaine ['a true faraway princess,' a familiar fairy tale figure]," taking over in his imagination the magical comforting function that his mother had provided during his childhood and that he wished to replace with the figures of Mary Stuart, Marie Antoinette, George Sand, and Sappho. As he gave up the image of the Virgin, he imagined Elsie as his own "damsel heightened by eternal bloom."

Experience and desire were dangerously compressed and confused in this glorification of Elsie. She became his distraction from carefully examining and questioning himself. He phrased her epithet in French. It was as though there were a part of him that knew what he made her seem was not what she was. She was an image, and the image was incompletely and incorrectly she. But his need was overriding.

His education and experience had brought him to the point where he could no longer find comfort in either his mother or in the religion she practiced and represented. He now found her, like the rest of the family, "dull and boring." Yet, like the female figure of "Sunday Morning," he still felt the "'need of some imperishable bliss'" (*CP* 68)—or at least the promise of it. He needed the indulgence of imagination he had early associated with his mother. He added female figures to his poetic pantheon. But they did not have the reality of the male figures since in practice his education had been directed and shaped by the rational turn of mind traditionally expressed in male voices. Even Goethe's seemingly more rounded elaboration of the idea of *Organismus* obeyed a deep sequential ordering. Until Stevens could truly integrate into his own spirit what he associated with the female—what he later named the "irrational element"—something that would take him years, he needed a female presence with whom he could identify and from whom he received approval. Elsie provided this. But it must have been quite difficult, if not impossible, for her, at barely nineteen, to discover herself or to live up to this image in reality. Without any experience in the world, almost no formal secondary education, and not reading very much because of her eyes, how could she have even a notion of the thing he had in mind—"The radiant bubble that she was" (*CP* 13)?

❧

A month after Stevens had left the city, his mood had not changed. He was still "drinking gin and courting the moon" (*SP* 147), in spite of his having noted just before he moved that perhaps his inability to experience "excessive delight" was a consequence not only of living in New York but of a "bad liver" as well (*SP* 147). Stevens's fear about his liver was more than an imaginative device linking him to the romantics, all properly affected with bilious temperaments. In June he made another resolution to stop drinking and to "be decent until autumn" (*SP* 147). Luckily, this one did not have to be tested in the austerity of his new—again—solitary situation for too long. A week later he was distracted by his first trip since his holiday in the Canadian Rockies almost two years earlier.

This time his trip was business connected. On it he visited the Midwest for the first time. Chicago, he found "cheap"; Kansas City, "a mere imitation of civilization," though the rest of Kansas he thought "glorious"; Colorado, a place where he could have kissed the ground. In New Mexico he experienced part of what he expressed poetically about Tennessee: "When the work was over, I went out onto the prairie + lay full in the sun looking at the sky stretching above Texas, which was at my foot." Last were Nebraska and Iowa, "a superb state." He also saw something he would never forget: "The best thing I saw was a lightning storm on the prairie. I leaned out of the smoking-room window and watched the incessant forks darting down to the horizon. Now + then great clouds would flare + the ground would flash with yellow shadows" (*L* 82–83; *SP* 148). Holly Stevens notes this memory as a possible source of one of the images of "Earthy Anecdote," the poem that opened her father's first volume (*CP* 3). An additional connection she does not note but that elucidates this poem comes from another kind of experience: a deeper, personal recollection reevoked at the end of this trip, when Stevens stopped in Reading for a "two-weeks loaf" before returning to East Orange and his job in New York.

During this two-week interlude he spent glorious days driving through rich, rolling farmland in horse-drawn buggies with Elsie close at his side (*SP* 148). He visited old denizens of his place as well as some of the favorite spots of his childhood. One almost Proustian moment nearly moved him to tears:

> I visited Ephrata. Old von Neida recognized me—same whiskers, same glasses, same U.S. M-a-a-i-i-l voice, but I think a considerably enlarged complaisance. His register is no longer bulky. Had I been more watery, I should have wept; for there was an ancient smell there, that I knew well. On the seat of one of the summer houses I found "W. Ƨ." done in wood—& I remembered what a monster of difficulty the letter "Ƨ" used to be to me—& my knife. Memory is too much of a pyre. I think human bones may be among my ashes. (*SP* 149)

The entry continued with a description that elliptically disclosed in flashes, like the lightning in the prairie, burning images from the past that disturbed his present in the same way the bucks clattering through "Earthy Anecdote" are disturbed in their course: "As for the rest, as one says at eighty,—

mother's sick, father's sick, John's sick, the house is a wreck, everybody's gone to the devil. Sometimes I care immensely. This morning I don't care a damn."

A few important background details illuminate both Stevens's incomparable state of mind at this moment and the significance of his later foregrounding "Earthy Anecdote" in *Harmonium* and eventually in *The Collected Poems*. In the poem the firecat intrudes into the Oklahoma landscape in the same way Stevens now felt himself to be intruding into his family constellation and the way R. L. Stevenson had noted that the traveler "lights up the contrasts of the earth" (see p. 121). His intrusion was aggressive. It both interrupted and shed light—like the lightning on the prairie—on the regularity of the life left behind, the life of bucks clattering. The association between his family and the "bucks" comes from remembering that "Buck" was his older brother's nickname. Stevens now, returning with fresh eyes from "clattering" on the railroad across the country, saw the whole family drama clearly. He saw everyone failing in one way or another. This failure was best represented by his brother Buck, who, from the time of dropping out of Yale ten years earlier, continued to fail in whatever he attempted; he had even been discharged from the army for an untreatable nervous disorder after volunteering for service in the Spanish-American War. Significantly, however, through all of Buck's inadequacies, Garrett, Sr., himself recently recovered from a nervous breakdown, kept on supporting him both emotionally and financially. And in his letters to Wallace through the Cambridge years and later he never hid his perception of Garrett, Jr., all the while stressing his constant interest in this first son named for him. It was as though Garrett, Sr., expressed for his eldest all the fears and pitying concern he felt but could not express for himself through the many years his own business enterprises met with failure.

The illumination of Stevens's difference—now a desired difference—from his brother and the rest of the family, as well as the accompanying uncertainty it raised once again, was as deeply etched into his sense of himself as the initials he had carved in the seat of the summerhouse. His following observation on memory reconfirmed this sigil's value. The noting of his difficulty in making the letter *S* and his calling it a "monster" inscribed the most constant feature of the years of his youth. He was the only one of his siblings not named for a family member. He was different from the others with whom he moved in the Cambridge circle. He was isolated from others in New York. All these facts contributed to the difficulty he still had in shaping the letter beginning his family name. This was evidenced by his signature on letters and on the flyleaves of books he acquired between the ages of about fifteen and well into his twenties. This letter remained a "monster." All through this period he wrote it in various, gradually more illegible ways until it finally became, in his mature hand, indistinguishable in most cases, except for context, from his capital *I*. This feature, together with his later calling his physical self a "monster," reveals how deeply the experiences of childhood and youth engraved his being. They produced an equivocal identity that could survive only by experimenting, as he did, with the various shapes of his *S*'s, and in following the various models of his "man-poets." This continued until a point when the *S* became *I*, though in an almost indecipherable scrawl.

Numerous observations Stevens made in his letters and journals about wanting to find a particular kind of nib show that he had more than a passing concern with the appearance of his handwriting. This would be expected of one who hoped to spend his life writing. Unlike the handwriting of his siblings, who imitated the models of penmanship offered both by their elementary schoolteachers and by their parents (Garrett, Sr., had an extraordinarily flourishing yet precise handwriting style, and Kate, that of the teacher she had been), Stevens's hand was always irregular and, well into his twenties, often immaturely so, his letters awkwardly managed and going in different directions. He most often used pencil, even at home (on his walks through the woods a pencil, of course, was dependable and easy to manage), to record his musings in his journal and to inscribe his name in books. The sloppy appearance of many of his earlier penned letters indicate that as a youth he had had a great deal of difficulty in the simple physical act of using pen and ink. This minor fact about someone who was to become one of the major poets of the century is perhaps accidental and unimportant. Yet for one who made this contribution through a long but hidden rebellion against past masters—at least partly out of a sense of not finding in them all he needed to know about how to live and what to do—it might evidence a connection between this reaction and the more immediate relationship with his father, the rest of his family, and his peers, in all of whom he had also sought, at various times, for guidance in directing his desires.

In this context, two major notes sounded that provided lasting tones for Stevens's spirit to play and transform into a music of his own. His strong attachment to male figures who served in his father's place and offered him approval has been mentioned. After Stevens had left Cambridge, the most important of these was W. C. Peckham. Curiously, after Stevens had worked in his law office and spent time with Peckham in British Columbia and at his home in New Jersey, there was a marked change in the way the young man shaped the letters that formed his name. He no longer even attempted to make his cipher fit the standard flourishing mode of late-nineteenth- and early-twentieth-century penmanship. Instead, he adopted for his signature Peckham's style in signing his own name. The man who gave him his first serious work as an apprentice attorney and who provided a model of what the good life could be also offered him a style of signing himself that, in turn, affected the shapes of all his later letters.

The second note, modifying this one with a sweet, less austere color, was provided by his mother and had to do not with the surface form of letters but with the deeper organizational form in which the letters shaped themselves into words, sentences, and understood paragraphs. In her letters Stevens's mother, Kate, jumped from thought to thought. She never indicated these leaps with new paragraphs, nor did she attempt to ease their abruptness with transitions of any kind. Similarly, in Stevens's correspondence with Elsie there were no transitions between thoughts or any paragraph indications. Though after one has read through all his letters and journals, patterns of both presentation and association may be discerned, there was never—until well into the thirties—a consistent attempt on Stevens's part to note major breaks between ideas. Though he used short dashes in place of periods—a device used by his father as well (and belonging to the loose stylistics of Victorian punctuation)—they do not follow a form that allows the reader to interpret them as paragraph breaks. This associative manner of relating perceptions later became one of the characteristic features of Stevens's poetry. Unless a reader places himself or herself in the context of the poem's occasion, it is nearly impossible to understand what accounts for the seemingly random connections between images.

As though unconsciously aware of the importance of the act of writing in his understanding of the world and himself, Stevens spontaneously used metaphors linked with it to describe his actual experience. When he returned to his home in New Jersey at the beginning of August 1905, just after his two-week stay in Reading, he wanted to "blot out" (*SP* 149) the memories of everything except Elsie, nature, and old acquaintances. These were memories of his family—"so dull that [they] affected [him] like an elegant phase of paralysis" (*SP* 149). In the same entry, after noting as one of the pleasant things, "Mrs. Smirk under a purple parasol" (a naïve image that seemed itself to come from a poem), he continued in his musing about the Smirks and wished to be like them: "What an immortal ascendancy the Smirks enjoy—and all the rest. I cringe by nature before them. I am not envious but I am consumed with vain longing. If these fellows *are* butchers' sons how *do* they *do* it?" (*SP* 149). Stevens felt himself on the outside both in the city and in his own family. He wanted to be one of the Smirks, natives of their place. But this was not possible. He moved instead into a "Jovian atelier," to become, at least, a part of the sky and weather.

Just three days later, on a Saturday—just five days before he moved from 11 Halstead Street to 24 Halstead Place and then left on the business trip that took him to the South and to Tennessee for the first time—a walk through the streets of New York, from his downtown office to Ninety-first Street and back again to the ferry that crossed to New Jersey, brought on a "vicious, dark mind." This he again blamed on his "New York gloom." The following day, because he felt moved by a need for purification, a drenching rain did not keep him from his ritualized Sunday walk, though he began the day intending to remain at home reading *Jane Eyre*. But rather than describe the effects of the rain or the details of landscape as he usually did, he focused on "many white shoes + stockings" and observed parenthetically that "the secrecy of a dress is a god-send to more than one woman" (*L* 83; *SP* 150). Preoccupied and tantalized by the secrecy of Elsie's dresses and by the secrecy of his desires, to which he had been sensitized by reading through Charlotte Brontë's lines her own hidden dreams, he saw himself once more projected onto the outside world. But rather than look at his past and carefully examine what made him dissatisfied and gloomy in the present, he looked toward the future and invested it with the wished-for words that would make his world.

Though only fragments remain of the letters from this early period of Stevens's courtship and though these fragments do not have precise dates indicated, it is possible to place them generally. After Stevens's death Elsie copied excerpts from his letters chronologically into a stenographer's notebook which she opened with the following curious "memorandum":

> Excerpts from letters of Wallace Stevens
> from 1904
>
> with this memorandum:—
>
> In an answer to a sonnet written by Wallace Stevens while at Harvard University—in which he took the point of view of a man whose impulses to good found their sources "say in Nature," George Santayana wrote: "The church is one's guide through the conflicting labyrinth of Nature and the inconsistencies of natural laws." (WAS 1772, Huntington Library)[8]

As here, other dates were noted, and some fragments have references that can be matched to dated material from the journals. These excerpts reveal how Stevens compensated for the lack he felt in his everyday world by completing it in the imaginary world he shared on paper with Elsie. Before we look at specific instances, a few broad observations about the most characteristic elements of this material and of the later, complete surviving letters will give a sense of the stage directions and costumes Stevens devised so that he could easily play the role he set for himself.

During the first year of this relationship shaped by words (a few years later, though still before their marriage, Stevens called it "an inky pilgrimage"), while still uncertain of Elsie's reactions, he carefully set to work painting backdrops for their projected scenes and acts. Like a good director, he meticulously delineated the outlines of character he would have them follow. For himself, introduced to her as "a poet from New York," he devised lines that were verses and poetic observations, similar to those he had earlier sent to his mother. And because he also wanted to impress the young woman with his seriousness in preparing himself for a secure future, he wrote prescriptions for attitude and behavior that were inversions of the admonitions he made to himself in his journal. In his letters to Elsie these were formulas for success in the world of fact, formulas that echoed the repeated advice he had received over the years from his father. What he wrote in some letters—

> I should like to make a music of my own, a literature of my own, and I should like to live my own life. (L 79)
> One of my ideals is to make everything expressive, and thus true. I would like to get out of line. (L 80)—

227

alternated somewhat uneasily with what he wrote in others:

> I mean to keep as busy as I can, so that in the end I shall have something to show for the trouble of keeping alive. (*L* 79)

> So long as the work is profitable and leads to something, I love it. The desperate thing is to plod, to mark time, to stand still. That I cannot endure. (*L* 79)

> The only brilliant things in life are friendship, self-denial and similar evidences of civilization, as far as men are concerned. (*L* 79)

Periodically, as if he sensed that she might perceive the contradictoriness of this up and down between his two postures, he momentarily revealed the artifices of both, as in the following two excerpts, in which the deeper sources of each, in turn, were laid bare:

> Perhaps I do like to be sentimental now and then in a roundabout way. There could be no surer sign of it than in my sending verses to you. I certainly do dislike expressing it right and left. (*L* 80)

> —the family to whom I send bulletins in regard to my progress. They call it progress. It is really nonsense. Once one is born, one does not progress again until one dies. The rest is all a waste of valuable time—or so it seems. (WAS 1772)

In sharp contrast with the duality he expressed about himself were the scenes he painted of the world he imagined inhabiting with Elsie and the constancy of the role he envisioned for her. The most important aspect of this world was that it was to be a "solitude," since it was only in solitude that he felt he could "know about [him]self, [his] world, [his] future when the world [was] ended": "I like to think that I do not bring a jaded fancy, or a cunning hand into this solitude of ours. It is as new to me as it is to you, and that is why, regarding it as a new world its colors are still bright and its horizons still wonderful" (*L* 80).

To ensure that she would come to live with him in "this solitude of self," which had been his most secure world before he met her, certain requirements had to be met. In spite of how he otherwise extolled the value of friendship, it became clear, even during this first year, that this primary virtue should be practiced only between the two of them and not be sullied by anything approaching intimate contact with others: ". . . not that you ought not to know things and people as they are, for you ought to—and the worst are only a very little from the best" (WAS 1772). He described their solitude in shining outlines: "A world of our own [complete with] certain scenes with which we shall associate one another, certain mornings, certain afternoons, certain nights" (WAS 1772). But he colored the rest of the world from which he excluded her in dark colors: "The world is only a trap. It can hardly have caught you yet" (WAS 1772). He believed he could create for them, from a "bucket of sand and a wishing lamp . . . in half a second a world that would make this one look like a hunk of mud" (*L* 80). He wanted her to see the "mud" world as old and artificial and invited her to climb with him into his "Jovian atelier": "Heaven is home, and the world is, all in all, only a doll's house. And the strong spoil most of the fun for the weak, and the weak disgust or bore the strong. There is only one good thing in it from beginning to end, and that is friendship" (WAS 1772).

To make sure that Elsie would feel that she belonged in this rarefied atmosphere, it was necessary to convince her that only he perceived her as she really was and that she already resided there, even if she had not been aware of it. Whatever changes occurred would be determined by the special demands of the "fluent mundo" of which he was the sole designer: "Few people have spirit enough to know when they're content. But E[lsie—the completing letters of her name she added later, using a different pen from the one she used to first copy this fragment] does" (WAS 1772); "I wanted to understand you, to give you confidence enough to make you reveal yourself" (WAS 1772). More, the creature that was being shaped under his tutelage had to have permanence so that she could sustain all of his imagination's wishes: ". . . if two people ever sincerely care for each other, they will care always" (WAS 1772). At moments when she must have, in the necessity of her youth, gently balked at so tight a rein, even if it was of gossamer, he calmly reassured her, using some of his well-learned rhetorical skills: "Six months more or less ought not to be the extent of our good will. We cannot be so shallow or changeable as that" (WAS 1772).

Through these fragments runs the thread of uncertainty, repeatedly noted as running through almost all of Stevens's young experience. But now the thread was being woven into the very fabric of the life he planned for the two of them. His need to have her help with the weaving was pressing. It translated itself into periodic refrains that urged her not to pull at it with questioning or reticence that threatened to unravel it: "We long ago passed into a world of our own, away from this one. I do not think you can fail to see why I write, or why I wait so impatiently to hear from you" (*L* 79); "Think of what a refuge affection is—from evil—from selfishness, from helplessness, and from adversity" (WAS 1772).

Elsie had ambivalent reactions to her constant, ardent lover. On the one hand, she was as captivated by the power of his attentions and gifts as the Moon was by Pan disguised in shining, white, thick fleeces, as we are by the poems. On the other hand, she was barely nineteen and felt more than a little hesitation at being so strictly directed. The young woman from the wrong side of the tracks naturally fell in the thrall of seeing herself as "une vraie princesse lointaine." Yet some inarticulate pang made her wince at the thought of a future immured in the construction of someone else's imagination. Consequently, her correspondence alternately reflected (as revealed by

229

references Stevens made in letters to her and in his journal) warm interest in him and in his poetic preoccupations and apparent indifference, shown in the more than occasional irregularity of her response. The young man of twenty-six did not see, through this ambivalence, the precariousness of the exalted position in which he placed her. But, then, the almost complete egotism of youthful perceptions and demands is not a novelty. Unusual, however, was Stevens's attitude toward Elsie. At least in his written manner with her, the voice he used was one of authority and dominance. What were really youthful exercises and experiments in role-playing seemed to spring, in his case, from a well of certainty fed by an elder's years of experience.

This archness of tone showed itself in contrast with the tone of the now-intermittent journal entries, letters to Elsie, for the most part, taking their place. Where, in the journal, observations of the external world were counter-balanced by observations of self or interjections of frustration, uneasiness, and uncertainty, in the letters these personal asides were transformed into moral directives to her. As the letters became more frequent, the ethical preoccupation with himself gradually disappeared from the journal, leaving simple recordings of externals. During his second business trip in August 1905, for example, while he was "Going South" (L 83), when the reality of Tennessee fulfilled his April dream of being "on a green mountain . . . simply green [on] an enormous continental ridge [where he had] windows," the journal entries themselves became windows, transparent forms framing the new world outside him. No comments on personality or purpose broke the surface descriptions of time and place, though certain repeated elements and an apparently unconscious sensitivity to sharp contrasts revealed the ineluctability of his true subject, which early established itself and continued to reflect the up and down of his relation to the world.

In these entries (see SP 152–53) "green" became an obsessive focal point, the apogee of Stevens's experience of the South. Against this background played a series of images that presented themselves opposingly. The alternating pattern was set even as he approached Tennessee, that "sunny-cloudy place." Following this, in the next entry, already in Mississippi, he recorded details of simple people in rural surroundings—"women chopping wood, wash drying on fences . . . bare legs . . . ox-carts, mule on kitchen doorstep . . . po' white trash leaning against things . . ."—around a central image of "black, white and yellow, [and] Greek temples." Rather than properly name the South's neoclassical structures as what they were—houses in imitation or reminiscent of "Greek temples"—he recorded an imaginary vision, unmitigated by reality, thus producing a naïvely surrealistic effect.

Even in the smaller things he noticed, what struck him was the same kind of severe juxtaposition. Of a razorback hog, he noted its "long nose & sunken face." Having observed that the umbrella tree shed its leaves very often, he followed his description of it with that of a precisely contrasting tree: "The live oak [which] does so only once." On a wagon drawn behind eight oxen, he commented on "a bag of flour," irregularly rounded, containing its uncontainable contents, and contrasted it with "a box of soap," which squarely mimicked the solid shapes of the individual bars. Elsewhere he noted a black girl's white sunbonnet being blown into a puddle.

Eleven days later he was back in East Orange. On his return trip he had stopped in Reading, where Elsie's way of taking his hand made him "feel wonderfully welcome" (*L* 84; *SP* 153). Before settling in at his new address on Halstead Place and reestablishing his city routine, he made a few more notes of what he had seen on his trip. "Green" again emerged as the metaphor for his recollecting in tranquillity: "[D]own there . . . at early twilight, colors—green I am thinking of—do not become obscure but stand out of the darkness." But now, within this memorial re-creation of reality, other kinds of observations interrupted and embellished the cold, external facts. Details were completed by comparisons the terms of which belonged to his well-educated sensibility: "The fan-like, starry palms on the marsh gutters, with the innumerable reeds (like a certain Seymour [Haden]) were new. So was the japonaiserie of pines now and then—when they were single and of strange design." Immediately following the inflections of experience, the innuendos of his studious ghosts whispered, now allowing him to leave reality uncompleted by metaphor.

Getting back into rhythm with his ritualized walk, on the last Sunday in August, he recorded external details in the same detached way, adding only another artful comparison to the familiar landscape along the towpath of the Morris Canal: "Delft-like reflections of sky in the water" (*SP* 153). The entry closed with a note that sounded its importance only years later: "Took lunch with Walter A[rensberg] at the Harvard Club. A fellow of most excellent fancy. Sat in the Park afterwards" (*SP* 154).

From this point until the end of the year, Stevens's journal entries became more and more peremptory. They served merely as notations of moments of internal or external transition. He had developed a shorthand that allowed him to reconstruct, in later circlings back when he reread, the sense of time as it passed while he was separated from Elsie. The one minor exception was an entry made on his birthday in which, after the beginning, one-third of the page was cut off before the closing words: "dark. And how active, how incessant!" (*SP* 154).

After he went back to Reading again on the Sunday and Monday of the Labor Day weekend, when he spent as much time as he could with Elsie, finding secluded spots in the gentle native woods, he recorded his decision to remain in East Orange through the winter. It was as though he wanted to ensure continued contact with a landscape somewhat closer to his pastoral dream than New York could provide. But just five days later, not having received a letter from Elsie, he decided the opposite, as though he wanted to move away from that "Faery" world he could not imagine inhabiting alone any longer:

September 15

No letter from Elsie for nine days. If I get none tomorrow, hanged if I'll be in haste to write again. This *cannot* be caprice—too much is excused on that ground, anyhow. I have this consolation, that we have had two inimitable nights—the moon in the trees, the sky blue all night long, and huge stars hanging in the branches like lanterns. The feeble are wearing overcoats. Next week I move to 6 University Place—as I understand the map. Somehow I am ambitious to work. One gets the best view of New York from a distance. (*SP* 154)

It is impossible to know what accounted for Elsie's apparent indifference at this point. But certain reasons can be guessed from the clues provided in this and in the previous entry as well as from the recollection of the general observations about her ambivalent feelings in regard to the position she held in the relationship. Though Elsie had responded openly in its first days and weeks, as the weeks became months that promised to become years, she seems to have had periodic misgivings, at least about how her position was understood by the others with whom she lived in the small provincial world of Reading. On the one hand, it was romantic and enviable to be courted by one who returned to this world, now just for her, as "the poet from New York," who was at the same time making himself into a successful lawyer. And there was the real verve of the romance, trysting down secluded paths, seeing the moon blue the sky "all night long." But there was a dark side, too, especially for her, who had held herself "so stiff and straight" against the background of the wrong side of the tracks. The consideration of those who held the conservative moral standard in this turn-of-the-century town played their part in her reactions to the situation they were beginning to see as compromising. It was not as though she could, as she might have had she been born fifty or sixty years later, leave this place and establish a life on her own where she could continue to act only on her feelings and on the practical concerns of the relationship. She had to remain for many reasons: She was only nineteen, did not have the educational preparation to sustain herself, and, more, felt she had a frail constitution that could not endure the stresses of harsher worlds away from Reading and the country—particularly if she were alone.

So she spent two days and "two inimitable nights" dreamily enjoying the company of this man who made her his princess. But left alone again, she shuddered amid the real or imagined whispers. In addition, there were openly voiced questions or advice from her mother, either to press her lover's implicit promise into a commitment to marry or to see other young men as well. Naturally Elsie felt confused and perhaps even angry at the one who caused these ups and downs. But she could not name the things she felt. The understanding and voicing of deeper, tenuous sources of motive were aspects of personality and behavior just beginning to be commonly explored as she began to explore herself and the world. Again, even if this were not the case, her youth and the inadequacy of her education mitigated against her being able to see herself with eyes that did not share the common view. She was a native of her place and could express her painful uncertainty only as what her lover could understand, in turn, as something more than "caprice."

He, for his part, was searching for stability. He needed an emotional buoy, both to mark his passage back and forth between imagination and reality and to offer him a resting place should he find his craft somehow destroyed. In the absence of such an anchor he could not even make necessary transits. He could not make the simplest of personal decisions. Months after deciding to move back to New York, but just after deciding to stay in New Jersey, he found himself wholly unable to fix his position. All he could do was comment on his "indefatigable . . . procrastination" and state of "bitter *far niente* [doing nothing]," though his *far niente,* for another, would describe an ideal life: "Smoking, reading [Henri] Murger's *Scènes de la Vie de Bohème,* improvising, writing and reading love letters, eating and drinking" (*SP* 154). In the ambiguity of his present relation to Elsie, unable to be secure in the knowledge of her approval, he implicitly turned to holding on to the set of values he had learned within his family of "good Puritans." He saw anything that did not directly contribute to his material progress in the practical world as nothing, *niente,* simply indulgence. As though quietly craving at least mild punishment for this, he described his feeling of separation from Elsie and wanting to see her as a "wonderful agony" (*SP* 155).

Adding to his uncertainty even more, the weather that late fall was summer-seeming. Well after Thanksgiving, when he again went back to see Elsie, and into December, "an air of truant summer" (*SP* 155) kept him in the imaginary pastoral he shared with her: "I cannot get the idea of summer out of my head." When the season slowly yielded to itself and rain and snow began, something changed in their relationship, as revealed in the journal entry of December 9, even in its expurgated state: "Snow and rain tonight. Elsie wrote to me today. 'I do not think [the balance of this sentence, less than one line, has been excised, either heavily crossed out or cut out].' She is quite right. Even reason aids her. She touches all my subtle stops" (*SP* 155).

The change was subtle but profound. Elsie had apparently voiced some admonition or suggestion, prompted by what she had adopted of the Reading chorus's attitudes. She was expressing something Garrett, Sr., would have expressed. Just as a few years before, Stevens had been persuaded not to travel to Paris, London, or Mexico but to stay, to go to law school, and to make something of himself by his father, who "always seem[ed] to have reason on his side," now he found himself persuaded of something else by Elsie, similarly with reason aiding her. Added to the role of muse she played for the pleasures of his imagination, she now took on as well the role of Athena-like guide for his progress in reality. He had urged her to do this: "If I were at your elbow I should prompt you. I'd say, 'Tell him to keep himself straight forward and to work hard'" (WAS 1772). With Elsie providing the voices of both imagination and reason, he could leave his mother and father behind and cleave to her. At this very moment the most important of his early metaphors, and the one that established the tone of his entire corpus, seemed to spring spontaneously from his being. He sensed himself an instrument, her instrument, as he had earlier been the instrument of his parents' expectations and dreams. He now became the organ of Elsie's wishes and desires: "She touches all my subtle stops."

The metaphor of an instrument for the self is not in itself unusual, especially since the romantics. What is interesting is Stevens's adaptation of the figure into the form it eventually took in his work, the harmonium. In light of how impressed he was by the words of others he read, it is not surprising that this adaptation had a connection to what he was reading during this period. Sometime earlier in 1905 he had read Thomas Hardy's *Under the Greenwood Tree* and recommended it to Elsie (*L* 85). Around this time, in December, he dipped into *The Trumpet-Major,* reading bits after dinner and as it pleased him. Stevens liked Hardy. He was sympathetic to the novelist's continually rephrased lament on the passing of the pastoral world as well as to his fine-tuned sensitivity to the effect certain women had on certain men.

This affinity seems to have made Stevens more than usually receptive to images he found in Hardy's pages. He easily associated these images with others he had come across and registered earlier. This description from *The Trumpet-Major,* for example, must have touched a responsive chord: "But she had been struck, now as at their previous meeting, with the power she possessed of working him up either to irritation or to complacency at will; and this consciousness of being able to play upon him as upon an instrument. . . ." [9] The evocation of an instrument here connected with an earlier note about a particular one which Hardy used as a controlling metaphor, as he explained in his 1896 Preface to *Under the Greenwood Tree,* a novel dealing with the changes industrialization brought to a group of musicians representative of an entire region and way of life:

> One is inclined to regret the displacement of these ecclesiastical bandsmen
> by an isolated organist (often at first a barrel-organist) or harmonium player;
> and despite certain advantages in point of control and accomplishment which
> were, no doubt, secured by installing the single artist, the chance has tended
> to stultify the professed aims of the clergy, its direct result being to curtail
> and extinguish the interest of practitioners in church doings. [10]

What Stevens hoped to do with his *Harmonium* more than fifteen years later was to replace religion with poetry. His journal entry of December 31, 1905, quoted below, referring to one of his installments of reading Hardy, provides the notes that, played together, fix this musical machine as the perfect instrument for Stevens's expression. The old world he had known was dying. Its religious values were stultifying, as he well knew. A new organ, one that would disclose the "control and accomplishment" of the individual in an uncertain age, was needed.

Four days before his end-of-the-year entry, Stevens briefly recorded how he had passed the time of the holiday. Two strong impressions set up the contrast he was experiencing between old and new: "Her cheeks were incomparable. In the evenings we chatted *etc.* on the sofa. That *etc.* means volumes. Everybody else stale as usual" (*SP* 156). He saw the object of his choice radiant and new against the "stale" family he was rejecting. Elsie was the one now concerned with him as the youth as virile poet, while they were still concerned only with news of his "progress," a notion he had already discarded as "nonsense" (his years at Harvard, in company with all those who had each debunked this deadening materialist idea, had gone a long way in shaping his dreams).

On the last day of 1905, then, accidentally but appropriately a Sunday, Stevens expressed his sense of things in a very different way from previous years:

A weighty day, of course. Walked to Montclair and back, in the morning, rather meditatively. Very mild air. My head full of strange pictures—terra-cotta figurines of the Romans, ivory figurines of the Japanese, winter birds on winter branches, summer birds on summer branches, green mountains, etc. Reflections on Japanese life, on specificness, on minute knowledge as disclosing minute pleasures, on what I should wish my wife to be, on my future. On returning, read a little of Hardy's "Trumpet Major" and after dinner read more. Pulled my curtains shortly after four and lit my lamp, feeling rather lonely—& afraid of the illusions and day-dreams that comfort me—and frightened at the way things are going, so slowly, so unprofitably, so unambitiously. I hope a few things for the coming year, but resolve nothing. (*SP* 156)

The first note of difference established a new key for the way Stevens now entered and encountered the landscape. Gone completely were the detailed recordings of what he actually saw. In their place, after just the briefest comment about the weather—"Very mild air"—were musings he saw in his imagination as he walked. The three particular pictures pointed to what came to be three general preoccupations of his poetry: the ancient world; the Orient; the changes of the seasons. It was, then, these *imaginings,* drawn from, *ab-stracted,* from the minute particulars he saw about him, *rather than* the elements of reality themselves, that prompted the *reflections* of his intellect. These reflections and their order, at first a seeming disorder, established major themes, each of which was later played out in all possible variations in and through the instrument of his work, the projected *Whole of Harmonium.* Hardy's metaphor marked the modern intellectual move away from the primary nourishment of a life still tied directly to nature.

Not yet conscious of the full effect this reading was having on him but obviously moved by what his spirit shared with Hardy's, Stevens went on to describe his feelings in a very different way from before. During earlier periods he had repeatedly maintained that his loneliness was not really "lonely" but a necessary and positive "solitude." But now he did not qualify it at all.

He was simply "lonely" and, more, "afraid" of the very things that had once soothed him—the indulgences of his imagination. Not satisfied that this first utterance was sufficient to express the depth of his loneliness, he added that he was "frightened" of the way things were going in reality. There was no holding ground, and so, in sharp contrast with all his previous end-of-the-year resolutions, which were periodically restated at moments of weakness during the year, he now only tremulously hoped but would "resolve nothing."

Though this uncertainty was painful, it was positive in that it prompted Stevens to question himself and things as they were in a deeper way than he had while at Harvard, under the guidance of instructors and acquaintances. This period of confusion meant openness. During its long swing he half circled for the first time things he had learned earlier but now wanted to understand more fully. This circling was later repeated at significant moments in his life. It was finally completed, in his own understanding of it as a movement, as he approached the end of his life. In his first poetic displays with it, it was metaphorically described both as the pattern of a bird's descent downward on extended wing, rounding its focus to light on various branches before meeting eventual darkness, and as the compass of a ship tethered on its mooring. Which of these images operated at any given point depended on whether the world was being seen from above—from a bird's-eye view—in its abstract pattern or from a fixed but circling lateral perspective, on a sea gently moving up and down—a more human point of view. Eventually both these images of circling were subsumed in a planetary metaphor, Stevens figuring himself as a planet, a rock, originally one with the mass of the sun, now moving in a predetermined orbit but changing its path and its nature almost imperceptibly with each revolution.

る

During this first rounding period during the winter of 1905–06 he went back to reading what had most impressed him while at Reading Boys' School and in Cambridge. He followed closely the order in which he had first met with these texts. But now he filled out the compass and curriculum of his developing thought by nosing into other works by and about authors who had earlier made some difference in the way he saw and felt. Conveniently reinforcing his present need to dwell, if only in imagination, in a pastoral world were the Greek poets and playwrights of the classical period. By the autumn of 1906 he had gone back to the poets of the archaic period. Then, working his way forward through history again, he found in the poems of the *Greek Anthology* sentiments he felt about the passing of an idyllic age.

Picking up the thread of Greek feeling and thought for the modern temperament, Stevens read Matthew Arnold again. He tried to get beneath his surface by giving careful attention to the *Notebooks*. His interest was keen enough that he not only recorded some of Arnold's observations in his own journal but began looking as well at authors to whom Arnold referred. He also

236

expanded his sense of his own and Arnold's aphoristic style by reading others who recorded and expanded their impressions in notebooks and journals. He wanted to collect a library of such things, and he later did (*SP* 160). By the end of February he had already gone through Arthur Schopenhauer's essays (*Parerga and Paralipomena*) and aphorisms and was reading Giacomo Leopardi's *Pensieri*. Each of these perusals affected his present state of mind and left strong impressions of both style and substance that he later modified and shaped into his mature work. Though he read other things during this time as well and began looking at paintings and listening to music much more regularly, he was moved by these in respect to how their effects could be translated into literary forms. The progress of Aleksandr Glazunov's symphonic arrangement *From the Middle Ages* (*SP* 160) contributed elements to the desired effect Stevens later achieved in "Sea Surface Full of Clouds." His response to Jozef Israëls' painting of a girl knitting by the sea provided one of his first sense of "exquisite prose" and the "poetry of fact" (*SP* 161). But these were single points of illumination, like the light of certain brighter stars in a dark but star-filled heaven. In contrast, what he read of the Greek poets, Arnold, Schopenhauer, and Leopardi, as of his other greater luminaries both before and after, was like moonlight gradually affecting the whole night sky. Periodically their presence made the world sublunary, their spirits variously combining with Stevens's own to provide the sustaining, repeated tone to his work.

From Arnold he learned to prize poetry, above all things, as the civilizing instrument. In Schopenhauer he found a philosophical basis, imbued with feeling, albeit morose and pessimistic, for believing himself and the world predetermined in some eternally illogical and inaccessible way. This is evident, for example, in an excerpt from the journal entry of February 5, 1906: "The difference between Keats and a long-shoreman is a matter of a drop or two of blood in their brains, or of the shape of their skulls or of something of the sort. Both are quite innocent of the merit or lack of it. Both are the results of an indifferent psychopathy" (*L* 87; *SP* 159). In Leopardi he found a manner of dealing with the sad human state in an ironic and playful way that broke down logical categories without leaving chaos behind. And underlying these and all the lesser shaping spirits was the Greek ideal to which Stevens aspired more and more with each of his revolutions. He, too, wanted to create a mythology of a region, an abstract fiction that explained the worlds of nature and of man. This fiction, animated by feeling and acting figures, would allow belief in something to continue and teach how to live and what to do.

Just as he had found models for behavior and attitude in what he read as an adolescent and as a younger man, so he was equally affected now, though not as obviously. Stevens had already settled into a professional and social role, and in its surface security he could look at himself with greater composure as the actor he had earlier discovered himself to be. In a letter to Elsie during this period, he revealed that he understood the function books served for him: ". . . in a book I escape realities" (WAS 1772). Near the end of April 1906 he picked up on this perception and noted the following in his journal:

There are no end of gnomes that *might* influence people—but do not. When you feel the truth of, say, an epigram, you feel like making it a rule of conduct. But this one is displaced by that, and thus things go on in their accustomed way. There is one pleasure in this volatile morality: the day you believe in chastity, poverty and obedience, you are charmed to discover what a monk you have always been—the monk is suddenly revealed like a spirit in wood; the day you turn Ibsenist, you confess that, after all, you always were an Ibsenist without knowing it. So you come to believe in yourself, and your new creed. There is a perfect rout of characters in every man—and every man is like an actor's trunk, full of strange creatures, new + old. But an actor and his trunk are two different things. (*L* 91; *SP* 166)

This came after an equally long passage about a walk during a "pre-Copernican" twilight that he would have liked to have shared "with some Queen discussing waves and caverns like a noble warrior speaking trifles to a noble lady." He went on to note that her absence prompted this grandiose imagining, that if he had had her, he would have been content with things as they were and would have no need for any of the costumes in the actor's trunk.

This entry disclosed the basis of what later became a major problem in his relationship with Elsie. Only in her absence did he feel the desire that moved his imagination to complete life perfectly. And what his imagination drew from, especially during these formative years, was what he was reading. It was still texts rather than experience that offered him terms for completing reality.

One of the sources Stevens retrospectively realized he had borrowed from in shaping his attitude toward Elsie during their first year was indicated in the above entry as well. Within a few months of their first meeting he had found, "in an East Side shop full of Tolstoy, Gorki, Heine, Ibsen, etc. [at] 1949 Bway,"[11] a copy of Henrik Ibsen's *Pillars of Society*. He noted many passages in both Havelock Ellis's Preface and the play itself that loudly echoed in letters to Elsie as well as in later poems. Ibsen's play unfolds the irony implicit in the notion of the "pillars of society" to show by its end that these pillars are, in fact, tools of society, incapable, as long as they fulfill expectations laid out for them in and by their roles, of any measure of autonomy.

In one of the passages Stevens marked in the Preface, Ellis pointed out that the only possibility for change within the social order rested with women and workmen and that clergymen and others strongly attached to religious systems were the "supreme representatives of [the] conventional morality."[12] These individuals made genuine utterance and uncoerced action impossible. It was not a long way from this to the shift in Stevens's focus which allowed women to join his imagined pantheon. It also seems to have prompted his guiding Elsie to separate herself from the rest of the world and to his being openly negative about Christianity for the first time: "The Christian fears life and loves death" (*SP* 164). He later developed the feelings implicit in such an observation in some of the strongest poems of *Harmonium* ("A High-Toned Old Christian Woman" and "Sunday Morning" are the most obvious instances). But more specifically, in terms of the way his relationship to Elsie evolved, two or three passages he noted both described aspects he recognized in himself and eerily forecast other things that sadly came to pass between them.

In the following quotation from Ibsen's *Ghosts* (which Ellis quoted in his Preface), Stevens seems to have found something close to his spirit; he drew a penciled line along its length in the left margin: "'I almost think,' Mrs. Alving says, 'that we are all of us ghosts, Pastor Manders. It is not only what we have inherited from our fathers and mothers that "walks" in us. It is all sorts of dead ideas and lifeless old beliefs and so forth. They have no reality, but they cling to us all the same, and we can't get rid of them.'"[13] Another passage, prefiguring Stevens's desire "to get out of line"—as he wrote to Elsie just after reading Ibsen—is this bit of dialogue:

> DINA: You don't understand me. What I want is just that they should not be so very proper and moral.
> JOHANN: Indeed? What would you have them then?
> DINA: I would have them natural.[14]

And the lines describing what was to become a sad truth for Stevens and Elsie were also prophetically marked in the margin. Ironically, it was expressed in words that Elsie could have used after they had been married awhile, when the imaginary longing and display that once filled his letters had been replaced by hesitation about their being together continuously for an extended period:

> Now you are frightened. You once loved me you say. Yes, you assured me so often enough, in your letters; and perhaps it was true, too, after a fashion, so long as you were living out there in a great free world that gave you courage to think freely and greatly yourself. You, perhaps, found in me a little more character, and will, and independence than in most people at home here. And then it was a secret between us two; no one could make fun of your bad taste.[15]

Unfortunately the desire and love Stevens expressed to Elsie all through the years of their courtship were replaced by greater and greater psychological and physical distance after their marriage. This showed itself in the letters he wrote to her on the many occasions he found himself traveling to different parts of the country or when he was at home in the apartment in New York and she was back in Reading, staying with her mother. Repeatedly he urged her either to go to Reading when he was about to come back to New York or to stay there longer when he was in New York. He sometimes pressed his point so forcefully that she felt she had been prohibited from coming home, and he had to write back and reassure her that there was a real and generously concerned reason for his wanting her to stay away. Usually either the weather or the apartment's not being quite in order was given as the justification.

In Elsie, Stevens had found someone "at home" in Reading who did not fit the mold, someone he hoped to mold himself. He wanted to provide her both with the wardrobe she needed to inhabit the imaginary world he was creating (in letters he often asked her to be wearing a certain dress, hat, ribbon, or slippers when he arrived to see her on one of the two-day visits that punctuated their five-year courtship) and with books from which she could learn to be, at the same time, the pastoral "Faery" princess and the revolutionary woman of the age. He also urged her, for the longest time, to keep their relationship secret. But after they were married and the secret was revealed, at least one of these roles had to give way. By the time evenings in Walter Arensberg's New York studio became regular occurrences during the early years of the Stevenses' conjugal life, he, the poet, piano-polished in his studied sophistication, must have felt more than a little fear that Elsie might be judged to be evidence of his lapse of taste. Unable to maintain either of the roles assigned her, she had retreated to the more familiar worlds of *Good Housekeeping*[16] and other women's magazines. It was much easier, then, if she went to Reading on another visit "for her health" or to see old friends (he no longer tried, at this point, to separate her from them or that world) while he stayed in New York keeping up contacts with those who now recognized him as a poet—something Elsie came to be at least ambivalent about after feeling betrayed when her husband published some of the poems she thought belonged only to her.

During these years of courtship, as Stevens continued to complete reality with imagination, the roles he designed for Elsie were modified by the various things he read, as they were as well by her responses in letters and when they were together on his periodic visits. And of course, his own feelings went on changing as he persistently kept looking for something that would suffice, something that would sustain him now that he had broken free of his moorings in his familial past. The marked passage in the Preface to Ibsen's play about the ghosts of parents inhabiting their children seemed to reinforce his sense of increasing alienation from his own parents and helped justify his seeing them as "stale" and "boring." But this separation from them was compensated for by his growing attachment to Elsie, though he did not address this directly. His parents obviously wanted him to become one of the pillars of society, and Elsie did not appear to them—at least not to his father[17]—as the suitable complement to this project. As their relationship progressed, Stevens began referring to her family as his own and saw his family less and less; eventually he did not even visit them when he went to Reading. At the final moment, when they married, no one from his family was present. In view of the extreme "solitude" he had created for him and Elsie, the desire to complete his world in imagination became more pressing, and his cries for faith, for something in which to believe, more understandable. This need became far more real, in a practical, everyday way, than what he had begun to experience years before in Cambridge.

ఢ

Stevens continued to review and expand what piqued his interest and offered his spirit temporary resting places. All through 1906 and 1907 he read voraciously. He filled his journal with aphorisms and maxims and with passages from the Greeks:

πάρθενον ἀδύφωνον ("sweet-voiced maiden"); γλύκεια μᾶτερ, οὔτοι δύναμαι κρέκην τὸν ἴστον, πόθῳ δάμεισα παῖδος βραδίναν δι᾽ ᾽Αφροδίταν. ("Sweet mother, I cannot weave my web, broken as I am for longing for a boy, at sweet Aphrodite's will"). (*SP* 168)

An Epicurean motto he copied expressed the ambivalence of his own desire: "ἔχω οὐκ ἔχομαι" ("I hold and am not held") (*SP* 168). There were also illustrations of the use of words from his nosings in the dictionary and comments on various essays and novels. The effects his reading had on him showed themselves in many of these comments and in the remaining excerpts from his letters to Elsie. The choice of his reading and the observations it generated reflected major preoccupations that later became central themes in both his poetry and his life. Expectedly these played on what he later named the greatest problem of his age: the "will to believe." His first inklings of their importance had touched him during his Harvard years. They now became constant scrapings of his spirit.

Out of these concerns emerged certain oppositions that reinforced his deepest sense of himself as moving forever up and down between imagination and reality. He found the same oppositions in those he read as he attempted to understand his uneasiness. The only comfort he could find through their lines was the shimmering picture of the ideal world of the Greeks. In his imagination he traced the way Christianity's development had moved the West farther and farther away from the trembling unity between beauty and goodness, καλοκἀγαθία, a virtue that could be cultivated only by a society that accepted physical, sensuous enjoyment. But there were one or two things missing from the Greek world for Stevens: "stockings and slippers," the tantalizing symbols of his own desire bred out of his "decadent" age:

. . . flute, a cup, a maid—there's a Greek idyll. One likes Anacreon for his roses, too—and gloomy grasshoppers. His maidens seem to have been about sixteen, whereas those of Horace seem to have been in the early twenties. Speaking of this (and it is a subtle matter) one cannot help observing that stockings and slippers are sadly missing from Greek and Roman poetry. Undoubtedly, stockings belong properly only to a decadent age. (*SP* 162)

In this short passage Stevens disclosed how intensely he had come to live in an imagined world. He completed *it* with elements of reality rather than

241

completing reality with elements of imagination. While he got Elsie to wear "slippers and stockings" in colors that teased his delight, to make reality approach a little more closely his imagination's paradise, to bring the rest of the world quite round required much more demanding manipulation. At the very least he had to clear from his consciousness the elements obscuring this dream. But he knew he could not do this without satisfying his intellect. He had already learned that imagination ungrounded in the particularities of reasoned experience was mere fancy, which led, at best, to art for art's sake. While still at Harvard, he had understood this to be "useless." Over the next few years his pattern of reading drew him deeper beneath the surface of the elements he now began to see as responsible for the fall away from the classical ideal.

Matthew Arnold, Goethe, and Schopenhauer had provided the groundwork for his present state of mind. But it was, again, lesser, contemporary figures that gave Stevens particular directions. These he followed to set the stage for his projected masque where he, as the Comedian par excellence, occupied a place in his poetic pantheon together with the other major actors, those he recognized as "man-poets." Among these lesser figures, two of the most important were Paul Elmer More and G. Lowes Dickinson. (Others included Arthur Symons and James Gibbons Huneker [SP 163].) Dickinson had been recommended to him by Russell Loines, his old acquaintance from Harvard. Loines had recently made a trip to Greece. (Stevens had been particularly struck by Loines's memory of the "eagles at Delphi" [SP 163]. This image seems to have contributed to Stevens's later image of crows—his version of the birds of Apollo—covering the face of the moon in "Red Loves Kit" [OP 31]). Loines's actually having visited places Stevens dreamed of inhabiting gave his recommendation to read Dickinson the hidden weight of passion at least imaginatively indulged.

In Dickinson's composite essay, intriguingly entitled "Letters from John Chinaman,"[18] written from the point of view of a fictionalized Oriental "everyman," Stevens found both precise descriptions of the ills of Western civilization that pained him and descriptions of Eastern alternatives that, in expressing the Confucian ideal, which revealed sources for the Greeks as well, suggested that the East, not the West, preserved the ethical basis of the classical world. Dickinson blamed Christianity for the decay of this ideal in the West because it stressed not the relation of man to his world—Stevens's later definition of poetry (OP 172)—here specified by Dickinson as the focus of Confucianism[19], but the projected relation of man to a world hereafter. One of the consequences of this difference, which Stevens noted in his journal, was that Christianity, unlike Confucianism, had much "less influence on society" (SP 163) since in reality, it did not have a practical purpose. Dickinson outlined the reasons for this in his essay.[20]

In building his argument and indicating another difference resulting from this opposition of aims, Dickinson reinforced his point with a description that must have made Stevens prickle in recognition. Showing how Christianity, in having a future rather than a present reality as its ground, affects the primary social unity of the family, Dickinson painted the following portrait:

> —To you, so far as a foreigner can perceive, the family is merely a means for nourishing and protecting the child until he is of age to look after himself. As early as may be, you send your boys away to boarding school, where they quickly emancipate themselves from the influences of their home. As soon as they are of age, you send them out, as you say, "to make their fortune. . . ." [N]o one is tied, also no one is rooted. Your society, to use your own words, is "progressive"; you are always "moving on." Everyone feels it a duty . . . to strike out a new line for himself. To remain in the position in which you were born you consider a disgrace; a man, to be a man, must venture, struggle, compete and win.[21]

Dickinson described in frighteningly specific detail the ethic so well illustrated and repeatedly voiced by Stevens's father. Garrett, Sr., followed this way in his own life and preached it in the form of advice. This had resulted in Stevens's giving up his dream of going abroad; he remained in New York "to make his fortune." In light of this, it is not at all surprising that just over two weeks after reading this, and prompted more immediately by reading something of an entirely different sort, Honoré de Balzac's *Le Peau de Chagrin*, Stevens indulged in a particularly violent suicidal fantasy that slowly slid into murderous wishes toward certain vaguely defined others:

> April 22.
> "Où trouverez-vous, dans l'océan des littératures, un livre surnageant qui puisse lutter de génie avec cet entrefilet:
> "Hier, à quatre heures, une jeune femme s'est jetée dans la Seine du haut du pont des Arts."* *Le Peau de Chagrin,* Balzac.
>
> Somehow, in this season, I like to get my pipe going well, and meditate on suicide. It is a splendid melancholy, and, mixed with a little beer and whiskey—divine. If only one could look in at the window when they found one's body—one's blood and brains all over the pillow. How terrible the simple books would look,—and the chairs and the curtains so carefully drawn! How empty, for a moment, the lawns would seem,—the Sunday twittering of the birds! How impotent all the people! Such a death is a death to everything—Then one would tap on the window and laugh and say, "It's all a mistake. Let me come in again. I know how foolish it all is. But what is one to do?"
> There's a robin's nest nearby and at twilight the trees are full of music.—There are three women I know—one in gray, one in purple, and one in green. I wish I could bury them all during the afternoon, and, after tea,

---

* "Where will you find, in the sea of literature, a book that can rival in genius a news-item such as: "Yesterday, at four o'clock, a young woman threw herself into the Seine from the Pont des Arts."

listen to the robin again. . . . [The entry in its present state continues at this point] are one: and one must begin to live out a certain, definite life. The horror of it is to be able to see the end of that life. That takes away all desire to live it. A clerk ends as a clerk—and so on. In ignorance of this plain destiny, a clerk, too often, imagines marvels for his old age, or even has some hallucination that supports a present pimp. At least, romantic clerks do. What a bore it would be not to!

Finally (for today) my opinions generally change even while I am in the act of expressing them. So it seems to me and so, perhaps, everyone thinks of himself. The words for an idea too often dissolve it and leave a strange one.

Has there ever been an image of vice as a serpent coiled round the limbs and body of a woman, with its fangs in her pale flesh, sucking her blood? Or coiled round the limbs and body of a man? Fancy the whole body fainting, in the distorting grip, the fangs in her neck—the victim's mouth fallen open with weakness, the eyes half-closed. Then the serpent triumphing, horrible with power, gulping, glistening. (SP 164–65)

Though he blamed the season, as elsewhere the city, for his mood rather than examine the particulars of his internal life, it was, he knew, these particulars that disturbed him. He was haunted by the horror of being able to see to the end of his life as a "money-making lawyer." How could he go on separated from the real value of life as taught by Confucius and now voiced again by Dickinson: existing in the harmonious contemplation of one's relationship to nature. To bring his point home, Dickinson repeatedly stressed the contrast between his Oriental everyman, who had "both the instinct and the opportunity to appreciate the gifts of Nature, to cultivate manners, and to enter into humane and disinterested relations with his fellows," and his Western counterpart, "isolated" in "a civilization which [had] manners so coarse, morals so low, and an appearance [as] unlovely as those in great [Western] cities."[22]

Stevens could not know his future would prove that even in conditions such as these he could integrate the contemplative attitude as well as teach it to others through his work. So, as he read Dickinson's description of the function and purpose of Oriental poets, he naturally despaired and resorted, in his suicidal fantasy, to a maturer version of the wish of a child who feels wronged by his parents: "They'll be sorry if I die." Here, like the child, Stevens wanted to punish the unnamed discoverers of his body with his unhappy end and have the satisfaction of seeing their suffering.

At this moment of macabre wish playing, Stevens completed another turn around the circle of associations that combined his childhood memory of painting the streetlamp with later experiences that contributed to "Disillusionment of Ten O'Clock." Here the ghostly women that dance in the poem in their gray, purple, and green appear almost as witnesses to his wished act. Years later, as he directed their performance through his poem's lines, it was as though in controlling them, he transformed his Erinyes—punishing his imagined murder in the following lines of the entry—into Eumenides. When we look further at this entry, which recorded his quick changes of opinions and how he perceived the words for an idea dissolving it and leaving a strange one, we can begin to see how directly connected these raw elements of experience were to the later poetic images of flitting metamorphoses.

Picking up the thread of violent impulse and shifting it to a direct attack on others, Stevens found another image that appeared years later. As Holly Stevens notes, the serpent in "The Auroras of Autumn" (*CP* 411) seems to have slithered out of this youthfully mournful moment of despair. The poetic transformation lacks the open murderousness of this early imagining but poses a central question about the nature and function of the serpent's image. The question surrounds the problem of evil connected with Christian belief. This was being raised for Stevens now both in what Dickinson wrote and in the essays of Paul Elmer More, which he began reading just a few days later (*SP* 164, April 9).

Unlike his response to Dickinson, Stevens was at first put off by More. Yet he remained preoccupied with him for at least the next two and a half years. Trying to understand him properly during this period, he diligently followed up on references More made in his writing. This involved him intimately with Christianity and religion. In an essay entitled "Tolstoy; Or The Ancient Feud Between Philosophy and Art,"[24] a subheading that certainly would have enticed Stevens, More referred repeatedly to Thomas à Kempis's *Imitation of Christ*. By early September Stevens was reading Thomas himself. He warmly noted two of his directives in his journal: "Read such things as may rather yield compunction to thy heart, than occupation to thy head" (*SP* 171); "The noble love of Jesus impels a man to do great things, stirs him up to be always longing for what is more perfect" (*SP* 171).

Stevens's interest in Christianity and in Christ did not stop here. By early 1907 he was reading the Psalms and Proverbs. In the case of the latter he followed a method of reading suggested by a newspaper item he clipped and saved. The advice promised the good reader that if he read one of Proverbs' thirty-one chapters every day, at the end of a month he would "be surprised to find how many problems of right and wrong [would] have been solved for [him]."[23] Stevens was trying to understand Christian doctrine by enacting Christian practice.

By March 1909, he was reading a life of Jesus (*SP* 214–15), and by May, after completing Dante's *Vita Nuova* (also referred to by More in the essay referred to above), he was reading the entire New Testament and still considering "the growth of our Western religion" (*SP* 220). He meditated particularly on how and why the Catholic Church made "so much of the Virgin" (*SP* 223–24). By this time Stevens had come to appreciate More. He had followed More's reading and had gone through other of his essays as well and even expanded his understanding with expressions of different thinkers' perceptions of religion. These ranged from Pythagoras' pre-Christian mystical approach (*SP* 170–71) to Élie Metchnikoff's contemporary theoretical exploration, focusing on the connections between religion and death (*SP* 184). Stevens thus broadened More's conceits and found in them resting places to which he constantly returned. They were like the particulates of a solution he attempted in mixing the elements he found in various writers he read. These points became central preoccupations. In the broadest and simplest terms, they were the feminine principle and the ideas of the East.

The feminine principle had long roots in Stevens's experience, which began in his early association of imagination with his mother. Tapping into these roots and running through them were the ideas of Goethe and Dante, two "man-poets" who achieved perfect apotheoses of the eternal female. Counterbalancing and stabilizing this principle was Stevens's deepening interest in the East. While in the West the preoccupation with the feminine virtues had been sweetly shaped into the Virgin, who evoked sentimental responses that even in their most secularized expressions were pathetic fallacies, in the East the same idea remained unattached to a particular form and so abstractly permeated all aspects of attitude and behavior. Over the years Stevens derived a great deal from cultivating this attitude and imitating this behavior. In the present, as he read More's *Century of Indian Epigrams* (a translation from the Sanskrit of Bhartrihari, which More published in 1898) and additional descriptions of the life and history of the East—like Kakuzo Okakura's *Ideals of the East* (1903)—he picked up certain ways of looking, which he quickly translated into his own in his journals and in some of the perceptions he expressed in letters to Elsie. These habits of mind were not entirely new to him. They had affected the thoughts of many from whom he had learned at Harvard. And in their essence they were very close to the ethic Matthew Arnold described as the Hellenic ideal, which Stevens knew very well.

Some of the most characteristic features of the Oriental attitude that made a lasting difference for Stevens were particularly highlighted by More. About Easterners' basic belief in the transitory illusiveness of human endeavor, More noted that the history of the world, no less than the individual's attempt to understand his or her place in nature, was really nothing "more than a desire of the imagination," something both the Greeks and the Hindus knew.[25] It was not far from this to Stevens's perception of imagination's function as a "completion of life" and to his tying imagination inextricably to desire. More also noted how in the decline of the classical world Plato and the philosophers following him attempted with only the "skeleton of logic" to fix the transitory and that this was an error.[26] In his "Adagia," Stevens responded to this, borrowing More's term: "Aristotle is a skeleton" (*OP* 168). At the same time, in his late theoretical essays (in "The Figure of the Youth as Virile Poet" and in "A Collect of Philosophy" [*OP* 183]), Stevens reexpressed More's argument for the primacy of art over philosophy, thus effectively reversing Plato's position.

Loudly echoing Arnold and extolling the chief Oriental virtue, More focused on contemplation, the nonprogressive, nonutilitarian way, and repeatedly illustrated its application. One of his most effective metaphors paralleled the "texture of art," the product of contemplation, to "the clouds that drift across the sky, veiling the effulgence of the sun and spreading an ever variable canopy of splendour between us and the unfathomed abyss."[27] Later, in "Sea Surface Full of Clouds" (*CP* 98), Stevens used the same metaphor and, through it, added to his personal experience of what happened "In that November off Tehuantepec," when his only child was conceived,[28] the aesthetic level that most have seen as the poem's only subject.

Another contribution to Stevens's understanding his relation to the world was More's tracing of the stages through which Western civilization passed on its journey from the East. He indicated how Christianity's idealization of the eternal feminine extended Plato's eschewing of the senses. He noted the particular moments and places when and where this deliberate ignorance was reinforced: in Pope Leo III's eighth-century iconoclasm and again in the Protestant Reformation, which became institutionalized and nationalized through American Puritanism.[29] More distinguished the features of a face turned only to an unattainable future and described a situation which Stevens himself had experienced and from which he turned away to try to face again the pagan ideal: "Christianity . . . produced its own legitimate form of art, different utterly from the brave parade of paganism, yet not without its justification. The artist did not seek for pure beauty, for that intimate harmony of sense and spirit which had been the ideal of Greece; matter [was] now constrained to express humility, the ascetic disdain, the spiritual aspiration and loneliness of the soul."[30]

Stevens had for a long time enforced, albeit with lapses, his own period of asceticism, his solitude. He was now receptive to understanding and going beyond the sources that had contributed to its making. He began exploring his limits and quietly prepared to display his own muzzy belly in the parade of his argument against religion that—particularly in "A High-Toned Old Christian Woman"—echoed what More described as "The Feud Between Philosophy and Art." In other later poems, like "Sunday Morning" and "Peter Quince at the Clavier," he dealt specifically with sensuous versus nonsensuous experience centered on woman and desire. "Le Monocle de Mon Oncle" and the celebratory tone of the whole of *Harmonium* were informed by Stevens's need to return to a way of perceiving reality that expressed what the mythology of the Greeks—"the greatest piece of fiction" (*OP* 178)—had expressed.

More's effect on the young poet—and the reason he at first reacted so strongly against him—resulted from how precisely he described the conflict Stevens was experiencing. The following passage, relating the parable current among the Greeks of Hercules' having to choose between two women representing virtue and pleasure, seemed to be directly addressed to him: ". . . the fable might be applied without much distortion to many an ardent young man who in his youth goes out into the solitude to meditate on the paths of ambition;—his choice lying not between virtue and pleasure, but between the philosophic and the imaginative life."[31] Stevens knew how difficult it had been and continued to be for him to indulge fully in the pleasures of the imaginative life. He had chosen a practical path, but he soon discovered that it could not satisfy his "instinct of joy" (L 296).[32] He had to find a way of filling this need. And he wanted it to be more than an exercise in "fancy" that would end in producing only the impressionism of art for art's sake. To do this while preserving the purity of his ascetic side meant he had to combine the philosophic and meditative aspects. But this was an aspiration More suggested to be vain for anyone in Western society. At precisely the moment when Stevens was reaching the climax of his own crisis of faith and wishing more than anything for something in which to believe—at best, his own possibility—he did not want to acknowledge that what he wanted might be an *im*possibility.

Though More painted this rather dismal picture, he nonetheless called for "a man of sufficient insight to present to the world a new and adequate ideal of the beautiful" and indicated that there was a model and an existing ethos that would, if followed, help this man to develop. These were Buddha and Buddhism. The followers of Christ disdained the beauty of the here and now and made of reality a vale of tears. In contrast, ". . . the doctrine of Buddha . . . is one of unspeakable gladness. . . . Only a reader familiar with the Buddhist books can have any notion of the overwhelming spirit of gladness and simple charity that pervades them."[33]

By the time Stevens came to accept More's thought, he had already begun exploring Oriental texts and practicing their opposing law. But he knew, too, that in order to make this knowledge available, he had to express it in a manner that was palatable to a Western audience. He continued reading in Western literature, familiarized himself with contemporary British and French periodicals, and kept up with current poetry. He noted lines and passages that voiced the thoughts and feelings he was coming to identify with the Eastern spirit. He also became more interested in knowing about the lives of figures important to him. During 1908 and 1909 he read James Boswell's *Life of Johnson,* John Keats's *Letters,* a life of Shakespeare, Arnold's *Notebooks,* as well as Herbert W. Paul's study of Arnold's life and work. In each of these volumes (now part of the Wallace Stevens Collection at the Huntington Library), he marked passages where he found either some aspect of himself reflected or some aspect of the other writer that he wanted to imitate in order to find a style, a manner to follow so as to be able to live his life and to set down in his work a practicable and sustaining ethic.

&

As Stevens was voyaging through both familiar and strange seas of thought, discovering himself in this intimate dialogue with his studious ghosts, his external life continued fairly regularly. His visits to Reading went on, though somewhat more frequently under pressure from Elsie (in her notebook Elsie observed that in October 1906 Stevens promised to come and see her once a month [WAS 1772]). And in spite of the failure of his partnership with Lyman Ward and finding himself out of work a few more times before finally securing the position with the American Bonding Company in January 1908 that, because of the professional contacts he established, ensured his permanent employment thereafter, these transitions bothered him less than the changes in his spirit that were occasioned by what he read, what he wrote, and what he wanted to write. In September 1906, after losing his job at the office where he found himself sometimes "engaged all day . . . on a sonnet—surreptitiously" (*L* 92; *SP* 170), he simply noted, "Out of work" (*L* 93; *SP* 171). After finding a new position during the first week in October (in the process of attempting to start something on his own, without a partner) and after finally moving back to New York (to Fordham Heights), he visited Cambridge once again to renew his acquaintance with things there, just as he had years earlier after similar changes in his external circumstances. There one of the things he remarked on was riding in an automobile. Its newness heralded the "new arrangement" of his life: "new office, new rooms—everything new" (*SP* 171). What he observed with marked concern, however, were his mind's movements nearer and farther from the center he sought. By the beginning of December he resented his new job's demands on his time and attention. He recorded his uneasiness and expressed the fear that he would not become the poet he dreamed of becoming:

> December 5th
> I am afraid to review the last two months. They seem to have changed me—I no longer read, and no longer think. The brain is like a worm that tunnels its way through everything—and leaves everything crumbling behind. Busy with many things—that's it—I'm *busy*. A walk now and then, a little music, a few pages, a trip home at Thanksgiving time—there's no Iliad in that. I feel strenuous, not lyrical. (*L* 93; *SP* 171)

By the beginning of January 1907 he made his feelings about the outside world explicit: "There's so little in reality." When he looked at the George Washington Bridge, instead of seeing it as an example of modern technology, he saw it as "Roman and wonderful" (*SP* 171). When he dined out, instead of commenting on the substance of what he ate, he fixed on its appearance: "very Fragonard" (*SP* 171). The only element of reality that entered was another aspect of his internal world, his feeling about his body, "that monster": "My tongue felt as large as a bull's" (*SP* 172).

As he lived more actively in his imagination, he gave almost all his attention to completing its landscape in his letters to Elsie. After the end of January these almost entirely "usurped" (*SP* 171) his journal. The shift reflected a growing need to feel his imagination's power responded to by at least one other. In his journal he might express all he liked, but it was essentially in "mute feeling." But Elsie reacted positively to the poet in him and, more, participated in the masque he was creating. She became, in turn, his "prin-

cesse de lointaine," the shepherdess of his spirit, his "Bo," and the Virgin
Queen before whom he, as jongleur wearing "cap and bells," tossed his words
like saucers high in the air. She was for the moment the one reader he
needed—"One does not write for any reader except one." He composed for her
poems that were parts of the first books he imagined; the "Songs for Elsie"
and the "June Books" collected for her birthdays were prototypes of final
shapes he desired. In addition, she offered him her spirit to be fashioned. As
the months passed into years, he transformed caresses he would have given her
were they together into the music his imagination's fingers played. He sent
her volumes of others' poems and recommended texts that would make her
respond to him more easily.

The excerpts and complete letters from this period trace the turns of his
spirit as it followed the various things he read. Around the time he was
occupied with the Proverbs, he included the following in a letter: "Whoso
keepeth the fig tree shall eat the fruit thereof: so he that waiteth on his master
shall be honored" (WAS 1772). And if not quoting from Proverbs directly, he
borrowed their form to express his early attempts at writing aphorisms: "Love
is a burden, like anything else; but a burden not to be cast off, but to be
carried gently" (WAS 1772); "Kindness is death to tragedy and all the elements of tragedy" (WAS 1772); "Respect breeds respect, desire breeds desire,
affection breeds affection, goodness breeds goodness" (WAS 1772). While
reading the New Testament, he used a reference to it to describe one of his
states of mind and his appreciation of Elsie: "—but sometimes when I am in a
haughty humor, the parable of the sower that sowed on barren ground repeats
itself to me, and in my gorgeous pride I cease to sow. But one seed must have
fallen on good ground for your last letter was like fruit in a wilderness" (WAS
1772).

During the beginning of March 1907 both his experience in reality and
his imaginative excursions in letters to Elsie reflected his reading a particular
volume, *Holiday and Other Poems* by John Davidson.[34] Later, in "The Snow
Man," in "Thirteen Ways," and in various associations of the image of the
"rock" and references to "fact," Stevens's rubbing against Davidson's spirit
showed itself again. He also found in Davidson's thoughts "On Poetry" some
ideas he recast as his own. The day Stevens began perusing Davidson's volume, it was snowing, making it seem like evening all afternoon. The lines
describing

> Trees of winter's nakedness aware
> Gleamed and disappeared like things afraid
> Dryads of the terraces and the square
> Silvery in the shadow and the shade[35]

stayed with him as he went out walking up the Bronx River to the Hemlock
Forest, "a huge clump of green and white [where he] stopped under an oak
still covered with dead leaves and noticed a whispering noise as the snow fell

on the leaves. And it was so quiet and lovely there" (*SP* 173). There the "snow man," hearing "the sound of a few leaves" (*CP* 10), began to be.

A few pages farther on in Davidson's volume, part of a short verse play appropriately titled "The Ides of March"—the time of the year Stevens approached himself—described

> The blackbird, he who sings
> At the top of his voice at once
> While the startled woodland rings:
>
> He peals his splendid song
> Loud and fluent and clear.
> For echo to prolong
> And all the world to hear.[36]

Transforming part of this pantomime into his own, Stevens on his walk noticed different birds in the greenhouses near the forest. They had built their nests under the dome above the tops of large palms. Like them, much later, building his nest of poems in the palm at the end of the mind, he recalled this experience, placing his own blackbird in a snowy landscape, prolonging his inflection into the echo of innuendo.

Similarly, fixing on Davidson's "No phantoms; facts: for facts I grieve/Authentic things that dreams abhor,"[37] Stevens drew this comparison for Elsie: "Facts are like flies in a room. They buzz and buzz and bother" (*L* 94). Near the end of his life, still bothered by these facts, he called for the ultimate poem in the language of fact, but fact not realized before (*OP* 164). Davidson also set up what became an important contrast for Stevens between

> Ancient snows
> About the poles [that] renew their sleep

and

> Ink to etch the rock
> Ethereal lye to blanch the snow.[38]

Stevens later used his own ink to blanch the snow, symbol of nature's cold dominion.

Stevens read Davidson's lines just before he observed to Elsie, in the same letter in which he described "facts," that he was "not in the least religious." He noted that he preferred feeling himself a god in nature to being simply a man in church, though he still said his prayers every night, "a habit: half-unconscious" (*L* 96; *SP* 174). This voicing of his antireligiousness followed his expressing that he had felt almost "insane" (*L* 96; *SP* 174) after that snowy afternoon's ramble first through nature as it was and then through the other season it was made to seem in the greenhouses. The feeling of insanity corresponded to the contradiction between being and seeming he described in his behavior vis-à-vis religion: He was not in the least religious, yet he prayed every night. He had reached the climax of his crisis of faith. Just over a month later he threw out his Bible: "I hate the look of a Bible. This one was given to me for going to Sunday School every Sunday in a certain year. I'm glad the silly thing is gone" (L 102; SP 177). It was only after the crisis, completed by this symbolic action, that he read the New Testament and the life of Jesus. He had separated himself from the herd and could, therefore, consider Christianity and the life of Christ in the same way he regarded the relation of Keats's poems and his life, Shakespeare's plays and his life, or the *Rambler* and Samuel Johnson's life, in all of which he also immersed himself during the same period.

Stevens's personal secularization was further strengthened on poetic ground by Davidson's observation that "Poetry is matter become vocal, a blind force without judgment." He illustrated this by noting that "Milton under[took] to justify the way of God to man in 'Paradise Lost.' [And that though he] may have done so in terms of his theology . . . that [was] not the point of his epic; the poetry of it [was] the love of Adam and Eve, and the rebellion of Satan."[39] In pointing out that Milton's power came from dealing with the irrational element of human experience, Davidson's perception helped Stevens clarify his thoughts on the true subject of poetry. Understanding how this was true for Milton gave Stevens the support he needed to attack the bases of Christian theology. This he did later in "Le Monocle de Mon Oncle" and in "Peter Quince at the Clavier," in which he evoked the erotic impulse, the irrational element, in the sounds and rhythms of the words themselves—"matter become vocal." The irrational element dominated the restraints imposed on it by religion and tradition. It showed those rationalized controls to be the source of evil, just as the elders watching Susanna, not she, created the sin. Stevens's preoccupation with religion and the problem of evil, which he had begun to explore in his journal a few months before, continued to direct his search through others' writing until he found at least a personal solution for how to live, what to do.

As Stevens cut the last of his emotional ties to the Christian myth, he indulged more freely in other imagined worlds and experimented without hesitation and without the admonitions that used to follow these indulgences. At the same moment he defined the play he envisioned for his life as a comedy and attempted to transform his earlier misanthropy into tolerance:

April 7 [1907].

One of my maladies is to rub the freshness off things and then to say— "So, how commonplace they really are!" But the freshness was not commonplace.

I must be gallant. One loses too much in going under the surface. Besides, it is all what one imagines, there. Take a lacquered cheek—why not let it go at that?

I must think well of people. After all, they are only people—The conventions are the arts of living. People know. I am not the only wise man.—
Or if I cannot think well, let me hide my thoughts.—It is of no consequence to explain or to assert one's self.—Nice people are nice.—It's a sore
delight to insist on the tragedy.—Life is not important.—At least let's have
it agreeable. (*SP* 175—76)

Of the things he was reading, Boswell's *Johnson* provided him with a most
fitting model for his new attitude. Throughout his three-volume edition (now
at the Huntington Library), Stevens marked passages illustrating how Johnson
saw beneath the surface of things without losing "freshness" by using his wit
and imagination to transform whatever was commonplace into comedy.
Johnson also offered Stevens a model for personal style. Like Stevens, he was a
big man, a kind of "monster," yet he displayed a delicate, fastidious sensibility. Johnson had a passion for tea. He carefully noted its effects and aspects of its blending. Stevens marked these passages in his volumes. Stevens,
too, eventually became a specialist on teas. He detailed not only its substantial
qualities but the permutations of its colors against Chinese porcelain cups.[40]
By the time he became a prosperous, bustling lawyer, he sent requests for the
rarest blends to growers and exporters in tiny towns in China and India, and
religiously observed his three o'clock tea ritual at the office.[41] Like Johnson,
Stevens was shy. Johnson counteracted his reticence in groups with piercing
observations voiced as quietly sparkling asides that nonetheless easily offended
those who did not understand the comic spirit behind them. This same quality was well noted years later by those closest to Stevens at the Hartford
Accident and Indemnity Company.[42]

Following his literary models helped Stevens cross the meridian of his religious crisis. Once he was on the other side, his uncertainty and hesitation
were replaced, for a while at least, by inquisitiveness and an almost childlike
expression of his excitement. He shared this new spirit with Elsie and showed
himself to her more and more as their "starry *connaissance*" moved closer to a
lifetime commitment. Before this point, in spring of 1907, he had, in his
letters, projected onto her his own ambivalences and accompanying resolutions
to be virtuous. These took the form of pleas for her constancy and rationalizations for her complete devotion. He voiced them both as descriptions of feeling and as prescriptions for behavior. But after this temporary easing of his
deepest moral conflict he focused on laying himself bare and addressed her
much more as an equal. The mental energy that had gone into shaping moral
directives was now channeled almost entirely into creating the fictional world
he wanted to inhabit with her.

From the end of 1905 through the beginning of 1907 Stevens had stressed
how important exclusivity was to their relationship. He had punctuated these
observations with improvised descriptions of the kind of behavior Elsie had to

cultivate in order to ensure the "secret" bond between them. This "secret" rested on a spiritual identity Stevens postulated for them. The following excerpts illustrate this perfectly:

I realize I have a second self in you. . . .

You are infinitely more a part of me than my family or than any friend I have ever had. So that you must be constant.

Aren't we happiest of all when we identify ourselves so that we live and think for each other? You are all that I have. If I could say to myself, "Elsie will stand by me always."

Judge me by yourself: we are too much alike for that test to fail. We could not be more alike if we were brother and sister.

Sometimes it seemed to me as if I were the only person in the world who really knew you.

—makes me want to stand between you and everyone else—I want to be the only person who knows what you really like and think and are. Then you would be my Elsie in reality and alone.

Just to have written last night was like recovering a part of myself that had been lost for a little. Do you realize how much a part of each other we have become?

Let us have faith together in the maxim that there is no good thing to be had without effort, without pain.

—and I should wish you to be as wise as you are good.

—for already you act the woman's part when you give comfort, and that is just what you do now.

I want you so much to desire to be good, that is the main thing. I don't mean religious or priggish—but kind, patient, unselfish. To be good, that's just what I want to be more than anything else.

What makes one worthy is goodness and kindness: "Be good to yourself; be kind to others—but be kindest of all to me."

You and I can have each other—if we must desire, do not let us desire other men and women,—but pictures and chateaus (sic) and honors and other desireable [sic] but unnecessary things.

If you had asked for the deepest pit we could dig for ourselves I should have said that it was feeling free to do as we like.

Each time we get a hair's breath [sic] apart we come closer together than ever before; and so it may be that your occasional defiances are only tricks that Nature plays on us—and so with my mistakes.

I wish no one knew about us. That would make it infinitely sweeter.

I trust you and have trusted you always—from the beginning because you understand instinctively that conduct, good or bad, is the source of happiness or unhappiness.

Peace is what you want, not pleasure; and peace is a matter of conduct.

Perhaps love is not so much adoration as understanding and being faithful nevertheless. (All the above are from WAS 1772)

But during the spring of 1907 Stevens broke through the restraints of religion and tradition. He had thrown away his Bible and now approached a starker, barer self. At the same time, one of his wisdom teeth was also breaking one of the physical limits of his being (WAS 1772). This was an accidental accompanying prod to the change he was experiencing. But there had been something else, too, that had forced him to forge his way through other kinds of limits. The letter excerpts from 1906 suggest that Elsie had begun reacting forcefully to what Stevens had been expressing. She no longer voiced dissatisfaction in terms found ready-made from her family or her circle but in terms that directly addressed her suitor and the reality of their relationship. Though there had been indications earlier of Elsie's remarking on the faults of her lover's nature that showed this eruption to be brewing—revealed in Stevens's apologetic explanations that he was one being on paper and another in reality (*L* 80) and in his promise to attempt being earnest (WAS 1772)—during 1906 she reacted repeatedly and specifically against what she now named as "criticism" of her. Stevens responded: "It is painful for me to think that you fear I am criticizing you. And why should you not satisfy me? If there were anything to criticize I hope you would find me true enough to defend you, rather than criticize you. My criticizms [*sic*] are only grotesque amusement to me.—They are instinct, no more" (WAS 1772).

Elsie felt he had been intruding. He answered: "Surely, I am falling into bad habits when I go peeping into forbidden doors, and tomorrow, and all tomorrows are forbidden doors" (WAS 1772). Before coming to the point of beginning his self-examination, by which he implicitly acknowledged the justifiability of her reactions, he attempted to soothe her both by admitting his transgression, as above, and, at least in one instance, by relating, rather insensitively, a description of other young women who pleased him and to whom he compared her: "Tonight I took dinner downtown. There were twelve people—four of them girls not much older than you. They played and sang and were pretty and had pretty manners. They were all rich. They satisfied me, the way you mean; but they are not different from you. They have only had a great deal more experience. At heart each one is so simple and personal as you" (WAS 1772). He followed this by again trying to ensure their identity, the base he had established for their relationship. In response to her having begun to declare her autonomy, her difference from him, he urged, "Let us be ourselves and not study contrasts." Nonetheless, he recognized the reality of one of the hesitations she had about the future life he envisioned: "I know perfectly well that to live in town would be a cruel disillusion to you" (WAS 1772).

Her reactions through 1906 coincided with his cutting himself off from his religious roots. During the next two years he attempted to bring her and the world he wanted to inhabit with her around. He tried to soothe her by stripping away the façade of certainty and authority he had until now maintained. He shaped the image of their future world by alternately pointing out the demands of reality, which would for some time mean that she would have to "live in town," and distracting attention from this necessity by describing in more and more detail the imaginary world where she was his "Bo" (the nickname he found for her, an abbreviation of Bo-Peep), his "Faery" Queen, and he was, variously, her sheep, pastoral companion, jongleur. But the only possibility for both of them truly to find a new world on wholly equal terms where she would not have somehow to conform to these necessities would have meant going off somewhere, away from the expectations built into the role of a "money-making lawyer." He had not been able to escape this role at twenty-one, and he could not do it now, though the idea of running away enticed him as much now as it did then: "Don't you like the idea of people who give up everything wildly, as Sylvia and Hilton [acquaintances] did? Instead of hanging on to dreary safety, they take a tremendous flight. That seems to be the New York idea. I'm glad some people do it though I shouldn't do it myself—nor recommend it" (WAS 1772).

Breaking the invisible thread of outworn religious belief was one thing. Having done that, he felt spiritually adrift. He had nothing on which to rely. It was too much to consider tearing up the costumes that were the only things that allowed those who had reared him to recognize him at all. Yet he realized that the kind of Laurentian dream of a man and a woman's complementarily forging a life sufficient to themselves demanded just that kind of rending. Only in such conditions could imagination and reality come together, imagination actively shaping the raw material of a new, common reality. Stevens's awareness of this had begun three years earlier, when he had noted expressions and illustrations of it in Ibsen's *Pillars of Society*. But he already felt the weight of society pressing down on him. Having been so well molded to the shape necessary to support it, he feared having no shape at all, being "no man" without his function. So, in April 1907, when he read Paul Bourget's *Une Idylle Tragique* and copied out in his journal the following passage reinforcing Ibsen's perception, he noted his rejection of it in his parenthetical closing remark:

April 23rd

Paul Bourget in "Une Idylle Tragique," p. 65—Je me dis: Il n'y qu'une chose de vraie ici-bas, s'assouvir le coeur, sentir et aller jusqu'au bout de tous ses sentiments, désirer et aller jusqu'au bout de tous ses désirs; vivre enfin sa

vie à soi, sa vie sincère, en dehors de tous les mensonges et de toutes les conventions, avant de sombrer dans l'inévitable néant.
("farouche nihilisme").* (SP 178)

Only years later, secure in his words and gray flannel suit would he admit his fear and finally dissolve into it, though only in imagination, in "The Snow Man"—*this no man.*

As though unconsciously attempting to ensure that this full break, which would mean real freedom for both of them, could never come to pass, precisely at the moment he cut his religious ties he strongly encouraged Elsie to bind herself. In this way she would become the check his father and family had been. In the same letter in which he announced himself to be antireligious, one of the first letters of spring 1907, when he began showing his inner self to her, he wrote:

I have never told you what I believe. There are so many things to think of. I don't care whether the churches are all alike or whether they're right or wrong. It is not important. The very fact that they take care of A.T.'s [a friend of Elsie's] "stupid" people is an exquisite device. It is undoubtedly true that they do not "influence" any but the "stupid." But they are beautiful and full of comfort and mental help. One can get a thousand benefits from churches that one cannot get outside of them. They purify a man, they soften Life. Please don't listen to A.T., or, at least, don't argue with her. Don't care about the Truth. There are other things in Life besides the Truth upon which everybody of any experience agrees, while no two people agree about the Truth. I'd rather see you going to church than to know you were as wise as Plato and [Ernst] Haeckel rolled into one; and I'd rather sing some old chestnut out of a hymn-book with you, surrounded by "stupid" people, than listen to all the wise men in the world. It has always been a particular desire of mine to have you join church; and I am very, very glad to know that you are now on the road—(L 96)

Elsie's following his advice accomplished two things. Not only would she thus become his conscience, but just now—as he had to begin admitting her difference from him, when he could no longer postulate her love on the basis of identity—having her yield whatever separate self was being born within her to religion allowed him to feel still somehow secure. Her becoming religious quieted his fear. If she didn't become one of the "stupid" people he implicitly named her, as she approached her maturity (she was nearing her twenty-first birthday) and began to realize and voice her autonomy in relationship to him, she might flee from him and their "Faery" world. He was afraid he would lose

---

*I tell myself: there is only one true thing in our world, to satisfy one's heart, to feel and go to the bottom of all one's feelings, to desire and go to the bottom of all one's desires; finally to live one's own life, one's sincere life, outside of all lies and all conventions before sinking into unavoidable nothingness.
("fierce nihilism")

his "chief possession," as he called her (WAS 1781). But dialogue about the function of religion even prompted her to write as often as he. Her conversion ensured him. Although she matured in years, if caught in the trap of the church's "comfort and moral help," she would not mature intellectually. He could thus keep her in his imagined paradise as his little girl. This was the ardent wish he expressed openly in a letter just at the time she was joining church: ". . . our Eden! Elsie . . . you will never grow old, will you? You will always be just my little girl, won't you? You must always have pink cheeks and golden hair. To be young is all there is in the world. The rest is nonsense—and cant. They talk so beautifully about work and having a family and a home (and I do, too, sometimes)—but it's all worry and head-aches and respectable poverty and forced gushing" (L 97–98). In another letter just the day before, he expressed the same sentiment even more specifically and at the same time playfully revealed one of the psychological devices he felt he could use to check his fear: "In October I shall be twenty-eight. Great Caesar! Can't we stop it somehow? You will be twenty-three when I am thirty. Thirty-three when I am forty, forty-three when I am fifty. Well, when you are forty-three I shall cease to worry—but not a day before; yet, even then, in New York, you may find some means to make me hot and cold—unless I keep you thoroughly terrorized" (WAS 1781).

In his now almost daily letters and cards to her Stevens recorded, as he had in his journal earlier, the changes in his spirit. He hid nothing from her he did not hide from himself. He depicted his external world for her as well—from a picture postcard with his house indicated by an inked arrow to expressing his delight that Barnum & Bailey's circus was coming (WAS 1772). It was the same delight he might have shown his mother when he was an adolescent. Instead of playing the paternal role he had until his "anti-conversion," he now wore the costume of a child, dependent on her love and approval. He felt free to relinquish his guiding authority to the church that would now take care of her.

It was as this transition took place that his handwriting took on the style it was to have for the rest of his life, the style imitating the signature learned from W. C. Peckham. He inscribed rhythmic patterns of peaked mountains that shaped letters and words nearly illegible except for context. Just as his fingers on the page made the music haunting their imagined world, the music played on his spirit, too. The surface of his words' appearance on what he once called "skyey sheets" hid their true subject, the fears and uncertainties of the boy who still crouched inside him. But he occasionally slipped and revealed them, as he did here, voicing once again his hostility about the perquisites of society—work, family, home—as he had before he met Elsie while he was still at Harvard. Revealing in another way, the very day he thought Elsie had joined the church, he shaved off his mustache, one of the marks he had associated, since his trip to British Columbia, with being a man (L 100).

He hid even from himself. He dressed the fearing, angry child still alive in him in various costumes from his actor's trunk. As he did this, Elsie changed, too. She took off the dress of "little girl" and donned that of "angel," Virgin Queen. With her in this exalted position, Stevens became a "penitent" before her (*L* 99) or put on "cap and bells" and juggled his words (*L* 100). Catching himself, unconsciously sensing that this reversal somehow revealed him as unequal to her, in a letter in which he had worn both these costumes, he switched, right before closing, and put the two of them back on the same footing, though not in reality but in a fantasized paradise where they both were children: "Oh, maiden, we are still in the land of the living, and we are still in the sun. Let us wear bells together and never grow up and never kiss each other: but only play, and never think, and never wish, and never dream.—Will that stop Time and Nature?—Let us trap Nature, this cruel mother, whose hand you have just taken, and whom I have known a little longer" (*L* 100).

Two days later he wrote another of his "after midnight letters." In it he referred to what he had expressed in this last letter, where the innocent world he staged offset grumbling protests about his unsuitability to the money-making bustle of New York. But while he stayed, he voiced his wish to be with her constantly in the country. There he felt he would be "writing verses and singing to [him]self," while as it was, he felt "there [were] bars in front of [his] windows" (WAS 1785). The prison metaphor of his early Harvard poems was still with him, barring him from reality. A few lines later he attempted to convince her—against her desire to shed the role he had assigned her—to continue playing his "angel": ". . . of course, you are not an angel, as you say: but aren't you different to me than to anyone else—aren't you like (in spirit) 'the young-eyed cherubim?'"(WAS 1785). The more reality pressed its demands, the more he pressed her to participate in his imaginary world. Reality included the needs of his nature as well. Ending this letter, he noted: "If you were here to-night I should kiss you like a madman. What a fate! But I should not be able to help myself" (WAS 1785). His exclamation expressed the reaction he expected were he to engage her in reality as he did on paper, where he felt like a "vigorous warrior" (*L* 116).

Stevens could not have continued to stage his play at all had not Elsie acquiesced, in spite of her periodic protestations. She complied not only because she enjoyed imagining herself in the various roles she played but also because playing these roles protected her virtue, something that became increasingly important as their courtship stretched to years and they were still unbetrothed. She had even joined church, becoming, at least in her own terms, a respectable member of the community. Appropriately she responded to even his verbal wish to "kiss her like a madman" with what he understood to be a "punishment" for what she thought was a "liberty": She denied him the favor of a return letter. They had come a long way from that first summer's seeming when she had yielded her warm mouth so easily.

Stevens went back to Reading for the Easter holiday the weekend following this "exchange." He found her "unmanageable" and his "family about as depressing as usual." On his return to New York, he wrote her the following letter:

Monday Evening [April 1, 1907]
DEAR ELSIE

This morning in the train I thought that we were like two people in a dark room groping for each other. Once in a while our hands touch and we get a glimpse of each other. Then we are lost again.—It is very hard to leave you this time, harder than ever before, because we both feel that we are becoming "all letters" as you said.—I can think of at least one way of changing that and, to say it at once, it is this: when I come, be all the time what you are on the sofa. You know how quickly we change on the sofa, and that is because you are yourself there, as you are in your letters. *Honestly,* are you yourself when we sit so primly, talking like strangers? I am not myself. I am "making a call." But you might laugh and talk just as you do on the sofa, and just as you do with one of your friends. You must let me know you.—When we were walking along Mineral Spring road, I said to myself, "I will never love anyone who does not love me. I will never try to make anyone love me that does not. All the delight in love is in being loved in return."—If you love me you will not wish to hide it. If I am your lover and if you are glad of it, you will give yourself to me, and not fear to let me know. You think that if I know I shall cease to care. If I did not love you, it would be just the opposite.—Now I must try not to speak of this again. It is unpleasant to me to speak of this. It is a thing not to be communicated in words, and words are like thorns in its wings. Poets and rhetoricians give it words, men and women, who are not poets and rhetoricians, do not. Let us hide it, not from each other, but from words. How subtle and sweet it was! We must keep it so. We must say that there has been a little winter in us, and we must watch it grow new and clear and wonderful again. You must return to the Elsie I knew and I must become the old Wallace. It must be Spring for us as well as for the fields.

Tuesday Evening

I have been reading all evening and it has refreshed me so that when I took up the letter again, it seemed a little lifeless and stale.—Then I happened to see in a bowl of odds and ends on my table the carnation you took from the table in your dining room the last time but one that I was home— and that you gave me. It is quite dry. I picked it up and smelled it.—There was still an odor of faint spice. So there is still life in what I wrote last night. I want Elsie to love me. How many, many times I have said that to myself! I want Elsie to love me—always. This quiet evening at home, with my lamp, is half-empty without you. If you were here, I should still be quiet. But you would be here.—I am in the mood for reading some big book and looking up and seeing you here.—Was it the sunset that made me so? It was clear and quiet and soft—like the shore of some island of adventure, and I looked at it for a long time.

Your,
WALLACE
(WAS 1787)

Elsie was pressing him, withholding herself both to maintain her respectability and to force him into making a firm, dated commitment to marriage. She used every device at her disposal, from periodically breaking off their relationship to complaining that her years were passing. But instead of the promise she wanted, he offered her poems expressing that in his eyes she would always be young. He also encouraged her to find solace in the elements and in books, as he did. On April 9 he wrote: "The love of books for the thoughts in them is like the love of the earth for its seas and distances. We must talk about books sometime when we are together. That will be quite as good as a walk on the hill, if we talk about the right ones" (*SP* 176). For him, among the right ones now were the *Notebooks* of Matthew Arnold and Proverbs, from both of which he quoted in the same letter and both of which, from this point on, provided him with models for how he kept his journal. It became a "notebook" exactly in the style of Arnold's, filled with quotations from what he read, with occasional epigrammatic additions.

In a letter five days later he strengthened his case for books. At the same time he voiced something that must have made Elsie cringe at least a bit: ". . . for if I have ardor left for anything at all, it is for books" (WAS 1789). He expressed a strong wish to have his walls lined with books and to devote himself entirely to them and to study. He remarked that lately he had "been buying almost any book that struck [his] fancy." Farther on he attempted to justify his delay in plighting his troth with what must have seemed to her, after an excursion through imaginary bookstores and stalls along Parisian quays, a feeble excuse. The beginning of this letter appears in *Souvenirs and Prophecies* (p. 176); the remainder follows:

In Boston and Philadephia it is different; and they say that in the bookstalls along the quays of Paris, it is different too. And it must have been different in Florence of Franceschini's. You remember the clipping I sent about him.—One gets in a way of looking at people (those beastly blobs [stains, ink? on paper] must stay: I have nothing to remove them) as one does of looking at houses or fields or stones and of feeling about them impersonally. And when you think that some old bald-head in a car may be humming: "Ce doux parler, ce cler tainct, ces beaux yeux." That is: "That sweet speech, that clear skin, those beautiful eyes" and know that he got it from a book: don't you feel ready to [illegible word] that men and books—life and books are all a wonderful jumble by this time? I wish I could fan the little flame for books that must be burn-[here Stevens revealingly forgot to complete this word with *ing* on his next line] in you. Then our winters would be as full of small miracles as our summers; and our summers would be more and more what they ought to be: a thousand summers in one. There are so many illustrations of that; but illustrations limit the imagination. But suppose on a summer day I quoted:

"Rest, and a world of leaves and stealing stream,"

I should be adding another day to the real one, don't you think? So I might ramble on, only suggesting things, not completing them. I do that too much; and I am afraid that sometime you must be at a loss for meaning in my scribble.—What will you do when you find the first line in your forehead? You know that you cannot possibly be old at twenty. No one says a girl is old until *she* says she is twenty-five. That is why she never says it. You are too young to be anything but a girl, but of course, you are not really a little girl, except in the sense that every woman is always a little girl, and that every man is always a little boy. That, however, is sentimental. Would it also be sentimental to say that I hope that I shall not always be writing you letters until you are old? Need I speak of this now any more clearly than we needed to speak during our first summer? We do not understand each other the less, I hope, for not speaking. You know I have a special dread of speaking of it tonight, because Mrs. Jackson had a piece of beef for dinner to-day that cost $2.25 and some asparagus, for salad, that cost .85¢ a bunch. Oysters are .15 and oranges .40 a dozen. It is frightful. Whenever the desire becomes so strong as to make one unreasonable, I find it a great help to inquire about the price of eggs and pine-apples and coal. And you cannot get a cook for under $25 a month; and (and, and) we *must* have a cook; at least I think so now. But you know my views. Meditate on the figures—and then put your right hand in my left hand and let us call down the wrath of heaven on all butchers, grocers, landlords, laundresses, tailors, seamstresses, and so on; and thank goodness for the present one can be happy without them. You must not scold me for saying all this. I think our notions of waiting until everything is ready before speaking of it is, *also,* sentimental. I have all manner of plans and as soon as vacation time comes around, we must put our heads together.—Now, surely, I have said enough, without running the risk of stirring your old-time rebelliousness; if, indeed, you still set any store in that green mood. At all events, no more tonight.—I have been dreaming since writing the last sentence. Will you be able to imagine what it was about? Or will you refuse to imagine and think me impudent for such liberty? But you are in a strange situation, understanding so well, saying so little.—After all, it is only myself that I understand. When I say "we," it can only be I. No; remember things you have said. We must settle it all between ourselves.—The wind is still blowing hard. It is a sign of my great age that I pay so little attention to it. If I were still young I should listen to it, wondering. Children dream in the wind. It makes a warm room sweet to them. It turns a rug by the fire into an Arabian Nights' carpet.—My adventures grow few and far between; and it is a great adventure to be writing to you tonight, calling you my little girl, yet knowing that you are a woman, almost—not that I should ever use the word. To think of you one way to-day helps me to think of you another way tomorrow.

With my love,
WALLACE
(WAS 1789)

This letter revealed many of the hidden elements contributing to what otherwise might seem evidence of "caprice" or even madness in Elsie's later hostility to her husband's involvement with poetry and books. (She not only became enraged at his publishing some of the poems she thought belonged only to her but never agreed to having a room of their house made a library. Most of Stevens's books remained in boxes in the attic.) Late in his life he one day returned home from having been awarded an honorary degree. He went into the house, opened a window, and waved the hood he had been given, shouting, "Look, another skull!" She did not even look up from the rosebed where she knelt, gardening,[43] like an aged "Ste Ursule" (*CP* 21). Not being a poet or rhetorician, she could not, like him, give words to her "old-time rebelliousness." It took the form, instead, of "blow-ups of the nerves" (*L* 422) or mute indifference—the only ways she had to express her individuality.

Though in his next letter Stevens acknowledged that he had been "spiteful and Dutch" in prating about the prices of things, he blamed her for having been "indifferent and coquettish" when he had been full of her (WAS 1790). To make up for this latest form of keeping her "terrorized," he related Arthur Clous's reaction to her (Clous had accompanied Stevens on one of his last visits to Reading): ". . . he said you were beyond his expectations. Remember that his expectations were high. He liked your voice and your manner. So he said! I shall not tell you what more he liked, because little girls should not hear such things about themselves" (WAS 1790). No doubt she would very much have liked to hear "such things" about how she was perceived, not as a "little girl" but simply as Elsie and not from Clous but from her lover. But this did not come—not here or in future letters. In place of these wished-for words, there was always something else from a book. Here, it was the voice of the turtle from the Song of Solomon that Stevens borrowed to sing to her: "The fig tree putteth forth her green figs, and the vines with the tender grape give a good smell. Arise, my love, my fair one, and come away." He was now reading around Proverbs: Ruth, Ecclesiastes, and the Song. It was three days after this that he threw away his Bible. In closing the letter in which the above appears, he revealed both that his utterance would be no more direct when they were together and that in appropriating these lines he had secularized them, made them simply part of "literature." As such he could use them to express his sublimated eroticism: "If you lived in a house with a

balcony under which I could serenade you, that would make a pleasant serenade in two weeks [*sic*] time" (WAS 1790).

On the same day he symbolically freed himself from his religious past he
again went into a paean about his books: "I wish you could see my new books.
They make me as proud as a peacock. . . . I want to surround myself with
them." But she had already begun to react against them, so he continued: "It
was thoughtless of me to recommend them to you. Most of mine would bore
you terribly. Besides, I ought not to thrust my own tasks on you. I am quite
content to have you write of blue clouds" (*L* 103).

It is not difficult to imagine Elsie's frustration now and over the years as
his passion for books continued to burn. It eventually became what must have
seemed an obsession to her. He bought special editions he never read. He
preferred not to own any book that another had owned or marked.[44] His
passion for her, on the other hand, was kept alive only in his imagination.
Her confusion finally broke into waves of increasing religious devotion and
practice. She lived by the most puritanical laws, banned alcohol periodically,
frowned at smoking. As he lived with books, she lived with the religion he
rejected. It did "exceed all Faery." The man he was did cease to be, and the
woman she could have been never was.

Years later, when the poet asked concerning his persona in "Sunday Morning," "Why should she give her bounty to the dead?" (*CP* 67), he already
knew the answer. He recorded it in some of the other poems he wrote then,
poems that shaped into a formal catalog the various devices he had used in
letters to distance himself from direct engagement with Elsie. These tropes
were abundant in the letters remaining from 1908 and 1909. Though the
excerpts recorded in "Elsie's Book" show that their correspondence continued
regularly, the next extant letter after the one dated April 22, 1907, was dated
December 2, 1908.

The April 22 letter leaves poignant reminders of Stevens's state of mind
that whisper through the remaining fragments. Just returned from a weekend
in Darien, Connecticut, at the home of his friend Charles Dana and his recent
bride, whom he found "very attractive," Stevens found himself quietly preoccupied with imaginings of the married state. What he saw and experienced at
the Danas offered him a model for the life he later attempted to create with
Elsie:

> . . . Sunday was a wonderful day. The house, where I visited, was quite as
> fascinating as the trees. On Saturday evening we sat by the fire and talked
> and read until almost midnight. The room was full of pretty things—every
> picture, every lamp, every chair. We slept late. When the church bells
> began to ring at nine o'clock, I was still dozing, or else half-listening to the
> frogs whistling or whatever it is they do. After lunch we walked . . . ,
> passing all manner of pleasant houses on the way. . . . My room was un-
> welcome when I returned. So, at noon today, I ran up-town and (to do what
> I could) bought a large photograph of one of Rembrandt's paintings. It is a

portrait of himself and of his wife, Saskia—*and she is sitting in his lap!* I might just as well have chosen a Madonna, but now I am glad I chose this, because it is just what I needed. And of course I bought a few more books: some pamphlets of lectures delivered at Oxford, and a translation from the Greek—Propertius. (Maybe it's from Latin—I know it's about love and that is really all I know.) . . . I came home . . . through the grounds of the University [Columbia], not at all a bad place at night. There is a dome there, and there are pillars and arches and quiet shadows and a suggestion of dark nobility. . . . (*SP* 178)

The next day he recorded in his journal his rejection of the self-centered, nihilistic values illustrated by Paul Bourget that would, if practiced, make the realization of his domestic dream impossible. To win Elsie, to keep her, he had to become, he thought, one of the pillars of society.

The images of gracious but sensuous domesticity, of love, of dark nobility flitting through his mind, like the quiet shadows he saw that night, showed themselves in the light his thought cast on them. These comforted him over the next two years and few months before his marriage. During this period, as he tried to bring the world quite round, to make these furnishings of his imagination those of reality, his doubts and fears beset him. The record he left in his letters and sporadic journal entries reflected his continued movement up and down.

VI

THE BOOK OF

DOUBTS AND

FEARS

1907–1909

To love her was a
liberal education.

—William Makepeace Thackeray,
Henry Esmond

It seems insincere, like playing a part,
to be one person on paper and another in
reality. But I know it is only because I
command myself there.

—From a letter to ELSIE MOLL, *Letters* (p. 80)

The century was well on the way to completing its first decade but crankily insisted on wearing the habits of the last. In New York Auguste Rodin's lyrical nudes provoked high-toned cries of scandal.[1] But Stevens announced that he would not play the flat, historic scale; he found Rodin's pieces the kinds of things that "ought to exist in abundance" and the world of high-toned old Christians who winced at them "a poor world" (*SP* 179). Not he but the time was out of joint. Yet he was caught in the cogs of its machinery. By June he was "in the mood for suddenly disappearing" (*SP* 179). By the end of July, he had—to Reading for a long stay. He was out of work again and would not find another position until the beginning of November (*SP* 185). He could not escape his time. The financial panic of 1907 called into question even faith in the model of strength offered by Roosevelt. The populace was now experiencing in practical terms the crisis of faith the intellectuals at Harvard and elsewhere had lived spiritually ten years and more earlier. The nation had to wake up from the dream of reason, the dream of the good life, the dream of finally becoming like an Old World aristocrat herself in order to prove she had come of age. No wonder Stevens had doubts and fears. How could the man arise in him?

As though he were carefully mapping America's trajectory, from its beginnings with lofty thoughts of reaching the glory that was Greece to its present disillusionment and actual decay, Stevens's attention gradually shifted from Greece to Rome. After finishing with John William Mackail's Greek translations, he moved on to Catullus, Horace, studies of Vespasian, and William Young Sellar's *The Roman Poets of the Republic* (*SP* 182–83). Thinking he had settled his own relation to religion, he abstracted himself and concentrated on it as simply a cultural force. He had begun to understand how religion had operated in his development. Now he applied what he had learned and started to explore the way he could use art to replace religion, putting into practice what he had internalized and continued to study in Matthew Arnold. ("I have become an intense Arnoldian," he wrote to Elsie [WAS 1772].) He was stirred by what he read of the world's greatest period of decadence. At the same time he feared his own. He hoped to become "new," and he made Elsie's name the spur to change: "I want to become a new person, a person separate from my tedious self, for you. I want your name to be a motive for me. I want you to be the last bit of good that is in me—whatever it may be: love you and never scold" (WAS 1772). Now Elsie would be the conscience binding his resolve. On October 4 he wrote to her: "I have determined to go ahead without the rum-bowl for a year—and probably always. The thing has never had any hold on me—it was a mistake to trifle with it" (WAS 1772). A short time later he reaffirmed his decision in almost exactly the same words and added yet another evidence of his attempt to become "new": "Well, here's news. I'm determined to go without the rum-bowl for a year—and probably always. I continue not to smoke but without any resolutions about it. It is an evil. All this self-control will make me a regular Roundhead—an old maid" (WAS 1772).

His summer at home had led to this attempt. These months were as important in helping him find a new sense of himself as the summers after his graduation from Harvard and after his graduation from law school when he met Elsie. He again walked and mused; he found his soil to be his intelligence and so was able to identify intrinsic elements of his nature. In his journal he recorded an overriding concern with the past and with change. Comments on graves and graveyards "full of soldiers and Dutchmen," abandoned sites, empty houses with their gardens full of weeds—all echoed the death of the pastoral world he loved. Together with this he mourned the loss of the classical ideal. As this dream slowly loosened its tenacious hold on his imagination, he loosened his hold on old patterns of behavior, especially in relation to Elsie. He spent at least one night with "some friends (all girls)" in one of the nearby towns and "Sunday mornings at the Tower [on Mount Penn above Reading]—with Elsie and without" (SP 181). The relaxation of his attention did not harm their relationship. By November he openly recognized her as his "strength" (SP 186). By then he had already invested her with the honor of serving as his conscience.

Back in New York by the beginning of September, he tried to put Humpty-Dumpty back together again after having dissolved himself—"disappearing." He fixed on the notion of "virility." He read and copied in his journal a descriptive comparison between the lives of the citizens of Athens and Florence. It based their difference on a distinction between what Schiller had named the "naïve and sentimental":

The Athenians' souls were close to part of nature and eternal mysteries and free men with even a found old cloak could sit at the feet of a master and participate in discourse. In Florence, by contrast, only certain rich and privileged citizens sat in elaborately manicured gardens, and, having despaired of ever reaching the ideal followed by the Greek sages, abandoned the *abstract* [italics mine], dream-filled contemplation that marks the *youth* [italics mine] of a people . . . [and] focused instead on that which marks its *virility* [italics mine], history and politics[2] (SP 182).

Ten days later he was still turning the idea of virility around in his mind. He added the note that the life of those who were "intensely bourgeois," like that of his family in Reading, was a life that was "really human—with the humanity of the bête humaine" ("human animal"), a life that was "somehow masculine—not in the bounding, virile way—but just masculine" (*SP* 182).

As he sifted through these perceptions, he further clarified what were already central preoccupations: the notions of abstract, youth, virility, human. He wanted to isolate each of these qualities, define them as precisely as possible, and recombine them at least in a fictive world that would be made up of all of them. The world in which he lived had only one or two of these virtues; he wanted all. If this world could not be, he would imagine it. He was not alone in his desire. On the other side of the Atlantic there were other individuals who were also engaged in taking reality apart, laying its acrid colors out, and putting it together again in new ways. These innovative attempts made what had been understood to be *seem* in all its shifting possibility. It was the year of the first cubist exhibition in Paris. It would be a few years before Stevens would meet and talk with some of these men of kindred spirit in the West Sixty-seventh Street studio of Walter Arensberg, Marcel Duchamp's unofficial U.S. patron.

By this time in 1907 Stevens had already begun what remained a lifetime habit of reading foreign, especially French and British, periodicals. "One must keep in touch with Paris, if one is to have anything at all to think about," he wrote to Elsie (*SP* 194). He found himself thinking about art for art's sake again, but in a very different way from what he had thought during his Cambridge years. Then and after—until his experience as a newspaper reporter chastened him—he somehow believed he could, as Stephen Crane had attempted and as Upton Sinclair had done more recently and effectively,[3] combine his gift for "painting pictures in words" with a practical end. Art for art's sake might have once seemed silly and empty, but now things had changed. In the face of personal and collective disillusionment, art for art's sake offered the only access to the beautiful and the true. Stevens copied the following in his journal: "La doctrine de l'Art pour l'art—c'est la doctrine qui professe à la fois ces deux principes, que le but d'art est de réaliser la beauté par le forme, que l'objet de l'art est la représentation du vrai"* (*SP* 184). About a month later he found another, more explicit solacing description, which he transcribed from the *Journal des Savants*:

This for heartsease:
"L'art pour l'art est aristocratique. Fidèle en cela à son heredité romantique, l'artiste pourra [word missing] le mépris et la haine des bourgeois, de leurs idées, de leurs goûts, de leurs institutions et, par suite, ces critiques en

---

*"The doctrine of art for art's sake—it is the doctrine that professes at the same time these two principles, that the aim of art is to realize beauty through form, that the object of art is the representation of the truth."

de la presse qui sont à leur service, ainsi, il se replie sur lui-même, s'enferme dans son argueil [sic] et son individualisme. Il dédaigne la foule et les genres littéraires qui lui plaisent, comme le théâtre: il se met au-dessus d'elle, elle n'est que la matière vile dont il tirera l'oeuvre d'art."* (SP 185)

Here was a way of expressing his frustration at the bourgeois values that he disdained yet that had shaped him into a man who could not separate himself from them. His many vituperative remarks about work, family, money-making were contradicted as he continued to plan and build for a future secured in these same things. Aestheticism offered him a way of rationalizing and acting through the pride and individuality for which he had often chastised himself in the past. Following it, he could give up extolling humility and the absence of personality. And this way was wonderfully tied to the Oriental ideal of the lotus growing out of the mire. He would make art out of his bourgeois soil. This doctrine comforted him. It replaced the religious faith he had recently abandoned. Being out of work, then, was not so important. He would find "something of consequence" or leave New York. In any event, he had higher things to contemplate. But there was Elsie, and he did want her, the home, the family. . . .

In November he took a "temporary situation . . . while other plans simmer[ed]" (SP 185). These other plans remain mysterious, but they seem to have involved following through on old Harvard contacts. During the last week in October Stevens went to Boston (where while waiting for the return boat to New York, he downed three martinis; clearly, his resolve to Elsie just a few weeks earlier was not long-lived). He then, on November 2, went to Washington. There, as he recorded in his journal, he "Saw Roosevelt and Bonaparte and talked with both.—Went up the Washington Monument—a very important thing to do, it seems. Ran through the Capitol and Congressional Library. The library [was] excellentissimus" (SP 186). Either Stevens by this time moved with the greatest of ease in the world of power, or he had already developed to exquisite perfection the straight-faced irony of the verbal sleight-of-hand man, one of the skills whose illustrations he had noted repeatedly in reading Boswell's *Johnson* a few months earlier. It was also a skill cultivated by François Rabelais, whose "Mieux vaut de ris que de larmes escrire, pour ce que rir est le propre de l'homme" ("It is better to write about laughter than about tears, because to laugh belongs to man alone"), Stevens had copied in his journal at the end of August (SP 181).

Holly Stevens believes the Washington entry to be straightforward and adds to it in brackets "[Theodore] Roosevelt and [Charles Joseph] Bonaparte." She further attempts to elucidate the mystery by noting that although the

---

*"Art for art's sake is an aristocratic concept. Faithful to his romantic inheritance in this, the artist will be able [to express] his contempt and hatred for the bourgeoisie, their ideas, their tastes, their institutions, and so for the critics who are in their service. Thus, he draws into himself, encloses himself in his pride and individualism. He disdains the crowd and the literary genres it admires, like the theater: He places himself above it, it is but the vile matter from which he will extract the work of art."

regular *New York Tribune* column listing White House callers did not list her father's name, on November 1, "the newspaper did report a presidential conference with Paul Morton, formerly Secretary of the Navy, and, at this time, head of the Equitable Life Assurance Society. Seven years later, in 1914, Stevens became vice-president of the Equitable Surety Company" (*SP* 186). It is possible that Stevens knew Morton at this point or had an introduction to him through one of his other contacts. It is equally possible that he was not listed as a White House caller because he met with Roosevelt and Bonaparte informally over tea or martinis. It is unclear what the still rather inexperienced young lawyer could have contributed to a discussion with the president and his adviser, preoccupied as they must have been with the financial crisis that would not be eased until J. P. Morgan stepped in and imported $1 million worth of gold from Europe.[4] Of course, they could have met and talked about their memories of Harvard and Cambridge, common acquaintances, instructors who had perhaps been lecturers in Roosevelt's time and professors in Stevens's.

But it is equally possible that in this entry Stevens described with mordant irony a situation quite the opposite of the one in which he actually found himself: out of work, looking up contacts, and feeling the "importance" of what Washington represented at the same time he sensed himself separated from its spirit as a result of the internal changes he was experiencing. "[T]alking with Roosevelt and Bonaparte" could be understood as a prototype for the kind of situation described, for example, in "Tea at the Palaz of Hoon" (*CP* 65), an exercise in hyperbole that expressed the contradictory aspects of a prideful self. This would not be unlikely, especially since when he had last been in Reading, staying with his parents, he felt his separation from them intensely. Their only desire, voiced by his father, was that he cultivate and maintain the very qualities he himself was calling into question.

It is impossible to know what actually went on during this visit, but in a November 4 letter of Garrett, Sr.'s he expressed concerns that could not have been very different from what he addressed during Wallace's stay. He opened with an explanation of why he had not said good-bye. He had not known Wallace would be leaving so soon and had gotten up earlier to go hunting— his election day "vacation." This was an example of the subtle and not-so-subtle devices Garrett used in his letters to impress his son with how severely he applied himself to the difficult task of supporting the family through the adverse situations in which he had found himself. He had lost both his steel plant and bicycle factory. The rest of the letter focused on Garrett, Jr. His father praised him as a "natural leader" whose "sensitive and quick-tempered" character was unfortunately responsible for his losing his job:"—he did not much like his work." Garrett, Sr., went on edgily equivocating about the "support" he felt compelled to give his eldest son, after noting that Garrett, Jr., had "never learned much of the Necessity of Self Support." This must have made Wallace at least momentarily ask himself how it had come about that he himself had learned this lesson so well. Garrett, Sr., then went on:

"He will get along if he actually does depend on himself and but for his family would not need my help. Of course he is entitled to that—and I should be glad to do more for him—but then the Lord's Lesson would not be learned. It is for you to sympathise with and cheer him up—He is sure of my confidence,—and I am sure he can eventually get there" (WAS 2164).

This was confusing. From his father's words it would seem that Wallace should be the one receiving praise and emotional, if not material, support. At the same time Stevens did not want to imagine being in the position of having a family and needing help, as his brother did. In his own eyes this would have meant that he could not be considered the man that he wanted to appear, especially to his father. He also sensed, through his father's solicitous concern, the soft spot he had for his namesake. In spite of chastising words, Garrett, Sr., accepted his first son. Even his worst faults were excusable. Wallace, on the other hand, had never been sure of his father's confidence, of his acceptance and love.

This is clear from Garrett, Sr.'s next letter, written ten days later. Its responses suggest that Wallace balked at the directive to sympathize with and cheer his brother. Wallace had also noted his difference from his bother. He had cited his own strength and self-reliance to his father, as though looking for explicit approval. Garrett opened his reply with a formula "Glad to hear . . ." (the last letter had opened with "Glad always to see you . . ."). He then went on:

> You, being alone, can of course always get along—All men rejoice in our success or at least congratulate us—but we want to tie closest to those who cheer us on in adversity and carry matches when the dark road seems mislaid—
>
> I am glad you feel strong and self-reliant. Many seem so constructed that they will starve rather than dig goobers under their feet unless somebody tells them they are here. . . .
>
> We are all well—Elizabeth home, Kate at School, John fairly busy and Garrett in good trim at Baltimore—resolved upon admission to the Maryland Bar—but must reside there one year and meanwhile does various stints and makes a little living—but the main good thing is his being away from Home props is that while he may wobble awhile will learn to make new friends and stand alone—it is in him all right and if you can say anything cheering to him write to him his address is. . . .
>
> The financial situation generally is rotten—it seems to me the Banks deserve a good scolding—the Public Utilities Commission will someday have to wrestle with a demand that private stock holders in National Banks be eliminated—that the Comptroller of the Currency be practically the U.S. Treasury, otherwise Great Central Bank and every Bank a branch.
>
> Love
> G. B. STEVENS
> (WAS 2165, November 17, 1907)

By offering his interpretation of the cause of the financial crisis, Garrett, Sr., subtly attempted to accomplish—no doubt unconsciously—two things. First, he wanted to blame his own difficulties on the national situation. Secondly, he wanted to communicate to Wallace that he now considered him his equal; he was discussing the situation with him as he would with a peer, a full adult involved in the life of the community and the nation. Significantly, after this, he sent his "love"—a very unusual feature of his letters to Wallace, not appearing in any of the others remaining in the Huntington Library collection. But in seeing him as an equal, Garrett also seemed to want to pass on his function of being the family's responsible figure. It was time for Wallace to attend to Garrett, Jr., as well as to himself and his future. From this point on Garrett's letters to his son were filled primarily with business matters. They now spoke the same language. The only minor interruptions to this professional man talk were continued progress reports about Garrett, Jr., one or two notes of other family news, and the usual reminders and mottoes urging attention to success and perennial vigilance of self. To a Harvard alumni notice he forwarded to Wallace (addressed to the class of 1901, asking for subscription to the alumni bulletin), he appended a note reading, "I would keep up with the boys" (WAS 2171). Another letter toward the end of March 1908 he closed with this little epigrammatic line: ". . . men judge others by their appearance of prosperity—apt to measure a man by his own yardstick— If he's cocksure he can do something they give him the chance—" (WAS 2170). This followed Garrett, Sr.'s attempt to be respectful of his son's privacy: ". . . not heard from you since your visit home on Washington's Birthday—. . . . From the fact that I hear nothing I may assume that you are absorbed in personal matters—and as you want your own way about them I do not want to butt in—. . . ."

Between November 1907 and March 1908 a great deal had happened. The change in the relationship between father and son, reflected in the letters, corresponded to a change in Stevens's external circumstances. In December, while still temporarily employed at Eustis & Foster, Stevens successfully helped someone Garret, Sr., had recommended to him. Wallace was praised to Garrett for his performance, and Garrett forwarded the kudos:

DEAR WALLLACE,

I am glad you were able to meet Kerper & client and to put them through so handsomely—as Genner put it—"went through with bells on."

Both were delighted and Kerper hypnotised by your readiness your energy and your success—and cannot get done talking to all his friends of how delighted he was with you in every detail including your manner both in Court and at dinner, says, "tell him to 'stick' he's all right and has now struck a gait that will land him wherever he wants"—Of course after all this I had to "get um up—" but was a mighty pleasant thing to hear him say— . . . . (WAS 2166)

Finally, reinforcing the approval he was getting from his father came what would prove to be Stevens's most secure success: On January 13, 1908, he joined the American Bonding Company of Baltimore. (After this his employment was uninterrupted until he died [*SP* 189].) Obviously pleased with his son's progress, early in March Garrett wrote and recommended that Wallace contact an influential "friend and kinsman" (WAS 2169). For the first time Stevens was safely on the road he had "chosen" to follow, the road that would provide stability for the wife and family he sometimes desired. At last he felt able to speak to Elsie about concrete plans for their future. These were the "personal matters" into which Garrett did not want to "butt." By November, when "Wall was in town," he didn't even go home (WAS 3970; also referred to by Holly Stevens). Garrett was not sanguine about his son's binding himself in lawful wedlock to the beautiful girl from the wrong side of the tracks.

But Stevens's successes in the outside world seemed to have made him certain of himself in a way he had not been before. His father's advice and attitude did not carry the weight they once had. His relationship with Elsie was like a rebellion against the values his father extolled. But as the distance between him his family increased, he was, nontheless, becoming more and more secure in the profession his father had urged him to choose. There was a tense contradiction in this. Under the strain, his imagination took on even more the function of "completing life." In his mind he could create delightful scenarios and costumes that distracted attention from what was problematic in reality. At the same time the details of his fantasies revealed that his trysting with Elsie indeed represented a rebellious escape. Promising that they would "make a dull world pretty for [them]selves" (WAS 1772) with these imaginings, he painted scenes like the following:

> And so when summer came they went in a boat to [a] quiet island, and on the way Pierrot pulled out a newspaper and read to Columbine a little news of the stupid world from which he was taking her. But Columbine didn't think it stupid. So Pierrot turned the boat around, and they drifted back to town. Yet even while they were drifting, Columbine thought of the quiet island and she knew that Pierrot was thinking of it too. (*L* 106; WAS 1772)

As he drifted farther away from his family and the everyday world, he made her even closer to him in spirit. He addressed her as "sister" and wrote: "What else have we to get and keep secret except each other's love? . . . We have only ourselves—and that is a very great deal—the most important thing in our lives" (WAS 1772).

He tried to make it easier for her to join him in his imaginary world by sending her copies of books that had stirred him. At Christmas 1907 he presented her with Bliss Carman and Richard Hovey's *Vagabondia* poems.[5] Years earlier, his reading Villon's poems and seeing the Portuguese ship *Elvira* had touched his desire to become a vagabond himself. These volumes now rekindled this desire. He borrowed their images to paint backdrops in letters he wrote to Elsie. Some of these he also used in poems he wrote to make up her "June Books" and in the inscriptions he made on their flyleaves (*SP* 187). Certain of the perceptions he found reappeared much later, reshaped into some of the strongest images of his major poems. While Elsie became more familiar with the gentle landscapes he wanted to whisk her to, their contours impressed themselves in his spirit.

Carman and Hovey's lines celebrated the countryside, spring sap stirring into summer on Arcadian hills, sexuality restored to prelapsarian purity. In them Stevens found his own feelings. The *Vagabondia* poets'

> . . . crickets mourning their comrades lost
> In the night's retreat from a gathering feast[6]

sounded their syllables again in the crickets of "Le Monocle de Mon Oncle" stirring in their mother grass (*CP* 15). The collaborating poets' attention to "Whiskey-jacks and tanagers"[7] made Crispin the Comedian more attentive to the birds he met in his imagination's new world, his

> . . . hawk and falcon, green toucan
> And jay . . .
> . . . raspberry tanagers. . . .
>
> (*CP* 30)

One of their "gaggled men with dissecting knives" who "[did] not find [his] way to Arcady,"[8] did, however, find his way into "The Man with the Blue Guitar," where he was imagined as picking the bitter colors out of his own brain. Even perceptions of Florida's "venereal soil" and sea seem to have been enhanced by Stevens's reading of

> The far-off orange groves
> Where Floridian oceans break,
> Tropic tiger seas.[9]

Carman and Hovey approved of "Bobbie Browning" because he "was the good boy [who]/Turned the language inside out."[10] They attempted to imitate him in lines like "Tropic tiger seas." In this, they were more successful with their second volume, in "Jongleur":

> Clons and cognomens
> Tomes, prolegomens
> Comment and scholia
> (World's melancholia)—
> Cast them aside and good riddance to rubbish!
> . . . .
> Rough and off-hand and a bit rub-a-dubbish.[11]

277

Here they exercised their sounds in the way Stevens later did with greater success in "The Comedian as the Letter C," whose "rude aesthetic" was indeed "rough and off-hand and a bit rub-a-dubbish." In defining themselves, Carman and Hovey playfully disclosed their provenance:

> Somebody says they have come from the moon,
> Seen with their eyes Eldorado,
> Sat in the Bo-tree's shadow,
> Wandered at noon
> In the valleys of Van
> Tented in Lebanon, tarried in Ophir.
> Last year in Tartary, piped for the Khan. [12]

Their imaginary map traced their path from the East. In another poem this was made even more explicit. In the persona of "The Sea Gypsy," the poets proclaim: "My soul is in Cathay." [13] The cover inscription of their first volume left no doubt:

> With the Orient in her eyes
> Life, my mistress, lured me on.

Stevens noted their mental itinerary. He had already begun nosing toward the East himself, and now Carman and Hovey's announcements of its importance to them made him even more attentive. Like him, they saw Robert Browning as a "man-poet." They were also fascinated by Robert Louis Stevenson, naming him the "prince of vagabonds." Paul Verlaine as well they acknowledged, as Stevens had while at Harvard and later. It was not surprising that Stevens felt their images to be his own. And because they were not "man-poets," he was not afraid that his voice would be muted by theirs. He could borrow from them freely and remake what he took in his own image and rhythm.

The number of these borrowings is astounding. In this case it seems appropriate to call them "borrowings" rather than "echoes." Stevens could be fairly certain by the time he wrote the poems in which his tranformed lines and images appeared that the *Vagabondia* books were not going to become part of the canon. It was unlikely that readers would hear their words in his lines. Unlike his thematic response to major poets like Milton, Spenser, or Dante— responses generalized over a long period of time, running through many poems, and, in some cases, through his entire corpus (this seems to have been the case for his reaction to Whitman and Mallarmé, for example [14])—the borrowings from Carman and Hovey were specific.

Stevens used particular collocations of sounds and images, as in the above lines, prefiguring what "The Comedian" elaborated into hundreds of lines, or certain lines picked out of longer poems. "Let it be!" and "Just to cease from seeming," from "Laura Dee," play their part in Stevens's "Emperor of Ice-

Cream."[15] "Laura Dee" turns around a central question. The poet asks his mistress:

> Why should all be heroes
> . . . Striving to be winning?
> Let the world be Zero's! As in the beginning
> Let it be!

The poem goes on to rephrase Andrew Marvell's urging to his coy mistress to seize the day. Then comes a crucial moment when the poet seems to wake from the dream that he was young and coaxing his lady, and he says:

> You and I together—
> Was it so?
> In the August weather
> Long ago?
> Did we kiss and follow,
> Side by side,
> Till the sunbeams quickened
> From our stalks great yellow
> Sunflowers, till we sickened
> There and died?

It is not a long jump from these lines to the following from "Le Monocle," though Stevens's attention to the lessons of the "man-poets" made his poem far more than the trivial trope Carman and Hovey's remains:

> Our bloom is gone. We are the fruit thereof.
> Two golden gourds distended on our vines,
> Into the autumn weather. . . .
> . . . .
> We hang like warty squashes, streaked and rayed,
> The laughing sky will see the two of us
> Washed into rinds by rotting winter rains.
>
> (CP 16)

After his rude awakening the poet of "Laura Dee" questions what he and his mistress were, whether what had been was a dream. The lines ambiguously express the doubt as wish:

> Were we tigers creeping
> Through the glade
> Where our prey lay sleeping,
> Unafraid,
> In some Eastern jungle?

279

Better so.
I am sure the snarling
Beasts would never bungle
Life as men do, darling,
Who half know.

He concludes that it would be better to be so, to

lose the human
Eyes that weep!
Just to cease from seeming
Longer man and woman!
Just to reach the dreaming
And the sleep!

These lines expressed precisely what Stevens at twenty-eight was feeling as he wrote to Elsie that he did not want them to grow old and sensed the futility of "striving to be winning." Like Carman and Hovey, like those at Harvard from whom he had learned to question the dream of progress, like Thomas Hardy, whose books he was also reading and recommending to Elsie, Stevens was breaking under the pressure of his time. The move from his idealized German peasants' pastoral life, timed by the sun's rising and falling and the soil's softness and hardness, was too abrupt. He was one of the first generation made to be on time by clocks. Machines, trains, industrialized city life demanded punctuality. No wonder he, too, dreamed of "tigers/In red weather" (*CP* 66) and of a return to a world in harmony with nature. No wonder he periodically reacted violently to New York and longed to "find a place to be in the country." It was not sentimental that he thought he could write poetry only there.

In spite of these feelings, his earliest successful poems, those of *Harmonium,* did not express this desire directly. The city man he was forced to become had to speak. Just as Carman and Hovey couched these same desires in clipped, ironic quatrains or in longer, parodically rhymed forms, Stevens voiced what he knew ironically. But for him this came through his various poetic characters rather than through stanzaic or line forms. Pound and Eliot had done the latter in their early quatrains imitating Jules Laforgue and Théophile Gautier. It was much more in keeping with Stevens's desire to keep himself and his tricks hidden to borrow subtler devices from comparatively unknown figures.

The first poem in which Stevens made his "rude aesthetic" the subject used the ironic mask of "Peter Quince at the Clavier." He referred not only to Shakespeare's "Quince" but more specifically to Carman and Hovey's from a poetic letter entitled "Quince to Lilac: To G.H." [16] The subject of the letter is the "prose" they share, which others call poetry:

. . . .
Our prose, I mean,—how beauty
Appears to you and me;
The truth that seems so simple,
Which they call poetry.

They put it down in writing
And label it with tags,
The funny conscious people
Who mask in colored rags!

They have a thing called Science,
With phrases strange and pat.
My dear, can you imagine
Intelligence like that?

And when they first discover
That yellows are not green,
They pucker up their foreheads
And ponder what it means.

And then those cave-like places,
Churches and Capitols,
Where they all come together—
Like troops of talking dolls,

To govern, as they term it,
(It's really very odd!)
And have what they call worship
Of something they call God.

But Kitty, or whatever
May be her tender name
Is more like us. She guesses
What sets the year aflame.

She knows beyond her sense;
Do tell her all you can!
The funny people need it—
At least, so says The Man!

. . . .

In Stevens's curious seeming reversal of Keats's "A thing of beauty is a joy forever," at the end of "Peter Quince"—"Beauty is momentary in the mind—/The fitful tracing of a portal;/But in the flesh it is immortal" (*CP* 91)—he added a most important element to what the romantic poet had expressed. Keats was younger, of different circumstances, and still lived in the heavenly orchard air of a moral order undisturbed by Darwin. He could contemplate beauty without specifically considering how it functioned in relationship to ethical questions. He could write, "Beauty is truth, truth beauty," without engaging in the dialogue in which truth and beauty represented antithetical positions. Stevens, on the other hand, had first to attend to the practical problem of how he was going to spend his time before he could afford to speculate about how human beings were to understand themselves and act well in a world without anything in which to believe. He could not avoid being preoccupied with the tensions between virtue and pleasure. This involved him in meditating on the central notion of aesthetic theory since the time of the Greeks—whether the good was tied to pleasure or to virtue.[17] From his years at Harvard, when he still thought art for art's sake silly, he had remained concerned with discovering a way to make pleasure virtuous. Though he occasionally despaired of succeeding—and even, at one point, described his "writing of verses" as "absurd"—he never abandoned the plight. But in order to effect this difficult synthesis, he had to find the proper catalyst, the element that would dissolve the didactic distinction between pleasure and virtue.

From the days of the pre-Socratics the didactic tradition held that "Pleasures are mortal, but virtues . . . immortal."[18] During the classical period, Plato, expanding what he presented of Socrates' scratchings against reality, could not resolve the difference and ended up equivocating, leaving behind, in various dialogues and parts of the *Republic,* various positions.[19] Stevens knew that the historical record since the Greeks showed that in the West, at least, under the increasing influence of Christianity, the didactic position held sway. But under the impact of Darwinism and the questioning of the myth of progress—which had fitted so nicely into the hierarchical world view—each of the positions maintained so long under its power was up for reconsideration. The notion of art for art's sake, then, did not belong to a discretely aesthetic ground. It was not simply an expression of decadence attached to a nihilistic philosophy, as it was derogated to be by those attempting somehow to preserve the hierarchical order. It represented, rather, a reassertion of value. In the absence of faith in God, faith in beauty, the abstraction of a radiant anthropomorphic deity, offered some solace.

It was with this implicit understanding and silent hope that Stevens looked again at the doctrine of art for art's sake. And with his strong Calvinist background, he sought the element that would make pleasure, beauty, the motivating force of virtuous action. In some way he had already experienced this transformational ability of beauty. Like Dante with Beatrice, he had made Elsie, even simply her name, his guide to the good. Between the time he had begun feeling this power now, while still in his youth, and the time of writing "Peter Quince" years later, Stevens became an alchemist of the spirit, experimenting with the various elements he had distilled from earlier magicians of words.

His experiment was successful. In "Peter Quince" he isolated the necessary element, and though he did not name it openly, he identified it by illustration. The "irrational" was the all-important element, as Carman and Hovey had playfully suggested in "Quince to Lilac." The irrational equaled, or contained as its motive force, sexuality. In Stevens's poem, sexuality is apparent from the first, from the name of the player, referring in veiled slang to both male and female parts, to the statement of desire as the subject of the poem, to what is one of the most exquisitely achieved renderings in English poetry of the stirrings of desire:

> . . . .
>
> The red-eyed elders watching, felt
>
> The basses of their beings throb
> In witching chords, and their thin blood
> Pulse pizzicati of Hosanna.
>
> (*CP* 90)

Brazenly exploring the effects of sound, Stevens laid himself bare. He not only disclosed a personally experienced connection between desire and the creative impulse (what Freud, by the time Stevens wrote "Peter Quince," had named "sublimation"[20]) but implied that if that same connection were not understood to exist—if, that is, desire as a motive were denied—one would end up like a hypocritical elder, denying feeling and replacing it with shame, evil.

It took Stevens years to get to this realization, years of desiring and denying. He came to understand that it was not enough to describe the "still unravish'd bride of quietness" elliptically before simply noting that "Beauty is truth, truth beauty." The central question had to be answered: "What is beauty, truth?" His answer was an elegantly phrased illustration: It was *feeling*, the irrational element, the experience of trembling in the moment. This was not different from Carman and Hovey's pointing to truth as what Kitty "guesses" at, what "she knows beyond her sense." But Stevens's answer was effective in being affective, while theirs was not.

It was not simply that Stevens reexpressed the art-for-art's-sake aesthetic in "Peter Quince." Metaphorically he did this, of course. He suggested that the poem, art, was like Susanna, and the stupid public like the elders; the song would live long after the readers were dead. In this, he also echoed Ezra Pound's directive:

> Go, little naked and impudent songs,
> Go with a light foot!
> (Or with two light feet, if it pleases you!)
> Go and dance shamelessly!
> Go with an impertinent frolic!
>
> . . . .

Ruffle the skirts of prudes,
     speak of their knees and ankles,
But, above all, go to practical people—
     go! jangle their door-bells!
Say that you do no work
     and that you will live forever.[21]

But much more than this, Stevens provided an ethical basis for the aesthetic by indicating, through recasting Susanna's apocryphal story in alternately twitching and relaxed rhythms, the hidden logical consequences of not acknowledging pleasure as legitimate and virtuous. Pleasure—"The measure of the intensity of love/Is measure, also, of the verve of earth" (*CP* 14)—was, for Stevens, the only measure of immortality. "It Must Give Pleasure." Generation after generation, trembling at these lines like Susanna's attendant Byzantines, will experience, in the flesh, the constant sacrament of praise, their common bond. There is nothing irrational about this:

Beauty is momentary in the mind—
The fitful tracing of a portal;
But in the flesh it is immortal.
The body dies; the body's beauty lives.
                    (*CP* 91–92)

Since early December 1907 Stevens had been living in the Village again, once more with a friend, Horace Mann, at the Benedick on Washington Square East. The move was another of the important changes that came about during this time. Coming back to a familiar neighborhood and, after getting his job at the American Bonding Company, being prosperous enough to be "Feeding at the Judson, Billy the Oysterman's [and] Fran Maurer's" (*L* 105; *SP* 188) sweetened the exile's return. This period, until his engagement over the Christmas 1908 holiday, was one of his happiest. It gave him the firm base he needed to face the serious self-doubts and fears he still had, which he later laid out systematically in letters to Elsie in 1909—from the time of their engagement until their wedding.

The evidence for his happiness during this period comes from the fragments of letters preserved chronologically in "Elsie's Book" (WAS 1772)[22] and from the tone of the poems written over the first few of these months and collected in the "Book of Verses" he presented to her on June 5, 1908, for her twenty-second birthday. The most effective way of communicating the sense of Steven's spirit through these months, for which there is only one journal entry on August 17, 1908, is to follow the excerpts preserved by Elsie. Rather than select just a few for the purpose of simply illustrating Stevens's state of being for this time, I have chosen to present the excerpts exactly as Elsie later recorded them. Though they may seem to interrupt the text, going through them in the way Elsie must have in the years after her husband's death gives us an opportunity to read her mind, as it were, as we read them. In view of the fact that we have so little direct evidence of how she perceived the world and so much evidence of how Stevens did, this intrusion of extensive quotation is, I think, justified. (Bracketed material indicates her additions.)

I am a man, after all, not a beau.

Politeness is the cure to subjection to moods—a desire to please others by anticipating their wants and wishes and studiously avoiding whatever might give them pain.

Politeness is superior to moods, as it is to circumstances, and, indeed, that being superior is the first condition of politeness.

[Read letter dated January 6, 1908 often.]

—if all the machinery of life could stop—if people could lay by their work, and rest, and recover all their lost ideals, they would all return quite simply to fundamental things—honesty, politeness, unselfishness, and so on—hiding in oblivion all the distortions that influence them now. Let the two of us always rely on these fundamental things.

What all the world agrees is good, pure, and the like *is* so, in the long run, and is the only law we have and the only comfort.

I have always one ally at home—Lady Nature, whose children we are, both of us, so completely.

Do you know what I would do if the world were made of wishes? I'd lock you up—in a large enough place, to be sure; a whole valley as big as a country, maybe—and I'd allow only the most unexceptionable people to come there.

But here's Reality—what harm, when all is said and done, has it ever done you? You have always had your own path to find and certainly you have found it. It seems to have led you away, when the time came, from every peril, and I trust it, and you.

The blessedness of being quiet.

It would be only proper for you to have your own private book of verses, even if it were very small and if the verses were very bad.

So I write, calling you sweetheart, and again calling you darling—out of my heart. I do not want to feel that those words are lost to us.

Night is a symbol of death. When one of the poets died Vagabondia lost its spell. So much of which was in the mere comradeship.

Get Charles Lamb's essay called "Old China" and others—for the sweet temper of them.

Look up John Burroughs. His pages on summer days, or like them.

Read Thoreau's "Week on the Concord and Merrimac [*sic*] Rivers"—and his "Walden."

I would rather sit here, with this button, these letters and the thoughts of you, than dine at all the queer places between the Hudson and the Yang-Shi-Kiang. Give me something sweet and clean. It is so little to ask, I mean to have it.

Peace shall play the viol for us, and Quiet her small lute.

Even if I did not know you, I should always find myself in what you are. I should be dreaming of some such—Elsie.

—the great trouble is to keep from being buried in work—It gives one a chance to "shine in use." That remains to be seen.

[1908] Try to stay home from now on. This summer we can tell your mother. You have so little a practical idea, or I think you have, of what home is. Goodnight my little Girl.

Our letters have told us more about each other than we could have learned otherwise. I should always know how, back of one Elsie, there is another—and you will know all the Wallaces.

Which is more important—that in some little thing I have vexed you, or that I desire so much to please you.

Love exaggerates the good in people.

A good opinion is more valuable than rubies—and I will purchase your good opinion at any cost.

We are like spiders spinning an immense web (in our letters) that glistens sometimes, and sometimes is all pitiful confusion. —However it glistens again now, and I am eager only to forget the snarl.

Back of all I say and do is the one desire that you should find in me, when you think of me, things to like.

The fact is, most people are a great nuisance, and my own disposition is not remarkably lenient in such things. Perhaps that is why my own likes are more often for things than for people, because of intolerance.

My society has always been an airy thing, not of men and women; books, music, quiet places, ye blue bird, ye country garden, quiet Elsie.

But since you call me knightly, my armor seems brighter again.

This is to be only a note—so small a celebrity must not come with too great a flourishing of trumpets [written just before a visit to Reading].

Elsie is my glory.

Shall I take off my purple and say, "I am what I am."—No I'll stand up in the purple you give me and say, "I am what it pleases my Good Angel to make you think me."

—till I reach for my purple, and hide her in it.

—little words, tricking me, tricking her—what are you but little creeping shadows, little thieves, after all.

I acknowledge how good it is in me to love you with all your faults. When I read one of your letters and come to the end smiling in spite of myself, I say, "How kind it is of me to like that so much!" Or when I see you and hear you, I say, "How nice it is of me to feel this way! How poetic it is of my blood to do that! What pretty manners my heart has! It is all very remarkable."

I don't believe in holding the microscope up to one's self, or to you, or to my friends—but only to the dolts and those whom I dislike.

Don't be too conscientious. I must have Elsie young and sweet and full of courage.

[Letter dated March 9, 1908 Too bad! Too bad! I am ashamed]

—writing to my Sylvie in the dead of night.

> Some power to make you love
> the poor thing that I am, forgetfully
> If I were king

The truth is I cannot endure friends whom I do not choose for myself, uncharitable beast that I am! But isn't it a sweet thing to have things one's way—quiet, clean, whimsical?

Trusting each other is the strength of us; and that too we must respect without failure. We must be able to say "Here we two stand together and all that one of us is, the other is."

I should rather have your letter than the sun every morning. It is true, it is true—but you won't believe it.

In a little while, when it is warmer they [robins] will warble at twilight with their red breasts turned toward the sunset. Does Elsie know that enchantment?

All of us want to express our moods: to be frank. It is not a brave or spiritual thing to do. Silence is the better part. It is nothing to assert oneself.

One's self is nothing except in pleasing.

April 10, 1908

> Quick, Time, go by—and let me to an end,
> To-morrow, Oh, to-morrow! But today,
> Poor draggling fag,—insipid, still delay.
> Flat drudge. Now let my feeble earth descend
> To violent night and there remend
> Her strength, not for a dream's affray
> But 'gainst slow death then up the sounding way
> Where vivid reaches of new blue attend.
>
> And many shadows of the whirling sun
> To greet her exultation thunderously!
> Let me be the first of living men to throw
> The weight of life aside, and there outrun
> Even the magic light—so swift to know
> Some passionate fate accomplished wonderously. (*SP* 187) [23]

April 23, 1908

Am I falling in love with you in some new way, from some new point of view? What a complication of motives!

Good night, my dearest, dearest Lady-Lady Little Girl.

Let there be a shower of grace because I want to sing for Elsie once more—be her Captain, King and Knight-At-Arms.

> I am so tired of holly-sprays
> Am weary of the bright box-tree
> Of all the endless country ways
> Of everything, alas, save thee.

We two—Elsie and Wallace—I could not explain it if I wrote and thought all night. You are so much a part of myself. It is as if we were the same person, only that you are the brighter part.

That elevated train coming home with its negroes and cheap people! Dearest, keep me from seeing all that. It is nonsense but it wrecks me. —It is a hideous, foolish, maddening world, and you are my only escape from it.

Take possession of me, fill my mind, my thoughts—if you love me it will be so easy, if you don't, so hard.

I will sing for you with the first bird you hear, and what he sings will be my song. I shall not be the mortal thing you think me, but that sudden warmth in your own heart.

And when I kiss you I shall lose all my thoughts, everything—just in kissing you.

I do not get on well with my equals, not at all with my superiors. Ergo, I have no friends.

Columbine and Pierrot. How aptly those two evanescent characters symbolize some aspects of ourselves!

It is such a blunder to call the main thing in you goodness. It is not that at all, but rather—delicateness. Certainly goodness would be very little alone. Perhaps it is both together.

The idea of neat, clean, sweet contented poverty—I confess that seems one of the best things in the world.

Write to me often and irregularly. If I may not have a letter every day, let me at least have the possibility.

—an odd play that I have just finished. The best things in it was the names of the women. I liked Selysette and Bellangere most—not as whisperable as Sylvia—nor as tinkling as Elsie.

I have found another name for you—Isolda. Elsie *must* be a form of that old name.
Elsie, Ilsa, Ilsolda-Isolda, Sylvia, Yseult—to embrace so many famous histories in your name alone.

I have become an intense Arnoldian [Matthew Arnold]—You recall his diary. Let me open it now and copy the first things I see—
"The happiness of your life depends upon the quality of your thoughts; therefore guard accordingly.
M. Aurelius"
Good Emperor,[24] I thank you.

—and to be poor, so long as you can be as rich as the richest in having leisure and the feeling of home, is no deprivation. My earnest wish is that you remain at home and do just what you are doing now.

I was wishing for a wise shepherd for both of us. —a shepherd more human than Nature—some innocent and true Confessor, some vigorous and consoling Guide to whom we could be gladly obedient, finding in such obedience irresistable sustenance and consolation.

Good-night, dear, good, happy girl.

In all the world, I am the only man awake. The Quiet says, "Come be part of me."

—but you will tame my savagery.

It is useful to understand such men [great men] as we understand other men. Their works are distant from them. There is no more reason for blinking at them in awe—at Keats for his poetry—than there is for blinking at a rose-bush for its rose. The poetry emanates mysteriously from some mysterious origin through Keats as, say, the rose emanates mysteriously from some mysterious origin through the rose-bush. It is all a delightful chemistry, to put it so.

The vital thing is that *Elsie* should be jaunty—well, happy, and think it a happy world, and never be sorry for anything—and now and then make dunce-caps for her lord (I am, I am, I am).

I have been away from home for eleven years—half your life. Yet it remains the only familiar spot in the world. My little sleepless trips home every little while do not get me in touch. I do not feel the strength of the place under me to sustain.

Life is a very thin affair, except for the feelings; and the feeling of the home waters the richest garden of all—the freshest and sweetest. Endure much for that.

We all, men and women, want so much more affection than we get from those around us. That, for example, is why my world centers about you, because you show me affection—because I cannot help showing my affection—and LaRue [Elsie's half sister, Dorothy LaRue Moll—at this point six years old; author's brackets] because she shows hers.

The deep centre [*sic*], of which you know, is under seal—except between two. It is a strange Law [author's brackets].

> The house fronts flare
> In the blown rain;
> The ghostly street lamps
> Have a pallid glare.
>
> A bent figure beats
> With bitter droop
> Along the waste
> Of vacant streets.
>
> Suppose some glimmering
> Recalled for him
> An odorous room[25]
> A fan's fleet shimmering.
>
> Of silvery spangle—
> Two startled eyes—
> A still trembling hand,
> With its only bangle.

That is to be in my second "Book" for you, which you will not see for a year—or almost—on your next birthday. But that's a secret.

—It has become necessary to have you near, or hear from you constantly. This is not only because I love you, but because you are, in such innumerable ways, my second self.

In an essay on Octave Feuillet, some interesting notes on romance—and hence on you and me. "Romance is the taste for the extraordinary. It is imagination in revolt against reason."—"The souls a prey to its influence are perpetually unsatisfied and disconsolate."

Adieu, dear Elsie (flippantly)—Good-night (in plainsong!)

You must not let yourself think that I am all virtue, and you all mischief. We are both alike. We can flippantly say to Saint Peter that what we are not, we hope to become. Then I read that mystics have pointed skulls; that man raises himself above the earth by two wings: purity and simplicity.

They have this drawback (books): They occupy your mind to such an extent that your mind ceases to be your own. But for a while, why not?

"Columbine is (historically) the flower of youth and beauty. Pierrot was pale, slender, dressed in white clothes, always hungry and always being beaten—the ancient slave, the modern member of the mob, the [illegible word], the creature, passive and disinterested who assists, gloomy and malign, at the orgies and frolics of his masters." That was all changed. Pierrot powdered his face with flour. He wore many disguises. As a marquis, "all in white satin"—made love to Columbine in other people's clothes, kissed her, "grew drunk with glory."

The plain truth is, no doubt, that I like to be anything but my plain self; and when I write a letter that does not satisfy me—why it seems like showing my plain self too plainly.

To bring me back to my pride—and to solace me I tell you that:

> What I aspire to be
> And was not, comforts me.

All the orchards are white—it is fantastic. Somehow, amid so many blossoms, one longs for dark woods, rain, iron capes. There is a great white cherry tree just outside my window.

[Nov 20, 1908 (About a diamond engagement ring for me)]

I shall not tell you, since it is unnecessary, that I should like to come in a week or two. The truth is, my dear, that I want to get you something for Christmas (it is no great secret) which requires a considerable degree of modesty in the meantime. Don't you think that we can deny ourselves this trip to make the one at Christmas all the better?

—But you are my "big tall girl" now aren't you, and tall girls, you know, don't bother tremendously about place and dignity.

The next entry is that of December 3, 1908, and will be dealt with a bit farther on.

An overwhelming tenderness comes through these fragments: tenderness for Elsie and for the self that Stevens was disclosing to her. Being loved by her, he could begin to be gentler with himself. This accounted for his ease, though there were occasional lapses into insecurity which prompted wishes like the one to lock her away or the reversions to his seeing her as his "little" or "big tall girl." The external changes between December 1907 and March 1908 had also contributed to the internal shift. Stevens's grounding in the everyday world allowed him to strengthen his commitment to Elsie sufficiently to ask her not to "go out" anymore. He assured her that they would tell her mother during the coming summer. Elsie obviously responded warmly and made him feel more secure in the relationship than he ever had before. This emboldened him enough so that he could even give her glimpses of the less than heroic side of his character. During the next year he went into each of the paltry details of what he saw as his "invalid personality" (CP 368). From the time of their engagement until their marriage he used every letter as a "microscope" turned on himself, even though he had written that he did not believe in doing this.

He was happy, too, because he had reemerged as a poet. Secure in his new job, knowing that this would secure him Elsie, whom he had made an inextricable part of his poetic endeavor, he composed for her his first volume. The crystallization of his lines over these months was also made possible by his having begun to clarify, over a long period of time, the issue of how poetry could be more than an indulgence. He had naturalized religion for himself and had begun to see through to the other side of art for art's sake. This freed him to become a poet "in more than mute feeling."

The poems making up his first "Book of Verses" reflect the integration of these various elements.[26] This was part of a larger composing of Stevens's world according to both the principles of the East and the female principle (now perfectly embodied in the way Elsie functioned for him) that he had been imaginatively exploring in his reading and musing over the previous years. In marked contrast with the poems of his youth, here the dominant tones were hope, fullness, and a serenity that belonged to an Eastern mood of contemplation and oneness with nature. Images of potency asserted themselves in more than half of the twenty poems—images like:

a world resolved

. . . infinite green motions [that]
Trouble, but to no end

the rising—"a second time" of "the pageant moon"

> . . . untroubled senses stirred,
> Conceived anew, . . .
>
> my two hands . . . strong enough
>
> more . . . triumphant fire.

The setting Stevens painted repeatedly was the pastoral countryside or wood that he also conjured in his letters to Elsie. He now could begin to imagine returning to the country in reality with his bride, even if they would have to stay in New York for a while. In one poem he mythologized the setting into an "Eden for the tired mind," complete with

> . . . misty vale . . . bending palm,
> Bright Orient reefs in Orient oceans rolled . . .

with her ". . . by his side [even] more than [this]." With images and other rhythms reminiscent of FitzGerald's *Rubáiyát*—"sing, on shores of lapis lazuli,/ A song serene"—Stevens created in his poems the perfect world in which with Elsie he could escape the "hideous, foolish, maddening world" of elevated trains full of "negroes and cheap people."

Elsie's spirit animated these poems. This was most perfectly expressed in the opening of the one sonnet of the group, which described the process of self-revelation and realization that belong to the letter excerpts as well:

> Explain my spirit—adding word to word,
> As if that exposition gave delight
> Reveal me, lover, to myself more bright.

The image of the potent Hoon in his purple was conceived during these months: "I'll stand up in the purple you give me and say, 'I am what it pleases my Good Angel to make you think me'. . . . I reach for my purple and hide her in it."

Though the most important text he learned from during this period was the one he himself was composing, Matthew Arnold also reemerged as a central figure. Stevens was now reading other things from which he borrowed and noted as well,[27] but it was Arnold's voice that he heard inside him. This gave happiness to his moments as they passed and promised sustained happiness in the future. Steven's marginal lines and checks in his heavily marked copy of Arnold's *Letters,*[28] which he read during the summer of 1908, indicate what he found to nourish him.

Beginning with the editor's introduction, Stevens noted a description of Arnold that gave him hope of succeeding in his aesthetic pursuit in spite of the daily demands that would continue to be made on him in the everyday world. The editor commented that Arnold "[q]ualified by his nature and training for the highest honors and successes which the world can give . . .

spent his life in a long round of unremunerative drudgery, working even beyond the limits of his strength for those whom he loved."[29] If, given this, Arnold still managed to leave behind what he did, Stevens was already ahead. Though he was working hard and it might seem drudgery, it was for Elsie, whom he loved, and it was not unremunerative. It had even recently earned him recognition from his father.

Reading on, Stevens marked passages where Arnold revealed things about himself that Stevens felt characterized his own spirit as well. (He had also done this in reading Boswell's *Johnson* and Keats's letters the previous year.) In an August 1858 letter to his sister Arnold complained that people did not understand the difficulties of expressing feelings, that if things were not very good, one concentrated feelings into the perfection of form. He added that this was to "tear [one]self to pieces," that it was extremely hard to do, and that of the moderns only Goethe had done it. Stevens also underlined passages where Arnold indicated, explicitly or implicitly, what the young poet saw as either models for writing or models for behavior. The following are the most revealing:

. . . a man is a just and fruitful object of contemplation much more by virtue of what spirit he is of. . . .[30]

The great thing is to speak without a particle of vice, malice or rumour.[31]

. . . to school oneself to this forbearance is an excellent discipline if one does it for right objects. . . .[32]

I shall never get over a sense of gratitude and surprise.[33]

I will go with meekness and contentment.[34]

If I ever come back to America, it will be to see more of the South. . . .[35]

. . . I enjoy my time here very much. I read five pages of the Greek Anthology every day, looking out [sic] all the words I do not know. This is what I shall always understand by *education* and it does one good, and gives one great pleasure.[36]

Stevens echoed Arnold in many of the letters to Elsie excerpted above. His sympathy for him was symbolically fixed in place by even their common interest in the South. Arnold's cultivation of a humble attitude before life appealed directly to the young poet's need to transform his own intrusive pride. More, Arnold's active interest in educating himself into his old age offered Stevens a model he followed until the end of *his* life.

Just after finishing Arnold's *Letters,* Stevens read Herbert W. Paul's study of him.[37] Here he found more specific ties. Paul focused on Arnold's glorification of the Greeks; Stevens marked this sentence in the margin: "Whatever was not Greek was barbarian."[38] It expressed not only the Greeks' point of view, Paul noted, but Arnold's; the English man of letters seemed to have wholly identified himself with their spirit. Stevens also had done this. In a letter to Elsie a few months later he expressed the same sentiment in different words: ". . . almost anything Greek is beautiful" (WAS 1802). He eventually memorialized his feeling in one of his "Adagia":

> The greatest piece of fiction: Greek mythology.
> Classical mythology but Greek above Latin.
>
> (OP 178)

He also marked Herbert's observation that "the chief lesson [Arnold] took from Oxford was the Platonic maxim βίος ἀνεξέταο·τος οὐ βιωτός,—'life without the spirit of inquiry is not worth living.'"[39] This Stevens took in as well, later integrating Arnold's beliefs into the transformational function and capability of poetry. In another of his "Adagia" he wrote: "The relation of art to life is of the first importance especially in a skeptical age since, in the absence of a belief in God, the mind turns to its own creations and examines them, not alone from the aesthetic point of view, but for what they reveal, for what they validate and invalidate, for the support they give" (OP 159).

More practically, Paul's stress, checked by Stevens in the margin, on Arnold's seeing "politeness" as the central "practice of life"[40] echoed and reinforced, or perhaps prompted, Stevens's emphasizing the same virtue in his letters to Elsie. Further, Paul's observation, also checked by Stevens, that Arnold's "poetic vein" was "dried up" by his becoming, at thirty-four, professionally involved as a professor and critic[41] with the life of letters soothed whatever fears Stevens still had about his professional choice. And one more revealing notation made by Stevens concerned Arnold's advice to his sister to educate her child in science, especially botany, "to cultivate perception." Paul commented, and Stevens continued noting, that this was perhaps because Arnold felt the want of scientific training in himself.[42] Here Stevens recognized a sensitivity to polarities he knew in himself. What he stressed as important was always a compensation for a lack, whether "politeness," "poverty," or the irrationality he thought poetry "must" have (OP 162) since his well-ordered life did not. In the same way his adopting Arnold as a spiritual father, one who saw poetry not as an "indulgence" or Sunday pastime but as the better part of life, compensated for heeding the advice of his real father, who "always [had] reason on his side." Now Stevens lived with both these paternal spirits. One ruled his days; the other, his nights.

૨▲

"I certainly do not exist from nine to six, when I am at the office. There is no every-day Wallace, apart from the one at work—and that one is tedious. —At night I strut my individual state once more . . ." (L 121) Stevens wrote to Elsie on the first anniversary of getting his job at the American Bonding Company. And almost every night, beginning in early December 1908, just before their engagement, until September 16, 1909, five days before their marriage, he recorded a station on what he called his "Inky Pilgrimage" (*L* 115). He felt he did not fully exist during his days, and the long nights of writing to her, often for five or six hours at a time, became his only real life.

As the months moved through winter into spring and full, green summer—until, on September 21, they consummated their five-year courtship of words—the letters reached a crescendo in detail, tone, and number. It was as though, as they drew nearer to "being together always," he wanted to assure her of his complete devotion and to allay her earlier fears about his habits, his company, his comings and goings. This became clear in letters written toward the end of the period, in which if he had missed one day of sending her at least a note, he made certain to say where he had been or what he had had to do. Since Elsie's correspondence is lacking, it is difficult to say whether this regularity was self-imposed or whether it was in part a response to her own far less frequent letters. There are more than occasional reassurances in his letters that respond to her questions or uncertainties. At the same time the self-validating, self-creating function of these letters is apparent. More than once he referred to her as his "second self" and to writing to her as "self-communion." By summer these letters, which he had earlier referred to collectively as a "History" or "Annals," became the "Mirror of Past Events," the mirror he used, as he had once used his journal, to see himself.

Roughly a third of the letters have been published, but the entire sequence gives a fuller sense of the increasing urgency he felt about his doubts and fears. Stevens had an overpowering need that Elsie herself as well as their relationship should meet the demands of his imagination. Before almost every visit to Reading he wrote and asked her to be wearing a particular dress or pair of slippers or to ribbon her hair a certain way. And repeatedly over these nine months he asked her to describe what she did, what she wore, how she passed her time at different hours and on different days.

I shall refer here to dated excerpts from already published letters and from Stevens's remaining unpublished letters for this period. These reveal the intricate and subtle dimensions of the relationship. Before I fit them into place, however, a few general observations and indications will be useful.

Apart from their human element, the most striking feature of these letters is that they contain in raw form, and in nearly exact chronological sequence, the germs of the major poems of *Harmonium*. A careful reading of all the remaining letters—those collected in *Letters* and in *Souvenirs and Prophecies* and those at the Huntington Library—shows that Stevens was aware of this. And in a much later letter to an inquiring critic, he noted that indeed, the order of his work bore a chronological relation to his life. With an additional bit of evidence—the admission in an unpublished letter to Elsie that after their marriage he looked forward to going through their correspondence and throwing away all the "bad ones" (WAS 1801, June 23, 1909)—it becomes clear that even in writing the letters, he intended to glean things from them, no less than from the journals. And as we have seen and as Holly Stevens notes, he revised entries in his journals as he did the letters. This extreme attention to the shape of what might one day be seen, were he to succeed as a poet, as part of the raw material out of which his work grew attests to the seriousness of Stevens's involvement with his craft as well as to his intention to create by one literary means or another the role he wished to assume. At the same time it sheds light on an important aspect of his relationship to himself and others. Tremendous self-conciousness and concern with image lay behind this editing and revising of personal material. His preoccupation was so great that when the letters to Elsie gradually took the place of journal keeping, he never seems to have considered how she might feel about having presumed intimacies regarded as just more *materia poetica*.

From periodic perusals of his journals and early letters Stevens gathered many of the images and perceptions he worked into poems (a number of these examples have already been presented). Stevens went back to these sources again and again, not randomly picking or searching out a particular reference but reading through the entire sequence as it unfolded past stages of his life, and the poetry that emerged after each rereading represented, in part, a revisionary cycle. Each reworking of the primary material included the previous reworking and additional experiences of the poet between the completing of one cycle and the beginning of the next. This was the movement of the planet Stevens imagined himself to be, revolving around its sun again and again in a path the same yet changing.

That Stevens wrote Elsie letters he knew he would then reread and exploit raises some interesting points about the extremity of his need to see her as one with or part of himself. His expressions of this need began early in the relationship and grew more intense as he became preoccupied with the significance of the Virgin for the Catholic Church and of Beatrice for Dante. He recorded in his journal that he found himself meditating on the cultural effects of religion when it had a female as the primary object of veneration (*SP* 223–24). This Catholic notion he connected to Dante's obsessive devotion to the figure of Beatrice. Within these historical musings he was trying to understand his own involvement with Elsie, trying to understand her effect on him, and it was perhaps easier for him to consider general and distant instances than to allow himself to feel directly and fully the complex of emotions stirred by her. Viewing his situation in a historical and mythical context protected him from having to confront her in her individual immediacy, and it protected him from facing the fear that he might be overwhelmed either by his feelings for her or by his not being able to comprehend her otherness, her femaleness. Using the model offered by Dante, no less than seeing her merely as an extension of himself, allowed him to rationalize his etherealization of Elsie in the implicit hope that he, too, might transform animal desire into a poetic sacrament of praise.

Stevens's attempts to rationalize and aestheticize his feelings were evident also in his increasing involvement with the painting and literature of the East—another of his major preoccupations during 1909, along with the New

Testament, the life of Jesus, and additional essays by Paul Elmer More, who had drawn certain parallels between Christianity and Buddhism. It was as though Stevens wanted so urgently to complete himself by making "the female" a part of him that he could not let his imaginative sense of Elsie be disturbed by allowing her her own reality. Hence, his directions that she should dress, feel, and behave in certain ways.

His conception of her was, he admitted, "old-fashioned." He wanted her to wear hats that were out of style, to appear the "country-girl," as he put it (WAS 1772). Disparaging the city girls' modish adaptations, he urged her to draw her hair back loosely as young girls used to. She was to remain his "Little Girl"—one of his most frequent forms of address—and more than that, she was to evoke the idealized image of his mother, the "country girl" who never left the "country." Looking at Elsie properly costumed, he could re-create through her his earthly earthy mother, smiling at him "in her hair," as she read him Bible stories and tucked him in.

Of course, none of this could be made explicit, not even to himself. In the name he found for Elsie ("I have been trying to think of a name of one syllable to call you by—some name between ourselves. It must be something natural you know" [WAS 1772]), the intimate name he searched his imagination to find, he encompassed all that he felt, all that he needed. It was "Bo," from "Bo-Peep," his shepherdess, the "country girl" par excellence. The name also evoked, as he later wrote her, "Bo-Pete" (L 118). Pete had been Stevens's college nickname, and he occasionally used it to sign letters to her. She went before and above him, their two names one, like their spirits. And she was a "Good Shepherd," caring for him, leading him. ("I was wishing for a wise shepherd for both of us—a shepherd more human than Nature—some innocent and true Confessor, some vigorous and consoling Guide to whom we could be gladly obedient, finding in such obedience irresistible sustenance and consolation.") "Elsie is my shepherd; I shall not want" sounded somewhere deep inside him as he read the Psalms that May. She nudged him when he went astray and always loved him. And together they returned to what he called "their Eden," saved from the clamor of the "maddening world," where from nine to six he did not exist.

"A Winter Night," Stevens headed a letter written on December 2 or 3, 1908 (SP 196–200).[43] It is characterized by all the mythic elements that were to sustain him through the long months ahead, even to the opening of his imaginary scene in winter. Beginning his "Inky Pilgrimage" on "A Winter Night," Stevens himself seems to have been aware of its mythic quality as well. He fell naturally into a pattern Northrop Frye later presented in his *Anatomy of Criticism* as one of the basic structures of literary description: that action beginning in winter and resolving itself in late summer marks the movement of comedy, where all the tensions presented as existing in the hero's relationship to others and to his society are eased in the fullness of the season just before harvest. Stevens, intellectually preoccupied with the idea of comedy—with Dante's *Commedia,* with Shakespeare's and Sheridan's comedies, with the contemporary musical comedies he so much enjoyed—was also emotionally drawn to this form. He wanted his own situation to be resolved in the months ahead as he presented Elsie with the details of his tensions. He wanted to be seen as he was; he wanted her to see through his disguises, to be loved without them. Appropriately his record would end just before their harvest; in marriage they could gather the fruits of their years of dreams.

He began the letter by announcing himself as the "sheep before [her] cottage door again," though he had not yet named her Bo. She took on this role for him because he felt a need for protection when, as he put it a bit later, he was "sheepish" and "forlorn" after one of his black moods. His mood, prompted by sensing himself different from other people, even the actors whom he had seen at the theater one or two evenings before (he had seen a Victor Herbert operetta and cried), had been reinforced by an argument at the dinner table earlier that day about "gold medal boys." Against the general opinion he had maintained that there was no reason why gold medal boys (those who won honors at school) should be expected to continue "on the front bench" as adults, as his father had urged him to do while he was still at Harvard. His dark mood now corresponded to his finding himself, once again, in the archetypal situation of the stranger/quester without a place unless he made one by distinguished performance of some kind, whether by chivalrous deeds accomplished for a "Lady"—his form of address to Elsie in this letter— or by winning gold medals at school.

His reluctance to acknowledge these doubts and fears and their source in his own childhood and adolescence is apparent in the camouflaged contradictions of his page-long ramble about "gold medal boys." First, he made a parenthetical comment about "the little Jews." Years earlier he had vented a similarly black mood after attending a concert by making a sniping remark about a Jew, preferring to fall into a cultural cliché rather than face the painful, personal reasons for his dark humor. Now, after a public performance of a different kind (the Herbert operetta), he used the same defense, but this time with peculiar ambiguities. Since he had also won prizes at school, his remark represented either his implicit identification with the "gold medal boys" or his desire to differentiate himself from "the little Jews," even while secretly competing with them. Buried in his ambiguity was his ambivalence about himself. In spite of the honors he had won at school, he was insecure about his "brains," as he put it in the letter. This was evident in his equivocations about what might account for a Cromwell or a Napoleon. It was even more evident almost two month later, when in another letter to Elsie he told her that he had taken "all the prizes at school"; it was not true. Not only had the "ubiquitous Erle Meredith . . . always [come] in first," but Stevens had, as noted in an earlier chapter, failed one term and then had had difficulty keeping up with his younger brother, in whose class he found himself.

Consequently, after asserting that "gold medal boys" should not be expected to distinguish themselves, he contradictorily added: "Brightness is so small an element of success. Brightness disillusions." This came just after his hidden expression of resentment at his father for pushing him to become "man number one": " . . . such an odd thing that bright boys should be expected to be successful." After going on with a definition of "learning" that became confused by his muddling of what "knowledge" meant, he cited Cromwell and Napoleon as examples of "dull scholars." Though he knew that he was not a "dull scholar," that he read voraciously and attentively in the attempt to make himself one of the "learned," he feared some future scholar, looking back at his school record—were he to succeed as he dreamed—would find the "idle fact" that he, too, might once have been considered a "dull scholar."

But nine years later, disillusioned about himself and his marriage and no longer confident about his future, he felt the curtain had fallen on a failed comedy. Trying in his spirit to balance the scale of middle age, weighing what was against what might have been, the "dull scholar" reappeared in "Le Monocle de Mon Oncle," squinting through his eyeglass at the standards he had used to measure himself:

> Like a dull scholar, I behold, in love,
> An ancient aspect touching a new mind.
>> (CP 16)

Preparing himself for Elsie, not as she really was, but as his imagination had fashioned her, as his "Lady," his "Queen," his "Muse"—for so he named her only about a month after his "Winter Night" letter—he had made himself a "new mind." This meant shedding old disguises, all the poses he had learned from the literary models of his youth and early manhood. These were the "studious ghosts" to be exorcised if he were to become himself.

The process of preparing himself for marriage was not different from the depersonalized "emptying" used by the ancient Chinese to reach the state described as "no-mind." It is not surprising, then, that these strange Orientals found their way into this poem about love:

> Is it for nothing, then, that old Chinese
> Sat tittivating by their mountain pools
> Or in the Yangtse studied out their beards?
> I shall not play the flat historic scale.
> You know how Utamaro's beauties sought
> The end of love in their all-speaking braids.
> You know the mountainous coiffures of Bath.
> Alas! Have all the barbers lived in vain
> That not one curl in nature has survived?
> Why, without pity on these studious ghosts,
> Do you come dripping in your hair from sleep?
>> (CP 14)

300

His preoccupation with the East and his female had, by the time he wrote this poem, become one; thus, he could replace her once all-important function with an abstract meditation on nature:

> It comes, it blooms, it bears its fruit and dies.
> This trivial trope reveals a way of truth.
> Our bloom is gone. We are the fruit thereof.
> Two golden gourds distended on our vines,
> Into the autumn weather, splashed with frost,
> Distorted by hale fatness, turned grotesque.
> We hang like warty squashes, streaked and rayed,
> The laughing sky will see the two of us
> Washed into rinds by rotting winter rains.
>
> (CP 16)

But hidden beneath this late acceptance was the identification made in his early letter between "dull scholar" and "hero." He beheld this "ancient aspect" and the other multifarious aspects of the world not as an ordinary man but as a hero, as the "Giant" he signed himself in many of his letters. Perhaps he was "grotesque," as he confessed to feeling on occasion, but he was nonetheless larger than life, above its affairs of "people and places," as he later put it, regretfully, in "Adagia." At twenty-nine he found that "the proper thing to do [was] to read one's paper at the table and pay no attention to them." At forty he wished to be a "thinking stone." At seventy-three he recognized himself as a "planet on the table." As he noted to Elsie in another letter during their courtship, he inhabited the "Jovian atelier," one of the forces of the weather.

In this "Winter Night" letter he disclosed further ambivalence about himself. Warning Elsie to take precautions during a local typhoid epidemic and to boil all her drinking water, he noted that he never drank "anything but spring or distilled water," as suited to an inhabitant of the "Jovian atelier" forced to spend time on imperfect earth. He went on to comment that he enjoyed her having spoken about the saxophone. His present observations about the saxophone, combined with his later use of its sound in "A High-Toned Old Christian Woman" and a final, much later remark in another letter to Elsie that he hated saxophones, together point toward an attitude toward himself as superhuman which was as equivocal as his feeling about "gold medal boys."

He observed to Elsie that the sound of a saxophone always brought images of a "German [or] rather Dutch Arcadia" to mind, complete with a "Dutch satyr" playing. Years after, in 1922, as Eliot was finishing *The Waste Land*, the poem that William Carlos Williams thought a "catastrophe" to American poetry for returning it by arcane references and oblique diction to high-toned academicians, the Dutch satyr reappeared to write "A High-Toned Old Christian Woman," a poem seemingly as frivolous and irreverent as Eliot's seemed recondite and solemn. In sharp contrast with the world of nervous and intro-verted sexuality in *The Waste Land,* Stevens imagined a world where sexuality was to be indulged and displayed like the sounds of the words themselves. This, he knew, would make the "widows," who are taunted in his poem, "wince" no less than the academics who would attempt to understand it. The man who wrote this poem knew that he was both the "high-toned old Chris-tian woman" and the "disaffected flagellant" he counterpoised against her. Early in his career he imagined himself as the satyr he had wanted to become before his marriage, romping with Elsie through the hills and vales of an Arcadia he wishfully peopled with the Dutch-German peasants from whom he fancied them both to have descended. But later, chastened by both the experi-ence of his marriage and by the frigid reception of his pagan playing in *Harmonium,* he retreated, drawing back into the darker self who hated sax-ophones. They could only remind him by then of another paradise lost.

Counterbalancing his wish to be a satyr in the hills and woods of an idyllic Arcadia, he felt during his courtship that he was, in fact, an "abandoned animal . . . living in a corner of a hostile house," as he put it in the same "Winter Night" letter. This was the animal of dark moods who needed pro-tection—the sheep at Bo-Peep's door. Between this reality and what his imag-ination projected lay a chaos of emotions attached to his selfhood and to his sexuality. The being he wished for would be both man and animal, mind and "that monster, the body." But he found instead that he existed as either mind *or* monster. Either he was the intelligence conjuring flowery words to dress the imagined "Lady" he would love, or he was the animal, deservedly rejected because of his intemperate indulgences, his periodically uncontrollable ap-petites. In each state the other part remained outside, unavailable, "aban-doned" for the time, though looking on and wanting the two parts to merge and become one. He required Elsie to help him complete himself and his reality in his imagination. After describing the Arcadia suggested by the sound of the saxophone, he went on, for example, to make two requests of her that would work toward this end. He wanted, first, a letter in which she would describe everything she did "some day from the time [she got] up until [she went] to bed," so that he could "peep" into one of her days "as if [he] were watching without [her] knowing it." Secondly, he wanted her to have a photograph taken of herself "facing [him] but not looking right out of the picture." He added that she could be wearing a hat, one of those "out of fashion when people no longer wear anything like them," a hat that would "mark an era."

The gentle voyeuristic desire expressed here reveals an additional, earlier source of the insecurity born in Stevens's past and lingering into his present. In a late journal entry, written during the time his mother was dying, amid a number of distracting descriptions of the room in which she lay and other cool observations of her actions and words, Stevens recorded one memory of her from his childhood. He remembered watching his mother buttoning her shoes while sitting on the floor of the upstairs room where she used to dress. Together with the strong visual impression, he also noted a synesthetic impression of her smell, of everything "she wore . . . so fresh and clean" (*L* 172). Still with him after thirty-odd years was the child's overwhelming desire to see, while himself unseen, his mother engaged in one of her private activities. The kind of late-Victorian household in which Stevens was raised, with parents who discouraged openness of expression, was not a climate in which a child would be invited to enjoy physical intimacy with his mother or father. In such an environment the child's natural curiosity about adults, about the different attributes and habits of male and female would be repeatedly frustrated over the formative years, and as Freud abundantly shows, such energy as that excited by Stevens's remembrances of his dying mother could be discharged only in substitute situations. Since attempted re-creations never perfectly match the inciting cause, imagination continues to create new scenarios.

The ways in which this compensatory mechanism shows itself obviously vary greatly according to individual circumstances. Nonetheless, there are some general and predictable patterns. In an adult who had experienced the childhood constraints common to a household like Stevens's, there would be a strong residual desire to see things ordinarily debarred from being seen. Alternately, in connection with the kind of experience being discussed here, there could be a desire to take on the characteristics of the object of initial curiosity, in a naïve attempt to gain full access to the knowledge excluded by the prohibition. Or in cases of extreme frustration at the initial situation and at the inadequacy of the imaginative attempts to re-create the experience, a desire to destroy the object of curiosity could emerge in the hope of entirely removing the cause of the frustration.

Before we consider the manifestations of these possibilities in Stevens, it should be noted that underlying the curiosity being discussed here is another, still more fundamental desire which centers on the sense of identity derived from a child's knowledge of his body. The need to see and know others is focused, understandably, on the child's discovering in what ways he is the same as or different from others. In an ideal situation parents acknowledge both the child's somatic similarities and his differences from each of them and give loving approval, thus affording him the opportunity for developing a strong identity. If, however, the child remains ignorant of these similarities and differences and does not get approval, the need to discover who or what he is remains. (In extreme cases, even this impulse can be deadened, and the person rendered practically incapable of breaking out of introversion.) Such an individual may grow into adulthood ambivalent about showing or wanting to show himself but still needing the approval not received during childhood. Depending on the degree of deprivation and the resources available to the adult, the result may be one or another variant of exhibitionism. Added to and complicating this is the child's simple animal desire to be physically close to another, larger, comforting presence. The greater the constraints put on these natural impulses, the greater the difficulty the adult will have in being fundamentally certain of his identity and in being open, in turn, about giving and receiving physical affection.

In Stevens's case the evidences of his various uncertainties are clear: his mixed feelings about seeing and being seen; his continued desire for approval as an adult; his uneasiness about physical expressions of emotion; his need to base his life on fictional models. In his relationship with Elsie he preferred imagining or observing her from a distance to meeting her in more openly, mutually engaged ways. This need, which he could not articulate directly, grew more pressing after their marriage. Unable to recognize and name the need and so perhaps to translate it into some kind of sexual play they might enjoy together, he instead encouraged frequent separations, during which he could again imagine her, complete her as he wanted in and through the words he wrote.

With his gift for "painting pictures in words," Stevens at least could transform even the absence of satisfaction into lines that gave pleasure. In "Peter Quince at the Clavier," for example, he poetically described how the very longing for completion became the "music" of his work:

> Music is feeling, then, not sound;
> And thus it is what I feel,
> Here in this room, desiring you.
>
> Thinking of your blue-shadowed silk,
> Is music . . . .
>
> (CP 90)

His need to transmute reality into the realm of imagination was immediate and pressing. It was clearly one of the main sources of his poetic inspiration; the transformations of desire are the marks of his genius.

For Elsie, on the other hand, things were different. Young, inexperienced, insecure herself, and without the benefits of a privileged education, she lacked the means with which to translate her own experience or to understand his. No matter how beautiful she might have found what he wrote about her, establishing a mutually satisfying relationship with him was going to be very difficult. How could they deal with each other as they were when he preferred imagining "The radiant bubble that she was" (as he described in the opening stanza of "Le Monocle de Mon Oncle" [CP 13]) to the real woman whose appearance and smell evoked once more all the confusion he had felt while watching his mother sitting on the floor, buttoning her shoes?

In stressing his identity with Elsie during the years of their courtship, Stevens exhibited another of the ways in which he still needed, as an adult, to incorporate or merge with what represented "other" for him. There are indications of this in a number of the published letters, but the unpublished letters at the Huntington Library, plus the unpublished fragments in Elsie's

304

notebook, show this need to have been expressed far more frequently and urgently than the published material suggests. His naming her with variations of names he used for himself reflected this, signing himself "Buddy," for example, and addressing her as "Dear Bud," or, as mentioned earlier, his incorporating their two names in "Bo-Peep" which evoked "Bo-Pete." This impulse, motivated by insecurity, was also one of the sources of Stevens's poetic sensibility, his extreme empathy. Being uncertain of a particular and delimited self prompts the search to find in other beings points of recognition and identity, replacements for the smiling approval of the mother whom Stevens described in "Sunday Morning" as "waiting sleeplessly." There she is ultimately associated with death, the extreme example of what we want to know about but cannot. And as Stevens knew by then and described there, it is from this desire to know that we invent and find beauty:

> Death is the mother of beauty; hence from her,
> Alone, shall come fulfillment to our dreams
> And our desires. Although she strews the leaves
> Of sure obliteration on our paths,
> The path sick sorrow took, the many paths,
> Where triumph rang its brassy phrase, or love
> Whispered a little out of tenderness,
> She makes the willow shiver in the sun
> For maidens who were wont to sit and gaze
> Upon the grass, relinquished to their feet.
> She causes boys to pile new plums and pears
> On disregarded plate. The maidens taste
> And stray impassioned in the littering leaves.
> (CP 68–69)

Obviously, however, this kind of positive transformation does not always occur, and it did not always occur for Stevens. When identity cannot be firmly established and nothing else ensures security, one often attempts to destroy or ignore the cause of the renewed feelings of confusion and uncertainty. This showed itself in Stevens's repeated and various requests that Elsie be not Elsie but someone else, his "Little Girl," his "Princess," "Lady," and, finally, "Muse." Though this desire certainly enriched his imaginative life, allowing him to use her to expand into the details of fantasies, it did violence to her as she was.

Stevens's insecurity about identity and his resulting need to display himself were intrinsic to his personality. They were also goads to his success as a poet, which was based on his inability to be satisfied by mere poetic competence. Had he gotten approval from his parents for what he liked to do, perhaps he would have settled for mere competence. But "good Puritans" were not in the habit of encouraging a child to do what gave pleasure. There had to be an edge of constant striving, for if this edge were blunted, there would be nothing to encourage industry, thrift, sobriety. Since Stevens's parents did withhold their approval, this denial became the core of later experiences that only further stimulated his need to distinguish himself. Stevens sought a place in the pantheon of "man-poets." Homer, Dante, Shakespeare, Tennyson, Browning were in his mind, and he wanted to join them.

While Stevens never resolved the tensions in his actual relationship with Elsie, he did attempt to resolve them in his writing; poetry was "a health," a "completion of life." Though he would never in reality fully satisfy the need to see and know, he imagined what he wanted and this created the poems that, in being part of what the world would see when he was recognized, also satisfied his need to display himself. But because these desires were worked out in a reality beyond words, Stevens remained, until late in his life, ambivalent about the display itself, worrying that his reputation as a poet might damage some of his relationships in the insurance business. At the same time, however, revealing his ambivalence in yet another way, he used his skill as a "word merchant" (as one of his associates at the Hartford Accident and Indemnity Company described him) to disturb those around him who were not comfortable with wit like his own.[44]

Stevens's poetry represented as well a mature form of the pranking for which he had been noted in his youth, a reflection of a need to call attention to himself, but covertly and in ways that invited at least mild punishment. In the end both the pranking and the poetry turned around an uncertain identity overburdened by a sense of shame since the fear that he did not deserve to be called a "boy" or a "man" remained. One response to this situation was, in some sense, to become both male and female. Hence Stevens's desire to be one with Elsie and to observe her, while himself unseen, in all her behavior; hence, also, his "indulging," as he put it, in the "lady-like" habit of "writing verses." But attached to this, of course, for Stevens was a different kind of fear and shame: that he was not what he was supposed to be in his social role, how he was seen. Naïvely revealing of this, too, is the "Winter Night" letter, in its disclosure of his contradictory uneasiness about "gold medal boys" and "saxophones" and his desire to "peep" at Elsie dressed as one of his imagination's props. In this letter Stevens signed himself "Sambo" (evoking the small, dark hero who watched his fears, represented in the story by tigers—reminding us of the "tigers/In red weather" in "Disillusionment of Ten O'Clock"— turn to sweet, liquid butter). Stevens could not imagine himself as Cromwell or Napoleon, someone who could change the world, but he could turn his fears into the sweetness of poems.

In the letter he wrote to Elsie on December 7, four days after the letter of "A Winter Night," he again revealed his need to be seen, in describing a conversation he had had with a little man of gentlemanly breeding on the subject of Michelangelo. In connection with this man's manner, he first remarked that "frankness," which he himself tried so hard to cultivate, characterized "people of good breeding" and that "generally . . . unimportant people . . . are secretive and full of dignity." Ironically, this is how he himself came to be perceived by those with whom he had regular contact. He also noted in his letter that he had gone with his friend Walter Butler on their "usual [Sunday] walk." This friendship was curious in that Butler was eleven years younger than Stevens; they had become "close companions" in 1905, when Stevens lived in East Orange and Butler was only fifteen years old. Butler moved to downtown New York about a year after Stevens had moved downtown again after his time in Fordham Heights. The difference in their ages suggests that it could not have been a friendship of equals; as Stevens wrote to Elsie, he did not get on with his peers or with his superiors. His relationship to Butler resembled Michelangelo's to lesser figures, obscuring, though masterful and guiding. As he put it to Elsie in this letter:

> And don't you agree with me that if we could get the Michael Angeloes out of our heads—Shakespeare, Titian, Goethe—all the phenomenal men, we should find a multitude of lesser things (lesser but a *multitude*) to occupy us? It would be like withdrawing the sun and bringing out innumerable stars. I do not mean that the Michael Angeloes are not what they are—but I like Dr. Campion. I like Verlaine—water colors, little statues, small thoughts. Let us leave the great things to the professors—substitute for majestic organs, sylvan reeds—such as the shepherds played on under cottage windows
>
> In valleys of springs and rivers
By Ony and Teme and Clun.
(L 110)

At this point Stevens had begun to declare himself a poet, at least to Elsie; at the same time he also disparaged the law as "mostly thinking without much result." Still, he was not comfortable wearing the poet's mantle. He, after all, saw his involvement with "verses" as "lady-like." He felt threatened, as he expressed indirectly here, by "man-poets" of the stature of Goethe or Michelangelo. The greater his need to become a "man-poet" himself, the greater the attendant fear that he would never succeed. Reflecting this ambivalence, his following association in the letter was to A. E. Housman, a less than "phenomenal" man whose studious ghost rose to whisper his prompting lines. In these Stevens found another of the suggestions that later went into the title *Harmonium,* an instrument somewhere between a sylvan reed and a majestic organ. On this he would play songs that communicated the same disillusionment with life, the same majesty of indifferent nature, the same stoic yet fatalistic acceptance of things as they are, though in more successfully achieved tones and syllables.

In the letter of December 7 he went on to note Gilbert Stuart's device of using dots of white in the eyes of his portraits; he noted, too, that he planned to go to the Morgan Library to see a manuscript of Keats's *Endymion.* Just after, he used an image of the moon and stars that could have been one of its lines. He then recalled the guitar-playing old lady in the Cambridge rooming house where he had lived while at Harvard; she sang a hymn with "thousands of verses" to the same repeated melody. This memory was evoked by his having played only a few chords over and over again on his guitar just that evening. The evocation reappeared transformed, as Holly Stevens points out, in "The Man with the Blue Guitar." Similarly, he later adapted to auditory effect Stuart's white-dot technique; in "The Comedian as the Letter C," for example, he experimented with repeating the various sounds of the letter *c* to focus attention. And his musing on the opening line of *Endymion,* which he quoted to Elsie in his letter ("A thing of beauty is a joy forever") years later elicited his response in the closing of "Peter Quince at the Clavier":

> Beauty is momentary in the mind—
> The fitful tracing of a portal;
> But in the flesh it is immortal.
>
> (*CP* 91)

Finally, as mentioned above, the association made between "majestic organs" and "sylvan reeds" contributed importantly to his eventual titling of *Harmonium.* Seeing how each of these elements relates to his later work makes it clear that Stevens did indeed go back and wander "far afield" in the letters he had written to Elsie. In them and in his journals he found the motifs and images around which he wove his poems.

The December 7 letter closed, picking up on his "Sambo" signature of the previous one, with a retreat into his "Faery" world and a fantasy most revealing of the desire connected to his uncertainty of self. In this fantasy he presented for Elsie's entertainment a male character, "Marse Sambo," who, on being ignored by the proud and pretty maid in pink slippers, acts gallantly. In so doing, he gets the maid's parasol, which, though the stage directions do not specify, he must have collapsed. He then comes down the road under the parasol that he has reopened and plays her part. At this point a tangle ensues. "Such scandal" Stevens called it because it disclosed his deepest "scandalous" wishes: taking the parasol, a conveniently protean instrument suggestive of both male and female sexuality; taking on her role; and, at the same time, getting beneath the parasol, thus provoking her into light grappling. Divulgingly the little scene culminates not in resolution between them but in a call to a "Constable" who will both protect her and punish him. All the lineaments of his doubts and fears were there.

In the following letter, written on December 8 and 9, he referred for the first time to "The Book of Doubts and Fears"—the "volume" he saw his part of the correspondence becoming. He also noted that it was not "desireable" [*sic*] to disclose so much of his spirit. But he had to reveal enough to assuage Elsie's obvious dissatisfaction about his not visiting her more often. She complained that in sharing only words, they were "shadows" at best, strangers at worst. Though when they were together, she did try to dress for the roles his imagination assigned her, the part of her that emerged in his absence to write her letters to *him* was healthily disturbed at being a shadow figure, a paper doll. ("Are you really fond of books—paper valleys and far countries, paper gardens, paper men and paper women? They are all I have, except you; and I live with them constantly," he wrote to her [L 80]. She was implicitly giving him her negative reply.) Had she been able to articulate, even in an unsophisticated manner, precisely what it was that unsettled her, she might have forced him to some kind of resolution of his feelings. If she had, their relationship might have been different, and it would be interesting to speculate about its effect on his poetry. As it was, however, it was all too easy for her "beau" to deflect her discomfort, her sense of things as they were, and to blame his reluctance to visit her on his feeling like a stranger at home in Reading. Though this was true (he had felt this even before he had met her), it was not sufficient reason to stay away. Nor was it in itself something that should have been left unexamined if he wanted to understand what he described to her in this letter as his "resentment" at the familiarity those he "once knew well enough" displayed toward him.

But had he examined his resentment ("I don't believe in holding the microscope up to oneself . . ." he had written to Elsie recently, and years later, to another correspondent, "I should probably not be able to stand up to a Freudian analysis" [L 488]), he would not have made up, as he did in this letter, his imaginary lists of "Pleasant Things" to distract him. In view of the result of this turning away from the painful aspects of experience, this troping that made his poems, it might be argued that we, too, should turn away. One piercingly ironic anecdote about an item in this first list of "Pleasant Things," however, calls this argument seriously into quietion. Pumpkin custards were one of the delicacies Stevens most liked. In *Souvenirs and Prophecies* (p. 202), Holly Stevens relates: "Pumpkin custards were something I suffered through, with my son, in my mother's later years—I do not remember them from my childhood, but after my father's death they made frequent appearances." As he withheld himself, out of fear of facing not his "studious ghosts" but his everyday phantoms, Elsie, too, learned implicitly to withhold what gave pleasure. Sadly, however, after his death, she seemed to want to feed his shade.

On the second evening of the same letter, December 9, Stevens continued his list of "Pleasant Things," prepared for a "change of masks," as he put it, and became "Tom Folio," a character prefiguring both "The Comedian as the Letter C" (Folio uses large spectacles to *see*) and "The Doctor of Geneva." He carries a collapsed umbrella, like Little Black Sambo, and, like the Comedian, later, a baton. Another curious fantasy followed; Stevens was sure he didn't know what it meant, he wrote, his only offering toward explication being that he had just finished "drawing up an agreement full of 'Whereas,' and 'Now,' and 'Therefore.'" He was so tired from this that he knew he could neither censor nor interpret. He went on, then, with yet another fantasy, but a more controlled one. In this he combined a thirteenth-century legend from Gonzalo de Berceo's *Miracles of Our Lady* with his own desire ("Now you have a blue [one of the Virgin's colors] ribbon in your hair"). The legend in question describes a monk who has nothing to offer the Virgin but his juggling. In spite of his initial hesitations about the appropriateness of entertaining her with his only, profane skill, she finds his performance immensely pleasing. Stevens, afraid of showing himself too directly, as he had mentioned at the beginning of this two-day letter, used this borrowed form, as he used others both earlier and later, and felt somehow protected, covered by it. Berceo's legend was his "cloak of Spain," the garment beneath which the Comedian later hid his identity.

But the rendering of what appears to be a neutral, "other" subject is precisely what allows the artist's irrational element to emerge unmediated, unselfconsciously. In dealing directly with irrational "up-pourings," rationality and self-consciousness too often intrude to dam or divert the source, just as Stevens here cut short his Tom Folio fantasy. The "more than rational distortion" that "reveals a way of truth," as Stevens put it, can occur and be communicated only if one describes the common ground of real facts in a particular manner (Stevens later developed this idea theoretically in connection with Marianne Moore's focus on "particularity"). In the very choice of facts to be imitated, the true particular is disclosed. Of course, at this point, in turning to the medieval legend of the juggler-monk, Stevens was not aware that he was revealing himself. But by the time he wrote "Cy Est Pourtraicte, Madame Ste Ursule, et Les Unze Mille Vierges" (CP 21) five or six years later, he was aware. In this poem he developed the same motif of the humble, spontaneous gift of joy being preferable to suffering for not having the requisite offering. Now sensitive to the covering/disclosing capability of borrowed forms, he distorted intentionally and rationally by replacing the juggler-monk, who could too easily be identified with him, with "Ste Ursule." Stevens could then imagine the "dull scholars" he covertly disparaged spending countless hours searching The Golden Legend, a possible source to which he pointed (through a reference to Jacobus de Voragine, the Legend's author, in another poem). But seeing that the titling of the "Ste Ursule" poem in old French belies that origin, the scholars would follow another false lead since the generating legend was versed not in old French but in Spanish. Nosing into what Stevens in "The Irrational Element in Poetry" called the "poetry of the subject," they would miss the "true" one, though the poem's last lines do reveal—"This is not writ/In any book"—Stevens's pranking.

Yet now, in the letters, there was only one reader. As she read these words—"my juggling, my dear"—did she smile? And how did she react to his including her in his category of "two sinners," as he did nearing the end of his letter? Did she mind that he showed himself "agreeably mad," as he put it? Did she forgive him for being "so flighty," or would she have preferred he had been "parsonical?" That would have been, as he went on, "just as easy" since he was both "disaffected flagellant" and "high-toned old Christian."

It seems she did smile, but whether in response to his juggling or to the news with which he closed the above letter—that he would be home for three days at Christmas (his usual stay was a day and a half)—is hard to say. What is certain is that she favored him, at least, with a return letter heavy with her scent; he commented in his following letter of Monday, December 14, that the "sachet was wonderful." In it she expressed her feeling in terms that belonged to the courtly conventions he had established: "I send my love to you monsieur, which you must not treat lightly." But instead of reacting positively to this, Stevens again voiced his fear of not being accepted as he was as well as his ambivalence about being seen. He voiced a dissatisfaction that must have made her reel at least a bit in confusion, addressed as she continually had been as "Lady," "Little Girl," and "Princess": "I wish that when you wrote, 'I send my love to you monsieur, which you must not treat lightly,' you had written instead, 'I send my love to you Wallace, which you must not treat lightly.' There is a difference to my re-acting [this word is somewhat illegible in the Huntington collection's manuscript] mind. Don't you, too, observe it?" (WAS 1796).

In this Monday evening letter he accounted to her, as usual, for his Sunday activities. He had once again spent the day with Walter Butler. Attempting to prove himself against yet another standard, he had exhausted himself racing him around the Central Park reservoir. He noted that he liked Butler because of his ability but that he, more than a few years Butler's senior, could still beat him. He was so "distraught" as a result of the race, however, that he could not write to Elsie that evening, though he had gotten as far as the second page of the letter. (He did not forward the false start or include it with this one.)

Stevens closed the letter noting that he was glad the typhoid epidemic, which had prompted his earlier precautions to her, was over, and he requested that on his arrival she wear a pink ribbon in her hair and greet him with her Christmas cakes. In describing this last wish, he made a comment on a most peculiar spelling error: "Imagine having a plate-ful of Elsie's own backing. I shall expect them—backing—what a singular word—bakeing or baking or whatever it is. The deuce with or-tho-graph-y. Cakes are much more important than spelling" (WAS 1796). Orthography was not the problem here. No phonetic confusion accounted for his slip, but rather, it would seem, a fear or sense of what he expected or desired; both her turning away from him, ignoring him as the pretty maid did "Marse Sambo," and her supporting him as he so much needed—"Elsie's own backing."

In the next letter, dated "Wednesday Evening," December 16, he excused himself for not having written on the intervening day. He then reiterated his desire for the cakes and made his stage directions for the coming visit even more explicit. After noting that he had received confirmation from Mrs. Keeley about his room—his separation from his family, prompted by their disapproval of Elsie, now being complete—he went on:

> I think it would be nice if we could just spend our time together quietly
> without attempting or wishing to do much—so that the time itself would

seem longer. But that is always so difficult. —I want to steep myself in you, if I may use so extraordinary a term—as if you were a South Wind and as if I were—well, a dingy fellow, as I am. You will not be too terribly ironed, will you? Just have a few comfortable things—perhaps pink slippers quite late [?], and that plate of cakes so that I won't feel at all as if I were making a call. Suppose we could pass quickly through some gates of the imagination and find ourselves? Yes—we must do that at once. —You must not look at me as if you had not seen me for a long time or anything. (A mandoline [*sic*] passes in the street.) Yet it is silly to lay down so many rules. They'll all be broken. There seem to be reservoirs concealed in all of us—even the most sedate—that break unexpectedly. I do not say they will break at this time or that. Fully! I simply say that they are concealed and that they break unexpectedly—and so much for the rules. —You will say, "The lazy vagabond wants his princess to salute him in the manner of a vagabond and not in the manner of a Princess." Oh my dearest Elsie, what a fib. I never said it and I shall be as royal as the occasion requires. —Still I want very much that pink ribbon and the pink slippers—or if you would rather be a snow maiden, white ribbon and white slippers and maybe a little white daub on the tip of your nose. —Yes, yes, yes. However, it is a week away. I could count the days. Fortunately, Sunday intervenes and will break up the week. Then Monday, Tuesday, when I shall begin to be ready. Wednesday, when I shall be almost ready, and Thursday when I shall start—hours before the train. Doesn't it make you tingle? —One ought not to think of it. I shouldn't especially except for you. —You are right in saying that the day itself is a kind of anticlimax. Yet it depends on the attitude of mind. . . . This is only to excite you, and to try to make you feel as I do. Acknowledge that you do. How delightful that would be. —Come, do throw your hat into the air—or whatever you do in lieu of that. —The Fast is over—the Dry Season—The Period of Pain [?], or whatever you choose to call it, and in a week I shall have you again. —But I'm a vain, assuming, dreaming—no, too late for that, and it's rubbish anyhow. —And we don't really care about the ins and outs of it, do we Elsie? I come unabashed without any philosophizing and proclaim myself

Your impatient,
WALLACE
(WAS 1797)

In addition to the details of desire and the description of how he expected to find himself and her in imagination rather than in reality, this excerpt illustrates how language works to concretize experience. The use of "reservoir" seems to have carried over from his experience of measuring himself against Butler a few days before. Here he used the word to name the source of his concealed feelings. This spontaneous, stylistic transformation of "reservoir" prefigures uses in poems. When a few years later he described a "deep up-pouring from some saltier well/Within" in "Le Monocle de Mon Oncle" or described the doctor of Geneva's tears bursting their floodgates as an "unburgherly apocalypse," references to the experiences undergone now, late in 1908, were implicit. "Reservoir" functioned here as reality imitated by the painter; it served as the "fact" through which the irrational element could show itself.

Bursting the word's literal meaning each time it was used directly, as here, or indirectly, in the poems to which it would lead, were Stevens's irrational fears of inadequacy, of showing real feeling to Elsie or to himself. It is even possible that each of these effects corresponded for him to a physical sensation, one that may be deduced from the sounds and rhythms of the words used when the idea of reservoir was conjured up in the poems. The effect of reading aloud either "The Doctor of Geneva" or the first stanza of "Le Monocle de Mon Oncle," for example, is a bursting through after a number of lines of constraint. In this last letter the same effect is felt in his description of how he imagined the days passing until he would see Elsie. The feeling of impatient tingling before breaking out unexpectedly was contained in his "reservoir," a concept deeply connected to his sense of vigor as a man (his beating Butler) and specifically to his sexuality. Later, in "Peter Quince at the Clavier," the sexual aspect of this feeling was communicated poetically in a variation of the image applied to Susanna:

> In the green water, clear and warm,
> Susanna lay.
> She searched
> The touch of springs,
> And found
> Concealed imaginings.
>
> (CP 90)

Just as he wished in the letter to have Elsie feel as he did, in the poem his wish is fulfilled. "Susanna lay" fully immersed, "steeped," as he wanted to be in Elsie. What he described to Elsie as "concealed" in his "reservoir" he revealed in these "imaginings."

Worn by his impatience and hidden psychical testing during these days, Stevens "caught cold all over [his] body" before the time of waiting was out. He recovered, however, and arrived in Reading with the Tiffany engagement ring Elsie had already "divined" as her gift. After these important three days he went back to New York and work, a happy man. On his arrival at the office on Monday morning he wrote her a short note in which he asked that she make sure to remind Mrs. Keeley that he would return on Friday morning. He closed with "Isn't it a corking day?" (WAS 1800). After that New Year's visit she had become his "Muse," as he addressed her in the first letter he wrote after coming back to the city.

"She was the occasion that awakened the poetic in him and made him a poet. That was why he could love only her, never forget her, never want to love another, and yet continually long for her. She was drawn into his whole being; the memory of her was forever alive. She had meant much to him; she had made him a poet—and precisely thereby had signed her own death sentence."[45] So wrote Constantin Constantius, the pseudonymous author of Soren Kierkegaard's *Repetition* about the fictional poet/self unable to love the woman he "loved" because of his romantic distortion of the all-too-human. The description fits what now began to occur in Stevens's relationship with Elsie. As he disclosed more of himself to her, he withdrew. Something had happened on this second holiday stay, only a week into their engagement, that made him want to "pull Silence over [him] like a cloak." He was unwilling even to indulge in fantasy and use *it* as a cloak. He was afraid of saying more about the "great sleepy jumble" inside him without first arranging it, setting it in order. In the first letter of 1909 (*L* 115–16) he jumped from one thought to another—"I do not attempt History. I shudder at Art"—and referred only obliquely to the characters that otherwise would have played out at least an imaginary act. The characters he suggested for them now were borrowed from fairy tales. In this New Year's letter they came from Kenneth Grahame's *The Wind in the Willows*. Soon he would be reading Hans Christian Andersen and using images from his stories. On paper, Stevens made his pastoral world more childlike as the "vigorous warrior" emerged in reality. He revealed this as he referred in his letter to what had happened on his New Year's visit. His uncertainty of self had been prompted and witnessed by Elsie. He felt shameful, as he admitted near the letter's opening: "I do not return placidly, as if it had never happened." Elsie had experienced his desire and his reticence: "—How soon we came together—after that first conquest of myself, so necessary to be made by me. Could you fail to see the prim letter-writer being mauled by the more vigorous warrior—yet still clinging to his wig?"

He covered what he could not express openly in a reference to Mole and Toad from Grahame's story. In a central chapter of *The Wind in the Willows* Mole and Rat find themselves in some strange *terra incognita* that is nonetheless familiar to them; similarly, Stevens described himself and Elsie as "half-native" in their *terra incognita*. In this eerie pastoral Rat and Mole meet the Great God Pan, the embodiment of sexuality as the life force of nature. Rat's reaction is appropriately "panic," confusion: "'Rat!' . . . 'Are you afraid?'

"'Afraid?' murmured the Rat, his eyes shining with unutterable love. 'Afraid! Of Him? O, never, never! And yet—and yet—O, Mole, I am afraid!'"[46]

This was the same reaction Stevens had to his own sexuality, his "vigorous warrior." By calling on these characters, Stevens, as the "prim letter-writer," could elliptically refer to what had gone on. Imagining he would need similar protection in the future, Stevens closed his letter describing his plans for long winter nights when they would be together after their marriage. They would skip "through all of Shakespeare" then.

Two evenings later he wrote again (WAS 1802) and claimed to have recovered himself. He voiced his uneasiness. He felt that she had probably found his state of mind in the previous letter "appalling." In his present state of composure he described his "usual" Thursday evening. He had gone through newspapers and pamphlets noting events of interest. He outlined activities he planned for the coming weekend: on Saturday evening a concert of two of his old favorites, Schubert's Unfinished Symphony[47] and Tchaikovsky's Fifth; before that the National Academy of Design for the last day of its winter exhibition—"which [he] never failed to see"—and the Metropolitan Museum of Art for the German pictures, for he was now becoming deeply involved in feeling his "kinship" with this "race" (see pp. 41–42); Sunday morning, work at home on a case with a friend; and then, in the afternoon, a ramble with Walter Butler.

He went on to respond to her "news." He was sorry she had finished *The Wind in the Willows*. He reassured her that he loved to hear her talk about "little things—over-shoes, slippers and so on—" because she didn't "seem so awe-inspiring then." He added parenthetically: "It's like sitting at the foot of the throne and talking about the weather." He followed up with a report of his activities of the evening before. He hadn't written because he had got home too late from dinner at the Columbia Club with a recently married friend whose wife was away. Across the table and on their walk later through the Automobile Show—which he found "tiresome beyond measure"—he had asked "all about it [married life]. It [was] thrilling!" Taking his imaginings home to his room, he fantasized about finding the perfect name for her.

Before closing the letter, he asked her to send him the folk song—apparently a Greek one—she had quoted in her last letter. He added a note that revealed how aware he was of the function of quotations with which he filled the pages of his notebooks: ". . . quotations have a special interest since one is not apt to quote what is not one's own words, whoever may have written them. The 'whoever' is the quoter in another guise, in another cap, under other circumstances. Now you shall be afraid to quote!" These sentences were most revealing. He attributed to her his fear of showing himself. He also uncovered how self-consciously he must have chosen quotations that appeared in other letters to her. His last sentence, prompting her to become as self-conscious as he, reflected how subtly he kept her "terrorized." Beyond the personal level Stevens here voiced his spontaneous rationalization for appropriating from others as easily as he did in making his poems. This belief also allowed him to feel stronger on the occasions when self-doubt was most intense. Finding a passage that reflected nobility of spirit and recording it in his notebook as his "own words" made him, for those moments a least, "man number one."

Finally, ending the letter, he compared their letters to "those mystical lanterns with their dim lights set in the dark gardens of the Japanese for the guidance of spirits." He had been reading Lafcadio Hearn's descriptions of Japanese life (in addition to volumes of collected pieces, Hearn's essays on the Orient appeared periodically in *Harper's* and in *Scribner's* magazines and others Stevens read). The Eastern resting places that he had contemplated were slowly taking on more reality.

Following the road to this faraway place in the next letter (partially in *L* 116–18, January 10, 1909), he remarked on one of the paintings that had moved him at the National Academy show: "a sunset from the roof of an Oriental house, so full of burning light that it looked like a city drowned in the Red Sea, perceived through placid water." His experience of this painting was heightened by its having been in a Paris exhibition, where it had won a "medaille." He felt that he stood in Paris looking at it rather than in New York, "far out on the bleak edge of the world." He recalled these evocations on this Sunday morning as he wrote a letter in which the words "Sunday morning" were repeated three times, while the sense of the morning itself was expanded in minute particulars. In this letter Stevens seems to have suddenly realized the centrality of "Sunday morning" in his consciousness. Over all the years of his journal keeping and letter writing, these words had been inscribed countless times, as he religiously recorded the experiences of his days of rest.

In the passage describing the "placid water" and "Red Sea" hue of the "Oriental" painting were the sonorous overtones of the "wide water, without sound" moving toward "silent Palestine" in his later poem. But there were other elements from this letter as well that suggest that "Sunday Morning" was indeed born on this cold morning in January, as Stevens imagined himself in Paris, fulfilling the wishes he had chosen—in following his father's advice—not to make real. (Ironically, just a few months later, as reality pressed Stevens even more, William Carlos Williams, right after his own far less formal engagement, was sailing to Europe, where he would spend time not only in Paris but in London and Germany as well,[48] all the places of Stevens's dreams.)

Of the already published portion of this letter, one of the most striking Sunday morning elements is Stevens's meditation on sound. This was prompted by his ten-year-old memory reawakened by the Schubert symphony he had heard the evening before. In his mind and for Elsie, he contrasted recollections with and without sound. He noted how sound reanimated lost time and immortalized it in the flesh ("Music is feeling, then, not sound"). In "Sunday Morning" he used this same contrast to key the poem. The reader strains to carry the "hush of ancient sacrifice" across the "wide water, without sound" (*CP* 67) as the very assonance and alliteration of the sounds of the lines animate the vision. Stevens's January realization is reexperienced in the reader's procession through the words of the poem. Later Stevens expanded this perception theoretically in "The Noble Rider and the Sound of Words" (*NA* 1–36).

Later in his letter, after an excursion through associations that reappeared in other poems of *Harmonium,*[49] he gave Elsie direct access to the spring of his poetic impulse. He disclosed the oppositional operation of his imagination, which transformed a gray winter morning on the edge of the world into a sunlit green one at its center: "Make your eyes round as the roundest saucers and marvel at the moon-colored night cap and all the candles set round the bed [another evocation that whispered later in *Carlos Among the Candles*]—that all come from looking out the window and feeling a shade bored by the mist and the possible rain—mist drives the mind back. Hence the confusion" (WAS 1803). When footsteps on the stairs intruded into his consciousness, he imagined following them to the park, which he would soon see on his way to dinner with Butler. In his mind he changed the park full of mist into a stage scene full of smoke from the firing of dueling pistols. This led him to a perception of self that forecast an image used in "Stars at Tallapoosa" (*CP* 71)—the lines between them plotted, in his imagination, as elliptically as the "plot" suggested here:

> We may go to the Murray Hill for dinner— . . . One is not a monk to live
> on bread and water, with parseley [*sic*—a playful evidence of his poetic
> preoccupation]—on Sundays. Only the monk—in the long run—comes out
> of it so nobly, so liberated, so much the master of himself. I say—three
> months of winter, of stern conduct—of work—and I start off with a dinner
> fit for a Bishop—Sometimes it is frivolous to be so much the master over
> self—The isolation is keen and clear ["The lines are straight and swift be-
> tween the stars."]—but the plot is pitifully thin. We are part of the world
> about us—that is the plot. Illimitable complications!—But why think it all
> out? The disorder is the mystery. The darkness we sit in to watch the dra-
> matic beyond the footlights. A lighted theatre is no theatre at all— (WAS
> 1803)

It was as though he were giving directions on how to deal with him and to read what he wrote: not to think, but to sit in the darkness amid the disorder to catch the dramatic. Now the directions were given to Elsie. As his muse she should at least be able to enjoy the fruits she inspired. But did he plot these lines for her alone?

It was in his next letter two days later (*L* 118–19) that he christened her Bo. He spoke of the evening before, when he had again enjoyed another couple's conjugal bliss, noting with relish its culinary benefits, and wove a rhapsodic fantasy using the thread of her new name. He tied together images of himself as the pilgrim continuing on his "Inky Pilgrimage" with suggestions she had provided in a verse she had sent. He added free-floating images to produce a short poem evocative of both his Poussin-like daydream and the spirit of the East. It was as though the compression of Paris and the painting of the Oriental house described in the last letter relieved itself in the outpouring of the lyric:

317

Under golden trees
I might lose desire;
Rest, and never know
The mortal fire.

In that golden shade,
I might soon forget;
Live, and not recall
The mortal debt.

The equivocation of "might" here, in connection with losing desire, pointed ahead to the many variations on the "as if" mode that characterize his mature poems. It also suggested why the ideas of the East were becoming more attractive to him: If he lost desire, he would no longer have to suffer the swings between wanting and feeling somehow inadequate, between indulgence and guilt.

This complicate harmony was prompted by his muse. Both the invocation of her new name and her offering of a verse "gave/ . . . motions to his mythy mind," (CP 67) which he here compared to a motionless sea, set undulating by "one mystical mental scene—one image." Later, another such mystical scene—an image of a marriage bed—set "Sea Surface Full of Clouds" in motion.

The next evening, Wednesday, and the evening after that he wrote as well (L 119–21). He described his German fascination a bit more—a fascination that was curiously linked with his interest in Japan and the East (see L 118 and p. 42 here). He revealed homely details of his at-home habits in the same way he had asked her to do for him. He sat in his rattan chair, one leg over its arm, wearing his soft deerskin shoes. He smoked a big cigar and read the Post before "scribbling" some lines that would find their way into Elsie's next "June Book." He described his "old prune" reaction to an Isadora Duncan-like dance recital he had seen.[50] He perused one of his old journals, one of the "Sacred Books," as he called them now, playfully evoking the Sacred Books of the East, the first volume of which had appeared in English (translated by Max Müller) in the year Stevens was born. With his interest in the Orient rising like the sun itself, this association rose as well. Later in the evening, carried all the way to Xanadu in his imaginings, he read Coleridge until midnight. He did not specify what he read, but from his comment to Elsie in his Thursday evening addition—"It is heavy work, reading things like that, that have so little in them that one feels to be contemporary, living"—it seems he searched in the "pure good of [Coleridge's] theory" rather than in the measured good of his poems.

Wanting something closer to contemporary living, on Thursday after work he stopped into several bookstores, looking for new things to read. He found Henry James's Washington Square, went home (fantasizing Elsie would be there), cut the pages, and then wrote to her, promising to send the book on "if it [was] any good." It wasn't, as he noted a few days later, on Sunday evening, when he wrote again (*L* 121–123). Stevens did not appreciate James's meticulous suggestions of the manipulative motivations underlying human relationships. Focusing on the surface alone, the young poet saw only "an exhibition of merely conflicting characters," just "an old story that the neighborhood was once suburban but that with the growth of the City has come to be very much 'down-town.'" He had read "quickly," as though he didn't want to look too closely into what could serve as a mirror for his own coercions of another's spirit. And he certainly did not want Elsie to become sensitized to what Henry's brother, William, called the "recesses of feeling, the darker, blinder strata of character . . . the only places in the world in which we catch real fact in the making."

On this Sunday, walking through the snowy park with Butler, Stevens had another experience of its being evening all afternoon. The circle of associations that would be completed in "Thirteen Ways of Looking at a Blackbird" was growing: "The sun did not shine directly and it was twilight before it was really clear." Later in the letter he noted the difficulty he had had with Maurice Maeterlinck's work. He had jumped to him from James. As Holly Stevens observes, in connection with the "blue bird" in her father's list of "Pleasant Things," Maeterlinck and his symbol—the title of one of his plays, which first appeared in 1909 and which Stevens probably saw—seemed to be associated with the blackbird in "Thirteen Ways" (*SP* 202). But Stevens had already established a personal link between bluebirds and blackbirds in substituting one for the other in one of his fantasies (see p. 218). In 1917, looking back at the events of his world from afar, as if from a bird's-eye perspective, Stevens went back over these letters and his journals. Their evocations moved him as he wrote that most cryptic poem, a poem as stripped of rhetoric as he would write. It was an approach to "white truth," a counter to Maeterlinck's obfuscation of philosophical perception with his display of rhetoric.

This Sunday letter revealed Stevens in one of his most open moods. He expressed his "delight . . . in the body," defined what he felt about the supernatural in accounting for Poe's success, defined his own concept of "bareness" and how books made up for it. He would dress the bareness of winter for himself by reading "violently all week," he wrote to Elsie. He also showed himself sensitive to her possible dislike of her new name, though he made her promise to wear her hair in the old-fashioned way he loved, at least once, only for the two of them to see, since she felt uncomfortable not following the current fashion. His temporary peace was reflected in his closing evocation of a "valley in Eden—[their] old Eden."

The next night, still feeling content, he composed two poems, as he told her on Tuesday evening, when he next wrote (*L* 124; WAS 1807). This evening, too, he was happy. He was playing everything in a "major" key. He again mentioned his work as a lawyer, not bitterly but simply as "the quaintest way of making a living in the world." He had found her letter that morning "bully" and was glad she had kept her new name, though he did not want it modified to "Beau." He also imagined the "dandy" time they would be having if she were with him; he would have her "practice the piano for seventeen hours [to] massacre . . . the noodles next door—one of whom [had] played like a mad woman a half-hour" before (WAS 1807). He described the most trivial aspects of his day, from having his razor sharpened, to what he ate for lunch "—sandwiches, milk and apple juice" (WAS 1807). After noting how long he had spent searching bookshops to indulge his passion (adding that in New York, as opposed to Boston, there were "few good bookshops" since "very few people read"), he observed how frivolous it was for damsels to spend all their money on fashionable clothes. Old things were better. Luckily Elsie made most of her dresses. But wanting to be fashionable herself, she must have felt somewhat perturbed by her fiancé's preferences. To please him she had to look like Little Bo-Peep, "in her hair," with ribbons and bows. She could not be as she wanted to be, part of the world around her. (After their marriage, however, as evidenced in photos of her from various periods, she seems to have followed her own bent and the latest styles she saw in magazines—at least until a certain point when she adopted a mode of dress suited to a withered old maid.)

As they approached the close of the first month of their engagement, Stevens wrote a letter in which he gave her some of the particular facts of his childhood (L 125–26; SP 206–08). He wanted to account for who he was, what he liked. He signed it using his childhood nickname, Pat. And like a boastful child, it was in this letter that he exaggerated the truth, announcing that he had taken "all the prizes at school." In it, too, he described the sharply contrasting uncle and aunt whose memories were later stirred into the making of "The Emperor of Ice-Cream" (see pp. 51–52).

In one of the excised portions of his next letter (WAS 1809, January 24, 1909) he described his love of ice cream. After commenting on Elsie's recipe for a gelatin she planned to make for him (he suggested she add a cup of coffee to her ingredients to make it more pleasing for him), he went on: "I detest pastry for dessert. They [eating places in New York] have rice pudding, too, which has a very queer taste in the evening. But on Wednesdays and Sundays [this was a Sunday] they have ice-cream! They give you a square piece. I like it in mountains—." He had had his usual Sunday with Butler. They had walked in New Jersey and on their return had eaten well at the Murray Hill, as was their habit. Elsie must have been bothered by her fiancé's spending on dinners "fit for Bishops" while he squinted Scrooge-like at the extravagance of fashionable damsels. But she had more troublesome things to consider than these subtle contradictions. A few sentences later she read of how harshly her mettle would be tested by living in the city. After he had noted that in New York "You become what you desire to be"—as though he had—he went on: "It will make a great difference to you coming here. For you will find immediately the necessity of adjusting yourself to many things now unknown. You will find your character either a torment or a delight, and *which* will depend entirely on your strength."[51] Poor "Two and Twenty," as he addressed her now, not only was she to leave behind everything she had ever known, but the man who waited for her presented himself as already having become what he desired to be. While she would just be beginning to ask herself what she wanted, she would have to adjust to the fixed product he was. But even these problems were not yet pressing. Besides, he tempered the picture with humor: "—and once a year we'll go to the theatre, and on Christmas I'll give you a box of cigars." He also distracted her with additions to her reading list and critical observations of his reading,[52] and sent her a poem in return for hers. For the moment she had only to consider whether she would like to accept the invitation with which Stevens closed his letter: Would she like to spend a Saturday with him in Philadelphia going to the annual exhibition at the Academy of Arts?

Before she had time to send her response, the next letter she received presented her with more considerations. A shift had occurred; their "Faery" world peopled with their various imaginary representations was suddenly replaced by a real one in which Elsie and Wallace would have to act. His letter of January 26 (WAS 1810) was different in tone from those in which he expressed romantic wishes for some lost or never-to-be-found paradise. Here he disclosed wishes he wanted to make real. He was aware of the change himself. He commented on wanting to keep to the facts of reality: ". . . for the present let us confine ourselves to black and white and keep radiance for dreams." He listed a number of pieces of music he was sending her to practice.[53] He promised "next time" to send her more Kenneth Grahame to read and made certain to give her a reason for the change in activities for a particular evening he had planned. He commented that he liked "to loaf in the evening" but didn't have enough books at present to do it happily. His solution was to occupy his imagination with the theater again. Just as during his first years in New York, when he swung out of a period of black moods and into one of comparative well-being, he indulged in bursts of going to the theater, now he did so again. Without books and unwilling to sit quietly at home and meditate on his state—something he seemed to do only in his dark phases—he lost himself in musical comedies. "Anything like a serious show would bore me to death," he wrote to her. He would call up Walter Butler the next day and get him to go in the evening to see *Kitty Gray*. He thought this English production preferable—with its agreeable music, bright people, and not so "beastly elaborate" set—to a "New York show . . . always filled with Jewesses singing solos and making dull remarks." Again, as his need to mix with others reasserted itself, so did his misanthropic bigotry.

Elsie read his letters as each day moved her closer to life in the coarse Babylon on the bleak edge of the world. At night she read books he sent, more fairy tales of golden ages and friendly woods and copses. Beneath the surface she wondered: If she pressed for more frequent visits to Reading, he pleaded economy, yet his slender purse seemed to stretch magically for more extravagances with Butler. He continued in the same letter in which he told

of his return to the delights of the theater to present more new realities for her
to encompass. These lay in a future farther off than the one she would meet in
eight months. Prompted by his observation about the superiority of the English theater, he described a new Bernard Shaw play he had read of. He then
went on to outline wishes he had once had for himself and that he now began
to imagine as realities that included her:

> Bernard Shaw has just brought out a new thing in London called "The
> Admirable Bashville." There is no scenery and the actors act in their every-
> day clothes. It is a burlesque on Shakespeare, I believe,—wouldn't it be nice
> to live in London and go, say, on Saturday evening? We'll be going over
> there one of these days, I hope.—I should mope in Paradise (possibly) if I
> were to die without first having been to London.—On Sunday, it was
> Berlin.—I have had my hours øf [sic] for Paris, too. —Where I could see
> the Street of Little Stables, and the Street of Beautiful Leaves, and the
> Bridge of Arts, and the Church of Our Lady, and the Arch of Triomphe
> [sic]—as clearly as I can see you looking out of that frame.—Good Fortune
> send us to them all.—We'll save for that. It isn't so impossibly expensive
> you know. People who go once go often—unless that once they go in stale,
> foolishly. —It seems much nearer, too, when the steamers start from the
> foot of your own street, as they do here.—I was well aware of that the other
> night in the fog when there was a continual whistling and bell-ringing all
> night long.—Perhaps it was that turned me into that salty billow rolling so
> far inland [see opening of letter of January 24 (L 127)]—foaming over the
> dazzling white shutters opposite you—white as blinds, say, in Algiers
> (where they are doubtless green or brown). So you have been sending kisses
> to me each night! My dear, I have sent you many, very often. But I must
> remember that you send them as you do, and wait for them, and send others
> in return. I have been thinking lately so many pleasant things of you. That
> will only be another. Bye!
>
> WALLACE

Here he was, expressing to "Bo" his desire to go to London, Berlin, and
Paris. She could not have any reason to object as his father had. At least she
could not have a reason he could perceive. Feeling her implicit compliance to
his needs, he closed the letter ebulliently, "thinking . . . so many pleasant
things of [her]" and spontaneously came upon another element that he later
transformed into an image for "The Emperor of Ice-Cream." The "actors . . .
in their every-day clothes" became the girls in dresses they were "used to
wear."

By Friday evening, three days later, Stevens began to have misgivings
about what he had revealed. He sensed that Elsie would have some questions
about his indulgences, so he sent a short note acknowledging his "dissipation"
and gave two justifications that were so weak that he could not elaborate on
them. One was internal and postulated on his need to reward himself for his

diligence. The other was external: He didn't want to stay home because his neighbors were always "drumming on the piano":

DEAR BO,

I'm in the midst of a fit of dissipation. When I have saved and cooped myself up for a month,

> There comes a night
> When we all get tight.

Well, I haven't been doing that, of course, but I've been to the theatre twice and am going again to-night, and to-morrow night too, possibly. . . . One . . . "The Blue Muse" was as funny as possible. . . . I think it will be "Kitty Gray" tonight though Maude Adams pulls me towards her. [He went on to describe the effects of the neighbors "drumming on the piano."] (WAS 1811, January 29, 1909)

On Sunday evening, January 31, he wrote again (WAS 1812; *L* 129–31; *SP* 208–10). He circumspectly opened this long and important letter by telling his "dearest Bo" how "intensely" he had wanted to see her the night before—so intensely that he had been tempted to send her a telegram asking her to fly to him. But in the next breath he gave the lie to his gallant device. Just after speaking of his "last night's" desire and that he had thought "at the last minute" of sending the wire, which she would have gotten at suppertime, he wrote, "Instead, I passed a reckless *afternoon* [italics mine] at the Library. . . ." His evening, he added, was even "more reckless." He spent it at the Metropolitan Museum of Art, visiting the German pictures again. He commented that *Kitty Gray* had been a disappointment but again praised *The Blue Muse* for how full it was of mistaken identities. Then, in a spontaneous burst, he revealed his confusion about his recent obsession: "Why I should so suddenly have taken to going to the theatre is beyond me." He followed this immediately with a statement of his new resolve to curb indulgence: "But I have already stopped going so it does not matter. . . ." Picking up the account of his first day of purification in the library and the museum, he told her he "then . . . went up to the Park and looked at the camels and the China pheasants and the polar bear." He noted that he "felt fairly brisk coming home and threw off the bad conscience that follows indulgence." Reflecting promptly but unguardedly on what this disclosed, he exclaimed: "What a deuce a fellow is to feel that way about going to the theatre!" Seeing his agitated state—perhaps for the first time—as indicating his separation from his feelings, he continued: "—Yet I am never so thoroughly content as when I pass my evening quietly (and, say, usefully) at home. . . ."

Though this pattern of moving up and down between periods of word-filled solitude and bustling indulgence in theater and dining was not new, now that Elsie was "a part of him," the nights he evaded the walls of his room were nights that he evaded her. No long letters unraveling the thread he followed out of the maze of his days would reach her waiting eyes from nights like these. Elsie had become involved in what he knew and didn't want to know about himself. He had made her into his secret sharer: "Writing to you is like whispering to you" (WAS 1772). When, after his death, she excerpted out portions of this long record of his confession into her stenographer's notebook, it was as though she were compiling a breviary that would justify God's way to the woman she was. The passages she copied, all headed by her inspirational memorandum of the guidance offered by Santayana, somehow explained things as they were. She used these to sustain her through her own last years.

In this same Sunday evening letter Stevens went on to tease her about the gelatins she had been making almost every night of the last week. He asked playfully whether her "father" hadn't yet begun to complain or suggest that she at least add "raisins." Stevens had just shown some of his shortcomings, and now he was gently hinting at some of her homely ones, though he transferred his judgment onto Mr. Moll. He didn't stop to think that perhaps she was trying to perfect at least one dish in preparation for living with the man whose *summum bonum* seemed to be as much a dish of peaches or pumpkin custard as imagined red-winged blackbirds. Reminded of the domestic scene, Stevens then moved quickly into responding to another kind of uncertainty Elsie had expressed in relationship to him. She felt that her family was inferior to his or, at least, that his family thought hers inferior:

> By the way, I don't in the least mind what your grandmother said about her relatives or mine. It is amusing to think of that washer-woman. Mother must be worried to death when she thinks of her. You know she is a Daughter of the Revolution and traces herself through two or three generations to an officer in the American army. You can imagine her crowding out the details. Father once told her that she was a shoemaker's daughter and that he was a farmer's son. That is true. But her father was an excellent shoemaker and his father an excellent farmer—not at all the kind of man we call a farmer at home, but a man of ability and character. They both belonged to large families and both were poor. It is very silly for people in a country town to bother about such things. Besides, you can't get around a washer-woman.
>
> On the other hand, we all have poor relations.—And as a last refuge, we can say that individuals rise or fall on their own merits. Their families are nothing.—The whole question is one of respectability.—We both come from respectable families—you and I. What more is there to be said? The rest depends upon ourselves.—What we inherit in our characters presents a question. What we inherit otherwise is unimportant. Nothing is more absorbing than to trace back the good and evil in us to their sources. At the same time, nothing is more unjust or more ungenerous. Our spirits are what we will them to be, not what they happen to be, that is if we have any courage at all.

I hate a man that is what he is—the weak victim of circumstances. That involves occasional hatred of myself. For example, no one loathes melancholy more than I, yet there are times when no one is more melancholy. And there are other traits besides melancholy. No one likes good manners more than I, or appreciates them more, and yet when I am blue—Lord! how blue, and bearish, and ill-mannered I am.—In defense: this is, quite likely, true of everyone, in a measure. It is particularly true of idealists,—idealists being, perhaps, the most intolerant form of sentimentalism.—By contrast, one likes those plain characters, always equable, that accept things as they are. Their simplicity seems so wise.—Unfortunately such characters commonly develop only in maturity and even in age.—The young are incorrigible. Personally, I am still decidedly young—not nearly so competent as I have an idea of being some day to be superior to circumstances. But there's no end to this. Let us avoid the beginning, therefore.

At the library yesterday, I skipped through a half-dozen volumes of poetry by Bliss Carman. I felt the need of poetry . . . . (SP 208–09)

Elsie clearly did not fit into his family's picture of how the young man suited to be "even President someday" should conduct his life. Stevens tried to soothe her uncertainty by admitting some of his faults and expressing that he was less than perfect. He hoped only to become "competent" someday at being "superior to circumstances" and at being able to "accept things as they are." How many times he had written that last phrase—almost as many times as he had "Sunday morning." Though it was linked to what he had learned and read, and belonged to the vocabulary of the age, it carried a particular meaning for Stevens. This refrain recapitulated different moments ambiguously. It suggested both stoic acceptance and transformation of what was through words. At each point that it appeared, Janus-like, uttered either directly or indirectly (as in "Let be be finale of seem" or in "The Plain Sense of Things" [CP 502]), it recalled both all that had come before and all that could come. It was a cipher for the evanescent present that punctuated the body of his work like a heartbeat.

A different kind of punctuation was offered by the reappearance of Bliss Carman. From "skipping through" his volumes, Stevens passed on to Elsie a sense of things that he later memorialized in the lyrical/sexual stanza of "Le Monocle." Stevens was particularly moved now by Carman's Sapphic poems. These were very different in tone from the *Vagabondia* books that Carman had composed with Richard Hovey. In sharp contrast with the iconoclastic and escapist atmosphere created in those volumes, quiet reverence and joy emerge from these. The appeal for Stevens reflected a real change in his own spirit. For the moment, at least, irony was out of place. With this displacement, he chose the comfort of diffuse "warm beauty" above "passion." His cool, cynical stance seemed to exist as a direct response to or defense against "passion," but when this (which would make widows wince) was absent, so was irony. In this mood, Stevens composed a sonnet around a line culled from one of his Cambridge journals:

IN A GARDEN

Oh, what soft wings shall rise above this place,
This little garden of spiced bergamot,
Poppy and iris and forget-me-not,
Oh Doomsday, to the ghostly Throne of space!

The haunting wings, most like the visible trace
Of passing azure in a shadowy spot—
The wings of spirits, native to this plot,
Returning to their intermitted Grace!

And one shall mingle in her cloudy hair
Blossoms of twilight, dark as her dark eyes;
And one to Heaven upon her arm shall bear
Colors of what she was in her first birth:
And all shall carry upward through the skies
Odor and dew of the familiar earth.

(SP 210)

As he grew older and his passion cooled, this quiet mood became more constant. Now it appeared irregularly, at moments when he withdrew from his feelings.

Prompted by having copied out this sonnet for Elsie and vaguely wondering how she would receive it, he thought of a review of a volume of poetry he had read the evening before in the *Evening Post*. His response to a comment about the vanity of poetry reflected the change that had occurred in him. He strongly asserted that though it might be vain, it was not hypocrisy and it was a delight. Now, without books, he could pass his evenings writing poems instead of escaping to the theater. He had found in Carman's form a way of withholding feeling—"Carman . . . has his morning planet, his garden *then* his longing"—that he adopted. He found this on the same day he had purified his dissipated spirit in the temples of learning and art. In the library that afternoon, amid volumes of words he used to attentuate his feelings, Stevens was gently moved by Carman's way of embedding Sappho's direct utterance of passion in layers of "warm beauty." Stevens responded easily and immediately to this device and learned from it how to embed in his own poems both the seed of his feeling and references to past masters and mistresses, as Carman did with Sappho.

As he moved to the end of this long letter, Stevens noted that he was tempted to learn Italian: "What with my whirling enthusiasm first for French, and then for German, I may expect sooner or later to be interested in Italy" (WAS 1812).[54] He had a vague memory of a Giosuè Carducci sonnet about Rome[55] in his mind. He asked Elsie to look "at home" for the volume in which he believed it to be. He gave her explicit instructions on precisely where in the bookcase upstairs she would find it. He wanted her to copy the poem and send it to him. He assured her that it would be well worth her trouble. His preoccupation with it had contributed to the images in the sonnet he had composed the week before and sent her now. His musing circled images of hair and eyes evoked in the opening of Carducci's poem:

> Date al vento le chiome, isfavillanti
> Gli occhi glauchi . . . (Give to the wind thy locks; all glittering
> Thy sea-blue eyes . . .)

In Stevens's poem the memory emerged in the image of "her cloudy hair/. . . dark as her dark eyes," a metaphor made powerful by his transposing and compressing Carducci's more expected terms of reference. What Carman had done consciously in constructing his poem around Sappho's fragments, Stevens had done spontaneously. Reading Carman's volume seems to have triggered his memory of having seen in Carducci something he knew had been one of the seeds of his latest poem.

He ended his letter with one of his periodic requests for a "picture" of her and offered a rather charming glimpse of himself. He also gave two additional details about what would fill his evening:

> What dress do you wear mostly now-a-days? The black one? And the hat I like? Tell me so that I shall know how you look when you go down for shopping.—Do your cheeks still—of course, they do. Paint a little picture for me so that I can see you. I still wear that abominable hat, and the dark suit: it is the warmest. . . . I seem to think of apples at ten o'clock every night . . . and a few more pages of "The Madonna of the Future" by Henry James.

James's tale was important for Stevens because it helped him clarify—in a very different way from Bliss Carman's work—another central aspect of personality and style that he forged into his American poetic voice. James's narrator relates the story of one Mr. Theobald, an expatriate American painter living in Florence, his name wonderfully descriptive of the modern type who, having lost faith in God, had placed all his idealism in art. Theobald completely loses sight of reality because of his imaginative need to conceive the perfect work, "The Madonna of the Future." He is talented but so lost in the pursuit of the ideal that he does not even notice the effect of time on the "perfect" woman he loves platonically and uses as his model. His preparation for rendering her image is so painstaking that the canvas, on which he has been "working" for years, remains blank. From the moment the narrator points out reality to him, Theobald begins to die. The account closes with his death and the reactions of the narrator and the model for the "Madonna." In contrast with the painter, the narrator is wry and looks on with dispassionate curiosity at this creature. He observes at one point: "There could be no better token of his American origin than this high aesthetic fever."[56] Though he, too, was in Florence, basking in the pure beauty of the place, he maintained a skeptical attitude that he voiced with humor, and he kept an ironic distance between himself and the ideal.

In his next letter to Elsie, on February 2, Stevens reflected on the theater and quietly disparaged the idealistic attitude. At the same time he made an important distinction between idealism and the function of imagination, which he wisely connected to the continued existence of the child's spirit in the adult. Making this distinction marked another phase of his disillusionment. While at twenty-one and twenty-two he had been wholly taken by the presence of Maude Adams on the stage, now "there was something about the lady [he did] not like. She has such a silly voice or something." He went on in his letter to articulate what he felt was missing from her and other popular actresses' performances:

> They are not the subtle dynamic creatures they should be . . . [I desire] something more vital, something with more illusion.—The stage is imagination, in a way. With them, it is invention. . . . The theatre is a puzzle. —If we are to believe in the theory that we are never anything but children (a theory supported by Fashion, Sports, our Armies, Work, everything)— then the theatre becomes no more than the most dazzling toy ever devised. —The most dazzling toy, the most absorbing plaything!—The frowning mask of Tragedy and the smiling mask of Comedy—put them by: they are the conceptions of a sincere and less knowing age. —Good Heavens. Yes! I'm content with "The Blue Muse" sort of thing. The rest is all pretense nowadays.—And I like the musical comedy immensely. The tragedies of the Greeks with their invocations and prayers and solemnities have evolved into "The Three Twins" and "Mr. Hamlet of Broadway." It is superb. It is modern. Sparkling dresses, Frenchmen acting the dunce, pretty songs, choruses acting like Persian armies—that's the ticket. I mean it.—I hate solemn things—unless there is enough genius to make them real. But all the genius lies the other way. Hence Broadway. (WAS 1813)

Stevens associated the child's ability to transform the real into an illusion with the marks of genius. The genius could make even solemn things real. The genius used imagination to see reality in a different light, unlike the idealist, who constructed a perfect model out of various, separate parts broken from the real, originating forms. Stevens saw the idealist as violating nature because he ignored—like James's Mr. Theobald—the integrity of the real, our imperfect paradise. But Stevens felt, for the present at least, this kind of genius was impossible. In his absence he approved recourse to the flash of parodic display, self-mocking comic deflation.

His observation about the theater was actually much more about the play he conceived his life to be. His analysis was a self-analysis. It described the motives and hesitations that later accounted for the tone of *Harmonium*. Resounding with self-mocking bombast and devices designed to deflate his masters, filled with perceptions dressed in sparkling words and choruses of sounds marching like Persian armies, this volume was Stevens's self-consciously "modern" offering, complete with a cast of characters costumed in the same closet as "Mr. Hamlet of Broadway" and the "Frenchmen acting the dunce."

The hidden mainspring of his "modern" stance was the fear of the man in his mid-thirties who had not yet made his mark, who could not aspire to be the genius who could make solemn things real. This fear had long and tangled roots in his personality and was sharpened by his having seen who had been greeted as geniuses during the years preceding and continuing into the war years and after. As Stevens announced in "Le Monocle de Mon Oncle," he knew no silver-ruddy, gold-vermilion fruits" (*CP* 17) like the transformed idealists of the Yeatsian persuasion, nor did his voice break in the adolescent throes of those who were seeking a pure American diction, like William Carlos Williams. Stevens's syllables followed studied lines and moved with mannered grace across the page.

But the enactment of the understanding he had now about something outside himself was still a few years away from beginning, though the other interests he indicated in this same February 2 letter revealed the necessary preliminary turning away from solemn things. Echoing his statement some weeks earlier that he preferred "lesser things" to the products of Michelangelos, he was now reading Thomas Campion[57] and Oliver Goldsmith[58] and indulging in apples rather than in the more exotic "other goodies—jars of marrons, figs, etc." that he saw on the shelves of fruit stores. He also noted, apropos of the visit he wanted to make with Elsie to Philadelphia for the Washington's Birthday weekend, that he looked forward to the exhibition they would see especially because unlike New York, where museum walls were graced only with canonized works, there everything would be "fresh" makings of new, as yet unsainted figures.

There were three weeks until the meeting in Philadelphia. Though he had been there as a child to see the zoo and historical sites, he described it as a city still unknown to him, "as dark as Carthage" (WAS 1819, February 17, 1909). In the weeks before this weekend arrived, both he and Elsie swung back into feeling their doubts and fears. They hadn't seen each other for almost two months and were afraid of meeting their real selves again. Stevens began his swing back with another series of escapes into the theater, the first less than a week after writing to her of his renunciation. He also fell back into his other indulgences—eating at the Murray Hill with Butler—and, whenever he was not lost in some diversion, giving into his "rash, tempestuous, horrid humor, beyond control . . . all nervousness and savageness," even at the office (WAS 1817, February 15, 1909).

She retreated into irregularity in returning letters and into pulling back from her commitment to join him in Philadelphia. Though she had written on the seventh or eighth that she would meet him, by the fourteenth or fifteenth she made keeping the date conditional: ". . . if I come . . ." (WAS 1819). Accompanying her withdrawal were physical symptoms, which she attempted to remedy with one of the patent medicines commonly used at the time to cure the unnamable ills that seemed to plague the new century's more sensitive types. Stevens was unhappy about this, committed as he was to the equally popular exercise/good living cure:

> The medicine was new to me. So long as it does you no harm I hope it will do you good. Personally I think one should only take prescriptions, nothing else. However, too many doctors are as bad as too many books, so I don't prescribe, particularly as I do not know the complaint. But I continue to harp on the advantages of walking on bright days. . . . This, I recall, was the winter you feared. Now that it is almost over—and the frogs are waiting to trill—you must not be behind them in celebrating. Yet leaves are two months away, leaves and shadows, for this is the shadowless season. (WAS 1817)

Though she had been trying, following his advice over the past few years, to walk more, to exercise, and had even considered learning to swim—something he had especially encouraged, telling her what a difference it had made in his life when he learned—this kind of therapy did not seem to be well suited to her temperament. Just as in joining church she experienced the comfort he derived from nature, she seemed to find another kind of opiate more soothing than taking "delight in the body." Though this was a period in which American women were first becoming conscious of possibilities of independence and strength,[59] most of these were city women, already aware of themselves as parts of the new kind of organism the modern, increasingly industrialized metropolis represented. In addition, beyond the disadvantages of her sheltered, provincial upbringing, the intimate facts of her difficult family situation made it impossible for Elsie to conceive of herself as one who could enjoy the strength of physical and spiritual self-sufficiency. She wanted to be protected, soothed. Though she had misgivings about the directions her soon-to-be husband gave her, her need overcame them, so she dressed the parts he assigned, tried to perfect gelatins, and learned how to do all the homely things that would win her the security she craved. Perhaps she would have been happier with another, one who would not tease her about her cooking or learning to embroider: "So you didn't want me to think that Mrs. A. had taught you how to embroider! Not that: you didn't want me to think that I knew. I bow my head, my dear.—But if you really embroider well, I shall have to call you Tabitha,—for it is the chief art of aunts and things.—But belts, of course, are different, especially ones of leaves and flowers. Only no 'God Bless Our Home' you know" (WAS 1814). Stevens not only was ambivalent about the kind of woman his imagination desired ("Little Girl," "Lady," "Princess," "Muse," "Shepherdess") but also was fascinated by the new kind of woman suggested by Ibsen and Shaw. His demands were certain to provoke conflict in the being who tried to fulfill any of these images. The signals he sent to her waiting there on the wrong side of the tracks in Reading were wholly confusing.

Stevens was no more aware of how his imaginative needs overlapped his real ones in relationship to Elsie than he was of how any of his imagination's products determined what he saw in reality. A fine example of this comes from one of the letters from this three-week period (WAS 1815, February 6–7, 1909). Stevens had gone with Butler to the Pratt Institute in Brooklyn one Saturday afternoon to see an exhibition of paintings by Charles Warren Eaton. The subject of these canvases was Bruges and some of its adjoining landscapes. Ending a long paean to the beauty of the place, especially to its waterfront and canals with their constantly varying reflections of shapes and light, a paean that included a line strongly evocative of Milton—"trees in an amethystine sky"—Stevens focused on the wharves: "And the wharves near Bruges! There is one called 'le quai du Miroir'—the quay of the mirror—a dock of glossy tranquillity with forms of blue and amber and rose swimming around idle shapes.—Bruges becomes important to me. I must whirl away there to-night in my chariot and never rest till I touch the Pont Flamand." Even before he reached home that night, his imaginings of Bruges had invaded reality and prepared him to see his own city framed as magically as Eaton's canvases: "Coming home I walked across the Brooklyn Bridge. It was clear and marvellously mild, except for a high wind. The harbor is certainly one of the great sights. To the Southwest it was a monstrous glare of sunlight in water, and then the innumerable ships, the fort, the huge silhouette of the city in the twilight."

He had other diversions during this period as well. Besides theater and dining out, Stevens made a trip to visit Arthur Clous, then living "as sincerely as a priest" in Jamaica, New York (WAS 1815). He went to another exhibition of paintings—these, Spanish pictures by Joaquín Sorolla at the Hispanic Museum. He liked these so much "for their effulgent sunshine in beach scenes . . . the realism of holiday, the external world at its height of brilliance" (SP 213) that he went again (WAS 1816). He attended a curious lecture on the "Savage South Seas," given by a "bald youth with familiar air" at the American Institute on Forty-fourth Street, "the oddest place for New York I have ever been in—looks exactly like a lodge room or library in a small town. I liked it," he wrote later that same evening to Elsie. He had also encountered a glorious recessional at Calvary Church. The hymn—"The daylight slowly fades"—he thought "the finest hymn in the world—The music of it" and tried later to find a copy of it for Elsie to learn to play (WAS 1815).

As the weekend when they would see each other drew closer, and the pressures at the office were not relieved by any of his evening or weekend escapes, he sought solace once more in the *thought* of Elsie. But it never occurred to him that this most recent attack of nerves might have something to do with actually presenting himself to her again. As though preparing his ground, on the Monday preceding their excursion, he wrote that it was only the *idea* of her that brought him "harmony": "Sometimes I am terribly jangled, full of clashing things. But always, the first harmony comes from something I cannot just say to you at the moment—the touch of you organizing me again" (*L* 131). The "harmony" was in what he could not say but *imagined* saying. Farther on he called her the "voice" of the "old world" that was his "reality." Another few sentences and he particularized even more what he felt: He called her his "genius."

Elsie seems to have lived up to his expectations over that weekend, though he had not been able to get rid of his "nerves." They were still with him the week after his return. He opened the first letter he wrote from New York on Thursday evening (WAS 1820, February 25, 1909) by apologizing for not having written earlier and accounting for why he had not. He called her his "Dear Delight" and his "Darling." He made no mention of what they had seen in Philadelphia. Though the exhibition and that evening's concert or play must have been "delightful," it was she who was at the center of his thought. He thanked her for how she had been once they were home in Reading. She wore the slippers he loved and kept them coquettishly hidden under her skirt so he could "not see them except by chance." He again urged her to walk regularly, adding that "The body answers good treatment and proper care like a fine instrument." Though he did not realize it consciously now, the "harmony" she provided was contributing to the complex of images that went into making *Harmonium*.

Interestingly in this context he sent her with this letter a clipping from the *Evening Post*. It described an encounter Goethe had with an Englishman who had come to see him in Weimar. On being refused entrance, he forced his way in. Goethe's response was to stand like a statue in the middle of the room. The Englishman took out his monocle and walked slowly around him without saying a word, then left. This anecdotal figure eventually joined certain monocled others in Stevens's imagination years later as he wrote the poem in which he, too, examined those who had been his great men, slowly moving around them in easily cadenced lines.

Stevens closed this letter observing that their next separation would be a long one—the forty days until Easter. He encouraged her to write more because he wanted "so very much more of [her] than [he] got." In the next letter, three days later (*L* 132–35; *SP* 210–12, February 28, 1909), he was clearly, as he expressed, in a spirit of "Lenten meditation." He opened with an excursion around death as sleep, another association that was reshaped in "Sunday Morning." The letter was an important one, another one of his long Sunday musings. In it he brought together the various elements with which he had been experimenting for a while. He drew on old sources—he had even gone to church that morning—and blended in the new. He spoke of Paul Elmer More, China and the East, the Eastern attitude toward nature. But everything was imbued with his perception of her and her mystery, so well suggested to him by that "certain pair of hidden slippers."

He preferred imagining fulfillment with her to actually engaging her: "Would I need to touch you to be happy? Only to know you were there would be enough to fulfill that 'Rose and gray/Ecstasy of the Moon.'" As long as he substituted imagination for direct contact, his thoughts came freely. From this emotional anchorage he swung into old and new fantasies. He donned and doffed old costumes; he was courtier and Pierrot. He now recalled the Philadelphia exhibition. He began articulating his perceptions about poetry, touching once more on pleasure and developing his ideas about it, "to give you confidence—because I do not want you to be frightened away by other people's mystery from one of the greatest things in the world." This major element of his later projected "Supreme Fiction" was involved in how he expressed his love for her. What was later addressed to the abstract "ephebe" was now addressed to her: "And for what, except for you, do I feel love?" (*CP* 380). He wanted beauty to touch her if he couldn't. But he could touch memories, perhaps his closest approach to reality. He recalled "a real evening—a real summer night when we lay in the clover and wild yarrow and noticed that soft witchery expand and fill a familiar valley—and I kissed you so often!" He also recalled Shakespeare's Seventy-third Sonnet ("That time of year thou mayst in me behold"). With its "Bare ruin'd choirs" adding to his sense of youth's having passed, the sonnet combined with Stevens's memory of the summer night he wrote of and seeded the imaginative cloud out of which "Le Monocle" rained years later:

. . . .
These choirs of welcome choir for me farewell.
No spring can follow past meridian.

. . . .
Last night we sat beside a pool of pink . . . .
                              (*CP* 13–17)

He went on in his letter to note to Elsie that he intended to write on every one of the next forty days and wanted her to do the same. Whether he fulfilled his intention is unclear. Though on March 11 he indicated that he had not missed a day in writing (WAS 1827), there are not letters from each day in the Huntington collection, nor do Holly Stevens's notations in *Souvenirs and Prophecies* refer to any others. Either Stevens or Elsie got rid of these others, or the "writing" Stevens meant was his writing "verses" every day. These he included with his letters. He wanted her to put them around her mirror in the sequence in which they arrived or were sent, without reading them until she fixed and primped her hair each morning. He called this a "game," and one of its rules was that the verse should be "crumpled" and thrown away ("Shall I uncrumple this much-crumpled thing?" [*CP* 13]) after it had been read. He wanted her to send him poems as well, as he wrote her on March 21 (WAS 1832), midway between this forty-day privation of her being, when he felt especially needful of some concrete reminders of her presence.

He opened this letter with an expression of his fear. This combined an eerie element from one of his college stories (see p. 92) with another leftover from his reading "The Madonna of the Future": "One of these days you will vanish—fade like a too delicate color into this rude canvas on which you are painted!—Stay real for me—send me, besides your letters, a pinch of sachet, for the odor of you, a thread from your dress, for the touch of you, another leaf, for the world about you." After this, writing that only the blue of the March sky had brought him "back to earth" from sojourns "in the sixteenth century, in China and in Spain," he asked her to grant him his wish: ". . . send a parcel of slips such as I sent you, with something of *your own* for each morning . . . that could make breakfast, say, like one of those old-fashioned bon-bons with a motto wrapped around it. . . ." He went on to explain his need: "It is not so much that I have been so far away that made me begin as I did, or that I have been so long away. I had a feeling that—well, so long as you do not misunderstand it, and I am ~~afraid~~ [*sic*] confident that you do not, my feelings may be regarded as imaginary—."

His confusion at this moment, well reflected in his "~~afraid~~/confident" error/correction, mirrored the change that was beginning to occur in his being and in his behavior. For three weeks before this letter he had been spending "long, studious evenings" at home "indulging in—with so ~~many~~ [*sic*] very much pleasure" books and imaginings and writing verses for Elsie. But the very next night after this letter, March 22, he was to go out with two friends to the Harvard Club and after that to the theater. On Tuesday night, March 23, he wrote to her again. He referred to that "wild night" and gave her an account of it that she felt to be laundered (as evidenced by his reaction to her return letter). He reassured her that that "kind of thing [was] a bore" to "a student of Chinese antiquities," into which he had been delving more deeply during those "long, studious evenings."

What accounted for his tension now was complex. The underlying difficulty was his shifting between the two basic modes of living. But added to this were the effects of his having made Elsie both his reason for being and his conscience. Complicating it even further were some of the things he had presented her with in his letters over the previous three weeks as well as his growing realization of her as a separate force to be dealt with. Not only had she begun sending *him* things to read and consider, but she was writing more verses of her own and also voicing her less than positive feelings much more openly than she ever had before. As the time of their marriage drew nearer, she, too, was less interested in fairy tales. She seemed interested in establishing the ground for real dialogue between them. As this became apparent, he, perhaps feeling threatened, presented her with some ideas that appeared to be his own but that he had actually drawn from others.

The best example of this is in a letter he wrote a few weeks before on March 3 (*L* 136). He expanded on the idea and effects of music and memory. These culminated in a perception that later reemerged in "Peter Quince": "So that, after all, those long chords on the harp, always so inexplicably sweet to me, vibrate on more than the 'sensual ear,' vibrate on the unknown. . . ." This realization, which he presented as his own to Elsie, was borrowed from an essay by Paul Elmer More, as evidenced by a journal entry he made in May (*SP* 220). In the interest of maintaining the preceptor's role he had for so long managed to hold in relationship to her, he had begun to misrepresent himself, even if evasively, calling the ideas he shared with her "a patch-work."

In addition, there had been some recent difficulty in his relationship with Walter Butler and his family. What it was is unknown, but they did break. The letter preceding March 3's and another about a week later indicate that there was friction between Stevens and Butler's parents (WAS 1822, March 2, 1909) and that Stevens had to see Butler in a new light. It seems his preceptor's role had already failed here.

Almost expectedly, with this new eruption of uncertainty, Stevens gave in, once again, to what seems to have been his favorite cultural prejudice. Of an individual Elsie described having seen or met somewhere near Reading, he responded:

> Your description of Mr. Austrian's [?] bower is more interesting. One does not often find a Jew in a nook; and that there should be one so near home is attractive in that it shows the softening influence of our green vales on one of the exiles from Jerusalem. Only the gold lettering in front of the cottage betrays the Hebraic occupant. I believe he married a Christian. The fancy revolts at a Christian and a Hebrew billing and cooing among the vines.— Still, that too is no concern of ours, and if the lady loves her Israelite, we must leave her to her fate—(WAS 1822)

Countering his weakened sense of self, as reflected in this latest outburst, he signed himself "Your own, Giant."

Since, a few years later, he extolled the Jew for "feasting" instead of "fasting" and even took on as one of his personae the "rabbi," as the man given to endless study (*L* 751), these early instances of unexamined attitudes must be considered in terms of the function they served in defending him against facing certain parts of himself that he later did incorporate. After weathering the storms of confrontation with his real self in relationship to Elsie and reaching the precarious balance of middle age, he looked back with a measure of equanimity and dispassionate distance at the circumstances that had gone into the making of his self. What he knew then that he didn't want to know now (just six months before his marriage) was how violently threatened he was by his own "billing and cooing," his physical "feasting" with the woman whom he had conceived not as any mother but as "Mother of Heaven, Regina of the Clouds" (*CP* 13). It was on this level that Stevens felt himself Christian and uttered his disgust at imagining the Jew-infidel fondling the pure idea of womanhood. Though he had separated his mind and spirit from Christianity, he had not separated his body, and it still had to suffer. The mortification of the flesh was more than a figure drawn in the colors of sun-beetled chapels for the man who died of a disease that consumed one of the organs of his delight—stomach cancer. The question Stevens posed in the voice of the woman in "Sunday Morning"—"Why should she give her bounty to the dead?"—remained in its deepest sense unanswered for him, just as it did for her, in spite of the motives for metaphor it provided.

The situation in which Stevens found himself was not unusual. This was 1909, the year of Freud's first visit to the United States. Though *Civilization and Its Discontents* was not yet written, the actual discontent that erupted in World War I, in Dada, in the exaggerated license of the postwar period already permeated the civilization. The seeds that burst into the sexual revolution of the 1960s had a long gestation; many have still not flowered. Ironically, Freud gave his series of lectures at Clark University during the same week Stevens and Elsie were on their honeymoon. It is impossible to know whether Stevens at that moment shared the negative impression that "Freud advocated free love, removal of all restraints and a relapse into savagery" or whether, as someone who had been at least indirectly influenced by William James, he shared the philosopher's enthusiasm for the Viennese doctor.[60] But it is equally impossible that what Freud expressed and represented made no impression on the newly wedded "prim scribbler in a wig" soon to realize himself as a "nincompated pedagogue" (*CP* 27). As their tracks crossed through the New England soil (both Freud and his party and the Stevenses were traveling in their glass coaches through the Puritans' first landscape over exactly the same days), neither of these giants knew the other in his particularity. Yet it was already clear to both of them why it was that Freud's eye was the "microscope of potency."

But this was still six months away. For the present Stevens had to deal with imaginary feelings and fears. Attempting to evade them until that "wild night" in late March when he yielded to physical appetite once more, he had filled countless "little slips of paper" (WAS 1824, March 7, 1909) with notes from what he had been reading. In addition to More's essays, he had gathered facts about China, Spain, the sixteenth century. There were also essays in French about a certain painter whom he wanted to understand fully so used a dictionary to be sure of deriving all the nuances of critical perception. He went to Thackeray again, *The Newcomes* and another novel. To these he responded ambivalently, sometimes enjoying the satirical amusement, sometimes finding it paltry and unsatisfying. Stevens was trying to be wise: "Solemn & Solomon" he signed one of the letters recounting his verbal explorations to Elsie. But he knew he was posing. As he commented, he was being "invincibly pompous when [he] ought to be [her] giant."

There was also an important evening with an old friend, Witter Bynner, whose enthusiasm for the Orient, now particularly Japan and Japanese prints, set Stevens's simmering mind spinning and hissing with oracular notations. Writing to Elsie of his evening with Bynner at the Players Club (WAS 1825, March 8, 1909), he was so full of the "eerie poetry of Japan" suggested by the prints Bynner had brought along that he was even able to dismiss her latest expressed fear of being called a "spinster" by those around her in Reading who did not know of their planned marriage since it was all still to be maintained as the "secret" he so enjoyed between them. He had asked Bynner that on his way back to Vermont through Boston he stop at Bunkio Matsuki's—"one of the best Japanese stores in [that] part of the world"—and get some prints for him so that he could have them for her. The interest Stevens had had as an undergraduate was burgeoning into a full-scale obsession. A few months later he would give "last winter's hat" for a particular catalog of Japanese prints from an exhibition in London (*SP* 235). He felt securely pristine in his Eastern mood and closed this letter to her with praise for what seems to have been one of her verses—"a link from Ego Flore's 'Necklace'"—as "quite in the Greek manner." He once again took on the role of preceptor and advised her what she should see and do: read and memorize for next month Browning's "Oh, to be in England/Now that April's here" (he quoted the lines this way) because, he noted, "It was written for you, Bo-Bo, my dear." He also expressed happiness that she had not gone to the theater; she certainly should not indulge in one of the vices he had so recently given up once more.

What was it about Japan and the East that particularly struck him? Simply musing about it gave him enough of a renewed sense of self that he fell into his old tone of authority. In the next day's letter, feeling the return of spring—for the first time without complaining that it set him into one of his black moods—he gave the answer:

> It is worth at least one night's studious candle to understand Spring—to realize that the sense of coming into one's own that grows as the season grows, is only the increasing satisfaction of the senses. They understand the senses better in the Orient (and hence, understand Spring better.) Bare Winter breaks [?] with thin shadows, small colors, the raw form of the Earth is lost sight of. The haze turns pink, blue, vivid green, golden—the April moon shimmers in a vague sky.—The emotions (which are only the effect of the senses) stir—and suddenly one's old spirit returns, subtly as
>
> > The mystic dew
> > Dropping from twilight trees.
>
> —My mighty Spring from the Holy Hill of the Muses.—But did I ever talk like this?—Pshaw! I meant only to send you a kiss and I did that first of all—and then wandered off on the influence of color on the senses, and of the senses on the emotions.—Yet it is worth pondering on, as the adaptation of clothes to character.—One can see oneself in a pile of clothes as plainly as in a mirror. (WAS 1826, March 9, 1909)

Stevens had understood something important in looking at the Japanese prints: the central discovery that the emotions were "only the effect of the senses." It wasn't necessary to chastise oneself for a gray mood. If the senses were satisfied, moods would be "pink, blue, vivid green, golden." Here was occasion for joy, a "mighty Spring." No, he had never talked like this. A way of stopping the old movement up and down seemed to offer itself.

Mirroring the shift in attention in his letter from senses and emotions to clothes as indicators of character, after his meeting with Bynner, his attention to himself shifted to the costume he had been wearing. He had felt like "a knight in his armor," as he noted to Elsie later in the same letter. But seeing the Japanese things and talking with Bynner had made a chink in that armor. Already deeply immersed in the thought of the East, Bynner turned his conversation with Stevens around a central theme: the necessary loss of the "invalid personality," a theme Stevens later picked up and developed (*CP* 368). The personality had to find and describe itself, however, before it could be transcended. In a letter Bynner wrote to another friend a few months after his return to Vermont, he delineated his position in explicating one of his recently published poems ("Open House"), no doubt one of the subjects he had also discussed with Stevens "until almost eleven o'clock" the evening they spent together:

> The very life of personality is desire of *completion;* every profound impulse, dream, passion, yearning manifests the need of the development of "personality" and its complete attainment. Moreover every fibre [*sic*] of the inner reason, deeper than self, responds to the idea that the only possible completion of any personality lies in the unification of *all* personality.—There seem to be two trends, two currents, one of the spirit upward, the other of matter downward, "Why?" is unanswered,—whether by theology, philosophy or poetry. It is enough to see at large and in particular, evidences of the opposing or passing currents. What is positive and permanent flows through all men and all things upward to the head of existence; what is negative and impermanent flows, likewise, downward to the foot of existence. The currents intermingle, seem to be one; we know not which we are in. By exertion of consciousness and will, we are enabled to partake more of the one and less of the other. There is joy, peace and understanding as we ascend. Once gained, the head is found to be fulfillment of love in the attainment of personality. It matters not what lonely bodies or blind forms personality may have lived through, losing arms, legs and all memories of what is separate and imperfect, its essential flame of love never dies but ever, consuming, absorbing, ascends. What it touches, it seems to destroy, but in that destroying touch, it gives light and is itself made visible. The desire to persist in our separate identities is nothing but inability to worship without images. We set up our weaknesses and cannot see our strength. The identity we crave we shall not find in separation; for as long as it is exclusive of anything good, it is not complete, not itself. We need not fear losing our personality. In becoming the greater personality, the lesser has nothing to lose, but everything to gain. In a word, completed personality, inclusive of all good, is God.

And there you have the "open house" [referring to the images in his poem] I have been building, against the cosmic chill,—the "little" poem! . . .

I can hear you say bosh at what you will think a new phase of my old unintelligible mysticism. Perhaps you're right. Meanwhile I continue to state that I have found the Pole and the Perrys may believe me or not![61]

This letter suggests what contributed to Stevens's current state of mind. Many of its terms later found their way into Stevens's personal poetic vocabulary: "personality"; "completion"; images of the North; the Pole; the center. Stevens took his friend seriously not only because he spiritually responded to what Bynner showed him but also because Bynner was being hailed both as the hope of the future for American poetry and as a foil to the decadents.[62] Unlike Stevens, he had been successful at a life of letters. He had lectured on poetry all over the United States and had been an influential editor at *McClure's* magazine for four years (1902–1906). He was the first to publish A. E. Housman in America. Later, on commission as a publisher's reader for Small, Maynard and Company, he also arranged Ezra Pound's first book publication.[63] The "Giant" listened carefully to what his onetime protégé said.

The confusion that culminated in his "wild night" had begun, prompted by silent questions about the postures he had been maintaining, questions raised by Bynner's commitment to a mystically pure understanding of personality that nonetheless was nourished through the senses. What more attractive way could there be for Stevens, preoccupied for so long with how to transcend the negative, romantic understanding of personality and exhausted from his periodic overindulgence and concomitant renunciation of the senses? The effects of opening himself were almost immediate. He first questioned the moralizing stance he had for so long held. Within a week after seeing Bynner, in "one of those frames of mind where [he started] a new letter every few minutes," he wrote to Elsie:

It worries me to be so much of a moralist, as I might seem to be from the sheets I sent you. I don't want to seem priggish and yet it is a little hard to take anything back—confusing. You know that the love of maxims is an aspect of idealism—of which I am not ashamed provided you understand that in my case (as I understand it to be in yours) the idealism is accompanied by a love of milk and honey, of moonlight nights, of good red earth, and a fund of many human frailties. I am not going to moralize for a long time. It is a creepy occupation. (WAS 1828, March 14, 1909)

The next day he went on even more emphatically. Unfortunately, this letter exists only partially, as a roughly cutout square, the detailed lines that would complete the following, written hastily on both sides of what remains, missing:

—I wish I could wish [or "write"] as fast as I think, but often while I am wishing [or "writing"] one thing, my mind darts to another, and the queerest jumble results.—It is just as well I tore up my last, because it had more about moralizing in, and i [*sic*] prefer to regard that word as ta-booed.—It is insisting, impertinent, ill-mannered, low-spirited, creeping, flat, weak, like the thing (not "think," be-jabers) it represents. Ugh! But no more of it—Heads up, Bo-Bo, and Mister!—Now for my green cap like Robin Hood's—and for some bright colored dress of yours. (I do like certain clothes immensely; that light dress with the . . .

[verso]

—To-gether, take a tremendous leap, out of all extracts [?], privations [?], parables, maxims, presedents [*sic*], proverbs and the like—and do not come down until you've found some grove of oaks, full of leaves, and of windy victims [or "visions"] of blue sky full of [illegible word], and sweet fragrant warmth. Now "old bogus" get ye behind us. We only want to have a good time. See that cap? Now you don't. See it now? P-r-e-s-t-o! Now you don't.—Are you fond of butter? I'll just hold a buttercup or two, and then a dandelion or two, under the chin of this poor philosophizing head. She loves me. (WAS 1829)

Though it is impossible to know how precisely Bynner had described to his friend the Eastern discipline for attaining wisdom, it is curious that in this letter Stevens wished to take "a tremendous leap" and that it is in exactly the same terms that Oriental sages and poets describe enlightenment. In his very next letter, the following day, Stevens made at least an imaginary leap, though he attempted at the same time to ground himself by drawing Western parallels, even searching one of his dictionaries for the French word that best expressed what this "leap" meant. After noting that moralizing "makes [one] an old maid"—like the "High-Toned Old Christian Woman"—he went on:

. . . priggish morality versus wisdom, as different as a goddess from an old hen in curl papers—think of Buddha directing millions of aspiring souls, fashioning a happiness for them: think of Plato with his powerful, clear thought—Well, you'll never read 'em (*no more have I*).—And I swear I feel a baby élan toward them. Élan according to my French dictionary means: "spring; start; bound; flight; soaring; burst; sally; impulse; etc. etc."—I propose, then, still to worship the wise and reverence wisdom, or as Solomon says, to "get wisdom, get understanding." Look for me in Sacred Pagodas; in shadowy temples, in groves hallowed by ikons . . . the voice of Socrates; by Ilyssus.—Now then, Master Green Cap, attend me. A curtsey to the noble lady wisdom—and bid her adieu for the evening. I've been galloping through books. One was a poem by so-and-so, full of excellent lines and images. From my notes:

> "O to cast off doubts and fears!
> To touch truth, feel it true!"
> (the second line is capital, I think)—

[noting that he was about to begin Okakura's *Ideals of the East*] . . . it soothes me to think that I'm reading the latest Japanese authors. Tho', the fact is, it is all enchantment, it is all wonderful, and beautiful and new— what a fine opal would be after a season of pebbles. (WAS 1230)

Especially interesting in this excerpt is his disclaimer about having read Plato and Buddha. Since he had clearly read at least some Plato, even buying himself a special edition to use as a "buoy" while still in Cambridge, his disclaimer about Buddha is also questionable. Perhaps in his newly imagined accepting state he was, for once, attempting to ease Elsie's feelings of inadequacy. He had made a leap and landed in an ideal precinct, at the same time both East and West. In his flight he discovered an image later particularized in "Le Monocle": He "galloped" through books, jousting with ghosts armored in words, "paladins" (*CP* 16). One of his trophies was the line he thought "capital": "To touch truth, and feel it true." Later he displayed it properly redressed in "The Man with the Blue Guitar": "To tick it, tock it, turn it true" (*CP* 166).

If he had not yet in reality read of Buddha, he soon would. After Okakura, there were others who instructed him in the intricacies of the East's opposing law. His closing comment above summed up his feelings quite explicitly; he had found something to soothe him.

Two days later, on March 18, his letter (*L* 137–38) was filled with lists of Chinese colors and traditional aspects. He particularly liked the "abstract" quality of these aspects. Of "The Evening Bell from a Distant Temple," he noted: ". . . it is so comprehensive. Any twilight picture is included under [it]." And of the poem of Wang An-shih which he copied for her:

> It is midnight; all is silent in the house; the
> water-clock has stopped. But I am unable to
> sleep because of the beauty of the trembling
> shapes of the spring flowers, thrown by the
> moon upon the blind[,]

he commented, "I don't know of anything more beautiful than that anywhere, or more Chinese." His enthusiasm was intense: "I am going to poke around more or less in the dust of Asia for a week or two and have no idea what I shall bring to light. Curious thing, how little we know about Asia, and all that. It makes me wild to learn it all in a night."

But then came the description of that "wild night" and dealing with Elsie's latest insecurities. These concerns temporarily displaced his sharing anything of what he unearthed in his poking—if, indeed, he poked at all in the next couple of weeks after his most recent breaking of his studious habit. One of the most revealing evidences of Elsie's doubts and fears and how Stevens dealt with them is a fragment of a letter he wrote on March 26:

> Be quite certain that your parents will not grudge you their aid.—I hope, too, that you have told your mother of our plans. Take her entirely into your confidence, if you have not already done so. I am putting aside money every week and by September I shall have all that we shall need to start with, and we must have some. Rely on me, trust in me. I do not care that you write, "I do not intend to marry one who is only nice to me," because I know that I love you—if that is what you mean. What nonsense about Abe Lincoln! Shame on you to say such a thing. Oh, please, never say things like that, and do not think them. I should not think of marrying you, no matter what had occurred, if I did not expect to be happy. . . .
>
> Be kind to yourself and me, darling. Do not [illegible word] yourself. Live your own life, and try to perfect it, by living unnoticed and kindly and faithfully. I will not protest that I love you, and you will know whether or not I do without my telling you. And believe, besides, in my friendliness, and in that of your friends.—I am not blind to the embarrassments of your position—we endure it, because it is best. It will soon be over.—Remember that you are not a stranger in your own home, and it is your home.—I am so sorry that you cannot be spared these anxieties, but they are unreal. Don't allow yourself to brood, keep up your friends, walk, read, work at home—learn to make your own life. (WAS 1834)

He wrote another note later the same evening (WAS 1835), which expressed his relief at receiving a note from her showing that she was in a better frame of mind, though still "frightened." He again reassured her that what he had drunk that "wild night" of March 22 was ginger ale. There was one more short letter before his Easter visit. He hoped she would be wearing one of his favorite dresses and reassured her that if she had not "found entertainment by that time," he would "stand on the piano and call [her] a silly goose and preach and shake [her], and scold [her] and kiss [her]" and "perhaps [even] bring a rabbit along," as king of the ghosts he had been fighting.

Two weekends after Easter he made another visit. This must have pleased her greatly. But after that, until the Memorial Day weekend, there was another long separation. With the exceptions of one or two serious and sincere expressions of self-doubt Stevens, at least, was less uneasy during this period of separation than during the last. As he recalled in a letter he wrote to her on May 2[64] (SP 216–17), his memories of that last weekend together soothed him. Elsie had been responsive and playful. She had even allowed herself to be carried piggyback by her "Giant." Her openness gave him a renewed sense of self, at least for a while. He had also moved again—nearby, to 117 West Eleventh Street. Shifts in light and sound occupied his imagination. This, too, played its part, as did another dinner with a married friend, proud of his wife's cooking. Stevens especially liked her homemade marmalade and wished Elsie would learn to concoct it. He also appreciated how clean their house was, she obviously cultivating this "fine old Dutch habit" (WAS 1839). Stevens was happy now, thinking of what his life would be like with Elsie, though he still doubted that his imaginings would become realities, just as he doubted that the memories he had of that last weekend corresponded to what had actually been. After evoking all the pleasant things they had done, he added, "[S]o it was.—Or have we been to Florida in our dreams? That seems most likely" (SP 216). Their sensual moments together, recollected as a dream of Florida, contributed the necessary element of reality to all his later poems celebrating Florida's "venereal soil."

As the May 2 letter also reveals, this was a period when Stevens began—notably, just after Easter—to examine the literature surrounding Christ, looking for the threads of Eastern thought and meditating on the function and success of the church and ritual. Though he once more denied that he was pious, he found he did believe in the *idea* of God, even if it was "no more than the mystery of life." He had, for the first time, understood the distinctness of the idea of God from that of Jesus (L 140; SP 215) and felt the connection his interest had with the experiences of his childhood in Sunday school. This was both freeing and comforting. His tempered expression of faith must have comforted Elsie as well. This sense extended to his beginning to become "competent" in accepting things as they were: both the "fell clutch of circumstances" and even the city. Though he perceived its negative aspects—the commonness resulting from its "teeming" numbers—he now saw it from an appreciative aesthetic distance. From the sacredly approved perspective of "a stranger on the earth," he appreciated "some interesting etchings of New York [perhaps some of the first examples of the ashcan school]—pictures of out-of-the-way corners, that [would] be more valuable in the future than they [were then]." This was something new added to his expected pleasure in looking at watercolors of flowers in bowls. For the first time he wanted to choose "praise and rejoicing." He was "sick of dreariness."

❧

In this new spirit of acceptance Stevens was busily composing poems, finishing up on the next "June Book" he would present to Elsie for her twenty-third birthday on June 5. He completed the twentieth and last poem on May 4. But though he was content, she was not. Just as he came, finally, to accept life on the teeming shores at the bleak edge of the world, she became increasingly anxious about her prospective move. Alerting him to her uneasiness, she sent him a clipping from the *Reading Eagle* which described in provincially fearsome terms a characteristic city scene. The writer had visited New York and, seeing a crowd huddled around the U.S. flag at Union Square, thought he had found his "brothers" within the foreign mobs. But "Lo! it was nothing but a Salvation Army squad trying to lure [those] Yiddishers from their synagogue." His proposed counter to attempted conversion and civilization in the American way was to erect around St. Mark's "ramparts of steel, topped with sixteen-inch rapid-firing guns and then, waving over it proudly every day the American flag, defy the foreigners forever" (WAS 1841).

In her next letter she sent another clipping disclosing another kind of anxiety (her letter is referred to in WAS 1842). It was an announcement of the engagement of Stevens's younger brother, John. Stevens's response was: "—And imagine John's being party to an announcement! But that, of course, is as the lady wishes, as they say—Personally, I am more secret. I should like our own engagement to remain our own secret, except in our families and among one or two, and I think that my desire and your desire are birds of a feather—" (WAS 1842). Though he periodically reassured her of his love, he had not been loving enough to imagine her situation, to put himself in her position. Consequently, he had not picked up the series of hints she had been dropping: She did not want to be thought a "spinster"; she, too, was a lady who wished to make her engagement known. He continued to want to consider his need hers—they were "birds of a feather." While he wanted her to be sure of her family's moral, if not financial, support, he did not realize what other supports she needed to feel secure in her acceptance of him. In his newly found mood of celebrating what was around him, he imagined a perfect future for them instead of facing the imperfect reality. In the same letter, after expressing his desire to keep their engagement secret, he went on about how beautiful Union Square and Washington Square were to him now. He then described his perfect fantasy: "—There is an apartment house on the West Side of Washington Square, where I often imagine we live. You often sit in the window-seat about six o'clock and I can see you as I come home, reading some wicked novel, you were there tonight, and looked up, and I waved my hand, and you threw me a kiss—." Part of her probably shared in the enjoyment of this fantasy, but another part no doubt could not understand why it was so important that their engagement be kept secret. He mentioned that *their families* should know, yet it seems that it was because he had not told his family of his commitment to marry her that the secret had to be kept. No other conceivable motive could account for this. Even if he did battle with his studious ghosts, he did not want to do real battle with his parents. Evidently just the suggestion to them that he was serious about Elsie had been enough to cause the rupture between them. Because he was unwilling to face his cowardice and did not trust his ability to argue against their case that Elsie was not the proper mate for him, he could not admit the legitimacy of her feelings or imagine how his need to keep what was between them hidden was affecting her sense of self. The secret fiancée would be carried over the threshold to become the sequestered bride, reclusive matron. It was no wonder she was unsure of his love.

As though deflecting his awareness of how, in ignoring her needs, he was violating her, in a letter written four days after, gently denying her overly subtle suggestion that they make their engagement public, he expressed his outrage at a different kind of violation. Apropos of a play he had seen, "a rather green comedy called 'The Climax,'" in which one of the hero's lines was "God put love into my heart," he wrote: "Isn't that kind of thing abominable? I cannot endure allusions to God in that way—and cries of 'My God' or 'Oh, God!' make me shudder" (WAS 1884, May 11, 1909). The psychic mechanism operating here was the same one that was set off whenever he was faced with the "pathos" of another's situation. In his youth, in the countryside with the Wily girls, he had turned his attention to nature. Now, in the city, unable to observe the minute details of a tree or bumblebee, he turned to the idea of God, which was, for him, equal to the mystery of nature and the current subject of his reading. As he wrote farther on, the New Testament was his "latest hobby." He was especially fascinated by the accounts of miracles. They were better than "Jules Verne or The Arabian Nights." In his escapist mood he was oblivious of how his comparison profaned the sacred name in the same way as taking the name of God in vain, to which he objected, and in the same way as his inattention to Elsie's spirit profaned love—another of the mysteries of nature.

But though Stevens could not look at these things directly, it did not mean that he did not carefully examine their shades. The springs of his behavior and attitude led him to Dante, the archetype of the poet obsessed with the transformation of physical desire into sacred contemplation. But as if fearing that following Dante's words closely would undo him and make him see himself too clearly, he only looked through *La Vita Nuova* once more, as he noted he had done many times, without reading to its end, though he knew "what it was all about" (SP 223). He also took up his journal again to transcribe notes from the slips of paper he had been using to collect others' thoughts. These pages (SP 219–23) provide a schematic but rich record of Stevens's preoccupations during this period of intense self-examination. This questioning became even more intense as he approached the day of his "mystic marriage" (CP 401).

The most striking elements had to do with his meditations on Christianity, the female, nature, desire, the philosophy of the East, which he now noted in its Buddhist aspect, the aspect that is a ". . . reproach of all that appeals to the senses and belongs to the transitoriness of miserable mortality" (SP 221). Another shift was occurring. Modified, no doubt, by his current involvement with Christianity, he was turning, in spite of his earlier attraction to the sensuous aspect, to the more ascetic Eastern form. This had all to do with a curious seeming title he included in the record he wanted to preserve: *La Réligion. La Guerre. La Sexualité.* With "war" in the mediate position, this triplet mirrored the conflict that was growing more violent as his wedding day approached.

The poems of Laurence Binyon also made their deep impression. One of the stanzas he copied together with all these other scribblings found its way to

345

that "saltier well" of memory deep within him. When its suggestions reappeared years later, they brought with them many of the others transcribed at the same time, now in 1909. It is not difficult to see in the three-line stanzas of "Sea Surface Full of Clouds" the transformed, developed versions of what came

> Out of suspended hazes the smooth sea
> Swelled into brilliance, and subsiding hushed
> The lonely shore with music.

In "Sea Surface," long regarded as the pure poem par excellence, Stevens actually grappled with the very problem he was facing now. The poem memorialized the conception of his only child. This was its "true subject," to which he referred through the haze of the "poetry of the subject," woven out of the elements of his personal mythology that had made him as restrained as he was. These elements had to do with the myth of the Fall and with Milton's fixing in inescapable rhythms and images the consequences of Adam and Eve's desire: their sexuality and knowledge. The child reared by "good Puritans," the child who had listened for years to his mother's Bible reading, gone to Sunday school, served as an altar boy, later listened to his friend's reading *Paradise Lost* in a shaft of sunlight, came to his own knowledge still fearing the Fall.

As his attraction to the Buddhist form of Eastern thought indicated, he could not get beyond his early steeping in the Christian myth. The more he attempted to get beyond it, feeling that he had transcended the need for what the church offered, the more he seemed to conflate everything under its law. As though naïvely attached to Blaise Pascal's notion that when one is in doubt, there is nothing to lose by believing, when he became even slightly aware of his fears, he fell into one of the familiar moods of Christian practice: self-chastisement or penitence. This is clear in a letter written to Elsie on May 17 (WAS 1847), a few days after his last journal entry for three years, where he cataloged his slip-of-paper notes. Just after elaborating on how life in a big city like New York "gets to be a terror" because "failure means such a horror and so many fail" (with the American Bonding Company now for only a year and a half, he could not yet be certain that he would not fail here as he had so many times before), he comforted himself with the memory of the country around Reading, a "kind of earthly Paradise," and then jumped to encouraging her criticism of his own critical spirit:

> What you call my critical spirit is my greatest enemy—and I say most sincerely that anything that helps me get the better of it is balm to my good will. —Sophocles, I believe, based everything on knowing one's self and you know the result. The cry

> I would that I might forget that I am I. The answer that
Jesus made to the lawyer,
> Thou shalt love thy neighbor as thyself
seems wiser.

He went on, after converting even Sophocles to the Christian attitude, to observe how hard he had to try to be pleasant and kind, saying that for him it was a "job for a spiritual Hercules." He asked her to send more "sayings to help him." But though in this frame of mind, he thought "it would be a sufficient achievement to make a little circle happy—so important it seems to me to live in the essential success, as distinguished from the various, vexing objects of ambition. What a pity that wealth and ambition should compose us so," it was, in the end, the vexing aspects of ambition that dominated him. What he did not realize was that his ambition was another aspect of the religion he thought he had outgrown. In view of his basic insecurity, it was impossible for him to give up the hidden hope of finally making a place for himself "on the front bench." The ongoing attempt was just as much the practicing of the religion in which he had been reared as praying or attending church. It is not surprising that in the wisdom of his later years he noted that "Money is a kind of poetry" (*OP* 165). Both money and poems were his prayers.

The remaining letters before his visit to Elsie on the Memorial Day week-end reveal his continued preoccupation with religion and his countering it with alternately puerile and paradisal imaginings and distractions. He thought of her as a "mermaid with seaweed and shells" (WAS 1848, May 19, 1909), prototype of his "Infanta Marina" (*CP* 7). He projected their Eden: "The seventy palms of Elsie are far better [than focusing on the reality of himself alone in his room] and I hope to find them some day. Next to palms are pools and wells. They speak of wells of sweet water in the sea. A well of sweet water in the sea would be pretty much what a palm would be in the desert" (WAS 1849, May 21, 1909). Though he was finding some of the central images of poems he later wrote—the palm at the end of the mind, the well of sweet water he could imagine causing the stillness of the sea in "Sea Surface Full of Clouds"—these images now deflected his attention from what was really at issue: his increasing tension at the thought of his approaching union with Elsie.

These letters also contained the usual directions for her costume: for one day, the pink dress and sun hat (WAS 1848); for another, Saturday evening, the white one. The last letter before his arrival is one of the best examples of how he evaded his feelings:

. . . been frivolling [*sic*] at the Phi Gamma Delta Club or something and walked home, feeling as if I should have had a much better time with Hans Christian Andersen's fairy tales, which I am reading now-a-days. Different people bring out different things in one and so knocking about has its excitements, yet how few people after all, bring out anything but gobble and gossip!—I had an argument about religion, my present *bête noire* (black beetle, says the dictionary) and it ended as all such arguments end: in a cigar.—Goodness, that's enough religion, provided, of course, that one has a vigilant conscience. But goodness must be defined since all people do not have vigilant consciences, and the tangle comes in the different definitions. . . .

[He described his route home and the weather, hoped the weather would be fine for the weekend, then planned their walking itinerary once he arrived.] . . . but it doesn't matter. The principal thing for both of us is to be together. What a full week of it we shall have! And you will see how glad I shall be to see you again—even if I should be pompous at first, you won't let me be pompous, will you? I don't want to be.—I'm not going to think that I haven't seen you for more than a month. I'll imagine that it was only last week. Don't forget to wear the white dress on Saturday evening. That's the one I like best. Well, I always like you in white best—for all that.—I liked your poetess—although her name was new. The "silver net of rain" was a pretty image; and as poetry goes a pretty image is a great deal.—It seems, however, that what counts in poetry is the "noble elucidation of a different world,—the noble criticism of life." The fortunate do not bother their heads about all that. I mean they are fortunate because they don't. Serious views are an offense. Therefore "silver nets of rain" is quite good enough from any point of view. I have, in reality, never read a great deal of poetry—a little. A little satisfies me.—In fact, a little of anything satisfies me. There are so many things and I am too curious about all of them to spend much time on one. Lately I have thought about Painting. There are pictures quite as wonderful as poems. It seems a tremendous discovery. Sometime, when it's possible, with the photographs in our laps, we can make some researches together,—There is a painting called "La Zingarella" by Correggio of which I have a photograph—that will be to you one of these days, when you see it, what that volume of Keats was on the river [?]. Do not look for it. Let me show it to you by and bye [*sic*]. You will understand then how nice it is for young rabbits to eat wild flowers—in the innocence of their hearts.—But Adieu! That hollow sound of the Elevated—late at night comes in at my open window—and my pillow is Peace. (WAS 1851, May 26, 1909)

Just as in his room, alone at night, he preferred giving his attention to Hans Christian Andersen's fairy tales to continuing to do battle with his "present *bête noire*," in his imagination he preferred contemplating Elsie's clothes to pursuing why he feared he would be pompous when he saw her again. In this letter he progressively moved away from real feeling with spontaneous tropes. These were: her costume; her "poetess," which even in the letter provided him with an occasion to assume a secure Arnoldian pomposity; painting; the Correggio reproduction he was saving to show her. It wasn't that these distractions were not in themselves valuable; they provided pleasure and helped him test and develop his aesthetic sensibility. But even he realized that his purpose in focusing on them represented some kind of weakness. He referred to those not preoccupied with similar things as "fortunate."

These concerns were lived versions of the evasions of metaphors. Like a metaphor, *La Zingarella,* was a beautiful device. He and Elsie would look at it together, he tenderly pointing out the rabbit nibbling the grass. Instead of lovingly nibbling at her earlobe, he would show her the delicacy of Correggio's lines and shading. All this would have been fine if it had brought them closer together. But the Elsie of his imagination who lost herself with him in "researches" was not the real Elsie, who in later years went into bookstores only to buy books for her daughter.[65] Though now eager to settle her "situation," she was still most attentive to her lover's enthusiasms and, under his tutelage, actually shared in many of them, after years of their living together, she found that these other concerns did not bring them closer together or satisfy her own "country girl" spirit. She probably realized, too, that in their common reality she could never fulfill the image of her that Stevens had, an image suggested particularly well by *La Zingarella,* the enticingly full-bodied, ever-young Virgin, resting in a glade, her earthly husband lurking almost unseen, observing her from the shadows.

The Memorial Day weekend, marking the informal beginning of summer, passed well. Once back in New York, Stevens immediately began memorializing it as part of their "History" (*SP* 226, June 1, 1909). His evocations were colored with tints from the East. The locust trees were "odorous as Asia." Their sofa became "an Oriental divan." The fanciful, recently built "dark Pagoda" halfway up Mount Penn, overlooking Reading, became a symbol for his meditative center. His senses aroused by the scents of the full season ahead and the promise of the heat in which he delighted (he hated the cold), he transformed reality into the Orient, seemingly taking on the attitude of the Orientals, who, as he had observed a few weeks earlier, enjoyed their senses. On June 9, after having gone to Reading again over the previous weekend to celebrate Elsie's birthday and present her with the "Little June Book," he fixed another "special memory" in thier "History": "That pond on the hill, with its population of frogs . . . here and there were goggle-eyes looking over the calm surface apparently blind to our being there" (*L* 144). Later, in "Le Monocle," he reevoked the order of these experiences. The Oriental hints developed into the stanza describing the "old Chinese," while the pond and frogs were painted in brighter and louder tones following his plaintive lament "If sex were all. . . ."

These memories sustained him until his next visit over the July Fourth weekend. As he noted his excitement to her about how the Wright brothers had collapsed real distance into record-breaking time, he mused (*L* 145) but was unable to imagine what real distance time would place between the nervous young man still anxiously wishing for the paradise full of palms he wanted to share with his bride and the disillusioned middle-aged man he would become, beholding in love only an ancient aspect. Until the actual testing of his wishes and dreams in the everyday world of their married life, he continued to soothe himself with memories and wishes whenever one of his darker moods intruded. Again he blamed these on the city, on having to be concerned with practical affairs, on smoking: "Smoking is really the source of all crankiness in me. The root of all evil" (WAS 1855, June 15, 1909). He realised that June, July, August, September, and October made him "home-sick," that he was usually all right in New York from then until May. So, as he began looking for an apartment for them, he also began imagining, for the first time, how wonderful it would be to move back permanently to Reading (WAS 1856, June 16, 1909). He elaborated on this newest wish many times over the month. While his attack of nostalgia was understandable, what was becoming clear was that no matter what reality offered, he wished for something else. From the time he had first left Reading until now, he had felt his senses stir in his familiar soil, but all through these years, when reality offered to fashion itself around his pleasure in the shape of a law practice in Reading, he could not stand the boredom of the place. Now that the reality of his marriage and a fixed abode in a high-class tenement beneath the stars offered itself, he wanted the other.

Though he seemed to be enjoying what the city provided during these days, he kept focusing his attention elsewhere. The more fixed reality became, the more he needed to escape into an imaginary world where, most important, he felt he would always be young. All the dreams of walking in the Reading countryside had to do with this. Repeatedly, when he mentioned the country, his wish to remain young came in the next breath: "On Saturday I wanted to come home in old clothes—without all that getting ready—and find you (without thinking of one kiss) and go off into that ever-dear wild wood—and have fun with you. And so to forget myself, and the contemplation of men and women and all that kind of thing, and be young. . . . I need an immense period of country-life" (WAS 1854, June 14, 1909).

Later in his life, Stevens remarked that as a boy he thought that reality proceeded by juxtapositions of contrasts that were never resolved.[66] Being young, being "romantic" in the sense he made his own, meant this constant movement up and down. It corresponded to what was most familiar from his childhood: He moved between his mother, all imagination, and his father, with reason always on his side. Then there was no pressure on him to resolve these differences. All he could do was accept things as they were. But as an adult, having internalized both ways of being, he was never wholly comfort-able acting through one or the other. During his days, practicing the most rational of professions, he wrote sonnets surreptitiously at his desk. During his nights he caught his most fantastic flights of imagination in webs of words built into poetic arguments as subtle as any he wove to win suits for the Hartford.

Being young became important as Stevens realized that he wanted to re-solve this basic tension but felt he could not. His attempt to make a career in journalism had represented a possible solution. It combined his imaginative gift for "painting pictures in words" with the reasonable end of making a living, but he had failed. His wish now to be forever young was a wish to return to a time when there was no question of attempting to bring his two parts together, to a time when he could simply observe, react, play, prank. He escaped into books or theater whenever he was not in some way fulfilling his wish by creating an Eden of words or walking through some patch of country where he lost the present and imagined himself either in his past or in a future paradise. On one of his walks he got so carried away that he completely lost his sense of direction and ended up coming back to New York very late, without enough money to eat along the way (*SP* 225).

Knowing that he had not resolved these opposing parts of his character, Stevens warned Elsie of his changing moods now that his real self was soon to stand before her without the protection the letters of five years had offered:

Be glad that your feelings are beyond analysis and description. What is it Santayana says—

Wretched the mortal, pondering his mood.

There is little dispute that anything like constant observation of one's own moods (experience being what it is) is a distress. My journal is full of law on the subject.—Be glad that you are beyond yourself—and never study anything please, except combinations of colors, varieties of powder, and other really interesting and amusing things.—Whatever life may be, and whatever we may be—here we are and *il faut être amiable:* we must be amiable as the French say.—The dickens with moods. They will be your chief difficulty with me. I am pretty grumpy now and then, although always sorry when I am, and more sorry afterwards.—The Dutch are all like that—as weird as the weather.—We'll find a way, however, and perhaps it won't even be necessary.—The dickens with that kind of thing, too. It is much better to try to hide our weaknesses than to point them out and say, "Beware." So, kind Miss, forget that I am "pretty grumpy now and then"—and depend on it that you will never find out. (*L* 146)

እ▲

The difficulties Stevens was experiencing were not wholly idiosyncratic. They belonged, too, to the broader cultural situation. As detailed in an earlier chapter and developed by Jackson Lears in *No Place of Grace,* the inability to resolve conflicting parts of the personality was a common problem around the turn of the century. It reflected a collective incapacity to face a future unsecured by the promise of transcendence that had been offered by a protecting godhead. Stevens's personal situation reinforced this one. At the same time, because this tension was a recognized aspect of the culture—discussed openly among the intellectuals at Harvard, for example—its personal motivations or causes could too easily be glossed over. Sensitive young men like Stevens could too easily account for their unsettled states by attributing them to the general *Weltschmerz*, thus conveniently binding themselves in an unspoken brotherhood as well.

The one thing the brotherhood agreed on as a good was beauty. At moments of greatest uncertainty Stevens found solace in creating a beautiful form of his own or sharing another's. Just before going to Reading on the July Fourth weekend, he further clarified his fairly recent assertion of the value of art for art's sake and also escaped once more into one of the poems that had impressed him most, Keats's *Endymion* (L 147). Both a particular paragraph from its Preface and the premise stated in its opening line, "A thing of beauty is a joy forever," had already predisposed Stevens to certain kinds of preoccupations. Now, as he read again, he expanded and used these to help him get through the next days back in the paradise he inhabited with his goddess. Stevens clearly understood the state Keats described in speaking of the imaginations of man and boy: "The imagination of a boy is healthy, and the mature imagination of a man is healthy; but there is a space of life between, in which the soul is in a ferment, the character undecided, the way of life uncertain, the ambition thick-sighted: thence proceeds mawkishness, and all the thousand bitters which those men I speak of must necessarily taste in going over the following pages."[67]

Keats's counter to this state was to imagine and forge "A thing of beauty . . . a joy forever." This also became Stevens's justification for almost everything. He used it as a fetish to focus his and his beloved's attention, as he used Correggio's *La Zingarella*, whenever he spent time with her. But something happened. Near the end of his July Fourth visit the charm failed, and he was left unprotected, "thread-bare," as he put it in his letter of July 6. This letter reflected an almost total dissociation of his personality:

MY DEAREST:

(So much dearer than I express—believe it, please). I have been worried today by the thought that, perhaps, I made a bad impression on you last night after we had reached home. And particularly while we were saying "Good-bye." I do not know just what it was, something vague.—You saw me thread-bare—as I am thread-bare when I stand beside you, dear, spouting these long sentences. You don't say much, but I don't think the smallest thing escapes you. And I don't like to seem thread-bare.—The purple robe must, of course, be laid aside now and then, but never, I hope, entirely lost sight of. —But if this is all my own imagination, re-assure me in your first letter. I shall send this to-night, so that you will have it tomorrow before you write. After all, let these little moments be swallowed up in our great ones. (Confound it, Prim [?] is a sleepy fellow to write to the tune of a street-organ and a bag-pipe? Does Puck, the comic spirit, intervene to spare further melancholy? A bag-pipe is the acme of silliness).—It is, no doubt, best; and I turn from my woe-begone self to that immense scene we drove around-about in for two days—a pleasanter thing to observe than the compunction of an uneasy lover. In May it was a place of new green; in June, of new flowers, in July, of wheat and wheaten fields. The first fruits of the ground which seem not so long ago to have been all snow, or all cold, barren rain. Sing a hymn to Ceres, the goddess of wheat and wheaten fields,—she that follows the ploughman and goes before the reaper; and to Priapus, the rugged god of gardens, now in the season of plenty,—and to all gods of summer and the long season, just beginning, that never goes before the hunter's horn challenges.—Yet it is true that the whole heart (in me) no longer join in such a hymn.

> Art thou less beautiful, or I more dull?
> O Nature, once my passion and delight
> How shall I win thee? . . .
> By me thy skiey [?] splendor are unmatched,
> By me thy changeful year unheeded flies. . . .
> Time was, I thought, that thou to me hadst given
> The dearest boon imported from above,
> The green meadow and the bluer heaven
> With the deep heart and wonder of love,
> But now, the sharer of a summer lot,
> I only wonder that I wonder not.

I could say two things of this, first, that it is not altogether true of me; and second that nothing could be more true. Holly-hocks such as we saw should be more than French-looking and pretty, and roadside patches of white snow should have more than a white smell. Yet should they? Should they or shouldn't they? I think I could argue successfully either way.—And our two July morns—one blazing like the very crown of heaven—one as red as the shield of the god Mars, yet I felt quite tranquil at the sight of them, even at the sight of the Silver River and the immense multitude of stars.—But I swear this is all nonsense. No, I swear it is the truth. Yet in both saw:

> The green meadows and the bluer heaven.

I would give a year of life to spend this summer at home with you—so that I might fall back into the "passion and delight" in so many well-remembered places. Books are a vexation—thought is a waste, work is idleness so far as living is concerned. Suppose I could walk in the country in the morning to-morrow and knew that morning after morning I should do the same. O Nature (horrid word)—then I should win you! One small indigo bird would be no more than one of all the birds of summer.—Dear, I am afraid I should keep all of this a secret, especially since it is about myself; but if I share a secret with you, it is still a secret—and you have your charity in keeping it.—Pshaw! what cannot be, cannot be; and I mean to go to bed early to-night and be at the office early to-morrow and toss things around. At thirty (or almost) one has to be practical. The deuce! I am going to write to you a little every day—not a word about myself for—a long time—and so gossip with you, if I may. I want to do it and I'm glad you liked it before, and I hope you will write very often to me.—By the way, if I said anything about September that you wish I had not said, believe that it was entirely thoughtless and I am sincerely sorry. I do not quite understand why we should not talk over even the small delights together and be absolutely in each other's confidence.—But we agreed not to, and it was an offense to have done so after that.—You must forget it. I expect to come home again towards the end of the month. Just when, I'll hide and surprise you, Bo-Bo.—Being tired seems to make me humble, don't you think? And so, humbly, I send you a good-night kiss, and every bit of my love.

Your,
WALLACE
(WAS 1866)

Interspersed here were many of the images that later reappeared, developed with the strength of self-acceptance and recognition, in *Harmonium:* his tossing things around the office in the same way the Comedian would toss words; Hoon's purple; cold, barren rain that hardened into "rotting winter rains" in "Le Monocle"; and, again, something for "Le Monocle," the feeling that his heart no longer joined in the hymn of renewal—"These choirs of welcome choir for me farewell." Like Eliot through Prufrock, Stevens had, before thirty, taken on the posture of middle age. Though he wanted to remain young in imagination, in reality, acting on his youth's natural virility was far too threatening. He could imagine mythological figures, Ceres and Priapus, refertilizing the earth but not himself approaching his woman, and so came all the evidences in the letter of his split into two:

> I could say two things of this: first, that it is not altogether true of me; and second that nothing could be more true;
>
> I could argue successfully either way;
>
> But I swear this is all nonsense. No. I swear it is the truth.

Of course, his training and practice as a lawyer had also prepared him to deal with himself as coolly as a case, seeing things from one side and the other without fearing the absence of a base. In view of his insecurity, however, this training in examining issues rationally and dispassionately did not enable him to voice these sides rationally and dispassionately. This was extremely significant.

But as many who worked with him observed, Stevens would not have made an effective trial lawyer.[68] He was not at ease talking to people. In person he did not seem to have the patience to persuade effectively; his early courtroom success with his father's friend seemed an accident. Only on paper did he remain the master of rhetoric he had first been recognized to be at seventeen. This inability reflected his reticence to assert himself directly with someone whose judgment he feared. This atavism, left over from his childhood, made it impossible for him to remain coolly rational when he actually voiced his position or perception. Both the causes and the effects of this showed themselves clearly in Stevens's relationship to his father, his first "superior," as well as in his relationship to his brothers, alternately and for different reasons also felt as superiors at various times in his childhood and adolescence. Later it showed itself in his observation that he did not get on with either his superiors or his peers. The consequence was apparent in the interaction between him and his father: He either yielded wholly to the one who "always [had] reason on his side" (as he had in choosing not to go abroad at twenty-one but to stay and "make something of himself") or he totally ignored that voice instead of attempting to engage it in open dialogue (as he did in completely separating from his family when they did not support his desire for Elsie). In the case of both these extremes what was at issue was the impossibility of truly *speaking* his mind.

With Elsie, on the other hand, it had been different. First, she was a woman; secondly, she was neither his superior nor his peer; thirdly, she had been pliant, shaping herself for so long to his needs. But even with her, as he noted many times in his letters, he had found it difficult, in her presence, to speak openly. Though on paper he had gotten closer than ever before to showing himself, it was because he could "command himself there," as he put it. It was no wonder that many of his letters to her took five or six hours to compose. Now, however, as the time approached when he would in reality have to prove himself the "vigorous warrior" rather than the "prim letter writer in a wig," his fear began to overtake him. He was afraid that she, too, would judge him, "cut" him, find him wanting. His sudden desire to make a life in Reading represented, in part, an attempt to conform to her wishes rather than enter into open dialogue. The alternative—simply ignoring her, separating from her as he had done with his family—was not a possibility he could consider. Elsie was, as he noted, his "strength."

The form of his uncertainty was reflected in both his letter writing and, later, his poetic styles. This style, characterized by quick dashes or turns around and away from one subject to another, related in some associative but not logically developed way, was his personality. But though the images seemed arbitrarily connected, the syntax of the sentences containing them was rigorously logical. His style mirrored the reality of the dreamy poet dressed in his lawyer's three-piece suit. While he himself observed that a change in style is a change in personality, he did not realize until much later that a change in style could determine a change in personality as much as result from it. The change in style from *Harmonium* to *Ideas of Order,* for example, represented a change that had occurred in his life, while the change apparent in *The Rock* was a rehearsal, a style *chosen* to try on death. Here, finally, there were no quick turns, no tremendous leaps or sleights-of-hand. In these last poems he stayed still and showed himself, slowly, deftly, as he never had before, almost without evasion by a single metaphor. By then whatever had once been meta-phorical was part of his common speech. The volumes between *Ideas of Order* and *The Rock* traced his gradual realization of how he could truly "command himself" on paper and change his being.

But at almost thirty he was still not fluent in this speech. Until he per-fected it, he rehearsed others' lines. Their styles were the costumes and cloaks he used to protect him from the weather of his moods. *Endymion* served him durably. The rereading he began on June 27 took him all the way through the next period of separation from Elsie after the July Fourth weekend. On July 21 he was still reading and commenting on how remarkable a piece of work it was for him. It had all the archetypal elements of his own mythology: the moon; the female; nature; springs; wooded glades; the ideal. Stretching it like a dream he did not want to wake from, he filtered his experience of this penultimate month before his marriage through it. He had reached the point where he exposed his "thread-bare" self, frayed, unable to hold together, and *Endymion* offered comfort. With it he escaped once more—in spite of his decision of a few months before to eschew idealism—into the contemplation of the ideal, of beauty. He tried to transform what he saw around him into illustrations of perfection. He recalled magical moments from the past. He wanted to observe things from a distance, "god-like," from "high places . . . to provoke considerable lofty philosophy and broad meditation" (WAS 1868, July 8, 1909).

His concerns about the future for this Keatsian month were accordingly impractical. He hoped that he and his bride would be settled in time for her to see the tricentennial celebration of Henry Hudson's sail in the *Half Moon* up the river bearing his name (WAS 1868). He clipped and sent her newspa-per items about certain birds that devoured large numbers of insects. Having this knowledge was preparation not for their life in New York but, as he wrote, for their imagined life "on Phosphor Farm, when our ship comes in" (WAS 1868). He again brought up travel plans. They would go to London and, after that, sometime, to Quebec and the Canadian provinces, a map of which he now followed with his finger, tracing the route they would never take (*SP* 238).

When he was not lost in fantasies, books, or work, his concerns were as trivial and mundane as these others were broad and whimsical. The most important was his stomach. He repeated his culinary orders to Elsie so many times that she finally made him promise neither to speak of "grub" again when they were together nor to mention it in his letters (WAS 1868). He apologized for his insensitive harping with the excuse that ever since he had been at college, the thought of being home had always been associated with food. But even after his promise he forgot himself again and one day got carried away about the size of carrots, as he described to her in a letter of July 23. Though it might have irked her, in this latest lapse he discovered another of the metaphors that went into creating one of his most effective figures. A barber had told him that carrots were small for the time of the season, but as Stevens walked home, he saw someone eating one "as thick as a thumb." His comment: "What lying knaves barbers are." Later "The Man with the Blue Guitar," a "shearsman of sorts," did "not play things as they are."

If Stevens's swings between the sublime and the banal had not resulted in the defensively painful situation of his everyday life with Elsie, they could be laughed at. But as it was, the grotesque became tragic. Never having examined the springs of his behavior, Stevens generalized his condition and projected that it was a normal state. He was even happy to find that Elsie, too, swung between extremes:

> Your letter of Thursday evening made me feel particularly cheerful. I'm such a contrary affair that when anyone else is blue, it always makes me feel in high feather. As a matter of fact you have probably felt the same thing by this time, for uncommonly low spirits are usually followed by a reaction to uncommonly high ones, and, as likely as not, I shall have a letter from my girl tomorrow in which she snaps her finger at that letter. I know that feeling, which in all experience, does not last long with you and that you have too much good will to let it influence you—(WAS 1872, July 18, 1909)

The double bind was set. Not only would he not question his constant moving up and down, but he would not question her doing the same. If there were to be moments of peace between them, they could come only accidentally as the arcs of their movements occasionally intersected.

Though the application of clinical terms is often a facile way of dealing with what is always an idiosyncratic and complex set of motives and actions, it does seem appropriate here, after our having seen in detail the various ways in which Stevens's personality manifested itself over the years, to suggest that his behavior bore manic-depressive characteristics. Knowing, too, that his older brother had been discharged from the army on the basis of what was then described as some form of hysteria and that his father had suffered a breakdown calls for our seriously bearing in mind the weight of the family history of the "good Puritans." Unfortunately it was a history that was not confined to them alone. The time was out of joint. Many suffered,[69] and the therapeutic possibilities of later years did not yet exist.

The "talking cure" was still a subject for snickering. From the point of view of "good Puritans" this was another invention of another unhealthy Jew, one of those beyond "the healing power of the sea" (WAS 1872, July 18, 1909). Yet in spite of this general defensive attitude and in spite of Stevens's personal reticence to engage himself or others directly, he did attempt a cure through words, even if unvoiced. The difference between him and his brother, who died a complete failure, ridden by psychosomatic ailments that had all too real effects, was that Stevens did somehow transform his irrational element, from the time of his youth filling pages and slips of paper with words shaped by it. If this cure was not strong enough to bring him to complete health, it was, nonetheless, an attempt. Poetry was health. With careful attention to how he engaged his irrational element, that "potent subject" (*OP* 229) this attempt could help show others how to live, what to do, and what not to do.

What remains unaccountable, however, is why Stevens, not his brother, found this possibility. Perhaps it was only that their father had noted his middle son's talent for "painting pictures in words." While his brother remained the prisoner of "facts," of "things as they were," Stevens developed his gift and used it to escape from them. He expressed this once again this July in another beautiful fantasy for Elsie:

> The pressure of Life is very great in great cities. But when you think of the ease with which people live and die in the smaller places the horror of the pressure seems self-imposed.—After all, a stout heart anywhere and everywhere!—Now, I wish we could rest after so much disquisition and listen to what we have never heard. The wind has fallen. The moon has risen. We are where we have never been, listening to what we have never heard. We are in a dark place listening—contentedly, to—well, nightingales—why not? We are by a jubilant fountain, like the one in the forgotten "June Book," under emerald poplars, by a wide-sailing river—and we hear another fountain—a radiant fountain of sound rise from one of the dark green trees into the strange moon-light—rise and shimmer—from the trees of the nightingales.—And is it all on a stage? And can't you possibly close your eyes and, by imagination, feel that it is perfectly real—the dark circle of poplars, with the round moon among them, the air moving, the water falling, and that sweet outpouring of liquid sound—fountains and nightingales—fountains and nightingales—and Sylvie and the brooding shadow that would listen beside her so intently to fountains and nightingales and to her?—If only it were possible to escape from what the dreadful Galsworthy calls facts—at the moment, no more serious than that neighborly bag-pipes and a dog singing thereto—All our dreams, all our escapes and then things as they are! But attend to that mysterious cry: "Have a stout heart against Fortune." Meditate on it long after ghostly fountains and ghostly nightingales have ceased their ghostly chants in the ghostly mind. Yes: for flesh and blood: "Have a stout heart against Fortune."—The curtain falls. The brief flight is at an end. (*SP* 238, July 20, 1909)

"Facts" were, paradoxically, Stevens's basic metaphor. Accordingly, he responded to the "facts" of his world in metaphorical terms. Just after he had gone through New York's newest tunnel on its opening day, deep under the dark river, he remarked in a letter to Elsie that it was "a great work, [of] enormous labor and art, the part of it one cannot look at. . . ." But his next thought was to "spread wing." He promised that the next day he would send her "a letter from the clouds . . . escape from things" (WAS 1874, July 19, 1909).

Whatever was had to be changed, turned by his or another's imagination. As he commented in a letter a few days later (*SP* 239, July 23, 1909), things as they were seemed "stale," a "vacuum." He needed the "stimulation" of new things: books; the morning newspaper; theater. "Man flies from nothingness," he wrote, able to see only the nothing that was not there, not the nothing that was. So, finishing *Endymion* and following and expanding the old Chinese advice "that a half hour's reading gives savour [*sic*] to the whole day" (*SP* 239), he began perusing a novel and then moved on to reading and translating some of the French poets of the sixteenth century (*L* 150–51).

Stimulated by all these evasions (as his readers would later be stimulated by the evasions of his metaphors), on the last weekend of July Stevens made his second to last visit to Reading as a bachelor. In a cart pulled by two horses he affectionately named Charley and Kate, he and Elsie rode through their native countryside. After jostling back to the harsher world of New York with the train's clanking rhythms, he memorialized this last idyll in words that later sounded the variations on *c* in the Comedian's mind when he wrote of "simple salad-beds": "The road-*s*ide blue with *c*ornflower*s* and the green *s*hadow*s* under the *c*orn with the *c*rumpled *c*ups of pump*k*in flower*s*—yellow a*s* pum*k*in*s* them*s*elve*s*" (WAS 1879, August 2, 1909; italics mine). Long before he sharpened his crescive words to wound—as they would, once shaped into poems—they slipped by, as here, softly describing passing scenes. And what he had liked as much as these, as he whispered into Elsie's "most private ear," were "all [her] dresses." They were a "charming" part of the pantomime he now staged in his memory.

Once back in New York, he lost himself again in his "cloister," as he put it (*L* 151). He began translating André-Marie de Chénier. He especially liked the last line of "La Flute": "A fermer tour à tour les trous du buis sonores"; (Stevens's prose translation was, ". . . how to touch in turn the stops of the deep-toned wood" [*L* 157]). Its sounds so low and fugal contrasted sharply with his own captious tones. But an unexpected visit from Walter Butler, who came to borrow money now that his "new friends [had] left him," disturbed Stevens's peace and forced him into an "icy Arctic" mood. The next day, as though willfully ignoring this iciness, instead of writing of reality at all, he composed a long and complex fairy tale. It was a bizarre account, tinged with more than a little violence, of the origin of "golden hair and blue eyes," the features of Elsie's that had enchanted him (*L* 152–53). The Grimm brothers might have been proud of such a tale, but Stevens's use of the various motifs of deception and castration suggested something other than pride. These motifs, too, reappeared with the "Comedian," who then revealed, as explicitly as he could, their motive—still hidden now.

This complete escape into the land of "Faery" had to do, too, with the fact most pressing on him: He had to find a place for him and his bride to live. How could he lend money to Butler? He regretted his iciness to him, but. . . . Instead of facing and dealing with his hostile feelings toward Elsie and the impending necessities of their marriage for not being in a position to lend a supporting hand to the friend he treated like a son, he wrote the "cutting" fairy tale and promised her another if she liked that one. But he also wanted to cut his friend—as the king in his fairy tale threatened to do to his messenger—for having come only because he was in need. He felt "cut short" by this and also "cut short" financially. With none of this spelled out, he continued during his days doing what he had to do and during his nights reading and writing letters and tales.

Without too much trouble he soon found a "befitting home." As he described it, it had everything they wanted and more than they needed (L 155–56). With this gift of "pure Providence" he felt happy, he said. He looked forward to going to see her on the following weekend—only two weeks after his last visit. But after an overnight stay with a friend in Whitestone, Queens, he caught another terrible cold, just as he had before the visit he made at Christmas when they became engaged. Suddenly he was writing only short notes and poor letters, for which he felt guilty (WAS 1884 and 1885, August 11 and 12, 1909). But he went and made his visit. He arrived back at the office in New York on Monday morning after an almost sleepless night on the train. He jotted another short note with excuses, reporting that he felt that they had "had a marvellously good time" which he would "flash up for Memory [the next] evening in the unfailing Mirror of Past Events" (WAS 1886, August 16, 1909).

This he did, but it was only a flash, an unembellished log of their drive. This flitted between an account of a Chinese dinner he had just had with an anonymous "fellow" (SP 239) and another apology; he would come back not in two but in three weeks: "I hope you will not be too much disappointed. . . . Don't scold me or anything. . . . I feel guilty about it—and all that—really.—But—but—but—but.—" (WAS 1887, August 17, 1909). To console her, he closed by noting that the next evening he would finalize the lease with Adolph Alexander Weinman, the landlord-sculptor who in a few years immortalized Elsie's image on the Liberty head dime and walking Liberty half dollar. Stevens also offered her his finished translation of the Chénier poem he liked so much (L 156).

The fragmentary state in which this letter exists, only partially quoted in Letters and Souvenirs and Prophecies, obscures an important element that reveals a central feature of Stevens's personality and of his mature poetic style. This is disclosed by restoring the portions that are at the Huntington Library. Stevens began this letter with "A cricket chirps in the rain." He went on first with the itinerary of his evening walk to the Chinese restaurant, then with the memorializing itinerary of their drive that past weekend and continued to looking at his calendar and planning his future itinerary, adding the note of apology that he would come in three instead of two weeks. He followed this with a closer itinerary, what he would do the next evening: sign the lease and continue translating. Finally came his offering of the translation, another itinerary, a record of his mental progress of past evenings. He closed, rounding the circle of his works and days, with "My friendly cricket still chirps—but not in the rain, for that seems to have stopped, for a time." In an earlier chapter a journal entry exhibiting this same kind of unity was discussed. But this quality did not belong to all or even the most part of Stevens's entries and letters. When it was used, as in these two instances, it served a particular purpose, and that was to help him contain and take safe distance from a painful feeling.

Here it was the guilt and fear he had about disappointing Elsie—something he wanted to escape from, evade. Earlier, in the case of the journal entry, it was to escape from the need he felt to escape in reality on a ship like the *Elvira*. In the same way, later, the extremely controlled form of "Sea Surface Full of Clouds," for example, helped him contain what were some of his strongest feelings, the complex set of emotions he had about the conception of his only child. The control and stringency of his lines and stanzas in that poem corresponded to the intensity of feeling.[70] In this letter to Elsie the overall cohesion provided by the cricket and the sliding metonymic connections from one itinerary to another were fairly loose; the feeling was difficult but not that intense. In "Sea Surface," by contrast, as in the earlier journal entry, in which the intensity was much greater, the overall cohesion was provided by a movement through time—a tighter control than the cricket in the rain—and the connections between internal items were metaphoric and contradictory, reflecting greater reticence, deeper conflict, and uncertainty.

Though this formal control worked at the precipitating moment to help him express his feeling, even in restrained fashion, as time came closer to the reality of their marriage, even such devices were not sufficient temperings. After this letter and until then, Stevens's letters became briefer and briefer, with less lyrical expansion of any kind and more notings of simple external events, like reports on the progress of arrangements for their apartment. Aware of this, he periodically apologized: "My crimes as a letter writer haunted me." "The real reason my letters were so bad last week was that I was depressed from too much smoking" (*SP* 243). While he reassured her now and then that she did indeed make him "tremendously happy," that even if she would be a "bother," he would "try with all [his] might to take the best care of [her]" (WAS 1890, August 23, 1909), it is evident that Elsie perceived something was amiss through his tautened lines. She responded with her own expressions of insecurity, perhaps feeling that it was his increased anxiety about loving and taking care of her that accounted for his new staccato tone.

He certainly was not at ease. The cold he had caught the week before his last visit was still with him more than a week later (WAS 1888, August 19, 1909). He mused in one of his later letters about how good it would be to have a "nurse" (WAS 1901, September 12, 1909) but was nonetheless edgy about revealing his needs. Attempting to recover his equilibrium, he returned to some old habits with an intensity he had not given them for a while. He stretched his Sunday walks to their past, almost superhuman limits: thirty miles and more. This exercise in itself then became another reason for his not writing: ". . . when I reached home I was too dusty and worn out to write, which you will forgive I know now that you know the reason. Next Sunday I hope to do the same thing" (*L* 158; *SP* 240). But his attempt to restore balance was unsuccessful. As he noted, though he went through the same paths, put himself into his favorite position—lying on a rock at the edge of a cliff, basking in the sun—he felt that his "sensibilities were numb—emotions sealed up" (*L* 158; *SP* 240). He closed the letter contradictorily revealing, in spite of himself, the reasons for his state: "It seems wonderful that you are coming—in a month. I shall have to buy a cane, I suppose, to live up to it. —But I'm not going to think about it, or about anything—." As he blocked the fear that he could not "live up to it," he also blocked the possibility of other feelings. He wished for a cane to use as the "Comedian" would later use his "baton" to "stem verboseness in the sea" (*CP* 28), to subdue and control the rumblings of his irrational element and hers.

In another attempt at balancing, he returned to his evenings at the Astor Library (*L* 157; *SP* 239), reading here and there, mostly poetry. Though this had a soothing effect and prompted a meditation on rhyme and a judgment concerning his own, by the end of the month his nerves were so agitated that he couldn't even read. He blamed his state on smoking and on the "mountains of work" at the office (*SP* 243–44), but since there had been other times when just these circumstances made him feel the solace of his library trips and reading and writing, it is evident that there were deeper disturbing causes.

Some of these were wonderfully and revealingly discharged by one night of old indulgences: an evening with friends; a play; smoking a big cigar. The result was a letter as playful as any he had written. It was, perhaps, because Elsie's letters of late had been "sweet" and had made him feel both "humble and glad," as opposed to feeling arrogantly prideful in one of his "black moods," that he felt he could reward himself with this night out. The indulgences came on the same day that the discovery of the North Pole was reported, as he noted in opening his letter. No doubt musing on the "facts" of this discovery, perhaps even playing with some of the images of the North, of cold, of the center, that he later developed in his poems, he spent the late afternoon and evening with two friends and business associates, James Kearney and Heber Stryker. First they went to the apartment Stevens had rented at 441 West Twenty-first Street, which, he happily reported, filled them with envy. They then went to see a comedy, *Is Matrimony a Failure?* He described his reactions to Elsie:

> . . . one of the most striking things I ever saw . . . I walked home *smoking a cigar*. How the deuce could I help it after such a riotous evening!—A fellow might as well be a priest as keep all his beastly resolutions. But heigh-ho— the cat and the fiddle and the tiger asleep, with 'em both in his middle.—So you're going to be too busy to write to me any more this week. B-e-w-a-r-e! —But then there's only another day.—Now if you wait a moment, while I put on my overcoat, ear-muffs and fur cap I'll run out into the wintry air

and post this at the corner, where I posted the last one. The other night, I saw an air-ship, with a light at either end—at least it was something. I sent a few stray post-cards this afternoon for LaRue [Elsie's younger half sister].

Bye-bye

GEORGE WASHINGTON

(WAS 1897, September 2, 1909)

Suddenly lightened like the airship, another of the time's wonders that he could delight in remembering, having seen that his spirit was soothed by laughing at the predicament which he feared and in which he was soon to find himself, he signed his letter as one of the avatars of the "man number one" he wanted to feel himself.

The rest of the letters until their marriage continued to be brief and were filled mostly with details concerning purchases and preparations. Though he wrote that he wanted her to think carefully about what she wanted and to express it precisely, he had taken care of almost everything. He knew even where to go for the coffee machine they had to have: ". . . today I found a store that deals in them altogether. That is one of the first things we shall need, because, while we won't want to bother about little dinners for ourselves, for the present, we shall have to get our own breakfasts. Everybody does, that lives that way—and it is great fun. The coffee makes itself (in the machine), while you thrill over the morning paper" (SP 243). He assumed her acquiescence about remaining purchases and other matters requiring a "mutual" decision. He didn't want to have "suites" of furniture; looking for odd and distinctive chairs and lamps was, of course, preferable (WAS 1889, August 20, 1909). He hoped to have the deer's head he bought in place over the mantel before she arrived (WAS 1898, September 8, 1909). Perhaps Teddy Roosevelt's image still mixed with W. C. Peckham's to offer him at least a partial model of how to live; a bit farther on he announced that he expected to go to Roosevelt's homecoming parade. Or perhaps he expected his memories of British Columbia to continue to be prompted by this addition. Specific recollections and images born during that first and last time of real freedom and self-sufficiency kept presenting themselves over these days.

Elsie seems not to have protested about any of this. Her misgivings attached to broader questions and less substantial things. During this last month she needed reassurance several times both about his general ability to take care of her materially and about the depth of his feelings for her. His responses were not insensitive but rather cursory:

> Don't worry about my being able to take care of you. That will be very simple—provided we are content to live modestly and without the envy of other people. I do not, however, propose to think of such things until the time comes.—In any event, with loyalty and courage we have nothing to fear. (WAS 1901, September 12, 1909)

363

So you are only a simple damsel, are you? Well you will be ten thousand times happy, then, for the simple are blessed as the pure in heart. I am perfectly sure that we shall be a great deal happier than we can imagine now. To have you always! What more could—no: just a kiss and my love—always. (WAS 1902, September 13, 1909)

On one occasion he accompanied another reassuring note with a mitigating clipping he found in the *Sun* written by Professor Élie Metchnikoff about the absolute necessity of women's maintaining the "three K's"—*Kinder, Küche, Kirche*—in those changing times. The item closed with another's observation that marriage licenses should be refused "if a girl can't cook." The *Sun* added a comment about hoping this terrible time would never come (WAS 1892, August 25, 1909). Though Stevens had also recently read an article elsewhere about the rights of women and women's suffrage (SP 242), it was the more banal, traditional line that he forwarded, even if playfully, to his bride-to-be. As though subliminally aware that this might not have been the most appropriate thing to do, he voiced an oblique apology for sending this in a "rather seedy envelope from the office."

As the recounting of his chores became almost frantic, he gave her the kind of meticulous instruction one would give a child. The letter best exemplifying this disclosed what was the deepest reason for his distraction: that he used these concerns precisely as distractions to keep himself from facing the "excited" feelings that he here completely denied. After noting the details of their wedding day, down to how much time they would have to leave themselves for changing in order to catch the 12:19 train, he went on:

I hope you are making your dress-maker hurry and will have things done on time. Don't forget, in packing your trunk, to pack only those things that you will not want right away—like that pink dress (the every-day one). . . . You will have to have things enough for about a week—because we shall go to Boston and then to the Berkshires in Western Massachusetts and then to Albany and down the Hudson by daylight—and I think it will take about a week—. Do you feel excited about it? I don't at all. My feeling is just gladness that you are going to be with me—and pride. I must think hard how to take care of that shadowy Elsie of long ago who is going to come to me. Take long looks at Reading while you can. Nothing there will ever be the same to you again—and resolve to be a patriot so far as the town is concerned. We shall probably not get back to it before Christmas—and then you will already be something of a New Yorker, and the little country girl you call yourself will have disappeared. By the way Smith has a fireless cooker. It looks like quite an idea. But we would care to use it for only certain things, such as baked potatoes for breakfast and that kind of thing. . . . it's all here [jumble] higgledy-piggledy. Haven't you a hundred and one things to think of? (WAS 1898, September 8, 1909)

"My feeling is just gladness that you are going to be with me—and pride." An indication that this was not all that he was feeling came the following week, perhaps after his thinking hard about how he would take care of "that shadowy Elsie of long ago." Just after noting that he felt "flitting regrets for the old time secresy [*sic*]," he expressed exactly the opposite feeling from the one above: "When I think that you are coming at last, I feel really humble and then I want to cover you with kisses" (WAS 1905, September 16, 1909). This was his last note as a bachelor, moving up and down between pride and humility.

Within another week, after a wedding ceremony shortened at his request, "since there [would] be so few there"—there being, as he put it, "No one at home whom [he] should care to ask" and not wanting to bother to ask any of his New York acquaintances to be best man because he did not want to have to travel to Reading with him (WAS 1902, September 13, 1909)— either the movement up and down would cease, or the tension would remain. The outcome was implicit. When he felt humble, he wanted to cover her with kisses. But with her exalted and him her suppliant, it would be quite difficult to feel himself "man number one." No wonder he had thought of getting a cane.

His last observation about the room he was leaving behind had the ring of an eerie premonition: "Yesterday's disorder has turned into the strict arrangements of emptiness" (WAS 1902, September 13, 1909). Within a few months he preferred returning, it seemed, to an empty apartment. He encouraged her absences so strongly that she came to feel forbidden to come back from more than occasional visits to Reading. And after years, when they finally moved into the spacious house on Westerly Terrace, its family rooms remained empty as Elsie, Holly, and he each retired to separate rooms after meetings at dinner, when Elsie repeatedly proved that she had followed the not so subtle directives of her once-hungry lover by serving copious, well-prepared meals.[71] Ironically, he died with his stomach blocked—killed, as it were, by her kindness in doing just as he had asked. "The Book of Doubts and Fears" served as his testament.

VII
THE GREAT GLASS
1909–1915

IN ORDER TO SURVIVE THE
SILENCE HE WOULD HAVE TO THINK
OF DARKLY DISTANT AND DISSIMILAR
THINGS: THE ANTARCTIC; CAMELS;
BOGOTÁ.

—WILLIAM GASS,
Omensetter's Luck

> There is no distance. We are intimate with people we have
> never seen and, unhappily, they are intimate with us. De-
> mocritus plucked out his eye because he could not look at a
> woman without thinking of her as a woman.
>
> —From "The Noble Rider and the Sound of Words,"
> *The Necessary Angel* (p. 18)

The "Inky Pilgrimage," the period of "Fast" was over. After five years of disclosing themselves through veils of words and manners, the "Giant" and his "Princess" opened their eyes in the same room, saw the light bend itself along the ceiling and wall, heard morning sounds scale the streets beneath their windows. For Elsie, the contours of the everyday world they began to share were far less familiar than the world of their honeymoon. After leaving Boston and Cambridge, where her husband proudly walked her through the streets of his youth, they traveled through the northeastern countryside much in the same way they had traveled around Reading. Elsie sent postcards home. "Having a wonderful time," she wrote, and though she did not complete it with the formulaic "Wish you were here," within a few months, when she was next traveling with her husband, she penned a card to her mother expressing just this: "It would be splendid to have you here with me" (WAS 4015, April 1, 1910). Between their honeymoon and this April trip, when Stevens had to visit his home office in Baltimore and used the occasion to travel around the area with Elsie for a few weeks, they had been in Reading together for the Christmas holiday, but Elsie had gone home days before and remained days after he left.

Elsie felt the need for contact with what was familiar, whether the comfort of her mother's presence when she found herself in a new surrounding or the relaxation of returning to what her husband called their "Native Earth," the earth "that [made them] giants." There, feeling secure, she could share herself with family and friends. But in New York, where she was locked inside by brick walls and threatened by the "maddening world" outside, her only possibility was to withdraw into herself and the relationship. This was difficult. She could not easily sustain herself, as her husband did; her inner resources were limited. The broadening she had been exposed to in the last five years represented a response not to her own curiosity but to whatever her lover desired her to know. Consequently, she could not draw on this material as out of her own reservoir of things chosen to satisfy spontaneous feelings. Nor could she draw immediate nourishment from the relationship since when they were together, neither of them was "in the habit of saying this or that" (*SP*

369

249). It was only when they were separated that he, at least, could express—and, again, only on paper—"how precious a prize companionship [was]": "I wish I could say how sweet you seem to me. I don't say it, mind you.—I only know it makes me happy" (*SP* 249). Life in New York, in their sparely furnished, though sunny, rooms, was more than a little empty for Elsie. Though he expressed what he felt in letters and occasional poems, it did not suffice. Elsie needed something more or something else.

He, on the other hand, was comfortable with what he had. He had been living in New York for nine years. He had his work, from which, though he might complain, he derived satisfaction. He knew almost every one of the city streets as well as he knew the country roads around Reading. All that was necessary was that this fairy girl whose spirit he had shaped should let it fall around him like an enveloping mist, a veil, a delicate cloak to protect and move with him. Of course, this was impossible. And as it was equally impossible for him to expose himself as he was, with his almost constant fears and uncertainties, there was no communication of the kind that would establish a firm basis of trust between them, from which they could grow together emotionally. Just as much as he needed the maternal comfort of being wholly accepted, so she needed the paternal comfort of approval. But as it was, neither of them could sustain his or her role for the other. Against their everyday rubbings in reality, imagination had no room to complete the desired reciprocal relations they had maintained over the past five years, when they made themselves out of words.

Again, however, this situation was far less problematic for Stevens. Whatever might go on between them, he walked the streets every morning and every night. He was affected by the exciting changes of his time. He was especially enthusiastic about airships and flying machines. The establishment of "world time" in 1912 was something that touched him directly.[1] He had to interweave his personal time with the world's. For his job, if for nothing else, he had to take into consideration the difference in transportation time for the herds his company insured. When he read of Henri Bergson's new conception of time, it was not as something wholly abstract. The French philosopher's distinction between *la durée,* the individual's intuited sense of his continuing evolution as perceived through memory, and *le temps,* ordinarily and arbitrarily measured time, seemed an extended description of his own experience. Stevens was a part of the world in which he lived. Though he did not support the futurists' program to "destroy museums, libraries . . . academies . . . and set fire to the bookshelves,"[2] he shared their sense of accelerated time and understood the need for a new way of looking at the world. All this belonged to the "stimulation" he so much enjoyed. His interest in these new developments helped him flee from his own uncertainty, an uncertainty that was ironically at the very center of the cultural experience he could not escape.

On the other hand, modernity's quickening movements only accentuated Elsie's sense of emptiness. Her direct experiences of the time's changes was limited to having electric lights extend the monotony of her days. Though she might have looked forward, finally, to getting away from Reading's provincial setting, where her identity had been fixed in its second-rate niche, as just one more "proof of the existence of simultaneous realities"[3] in the city her identity suffered even more. To compensate for her increasing sense of isolation, she concentrated on what she knew she could control, the household. She established laws for its running that became the order of her universe, one that her husband had to observe if there was to be at least a polished surface of domestic harmony. So, for example, when she was away on trips back to Reading, he dutifully reported having performed the necessary tasks: He had been a "good boy" and gotten the black marks off the floor (WAS 1906, December 23, 1909); he attended to the plants (*L* 167; WAS 1916, December 28, 1909); modifying her "housewifely injunction," he got mothballs instead of camphor to protect the stored woolens (*SP* 248–49). As time passed, both her enforcement of these laws and his observance and manipulation of them served as subtly aggressive defenses that protected them from dealing with each other directly.

Stevens's manipulation was instanced even in the marriage's first year. Unable to face the deeper reasons for their life's not having "exceed[ed] all Faery," as he had promised her it would years earlier, their separations offered him spiritual respites. He could fall back into his solitary habits of walking all day, going to museums and the library, peacefully reading at home at night without feeling any obligation to her (*L* 166–67; WAS 1916). He could once again recompose himself, "on paper," in letters to her. He could rationalize this and their separations as exercises in being protective since he was allowing her to renew herself by going back to Reading and the countryside. This was a relief for her as well. But often, when she wanted to return, he used some excuse derived from the rules for running the household to keep her away until he was ready to receive her:

> If you are going to stay away next week (and I want you to have a long loaf) [this gentle encouragement would extend a separation of what was already over two weeks]—try coming back on Saturday afternoon of that week and getting home about four or five o'clock in the afternoon if there is a train.— You would give me the opportunity to brighten things up a bit. It is so much better to find things shining,—cheerful etc. (WAS 1913, June 14, 1910)

The other concern he used, at least in summer, was the weather. To stretch the above stay another week, just before she was to have returned he wrote: "I hesitate to ask you to come back—it has been so hot here. . . . [It] would be a hundred times better for you in the country." But in the same letter he also wrote: "You know I want to have you here again" (WAS 1915, June 22, 1910). He suggested she write her mother and sister to come to New York, though in the next breath he told her to tell them "how fortunate they

[were] to live among so many mountains [like the blackbird that later moved among them in his poem] and so much pleasant countryside," thus alerting her to what she would be leaving behind in returning to New York.

And six months later, when certainly summer heat would no longer disturb the delicate balance of her constitution, it was again another domestic chore—the rug he had sent out to be cleaned, not yet returned (WAS 1916, December 28, 1910)—that was the excuse. He urged her, then, to "Take the opportunity to rest and breathe native air" and attempted to deflect any uneasiness she might have about his intentions or actions in her absence: "And don't be restless, please. I expect to spend the evening at home with a book." Subtly shifting his role, he signed this letter "Your[s?] Buddha," extending with a variation on a verbal pun the nickname he had used most often during the previous sixteen months, "Buddy." This epithet, first taken on during the year preceding their marriage, but then still vying with others—"Giant" and "Bold Youth"—seemed appropriate to the ideal relationship he imagined, in which they would exist, as they did on paper, in perfect harmony, her attentions balancing his needs and his attempts to take care of her being successful. But as it became apparent to him that despite his intentions and assurances—". . . come to your Buddy with the knowledge that he will do all he can to make you happy" (WAS 1915)—they could not achieve a balance based on reciprocity and friendship, on being "buddies," he moved quietly toward an alternative he had already explored. Becoming Buddha, if only in play or wish, would mean transcending desires he could not otherwise ignore. This would mean he could retain his equanimity even when they were together. Whatever went on or didn't go on, he could find satisfaction in the trembling present, contemplating a dish of peaches or a memory of lightning flashing across the plains as he perused his earlier journals during a New York storm.

Before beginning to make this gentle transition with her, he had understood quite fully the important function that desire served for him. In a letter written about midway through their long summer separation while she watched "Spring change into Summer" (SP 250) and searched the night sky for Halley's comet, after he had observed that he did not feel like reading, that it didn't "seem to be in the air in June," he went on:

> But I *do* like to sit with a big cigar and think of pleasant things—chiefly of things I'd like to have and do. I was about to say "Oh! For a world of Free Will!" But I really mean free will in this world—the granting of that one wish of your own: that every wish were granted.—Yet so long as one keeps out of difficulty it isn't so bad as it is. For all I know, thinking of a roasted duck, or a Chinese jar, or a Flemish painting may be quite equal to having one. Possibly it depends on the cigar. And anyhow it doesn't matter. (L 168)

Unfortunately this equation of "thinking" and "having" extended to her. The realization itself seems to have been prompted by a feeling he had about her that he expressed only a week earlier. Though he had obviously thought that in writing, "The longer you are away, the more I desire you," he was expressing his love and that this would be reassuring, he was actually pointing to the sources of one of the main problems between them. This expression of desire came up in a letter written to assuage her feelings of discomfort at being so long back in Reading and hearing of the neighbors' whisperings. In this context Stevens's ambivalence was made all the more clear. Instead of offering to come see her often or suggesting that she, at least, come to New York for occasional midsummer days—two possible solutions that would have eased a great deal of her tension—he offered the following curious aids to help her reach the state of his own blissful indifference to such things:

MY DEAREST:

Don't let that scare-crow next door worry you. I know what is in your mind and it only amuses me. Why in the world Mrs. Althouse or Mrs. F. or Mrs. Longnose or Mrs. Long-ear should gossip as they do is beyond me. Such rot! Tell them that, if they want to know it, I think more of my girl than I could ever think of them by the thousands—and be content in feeling that I love you with all my heart, and am proud of you and that I don't care a crumb what they think about it. The truth is that people only see in other people what they know in themselves. They do not, and cannot see, the little more or the little less. Nor would they recognize it if they did. You remember who it was that said that you were not affectionate. Pshaw! The ~~blessed~~ [*sic*] old lady who said you were "sweet"—what a blessed old lady to be able to see it! But I will not tell you what you are. It is a balmy thought! but balmy thoughts sometimes make serious reading.—Sweet—sweet—sweet—

You give brooks a tune
A melody to trees

I never felt free, or strong, until I had cried "Farewell to my elders!" and their beastly ideas—and why should a girl not go home for two or three weeks and be at ease and think pleasant things in the Spring? Oh, because her lord and master cannot care for her if he gives her so much liberty. But, ladies, the damsel is not my prisoner, nor my slave. . . . The longer you are away, the more I desire you—I think that you will be all the gladder to get back then . . . . (WAS 1912, June 10, 1910)

Not realizing how guilty he was of the very projection he noticed about "people"—most obvious in how he followed up the justification that she would be all the gladder to return because of it—he ignored the feelings she had expressed, and so he offered his ridiculously feeble suggestions. She should tell the neighbors how he thought thousands of times more of her than of them, as if there were some relevance to the comparison. Even if he did not mean this to be taken literally but used this form only to express that he did think well of her and was proud, the comparison was still strange. He didn't "care a crumb," so why should she? She should implicitly follow his model and cry "Farewell to [her] elders!" simultaneously making a distinction between those like Mrs. Althouse and those with whom he wanted her to remain, her parents, the elders who really mattered in the sense he was describing. All this was confusing for Elsie. Added to the strain she was already feeling about her situation, it must have made her quite unhappy, even angry. She made her discomfort known in failing to answer more and more of his letters, in spite of his reminders and urgings (WAS 1909 and 1913).

He revealingly ended this letter expressing a concern with appearances. He directed her not to let the dentist "put a gold cap where it [would] show under any circumstances" but to "require porcelain" and not to "let him tinker with front teeth." He also noted that the apartment was all clean and orderly and that he had a "new straw hat" and would be "going for some other stuff" the next afternoon. Somehow there was never a question of money when it came to books or to being dapper, yet there was a question about too many trips or, much more seriously, about what Elsie really wanted. A child would fill the spaces of her New York days. She probably had this in mind even during this first year and saw not being pregnant through the eyes of old Reading mothers, as an indication that something in her marriage was wrong. Certainly, another reason separation and desire at a distance were better for Wallace than intimacy and desire in her presence was that it was easier to control the issue that way. He would not feel ready to have a child until he thought himself fully secure in being able to support household and child in the fashion of a true burgher.

The tensions of their situation did not cease. But toward the end of the first seven-year period of their marriage—the New York years—Stevens at least had begun to understand both some of their generating aspects and their consequences. Three or four years after their marriage, when he wrote "Peter Quince at the Clavier," he focused precisely on the feelings he had uncovered in this 1910 letter. The sensuality and pleasure of the poem come from desire:

> Music is feeling, then, not sound;
> And thus it is what I feel,
> Here in this room, desiring you,
>
> Thinking of your blue-shadowed silk
> Is music. It is like the strain
> Waked in the elders . . . .
>
> (CP 90)

The consequences played out by Peter Quince at his clavier on the surfaces of paper and the ear, though beautiful, were as deeply and perversely painful as those intended by the elders for Susanna. The very being who offered immortal beauty in the flesh was too threatening. She had to be defended against and punished.

When Elsie did return to New York later that summer, she reported in a card to her mother, expressing again a strong wish that they could be together, that though she knew how fortunate her mother was to be able to enjoy the country now (she was with relations of her husband's in the Pennsylvania mountains), she was not "having such a 'bum' time of it" (WAS 4017, July 22, 1910). Either she did not want her mother to be concerned about her state of mind or health, or she was truly happy to be back with her husband, however lonely the rooms might be during the days, when he was gone. Either she maintained a different attitude about her state of being before her mother and her husband—reassuring one and complaining to the other—or the image her husband had of her as being delicate and needing the country, unable to bear the city in summer, was a distorted one, induced to justify his own inability to be with her continuously and at the same time to be himself.

Between the Christmas 1910 holiday—when it was the rug's being cleaned that was the reason why she should not return—and New Year's, Elsie's grandmother died. Stevens sent a night letter expressing his surprise and condolences and added that she should "stay until Thursday at least" (WAS 1917, December 30, 1910). On New Year's Day he sent another, wishing her "A hundred happy returns of the day with love" (WAS 1918). And the next day he sent a special delivery letter (*L* 168–69) describing how he had spent part of this day walking and at the museum looking at sculpture. (He especially liked a Henry Bouchard of a girl feeding a fawn, a John La Farge, and Chinese and Japanese jades and porcelains.) It had been a day out of his lost bachelorhood. Why he sent the report of it special delivery does not become clear until the portion of it excised from *Letters* is restored: "—I have sent you during the last few days several messages. I shall not be certainly ready for you before Thursday. It is quite likely that the rug may be a day later and the place looks quite shocking without it. Unless I hear from you to the contrary, I shall expect you Thursday evening. The train leaves the outer depot at 5:57. I shall meet you in Jersey City" (WAS 1919, January 2, 1911).

Whether to comfort her mother in her bereavement or to protect herself from the extreme shock of seeing a bare floor, she should stay away until Thursday. He was reiterating what he had written only five days before about the rug and her staying away, making sure with the special delivery letter, as with the comforting night letter of three days before, that she got the message: DO NOT COME HOME BEFORE THURSDAY AT LEAST. It is impossible to know if there was anything more than the rug accounting for his insistence. If her grandmother's death had not also been used to keep her away until the same day, it might be reasonable to accept his concern for her reaction to a less-than-perfect surrounding as the real reason for wanting to delay her return. And if Thursday had not been the limit set in both cases, it would be reasonable to see these as simply manifestations of his desire to remain alone and enjoy the sense of being a bachelor again a bit longer. But as it was, the rug must have seemed a feeble excuse for Elsie, unless she really would have been seriously unnerved by the naked floor or unless she wanted to remain in

Reading as much as he wanted her to remain. In the end the devices worked. She did not return that week at all, but the next. In a photo postcard showing the General Theological Seminary and their house beyond with an arrow drawn in pointing to their apartment, postmarked January 8 (Thursday had been the fifth), he noted, "I shall meet you in Jersey City. Glad you're coming" (WAS 1920).

In the next six or seven months it became clear to both of them that Elsie was not going to adjust to living in New York. Though she might have wanted to be with her husband, she was unhappy in the city. Unfortunately, just as this became apparent, the consequences of Stevens's rupture with his family began to show themselves as well. He had made no attempt to contact them since the storm broke around the time of his engagement, but overtures had been made to him. A few months after his wedding his mother sent her love to him through his sister Elizabeth, who was going to be in New York. Elizabeth was going to see Garrett, Jr., and his wife, who had moved to the city recently. Between this time and 1912, when he relocated, Garrett, Jr., and his wife, Sarah, had attempted to establish a relationship with Wallace and Elsie but had been coolly rebuffed.[4] Then, on July 14, 1911, Garrett, Sr., died, and Wallace went home for the funeral. (Although Elsie went to Reading as well, it is unlikely that she went to the services, for she did not go to her mother-in-law's the following year.[5] Stevens had not spoken to his father since their blowup. The silence they had established he extended now, not mentioning a word about his feelings concerning the death or about the man Garrett was, either in the letters he began writing to Elsie on his return to New York within a week after the funeral or in his journal, in which he did not make an entry again until the following year, when his mother died. At that point he simply referred in one line to his father's death the year before (L 172–73).

But even though he neither addressed nor expressed his feelings about his father, they found their way into the spaces between his breaths and words. They showed themselves in the short note he wrote to Elsie on his return to New York from the few days in Reading at the time of the funeral:

> The apartment looked a little dusty and was as hot as India. But I "dusted" a bit last night and before breakfast this morning swept the middle room and the bedroom. Wasn't I a good boy? I shall be quite comfortable and you must try to have a pleasant visit and not think to much about me. I mean to spend my evenings at home reading and trying to think a way through the future, that will lead us through pleasant places. Be sure to let me hear from you.
>
> With much love, Your
> BUDDY
> (WAS 1921, July 22, 1911)

For the first time in the correspondence as it remains, Stevens revealed himself vulnerable to her concern. He tenderly and playfully expressed a need for approval: "Wasn't I a good boy?" And he took on the "reason" his father had always had on his side to "think a way through the future" that would make her happier.

On August 6, Stevens wrote another letter (*L* 169–70) the first part of which showed him to have temporarily taken on other attitudes that belonged to his father. In its second part—which he added after he had kept the letter an extra day, sending Elsie a postcard on his route home on Sunday evening after he had written the first half and then gone out walking (WAS 1923, August 6, 1911)—earlier specific images and themes returned that reevoked the musical structure both of Stevens's perception and the way he recorded it.

Sunday Morning [August 6, 1911]

MY DEAREST BO-BO:—

I was so glad to get your letter last night and to find you in such good spirits.—I was in rather a low humor, to put it so; for I had learned during the day that Connie Lee [J. Collins Lee, an insurance colleague with whom Stevens was in competition for a promotion] had got a fairly good thing that I was after—although Lee and Kearney and Stryker [James L. D. Kearney and Heber H. Stryker, other insurance colleagues and friends mentioned near the end of the previous chapter] do not know it, yet, to be honest. You will recall that I always said that Lee stood in my way—and I know that they are all loyal friends of mine. Only now that Lee is taken care of, I should be next in line [for a promotion]. However, the assistance of friends is at best auxiliary; and progress depends on one's own energy.—Your dream of a home in Reading is most fanciful. To be sure, if I succeeded here, we could have an inexpensive place there in summer. I think that possibly I should have been well advanced if I had stayed in Reading. If I should come back I should want to go into a business—and that requires capital and experience and a willingness to make money 1¾ cents at a time. I fully intend to continue along my present line—because it gives me a living and because it seems to offer possibilities. I am far from being a genius—and must rely on hard and faithful work.—It is not hard to see why you are discontented here. It is undoubtedly lonely—and if by nature you are not interested in the things to be done in a place like New-York, you cannot, of course, force your nature to be happy. If I could afford it, there are many things you might do. But there are many thousands of us who do not look too closely at the present, but who turn their faces toward the future— gilding the present with hope—to jumble one's rhetoric. And then, you know, there is no evil, but thinking makes it so.—I hope to make next winter a little more agreeable for you.—There's the sexton announcing morning services with his bell. After an hour at church, I am going out into the country somewhere—haven't had any fresh air for a long time. I may go to Yonkers, cross the river and walk down the Palisades among the locusts.

With my love, Your
BUD

WUXTRA!

There were no locusts. I saw *one* thing distinctly pleasant. A path in some woods was surrounded by black-eyed Susans—(flowers, of course). Three yellow birds in a group were swinging on the yellow flowers—picking seed, or something, and chattering.—But in mid-summer grandmother Nature is not specially interesting. She is too busy with her baking.—To-night as I came out of the Earle, I saw the moon beautifully soft over Washington Square. The Weinmans have been up on the roof—gazing.—Such nights are like wells of sweet water in the salt sea (to repeat an ancient fancy)—like open spaces in deep woods.—Why cannot one sit in such rich light and be filled with tableaux! At least, why cannot one think of new things and forget the old round—past things, future things? Why cannot one be moonlight through and through—for the night?—The learned doctors of men's minds know the reason why. I read it all once in the *Edinburgh Review*. Psychologically, the obscurity of twilight and of night shuts out the clear outline of visible things which is a thing that appeals to the intellect. The clear outline having been obliterated, the emotions replace the intellect and

> Lo! I behold an orb of silver brightly
> Grow from the fringe of sunset, like a dream
> From Thought's severe infinitude—

I swear, my dear Bo-Bo, that it's a great pleasure to be so poetical.—But it follows that, the intellect having been replaced by the emotions, one cannot think of anything at all.—At any rate, my trifling poesies are like the trifling designs one sees on fans. I was much shocked, accordingly, to read of a remark made by Gainsborough, the great painter of portraits and landscapes. He said scornfully of some one, "Why, the man is a painter of fans!"—Well, to be sure, a painter of fans is a very unimportant person by the side of the Gainsboroughs.—I've had one of the candle-sticks over at the table to write by and find that the wax has been melting over the table. Poor table-top—as if all its other afflictions were not enough!—Adieu, my very dearest—and many thoughts of you—and kisses.

W.

The tone of the first half is almost wholly Garrett, Sr.'s, its archness and artificiality marked by contrast with the second half, magically conjured, as it were, by "Wuxtra!" In having lost a promotion to J. Collins Lee, Stevens was once more shuttled back to feelings of childhood and adolescence: not measuring up to the performance of his brother or the "ubiquitous Erle Meredith" or to Garrett, Sr.'s expectations of him. He addressed himself the way his father would have: "I am far from being a genius—and must rely on hard and faithful work." He even generalized one of his most problematic personal traits by using the collective subject "thousands of us," imitating one of his father's most common stylistic devices. This was further reinforced by the quick switch from that observation to the aphoristic mode Garrett, Sr., felt so comfortable using: "And then you know, there is no evil, but thinking makes it so." Here Stevens was trying subtly to persuade Elsie to look toward the future, as he did, rather than to examine present dissatisfactions.

He also took on Garrett's manner to address Elsie's desires and complaints. Obviously forgetting his strongly expressed premarital wish to find and do something in or around Reading, he shifted it to being only *her* dream. He told her it was "fanciful," not at all realistic, though he might—again voicing the advice his father would have given—eventually think of a small summer place if he worked diligently where he was.

The motif that returned in the letter's first part was the "gold medal boy" theme. While years before it had been prompted by a dinner-table conversation about performance and excellence, now it was directly connected to real performance and external recognition of superiority. Appropriately, in the earlier statement he had generally observed aspects of how people gauged "brains" and only tangentially revealed his own uncertainty. But now, pressed by a real reversal, he explicitly stated the feeling he skirted then: "I am far from being a genius." What made this even more poignant was how deeply failed he felt in relationship to Elsie and to the dreams he had preserved for so long. In the letters just before their marriage he was full of enthusiasm for the sunny rooms he had found for them and promised that they would be happier than she could have begun to imagine. Here there was only a feeble wish: "I hope to make next winter a little more agreeable for you." It was, perhaps, this profound sense of failure that led him to take up going to church once more. Though there was a church just across the street, more than proximity motivated him. He no longer felt like a god in the temple of nature; he felt too much of a man and so participated again in the church's more mundane worship before going out into nature.

After his communion in the woods he returned renewed—or at least free of his father's ghost for a while. He announced the difference with "Wuxtra!" and more specifically with "why cannot one think of new things and forget the old round—past things, future things?" Though he knew he could not completely escape past things and gave a provisional explanation, loosely borrowed from something he had once read in the *Edinburgh Review*, what returned now were reverberations of his own voice instead of his father's. These echoes provided the repeated themes of this second section. The order in which they appear is both regressively chronological and associative. First is the image of wells of sweet water in the sea. This resurged from more than two years earlier in May 1909 (letter of May 21; see p. 347); he recognized it as a repetition "of an ancient fancy." Following this, as though from one of those wells within him, up-poured the memory of what he had read in the *Edinburgh Review* about night and the effects of light and shadow just a week before he had first come across the image of wells of sweet water in the sea (see journal entry of May 14, 1909 [*SP* 223]). In other words, he had returned in his imagination to the last period before his marriage, when he did not yet feel overwhelmed by its impending occurrence and the uncertain feelings he had. That was, in fact, the last time he had been "poetical," copying things in his journal that he wanted to have for future reference and finishing up Elsie's last "June Book" while thinking of her like a mermaid, seaweed dripping in her hair.

But now, because of his present state of mind, he felt himself a failure. Appropriately, his return to being "poetical" was tainted by the reevocation of David Gray, who, though he had written beautiful lines like the ones quoted, was one of Stevens's strongest models for the failed poet. The pattern of regression and association had brought him full circle, back to his feeling of inadequacy but now linked to his deepest fears of inadequacy about what mattered to him most, "being poetical." His closing judgment, that his "poesies" were "like the trifling designs one sees on fans," expressed his worst fear about himself in the form of what he distortedly imagined his father would have thought. This deflected his attention from the situation in which his father had most recently and strongly expressed his disapproval: about his binding himself to Elsie.

But rather than face the pain of having the memory of this as the last contact they had had, he subtly shifted the disapproval onto his involvement with words. This was safer since the incipient anger he felt at Elsie as the object that ultimately separated him from his father—this kind of anger being the other side of guilt, with which it operates in a constant but varying reciprocal relation—was much more easily expressed at poetry, as here in his trivializing it, than it was at Elsie. It was at the same time more honest to do this since Elsie was not really to blame for the choices he had made, even if he had begun to realize the validity of his father's concern about her being the proper partner for him. Things were not working out the way he had imagined. As for her involvement with his poetry, if he had not already withdrawn to the closet of their apartment in order to recite,[6] it would be only a matter of months before he did. Perhaps it wasn't unreasonable to want her to stay away more and more. With her gone, not only could he read aloud or even quietly as he liked and where he liked, but he could also have his cigars at home without fear of disturbing their heavenly, orchard air. Within a year even the tone of his letters had changed. He no longer felt in the least compelled to reassure her when she felt uncertain or unwanted. He simply told her to stay away.

The contrast between the rest of the letters of this summer of 1911 and those of the summer of 1912 is sharp. Something deep inside him had changed. The change began with his father's death and culminated in July 1912 with that of his mother, after a long and increasing disability that had begun after her loss of Garrett, Sr. With them Stevens lost the worthy opponents who had vied with his studious ghosts in being the targets for his feelings of antagonism. Once they were gone, Elsie easily slid into their place. He had unconsciously but cleverly prepared for this long ago by investing her with his conscience. Now she had an additional qualification for becoming the butt of his anger: It was because of her that he had broken from his "poor mother" (*L* 175) and father, now dead.

The remaining August 1911 letters, after that last wonderful two-part invention with its echoing themes, were solicitous and apologetic in tone, even in the expression of his differences from her and in his assertions of contrary desires. His unexpressed guilt about his father spilled over a bit, coloring what he felt and wrote. He was still preoccupied with his familial situation about a month after his father's death. On a picture postcard showing the South Branch of the Raritan River, which he wrote to Elsie on August 10 from High Bridge, New Jersey, where he had gone for the day on business, a card he sent apparently simply to share part of the view with her, he scribbled just the pertinent details: He had come on business; it was "Beautiful country" (WAS 1924). After writing her name, he continued the address with his own old home address but made a mistake in this. Instead of writing "323," he wrote "322." He then crossed out the whole thing.[7]

As though imaginatively returning to a time before a problem had existed between him and his mother, Stevens recaptured and held on as tightly as he could to the rhythms of the solitary life he had had before meeting and marrying Elsie. Writing a card to "Mrs. Stevens," he addressed it first to the mother to whom he had sent similar notes about his travels and what he saw when he was still free. In his reality now he was keeping Elsie away and cultivating all his past pleasures. At the same time, in his letters to her, he went back to using his old authoritarian tone, as he justified his habits and activities. This was the tone he had used in the early years of their correspondence—before he was assaulted by his doubts and fears. He was recreating the way of being he had followed before his marriage, a way his father and mother would not have disapproved of, a way that allowed him to explore the curiosities and contacts that would lead him to a place "on the front bench." With Elsie around, this seemed impossible. She had begun to resent what she could not understand, and though she wanted company, evidenced in a reply Stevens made to her in a letter we shall look at shortly, it was that of neither the studious ghosts with whom her husband still held mysterious conversations nor the occasional old Harvard pal or business colleague he found himself drawn to in his less reclusive periods.

The letters of August 16 and 20 (WAS 1925 and 1926, partially in *L* 171–72) are excellent indicators of this return to an old mode. The first will be quoted in its entirely; from the second, only those sections (in neither *SP* nor *L*) that illuminate how significant and ultimately productive this retreat was.

Wednesday Evening [August 16, 1911]

MY DEAREST:

I am writing this by candle-light [indeed, his handwriting in this letter was extremely shaky perhaps because of the quality of the light]. The electric light, you remember, does not reach the table.—I found your letter, as I came upstairs. Just so you are happy. Only, you must not allow yourself to think too badly of us over here. We lead rather severe lives! Who in the world would see the truth in that remark? People in the country think it is one unbroken round of holidays here. The fact is, it is all work. The amusements are "quick": grab a bit of fun and then back to work—to use such language. . . . But personally I find pleasure in too many things not sociable. This is largely the result of many years of isolation and of tastes formed under such conditions . . . (notice my Frenchy way of punctuating? Très chic, n'est-ce pas?) . . . But for all that, I see your side of it, too. The society of friends is the sweetest of all pleasures . . . and the one you enjoy most. My dear, you know I do not willfully forego all that. But all my hopes lead me to expect most from life in the end by doing as I am doing. For the present patience and good-will are our greatest wishes. All the time you know how much I love you and how much we have in common deep down . . . I had thought of running over to see you but will not do so at present. There are so many things we need here and so much besides that it would be agreeable to have. I don't think I have seen Mrs. Weinman since the day I came back. They use the porch in the evenings—I mean the roof. If we had some place out-of-doors to loaf in on summer nights a part of our problem would be solved. You would be surprised to find how pleasant a candle on this table makes this room. It gives such a quiet,—uncertain light—very favorable to meditation and the like that.—Have a good time, Bo. We'll have a good time when you come back, depend on it. Remember me to your mother, please, and to the rest of the family.

Your own,
W.

Here, again, hidden contradictions were contained uneasily by a controlled unity of form. The candle on the table lighting the room was the holding device. Beyond providing the frame for the letter, what Stevens wrote about it revealed how controlled he was when Elsie was around. He experimented with the candle only when she was not around. They had been living together for almost two years, and he had never done this, though he had done it many times as a student and when he was living on his own. The first Elsie knew of how beautiful the room looked lit this way was in his writing to her about it, not in his sharing it with her. Within this flittering frame he first reassured her that he had more or less returned to his monastic habit: Whatever amusements there were were "quick." They had been living together long enough that it was unlikely that she would have had the sense that he had been out indulging himself in a way she would "think too badly" of if she had not had some evidence that he had a tendency in this direction—unless she was totally irrational in her fears about what he did when they were apart. But she did have the evidence of how he had acted before their marriage. She knew that his periods of solitude alternated with periods of indulgence, of nights out, dinners with acquaintances, theater, cigars. Perhaps she felt that his periods of relative asceticism now coincided with his time with her. She would expect, then, that he satisfied his other side whenever they were apart.

His transition to the letter's next section—"But personally I find pleasure in too many things not sociable. This is largely the result of so many years of isolation and tastes formed under such conditions [ironically, one of the passages Elsie copied out into her special book as a reminder of his spirit]"— must have touched a sense of him that she knew quite well and, at the same time, alerted her to the fact that he was somehow dissembling in order to mark his difference from her since she obviously enjoyed the "society of friends." She had to have understood that part of what he was really saying here was that he did not want the society of *her* friends. Though it might have been pleasant that first summer when they had met and he had entertained them all with his songs and recitations, now he had more important things, solitary pursuits from which he expected to get the most out of his life. But he could not tell her directly that he valued his solitude more than he did their common life, that he did not enjoy conversation with her as much as silent interchange with one of the inscribers of the magical ciphers with which he filled his nights. Consequently, he ended up with this contradictory letter.

But as he began to be vaguely aware of his dissembling, he signaled. He directed attention away from himself to his "Très chic," "Frenchy way of punctuating." He had come close to revealing himself and was now taking distance. He adopted the ellipsis to replace the usual short dash he had picked up from his father. This new pause mark somehow became "Frenchy." (Though it was not a widely employed stylistic device in English prose until a few years later in the century, it did not have a much wider currency in French.) His using it here and there in his letter represented at least a sentimental turning away from the harsher dash associated with his father and the more stringent tradition in which he had been raised. He was going to Paris at least in punctuation, rejecting the good burgher's habit.

The first passage omitted from the letter of Sunday, August 20 (*L* 171), announced that he had gone to church once again and had heard a "thundering good sermon." Then, after a walk uptown along the west side of the park, he found himself in the "confounded museum" looking at seventeenth-century Dutch canvases. He had especially liked an ice-skating scene (". . . by a monkey whom people call Beerstrooten . . ." [WAS 1926]) in which one Dutchman was pushing a fat Dutch woman in a sled on the ice. He bumped into a stump and sent her spilling out onto her nose; nearby another Dutchman was drunk. After enjoying this, though he had intended to continue walking, Stevens found himself in the library where he fell asleep over a French book and had a delightful dream, which he unfortunately did not record.

The second omission described something else he had found most interesting the day before. He had been musing on the wise sayings of the Chinese. This was prompted by an excerpt from "The Noble Features of the Forest and the Stream" which he had come across and clipped, together with an editorial comment, from the newspaper that day or the day before (in WAS 1926 folder).

These passages revealed the reemergence of Stevens's interest in the Dutch (expressed in his sympathy for the homely yet boisterous nature of the painting's subject) and of his preoccupation with Oriental ideas. As in the previous letter, in which his references returned him to the period before his marriage, so did these. But the time evoked now was even earlier. It was the period during his first years of living alone in New York, when he had begun to search out both his blood ties to a European past and his spiritual ties to the Eastern tradition that seemed to offer a healthier, alternative way of being in the world. Now, because of his father's death, he again felt himself new and separated from his roots in familiar soil, and thus found himself once more suspended between these two poles.

Further, his newspaper clipping suggested a mode of contemplating oneself in the world that he later translated into one of the basic features of his poetry. This was the focus on landscape imbued with feeling:

> Nearly a thousand years ago the critic, Kuo Hsi, in his work, "The Noble Features of the Forest and the Stream," expressed once for all the guiding sentiment of Chinese landscape painting. He takes it as axiomatic that all gently disposed people would prefer to lead a solitary and contemplative life in communion with nature, but sees, too, that the public weal does not permit such an indulgence.
>
> "This is not the time for us (he writes) to abandon the busy worldly life for one of seclusion in the mountains—as was honourably done by some ancient sages in their days. [Here was something else that would be echoed in Stevens's lines in "Le Monocle": "Is it for nothing, then, that old Chinese/Sat tittivating by their mountain pools. . . ."] Though impatient to enjoy a life amidst the luxuries of nature, most people are debarred from indulging in such pleasures. To meet this want artists have endeavored to represent landscapes so that people may behold the grandeur of nature without stepping out of their houses. In this light painting affords pleasures of a nobler sort by removing from one the impatient desire of actually observing nature."
>
> Such a passage yields its full meaning only upon very careful reading. One should note the background of civilization, quietism and rural idealism implied in so casual an expression as the "luxuries of nature." Nor should one fail to see that what is brought into the home of the restless worldling is not the mere likeness of nature, but the choice feeling of the sage.

Stevens had repeatedly expressed his preference for a solitary life in nature, but at the same time he felt that in the social world in which he actually lived, this was an indulgence he could afford only on his Sunday walks, though he could not even afford this when Elsie was with him, for she needed his full attention at least one day of the week. The Oriental model suggested

THE HUNTINGTON LIBRARY

SPENDING HONEYMOON
IN MASSACHUSETTS

Mr. and Mrs. Wallace Stevens (nee
Miss Elsie Viola Kachel), who were
married on Tuesday morning at 11
o'clock in Grace Lutheran Church,
are spending their honeymoon in the

MRS. WALLACE STEVENS (NEE KACHEL.)

western part of Massachusetts. The
couple were accompanied to the
depot by a number of friends. They
will be "at home" at 441 West
Twenty-first street, New York, after
Oct. 1. Mr. and Mrs. Stevens were
the recipients of many gifts of silver-
ware, chinaware, linens and cut glass

This was their ceremonial hymn: Anon
We loved but would no marriage make. Anon
The one refused the other one to take,

Foreswore the sipping of the marriage wine.
Each must the other take not for his high,
His puissant front nor for her subtle sound,

The shoo-shoo-shoo of secret cymbals round.
Each must the other take as sign, short sign
To stop the whirlwind, balk the elements.

"NOTES TOWARD A SUPREME FICTION"

The announcement, as it appeared in the local Reading newspaper, of Wallace Stevens's marriage to Elsie Viola Kachel Moll. The photograph of Elsie was one of the poet's favorites, of her "facing [him] but not looking right out of the picture," that he had asked for as a Christmas gift in the letter of "A Winter Night."

THE HUNTINGTON LIBRARY

It is the celestial ennui of apartments
That sends us back to the first idea, the quick
Of this invention

"NOTES TOWARD A SUPREME FICTION"

A photo postcard of the General Theological Seminary and Chelsea Square with the Stevenses' New York apartment at 441 West Twenty-first Street indicated by an arrow penned in by the poet

THE HUNTINGTON LIBRARY

Stevens's letter to Elsie dated July 17, 1912, shortly after the death of his mother. Note the large, jagged "W" beginning "Wednesday" as one of the indications of his state of mind (discussed in Chapter VII).

THE HUNTINGTON LIBRARY

"Well,1 I think I have found the
befitting home. . . . There are two
very large rooms with abundant
light (they occupy almost an entire
floor.) The front room looks out over
the General Theological Seminary"
(*Letters*, p. 155).

A partial view of the interior of
the living room after the 1913
acquisition of the piano

THE HUNTINGTON LIBRARY

THE HUNTINGTON LIBRARY

She will speak thoughtfully the words of
  a line.

She will think about them not quite able
  to sing.

"DEBRIS OF LIFE AND MIND"

Elsie in the apartment on West Twenty-
first Street, holding something that appears to be a small musical score

Poet, be seated at the piano.
Play the present, its hoo-hoo-
  hoo,
Its shoo-shoo-shoo, its ric-a-
  nic,
Its envious cachinnation.

"MOZART, 1935"

A formal portrait of the piano

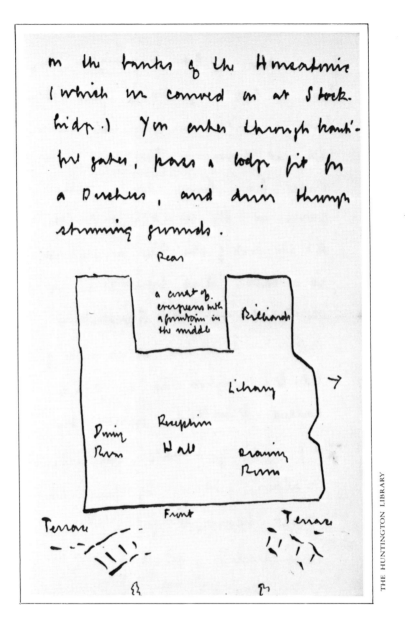

THE HUNTINGTON LIBRARY

Two central pages from the letter to Elsie in which the poet described his visit to the Vitales, from whom he purchased the piano. Here, he detailed as well the day-visit to the house of "old man Walker," which he found so "bee-you-ti-ful." Note his drawing of the house's layout and on the next page, slightly below the center, the curious ambiguity of his handwriting that made "Old man Walker" look like "Old mom Walker."

The house is a mass of beautiful
things: 200,000 worth of rugs
on the first floor alone! In the
library is a whopping organ.
But bother all this. In front of
the house is a circular garden
full of seats, statutes, flowers,
a fountain and I know above
the steps leading down. We
sat here in the twilight. Old
man Walker showed me everything
he had from dish-warmers
to tapestries. My, my, your
eyes would have melted. Then
bye and bye, when the moon
rose, we went in the direction

THE HUNTINGTON LIBRARY

PHILADELPHIA MUSEUM OF ART ARCHIVES

A partial view of the interior of Walter Arensberg's New York apartment, showing some of his collection. Over the fireplace hangs a Matisse, *Mlle. Yvonne Landsberg* (1914); below it, on the mantel, from left to right, Constantin Brancusi's *The Prodigal Son* (c. 1915), an African figure, Paul Cézanne's *Still Life with Apples* (c. 1880–85), an African figure, Cézanne's *Group of Bathers* (1892–94), an African figure; to the left, hanging on the wall, from top to bottom, Marcel Duchamp's *Chocolate Grinder, No. 1* (1913), Francis Picabia's *Physical Culture* (1913), Duchamp's *Yvonne and Magdeleine Torn in Tatters* (1911), Cézanne's *Landscape with Trees* (1890–94); to the left of these last two hangs another African figurine; to the right of the Matisse, on the wall, Georges Braque's *Musical Forms* (1913) and Charles Sheeler's *Barn Abstraction* (1918); to the right, on the wall perpendicular, Braque's *Still Life* (1913), his *Musical Forms (Guitar and Clarinet)* (1918), and on the floor, in line with the right edge of the fireplace, an Aztec figure. This photograph and the two following were taken by Charles Sheeler.

PHILADELPHIA MUSEUM OF ART ARCHIVES

Another view of the Arensberg apartment, showing, in addition to the two Braques already noted before the Aztec piece detailed in the previous photograph, Duchamp's *The Sonata* (1911) above the door; to the right, above the chair, another Braque still life (1913) and Duchamp's *Chocolate Grinder, No. 2* (1914); to their right, from top to bottom, André Derain's *Woman* (c. 1914), Cézanne's *View of the Cathedral of Aix* (1904–06), and another African figure with Joseph Stella's *Chinatown* (c. 1917) to its right; above the secretary, Duchamp's *Nude Descending a Staircase, No. 3* (1916)

PHILADELPHIA MUSEUM OF ART ARCHIVES

Another view of the Arensberg apartment, showing, above the bureau, Joseph Stella's *Landscape* (1914) and Derain's *Nude* (c. 1909); above the sofa, clockwise from lower left, Pablo Picasso's *Violin and Guitar* (1913), Braque's *Fox* (drypoint, c. 1912), Duchamp's *Nude Descending . . . , No. 3,* apparently rehung, Picasso's *Still Life: Bottle* (drypoint, c. 1912), his *Female Nude* (1910–11), and Pierre-Auguste Renoir's *The Bather* (c. 1917–18); on the wall perpendicular, above the phonograph, Morton Schamberg's *Mechanical Abstraction* (1916), Sheeler's *Barn Abstraction* (1917), and his *L'hasa* (date unknown)

The Florist Wears Knee-Breeches

My flowers are reflected
In your mind
As you are reflected
In your glass.
When you look at them,
There is nothing in your mind
Except the reflections
Of my flowers.
But when I look at them
I see ~~only~~ the reflections
In your mind,
And not my flowers.
It is my desire
To bring roses,
And ~~place~~ them before you
In a white dish.

THE HUNTINGTON LIBRARY

Penciled manuscript of an unpublished poem, "The Florist Wears Knee-Breeches," written in 1916, the period of Stevens's visits to the Arensberg apartment

THE HUNTINGTON LIBRARY

THE HUNTINGTON LIBRARY

Front and back of the postcard from Walter Pach, dated March 14, 1917, that Pach was "afraid" to send without an envelope to Stevens at his office; Pach did not want to shock the other insurance-company employees, he noted. The kind of humorous Italian greeting was nothing compared to what the Society of Independent Artists' Exhibition would show the following month, he commented to his avant-garde friend.

THE HUNTINGTON LIBRARY

If any duck in any brook,
Fluttering the water
For your crumb,
Seemed the helpless daughter

Of a mother
Regretful that she bore her;
Or of another,
Barren, and longing for her.

"SONATINA TO HANS CHRISTIAN"

Elsie in Elizabeth Park, feeding the ducks, c. 1919

THE HUNTINGTON LIBRARY

THE HUNTINGTON LIBRARY

Two things of opposite natures seem to depend
On one another, as a man depends
On a woman, day on night, the imagined

On the real. This is the origin of change.

"Notes Toward a Supreme Fiction"

Wallace and Elsie Stevens, in light and shadow, in Elizabeth Park, c. 1921

THE HUNTINGTON LIBRARY

One is not duchess
A hundred yards from a carriage.

"THEORY"

Elsie entering the apartment house at 210 Farmington Avenue in Hartford, Conn., where the Stevenses lived from 1917 to 1924, the years during which most of the poems of *Harmonium* were written

THE HUNTINGTON LIBRARY

And these two never meet
in the air so full of summer
And touch each other, even
touching closely,
Without an escape in the
lapses of their kisses.

"TWO AT NORFOLK"

Wallace and Elsie Stevens walking in Elizabeth Park, c. 1921

THE HUNTINGTON LIBRARY

Elsie (foreground) and an unidentified woman, c. 1922

These two by the stone wall
Are a slight part of death.
The grass is still green.

"BURGHERS OF PETTY
DEATH"

Elsie with her half sister, LaRue,
c. 1918

THE HUNTINGTON LIBRARY

THE HUNTINGTON LIBRARY

Nomad Exquisite

As the immense dew of Florida
Brings forth
The big-finned palm
And green vine angering for life,

As the immense dew of Florida
Brings forth hymn and hymn
From the beholder,
Beholding all these green sides
And gold sides of green sides,

And blessed mornings,
Meet for the eye of the young alligator,
And lightning colors
So, in me, come flinging
Forms, flames, and the flakes of flames.

The Long Key Fishing Camp in the Florida Keys where Stevens spent time, as in January of 1923, when he sent Elsie this card. He, Judge Arthur Powell, and other friends were "roughing it." The camp had no running water; pitchers of fresh water for washing were placed outside their doors each morning.

THE HUNTINGTON LIBRARY

MORAVIAN FUNERAL OF THE OLDEN TIMES.   BETHLEHEM, PA.

POST CARD

The Albertype Co., Brooklyn, N.Y.

Post Cards of Quality.—

THIS SPACE FOR MESSAGE.

THIS SPACE FOR ADDRESS.

THE HUNTINGTON LIBRARY

Front and back of a postcard Stevens sent to Elsie while he was traveling in September of 1923. The humor expressed, apropos of the Moravian funeral depicted in the drawing, perfectly illustrates Stevens as the comedian he aspired to be.

that he could transform his desire for solitude in nature into the words of poems. This, then, offered a solution that was both satisfying and ethical. From this point on, in his mind, there would be a purpose to his indulging in what he had considered, until now, the "lady-like" and "absurd" habit of "writing verses," a purpose that transcended his personal need: He could paint pictures of landscapes in words so that people could behold the grandeur of nature without stepping out of their houses.

Having come to this subtle realization, having a sense of how he could both be true to himself and do something worthy in a social context—something that would have pleased his father—Stevens was able to express more openly than before some of the feelings he had for those closest to him. A little more than a month later, in a letter his mother wrote to his sister Elizabeth, she noted that she had, within the week, received two letters from Wallace (WAS 3975, September 24, 1911). In another letter to Elizabeth in February she added that in his last letter Wallace had written that he would be coming to Reading for his summer holiday. Stevens also became more responsive and accessible to his siblings. In March 1912 Elizabeth wrote to him asking if he could help her financially. Though he was not able to, as he wrote back to her in a note dated April 1 (WAS 1092), he said that he was always glad to hear from her and assured her that when he was more solvent, he would be happy to make her a present of the amount she had asked to borrow.

᳁

A few days after this, on April 14, the *Titanic,* speeding to break the transatlantic crossing record, hit an iceberg and sank. It was like a premonitory metaphor for the century and for the individuals most caught up in its exhilarating but dangerously quickened pace. Sensitive to what the changes brought with this acceleration meant, Stevens bemoaned each new advance of the machine age, especially when it encroached on the pristine solitudes where he liked to walk. In the city he seemed to enjoy seeing and contemplating the new machines, as if they were toys invented for the pleasures of his imagination. He particularly liked thinking of the air machines. He enjoyed the reveries of seeing the world from a bird's-eye perspective—the view of his later imagined blackbird, so closely tied to Hiroshige's depiction of a bird in flight casting its eye down obliquely on a geometized landscape. But in spite of this fascination, just the thought of machines trespassing in his sacred groves was enough to keep him from indulging in his walks (L 171).

This conservative strain in relation to modern technology set Stevens apart from other major contemporary American figures, like William Carlos Williams, who appreciated these advances and translated the speeded-up pace of life into the forms and meters of his work.[8] This atavism of Stevens's was tied to the deeply unresolved situation with his parents, his family, and his place in his native soil. He had negative feelings about his father's having overextended himself and failing in the steel plant. This was a circumstance which could not but be connected in Stevens's mind with Garrett, Sr.'s breakdown and the resultant increased pressure he exerted on his son to succeed and be responsible not only for himself but also for Garrett, Jr., and the others, like Elizabeth, who might at different times need help.

In addition to this personal association, there was the more generalized problem of the disruption brought to integrated family and community life by the advances and necessities carried by the railroads and other new forms of transportation and communication. For the young Stevens (and for others with his possibility who belonged to the same class and situation in a rural, provincial environment that was undergoing the abrupt dislocations of industrialization), this had meant having to develop an identity in a setting completely cut off from the emotional and physical connections with which it had developed until late adolescence. It was understandably much easier for the patricians who had gone to Harvard from Boston or one of the other major eastern cities to consider the fruits of the myth of progress even if they did find them poisonous. They could freely return to their city homes on holidays, on weekends, or whenever they wished, making Harvard, as it were, simply the new center of their nests. Unlike them, who, while railing against the evils of industrialization, could at the same time be fascinated by the speeding gleam of glistening engines as they waited on the platform for their trains to stop, Stevens could return home only when his father could afford the fare. This he had not been able to manage very regularly. It would have been difficult for Stevens, then, already reticent to express any of his tender feelings directly, to regard the railroads and what they represented with joy or with any kind of objectivity. Riding in a glass coach, he was pierced by fear.

This early situation was further complicated by the exigencies of his job as a claims attorney after his marriage. His frequent traveling, made possible by the wonderfully efficient railway system, was the wedge that allowed him to keep his distance from Elsie and the possibilities that constant contact might have fulfilled. With separation, and so desire, waiting in the wings, there was always a reason for his repeated evasions, the evasions that reflected his inability to face his painful and frightening feelings.

Paradoxically, though he could use these dislocations as defenses, his state was the result of them. In not responding positively to the materials and machines that made these disruptions possible, he showed that he was somehow aware of them as at least partial causes of his situation even if he was not aware of how they fortified his defenses. It was not only when he spoke about the contamination of the countryside by steel plants and automobiles that his feelings became apparent. A revealing instance in another context is in the journal entry he made on June 25, 1912, almost a month after having last seen his mother. He had gone home in response to having been told that she was about to die. This entry, written between this time and the next month, when she did die on July 16, disclosed Stevens at one of those moments when he balanced himself precariously between acknowledging the causes of his painful feelings and acting in ways that might have alleviated his suffering.

He kept his balance by concentrating on surface details of the reality he faced and by reflecting on paradisal memories. These last he used to dissipate the unsettling effect the details otherwise would have produced.

He had just returned to keeping his journal. This relaxation into another old habit in Elsie's absence (she had left the city earlier in June and did not return until after the beginning of September) mirrored his search for a deeper sense of himself now that his mother was dying. It also announced an internal separation from Elsie. He was entrusting his perceptions and memories in letters not to her but only to himself and to the ideal future reader he might have imagined, a reader who would profit just as much as he did from reading and rereading his journal entries periodically over the years to follow. Here, then, is the entry:

June 25, 1912

About a year ago (July 14, 1911) my father died. And now my mother is dying. She was thought to be gone about a month ago and I went home to see her. I have not been able to see her often for ten years or more. During that time, she has changed, of course, but only in growing thinner. Her present sickness has aged her more than many years; and when I saw her a month ago she was much whiter than I expected. When I went home, I saw her sleeping under a red blanket in the old blue-room. She looked unconscious.—I remember very well that she used to dress in that room, when she was younger, sitting on the floor to button her shoes, with everything she wore (of summer evenings like these) so fresh and clean, and she herself so vigorous and alive.—It was only a change for her to be in the blue room. After a while, she walked, with assistance, into her own room and either rested in her chair by the window or in bed. Many unconscious habits appeared. She wanted her glasses to be on the window-sill by her side. She would reach out her hand to satisfy herself that they were there. This was at a time when her mental condition was such that she could not form a question: when she would stop midway in her questions out of forgetfulness of what she had intended to ask. She would pick up anything strange on the sill and examine it.—After some days, her mind (and body) cleared somewhat; for she was still powerful enough to resist, although to the eye she seemed so often at the point of death, with her dark color, her fitful breathing and the struggles of her heart. She liked the flowers that had been brought. She asked for Mrs. Keeley, an old friend, who came to see her. She watched the parade of the veterans on Decoration Day in a sort of unrealized way. It encouraged her to be taken to the porch and to remain there for long periods. She seemed to be perfectly conscious of her surroundings. She smiled and nodded her head, but seemed to be trying to gather her thoughts—or else to let them wander far away.—All the feelings that are aroused create a constant desire or hope of something after death. Catherine [his sister, Mary Katharine, referred to by the family as Katharine; Stevens always spelled her name with a "C," and sometimes with an "e" as here and

387

sometimes with an "a"] writes that mother wishes it were over. Fortunately for mother she has faith and she approaches her end here (unless her mind is too obscured) with the just expectation of re-union afterwards; and if there be a God, such as she believes in, the justness of her expectations will not be denied. I remember how she always read a chapter from the Bible every night to all of us when we were ready for bed. Often, one or two of us fell asleep. She always maintained an active interest in the Bible, and found there all the solace she desired.—She was, of course, disappointed, as we all are. Surely, for example, she endured many years of life in the hope of old age in quiet with a few friends and her family. And she never had a day of it.—In the bed she is in now all of her children, except the first (and possibly him) were born. And there are a thousand things like that in the old house—certain chairs, certain closets, the side-board in the dining-room, her old piano (she would play hymns on Sunday evenings and sing. I remember her studious touch at the piano, out of practice, and her absorbed, detached way of singing). At one period, say twenty years ago, she made efforts to get new things and many such objects remain, things in the parlor, etc. Her way of keeping things, of arranging rugs, of placing pieces of furniture, remains unaltered. A chair is where it is because she just put it there and kept it there. The house is a huge volume full of the story of her thirty-five years or more within it. (L 172–73)

Important here is the subtle embedding of the fourth sentence in the context of the other seven purely descriptive sentences preceding the first dash (notably Stevens had reverted completely to this old form of punctuation linking him to his father's spirit, having either forgotten or abandoned the "Très chic . . . Frenchy" ellipsis he had recently adopted): "I have not been able to see her often for ten years or more." Most revealing was his verb choice. He did not simply state, "I did not see her often," or, "I have [or had] not seen her often." Instead, he used "have not been able," as though there had been some constraint accounting for his not having gone. The sentence showed that he felt apologetically irresponsible at the same time as it attempted to shift the burden of responsibility onto some external factor that had prevented his acting the loving son. As long as he perceived that he "had not been able" to see his mother often enough over the years, he could fit any blocking factor he chose into the place of the reason why. There had been the demands of applying himself in law school; later, the demands of his work; his not having a surplus of funds for traveling (even though he had gone on his long holiday to British Columbia with Peckham and though he had visited him at his New Jersey home on many weekends when he could just as easily have gone to Reading). Finally, when he had begun going back more or less regularly to see Elsie but before the rupture with his family around the time of their engagement, he had Elsie as his internal excuse. He could tell himself how demanding she had been of his company and attention.

Now at the moment his mother was dying he forgot how "boring" he had found his household over those ten years or more. He did not then or now stop to uncover and analyze the confusion of feelings his attribution of that quality covered. Not having done this, he did not understand how insidiously the train of progress had intruded into his sense of who he was, how difficult, nearly impossible, it would have been for anyone in his circumstances, separated from his family and moving into a wholly foreign physical and spiritual environment, not to see them and feel himself painfully different. The changes of his time had made both this and his opportunities possible. It was no wonder that the marks of modernity intruding into his familiar landscapes disturbed his thoughts and troubled his sleep. But not having any understanding of this yet somehow feeling, justifiably, that he was not wholly responsible for having been inattentive to his mother, he could neither state simply that he had not gone home often enough for more than ten years nor fix on any one reason why he had not. He had simply been unable, and given this vague sense, he could flit from reason to reason as it corresponded to his mood or to whatever else was going on in his present life. If he felt disturbed at Elsie, she could slide into place as the reason he had not seen enough of his mother. If he felt perturbed about his work, it could retroactively take on the constraining role. Thus, the unresolved, unexamined feelings remaining from childhood, adolescence, and youth found at least partial expression in fictionalized causes.

When we look back at the journal entry, the next striking feature of its opening seven sentences is the abstraction of his perception of his mother into a figure representative of America: She was *white,* sleeping under a *red* blanket in the *blue* room. Of course, this setting was not invented or constructed, yet in selecting these details as the unifying elements of his memorial tableau, Stevens disclosed both a central aspect of the associative contents of his mind and a central aspect of the process whereby he protected himself from his feelings. Rather than express the dread prompted by seeing his mother whitened, frail, already lost to his needs, Stevens deflected his attention, as he had learned to do so early in his life, onto surrounding details. Proportionate to the distance he took, these details were not merely random, nearby elements but the broadest symbols of what the concept of "mother" meant for him: The associations moved from his mother, Daughter of the American Revolution, to his motherland, his mother earth, America, the colors of its emblem.

He turned away into his tropes because he could not face the guilt he felt for not having seen her more often. This was connected to his deeper inability to face directly any situation that filled him with pathos. Composing himself with his American *tableau mourant* after his covert sentence of apology, Stevens again used his dash and was then able to go on to remember a poignant instance of childhood intimacy with his mother. He had watched her and had been stimulated by both the sight and the smell of her, "so fresh and clean." Again, now, as he was brought to the point of being overwhelmed by feeling, came another dash, followed by the strange syntactic arrangement of the next sentence: "It was only a change for her to be in the blue room."

From this point until the end of the entry Stevens mentally followed his mother through her present to gradually broader ranges of things and ideas associated with her. He made a slow withdrawal from the close focus on her face opening the entry to the panning shot of the house and all the objects in it which she had arranged. This culminated in his closing metaphor of the house as "a huge volume." He recollected parts of himself as he recollected her. In this movement he merged with her, evidenced by the sentences in which tense shifts or prefigurings of what appeared in later lines of poems marked the merging of his inner and outer experience. The first of these is in the sentence where the verb "seemed" disclosed that what was to follow was Stevens's attempt to place himself inside his mother's fading consciousness: "She smiled and nodded her head [still an externally descriptive statement like those preceding], but seemed to be trying to gather her thoughts—or else to let them wander far away." His uncertainty about whether the expression he observed reflected a contraction or dilation of her consciousness stayed with him over the next three years, at least, to reemerge as the informing motive of "Sunday Morning," in which the thoughts of his female persona wander far away across the wide water as she tries to gather and focus them around the pungent fruit and bright green wings of earth.

After this sentence, where once again his feelings had begun to emerge, another dash, another evasion, followed. The next sentence about "feelings" was generalized and removed: "All the feelings that are aroused create a constant desire or hope of something after death." Here was a concise thematic statement of what developed into "Sunday Morning." Added to the contracting-dilating movement, it provided Stevens with the basic structure around which he wove the religious images remaining from his early childhood and the pagan ones learned somewhat later in an attempt to resolve his uncertainty and fear about belief. Within the entry this sentence strikes the ear and eye because of its cold ambivalence. At first it is unclear whose feelings are being described: his or his mother's. But the present-tense copula very quickly points out that it could have been only about his feelings that he was speaking. And so it becomes equally clear that at almost thirty-three Stevens was still, in spite of all the questioning of his Harvard years and after, yearning for some imperishable bliss. It would have been difficult to phrase this personally and directly. Regardless of all his pronouncements about how nature made a god of a man while the church kept him only a man, he found himself now, at the hour of his need, wishing for heaven. Unable to express his genuine feelings of dependence on the mother he was about to lose, he shifted back, instead, into dependence on the religion in which she had reared him.

In the following sentences, beginning "Fortunately for mother," Stevens attempted to extricate himself gently from the category of believers by speaking only about his mother's faith and expectation. But he gave himself away once more, though he again tried to cover himself with a qualification: ". . . and if there be a God, *such as she believes in* [italics mine], the justness of her expectations will not be denied." In this construction he did not use the conditional "if there were a God . . . would not be denied," which would have indicated his separation from the belief. Though he added the qualification, pointing to her alone as being the believer, here again the verb tense exposed him[9] and his joining with her in ways seemingly beyond his rational control.

A repeated indication of his identification with her is the sentence following the next dash: "She was, of course, disappointed, as we all are." Though still a young man, married for only three years, Stevens was experiencing, or thought he was experiencing, the disappointment with life that his mother had soothed with her interest in the Bible. He was doing the same thing in covertly adhering to his belief. But the difference was that beyond cultivating his interest in the Bible, which he again did in the months after her death, he would attempt to create a Bible of his own in the "whole" work he intended to compose. His "Great Work," the "Grand Poem," would include all the elements that would teach, as the Bible did, how to live, what to do. But his histories, gospels, and parables would be colored by his moment in time—no longer heroic and epically naïve but fallen into irony, with the only possible hero a comic one. Over the next few years Stevens began filtering from everything he read, heard, and saw the elements he needed to create his new vulgate. This process began within a year of his mother's death. It was from her that he felt he had gotten his imagination. Indulging in it after she died was a way of maintaining contact with her spirit.

On June 29, four days after this last journal entry, Stevens went home to Reading. Fortunately his mother was very much in possession of herself. So this, one of their last contacts,[10] was as full of affection as any of the tenderest moments of his childhood. The entry describing this visit, written on his return to New York, Monday, July 1 (*L* 173–74; *SP* 255), reflected the peacefulness of the encounter. But it did so precisely because in it Stevens focused not at all on himself but wholly on his mother, who faced her end with acceptance and faith, recalling the joyous moments of her motherhood when Stevens and his brothers were still "her boys." With the exception of three sentences, it was "she" who was the subject of the passage. Of the three sentences not centered on her, one had to do with the minister who had come to give her last rites; the other two touched on his feelings but only tangentially—"It was a terrible thing to see"—and: "After all, 'gentle, delicate Death' comes all the more gently in a familiar place, warm with the affectionateness of pleasant memories. [This is an observation made sadly ironic in light of Stevens's himself dying in St. Francis Hospital, unwilling to burden Elsie in his last weeks.]" He seemed to have returned to the style he had learned as a young reporter, describing even the terrors like the two-headed Hebrew child with compassion yet distance. This was the only way he had of not being "bathed in tears."

As all this was going on, Elsie was in the country, at Park Mansion in Vinemont, Pennsylvania. In picture postcards of the place which she sent to her sister, LaRue, she commented on hearing the frogs croak every night. Borrowing one of her husband's often-used adjectives, she added that she liked it there "immensely" (WAS 3981 and 3982, June 28, 1912). Whether because of her unwillingness to dissemble or because of Stevens's desire to be alone with his mother in her last days, or because he or she felt that Elsie's fragility demanded that she simply rest in the country untroubled by anything, she was not with him during any of the trying moments surrounding his mother's death. In all fairness, however, from the evidence of what he wrote to her over these days, there was no reason for her to think that she was needed. She was so unconcerned, in fact, that she had not even been sending letters or postcards to him, though she had thought of writing to her sister.

Stevens quietly voiced his disturbance at this—"Am I to have no postals?" (WAS 1927, July 7, 1912)—in describing his activities since his return to New York from his last visit to Reading when his mother had said, "Goodbye" (she did not die, however, until more than two weeks later). Yet he gave no indication of need or of missing Elsie, apart from complaining that his "dinners [had] been a great bother to [him]." But his young wife could not read through his renewed concern with food that he felt abandoned. Even if she did remember what he had once written her about how ever since he had left Reading for Harvard, thoughts of home were always associated with food, she could not have understood how his feelings for his mother had been translated into his concern for good dinners. She probably found this preoccupation annoying, especially since he did not comment on any other aspect of their common life.

The excised portion of this letter quoted above also mentioned his having been to dinner two or three times at the Strykers since she had been gone— the last time being on his return from seeing his dying mother, to whom he did not even refer. He added that he would read John Galsworthy's *The Patrician*—which Elsie had forwarded to him—and that he would return it to the Strykers in the next two or three days. He noted that he especially liked dinners with them, commenting that the conversation last time on the subject of the advancement of women had gone on until midnight and that Mrs. Stryker was "very *live* on the subject." He then continued with his description of where and why he had been having his other dinners: "The office closes too early for me to stop down-town; and I cannot bring myself to go to the cheap places up-town; so that I've been going to pretty stiff places for an entrée and a dessert. But bosh! I like variety and I think I may telephone the Earle tomorrow and go back there. The thought of iced-tea would, of itself, tempt me" (WAS 1927, July 7, 1912). At this point the letter continues in *Letters* (174). He had had a "slapping walk," he wrote her, adding pointedly, "If you care to you can read about it when you come back because I've taken to my journal again." Losing his mother and feeling somewhat abandoned but unable to express his feelings for Elsie in a way that she could understand, he imagined a loss of interest on her part. It was true that she did seem to be unconcerned, yet from the manner he had taken on in relationship to her after their marriage, it is clear that it was he who continued to set the stage and direct their roles, as he had during the years of their courtship. This was quite natural. He was the one with the actor's trunkful of old costumes gathered from his reading, and he was the one with all the words in the world at his disposal, words that he could juggle either to please her or to manipulate her, like a sleight-of-hand man, to induce just the right amount of guilt, as here. Angry at his mother and at himself but unwilling even to recognize the anger, he simply did what most do: turned it inside out and flung it, as guilt, at her.

He then went on about his library visit and his fascination with the Comtesse de Noailles, her "goût d'azur" ("taste for blue," "hunger for blue," metaphorically, "yearning for the sky") and its associations for him with his feelings for the countryside. Here another kind of displacement combined with his now poeticized hunger, *goût,* for what his mother represented, with his love of nature, *mother* nature, the countryside in which he felt free and about which he felt free to express his feelings. Evidence for how effectively this tactic worked was how happy he felt after his walk, in spite of his mother's dying: "Nothing proves it more certainly than the charm I felt all day to-day. I sated myself in it."

Strengthened by recollecting this in writing to her, Stevens went on to express his warm desire that Elsie, too, enjoy nature to the fullest extent. He voiced this in a caring way; the meaner mood had lifted. He even returned, in mentioning that he had been to the Murray Hill for dinner, to the playful "hey-diddle-diddle" refrain of his courtship letters. But just after this came the nagging question noted above: "Am I to have no postals?" He was moving back and forth between thinking of his dinners and dropping guilt-inducing statements—both self-protective devices of different kinds—and warmly expressing concern for her, desiring her to stay and enjoy what he would have liked for himself. These conflicting messages were confusing, at best. If Elsie slowly withdrew into reclusive defensiveness over the years of their marriage, it was not only because of her own weakness or lack of preparation to meet the demands of the sophisticated world into which she had moved.

In retreating from that world, Elsie all too easily remained Stevens's "Little Girl," the role in which she was fully open to the effects of his alternating behavior. She was treated best when she elicited her husband's paternal instincts. If she was frail and sickly, his behavior toward her was more likely to be warm and caring. If, on the other hand, she acted strong and independent, she would be inviting the more severe forms of behavior that would keep her "terrorized," as Stevens had so acutely yet naïvely warned her long before their marriage. Unfortunately, the more pressure was exerted on them from the outside world, the more necessary and likely it was that they would act in these familiar roles in which there was least friction. So now, as his mother died, before he left the office to go to Reading, he sent Elsie the following note:

WALLACE STEVENS

Wednesday [July 17, 1912]

MY DEAREST BUD:

I opened this by mistake—so it is all a secret—spite of the cut in the envelope.—Your letter came last evening. I am always glad to hear from you. Dont [*sic*] stop eating meat. You've gained two pounds on it, haven't you? Dont [*sic*] adopt other people's ideas about food. You need strength and blood, and you'll get them from meat, not from string beans. Will write some evening soon.

With love,
WALLACE
(WAS 1929)

Though he made no mention of his mother, a number of curiosities here pointed to what was going on beneath the surface of the fatherly role he at this moment took on so blatantly. The first was the way the *W* of "Wednesday" was shaped: huge and jagged, greatly out of proportion to the rest of the word. It seemed to indicate that indeed, something was out of control for Stevens, even though he tensely was attempting to make things seem to be as they always were. Unlike other instances of his making capital *W*'s, where they were different from the *W* he shaped to sign his name, it appears that with this one he had begun to write his name in place of the date, which he no doubt, in part of himself, wanted to forget. This was, after all, the first day in his life that he existed wholly cut off from those who tied him to the past.

The next indication of his state of mind was his addressing Elsie as "Bud." This return to a form he used when he felt the desire for total identification with her—as he, too, was "Bud" or "Buddy"—echoed his need. Now that he was separated from those who had brought him into the world, this was understandable. Moreover, sensing this and considering the extremely protective tone he took with her in this note, it seems that what he was doing was treating her the way he would have wanted to have been treated himself, at least the way the child in him, still longing for the absolute attention of his mother, wanted to be treated. At this moment of transition all the lingering, unresolved feelings of childhood reemerged. But Stevens, unwilling to admit and express his feelings, even in less emotionally loaded situations, was not able to question the causes of those feelings. Instead, he simply acted out, in a curious loop projection, the role his mother had taken on with him more than once when he was sick as a child: "Eat your meat"; "You need strength and blood"; "String beans aren't enough."

As we see how the internalization of his mother's role operated now, it is worthwhile to speculate on the broader parental internalizations and how they subsequently affected Stevens's behavior. We look at this in him not because it was peculiar to him but because he is the subject here. Indeed, whatever is observed about him in this respect applies to any of us as part of an updated consideration of how the sins of fathers and mothers are visited on children.

Since we have witnessed the many variations of Stevens's swings—between two kinds of behavior toward Elsie; between imagination and reality; between indulgence and asceticism—it is not farfetched to suggest that at the most primary level what accounted for this duality was Stevens's early incorporation of his parents' antithetical patterns of behavior. As an adult he acted out what he had experienced over and over again as a child, moving constantly between his dreamy, loving mother and his cold, distant, and judging father, who always managed to make him feel guilty about not having measured up to the standard he had set. It was from these parents that Stevens learned to love. Each one loved in his or her own way. Their son would love in both ways. He could no more choose to exclude one of these ways than he could have chosen not to grow, unless, that is, he had met someone much more experienced than Elsie, someone who would have forced him to listen to her as an "other" and so would have prodded him into learning to love in a way not determined by the past.

The next remaining letter to Elsie is dated July 29 (*L* 175), a week after his return to New York from the days spent in Reading for his mother's funeral. This letter, considered with the portion excised by later editing, further instanced the effects of the alternating roles Stevens took on in relationship to Elsie. Though he opened by mentioning that for several evenings all he had done was sit around thinking about his "poor mother," the only indication of how he felt was in his choice of that adjective. He then went on to describe once more what could have been one of his bachelor weekends. He had walked, gone to dinner at a friend's, walked again, gone to the beach with another friend, read about Eugène Delacroix, and smoked a cigar at home—something he had not done in a year and a half, as he was careful to note, inscribing even the month and year since that last indulgence. He added that he planned to do this more over the next month until Elsie came home. After this, he promised, he would not do it again until the following summer. He next moved, by way of fingering himself as the cause of all this "ado," into an attempt to assure her that he had, through all this, not forgotten her, that he had many thoughts of her and wished for her often, but that in spite of this, he wanted her to stay where she was.

As he pointed to himself as the cause of the "ado," Stevens began shifting roles uneasily. His uncertainty was triggered by a slight feeling of guilt. There he had been, describing himself alone in New York, without her, without his love object, not having to be loving. Not having to play the role of either mother or father, he was simply "Wallace," the child he would have wanted to be—self-indulgent, self-assured. But as he became conscious of Elsie once again, thinking of her coming home, he first switched into another transitional role, that of acting the penitent child and then, through that, alternately of acting the stern and guiding father and, finally, by the end of the letter, the loving mother:

So sorry about the back board! I'll come to the rescue on Thursday when I shall send you Forty dollars. This you will need to pay this week's bill and the bills for the next two weeks to come. That will leave you only Ten dollars for your laundry and pin money. But I want you to try to make it reach. It will if you are careful and independent. If it does not, let me know promptly, (do not be afraid to) for I do not want to think you are pinched and more particularly I do not want you to borrow or to run up bills. Mind! (WAS 1930)

His sense of irresponsibility for not having been more attentive to his mother gently extended to Elsie: He had forgotten to send her money. This subtly hostile omission rebuked her both for being the cause of his break with his parents and, beyond that, worse, for actually being the less than adequate mate his father had warned him about: She was frail; she no longer took an interest in what he saw and felt on his walks; she was not happy in New York. Momentarily feeling his penitence, though not his anger—"So sorry about the back board!"—he quickly transformed it into control over her. She would have to exercise restraint and act responsibly since he was sending her just barely enough to get by—"But I want you to try to make it reach. It will if you are careful and independent." In the next breath, having already terrorized her, he told her "not [to] be afraid to" ask him for more money. If she had been truly independent and strong, these contradictory signals would have made her furious, but she was dependent, child-like and so only felt more dependent and afraid not to meet the standard he set—just as he so long had been afraid not to meet the standard his father set. Meanwhile, in the weeks before, when he should have been thinking of how much he would have to send for her board, he had been dining out night after night at "stiff places" and saying, "Bosh, but I like variety." And now he was even back to buying cigars while she had to think twice about having her laundry done.

Stevens moved on to close with a note of caring, thinking of Elsie in the country he imagined and wishing for her what he wanted for himself. He did this after fantasizing himself in his most particular setting, the house where he had been born and lived for eighteen years that now would be sold. The August calm he conjured for Elsie he needed as solace for himself.

Though he had planned to go to Reading to spend a last few hours in that house and from there, perhaps, make a day trip to see Elsie in the nearby countryside sometime around the middle of August, by the eleventh of the month he wrote her that he could not possibly afford it (WAS 1931). Fortunately Elsie was not pining for him. She was, in fact, "growing stout . . . on the waffles and pine apple ice cream and mountain air" (WAS 2054, August 2, 1912). This pleased Stevens, who was also indulging himself, feasting on "capons and fresh peach pie," while he wrote to her about the "monastic life" he was leading in her absence (L 176). True, he had acted monklike in spending hours in the library, investigating various biblical figures referred to in a sermon he had recently read. He was particularly interested in finding out who St. Anthony really was, feeling a special sympathy for this being tempted so enticingly yet painfully by his demons. He had also "punished" himself by spending time in that "confounded" place he "hated," the "M-tr-p-l-t-n M-s-m of -rt" (*L* 176). He curiously spelled it in the way one would spell the sacred name in Hebrew. It was as though he had subliminally substituted the temple for the God, beauty for divinity. In so doing, he could use it as his object of anger.

The steps leading to this substitution moved through various associations he had established over the years between art and religion, as he attempted to replace parochial devotion to an anthropomorphic deity with a secular appreciation of the beautiful. In this movement many elements overlapped and became confused. First, there was the tie between religion and his family. When, in his years at Harvard, he had begun to question the bases of religious belief and to separate himself intellectually, at least, from its hold, he was also separating from his family. "Art," "beauty," quietly took over the family's comforting function. In his mind, beauty became the standard to which all the makings of his self aspired. In lines of poems he found the voice of an authority far easier to accept than the voice of his father or the church. Beauty also became the mystical mother always waiting, sleeplessly, to soothe him whenever he felt the need for some imperishable bliss.

At this moment he had lost both his father and his mother but had not begun to express, or even to recognize, the full range of his feelings about them or about himself in relationship to them. The museum, symbolically the container of his parents' solacing and guiding roles, became the butt of his inarticulate pangs. He was angry with that irrational anger we have for the dead, who, in having departed, leave us alone. He "hated" the "confounded" museum. But he was as ambivalent about it as he was about his parents, so he went there and loved what he saw: the Dutch paintings of the seventeenth century, which he found "a very remarkable period in modern history." And he honored the temple's name in the same way he honored his parents—in spite of what his feelings were—in the same way the Hebrews honored the unutterable name of their God, the perfect parent, source of all life, beauty, and creativity.

Though his state of mind might have made him feel as if he were living monastically; though he might have wished to believe that he was in some way mortifying his flesh, "that monster," and approaching more nearly the state of pure spirit; though he might have wanted Elsie, too, to believe that he was being monastic, not seeing friends or spending money on elaborate dinners and evenings at the theater while she was being told to pinch pennies and being offered the excuse of money for his not going to see her, in reality he was as far from being monklike as he would ever be. He was, after all, full of capon and fresh peach pie and had only a few days before written about his other indulgences and his cigar at home and only a few days later would be writing about indulging again in a "Belinda perfecto" (*L* 177).

In his next remaining letter, written on August 26 (*L* 177), Stevens found himself in another familiar guise—the poet. It was not only in describing the way he was dressed and how he moved and in comparing himself to "le grand Byron" that he announced this return. The letter itself was the first "poetical" one he had written in years. After he had imaginatively conjured himself back to the past, reopened his actor's trunk, and donned the monk's costume, which he used to cover his feelings, he put on the poet's mask once more as well. He had figuratively expressed his penitence. He had flagellated himself by going to that "awful place," the museum, and was suffering through life in the city. But the period of fast was over. He had reached one period of his arc; it was time to swing back.

The swing back into being the poet meant once more turning away from religion and toward nature. Whereas two Sundays before, still playing the monk, he had gone to church, this Sunday he took to the roads for a walk of about thirty miles. He felt "proud" of himself, and his imagination took flight like a moth fascinated by the lantern of the moon, his "flame." The images came from his old infatuation with Japan and the Orient. His description of the moon in the trees and hearing the evening bells evoked both some of the titles of Japanese and Chinese paintings he had once listed for Elsie and in his journal, and the traditional Zen garden he had once described to her, with its "mystical lantern" hung in the darkness. He was open, allowing himself to be metamorphosed into the various shapes produced by the interaction of his present with what it called forth from his past associations. The transitions he made while walking, as he recorded them, were sharp, as contradictory as the antithetical parts of his being learned from his parents, as contradictory as the attitudes and expectations expressed in his letter to Elsie, as contradictory as the roles of monk and Byron-like poet, displaying his fuzzy chest as he paraded along, his "shirt turned back . . . chemisette flung back." He changed from moth to lion, roaring for his meat, and beautifully transformed the human syllable of celebratory exclamation "Wow" into the onomatopoeic animal voicing "Wow-ow-oo-oo-ruh-r-r-r!" The poet did this. Feeling the pressure of his animal appetites mounting as he entered the city where he would be pent and wanting compensation for the natural habitat he had just left behind, he created language for his feeling.

He felt intensely the change from country to city. He expressed it in one way by transforming himself from moth to lion; in another, more direct way, by describing how he felt the "corsair of hearts" to feeling as though he had "put a noose around [his] neck." Putting on his coat instead, he sensed himself change from the rebellious devil-may-care romantic poet to a "Spanish gentleman," still touched by romanticism but complacent in his self-possession.

This letter was characterized by the kind of unity belonging to a few of the early journal entries and letters, in which his frame of mind was such that on certain days the world seemed to arrange itself into a poem. On days like this his need for order dictated that the world and his words take shape. In this letter, unity was provided by the image of the moon, the flame he continued to follow even after his various permutations from moth to Spanish gentleman. Moreover, this account represented a metaphorical attempt at experiencing something of which he could have no knowledge—death: "Walking through the dark, to a strange place." Just after he wrote this, his description moved from straightforward reporting about place and distance covered to the lyrical sequence that imaginatively projected his spirit into its various shapes. It was as though he had unconsciously identified with his parents, who had gone "through the dark, to a strange place." In this symbolic action he liberated his own creative power. Dealing with mortality prompted his coming to terms with his own limits in the world and contributed to his serious return to poetry the following year. Facing the reality of his own end forced Stevens to set his own priorities and values. In this ordering poetry was to take first place.

૨▲

But there were many other factors contributing to Stevens's fulfilling the wish to be a poet. A number of extraordinary developments affected him between midsummer 1912 and midsummer 1913 and helped bring about the change from a life that ran along "obscurely . . . without incident," as he wrote to his sister Elizabeth on November 30, 1912 (*L* 177–78), to a life full of stimulation from the exciting currents of his time. As he diverted himself that fall, after Elsie had returned, with a "raft of plays," which she enjoyed at least as much as he (their life consisting, as he noted to Elizabeth, of "Nothing picturesque," just "keeping house"), events that were profoundly to alter him and the way he lived already sparkled beneath the surface of things as they were.

Poetry magazine was founded in Chicago in 1912. (Two years later Harriet Monroe would select four of Stevens's poems for her "Poems of War" issue, thus helping launch the poet in his career.) It was also during 1912 that Walter Pach and Walt Kuhn were roaming artists' studios in Paris selecting pieces for the Armory Show, which opened in February 1913 and revolutionized the way art was understood no less than the way people looked at "reality." It was also in the same year that the political situation in Europe began crystallizing into the events that culminated in the outbreak of World War I. Montenegro declared war on Turkey, which, in turn, asked the Great Powers to intervene, while Bulgaria and Serbia mobilized their armies. Later in the year Woodrow Wilson was elected president of the United States, and the stage for the war that was to end all wars was fully set.

In his November 1912 letter to Elizabeth, Stevens had also mentioned that neither he nor Elsie was reading particularly. He had been trying to get through *The Winter's Tale,* for weeks, he wrote. This shift from his habit of reading omnivorously when he was alone also contributed to his finally finding and declaring himself a poet in the following two years. A long period in which his mind was not like a hall in which he heard someone else's voice intoning was necessary for him to begin hearing his own. While their marriage nourished him at least in terms of food ("Elsie is a stunning cook—quite the best in my experience," he noted to Elizabeth), it did not nourish his spirit with the things he had grown used to feeding it for so many years when he was alone. Elsie probably felt that books usurped the attention she required or desired when her husband came home from the office. The only agreeable compromise was the theater. At least they could enjoy it jointly, laughing or crying at the same things.

Although there is no direct evidence that Stevens attended the Armory Show—after the November letter to Elizabeth, the remaining papers do not pick up again until April 1913—Holly Stevens relates that he did,[11] and it is impossible to imagine that he did not. Years later Stevens wrote of its impact on Walter Arensberg in terms that suggest that he had more than a passing familiarity both with what it presented and with its cultural impact (L 821). Stevens probably went more than once. Someone as concerned with "stimulation" as he could not have ignored the brouhaha surrounding the show after it had opened if indeed he had not been one of those discussing it in the months of its preparation. Since he was a "good friend" of Arensberg (L 850), who was, in turn, a good friend of Walter Pach, one of the organizers of the show (whom Stevens met through Arensberg and with whom he established his own relationship, often visiting him in his Washington Square studio), it is even possible that Stevens had access to news of the developments surrounding the show and even, perhaps, to the works themselves, before the show opened on February 17. It would have been highly unlikely that Arensberg, so excited by what he heard from Pach and others about the Steins' studio and other Parisian ateliers—like that of Duchamp-Villons—would have excluded his old Harvard friend from whatever he knew of its preparations.

Stevens's relationship with Arensberg, like that with Witter Bynner, seems to have had a basis in mutual respect that prompted each of them to keep the other abreast of what he felt to be the most important aspects of the spiritual life of the time. Neither spatial nor temporal separations—during this period and until 1914 Arensberg and his wife Louise were living outside of Boston, at Shady Hill, which had been the residence of Charles Eliot Norton—prevented them from somehow, at various points, communicating what was new or noteworthy. This probably had to do with the similarity in the kind of bond that existed between Stevens and Arensberg and Stevens and Bynner. All had worked at directing Harvard's literary journals. Bynner had succeeded Stevens as editor of the *Advocate,* while Arensberg was editor of the *Monthly* at the same time Stevens was editing the *Advocate.* Perhaps what continued to privilege these relationships was the sense of responsibility all had in connection with their functions on the publications. All had had to have knowledge of current social, cultural, and aesthetic developments, and all had had to make selections based on subtle discriminations about purpose and importance. Focusing this kind of attention over a long period of time in the still-formative period of youth could not but predispose these sensitive types to being, as mature adults, consistently on the lookout for what was central in their time. There was naturally satisfaction in sharing what they perceived with those few others whom they knew would be equally concerned and sympathetic.

In the unlikely event that Stevens did not attend the Armory Show,[12] he would still have known a great deal about it. Not only did countless newspaper and magazine reports cover it, but in the studio of the Arensbergs' at 33 West Sixty-seventh Street in New York where they moved within a year of the show, Stevens not only had direct access to some of the works that had hung on the Armory Show's cleverly divided and arranged walls but had access as well to some of the artists: Marcel Duchamp, Francis Picabia.[13]

Coming into contact with this group and these works was as important a single factor as ever played a part in Stevens's development. Some of its implications showed themselves almost immediately, while others continued to vibrate beneath what appeared on the surface of his work and behavior. In one sense, it is unfortunate that there is no direct evidence of Stevens's reactions to particular events and objects. But in another, it is better that it is this way. Knowing simple and containing "facts"—for example, that Stevens was delighted by the arrangement of works at the show or that he especially appreciated the Matisses but not the Redons (which were among the few things the public found palatable)—would allow the easy registration of its influence. This, in turn, would force certain evidences of that influence to make sense in an almost commonplace way. But not knowing the facts stimulates a questioning sensitivity that demands engaging the remaining texts openly and actively, quizzing all sounds, all thoughts, for the music and manner of resemblance to the thing borne in mind.

In the case of the Armory Show and the other events and individuals associated with it, there is no question, after we look at the later "facts" of Stevens's life and work, that it was for him, no less than for America, the most important single exhibition ever held. This importance included the intention with which it was conceived and the broader concepts and aesthetic developments related to it. From its most general aspects—that it broke entirely from the realist tradition and that it represented the public's recognition of art's complete break with social or political concerns—to its particular ties, especially through the work of Duchamp and Picabia, to the Dada attitude (which would not be named as such until a few years later in Zurich's Café Voltaire), this event left its strong imprint on Stevens. It was not so much that it presented him with a new way of looking at the world as that it trumpeted confirmation of tendencies in himself about which, until this moment, he had been uncertain and reticent.

Beyond the show itself there was its "genius,"[14] Walter Pach, singly most responsible for translating the project's underlying concept into reality. Having lived in Paris, painting and writing about new developments in art, he had a wide acquaintance with both artists and dealers. Since 1909, in New York, he had known Arthur Davies, a painter as well and the man who secured the necessary financial support for the exhibition. The idea began in

1911 with Kuhn, Henry Fitch Taylor, Jerome Myers, and Elmer MacRae.[15] Hearing of the plans, Pach wrote to Davies and offered to gather a "representation of the men for whom they were looking." He introduced Davies and Kuhn to the avant-garde collection of Gertrude and Leo Stein and took them to the studio of the Duchamp-Villons, where Davies was greatly moved by the work of the three brothers, especially Marcel Duchamp, of whom he said, "That's the strongest expression I've seen yet." Davies was also taken with the Rumanian sculptor Constantin Brancusi and announced, "That's the kind of man I'm giving the show for." He also loved the work of Odilon Redon, lining the walls of the show with 83 of his pieces (there were 312 or 313 pieces in all); he eventually bought his *Roger and Angélique* for himself. Through his friendship with Ambroise Vollard, the well-known dealer immortalized in Braque's and Picasso's portraits, Pach also helped the show's organizers acquire the rest of the pieces that graced the armory's walls.[16]

Stevens's exposure to Pach no doubt familiarized him with at least some of the concepts and new directions in art about which Pach was passionate. During his visits to Pach's Washington Square studio after the latter's return to New York, discussions almost certainly focused on these matters and must also have touched on Gertrude Stein, who had already published *Three Lives* (1909) and her verbal portraits of Matisse, Picasso, and Mabel Dodge (in Alfred Stieglitz's *Camera Work*, August 1912 and June 1913, respectively). From a later letter to J. Ronald Lane Latimer, the publisher of two of Stevens's limited editions in the mid-thirties, it is clear that Stevens was familiar with and admired Stein's style (*L* 290). Its most characteristic features mirrored the plastic form of the work of many of the painters represented both in her collection and in the Armory Show. Stevens would have carefully considered these in terms of their efficacy in communicating what he felt to be expressions of the modern sensibility. Whether he became knowledgeable about these techniques through reading Stein and seeing the Armory Show or in talking with Pach, as well as with Arensberg, and later, Albert Gleizes, Jean Crotti, Duchamp, and Picabia, their impact on him became evident in the poems he began writing sometime in 1913 and 1914 and continued to be evident over the next few years as he wrote the poems eventually collected in *Harmonium*.

The most general and striking of these features was the apparent irreverence for the past displayed in the break from the traditional forms of representing reality, while the most subtle feature was a pervasive undertone of irony that colored even what seemed to be the most purely aesthetic, abstract renderings. The particular ways in which the move away from the realist tradition showed itself had a direct impact on Stevens. The most obvious of these stylistic shifts was the breaking up of surface into several planes that characterized cubism. The strongest effect of this device was to destroy the distinction between background and foreground, decentering the "subject" from the privileged position it had enjoyed in perspectival renderings. From one side this represented the subtle external change in the way human beings saw themselves in relationship to the historical and natural orders and to their personal, unconscious order, hidden from yet motivating them. In this sense, the decentering symbolized the actual feeling of dislocation experienced by those who allowed themselves to remain open to what the discoveries of Darwin and Freud meant. The individual could no longer be understood as something separate from the background that had produced him or her. Cubism reflected this breakup of an integrated identity.

Seen from another side, this reflected the aesthetic translation of Kant's perception of the indivisibility of inner and outer realms: that the understanding of reality must come not from placing inner against outer but from understanding the fused and interdependent relation between them. Since the bases of this relation were time and space, the relation was constantly changing, shifting in the way cubist presentations attempted to depict. It is impossible to see all the aspects of a "subject" of a cubist canvas at once, in the same way as it is impossible to see both chalice and two facing profiles in the illustration so often used to make this point about perception,[17] the point often taken as the meaning of a "relativistic" view of the pictorial plane.

In terms of cubist aesthetic and method, this was articulated in two fundamental ways, one having to do with time, the other with space, each with devices appropriate to it. The primary understanding concerning time was that no subject or object could be experienced fully if the subject or object were separated from past knowledge of it. The representation of reality was "truer," as Stevens's friend Pach expressed it,[18] when the thing known was presented incorporating some record of previous experience. The various intersecting and juxtaposed forms depicted on a cubist canvas were intended to mirror this constant movement of consciousness, aware of itself, as it observed something external that temporarily focused attention.

Extending this understanding to its extreme, Marcel Duchamp eventually abandoned even the canvas that created a barrier between observer and ground beyond the work. *The Bride Stripped Bare by Her Bachelors, Even or The Great Glass* (now in the Arensberg Collection at the Philadelphia Museum of Art) includes the ever-shifting present background seen through the glass but incorporated by its frame. In a sense the intention behind this work is parallel to that behind Stevens's use of the harmonium as his dominant figure. The suggestion of the instrument's tone and function works to make the reader aware that as he or she goes through the poems of Stevens's "Great Work," his/her playing/reading is, of necessity, different from another reader's, even though controlled by the individual and collective arrangement of the notes/poems themselves. In the same way the frame and subject of Duchamp's *Great Glass* are fixed, sustaining the viewer's attention and providing the holding tone. Both work like updated but comic continuos.

The literary application of this understanding began, at least chronologically, with Gertrude Stein's stylistic innovations. The introduction into prose of the repetitions and variations of poetry, different from their use in poetry because of almost endless qualifications (equivalent to the many juxtaposed and intersecting planes describing the same object in painting); the extraordinary extension of the sentence; the implicit and explicit contradictions pointing always to the opposite or stating the negation of the given statement; the subtle sequencing of time beneath the heavy preponderance of present participles—all these features combined to produce the dizzying effects of uncertainty, produced as well by the cubists' rendering of objects decentered and broken into various constituent parts, both memorial and possible. These works were also the equivalents of the analytic experience; it was no accident that cubism had its "analytic" phase (1907–1912). Though Henry James had already experimented with varying, it seemed to infinity, possible points of view in a narrative, he had not, in the same way as Stein, incorporated into his form the phenomenal content he was describing. Narrative still progressed along the trail of plot with none of the hairpin turns, deliberate repetitions, or apparently lunatic or silly qualifications Stein produced long in advance of the accepted uproarious stylistic effects of Samuel Beckett or Eugène Ionesco.

When, then, in Stevens's work, the same devices reappeared modified and adapted to the different requirements of poetry, it was more than coincidence. His most direct application, of course, was in "The Comedian as the Letter C," where the letter *c,* punned on its semantic homonyms and sounded and conceptualized in all its possible variations (including additional puns on the eleventh and twelfth meanings of certain words beginning with *c* used in the poem), is treated like the "subject" of a cubist canvas and like one of Stein's central words (as in her portrait of Matisse, "struggling" and "expressing," and of Picasso, "charming" and "working," and in her famous poem on the "rose"). "The Comedian" clearly expressed *Harmonium*'s dominant tone. In it, his longest poem, Stevens provided the program for his "rude aesthetic," an aesthetic intrinsically allied with cubism.

The most characteristic features of this mock mock epic repeat those Stein adopted for her prose from the canvases she and her brother loved and collected.[19] Besides the repetitions and variations, opposition, syncopation, and contradiction run throughout the poem. Time sequences subtly shift back and forth, while present participles maintain constant movement. In addition, sentences expand and contract irregularly, as in Stein's portraits, following the alternations of excitement and fear that attend uncertainty. These same irregular rhythms were also being heard in jazz and in jazz-influenced "classical" compositions like those of Erik Satie, Igor Stravinsky, Claude Debussy, Francis Poulenc, Darius Milhaud, Arthur Honegger, and others in Paris. For Stein, the uncertainty was, in part, a function of confronting the newness of Matisse's and Picasso's works and representing in both the form and the content of her pieces the vacillating and vague overqualifications of critics' responses. The works and the responses to them were raised against a background colored by Einstein's theory of special relativity and Freud's investigation of the wells of unknowing within each individual.

For Stevens, too, the sense of uncertainty derived from the general cultural situation. But a deep personal doubt about his own effectiveness overlapped this and called into question all he had learned that had gone into making him who he was. Crispin in his situation, at sea-*c* and "seeing," was the perfect figure to express all aspects of this uncertainty. Stevens's naming his hero a comedian pointed to his desire to achieve the kind of effect derived from reading aloud one of Stein's portraits or from fully engaging Duchamp's *Great Glass* and imaginatively playing through the kind of Rube Goldberg[20] interactions depicted there.

Counterpointing the attempt to represent the new perception of space with new forms was the attempt to represent the new understanding of time. Though both these approaches had begun as early as the end of the eighteenth century, in Mozart's restructuring of phrasing, for example,[21] not until the early twentieth century, as art became as self-conscious as consciousness itself had become with Kant and Hegel, were these aesthetic developments formalized. The philosopher who first handled these effects in a direct and practical way, examining them from various angles as if he himself were one of the cubist painters, was Henri Bergson, who appropriately wrote seminal pieces on time and on laughter. Stevens himself was preoccupied with both these subjects in ways inextricably connected to how their functions were being perceived and applied by European contemporaries in the early years of the century.

In translating this new understanding into formal artistic elements, painters, writers, and musicians focused primarily on intervals and how varying intervals could be used to approximate the distinctions between the different kinds of time that were now being discussed. In poetry this meant that in addition to the attention traditionally given to meter and refrains, which rhythmically punctuate the sense of the poem, there was an attempt to create other kinds of time intervals. Using a title that was puzzling, Stevens hoped, in part, to force pauses or rests, spaces where the reader could attempt to figure out the relationship between title and poem. Stevens exploited this device to its fullest, drawing on lessons he had learned from the Oriental masters who established the same kind of tension in their koans. This aspect was also linked to the comic element. For Zen masters the illogicality of a koan is intended to produce the laughter accompanying the realization of reason's limits; this experience is a moment of enlightenment, when according to one of their standard texts, the individual has the experience known as the "snow man," which means melting into perspiration at the moment of illumination—a moment when the ego dissolves.[22] Though Stevens did not weave all these threads together until a few years later, when he wrote his "Snow Man" poem (*CP* 9), being exposed during this period to the playful experiments of some of the proto-Dadaists, like Duchamp, spurred him to look once again at his own comic bent—evidenced early in his mocking "Ballade of the Pink Parasol"—and to consider ways of transforming it into a formal mode.

Other experiments with time intervals in poetry had come long before the cubists' manipulation of visual time in their canvases. The most notable was, of course, Stéphane Mallarmé's "Un Coup de Dès Jamais N'Abolira le Hasard," in which the words were set on the page in the manner of a musical score. This, too, had not been lost on Stevens. Though he never broke the traditional appearance of poetic forms, his use of images over the years imitated in an abstract way this musical project. Images reappeared over time, enlarged or diminished in the internal time of his being by his passage through actual time. The ultimate effect paralleled what Proust had done and was doing in prose, specifically illustrating Bergson's ideas.

All these innovations, including the stress on the comic element, had behind them a serious philosophical intent. In the most general terms, this was to dissolve the distinction between subject and object, to solve the problem Descartes had set three centuries earlier; the attempt continues today. Though Stevens probably did not discern his own intention theoretically early in his career, his conversations with Walter Pach, Walter Arensberg, and the others who moved in the Arensberg circle over the years surely touched on specific manifestations and issues connected with this deeper search.

Stevens did not keep a nonpoetic record of the particular subjects discussed during his evenings with the group or with individuals attached to it, but others did. From the writings of Walter Pach, the essays on cubism by Gleizes and Jean Metzinger, or, later, on Dada, by Picabia, from some of the reminiscences of William Carlos Williams and Witter Bynner, for example, as well as from subsequent scholarly studies,[23] the nature of some of these discussions can be deduced, and a number of specific elements that appeared in various forms in Stevens's work can be isolated. In connection with the blurring of the boundary between subjective and objective realms, subject and ground, there are several descriptions from some of these sources that have direct parallels in Stevens's conceptual framework and developing vocabulary.

In his *Masters of Modern Art* Pach gave a coherent account of the historical evolution of the new forms and named the different features of these forms, all of which play around the underlying theme of the identification of inner and outer, time and space, what is and what seems. In discussing the genesis of the modernist movement, he compared the early twentieth century to the Renaissance, noting how contemporary painters went to museums to broaden their bases of reference in the same way that the fifteenth-century painters looked to the classical past. This represented an intuitive attempt to obviate the limitations derived from the eighteenth century's mannered extension of one side of the Cartesian duality, which had, then, to be compensated for by the antithetical romantic excesses of the nineteenth. The extreme separation of the thinking subject, reason's instrument, from its organic sources prompted the romantic reaction, which, when it was later empirically evidenced and argued for by Darwin, in turn prompted the disguising reaction described by the term "Victorian." Imitating the Renaissance model represented, in large part, a desire to return to a point before the disjunction between man and nature, mind and body was made, in the hope that a synthesis could be achieved. By the end of the nineteenth century this attempt had produced the symbolist aesthetic, which, more than anything else, stressed what Charles Baudelaire popularized as a system of "correspondences," linking the individual to nature and the universe in a way that echoed the fifteenth- and sixteenth-century neo-Platonists' interest in the Cabala and Hermeticism, both of which offered, in different form, magical or mystical keys to unlock the secrets of the universe and the individual's connection with it.

Furthermore, Walter Arensberg, by the time Stevens and the others came to spend hours in his famous studio, was deeply interested in the work of Francis Bacon.[24] Stevens must have often heard him extol the utopian view described by Bacon in his *New Atlantis,* in which the applications of reason in science grew out of and served the senses' determination of human good. Arensberg, it seems, even patterned his "group" on Bacon's model of thinkers working together in a community gathered to solve the riddles proposed by the universe. Bacon's view, unlike Descartes's expansion, did not separate matter from spirit, contemplating subject from its position in a friendly ground, part of the objective world it wanted to understand.

Associated subjects discussed by Arensberg's circle included defining "impersonality" in modern art. For them, this notion derived from painters like Delacroix with his use of color. This quality was best expressed by seeing any particular "modern" work as a "meeting place of instinct and experience."[25] This paralleled the return to both a Renaissance and classical ideal since the artist was to abandon himself to the "deep sources of his nature" in order to express the instinctual "irrational element" while at the same time using logic to control the violence that without it might destroy any possibility of form.[26] This balance represented a new classical moment, modern art reflecting not external appearances but thought as it addressed itself to nature and the senses. Where the Greeks had abstracted perfect individual elements from various models to present the ideal, modernists were abstracting the harmonious movement of thought itself. All these elements were combined in the cubists' formula expressing the relation of the thing as seen to the thing as known[27]; in so doing, they believed they were hearing "real voices," not echoes.[28] This meant that their work attempted to abolish the distinction between "essential and apparent subject matter."[29] Another of the formulas they used to express their aesthetic was directly connected to all this but was decidedly more cryptic: "Nothing comes from nothing." This slogan, adapted for their use from Socrates, Marcus Aurelius, and Shakespeare's Lear,[30] perfectly contained their various considerations, as described here, while to outsiders, not of the elect, it would appear tauntingly nihilistic, attached, at best, to a decadent late-nineteenth-century aesthetic.

This ambiguity raises a number of interesting points touching on the comic aspect noted above, for this group given its fullest expression by Bergson. Considering this in the terms carefully laid out in his essay on the subject illuminates how the modernists rejected the "decadent" attitude and at the same time illustrates how Dada was a natural outgrowth of a positive "classical" aspiration described by Pach as held by the early modernists. Stevens was familiar with this rationale, as he was with these perceptions, formulas, and slogans. Whether or not he consciously intended to align himself with this group when he shaped his own most characteristic poetry, the parallels between many of them and these particular expressions cannot be ignored. At the very least they reflect an unconscious participation in the spirit of his age.

"Let be be finale of seem," from "The Emperor of Ice-Cream" is certainly not far from the cubists' stated intention to express the "relation of the thing as seen to the thing as known." The observation of the "Nothing that is not there and the nothing that is" in "The Snow Man" is similarly a brilliantly culminating development from "Nothing comes from nothing." The cubists' focus on integrating the "deep sources of nature" into their representations—following their realization of the tremendous import of Freud's and William James's more restrained stress on the part played by the unconscious in perception and action—was also given a central place by Stevens. Though it was not until later in his career that he named his "irrational element," once he did and described its operation in the essay which it titles, it became clear that he had been working with a full understanding of its function and effect since the time he began composing the poems in *Harmonium*. The distinction made in that essay between the "true subject" and the "poetry of the subject," two aspects that the poet was always writing about at once, shares the aesthetic bases of the cubists' recognizing that there is both an "essential" and an "apparent subject matter" yet that the boundary between them is collapsed in the work of art.[31]

These common elements, playing on the ambiguity between essential and apparent subject matter, were involved in the idea of comedy as it was laid out by Bergson. Stevens had been interested in the theoretical aspects of comedy at least as early as the time he was at Harvard, when he first read George Meredith's essay on the subject.[32] Later in his career he even referred Robert Pack, one of the critics interested in explicating the sources of his poetry,[33] to that piece (L 838). Stevens's reading of Bergson, later, was reinforced by his contact with Duchamp, Picabia, and their work.[34] The cardinal point about comedy made by both Meredith and Bergson[35] is that it is both a social and a socializing force.[36] Indeed, Meredith perceived Byron to have been rebellious and antisocial precisely because he lacked comic spirit.[37] It is unnecessary to go into the tautology implicit here; Bergson, in analyzing this connection in its generality, laid bare the interrelation in his clearly reasoned exposition and in doing so recapitulated the history of the comic mode from the time of the Greeks to the present. It was as though he had provided the companion piece on comedy for Aristotle's *Poetics*, which had existed but, according to one tradition, was lost.[38]

Bergson's basic premise, articulated into its various applications and manifestations, was that comedy is produced by and depends on the possible unity of the accepted duality of personality. This unity is elsewhere described as follows: "This unity [is] seen in the tendency of the comic sense to bring the deviating individual into accord with social norms, or to bring the deviating society to awareness of the ideal, or, finally, to reconcile the individual and his social milieu with the ideal by way of a productive and unifying insight into a more authentic vision of human possibilities."[39] Bergson saw this attempt at establishing a balance, a harmony of forces, as a movement toward the classical ideal, an equilibrium of man's relation to both society and his understanding of the universe. Stevens's later description of his poetry as the expression of the relation of a man to his world (*OP* 172) set his entire corpus, not simply "The Comedian" or the poems of *Harmonium,* in this category. But it is only by our looking carefully at Bergson's anatomy of comedy, which shows how its various elements develop and interrelate, that Stevens's movement through the different tones in his volumes can be understood as comic.[40] It is important to see in this connection both that his project for a comedy, at the same time "divine" and "human," could not be realized until he had given completion to the form he envisioned with what he felt were his last poems and that the intention for the project began to take shape at least forty years before this closure that marked it as a real comedy. Stevens's understanding of and involvement with the comic element helped him resolve the tensions he had been experiencing all his life. But until he found a vehicle for transforming these strains into an aspiration toward the ideal—comedy's classical aim—he continued his uneasy movement up and down between two elements. The importance of this period in his development cannot be overstressed. The year 1914 was the watershed of his personal experience as much as it was of the century's.

Like *Creative Evolution,* Bergson's work on comedy appeared serially in *Camera Work,* one of the required texts of the Arensberg circle. One of its most striking points and its controlling metaphor, which appeared in countless variations and contexts throughout the essay, was Bergson's comparison of the comic to what is mechanical or machinelike in human experience. Whatever is done repeatedly, without thought or attention given to the continual permutations of the present, is comic, "ready-made"—a perception that Duchamp seems to have used in naming some of his absurd constructions. In later, existential terms, this unthinking, mechanical way of being was described as the antithesis of engagement, where the individual must at every moment confront the abyss of changing moments and create himself or herself anew by choosing and acting in the way that the ever-new present demands. Whatever is laughable is, on some level, a measure of the inappropriateness of a response to the present. Whether out of fear, out of laziness, out of preoccupation with the past, speculations about the future or about the purely abstract realm of ideas, when the prompting is not something in the immediate present, the "absentmindedness" (Bergson's term) that causes either slipping on the banana peel or the conjuring of utopias no human being could ever happily inhabit—since the imperfect is our paradise—produces laughter.

Looking at humans in the industrial age this way was precisely the opposite of the pessimistic, even tragic way of those at Harvard who had left

America and gone in search of better solutions to the modern dilemma than the myth of progress. While Stevens and others like him had been touched by many of these disheartened men after their returns to their native ground, writers like Thomas Hardy and, later, D. H. Lawrence presented this bleak world view to a much broader segment of the population. If this view were taken seriously and followed logically, the only possible solutions would be either to return to a kind of Rousseauian "natural" state or to accept total despair—in other words, nihilism. Many did follow these ways. For those unable to transcend the sense of despair and to arrive at an updated stoicism, this attitude resulted in either escapism—whether literal or metaphorical, through drugs or alcohol—or complete apathy. These last became, at best, "disaffected flagellants" (CP 59). But neither of these postures could accomplish any melioration of the modern human condition.

The comic view of the contemporary situation, which first began to be apparent with the cubists and proto-Dadaists, reached its popular form in Charlie Chaplin and Buster Keaton films. While at first this comic view seemed to present a satirical and nihilistic opposing law, it was actually a natural development of the previous generation's pessimism. Though Bergson was chronologically part of that generation, it was as if acting the philosopher in the best sense, he had surveyed the general cultural situation and taking it as his beginning term, his thesis, had worked out the dialectic issuing from it. His predisposition to do this was part of his own cultural baggage; it was France that had produced as its monumental document of social history Balzac's *Comédie Humaine*. Too, Bergson, like Freud (born in the same year) was a Jew; he was part of the French culture and also stood a slight distance from it. He was thus able to see it in a perspective that allowed him to abstract its prominent features. Both his and Freud's focus on comedy, jokes, their formal and unconscious aspects, developed from feeling in some way separate from the society in which they lived. This allowed them to regard it in its distinctness as an integral form. They could then easily see and comment on exaggerations within it or eccentricities from it—the seeds of comedy.

Bergson's position was that the comic attitude represents a more mature stance in relationship to a culture because it presupposes that all the structures shaping it are social products and consequently subject to being changed. While those who mourned the birth of the industrial age fearfully prophesied that the machines they created would, Frankenstein-like, destroy them, these others—like Alfred Jarry, Duchamp, Picabia—accepted the new machine monsters as simply other forms created for particular uses and tried, in their art, to cast the machines in ways that would remind people of how ridiculous they could become if they lost sight of this. The sexual machine pastiches of Picabia (particularly his terrifying *Rock and Drill*), of Duchamp in *The Great Glass,* and Fernand Léger, share this purpose, a purpose fully understood by Stevens. He bade his "Emperor" "whip/In kitchen cups concupiscent curds" (CP 64), and he echoed the same reminder about the possibility of dehumanization if people saw themselves only as determined mechanisms sprung from the first "machine' of ocean" (*CP* 102):

> If sex were all, then every trembling hand
> Could make us squeak, like dolls, the wished-for words.
>
> (*CP* 17)

Sharing this comic sense of life, Stevens attempted to shake off his dour Puritan spirit, a spirit colored by the gray weather of the northern climates where it found its home. He allied himself instead with a Mediterranean spirit inherited from the various itinerant groups that had, over the centuries and for various reasons, explored its shores. This was the spirit of Odysseus and, in another form, of the Jews of the Diaspora. It was also the spirit of the nomadic Moorish tribes that made their way into Spain, and it was also the spirit of the troubadours. Each of these, moving through different places, adapted, integrated themselves, and ensured their continued welcome with entertaining yet edifying poems or stories as they took on different postures or donned disguises. Their rubbing against changing realities, always aware of themselves as outsiders and of the mores they had to learn to manipulate, made them naïve and native ironists.[41]

❧

That Paris in the earliest years of the twentieth century became the center where a new group of outsiders gathered is partially attributable to the Balzac of the *Comédie Humaine,* the Flaubert of *Bouvard et Pécuchet,* and others who prepared the ground for the French themselves to look with ironic distance at various aspects of their culture. But the allure of Paris for these artists was probably more directly connected to Napoleon's conquests and pillaging. As a result of the latter, the Louvre had developed, through the greater part of the nineteenth century, the best collection both of works of antiquity and of more contemporary European productions. And the artists of the modernist persuasion had substituted immersion in museums for immersion in the world of people and places, as the camera slowly usurped what had been the painter's major social role. It was Paris, too, because in France the Industrial Revolution had not been as intensely disruptive as in England, which did have, after all, the British Museum and the Victoria and Albert. Though their collections could not rival the Louvre's in range, they could equally have made London an international hub were it as pleasant to sit inside a pub as at an outdoor café near St.-Germain-des-Prés. But the truly horrible elements of exploitation and dislocation that were an everyday part of London life were not as obtrusive a part of Parisian city life.

Had Stevens followed his instinct to go to Paris in 1900, he would have found a stimulating cultural atmosphere congenial to his spirit many years earlier and, perhaps, would not have had to wait until thirty-four to begin resolving the tensions of his personality and experience into the shaped forms of art. But in 1913 it was as though Paris had come to New York, so he began then. In August 1913, as Stravinsky, in Paris, completed the trilogy of modern dance music of *Firebird* and *Petrouchka* with *Le Sacre du Printemps,* Stevens attempted to put together a little collection of verses once more (*SP* 257). The following year, goaded by his contact with Alfred Kreymborg and those who would become the "Others" group, he began publicly showing himself as a poet. The "Others"—borrowing their name from the magazine that Kreymborg and Arensberg began after the failure of Kreymborg's *Glebe*—committed themselves to forging an avant-garde of the avant-garde aesthetic, more imagist than the imagists, a purely modern idiom. They saw Stevens as their herald and hero.

At what level Stevens's early commitment to comedy represented a fully reasoned choice cannot be known. But by the time he wrote "The Comedian as the Letter C," he was consciously fashioning a comic persona. And later, when he chose the rinky-tink-sounding harmonium as his controlling metaphor, he clearly reiterated his adherence to comedy's "rude aesthetic."

As all the new things he was seeing began percolating beneath his surface of "barrister," Stevens was still giving the greater part of his energy to succeeding in the practical world. And as he became more deeply involved in following the threads of the connections he was establishing in the business world and in the world of colors and words, he attempted to make for Elsie another world where she would be as comfortable and happy as she could be in New York. It is unlikely that she accompanied him to the Armory Show. If she did, she would have been as mystified as most of the public, and it would not have been only because of her lack of sophistication. Theodore Roosevelt, well educated, familiar with the European cultural scene, and easy with the ways of the world, attended the show—on March 4, 1913, as President-elect Wilson was taking the oath of office. His comments, reported in the newspaper, under the title of "A Layman's View of an Art Exhibition," were as derisive as the common man's: "Yet we have to face the fact that there is apt to be a lunatic fringe among the votaries of any forward movement. . . . Cubists are entitled to the serious attention of all who find enjoyment in the colored puzzle pictures of the Sunday newspapers." He closed with a comparison of Duchamp's *Nude Descending a Staircase* to a Navajo rug, to the great advantage of the latter.[42]

Elsie must have found it difficult to reconcile her husband's staid, professional surface, modeled to a large degree on Roosevelt's, with his enthusiasm for the products of the "lunatic fringe." Even the more formally traditional Redons had subjects reflecting what the eye saw when it turned inward rather than an externally verifiable reality. For someone like Elsie, these works had to seem bizarre. She was untrained in the subtle shifts of her time, the shifts brought with the discoveries of Freud and Einstein that coincided with and prompted the inner eye's imagining what could not be seen. Other kinds of entertainments and diversions, then, had to fill hours and days she spent with her husband. Of the New York offerings, it was the theater they shared, as they did a great deal during the fall of 1912 (*SP* 256). And the following spring, trying to include her in at least the part of his life she could understand, he asked her to accompany him on a business trip to Atlantic City. There she did find things to interest her, flowers and gardens, as she related in a postcard to her mother where, in referring to her husband, she naïvely and spontaneously disclosed a sense of distance from him: "Plenty of hotels here— but lots more things besides. Gardens—plenty of flowers in beautiful beds— trees—grass. We're trying to get all of Spring we can in a few days. Poor Stevens talks business—while I do just as I like to my heart's content" (WAS 4018, April 26, 1913). It was "Stevens," not "Wallace" now, and she simply did as she liked while he engaged in his "business." In a few more months they would again be separated for the duration of the summer, he doing what he liked and she busying herself in the country with more flowers, trees, and birds.

That summer of 1913 Elsie went to Pocono Manor, high in the hills of Pennsylvania (*SP* 256). There Stevens hoped she would find what she needed to enjoy herself. He hoped there would be young people to add to her pleasure in the countryside (*L* 180). He wrote her fairly often from New York, reporting on his comings and goings and on the vagaries of the washerwoman, who, it seemed, planned to abandon him, leaving him with only "bath-trunks" to wear until Elsie returned (WAS 1933, July 2, 1913). He also tried to visit her on weekends as often as he could, though this depended, as he noted more than once to her, on whether or not he could afford it and on whether he had been invited elsewhere by one of his business associate friends who might be instrumental in helping him improve his position. He did not visit her on the July Fourth weekend, when he could have spent an extra day with her. It was because the visit he made instead to the Strykers in Hartford would mean, he hoped, as he made certain to tell her, a raise (WAS 1933).

Accidentally prefiguring the ultimate outcome of his wished-for raise, the Strykers' house in Hartford was, as Holly Stevens notes (*SP* 256), just around the corner from 735 Farmington Avenue, where Stevens and Elsie were to live from 1924 until 1932. In the letter he wrote to her on his return to the city that Monday, July 7 (*L* 179–80), he described what was most notable about the weekend: a 130-mile "auto trip in [a] machine (a big six-cylinder car)" with the Strykers' neighbors and one celebrated Miss Trumbull (an old maid of fifty, he was careful to add); dining in the open air at the Hartford Country Club and especially enjoying "mint juleps and cigars" (their plurality stressed); and simply being in and around the Strykers' house, the charms of which he re-created now in words for Elsie and years later, in actuality, when they, too, would have a house with walks bordered by flowers, where blackbirds and robins, sparrows and wrens could gather. It was as though the Strykers now offered him a model, just as the Peckhams had when he was younger, for the kind of life the "barrister" in him wanted. And what better setting than Hartford, where the Puritan ethic prevailed in a good Yankee attitude toward success and material prosperity? Although it was important to strive, to achieve, to reap monetary rewards, it was uncalled for to flaunt the material symbols it engendered: large but not ostentatious houses, well-manicured but simple grounds and gardens with homey azaleas, roses, and other blooms, no baroquely carved marble fountains or dwarf fauns lurking in the shrubs. This way of life was as congenial to the part of Stevens that followed his father's voice of reason as the New York City way of the "lunatic fringe" was to the part of him that wanted to break loose, "to get out of line," as he had written to Elsie in the early years of their relationship. The successful barrister's life, however, offered a distinct advantage over the adventuring visionary's: Success in it was immediately measurable and visibly corrobaroted in the here and now, while success as a seer or artist of any kind, part of what Roosevelt had called a "forward movement," could not, because of the very nature of the endeavor, be recognized and weighed until the rest of society at least learned how to read the map carried back by the avant-garde.

In Stevens's case, witnessing the public reaction to the Armory Show must have made it plain that following his poetic proclivity and participating in the modernist spirit were not, for the present, going to provide him with any of the external signs of success or with the mode of life he needed to satisfy the part of him that was still a "good Puritan." Moreover, the high-toned life of the Connecticut Yankee, because it played on the duality of having, but not acting as though one had, appealed to Stevens at all levels of his personality—from his deep ambivalence about wanting to be seen, to the surface morality he had learned from his parents as well as from those good old American types with whom he had come into contact at Harvard (whose trustees, in fine Yankee spirit, even turned their collars as they prospered).[43]

But as though out of an intuitive sense of how stultifying some aspects of the kind of "good life" led by the Strykers could be, Stevens noted something else that impressed him about the Independence Day weekend he spent with them: "How unpleasant Mrs. S. was after all with her infernal invalidism!" With Elsie's weak nerves, her inability to take the New York summer heat, his being periodically concerned that she eat well to build up her strength, he could not have made this observation to her without at least a twinge of fear or premonitory recognition. It was no wonder that a few years earlier—before they bound themselves in marriage and plans for a common life—he had expressed to her how much he admired a couple who had abandoned everything and gone off to live a life unfettered by social convention of any kind. Now, married, with Elsie reinforcing his own need to fit into an approved social role, convention would play an all too important part. Stevens unconsciously knew the price that would be paid: In spite of the flowered walks leading into it, eventually no one would enter the house where Elsie led the life of a recluse.[44]

Even if this perception had been wholly available to his consciousness, it would have been difficult for him to effect the changes that would have been necessary if he and Elsie were to escape the perils of living a life in which choices were determined not by them as individuals but by their place within a fixed social and economic framework. Security was far too weighty a consideration for Stevens, who not only had been reared to have it occupy a central place in the structure of his mental economy but had to contend with the spectral memory of his father in a state of mental collapse in the face of economic failure. Because of all this, Stevens even constructed for himself the fiction that he was "a man of fortune greeting heirs" (*CP* 13) when there seemed to be no possibility that he would ever have even one. Yet he lived the life of a man amassing substance he could leave behind. And Elsie, who had, all her life before she met him, experienced nothing but economic strain and deprivation, would want the ease she must have wished for countless times. She would naturally encourage anything that would foster this ease and discourage anything that might preclude it.

In addition to the long-range threat to personal freedom that this overconcern with security presented, its particular effects were often damaging to their everyday relationship since some penurious consideration could always be offered for not doing something that might in some way be psychologically threatening. With this exaggerated focus on "having enough," until real affluence was attained, there was always a ready excuse not to do or not to buy. And since, with the peculiarly deceptive habit of not showing what one had that was part of the "good Puritan" background, Stevens could never admit to having achieved real affluence, the situation generated out of these considerations ultimately ensured his absolute control over external reality and those who moved within its reaches. As such, the power affluence kindled in him represented the fulfillment of a childhood wish never again to be enslaved to the feeling of helplessness. Whether at the core of his being it was the residue of his serious bout with malaria when he was still quite young; whether it was the birth of his younger brother, John, that made him feel deprived of the full attention he wanted from his mother; whether it was the spill from his velocipede that injured his back and resulted in his absence from school; whether it was when still in primary school he had no control about being sent away to live with the aunt and uncle who were virtually strangers to him in spite of the familial connection—whether for any one, all, or a combination of these factors, Stevens was extremely afraid of once more losing control as an adult.

One of the things Stevens felt he could not afford during the summer of 1913, when he visited Elsie at Pocono Manor, was a double room; she had her single room for the season, and he took another (*SP* 256; WAS 1935, July 10, 1913). After a subsequent visit (Saturday and Sunday, August 8 and 9), when Elsie *had* persuaded him to book a double room, though he responded with ". . . go ahead. It will be like forty-eight hours of home" (WAS 1940, August 4, 1913), he later complained of its cost, warning her not to do it again for his next stay: ". . . don't let them give me an expensive room again. They soaked me last time. Be sure I have a single room without bath" (WAS 1945, August 8, 1913). What made this already seemingly excessive burst of thriftiness even more exaggerated was that they appeared to have especially enjoyed themselves that weekend, he noting unusually to her his residual excitement in the letter he wrote on his return to New York: "What a heavenly time we had together. It was particularly nice not to have met *too* many new people. I wish, however, it had not been (as it was) too hot for us to exercise ourselves a bit. Exercise in the open air is what both of us need most" (WAS 1942, August 12, 1913). They had, it appears, spent most of their time indoors and without much company.

On the other hand, one of the things that he even economized on his dinners out in New York to be able to afford was a piano, for which he began negotiating that summer. Stevens was very enthusiastic about the prospect of having a piano. He wrote Elsie how much he looked forward to winter evenings when their New York life would be sweetened by her playing. His intention to buy the instrument and his excitement about it coincided with his return to poetry. These yieldings to the softer parts of his nature that he associated—at least in connection with his "absurd . . . writing of verses"—with being "positively lady-like" coincided as well with certain signs of identification with his mother (who, as we remember, had also played the piano and from whom he felt he had gotten his "imagination"). These signs were minor but distinct. In one of the letters he sent to Elsie that August, he announced that he was to see the piano for the first time that evening and planned to "treat" its owner to "a sonata before the evening [was] over. . . ." The letter was written in the very same and unusual manner that had been his mother's habit. There is no earlier or later letter in the Huntington collection that is written in this way. Though the letter paper was the same size as he usually used and was folded in the same way, he covered its faces differently. Stevens had always written on all sides horizontally from left to right. If the paper already had a fold, he wrote first on the front, then on the inside facing the verso of the front, then on the verso of the front page, then on the back. But on this occasion he wrote on the folded sheet, a small folio, first across the front horizontally; then, on the inside, he turned the unfolded sheet to its double length and wrote across, down its full length, so that when the folio is opened, the writing is vertical (WAS 1946, August 20, 1913). This was exactly Kate's style in her letters.

In addition, in an earlier letter to Elsie, describing the visit he made to Great Barrington to meet the owners of the piano (these were friends of the Strykers, the Vitales, who had invited Stevens to come up and stay), he wrote the word "man" in a way that was indistinguishable, except for context, from the word "mom." He had written the word this way in describing "old man Walker," a wealthy friend of the Vitales, who had asked them all to spend the day with him at his home, which he had named Brookside, just across from Great Barrington. Walker had, "by far the most beautiful place [Stevens had] ever seen," a house "full of beautiful things: $200,000 worth of rugs on the floor alone! In the library . . . a whopping organ," all of which had impressed him as much as the elaborate circular and Italian gardens. "[B]ee-you-tiful," he added (already having used the same word twice in his description, still too awestruck the day after the experience to find alternative adjectives) where they sat "in the twilight." At first it might seem unusual that in referring to Walker, Stevens would have nervously shaped letters mimicking "mom," yet beyond the associations to the piano that was the occasion for his having made Walker's acquaintance, there was something else operating here that could easily explain the doubling palimpsest of his penmanship.

As noted earlier, in connection with Stevens's desire to internalize "the female" and with how this desire was tied to the vestiges of this childhood wish for the mother, "old man Walker" also represented what Stevens most desired. As he commented to Elsie apropos of another invitation Walker extended to him to visit at his New York City residence, she would accompany him and they would "toddle up there . . . and weep with envy. . . ." "Sure as your [*sic*] born," he added, playing again with another word form. While for the child he had once been, his mother had embodied absolute security and comfort, for the man who wanted, as much as anything else, to become "man number one" in the society he had come to know more and more intimately since his years at Harvard, "old man Walker" embodied the ultimate in that society's ideas of security and comfort. Aspiring to this ideal himself, wanting to provide security and comfort for himself and for Elsie as the child he had made her in his imagination, the child whose feelings he could understand since he had them as well, he closed the letter signing himself "Your, Old Man" (WAS 1945, August 18, 1913). Ironically it was just before this closing that he warned her not to book an expensive double room for them on his coming visit. He couldn't yet begin to think of himself as measuring up to what he wanted; it would be better if they stayed as children, dreaming in their separate rooms.

But it wasn't only on his little vacations out of the city that summer that Stevens dreamed. Dreaming was part of the poet's indulgence, one of the sources of images and rhythms that welled up to be shaped into fine lines limning coincidences of fact and feeling into the chapters and verses of his new vulgate. Assuming the role of poet once more, he found himself musing on topics that for a long time he had thought childish. He had, over the years of his relationship with Elsie, been sending her half sister picture postcards of various places for a collection she kept. Just before announcing to Elsie that he had again begun to write poetry, he related to her how he had spent an evening going through their New York landlord's collection of "photographic cards" of Paris, getting a "better idea of the Louvre, the Pantheon, the Luxembourg than [he] had ever had before" (WAS 1938, July 30, 1913). And in another letter expressing the wish that he, too, could be in the country beneath the "clair de lune" ("light of the moon") he remarked how he planned to spend the evening on the roof in his "white tent," camped like an urban Arab, conjuring the stars he could not see beyond those he observed (WAS 1944, August 15, 1913). Yielding to his imagination this way, he became one with the moon, symbol of Apollo, patron of poets, the moon he had once referred to as "that Arab in [his] room." Many years later he returned to sound his "hoobla-hoo" in the poem celebrating his "Supreme Fiction."

One of the immediately visible products of this indulgence was a new playfulness with language in his letters to Elsie during this late summer. In one note he told her it was not necessary to meet him at the "day-po" (WAS 1935, July 10, 1913); in another, he again communicated his disappointment at her not writing to him frequently enough, commenting that she was "a nawfully poor correspondent" (WAS 1956, September 13, 1913). Though he was happy she was learning to play golf, as he, too, was that summer, in true American businessman fashion (WAS 1939, August 1, 1913), pleased, also, that she had found company to amuse her, he still felt somewhat neglected. Finding a gently humorous way—through *breaking* words into sounds—to express his feeling *broken* when she did not respond in ways he needed to help him feel secure was a discovery that went a long way in teaching him how to deal with other, deeper ruptures in his spirit over the years. As though mimicking this breakup of linguistic forms, which itself reflected a dissolution of the bonds of his being, in another letter of this period he signed himself for the first time "Wally" (WAS 1950, August 28, 1913), the natural diminutive, boyish form of his name. The formal "Wallace" and all his other nominal guises were, for the moment at least, gone.

So many factors had contributed to this summer's exuberance. His mother's death the previous summer, which again raised the feelings surrounding his father's death a year before, had prepared the way for Stevens's finally establishing his independence. He set out his priorities, his values, without having any longer to consider what either of them might think or say. Then there was the Armory Show and his coming into contact with individuals who were excited about the purpose and state of art. Through them he was exposed to new literary forms as well. Besides Gertrude Stein's bold experiments, there was the work of other writers less immediately striking but as complex in their attempts at expressing the still-young century's grappling with the new concepts of reality, even in their critical writing. Romain Rolland's piece on modern art, "The Unbroken Chain," for example, in the *New Republic* (Vol. III, No. 39, July 31, 1915) Stevens found "uncommonly well-written" (L 186).

In addition, there were the generating ideas themselves: evolution; the unconscious; sexuality; the death of God; relativity; quantum leaps; the discoveries of what had been thought fictional civilizations and of uninhabitable places like the North and South poles. By 1913 each of these new frontiers had been explored enough that it was given attention outside its specialized field. People curious about the world and their place in it could begin to imagine it and themselves in ways wholly different from those that had dominated Western thought for at least 300 years. There was both tremendous exhilaration and trepidation in this. In general ways Stevens and Elsie represented these two contrasting positions.

For those who felt themselves to be instruments through which these discoveries could be shown, those who, if they had not done the actual exploration, experiment, or calculation nevertheless were translating their understanding of these results, the fear attendant on being at the edge of a universe entirely changed in conception was played down. Most of their energy went into shaping their new expressive forms. Though analogues or echoes of fear might find expression in discordant tones of even Stravinsky's popular music for the dance or in the images of some of the early expressionist paintings, like Edvard Munch's *The Scream,* there was a sense of control growing out of having managed to shape a form that superseded these signs of fear. But for others, who did not create new forms yet were familiar enough with the details of the modified views of the world and its human inhabitants to understand that all they had learned about it and themselves had, within five to ten years, become obsolete, the fear could be paralyzing. Reactions to this, in turn, ranged from total anesthesia and apathy through escapism to intense anger that could not be justifiably directed at anyone or anything.

Probably, one of the reasons the piano became such a focus of attention and hope for Stevens was that it could serve as a bridge between at least some of the manners of the old, lost order and the particularities of the new. On it he could both play sweet melodies of leftover Victorian sentiment—or listen as Elsie played from the sheet music he bought for her[45]—and experiment with random sounds and chords of his own invention. She, in turn, could practice some of the new music of Continental composers to ease her into a sense of things in this new world. The piano would be the instrument of their equality, the sole object of their joint life, which they both could come to out of more or less common impulses and on which Elsie could excel and thus lend her weight to the balance of contributions to their relationship. Knowing this at a level he did not have to spell out, Stevens looked forward to the difference the piano would make in their lives. He referred to it in almost every letter to Elsie from the occasion on which he first told her that he intended to go look at it until she came back to New York in late September. The only others of his letter subjects that had ever sustained or would ever again sustain his attention so constantly were weather and, when he traveled, landscape. But as much pleasure as he foresaw deriving from the piano and as much as he probably did derive once it had taken its place in the household, there was for the duration of the next year as much painful belt- and penny-pinching, with the by-now-expected reminding strictures communicated to Elsie.

But, as would also be expected by now, there were several occasions in which he relaxed his tight grip on himself, confessed and rationalized his indulgences to Elsie, and once more resolved to follow the straight and narrow. One of the factors now adding weight to his periodic yieldings to temptation was his having begun to travel a great deal for business. Even before he found himself in a new town or city, where he searched out the best eating places and out-of-the-way bookshops, there were days passed riding through the country in the still marvelously luxurious trains,[46] where in addition to feasting on well-prepared dinners that reflected the various cuisines of the regions through which he passed, he could, if he liked, hire a manicurist to pare his nails gently while he sat in the barber's chair with his face wrapped in fragrant warm towels. Though the company no doubt reimbursed him for his necessary per diem expenses, there were items Stevens would not have begun to think of charging to the account, especially not now, when he was so concerned about maintaining the position that seemed to promise advancement. There was another consideration as well. The insurance company branches for which Stevens worked during these years were still establishing themselves and expanding. They could not provide extravagant expense accounts, perhaps not even reasonably generous ones. And even if they could have, their executives, in good Connecticut Yankee spirit, would not think this good policy. So if Stevens wanted to dine on grouse or venison, he would have turned in a voucher for chicken or chops and paid the difference out of his own pocket.

At the same time, as befitting one who aspired to be an executive, he wanted to appear the suitable candidate. One of the ways he demonstrated that he had the requisite external qualifications was to send Elsie to resorts like Pocono Manor for the summer months. But he could not afford to do this the following summer of 1914 largely because of the expense of the piano, so Elsie went to Reading instead. By summer 1915 he was again able to send her away to the mountains. Indeed, he noted to her that the appeal of being able to do so had supplanted his need to be alone:

> I think that it is not only my desire for solitude that suggests vacations to me. It appeals to my pride to be able to send you away. I have not made much progress as the world goes; but I forget that, when I can feel that you are away in the country like everybody else, doing pleasant things. When New York is empty and dull I should feel as though I were of no account to have you here and be unable to make things pleasant for you. (WAS 1966, August 30, 1915)

Between August 1913 and August 1915 Stevens became more comfortable both in his roles as businessman and as poet. Not only did he work hard at his two endeavors, but he also actively cultivated those who could be instrumental in his advancement. He had learned to play golf and encouraged Elsie to practice hard while she was still at Pocono Manor. And on his weekends with associates he became more familiar with the ways of the good life he had chosen. On another of his trips to Connecticut in August 1913, for example, again as a guest of the Strykers, he accompanied them on a visit to one more of their acquaintances at Eastern Point. Together they spent a good part of the weekend sailing, going to Watch Hill, Rhode Island, and Fishers Island (SP 256–57), though not landing and with Stevens missing much of the view and adventure, hiding most of the time "under canvas" in the cabin since, as he noted to Elsie, "spray doesn't go well with clothes" (WAS 1940, August 4, 1913). One of these evenings he spent fully dressed in formal attire, eating, talking, and sipping after-dinner drinks until midnight, getting a rich taste of how the other half, whom he was rehearsing to join, lived.

But this was the first summer of the great piano expense. While he had both to pay for this (he paid half the purchase price[47] on September 2 [WAS 1952, September 2, 1913] and the balance over the next year) and to make sure that he attended carefully to his wardrobe and habits so as to be ready for similar social occasions, Elsie was urged to be thrifty and praised when she was. He usually added notes exclaiming at the cost of some of his most banal requirements, after confessing one of his less than necessary indulgences, like spending a night at the Turkish baths and getting a good rub (WAS 1939, August 1, 1913). He was also once again treating himself and Walter Butler—recently engaged to a Miss Caird, whom Stevens hoped Elsie would meet and like ("She might be nice for you to know. Everybody helps in a way," he added)—to a lavish night out. It was perhaps with this indulgence that he repaired his relationship with this old friend. He commented later in the evening in his letter: "I haven't blown myself this way for years and heavens! how it hurts. I suppose I'll sulk like an old Dutchman until I have forgotten it."

With all the piano—a beautiful baby grand—represented, it is not surprising that it, too, became one of the devices Stevens used to urge Elsie to stay away longer than she seemed to want. On Labor Day weekend, the end of the 1913 summer season, he had arranged to meet Elsie at Pocono Manor and travel with her to Reading. But there was some kind of change of plan, and he advised her at the last minute that he would not meet her at the train station as he had originally intended. It is unclear how Elsie got to Reading or if she was with him there over that weekend, though Holly Stevens indicates that they were together (*SP* 257). Back in New York the following Tuesday, he began a letter to her which he sent to her mother's address; it opened with an apology: "Well, I suppose you think I am a hyena in human form. I know just how you are thinking of winter things. It was simply a piece of bad luck to have this unseasonable cold snap right now. However, this time next week, you'll be here—and then all will be forgiven, I hope . . ." (WAS 1952, September 2, 1913). Either they had missed each other, or he had forgotten to bring warmer clothes as she had asked, or he had insisted she stay in Reading while he came back to New York. Enclosing money for her in the same letter, he went on urging her to be mindful of it:

I send you $5.00. Will you hold on to this as firmly as you can? I paid half the piano today and $5.00 looks like a six-cylinder motor car to me. I wish that you would just keep it in your pocket so that it would be unnecessary for me to send more; but it will take almost that much for your fare and trunk. Write to me about this at once, because I'll have to send whatever else you need on Friday . . . Be brave, Missus, and make the most of the honor of luxurious poverty, for when you have the piano you will leap for joy. . . .

Since he had to *send* her five dollars and since in the next letter on September 4, two days later, he evoked Reading and his rather Proustian impressions about having gone to church the Sunday before in a way that appears to indicate that she had not shared the experience (*L* 181), it seems that they had somehow missed each other. This letter is particularly interesting because it reflects how he had again begun to filter his experience through others' earlier literary descriptions. Having put on the poet's mantle once more, he returned his terms of reference to the poetic. Here they were borrowed from a Joachim Du Bellay sonnet he had translated during the summer of 1909 (*L* 151). In doing this, he memorially recreated as he had before when under stress, the period just before their marriage. It was as though in his contemplating her coming home and the resumption of everyday domestic life, he reexperienced the same kind of hesitant anticipation. This was reflected as well in a more personal observation made earlier in the same letter. Having complained that he had been somewhat out of humor since getting home from Reading, he went on: "[I] expect to be all right again in a few days. The fact is, I think our own bed better than a health resort. True, I swish around like a ship at sea before going to sleep. But when I sleep, I sleep like a monument—. And then it is so nice to look out and see a familiar chimney or two" (WAS 1953, September 4, 1913).

Soon he would be sharing his bed with her again and felt at least somewhat ambivalent about it, else there would have been no need for him to describe self-consciously how he tossed and turned before sleep. With these words he was preparing himself and her for their renewed conjugality. So though just two days before he had told her that in a week she would be back and added that she would be "a thousand times welcome" (WAS 1952), almost three weeks passed before she actually did arrive. All through the interim he reiterated that he looked forward to her being with him again but usually attached to his declaration another of his reminders of how financially pressed he was. "You might want to linger there a day or so more," he noted, "but if the weather is still bad, you might as well be here, for you'll be happier here (I hope). I am going to be *uncommonly* hard pressed until the 1st of October, after which things will run along as usual" (WAS 1954, September 6, 1913). Even though one of the apparent reasons for extending their separation seems to have been that he had to be traveling again a great deal of the month—to Troy, Albany, and Baltimore—he used the piano as the reason. It was perhaps because he could not afford to send her fare, choosing instead to have the piano polished before she came home. She would then be in the situation in which he had been while still a student at Harvard, unable to visit Reading for the holidays because his father could not afford the price of his ticket. On the other hand, unlike him, who could not then go home until months later, Elsie would be delayed only a matter of days or weeks.

(This he could have used as an unuttered rationalization to himself.) On September 13, for example, after noting that he was going to Albany by boat the next day, he added:

> If you could stay until Monday, September 22 and come back on that day, it would just suit me. Couldn't you, Bud? Then I shall surely have it [the piano] polished and have one other little thing done that I have thought of. In fact, I think I'll have it polished anyhow [he had been debating whether to do it himself or to hire someone]—Although it will make things close.
> . . . You have been a real help by not wanting anything these last two weeks—. . . I have been devilishly economical too. Several times last week I went to dinner in an interesting Italian hole on Grand Street called the "Villa Penza." I have been making researches on spaghetti. But I made up my fasts in Newburgh. The humors of practicing law in New York . . . However, the ups and downs are the salt of life. They give a relish to the periods of indulgence. Personally, I do not mind in the least, since there is so much to gain; I hope that you, too, between walks etc. continue to be cheerful. . . . (WAS 1956)

Just as in an earlier separation it had been the floor he wanted to have polished and the rug he had sent out to be cleaned returned, now it was the piano. Nonetheless, he was preparing. He had bought her "several waltzes" she could begin practicing when she returned. But once she was home, he would not be able to play as much himself. Exaggeratedly, no doubt, he reported to her that he had been playing for seven hours every night (WAS 1957, September 20, 1913). Perhaps he simply did not want to share the piano with her at all.

Though he had intended to meet her train from Reading at Jersey City on the afternoon of Tuesday, the twenty-third, he apparently did not. Two days after her arrival she reported in a note to her mother that he had only gotten back from Baltimore late Tuesday night (WAS 4019, September 25, 1913). It is impossible to know how Elsie felt coming home, but it is fairly safe to assume, in view of the delays and his ambivalence, that she must have felt at least a little uneasy, uncertain of how welcome she really was.

જ

The next remaining letter in the Huntington collection is dated August 11, 1914; portions appear in *Letters*. With this interruption in the correspondence and because he no longer kept a journal, it is not known whether he traveled a great deal in the intervening year. But though there is no evidence of what he did and where he went during this period, it is clear that he had been pursuing the "literary life," as he once called it, as energetically as he was his life in the business world, where by August he had made the switch from the American Bonding Company to the Equitable Surety Company, of which he became resident vice-president (*L* 182). From here the move to the Hartford two years later was almost automatic because of the professional relationships he had cultivated.

In the literary world he had been in contact with his old college acquaintance Pitts Sanborn, who had asked him to submit some poems for *Trend*, a magazine he edited. With this encouragement from one who was part of the old Harvard boys' network, in early summer of 1914 Stevens submitted a group of poems titled "Carnet de Voyage," which he anxiously expected would appear in the August issue—it was like "waiting to hear a will read," he noted. He was disappointed to find that his poems did not come out in that number (WAS 1959, August 13, 1914). But they did come out in the September issue, much to Elsie's consternation. It was not that she was unhappy about her husband's success but that she had thought most of these poems belonged to her since they had been made as offerings to her, parts of the "June Books" presented on her birthdays in the years before their marriage. Soon after Elsie came home from Reading that summer, again having had her intention to return gently postponed by her husband—"It would be the devil for you to be here just now [it was August 11]. Do as you like, however. I am thinking only of your comfort and my own" (L 182)—there were difficulties that even enjoying the piano together would not be able to soothe. Just when things in the outside world were beginning to meet the requirements Stevens had established for himself during years of dreaming, the implicit tensions in the inner world of his relationship with Elsie stretched to explicitness.

The publication of the poems in *Trend* that September was followed by the publication of two more groups, "Phases"—in the November issue of *Poetry*—and another two poems in the November issue of *Trend*. Stevens was also becoming more successful in the insurance business. In February 1914, he had been named resident vice-president and second in charge of Equitable's New York branch. His skill as a lawyer in the bond department, specializing in both fidelity bonds and surety bonds, had earned him recognition. He outdid his superior that August (WAS 1959) and maintained even closer contact with Stryker in Hartford. On one visit to Hartford in August that pleased him tremendously because the weather was so much more pleasant than in New York, he noted to Elsie that he had walked with Stryker through an uninteresting cemetery distinguished only by the remains of J. P. Morgan. Here, the Cedar Hill Cemetery, forty-nine years later, Stevens would be buried, by his own request. In spite of the signs that he might one day become "man number one" according to the standards he had set for himself, there was a deep sense that things as they were were not as he wanted them to be.

This underlying sense is detectable both in the change in tone of the few remaining letters to Elsie from August 1914 and in the poems that Stevens wrote during this period. Though it is impossible to date them precisely, it is clear that those appearing in *Poetry* and one of those printed in the second *Trend* issue ("From a Junk," SP 260) were composed between the summer of 1913, when he related to Elsie that he had begun "writing verses" again, and late summer of 1914. Following these, "Sunday Morning" appears to have been written or completed sometime between November 1914 (after the poems Harriet Monroe had chosen for the war issue of *Poetry* had appeared) and late spring of 1915 (when he sent her the poem that was published in the November 1915 issue). Stevens arranged the five of the eight sections Monroe chose in the order of: I, VIII, IV, V, VII (*L* 183–84). During this same period "Cy Est Pourtraicte, Madame Ste Ursule, et Les Unze Mille Vierges" (*CP* 21), "Tea" (*CP* 112), "Peter Quince at the Clavier" (*CP* 89), "The Silver Plough-Boy" (*OP* 6), and "Disillusionment of Ten O'Clock" (*CP* 66) were also written and appeared in various magazines.[48] "Blanche McCarthy" (*OP* 10), too, was composed at this time, though it was not published; since it did not appear until after his death, it seems Stevens did not find it satisfying enough to send out.

Both in letters to Elsie and in these poems the most marked difference is a cool, clipped tone. In the poems this was achieved by sharp contrasts established between images. The attitude toward what was presented was an almost macabre and distant snickering, reminiscent of the feeling of some of Poe's stories. There was a stinging distinction between these poems and those he composed for Elsie's "June Books" (these appear in *SP* 227–34). This cannot be accounted for only by the fact that the earlier verses were addressed to her in a spirit of tenderness while these had no particular addressee. One of the most constant features now was a change in perspective. Whereas the greater number of the earlier poems (with the exception of "In the Sun," where it was, as it were, the eye of a young Hoon that regarded the world) described some impression from a wholly human point of view, these poems reflected the perspective of an observer no longer content to accept mere sublunary existence. In "An Odor from a Star" (*SP* 259) the point of view imagined encompassed knowledge of angelic realms, while in "One More Sunset" (only in *Trend* issue and Buttel, p. 156) and "From a Junk" the eye was imagined as seeing beyond what it could actually see. Already, then, by 1913 and 1914 Stevens had assumed that planetary perspective so characteristic of his mature style. This perspective suggested that *sub specie aeternitatis,* the mundane details of the everyday world, of troubled individual lives, did not overtly matter. This excellent defense against confronting the painful problems of both personal relationships as well as his individual relationship with the world (World War I had begun that summer, the archduke Franz Ferdinand's assassination on June 28 being followed by Germany's declaration of war on Russia on August 1 and on France on August 3; on August 4 Great Britain declared war on Germany) reflected the monumental shift in the broader cultural situation. Since the discovery of the X ray in 1895, attention had been turning more and more consistently toward knowing what could not be seen, heard, or touched directly.

One of Stevens's most effective early figures for this awareness was an image he used in the second of the "Phases" poems: "an eyeball in the mud" (*OP* 3). This synesthetically echoed some of Odilon Redon's stranger depictions inspired by Poe, like "L'oeil comme un ballon bizarre se dirige vers l'infini" ("The eye like a bizarre balloon moves toward infinity"). Stevens might have consciously or unconsciously remembered having seen a print or reproduction of this lithograph, perhaps in the private collection of Arensberg or Pach. It carried his own sense of things as they were. It communicated, at the same time, the post-Darwinian description of human beings' shifting their awareness of themselves from being creatures stretched midway between soil and heaven, yet moving ever closer to heaven, back to an awareness of themselves as parts of the muddy slime. It also expressed the sense of what the landscape of war really was (the "Phases" poems were those submitted for *Poetry*'s war issue) and the surrealistically dissociated but accurate sense of what could be seen of human nature in things that seemed to block vision, like mud. Much later in his career Stevens again played with the image of the severed eye in his epigrammatic "Adagia": "The tongue is an eye" (*OP* 167); "The eye sees less than the tongue says . . ." (*OP* 170). But it was not only in these particularized uses that the image worked. The planetary perspective Stevens mastered indeed depends upon the metaphor of a free-floating eye, moving like one of the heavenly orbs circling both familiar and strange locales. One of the most powerful poems of *Harmonium*, "The Emperor of Ice-Cream," exemplifies this beneath the surface playing in the pun of its title. The poem describes what the emperor of "I-scream" or "eye-scream" sees, having collapsed into one the two most primary senses of eye and tongue.

This seemingly eerie sensibility, apparently so much a part of the new century, actually had roots running deep in American thought. In *Nature*, Ralph Waldo Emerson had imagined himself as a giant eyeball moving through his world, taking in all that was around him in exquisitely excruciating joy: "I become a transparent eye-ball; I am nothing. I see all; the currents of the Universal Being circulate through me. I am part or parcel of God."[49] As noted earlier, Stevens was familiar with this and with other texts of Emerson's but as yet had no access to the transcendental happiness experienced and described by him, hard as he might have tried to attain it. Not having been able to follow Emerson's prescription that a man stand "erect" before nature[50] disturbed him, so it is not surprising that Stevens never mentioned being familiar with a specific Emerson essay. One of the easiest ways Stevens would have had of explaining to himself his difference from Emerson was to attribute his own inability to stand "erect" before nature to the changes in the world since the time Emerson had written.

One of the most immediately observable changes, as Stevens again began to write poems, was the outbreak of World War I. It coincided with his having to begin to come to terms with the smaller yet nonetheless painful war that existed between himself and the woman he had married, who, in the end, as he had conjured her, represented a part of his own personality. The war became the occasion for the group of poems that, because they were published in *Poetry*, remained as the foundation on which his future literary career was based. Though the terms of reference in these poems belonged to places he could only imagine, places he had dreamed of going to—Paris and London, now the centers of the European theater of war—the sensibility expressed belonged to what he had been experiencing himself in America since the death of his parents and the growing realization that his marriage was not made in heaven.

In the first and second poems of "Phases," though the apparent subjects are soldiers in a square in Paris, what "they" perceive is precisely the world from which Stevens had recently felt himself separated on his last visit to Reading in September 1913:

I

There's a little square in Paris,
Waiting until we pass.
They sit idly there,
They sip the glass.

There's a cab-horse at the corner,
There's rain. The season grieves.
It was silver once,
And green with leaves.

There's a parrot in a window,
Will see us on parade,
Hear the loud drums roll—
And serenade.

II

This was the salty taste of glory,
That it was not
Like Agamemnon's story.
Only an eyeball in the mud,
And Hopkins,
Flat and pale and gory!

(*OP* 3)

The "parrot in a window" image is recognizable as "Madame's parrot from Madagascar" which Stevens imagined listening to in Paris in his September 4 letter to Elsie (*L* 181), in which he described how he had felt in church that last Sunday he had been in Reading. This was earlier noted as being framed within his recollection of having translated a Du Bellay sonnet, "Regrets." In these and in the other four poems that complete "Phases" ([*OP* 4–6]; the last two were not published in *Poetry* and did not appear until after his death), Stevens's consciousness of leaving behind all that had ever been familiar, his awareness of death, his unrealized desire to have gone to Paris, and his having naturalized Du Bellay's sensibility to his own region and to his imaginings of the classical world evoked in "Regrets" all combined in a wholly new diction and rhythm, mimicking the sound of soldiers' marching, accompanied by drumrolls, through Paris streets. This imagined scenario, "Winding/Through [his] heavy dreams" (*OP* 4), replaced actual experience much in the same way that focusing on the landscape had substituted for his facing the pathos of the Wily girls' situation when he was younger or that making lists of "Pleasant Things" was used more recently to distract him from feeling overwhelmed by his complex sentiments for Elsie.

Remarkable in this sequence of poems is how effectively and subtly earlier traces of Stevens's perception revealed themselves. His ability to conjure himself as one of the soldiers on parade derived from the broader imagining of himself as a returning hero in the manner of Odysseus, evoked in Du Bellay's sonnet. This borrowed one of its most powerful images from Homer's touching description of his hero, pent on Calypso's isle, yearning nostalgically to see even the smoke rise in tender curls above his own island. Stevens fused his vision of what the soldiers must have felt marching off to the Great War with his own hidden desire to return to a time in his life before his internal war had begun. This reminded him of his last nonpoetic expression of this feeling in that September 4 letter with its closing image of the parrot, the letter that had borrowed its points of reference from his memory of having translated the Du Bellay sonnet. In the time before his marriage he still could imagine that he might appear as a hero to Elsie. Now he knew he did not, but he could begin to imagine—after Sanborn's and then Monroe's acceptances of his poems—that as a poet he might put on the laurel wreath and return triumphant.

Following Du Bellay's use, Stevens conjured Odysseus' wish fulfilled in the fifth poem of "Phases," "Belgian Farm, October, 1914":

> The vaguest line of smoke (a year ago)
> Wavered in the evening air, above the roof.

At the same time he pointed back to his own last experience of returning to Reading—"a year ago." This memory, in turn, was tied with his pleasure, as expressed in an earlier letter to Elsie, at being "home" in his bed in New York, looking out at familiar chimneys. But though the contours of his lines recalled Odysseus, the hero he pointed to in these poems was Agamemnon. In this substitution, much was both revealed and hidden. While Agamemnon returned as a hero, he had been betrayed and was murdered by his wife, Clytemnestra, in retaliation for his adherence to a superstitious code that had demanded the sacrifice of their daughter, Iphigenia, to ensure the success of the war. At this point in Stevens's life he had begun to experience the death of the man he had hoped to be for Elsie. He no doubt felt this to have resulted, in part, from a kind of betrayal: She was not what he had thought her to be. But now he could also begin to see the death of the man he had hoped to be as deriving, too, from his own adherence to a code of behavior that belonged far more to the age of chivalry than to their own time. The association to Agamemnon was more than understandable.

Compensating for the distance it allowed from his actual situation, this flight of his consciousness to worlds described by earlier poets and across the sea he would never cross gave his mind's eye extraordinary freedom. "Phases" contains beautiful images couched in rhythms of exquisite sensitivity, some of which were used again, though transformed, in some of the major poems of *Harmonium* and other later work.

> Arabesques of candle beams
> Winding
> Through our heavy dreams;
> (*OP* 4)

reappeared in the most expressionistic of his plays, *Carlos Among the Candles* (*OP* 144). Its controlling image was originally drawn from his delight at seeing his room transformed by candlelight, as he had portrayed it in one of the letters to Elsie in the first years of their marriage. And

> Vines with yellow fruit
> That fell
> Along the walls
> That bordered Hell.

resurfaced a few years later to combine with others as he composed "Le Monocle de Mon Oncle," with its image of "golden gourds distended on [their] vines" (*CP* 16). This poem laid out the connection between the outworn forms of behavior he had learned as a child and from the poets of the past who had assumed the heroic stature to which he aspired and the disillusionment he felt about his relationship with Elsie. In the few years between "Phases" and "Le Monocle de Mon Oncle," hell had been naturalized into simply another process.

In addition to the above instances, the last poem of "Phases"

> VI
> There was heaven,
> Full of Raphael's costumes;
> And earth,
> A thing of shadows,
> Stiff as stone,
> Where Time, in fitful turns,
> Resumes
> His own . . .
> A dead hand tapped the drum.
> An old voice cried out, "Come!"
> We were obedient and dumb.

contains images that reappeared slightly altered in two later poems of *Harmonium*. The heavenly masque projected beyond the spheres in "A High-Toned Old Christian Woman" was a more generalized form of the heaven here, "Full of Raphael's costumes," an image that was itself an elaboration of another of the images he recalled from his Du Bellay translation, the peristyle on the façades of Roman palaces. The rhyme of the last three lines of "Phases" echoed in the fifth and sixth lines of the second stanza of "The Emperor of Ice-Cream":

> If her horny feet protrude, they come
> To show how cold she is, and dumb.
>   (*CP* 64)

One more image that reappeared later was the "Old Man" in "Belgian Farm, October, 1914." In "No Possum, No Sop, No Taters" (*CP* 293), the "old man" was identified with the sun. This image had direct ties to Stevens's personal experience. In it he brought together a vague evocation of his father; of himself as he hoped to be one day, like "old man Walker" whose home and manner had so impressed him; of the playful yet serious way he sometimes signed himself now in letters to Elsie; and the image of the smoke signaling home, the resting place, here in the poem, as the "Old Man of the Chimney" (*OP* 5). These all were wished-for completions of himself. By the time the "Old Man" became identified with the sun in "No Possum," Stevens had removed himself entirely from the everyday world to enjoy instead the pleasure of merely circulating above it all, like the sun, part of the "planetary pass-pass" (*CP* 425), as he called it very near the end of his career.

Finally, beyond these later reworked elements, there were images that found their resting places here in these first evidences of his mature style. These extended others lingering in his mind from earlier poets. Stevens's elaboration of the image Du Bellay borrowed from Homer, of the smoke above Odysseus' island, announced that indeed, he had become an author in the fullest sense of what that all-important name implied. In its derivation from the Latin verb *augere,* meaning "to add to, augment," it suggested that the work of the individual with talent was to add to the tradition by using and modifying it. T. S. Eliot laid out this perception theoretically a few years later in "Tradition and the Individual Talent." To the image of the smoke rising, which had obviously touched him deeply, Stevens not only added the particularity that it rose from chimneys but extended it into the personification of the "Old Man" and imagined him having "Stretched out a shadowy arm to feel the night" (*OP* 5). He continued, to combine the personification with a description of the wind which produced the effect. Seeing the poem in its entirety provides the perfect illustration of Stevens's early mastery. In his hands the pathetic fallacy usefully augmented a traditional image passed down from Homer, through Du Bellay, Tennyson, and other poets. The image was catalyzed by a modernist sensibility, all too aware, after Darwin and then Nietzsche's proclamation, of the loss of the image of the "Old Man" as God:

BELGIAN FARM, OCTOBER, 1914

The vaguest line of smoke (a year ago)
Wavered in evening air, above the roof,
As if some Old Man of the Chimney, sick
Of summer and that unused hearth below,

Stretched out a shadowy arm to feel the night.
The children heard him in their chilly beds,
Mumbling and musing of the silent farm.
They heard his mumble in the morning light.

Now, soldiers, hear me: mark this very breeze,
That blows about in such a hopeless way,
Mumbling and musing like the most forlorn.
It is that Old Man, lost among the trees.

(OP 5)

Monroe published neither this nor the sixth and final poem of "Phases"— probably because they seem to interrupt the narrative sequence of the other four. Yet, when they all are read in order, it becomes clear Stevens intended that they constitute a unified whole; his method of juxtaposing stanzas in the later poems is announced, as it were, in this sestet. These poems marked the beginning of Stevens's career as a poet in their expression of a new aspect touching the ancient mind of tradition. Monroe recognized the power here, and she was not alone. Alfred Kreymborg, William Carlos Williams as well as Walter Arensberg and the habitués of his salon were all listening carefully to the "Giant" of a man with, as Arthur Ficke put it, "a voice on tiptoe at dawn."[51] In them Stevens saw his effects. Now these literary friends functioned as his mirror, his own great glass, as they replaced the Harvard circle and Elsie. With them he could go on.

He did, and as he did, having replaced the smaller mirror Elsie had provided with this larger one, his expression broadened. In the idiosyncratically contradictory and ironic diction with which he became increasingly comfortable, he began addressing even the concrete sources of his painful situation with Elsie, now that he no longer used only her to test his image. In this separation from her he confronted himself more objectively. The poems he wrote during the 1915 and 1916 period touched closely on his disillusionment and pointed to the association sexuality had to his sense of loss. As though marking this transition, "Blanche McCarthy," one of Stevens's first strangely titled poems, addressed a female—one of the devices he was to find most congenial—and told her, with a mordant bitterness derived from his juxtaposition of her commonplace name as title and the heavy, assumed seriousness of the lines themselves, to do just as he had been doing in looking away to the world scene and the sky instead of into the "dead glass" reflecting his personal predicament:

> Look in the terrible mirror of the sky
> And not in this dead glass, which can reflect
> Only the surfaces—the bending arm,
> The leaning shoulder and the searching eye.
>
> Look in the terrible mirror of the sky.
> Oh, bend against the invisible; and lean
> To symbols of descending night; and search
> The glare of revelations going by!
>
> Look in the terrible mirror of the sky.
> See how the absent moon waits in a glade
> Of your dark self, and how the wings of stars,
> Upward, from imagined coverts, fly.
>
> (*OP* 10)

Forecasting the closing of "Sunday Morning" in its last line, the poem itself functioned as a mirror for Stevens, and what he saw reflected was not wholly pleasing. It revealed the evasiveness that was at the core of his problematic relationship with Elsie.

In the poems he wrote after "Blanche McCarthy" Stevens addressed the sources of his pain more directly. To conceal from others how involved he was in what he wrote, he began using references that pointed away from himself. In doing this, he began weaving the rich fabric he later named as the "poetry of the subject." With this he addressed his "true subject," himself, grappling unceasingly with his irrational element while at the same time trying to win another battle with the "necessary angel of reality," the pressure of the actual, the "confounded" reason of his father.

In this spirit, he wrote "Cy Est Pourtraicte, Madame Ste Ursule, et Les Unze Mille Vierges," the poem referred to earlier as being so misleading in its suggestion of sources (see pp. 000). Thinking to throw anyone who might be curious completely off the scent, Stevens again used a female subject. Perversely her legend has nothing to do with the situation of humble offering described in the poem. By appearing to present a version of a medieval legend about St. Ursula, Stevens depicted, in extraordinarily suggestive images, a sexual scene with which he was quite familiar, though he transposed its terms of reference to accord with the imaginary female he had created:

> Ursula, in a garden, found
> A bed of radishes.
> She kneeled upon the ground
> And gathered them,

With flowers around,
Blue, gold, pink, and green.

She dressed in red and gold brocade
And in the grass an offering made
Of radishes and flowers.

She said, "My dear,
Upon your altars,
I have placed
The marguerite and coquelicot,
And roses
Frail as April snow;
But here," she said,
"Where none can see,
I make an offering, in the grass,
Of radishes and flowers."
And then she wept
For fear the Lord would not accept.
The good Lord in His garden sought
New leaf and shadowy tinct,
And they were all His thought.
He heard her low accord,
Half prayer and half ditty,
And He felt a subtle quiver,
That was not heavenly love,
Or pity.

This is not writ
In any book.

(CP 21)

Here was a concise poetic record of his relationship with Elsie. The bunch of roughened radishes dug from the soil, surrounded by wildflowers with curling tendrils, is an image strongly evocative of genitalia, ambiguously suggestive of both male and female parts (like, though in a different way, the umbrella carried by the pretty maid and stolen by Marse Sambo in the fantasy painted for Elsie in the letter noted earlier). Carrying her feeling through to modify her appearance so that it would reflect her courting, seductive desire, his "Ste Ursule" dressed herself in "red and gold brocade," imitating the radishes surrounded by flowers. In other words, she did what Stevens had done in dealing with his response to Elsie over the years of their courtship. He transformed the strong sexual urge of the young man he was into bouquets of words and manners—manners suited to one dressed in the gentlemanly "red and gold brocade" that was worn and displayed, like bird's feathers, in the elaborate mating dance he choreographed.

In quoting the words of "Ste Ursule" to her imagined Christ, Stevens articulated what he could have said and did often say in similar words in letters to Elsie in the moments he had taken on the role of the monk or penitent and made her his "Lady," figure of the Virgin. His using the familiar "My dear" revealed this parallel perhaps more than any other single element in the poem. But at the point where the poem completed reality in imagination, at the point, that is, where the fiction compensated for what was absent in reality, the parallel between Elsie imagined as Virgin and the "good Lord" of "Ste Ursule" veered, since the Christ evoked here fulfilled the wish Stevens had about Elsie: that she would "quiver," as he did in reaction to her.

At this moment the identity to which Stevens's identity attached itself shifted. He became the "good Lord" who sought nothing more keenly than "New leaf and shadowy tinct." These sexual offerings "were all His thought," as would be expected of anyone who bore the frustration of impulses as much as he did—whether because of his own inner constraints or another's. But in taking on this other, responding identity, he maintained the first as well: the "low accord" of "Ste Ursule" was his own poetry, "Half prayer and half ditty." This sublimation, which produced a "subtle quiver," would take the place of the primary contact that seemed to be impossible. He closed the poem playfully pointing out that this conjuration was not what it appeared: "This is not writ/In any book."

One of the other interpretations the poem offered itself to most easily was that it was and is simply about the act of writing poetry, that the bunch of radishes represents the poems of one who "makes silk dresses out of worms" (*OP* 157), and that in their simple rudeness they are a humble but worthier sacrament of praise than the expected hymn, the traditionally well-wrought poem. There is no doubt that indeed, this is what the poem is about, yet it is not enough to leave it there. Stevens tied it to sexuality and to Christian figures for particular reasons. Not to deal with those associations would be to miss the "true subject."

Attributing to religious figures, particularly Christ, the most primary of human impulses and responses, even in jesting, was sacrilege. What was Stevens announcing in doing this? Beyond whatever it implied about his separation from or secularization of the religious tradition in which he had been reared, and in that separation joining the future ranks of other modernists like James Joyce and D. H. Lawrence, who also pointed out the horrible restraints Christianity had placed on the human possibility of experiencing pleasure, this poem prepared the way for "Sunday Morning." It made quite clear—in spite of the ambiguities that its title or its figure's imagining might suggest—that Stevens's vision of a healthy and satisfying reality depended on abandoning a Christian conscience.

"Sunday Morning" opened with an evocation of both the memory of his mother in death (as indicated earlier, see p. 390) and the reality of Elsie in her "peignoir":

Complacencies of the peignoir, and late
Coffee and oranges in a sunny chair,
And the green freedom of a cockatoo
Upon a rug mingle to dissipate
The holy hush of ancient sacrifice.
She dreams a little, and she feels the dark
Encroachment of that old catastrophe,

(CP 66–67)

"Peignoir" is the key word disclosing the presence of Elsie in Stevens's consciousness here. As the name of the gown worn by a woman as she combs her hair (*peigner* in French), it evoked her, so often referred to in his poems with a mention of her hair. The associations to Elsie and his mother pointed to one of the reasons "Sunday mornings" had become so weighted with importance for him, from the days when he had gone to Sunday school and been an attendant at Sunday services until now, when he still found himself ritually observing its hours on long walks communing with nature, in writing to Elsie when they were separated, or by going to church in spite of his expressed feelings about doing so. "Sunday morning" and the religion it symbolized had always been and still were connected to the primary female in Stevens's life. Elsie, following his urging, had become, like his mother, a devout churchgoer. And both of them displayed the contradictory enticement of their sweet-smelling presences and the prohibition, at different times and for different reasons, against being touched. Mingling in his consciousness, then, as he composed the poem, were memories of his mother and her words as she lay dying and hidden wishes about Elsie; in a way he would prefer Elsie dead rather than alive and unattainable. At the same time, in conjuring the poem, he could try to imagine being either his mother or Elsie. This would help him understand them. If he did, he could be more sympathetic and contain the frustrated anger that otherwise would be expressed in disguised viciousness or cold withdrawal. In addition, the female figure was himself, still attached, despite his sardonic gibes against it, to the idea of imperishable bliss that Christianity offered the inhabitants of an imperfect paradise.

Certainly the most complex of the poems he had written until this time, "Sunday Morning" trumpeted Stevens's major preoccupation with the "will to believe" that he later attempted to generalize as simply being the problem of his age. As he wrote to Gilbert Montague (a classmate of his at Harvard) almost twenty-five years later apropos of the theme of "Notes Toward a Supreme Fiction," he was still as concerned with this problem then as he had been during his Cambridge years (L 443). Contrary to what he suggested to Montague, this was not a central consideration of others who shared the spirit of his age. It did not become the focus of attention for William Carlos Williams or other important figures, whether those frequenting the circles in which Stevens moved or those across the ocean, who were his contemporaries.

Neither Ezra Pound, Witter Bynner, Marianne Moore, nor Mina Loy found themselves preoccupied in their poetry with the problem of belief or with the residues of their Christian upbringings. Only T. S. Eliot, perhaps because he, too, had been long exposed to the problem while at Harvard, shared an equally deep concern about faith and about Christianity, as he shared as well the problems of a devastatingly unsatisfying relationship with women and of his own sexuality. These common features are significant. Both these men, in different ways among the strongest poets of the century, sensitive to their poetic gifts from early ages, lived with a fear they could never quite escape, one reinforced by the Puritan tradition with which they identified themselves. They were afraid that in being or becoming poets, they truly were—as, ironically, was Whitman, the strongest poet of the generation in which they matured—or would prove to be "lady-like." Whether or not there had been any individuals while they were at Harvard who recognized the greatness of Whitman or of Emily Dickinson—actually a "lady"—Stevens and Eliot, themselves strong poets in the making, undoubtedly felt the power they wanted to take on in these figures. Stevens's frequent use of female personae was not simply a distracting device chosen to deflect attention from himself but something that revealed the innermost tension of his relationship to himself as the poet he conceived himself to be—moving up and down between two elements. The same tension is apparent in Eliot, who also took on female voices and masks easily. But in having Tiresias as the persona of *The Waste Land*, he made the conflict that much more explicit, calling attention to the very ambivalence itself.

For Eliot and Stevens, the female represented what was unavailable yet always there to be striven for, alluring in the very appearance of impossibility. To both of them it seemed that Christianity was inextricably involved with the female and this unattainable goal. More precisely, it seemed that Christianity was the block to achieving the desired end. And so the two poets attempted to circumvent the obstruction by calling for, at some point in their careers, a return to some kind of pagan understanding of morality and the practice of life. Eliot did this through Tiresias, and Stevens did it through the imaginings of the female in "Sunday Morning."

In excluding Sections II, III, and VI from the poem as it was published in *Poetry*, it was as though Harriet Monroe spoke with the voice of a chorus from an American tragedy just beginning to be outlined. She heard in her mind the censorious comments of the commonsense society were the excised stanzas to appear. Without them its remaining sections arranged in the order of I, VIII, IV, V, VII, the poem presented itself as a more or less straightforward, though fictional, narrative of the imaginings of an anonymous female as she confronted death, her fear of death, or of simply falling into a daylight sleep, disorienting in its inappropriateness yet familiar: "the dark/Encroachment of that old catastrophe." With the specified portions deleted, the reader or listener could remain easily suspended in these imaginings without regard to disbelief. Even though the closing stanza called for a chanting ring of men celebrating a naked, savage god, the wish could be attributed to the unidentified, unidentifiable woman, whose irreverence was, in any case, already announced in the opening, where she sits hedonistically enjoying late coffee and oranges dressed in her peignoir, while across the street—or nearby enough so that she could hear—the devout participate in "The holy hush of ancient sacrifice." Whatever it was, then, that this figure dreamed, fantasized, or desired could, in the absence of the questioning stanzas interrupting the narrative of her states of mind, be considered part of the idiosyncrasy of a character about whom her creator's attitude was unknown.

But with the originally omitted sections returned and arranged as composed, the situation was entirely different and most problematic to the consideration of those still feeling tied themselves to "The need of some imperishable bliss." The difference, which Monroe in her editorial astuteness must have sensed, was this: The sections she cut presented all too clearly—in the mode of direct interrogation followed by an equally directive response—an open challenge to a Christian view of life. An attack on this, just at the moment when across the ocean, for far-distant cousins of the same blood and tongue, the standard of war was being raised to the accompaniment of appeals to God and country, could not have been felt without at least an inarticulate pang—in spite of the fact that Monroe echoed the sentiment of the enlightened opponents to the war itself, as was made clear in the editorial comment of the war issue of *Poetry*.[52] Though the drama of the century would continue to unfold and show the tragic flaw Darwin found in the richly woven fabric of Christian belief, the conservative voice of society's practical sense, if not reason, would naturally attempt to point out how dangerous total disillusionment would be at this moment when everything that had been held so dear in the modern, progressive civilization was about to be weighed in the balance.

The world was not yet ripe enough to fall into the existential abyss of Camus's "Stranger," who even more than thirty years later had such difficulty on Sunday morning. In his disaffection Meursault was unable either to participate in its outworn ritual or to accept—until confronted by his own imminent death—the "benign indifference of the universe."[53] This image carried precisely the same sense of Stevens's line of "dividing and indifferent blue" (*CP* 68) in his poem, from which Monroe intuitively protected her audience. It was no wonder that "Sunday Morning" became Stevens's most characteristically representative, praised, and explicated poem, but achieved this wide recognition only in the later years of his career—after, that is, the politicizing of the existentialist position and Sartre's attempt to neutralize it. By showing that it was not incompatible with Christian humanism,[54] the French philosopher popularized it enough to make it at least palatable to American intellectuals, who were, in effect, those responsible for Stevens's eventual acceptance as a major figure. Until then Stevens's success would have to remain limited to those who formed part of one of his circles and to the occasional foreigner, like the Irish poet James Stephens, who immediately recognized the author of "Sunday Morning" as "A great poet, a great spirit, one of the leading spiritual interpreters of our age."[55]

The restricted appeal of Stevens's work was clearly evidenced in the unpopular reaction to *Harmonium,* in which not only the complete version of "Sunday Morning" but "A High-Toned Old Christian Woman," "The Doctor of Geneva," "The Emperor of Ice-Cream," as well as the shorter but no less mocking poems appeared explicitly and implicitly to attack the Christian tradition in their questioning and in their presentation of the flaccid underside of any dogmatic position. The easiest and perhaps the most generous, gentlest way of parrying this poet's thrust was to question the very basis of his being, the source of his voice. Simply call him a dandy, a leftover nineties decadent imitating French frills and affectations, an aesthete cut off from his roots in the good, old American soil, and he would not have to be dealt with more harshly. Let him have his place among minor poets singing to the sad or mad strains of gay waltzes. What the age demanded was a singing strength it could recognize in noble accents and inescapable rhythms.

It was fitting and proper, then, that Harriet Monroe rejected the packet of poems Stevens sent her after "Phases" had appeared and before "Sunday Morning" was submitted. While "Cy Est Pourtraicte, Madame Ste Ursule" (as the "radishes poem") and "Tea" were accepted for the premier issue of *Rogue* (March 15, 1915)—in seeming appropriateness to what the journal's title promised—Monroe felt she would be "blamed" for publishing some of the other instances of Stevens's temptingly sacrilegious sensibility. I am uncertain which poems were in this packet, but from the fact that they were submitted before January 27, 1915, when Monroe wrote her responding note, and from the fact that the only other poems to appear before "Sunday Morning" were "Peter Quince at the Clavier," "The Silver Plough-Boy," and "Disillusionment of Ten O'Clock"—the first two in the August 1915 issue of Alfred Kreymborg's *Others* (a magazine financed by Arensberg) and the third in the September issue of *Rogue*—it seems safe to assume that it was to these poems Miss Monroe reacted and that after this Stevens wisely sent them to these two newer, more adventurous, or less programmatically self-conscious journals. Though there is no way of knowing, it is possible that he also sent "Blanche McCarthy" for consideration to one or all of these as well.

Looking at Harriet Monroe's reply to Stevens provides an excellent insight into her acuity in perceiving the earlier-noted peculiarly macabre but modern quality of his comic manner, at the same time as it indirectly reflects the difference between what she wanted *Poetry* to represent and what the editors of the other journals like *Rogue* and *Others* felt to be reflections of modernism. In addition, noting the point where Miss Monroe's message was continued on the reverse side of her card privileges us to a momentary re-creation of an experience Stevens had to have had as he eagerly read:

I don't know when any poems have "intrigued" me so much as these. They are recondite, erudite, provocatively obscure, with a kind of modern

438

gargoyle grin in them—Aubrey Beardsleyish in the making. They are weirder than your war poems [here the message is interrupted and continued on the reverse of the card], and I don't like them, and I'll be blamed if I print them, but their author will surely catch me the next time, if he will only uncurl and uncoil a little—condescend to chase his mystically mirthful and mournful muse out of the nether darkness, in other words, please send more. Yours sincerely and admiringly,

HARRIET MONROE
(WAS 29)

It could have been the apparently accidental, ironically gratuitous arrangement of words in the space of this card that prompted Stevens to give his poems to others in spite of Miss Monroe's dislike. In any case, he did not relegate them to a drawer, as another in his position, just at the beginning of his poetic career, might have done. But perhaps this was because Monroe made her continued admiration and interest as evident as she did. Or perhaps he read one or all of these poems aloud to hushed but wondrous acclaim at one of Arensberg's soirées, though it is unlikely, unless one or two martinis with intimate company overcame the reticence Stevens had developed about reading in public. Even if he did not read them aloud, however, it is more than likely that they had been read by some of the individuals in Kreymborg's and Arensberg's groups and that they had praised these poems, so strongly attached to images of death seen through the eyes of a grinning gargoyle. This attitude would have been especially appreciated by those in the Arensberg circle, affiliated as they were with the European consciousness of the necessary death of the old order. It was out of this awareness that black humor grew, and central to it was the ability to look at death, so long romantically sentimentalized into transcendence of some kind, with cool and conquering irony.

Interestingly, in these three poems—all turning around the idea of death—Stevens moved from a late romantic, early symbolist attitude as expressed in "Peter Quince"—"The body dies; the body's beauty lives"—to a simple, irreverent irony in the face of death's effects, as in both "The Silver Plough-Boy" and "Disillusionment of Ten O'Clock," in which ghosts eerily cavort and disappear back into their birthplace in the ground of imagination and dream. Stevens's long preoccupation with physical death—from the time of his parents' demises in 1911 and 1912 until 1914—overlapped with the spiritual death of his hope for transformation in marriage and prompted these strange poems that Monroe was afraid to print. With the edited version of "Sunday Morning" it was different. Though also focused on death, it at least suggested the outlines of possible nonaesthetic transcendence, as Stevens made sure to indicate in his letter to her about its meaning: "I mean . . . that death releases and renews" (*L* 183). And with this acceptance Stevens was renewed as well. Through 1915 and into 1916 he continued working diligently on his poetry, as he periodically noted to Elsie in letters to her while she was away that summer at Byrdcliffe, an "artistically-minded" resort in Woodstock, New

439

York that he was happy to be able to afford. (He encouraged her to take painting lessons and "go in for everything" as part of her cultivated holiday pastimes [WAS 1960, July 21, 1915]).

As he read of the war raging on the other side of the Atlantic and forwarded clippings from domestic and foreign newspapers and periodicals to Elsie, his major concerns were not the battle lines but his own. These he drew in his renewed struggle with his studious ghosts and with the ghosts of himself and Elsie as he had once conceived them to be in the imaginings of his desire. He dressed them now in frail colors and had them play in the dark, empty places of his mind. How many nights of his own disillusionment of ten o'clock as he prepared once again to climb into their marriage bed were captured behind the lines of his poem? And how many half-perceived wishes haunted him for the death of the woman who caused him the pain of continued longing and remorse for his own part in having created her in the image of his hidden self? The studious ghosts, too, that had played their part in making him who he was were being wished away. When the wishing failed, they were more directly attacked. In the years to come, with the confidence won from his continued acceptance by his avant-garde friends and more publication in *Poetry, Others,* and, later, *Soil,* the *Little Review,* the *Modern School, Broom, Contact,* the *Dial,* and even the *New Republic,* Stevens took on each of the "man-poets" whose voices he once feared would dissolve his own. By 1922 he was even ready to trace his journey and accomplishments and wrote, in hidden pride, his mock heroic epic, "The Comedian as the Letter C."

But with these feelings raised—stronger and perhaps more negative feelings than he had ever had—he turned once more to nature and "Lists of Pleasant Things." Domesticating his interest in keeping with the contracted compass of his experience, as he spent more time hard at work and in cities (both New York and those he visited on business), he became interested in hothouse flowers raised and kept in botanical gardens, like him and Elsie enclosed in their urban life. He wanted more flowers at home. He particularly liked cyclamen. He wrote to Elsie when she was away that he wished he could find out how to make geraniums bloom. He commented on the wonderful ivy the people downstairs were growing over their windows and shared with her the exotic name he had discovered of one of the flowers they had had at home the previous winter (L 184). Their colors delighted him.

But in translating the impressions they made, Stevens disclosed their true function. These colors from his mental lists were the ciphers for his pains. He used them to plot against himself, against exposing his needs and yearnings. In "The Plot Against the Giant" (*CP* 6–7), they, as the cloths spread before him—as the "civilest odors/Out of geraniums and unsmelled flowers," as the heavenly labial sounds of their names—first check, then abash, and finally undo him. And as he undid himself, unraveling the twisted skeins of the fabric of illusions and beliefs out of which he had woven the costumes he was used to wear, he saw himself reflected in the great glass of his words. He trivialized what he saw, as though still seeing himself with his father's eyes:

I am quite blue about the flimsy little things I have done in the month or more you have been away. [This letter is dated August 29, 1915.] They seem so slight and unimportant, considering the time I have spent on them. Yet I am more interested than ever. I wish that I could give all my time to the thing, instead of a few hours each evening when I am often physically and mentally dull. It takes me so long to get the day out of my mind and to focus myself on what I am eager to do. It takes a great deal of thought to come to the points that concern me—and I am—at best, an erratic and inconsequential thinker. (*L* 186)

At the same time he drew persistence from the encouragement he was receiving from those who enjoyed contemplating his images. That summer of 1915 Walter Arensberg helped in this a great deal. He made a special point of introducing Stevens to Marcel Duchamp, who was being heralded by the group as the most important modernist painter. In putting them together, Arensberg was announcing his esteem of his old Harvard friend, though Stevens, in characteristic manner in writing to Elsie, presented himself as not equal to understanding what Duchamp was all about: "After dinner, we went up to the Arensberg's [*sic*] apartment and looked at some of Duchamp's things. I made very little out of them. But naturally, without sophistication in that direction, and with only a very rudimentary feeling about art, I expect little of myself" (*L* 185). But in spite of himself, he transformed the experience into a beautiful image of his own: "When the three of us spoke French, it sounded like sparrows around a pool of water."

Sadly, as Stevens began to see himself more clearly, and as others enlarged his audience and mingled in his reflection, Elsie began having more problems with her eyes. "Personally I think the whole trouble is with your eyes," Stevens wrote her on August 30, 1915. "The strain in them gets on your nerves and I'm a firm believer in the deviltry of the nerves" (WAS 1966). She would not see, could not see what others saw.

VIII
THE ICONOCLAST
IN THE GLASS
SHATTERING
1916–1923

. . . HE WHO DESTROYS A GOOD
BOOK, KILLS REASON ITSELF, KILLS
THE IMAGE OF GOD, AS IT WERE, IN
THE EYE.

—JOHN MILTON,
Areopagitica

> Is it the case, as it seems to be, that there is no vanity in
> China? There is, of course, since China has its own clas-
> sics. . . . Gathering together the things for my book has
> been so depressing that I wonder at *Poetry*'s friendliness. All
> my earlier things seem like horrid cocoons from which later
> abortive insects have sprung. The book will amount to noth-
> ing, except that it may teach me something.
>
> —From a letter to Harriet Monroe,
> October 28, 1922,
> *Letters* (p. 231)

While the first seven years of Stevens's marriage had been lean, as he struggled
to make something of himself, the next seven were fat with the fruits of his
labors. Though the unexpected and abrupt failure of the New England Equitable Insurance Company in February 1916, in effect left the poet without a
job, because of his friendship with James Kearney, at that point head of the
bond department of the growing Hartford Accident and Indemnity Company,
Stevens was able to move immediately to a more promising position. By
March 15 he was installed to handle surety claims—an area in which the
Hartford was expanding—and to oversee the legal affairs of the also expanding
bond department. At the same time, since this was a fresh branching for the
company, during his first months at his new post, Stevens also dealt with
casualty claims. Within two years, a separate fidelity and surety claims department was established; this Stevens headed until 1955. The poet was well on
the way to earning his reputation as the "dean of surety-claims men in the
whole country."[1] But beneath the smooth surface of things as they seemed,
"the unconscionable treachery of fate" (*CP* 17) was still at work. As he became
firmly established in both his poetic and his business careers, with editors
asking for the products of his evenings' devotion and superiors and contacts in
the insurance world rewarding his daily skills as an attorney, in his most
intimate and important relationship he was unable to draw sustained joy and
confidence. In spite of external successes, and in spite of the change offered by
the move, in May 1916, out of New York to Hartford, Connecticut, where,
he hoped, Elsie would be happier in a city scaled to human proportions and
closer to nature and the way of life left behind in Reading, emptiness remained.

But now, for Stevens at least, poetry completed life. Imagination provided
satisfactions reality denied. The rhythms of lines he murmured answered his
need for companionship. They comforted him in cadences evoking the mem-

ory of his mother's voice as she read to him before bed or sang her Sunday hymns. Though he often broke these rhythms as he wrote, as though revealing intrusions of his imperfect present, the constancy he required always returned with his resolution to turn back to their regularity. While other poets in his circles—like William Carlos Williams, Mina Loy, Alfred Kreymborg, and Walter Arensberg—experimented with new rhythms and meters, Stevens held on to familiar sounds and the traditional forms into which breath was shaped to be spoken to multitudes hungry for spiritual guidance. These were forms borrowed for centuries by poets knowing the power of biblical incantation. Stevens didn't announce this. Perhaps he was not even fully conscious of it. Within the secure frame these familiar forms provided, he experimented with rhythms of different kinds.

Stevens became a master of spatial rhythms. He created pauses where the mind could play on resonances of certain sounds, on the curious relationship between titles and poems, or on puns suggested by arcane references. He also rephrased and echoed earlier poets who had been moved by the same feeling for the language of the English Renaissance. This was the idiom perfected by William Tyndale in what became the basis of the version of the Bible authorized by King James. In Stevens's imaginary pantheon Spenser and Milton held first places. Milton had enriched the language with the products of his delight in Latin, while Spenser had added French forms to the already rich tongue used in the biblical translations. When Stevens later noted that French and English constituted a single language, he pointed back to the long historical moment when in the centuries after the Norman Conquest French and English blended into the language mastered by these "man-poets." He also had Shakespeare in mind. He had brought English to its fullest popular form without losing any of its resonance. And though Stevens never mentioned him—perhaps because he was too close—there was Whitman with his lines so clearly imitating the Psalms and voices of the prophets.

As Stevens worked with this material, his *materia poetica,* perusing *Webster's,* the *Oxford English,* and Lewis and Short's *A Latin Dictionary*[2] for the various appearances of usages and musing about how they derived from the origins of words, he pondered his own derivation and origin as well. As he searched out his spiritual and literary roots, he sought his simpler, biological ones too. By the time he reached his early sixties, Stevens was pursuing his precise genealogy almost obsessively. He hoped to be able to trace his ancestry back to the elite group of first Dutch settlers in America. Becoming involved with his roots also made the study of history itself come alive.

As he became more of a poet, Stevens became involved with words in the way others might become involved with children. He played with them, he fondled their sounds, he helped them grow into strong, commanding presences, and he sometimes grew impatient with their recalcitrance. All this was quite demanding. Added to his already rigorous business schedule, it meant he was almost always occupied—at least when he was at home in the North, in the climate congenial to hardworking "good Puritans." While his tremendous capacity for work had to do with his still-unabated striving to become "man number one," devoting himself entirely to his various labors also protected him from having to confront how he might resolve the seemingly uncontrollable situation with Elsie. Giving his attention to work also protected him from having to confront the larger, equally uncontrollable political situation surrounding the war. Though he was observant about the surface features of these situations—to Elsie's watering the plants and keeping after the moving men when it was time to relocate and to the exercises of recruits in the various cities he visited on business—he rarely probed beneath these surfaces. He commented only occasionally on what lay at deeper levels.

But around this time there began to be longish periods of holidays in reality, respites from the demanding rhythms of the everyday world he had fashioned. They belonged to a different place, however: to Florida and the South. These times were, for the most part, spent away from Elsie and so were replays of a situation that had existed before their marriage. From his safe distance he wrote her elaborate letters full of passionate descriptions of place. In the past he had detailed the landscapes of Sunday walks. Now he rhapsodized Florida's swaying palms and venereal soil.

But before ever going to Florida—"one of the most delightful places [he had] ever seen" (L 192)—he traveled to some less pleasing locations. This was a result of his new position with the Hartford Accident and Indemnity Company. For the first two months Stevens remained in New York working at the company's office there, handling mainly casualty claims. By May, with insurance companies expanding into broader areas, the Hartford formed an additional subsidiary, the Hartford Livestock Insurance Company, of which both Kearney—acting like his friend's necessary guardian angel—and Stevens became officers. This then occasioned Stevens's move to Hartford, where the branch had its base with the parent organization. After beginning at this new post, Stevens loyally continued for a while with the casualty division as well. With the demands of both jobs, he traveled the greater part of the year (L 189).

His first trip after starting to work for the Hartford was to St. Paul, Minnesota, where the company had another of its major offices. While he was away, Elsie had her mother and LaRue come to stay. On March 23, four days after his arrival, Stevens wrote from his "Absolutely Fire Proof" hotel that he expected to be home the following week but that should her mother and half sister be planning to leave, she should think of going home to Reading with them for a few days (WAS 1968). On April 3, he was still not back, not even on the way. He was in Chicago, where he had expected to stop before making the last lap of the return trip to New York. He noted that his delay resulted from things being far busier than he had anticipated, and in addition, Kearney had telegraphed him from Hartford about stopping in Chicago, though in an earlier letter he had already written that Chicago was on his itinerary. There is no record of Elsie's reaction to this indeterminately lengthened stay. But it had to have made her uneasy since she, too, was being periodically telegraphed about the various changes of plan. Expecting a husband but getting a wire—no matter what the relationship—is disturbing.

And his letters during this particular trip were not at all intimate. They didn't even have the usual lyrical descriptions; there were only cursory reports of things and people seen. In St. Paul he had visited his uncle Harry and his wife, though he had put it off at first, he noted, because he did not want "personal matters to take [his] time until everything [was] in good order." His uncle and aunt wished Elsie would go out to visit, and so did he. Chicago was new; he would not mind living there, though by comparison, New York was "much more varied, much older and far more full of things" he liked, in spite of a "loan exhibition of modern French paintings (Renoir, Monet etc.) superior, as a group, to any in New York" (WAS 1969, April 2, 1916). Though while in Chicago he had attempted to see Harriet Monroe, whom he unfortunately missed (L 191), he did not mention *this* to Elsie. Yet it was this intention that had probably been the reason he originally planned to stop in Chicago; getting the telegram from Kearney telling him to go there simply made it an "official" stop. Perhaps only coincidentally, in this letter, which he must have written fully imagining Elsie annoyed at his keeping her dangling in wait for his return, Stevens's handwriting most closely resembles not English but Arabic. This peculiarity was something that had begun to happen the year before—the first instance of it (in the letters as they remain) being another letter which he wrote during a circumstance that would also not have been wholly pleasing to Elsie.

By the time he got to Chicago, he wrote that he was "growing fairly keen to get home." When he did arrive, late on the fourth or fifth of April, he found that he had to leave again almost immediately to go to Albany and Hartford. This must have disturbed him. He had already extended his midwestern stay and was probably feeling neglectful of Elsie. But business was business. After being home no more than a week, he was on the road again, this time heading south, on his way to Florida. On April 15 he stopped in Atlanta, Georgia, where the Hartford had its southern branch, for which Judge Arthur Powell (who was to become one of Stevens's closest friends) was legal counsel (L 189). The first note Stevens wrote Elsie from Atlanta opened with a particularly tender address: "My dear old Duck." He then went on to describe very briefly some of the "beautiful things" he had seen on his trip down: "Dogwood, apple blossom, cherry and peach blossoms, irises in the garden, laurel in the woods. The country . . . full of barefoot boys, girls in white, boys in white trousers and straw hats" (L 191). Stevens's romance with the South was beginning to get serious. But at the same time he wanted to protect what was left of the one in the North, so he took care to be especially affectionate in greeting her.

He had to be encouraging, too, because while he was away on this trip, she had to begin preparing for their move out of New York to Hartford. His last underlined sentence in the short note he sent her four days later from the Hotel Mason—"The Hotel Made Possible by the Travelling Man"—in Jacksonville, Florida, was *"Keep after the moving men"* (*WAS* 1971). (On his trip the month before to St. Paul his last underlined sentence was *"Water the plants"* [*L* 190]; she had obviously not yet become the gardener he seemed to be trying to train.) In the correspondence as it remains, there are no indications during this period—which had to have been a most stressful one for Elsie—of Stevens's concern for what she might be experiencing or for the real pressures she was under. He treated Elsie much in the same way he treated himself. He did not allow himself to feel and express his fears and uncertainties directly; he could not afford to imagine himself in her place and feel her weaknesses either. This would have provoked the same sense of being overwhelmed that he refused to admit in the face of his own prompting circumstances. Instead, there were rather brusque reminders of duty. They were the kinds of reminders his father would have made, though he would not have softened them with tender forms of address. This, it seems, was Stevens's concession to his wife's womanhood.

Two days later he was 400 miles farther south, in Miami, at the Hotel Halcyon, "On Biscayne Bay and the Sea." He had spent the "entire afternoon in an automobile with a hustling youth" who represented the company there. He had seen the sights and been filled in on necessary business details along the way (*L* 192). Stevens described what had impressed him that afternoon to Elsie. He named the "tremendous quantities of flowers" he saw spread on the grounds of fine but "unpretentious" houses. He was struck by the rich, junglelike soil so different from the North's. He was fascinated and surprised by the sun, "the most important thing in Florida," which went down so "abruptly with little twilight" that it allowed little time for ambivalently shaded perceptions. He also wrote her the more mundane details: He described the hotel and its hours; the food at local "tearooms," much better than New York; his projected timetable—though he had been getting up at five in the morning to stick to his schedule, he would not be home before the end of the following week.

Two days after this it was Easter Sunday, and he wrote again. He communicated that his thoughts were with her in New York but in a rather impersonal manner. Following his "Easter greetings, as the old song goes," all he noted about being conscious of her, far away, was "There will be a stiff parade on Fifth Avenue today" (*WAS* 1923). Again, revealing an agitated state of mind—or perhaps poor light, or writing after dinner and drinks—his handwriting once more seemed to be imitating Arabic. There was also a return of that old "Frenchy" way of punctuating—the ellipsis—which he used in variations of two and three dots to separate his thoughts or announce rest pauses. Florida seemed to have evoked something French. The previous letter had opened with a play on the French connection of a commonly used English word: "This is a jolly place—joli" (*L* 191). Perhaps it was "Biscayne Bay" that prompted imaginings of the Bay of Biscay from where Crispin soon would begin his voyaging. In any case, unless she was truly indifferent, Elsie must have felt a tinge of hurt frustration at the marked distance of his concerns. Yet this removal itself pointed to his having been touched all too deeply by something. This was revealed in part by the idea of France brought up from that part of him where his wishes and dreams mingled with memories.

The strongest feature of this letter is the unusual directness with which Stevens expressed his perceptions about Easter observance:

> Unfortunately there is nothing more inane than an Easter carol. It is a religious perversion of the activity of Spring in our blood. Why a man who wants to roll around on the grass should be asked to dress as magnificently as possible and listen to a choir is inexplicable except from the flaggelant [*sic*] point of view. The blessed fathers have even taken the rabbit, good soul, under their government. (*L* 193)

His voicing such vituperation about religion to Elsie, whom he had so strongly urged to join a church, calls into question how much, if at all, Stevens took into consideration the "other" to whom he addressed his communication and who should have held a place in his consciousness equal at least to the letter's subject. At the same time it disclosed how unresolved his relationship to religion and the problem of belief still was. Perhaps it was "the absolute midsummer of the place" that triggered a temporary madness, expressed here as the anger against the Christian ritual. Perhaps it was the memory of Reading evoked by the choir's singing, a memory he did not want to have to deal with at this moment, resisting it because he did not want to feel the pathos of looking back at the irretrievable past. Nor did he want to reexperience the feelings he had had in that past, uncertain as he was then— surely, more than now—of his capability in the world, though still innocent and hopeful in respect to the country girl he conjured in various guises as he made something of himself for her. Perhaps it was the reminder, too, from one of those lost moments, of his father's voice of reason, persuading him not to go to Paris but to stay and apply himself to something practical. This feeling would almost certainly have been there, especially with Biscayne Bay nominally pointing to the wished-for place where, at the same moment that Stevens was working hard for the insurance company, his friend Pitts Sanborn was thinking of going to travel, observe, and write. This he did, sending Stevens postcards from, notably, Bordeaux, Crispin's home port, as well as from other cities on his route. Later in 1916 Sanborn published his *Vie de Bordeaux,* dedicating it to Stevens, his stay-at-home friend, as well as to five others.[3]

It was in the broadest terms, Stevens's religion, secularized through his father as the work ethic, that was at the core of how he had made and continued to make major decisions in his life. No doubt feeling incipient guilt about not having been home enough in the last month to give Elsie proper attention, no doubt also feeling somewhat displaced in a strange city and new climate on a day when people gathered with their families, he understandably retreated into protecting himself from acknowledging these responses by unconsciously lashing out at the originating cause of the whole situation. Unfortunately, however, Elsie had become inextricably bound up with religion as he perceived it, largely because of his having invested her over the years with the function of conscience his parents had once served. So she now bore the brunt of his reactions. Though he had already begun to write the poems expressing his anti-Christian impulses, the exercise was not sufficiently cathartic. There was still, probably because of the more immediately painful frustration he experienced in his relationship with Elsie, a deep pool of violence from which he drew his periodic indirect attacks on her—as here—and from which he also drew particular attacks on others, whether earlier or contemporary poets whom he saw as too strongly tied to their orthodoxies, or simple individuals around him, devout and respectful of myths that kept them from full enjoyment of their senses.

His anger on this Easter Sunday also had to do with his own inability to indulge in his senses fully. Although his eyes celebrated everything around, feasting on varieties of colors and shapes and although he was in a period of feasting on good food and drink, he was still not able, as it were, "to roll around on the grass" and delight in the "activity of Spring in [his] blood." He wore his own magnificent dress not only on Easter Sunday but almost every day, and in the service not even of God but of Mammon, though his own service was now rationalized as supporting Elsie and making enough to be able to provide for the family she wanted. But what he was really "eager" to do was give the better part of himself and his time to writing poetry, as he had expressed to her only a few months before. With her now his excuse for having to work at business as hard as he did, it is not surprising that he did not consider her feelings when he wrote about the "inanity" of the observance in which she was no doubt participating, if in another place, while he "lay abed listening to the birds," as he reported doing that Easter Sunday morning—in spite of the noise of the choir's singing. It is also not surprising that his memories of having wanted to go to France were evoked at this moment when Elsie's reality checked him and the possibility he imagined of giving himself up to the literary life and to complete physical enjoyment in places of "absolute midsummer."

As he was about to leave Florida, once more in Jacksonville, while waiting for the train to Atlanta, he signed a card he sent her from the station, penciled in a very shaky hand, with only his initials, "W. S.," shaped in the same tortuous way a child would carve them into a tree or table (WAS 1974, April 24, 1916). He seemed to be having the same kind of difficulty being "W. S." as he had once had shaping the letter *S*. And the difficulty was not helped by all his absences from home. Yet being away prompted the strong need to complete himself, to ground himself in the continuity of the poems and plays he wrote. Even with his heavy business schedule, he continued writing poem after poem, just as he had, over the months of transition—moving first from one company to another and then from New York to Hartford—written many poems and *Three Travelers Watch a Sunrise,* the anonymously submitted play for which he won a prize for a one-act play in verse.

Though Stevens focused extreme concentration in managing both his careers, there were moments when his attention lapsed. Quick slips occurred. As might be expected, they usually showed themselves in relationship to Elsie, the only person to whom he could reveal himself at all unguardedly. One of the most interesting again happened in connection with his addressing a letter to her, this one from St. Paul, Minnesota, where he found himself once more within weeks of finding out from Harriet Monroe that his play, which she would publish in *Poetry,* had won a prize. The letter mockingly yet seriously played on his recent success and disclosed that at this point, Stevens saw himself not as poet but as playwright:

Eminent Vers Libriste
Arrives in Town
Details of Reception

St. Paul, Minn. July 18, 1916. Wallace Stevens, the playwright and barrister, arrived at Union Station, at 10:30 o'clock this morning. Some thirty representatives of the press were not there to greet him. He proceeded on foot to the Hotel St. Paul, where they had no room for him. Thereupon, carrying an umbrella and two mysterious looking bags he proceeded to the Minnesota Club, 4th & Washington Streets, St. Paul, where he will stay while he is in St. Paul. At the Club, Mr. Stevens took a shower bath and succeeded in flooding not only the bath-room floor but the bed-room floor as well. He used all the bath-towels in mopping up the mess and was obliged to dry himself with a wash-cloth. From the Club, Mr. Stevens went downtown on business. When asked how he liked St. Paul, Mr. Stevens, borrowing a cigar, said, "I like it."

DEAR BUD,
The above clipping may be of interest to you. (*L* 196)

This generally ignored point about how Stevens identified himself in 1916 is extremely significant. In terms of his personality, his romance with playwriting showed how fragile he was. A little more than a year later, when a production of another of his plays met with failure, he turned completely away from the theater. In terms of his work, though he turned away from this activity, the success or failure of which was felt too immediately and publicly on opening night, he nonetheless continued to explore what he thought to be the most important aspects of dramatic form. These he incorporated into the structure and interrelationships of his poems. Both these effects of his involvement with the theater will be explored fully farther on, when the impact of that first major failure is described.

This was still in the future, the future Stevens now anticipated with more eagerness after winning "Arriet's prize" (as William Carlos Williams called it when he wrote his note of congratulation [WAS 12, June 8, 1916]) than he had in years—probably not since winning "all [those] prizes at school" that he had made so much of to Elsie. Reflecting his excitement, Stevens made two proleptic numerical mistakes in the addressing and dating of the above letter. The first was writing "July" instead of "June." Perhaps he looked forward to the following month, when he would be home again. The second error was in his writing Elsie's mother's address. (This was another summer Elsie was visiting Reading; their finances after the move were not in a state that would support her spending the summer at a resort.) While a few years earlier, Stevens had mistakenly reduced the number of his mother's address, he now increased Mrs. Moll's from 231 to 239 South Thirteenth Street (WAS 1976, June 19, 1916). In spite of the error, the letter reached its destination. That he made two such similar errors in the same letter suggests that there was something more amiss than just excitement.

Everything about the letter and the experience described was contradictory. No less was what he was going through internally. It seemed that at last his career in the life of letters was leaping ahead—like the numbers he wrote. At the same time to the part of him that examined himself and what he did, burdened with judgments left over from his youth, this—like the resulting wrong date and wrong address—seemed wrong as well. He somehow felt this jump forward had to be a mistake. Though he wanted success very much, it was probably far too much. As a result, there was a self-consciousness about it that turned to mocking self-deprecation. Though Alfred Kreymborg thought that Stevens "wore his self-deprecation as a protective mantle,"[4] for the "Vers Libriste-barrister" it felt more like the wet washcloth he described in his letter: inadequate and inappropriate.

It is also possible that these slips resulted from Stevens's having written this satirically playful note in a state of extreme relaxation. Perhaps he had had a few drinks and settled into an easy chair before dinner to report his activities and location to Elsie and felt reluctance about having to do this at all—hence, the mistakes in date and address. He did not want to report the correct information or to have to be accountable, and once he had done his duty, he did not want her to receive it. The exaggeration of his importance, then, as "Eminent Vers Libriste" would stress and counterbalance what he felt to be the inappropriateness of keeping Elsie fully abreast of everywhere he went and everything he did, as though he were a child having to ensure that his mother's mind was at ease about his activities and well-being whenever he was not with her.

In view of the way he had shaped the roles for the tragicomedy they played, this scenario was probably close to reality. The roles that Elsie and he needed the other to fulfill were parental. And though they could not succeed in playing these out as desired, perversions of them, forced by the circumstances of their lives, ensued. They each wanted the unequivocal approval from the other that they had never experienced in childhood and youth. Because of the very nature of an adult relationship in an everyday setting, this was impossible. But the need for some kind of parenting persisted and was filled by whatever behavior was most easily called for, considering the individual proclivities of their personalities. Like his mother, Elsie cooked well, kept a spotless house, and played the piano, but she also acted out her possessive need and insecurity, making him account to her as the worst kind of mother would. Like the father Elsie dreamed of having, Stevens provided even more than she thought of wanting, though at his determination. He showed concern for her health—particularly for her eyes, as her mother and Mr. Moll could not—and was thought of highly so that she had no difficulty idealizing him when she felt the need. But he also acted out his insecurities and constraints. He directed her, made her implicitly accountable for every penny she spent, the way the worst kind of father would. Stevens observed concerning the prime effect he was trying to communicate in his plays that "people are affected by what is around them" (L 201n.). In the same way as the subject of a cubist canvas reflected in its fragmented planes what was around from the past, as well as in the present and suggested future, Wallace and Elsie Stevens, as subjects of their lives, reflected the complicate disharmony of their time and circumstances as well as that of their parents and the culture, still searching, as they were, for approval and identity.

આ

Stevens's prizewinning play, *Three Travelers Watch a Sunrise*, appeared in *Poetry* in July 1916. Among the poems that were written during the same period, "Bowl" (*OP* 6) is important to consider with the play since both seem to have been prompted in part by Stevens's meditation on a porcelain object that functioned for him in much the same way as Keats's famous Grecian urn. In Stevens's play and poem, the bowl and bottle respectively represent earth and differ from Keats's urn in that they have no narrative surface decoration, though like the Grecian urn, they generate preoccupation with death, change, and immortality. In "Bowl" and *Three Travelers* these objects are connected to the Orient, as opposed to Keats's connection of his object to the classical world. Keats's contemplation freezes the passage of time suggested by the pictorial narrative on the urn, a narrative already frozen, immortalized. In contrast, Stevens's polished surfaces constantly change with the coming and going of light, whether natural light, like the reflections of the "various obscurities of the moon" (*OP* 7), or the human light of imagination, symbolized in the play by the light of a candle. At the beginning of his poetic career, then, Stevens announced his difference from the romantic poets in projecting a world understood from a relativistic point of view. He wanted to set out a vision of reality washed clean of all past narratives, a tabula rasa, a shining bowl or bottle beautifully shaped by human conception, blank but ever-changing, capable of being understood from as many perspectives as the subject of a cubist canvas:

> There are as many points of view
> From which to regard her
> As there are sides to a round bottle.
>
> (*OP* 136)

Significantly, during these first months of presenting himself and his modernist view, Stevens pointed directly to the Orient as one of the sources of his perception. It was not only the recently constructed Pagoda on Mount Penn in Reading behind Elsie's parents' home that focused his attention, as he indicated with the setting of his play. In a different way from William Butler Yeats, who was affected mainly by the structure and dramatic effects of Oriental drama, being especially attracted by the mask element in the Noh of Japan, Stevens was primarily interested in the epistemological and ethical differences Oriental thought offered to a Western audience. The major difference had to do with the Orientals' easy acceptance of change as the only permanent or "true" aspect of reality and with how this acceptance affected attitudes toward death. Death was neither something to be feared nor the liberation to an ideal, eternal way of being but simply another fact of nature. The dead body hanging in the tree in *Three Travelers* does not cause the Chinese characters in the play any alarm but is regarded as a leaf would be, a leaf that will fall. Though one character, the only female, feels the death to be an "evil" because the dead man has hanged himself, there is no support from the others for her judgment, nor is there any grieving or despair. They can perceive the beauty of the world, of the porcelain bottle, and they can also accept that another human who "wanted nothing" could choose to end his life. In this little drama Stevens quietly annulled one of the most basic of Christian values, that concerning the sanctity of human life envisioned as being a gift of God which only He had the right to take. But he managed to do this so subtly that Harriet Monroe not only accepted the play but supported it for the prize it won from *Poetry*'s donor (Max Michelson) and staff who were the judges.

Stevens was very pleased about this, as he noted to Miss Monroe (*L* 194). Naturally, he was pleased, as Elsie was, too, for the recognition. (She had telephoned her husband in his hotel room to tell him of it, even though he would be home in two or three days.) It was an acknowledgment that he was not spending ink and evening hours he could have devoted wholly to her in vain. But he was pleased more because the acceptance of this symbolist piece, which forecast the later theater of the absurd, suggested that he could continue in this spirit, a spirit enlightened with a new and, as he hoped, better way of looking at the world and the place of human beings in it. His years of preoccupation with Oriental poetry and thought were now affording him the possibility of articulating an alternative to the Western myths with which he had been reared. It was as though he were calling for a return to the period in history when skepticism yielded to the promise of transcendent security promised by Christianity and suggesting that truth should be sought instead by one's turning to the East. Reflecting this idea, his play opens with a Diogenes-like figure, the "Second Chinese," who looks not for an honest man but for poetry, feeling certain he can find it with a lantern. Though this was, on the most essential level, an expression of Stevens's personal trust, his hope, it was also an expression of hope for the culture. This hope was ultimately a belief that through the civilizing force of poetry, found by and including imagination—the lantern—rather than through the force of pure reason alone (the force on which Western culture was based and depended), individuals would come to know the same peace and acceptance that Orientals seemed to have.

This turn to the East did not develop from his reading alone. All through this period Witter Bynner, moving between the Midwest and New England,[5] periodically stopped in New York, where he saw old friends and talked at length about the superiority of Oriental to Occidental attitudes and their difference from the romantics' excessive "indulgence" in imagination severed from the particulars of reality. By the beginning of 1917 Bynner was in the Orient, traveling with, among others, Arthur Davison Ficke, another of Stevens's contacts and admirers. They visited China, Korea, and Japan, where they stayed with Lafcadio Hearn and his wife, daughter of a samurai. Though there is very little correspondence between Stevens and Bynner, and none from this period, there is no doubt that Stevens kept up with Bynner, whose talent he had early recognized, having invited him to join the *Advocate* staff when he became its editor. It is possible that it was Bynner (in 1913 and 1914, already an established poet, invited to read and speak all across the country), returning the recognition, who alerted Harriet Monroe to Stevens's name, so that when she saw his "Phases" in her pile of unsolicited manuscripts after her war issue of *Poetry* was already in proof, she picked out the poems and tore apart the page proofs to include them.[6] Bynner and Monroe were "good friends," if not "close," their natures being quite different, he nothing like the "careful, humorless puritan" she was characterized to be, except in also having a "passion for verse."[7]

In addition to being included in *Poetry*'s pages, Bynner had been published in various other periodicals. Since 1911 sections of *The New World*, its greater part first delivered as "An Immigrant" to the Harvard Chapter of the Phi Beta Kappa in June 1911—as almost forty years later Stevens would deliver "Description Without Place" (*CP* 339)—appeared in *Poetry*, the *Bellman*, the *Boston Evening Transcript*, and the *American Magazine*.[8] Though derivative, in fact, intentionally imitative, of Whitman in a not entirely successful manner, the poem and Bynner were celebrated for the patriotic and transcendentally secularized religious sentiment expressed in his lines. Because of its overly self-conscious bombast, this was not poetry Stevens would have found congenial, yet it offered him something quite attractive that the imagist pieces, by contrast, appearing in journals over the same period, did not. This was its direct appeal to a humanly shaped spiritual element, as opposed to the depersonalized, strictly formal spiritual sense urged by Pound and the later followers of T. E. Hulme, also expressed in relation to painting, as Pound noted, by Wassily Kandinsky in *Concerning the Spiritual in Art.*[9] While Pound and the first *Imagistes*—and later Amy Lowell—stressed "hardness" and the kind of chiseled classicism perfected, they believed, in French poetry by Théophile Gautier in *Émaux et Camées,* Stevens not only appreciated but yielded himself to almost all the "soft" characteristics the imagists eschewed: elaboration and ornamental frills; high diction; abstract concepts and terms; lofty subjects, instead of those reflecting Pound's praise for John Gould Fletcher's "daring" search through the "dust-bin"; lines and stanzas in metrical, isochronic measures rather than in new "rough" imitations of the "contours of things."[10]

Perhaps it was precisely because Stevens had not traveled to Europe that he remained so strongly attached to these "soft" forms. Though Bynner had been in Europe, it had been in 1902, long before the rumblings of change heralded by the first cubist exhibitions in Paris and, later, by Roger Fry's postimpressionist show and the futurist display in London in 1910 were carried into the discussions of the early imagists sitting in the Eiffel Tower or wherever they gathered after that little Soho restaurant. The difference in moment is perfectly reflected in the difference between the poetry of Bynner and William Carlos Williams, who visited Pound in London at exactly this later time, a time ripe for loudly announcing the change in tone T. E. Hulme identified as a renewal of a "pure" unsentimental stance before reality, one close to both the classical ideal of the Greeks and the geometrical abstractions of primitives. In spite of its Whitmanesque evocation of the immigrant experience, which represented primitivism of a kind, Bynner's perception, as expressed in *The New World,* was loaded with a sentimental call for transcending personal identity through love and merging with the *all.* Though Stevens would have been loath to admit it, he liked this sort of thing in spirit. He found in Bynner's work either elements he had begun to explore already himself or some he could transform in the same way he did elements from other poets who touched his responsive chords.

In *The New World* and in some of the poems that appeared in *Poetry,* there are more than a few features that are paralleled in Stevens's work. More than the particular lines or images where the similarity is clear,[11] there are thematic and attitudinal identities and, in the case of *The New World,* an idea for plot that Stevens developed to the fullest in "The Comedian as the Letter C." A repeated theme in Bynner was the transcendence of physical, not ideal, beauty. It appeared in variations throughout *The New World* and paradigmatically in a poem like this one:

GRIEVE NOT FOR BEAUTY

Grieve not for the invisible, transported brow
On which like leaves the dark hair grew,
Nor for the lips of laughter that are now
Laughing inaudibly in sun and dew,
Nor for those limbs that, fallen low
And seeming faint and slow

Shall yet pursue
More ways of swiftness than the swallow dips
Among . . . and find more winds than ever blew
The straining sails of unimpeded ships!
Mourn not!—yield only happy tears
To deeper beauty than appears![12]

But while in Bynner's lines the theme was almost emptied of meaning because of being overly stated and restated, in Stevens's hands the same theme was resolved into the hauntingly paradoxical and transfixing coda of "Peter Quince":

Beauty is momentary in the mind—
The fitful tracing of a portal;
But in the flesh it is immortal;

(CP 91)

In the same way Bynner's controlling image in *The New World*—which depicts a voyage to America and collapses into a universal crossing all voyages to her shores, from Columbus's to the latest influxes of immigrants as they came in increasing numbers in the first twenty years of the century—was used to masterly advantage by Stevens in creating the epic of Crispin. There the initial *C* called forth not only Columbus as hero but the sea itself, the natural mother who bore all life to welcoming shores as well as the primary sense we use to understand and record our voyage through becoming—"to see." The unitary Eastern sense that Bynner communicated all too discursively in his poetry, which made it both accessible and popular, Stevens actually forged into images and sounds bodying their meaning forth in a way even Pound would have approved, had Stevens, too, completely broken from the tradition Pound wanted to blast. If Pound had not so "detested" Stevens and the New England sensibility he disliked so much in Amy Lowell,[13] he could have seen that Stevens was as revolutionary as, if not more so than, he and that his particular and major contribution to modernism lay precisely in filling the traditional forms with a wholly unexpected content.

Stevens had not forgotten the lessons he had learned from Goethe and Heine about the effectiveness of regular meters in insinuating themselves into the consciousness of audiences. His desire to write plays in verse was connected to his knowing how powerfully *Faust* could move an audience. While *il miglior fabbro* appreciated and guided Eliot's talent, sympathized with him as an expatriate, without criticizing his exploitation of Elizabethan rhythms to their fullest effect, he rejected Stevens out of hand because he did not see the "true subject" beneath the "poetry of the subject." This may have been, in part, a result of Harriet Monroe's careful editing that had presented "Sunday Morning" in a way that did almost entirely obscure its "true subject." Or it may simply have been Pound's orneriness that closed the door on anyone who seemed to affect Harvard airs and Boston manners. Fortunately, as Daryl Hine recently expressed in his Introduction to the *Poetry Anthology*, in spite of her puritanical editor's eye, Monroe did exist for poets like Stevens who needed encouragement to withstand the judgments of others like "the Pounds of this world,"[14] who proclaimed advertisements for themselves and new movements that, ironically, stood on the base of impersonality.

By the time Amy Lowell, having wrested the imagist standard from Pound, who moved on to vorticism with Wyndham Lewis and *Blast*, announced in 1917 that the last of her three imagist anthologies had done its work, the broader modernist movement and the Great War were both well under way. The United States declared a state of war on April 6, 1917. By that time, if not the myriad Pound soon mourned in his lines from "Hugh Selwyn Mauberley," some of the best poets and artists of Stevens's generation were already dead: Rupert Brooke and Henri Gaudier-Brzeska. T. E. Hulme and Edward Thomas would not make it through the end of the year. By the war's end many others had joined them. But Stevens, on this side of the ocean, not only had not known them but had no idea of how constant a presence war had become in Europe's everyday landscape, how the glow from the shells exploding over the trenches in Belgium and France could be seen as evening darkened over London—the sky no longer "a dividing and indifferent blue" but threateningly reddened like the diminishing vision of "a patient etherized upon a table."[15]

&

"Yet the absence of the imagination had/Itself to be imagined" (*CP* 503) on this side of the Atlantic. Almost as though protected by the childishly utopian myth pointed to by the ocean's name, people could still imagine the perfection promised by idealists in this New World—even better than a New Atlantis. As bullets and shells syncopated the longer measures of moving tanks and machine-gun fire, here, during the nights of those same days, first in the South and then in cities across the country, the strange, sweet notes of jazz syncopated unheard melodies. There was both innocence and the brutal wisdom of experience in this music of black musicians who simultaneously mourned and celebrated with their rhythms. The rhythms intruding into those Stevens heard intoning in his memory were these, and they carried the same kind of "black humorous" attitude toward death and change as the sources of jazz. This was the spirit of songs like "When the Saints Go Marching In" and of poems like "The Worms at Heaven's Gate" (*CP* 49), "The Emperor of Ice-Cream" (*CP* 64), "Domination of Black" (*CP* 8), "The Silver Plough-Boy" (*OP* 6), "Metaphors of a Magnifico" (*CP* 19), "Cortège for Rosenbloom" (*CP* 79), and other poems in *Harmonium,* in which irregular rhythms, mimicking Stevens's present preoccupation, broke through the regular pace of pentameter lines, the meditative meter appropriate to occasions evoked from the past or wished for in the future. It is not surprising that these irregular rhythms largely disappeared from the poetry written after

WALLACE STEVENS

Harmonium, when Stevens separated himself more and more from the present to reside in imaginings of past and future.

Stevens was also experimenting with distinctive rhythms to establish his particular modernity among those whose printed voices were appearing simultaneously in *Poetry* and other periodicals as well as in editions of their own. Pound's *Cathay* translations came out in 1915, adding a new tone to his earlier personae and countering the harshness of *Blast*'s 1914 poems. In 1916 Arensberg's *Idols* was published.[16] In 1917 William Carlos Williams published *Al Que Quiere!* and T. S. Eliot published *Prufrock and Other Observations*, providing a wonderful counterpoint to Amy Lowell's *Tendencies in Modern American Poetry*, which also came out in the same year. While Arensberg and Williams were attempting to forge an entirely new, quick-paced American idiom, Eliot and Pound—like James Joyce, who in 1916 published *A Portrait of the Artist as a Young Man*—seemed to be consciously turning toward a ritualistic assuaging of what they were perceiving. Eliot immersed himself in Elizabethan rhythms or bitterly ironic quatrain forms imitative of Jules Laforgue and Théophile Gautier. Pound, too, toyed with mocking quatrains while turning back pages of Eastern and Western history, searching in China, Japan, Greece, Rome, and Provence for rhythms to soothe violated senses. Joyce attempted to transcend the very rituals with which he had been reared by using their very same meters and cadences to express his cold criticism of the religion that used these rituals to imprison its faithful.

As Arensberg, Williams, and the rest of the "Others" established their camp, opposing Pound and Eliot, who had retreated to older forms, Stevens found himself, once again but now in a particularly poetic way, moving up and down between these two elements. Deeply attached, like Pound and Eliot, to traditional rhythms, which he also used, like them and Joyce, to parody the earlier content that filled them, he did not witness with them the violent death throes of that "old bitch gone in the teeth, [the] botched civilization"[17] that had refused for too long seeing things as they were. Stevens addressed, then, like the other "Americans," the peculiarly American problem of individual identity and voice against the background of "the wild, the ruinous waste" (*CP* 24), the nation's comparative "uncivilization."

In poems of the late 1910s and early 1920s, Pound and Eliot addressed broad questions concerning civilization and its destruction because they were directly in touch with the negative social and cultural effects of a class system still attached to a feudal world view and the idea of a great chain of being, dependent on preserving the Christian myth. Stevens, on the other hand, understood the inappropriateness or inadequacy of the Christian myth primarily from personal experience. American society and culture were still thriving, it seemed to most, on the pap that myth offered. This was evident even in the attitude of astute literary critics like Paul Elmer More. Though Stevens, through his contact with the Harvard circle, had learned to question the basis and nature of belief, this kind of openness was not at all characteristic of the rest of society. Not even simply considering alternative myths, no less

460

mockingly criticizing consequences of the Christian one, was acceptable. In this puritanical setting Stevens closely addressed immediately recognizable aspects of religious and cultural life rather than large, already abstracted issues couched in gnomic, historically weighted references, like those of *The Waste Land*. Of course Stevens was going to provoke a very different reaction from that prompted by his expatriate compatriots. As the war raged and ended, America's powers-that-be attempted to strengthen its moral consciousness. They breathed new life into the myth of the Puritans' mission, even passing a Prohibition amendment that formally announced this reassertion. Against this background Stevens continued writing his irreverent, sacrilegious poems.

Much of Stevens's ability to persist in his resistance was connected to the support he received from both the Arensberg circle and the "Others" group.[18] The importance of this cannot be stressed enough. The Arensbergs and their entourage were the "avant-garde of the avant-garde"[19] and, with their international representation, provided Stevens with a full range of terms of reference. These delighted his imagination, satisfied his need for stimulation, and offered him the assurance, which could come only from an Old World attitude, that revolution was really only evolution. Their collective function—inciting to change the way human beings saw themselves and the world—was really only the age-old function of the prophet. Their errand into the wilderness was clear: to create contexts, worlds within worlds, in their works of art, in which and through which those who were willing to submit themselves to the process illustrated and demanded by these works could perceive what it meant to live on the edge of experience in an ever-transforming present. This meant living without the encumbrance of certainty provided by the various versions of the Western myth of progress, which for nearly two millennia had kept human beings' minds separated from their bodies. The myth had succeeded so well that the mind's technology was in the process of sacrificing the bodies of 8 million young men at its altar.

Though there is a general tendency to trivialize the activities and snicker at the personalities of those involved with an avant-garde movement—especially one celebrating as one of its heroes, Marcel Duchamp, a man who drew a mustache on a reproduction of the *Mona Lisa* and added beneath his carefully shaped rebus letters advertising her, if pronounced in French, as a "hot piece"—it is imperative to recognize, particularly in this instance, the high seriousness of these activities and personalities. The purpose of those who met in Arensberg's studio was not simply *épater les bourgeois,* though this was naturally one of its side effects. The group felt a strong and sincere desire to restore to human beings what Stevens once called the "instinct of joy" (*L* 276). Indulging this sense did not mean taking an easy step into laughing at the surface details of experience or even at the deeper, ironic condition of human life. What these individuals perceived was that the closer one could approach pure *being,* without the interference of distracting appearances—"Let be be finale of seem"—the closer one came to joy, the pleasure of merely circulating. The more often and the longer this state could be sustained, as Walter Pater had suggested,[20] the more likely it became that one could understand something about the nature of nature—not regarding it only from outside as an object of contemplation but knowing it from inside, as one with it, experiencing the self as matter being continuously transformed into spirit, feeling the waves of energy that are the universe move in and out, pass through the temporary container of the body. Though this may seem mystical, it is not and was not perceived in that way by Stevens or by any of the others also working with the same consciousness to provide, through their carefully constructed works, an access to this understanding.

The stress Duchamp laid on eros is at the center of this understanding since it is usually through eros that human beings first come into mature contact with their oneness with the universe. Duchamp was not alone in having this perception. Plato and the "old Chinese" sages knew it, and, among Duchamp's contemporaries, D. H. Lawrence, Sigmund Freud, and Havelock Ellis began from this premise. T. S. Eliot, too, began from it, seeing the Victorians' extreme divorce of mind from body as the cause of his then present personal predicament and the largest single feature contributing to the conditions that gave birth to World War I. Out of his perceptions Eliot drew his early emphasis on the importance of senses and sensuous elements.[21] But being the product of the American Puritans' culture, like Stevens, he never became more explicit than this in his work, though the details of his life testified to the inextricable connection between keeping senses open and sexuality.

Marcel Duchamp, by contrast, was the son of a French provincial notary, steeped in a tradition that praised Rabelais as much as Pascal. He grew up in the same town instanced by Flaubert in *Madame Bovary* as a typical center of hypocrisy and repression. Duchamp, having witnessed examples of these less than pleasing aspects of social behavior and having had the benefit of being exposed to Flaubert's attitude and implicit judgment about the situations created out of these aspects, simply left France after the outbreak of World War I. He had no compunctions about leaving the country he saw as one of the centers of bourgeois duplicity and complacency. He came to America, where he felt he could put his experience to good use in making people aware of what was at the core of their experience, the core they tried so hard to deny. When Duchamp—alias Rrose Sélavy (a homonymic pun for "Eros c'est la vie" ["Eros is life."])—arrived and began presenting his work, it seemed that he had experientially understood what Freud had started to lay out abstractly and clinically in his *Three Essays on the Theory of Sexuality*, subjects he would make both broader and more specific in *Civilization and Its Discontents*. Duchamp seemed to be illustrating, with two- and three-dimensional examples, precisely the problems and consequences that Freud delineated. And enriching and reinforcing this consciousness, Duchamp also drew on a longer tradition, considered arcane by some, but nonetheless a tradition out of which the most important scientific discoveries from the seventeenth to the nineteenth century had been born. Duchamp was more than familiar with the theory, practice, and history of alchemy; he became expert in translating the viable points uncovered and employed by the alchemists in his own description of reality.

Though Stevens, on meeting Duchamp, claimed that he could not pretend to understand what he, or any other painter for that matter, did, it is clear from the evidence of *Harmonium* either that if he, indeed, had not understood Duchamp's work, he certainly made it his business to do so within the five years after their first encounter or that he was being characteristically disingenuous about what he understood because he saw or felt in Duchamp's work an intention and method very close to his own and therefore did not want to admit the possibility of influence. In the same way he often expressed that he did not read poetry—though it was clear that he did—because, he noted, he was afraid the voice he would hear intoning in his mind's corridors would not be his own (*L* 575).

One of the strongest points to come through Duchamp's work is a comment on the attitude toward sex of the Western, civilized individual around the period of the First World War. This showed itself in the content of the most important canvases of this period, done in the quasi-futuro-cubist style identifiable with Duchamp, for which he received so much attention. Unfortunately this concern with his style diverted attention from the content, from which the style should not have been divorced. This same situation has also existed in relationship to Stevens's work, where critical attention was directed toward the "poetry of the subject" rather than to the "true subject." Though Duchamp's *Nude Descending a Staircase* evoked the greatest response because it was one of the most controversial contributions to the Armory Show, it was in the other paintings—done in the same style during the same period—that the artist's intention showed itself more clearly. In *Bride,* for example, as in the later *Great Glass,* what was delineated in the work was a sexual act: in the case of *Bride,* intercourse itself, while in the case of *The Great Glass,* the beginning causes of desire, described in wholly mechanical terms that are, at the same time, allegorical forms for alchemical processes.[22] When these are considered together with his other work, the related *Nude Descending* and *King and Queen Surrounded by Swift Nudes,* as well as with the production of his later years, it is plain that Duchamp was translating into the symbolic forms he depicted his observation that the only way human beings of his generation seemed able to accept and deal with their sexual appetites—what Aristotle called and Stevens referred to, pointing back to him, as "concupiscence"[23]—was in dissociated, mechanical terms. This protected them from having to look closely at and admit, with the full range of feeling entailed, their animality.[24]

Although the way Duchamp used alchemical symbols and references in his long project, *The Bride Stripped Bare by Her Bachelors, Even, or The Great Glass,* reinforced his point to those who had recognized his intention from earlier works, to those who were not familiar with the progress of his ideas as recorded in these works, the piece appeared as the absurd product of a madman. But even this was in keeping with the Hermetic tradition[25] with which Duchamp, Arensberg, and the rest of the circle were involved.[26] The lore they were dealing with was arcane, required serious application, and was not, therefore, accessible to all. The function of a circle like the one Arensberg put together, following a model Francis Bacon had imaginatively suggested in *The New Atlantis*, was to relate this privileged body of knowledge to particular facts of nature and human experience, of which they became specialized observers, their participation in the circle strengthening and clarifying their skills. Their reading and discussion of the new intellectual and artistic contributions in Alfred Steiglitz's *Camera Work* and of Freud's *Interpretation of Dreams*, for example, were parts of their commitment. Duchamp's application of the idea of the alchemist's "Great Work" in constructing and naming his *Great Glass*, just like Stevens's application in projecting the "Grand Poem," reflected the high seriousness of their endeavor.

The original purpose of the alchemists' "Great Work" was to discover the philosopher's stone, the catalyst that would transform base metals, like lead, into gold.[27] By the fifteenth century, after Paracelsus, this pursuit had already become a metaphor for finding the gold understood as a medicinal unguent that would cure human ills. By the time the idea itself became transmuted over the centuries separating the early alchemists from twentieth-century initiates, the literal aspect had crystallized and been transformed into chemistry, while the metaphorical aspect had sublimed into the search for a spiritual catalyst that would change the base elements of human experience into a golden rule to help individuals live their lives in a better way. One of Stevens's particular phrasings of this end was "The gold dome of things is the perfected spirit" (*OP* 168).

But becoming more involved with the preoccupations of the Arensberg circle meant that Stevens had to confront his own attitude toward sexuality and the reality of his relationship with Elsie. Though he no doubt preferred toying with associations to various alchemical symbols and playing, like Duchamp, with puns, anagrams, and mixtures of French and English,[28] he could not ignore the intent behind the group's interest in primitive art and in the work of certain other contemporaries who were also making the point about the importance of sexuality. Arensberg was one of the first collectors of pre-Columbian pieces,[29] which he added to his African examples. He also had a special interest in the primitivism of Henri Rousseau. Rousseau's *Merry Jesters*, which hung in Arensberg's studio, was an intriguing piece for the circle. It is a huge canvas, depicting, in the midst of one of the French master's distinctive jungles, curious kinds of primates, which seem to be humans in primate costumes, doing very mysterious things. The painting challenges the viewer to make sense out of its primitive/mechanical confusion. A curious object in the center foreground focuses this provocation. It appears to be an invisibly suspended milk bottle pouring out its contents to reveal, through its transparent surface, what appears to be a baboon's misplaced breast. Stevens once observed that Arensberg could stand in front of a work for hours waiting for disclosure of meaning (*L* 823). It is easy to understand, when one looks at this Rousseau, how and why he learned to do this—something he must have invited his friends in the studio to do as well. This painting, and certainly the paintings and constructions of Duchamp, absolutely demanded long attention if they were to yield to interpretation. What was presented was a puzzle. The key had to be found if it was to make sense. At the moment it did, the joke realized, the skill of the maker was appreciated and a bond formed between artist and audience.

This pleased Stevens a great deal, and he learned to think and imagine in these terms. This allowed him to deflect immediate attention away from the painful aspects of his personal life and, at the same time, put these same aspects at the center of an elaborately constructed puzzle. In this way he could unburden himself, place the unpleasant secrets outside, and do to them whatever he wanted through the symbolic forms of the poems he wrote. In keeping with the idea of the "Great Work," it would be necessary, he projected, for those who would unlock the puzzle—discover the puns and follow their cues—to devote themselves to his whole corpus over a long period of time in the same way as the practitioners of arcane knowledge.

Stevens was not the only poet of this circle to be fascinated with playing cryptically with letters and words. Mina Loy also frequented the studio when she was in New York. Described as a "coil of wit,"[30] she must have both delighted and threatened Stevens the way Sybil Gage once had—if, that is, Stevens met her at all.[31] But whether they actually knew each other or knew each other through their work and reputations in the group, he must have been enticed by her passion for "anagrammatically and numerologically derived pseudonyms" and her reticence—far more extreme than his—about indulging personality, her vision of herself being that she was a "sort of moral hermit."[32] Pound and Eliot praised her (one of her poems appeared in the famous *Dial* issue in which *The Waste Land* was printed in November 1922[33]), and Carl Van Vechten (then editor of *Trend,* who also sought out and encouraged Stevens) together with Kreymborg and the "Others" group tried hard in 1915 to draw her out, urging her to take on her persona as a poet. Her response was to hide behind that persona. Her feeling about this could just as easily have been uttered by Stevens: "To maintain my incognito the hazard I chose was—poet"[34] Ironically, or perhaps not, her first volume, like Stevens's, appeared in 1923 and fared even worse than his. She maintained her silence after this well beyond the six years he did.[35] Something else they had in common was the project to write the "Grand Poem"; hers she thought of as the "Long Poem," and like Stevens's, hers needed a key. Her "Anglo-Mongrels and the Rose" was her key,[36] just as "The Comedian as the Letter C" was Stevens's.

It is interesting that in plotting to counter Harriet Monroe's canonical *Poetry* with a magazine that would truly announce the message of the avant-garde, Arensberg and Kreymborg, devising their scheme all through a long night at the studio, agreed that their intention would be best achieved by featuring Loy and Stevens in the first two numbers of *Others.*[37] With the delight he took in playing on the differences between various seemings and being, Stevens must have been particularly tickled to be representing both Monroe's more traditional end and Arensberg's iconoclastic one.

While his first poems in *Poetry* showed Stevens's concern with moral issues connected with the problems of the age—war and belief—those in *Others* dealt with more primary human problems: death and sex. Voicing this concern with fundamental subjects was what Stevens had in common with Loy. Both illustrated what Kreymborg offered as the magazine's contradictorily cryptic motto: "The old expressions are always with us, but there are always *others*."[38] Stevens and Loy were preserving "old expressions" in their references to, for example, biblical narrative or Homeric epithet, yet both were also giving shape to new forms of expression for age-old concerns. Their otherness was subtle, neither turning completely away from traditional forms as Williams was doing nor accompanying their image breaking with the anger of Pound or nervousness of Eliot. In spite of the revolution in which they were involved, they remained complacent. This made their irreverence all the more powerful. Their complacency showed itself in an ability to evoke what Stevens later called the "gaiety" of language (*OP* 174 and 178), the sense and sounds of words themselves asserting their curative, comforting potential. They saw poetry as the "cure of the mind" (*OP* 176), the twentieth century's philosopher's stone.

This commitment to what Stevens understood as the function of the "Comedian" allied him to Loy and, in the previous generation, to Emily Dickinson. Marianne Moore, also connected to the Arensberg circle, shared this as well. What all these poets had in common was the capacity to withhold forcing any moment of perception to its crisis in the despair or futility it seemed it must reach in the face of what had come to be known about the world and human beings' relation to it. Each of them wrested continuing possibility from the threat of conclusions. They did this by forcing attention on the particular, expanding the instants of being, investing any and every object considered with the quality of sacredness. This was strongly bound, especially for Stevens and Loy, with the sounds of words they chose. Each of their poems, like Dickinson's before them—some of which they may have known during this period as they carefully shaped their syllables—was and is a prayer, a celebration exquisitely attenuating the lived moments. In one sense of time, as Bergson had pointed out to them, moments passed regularly and consecutively, but in another sense there was only one extended moment created out of extreme attentiveness to the overlappings of sensations, memories, associations—the constant returns that were at the same time points of departure in the ebb and flow of consciousness.

Though the external march of events continued with the war, his trips every day to and from the office, the longer trips to new and already familiar cities, the periodic "blow-ups of the nerves" (*L* 422) with Elsie, Stevens did not measure his life in these broad steps. Nor did he, even in the face of sexual dissatisfaction or reticence, like Prufrock, shrink into despair and measure it out "with coffee spoons."[39] This was because, in spite of turning away from its particularly Christian form, he had never lost what he had named in his youth the "instinct of faith," the sense with which he had been reared that there was something that would suffice, even though at the moment he had intellectually rejected his family's religion while at Harvard, he understandably *thought* he had lost it. His substitution then of art and beauty for religion returned now, as he again felt himself the poet with the full vigor evoked by emotional necessity. He had not been wholly disillusioned then; he was now. But instead of avoiding it, he entered it powerfully, examining with a "microscope of potency," which he carefully focused—following what he learned from "Freud's eye" (*CP* 368)—on each detail of every veil of illusion he had had, many of which he still maintained since he had used them to dress another who could not so easily strip them away. Elsie waited at home in "such dress/As [she was] used to wear" (*CP* 64).

Stevens's real double life had begun. The up and down between imagination and reality was no longer confined to internal perception or alternating forms of behavior, sometimes ascetic, sometimes bawdy. It was now constant, like "a duet/With the undertaker," as he expressed it poetically in "The Man with the Blue Guitar" (*CP* 177). He figured himself playing or singing with the undertaker because he had devised his solution under the pressure of death. Living this way was the only solution he could derive, given things as they were, if he was not to live as one already dead, not experiencing any of the sensual delights for which "that monster, the body" yearned, the animal appetites that he thought perverted by Easter carols and the like. If being in the company of the Arensberg circle—where it was neither thought unusual nor hidden that Mina Loy spent a night in Duchamp's bed in the company of four others[40]—he did not wince, he also did not participate in kind. He preferred sitting on the sofa, whispering and giggling, perhaps at nothing more titillating than a word. While he had understood the legitimacy of the demands of the body, he understood, too, that "If sex were all, then every trembling hand/Could make us squeak, like dolls, the wished-for/words" (*CP* 17). His solution—considering who he was, the choices he had made, the woman who depended on him, and the realization that in spite of it all, it was necessary to live as well as one could—was to make and take sensual delight from the primary human element, words. His joy would come from transforming into an opposing law the very same things that had shaped him. In doing this he could at least show others why he had had to become only a man made out of words and at the same time point a way to go beyond them and him.

Though before they moved to Hartford, Elsie occasionally joined her husband for dinners with Walter and Louise Arensberg (in spite of being hosts of the extremely "artistic" evenings, the Arensbergs were the most conventional couple of the group), Stevens did not feel comfortable including her in the company gathered in the Sixty-seventh Street studio. This was a necessary concession to things as they were. He no doubt remembered one evening in November 1915 when he had invited her. He was to read his latest work; "Sunday Morning," "Disillusionment of Ten O'Clock," and "Peter Quince" were some of the poems from which he had to choose. As the guests gathered around the fireplace, he "prefaced his reading by remarking that his wife, who had hinted disapproval before he began, did not like the poems. 'I like Mr. Stevens' things,' she said, 'when they are not affected; but he writes so much that is affected.'"[41]

So, though her physical appearance would have continued to delight the painters and sculptors, as it had Adolph Alexander Weinman, their New York landlord-sculptor who had already immortalized her on the dime and half dollar, Elsie was too different from the sophisticated, extravagant types who were her husband's admirers. If she found his work "affected," she certainly would not have shared the group's appreciation of Picabia's latest issue of *391,* nor would she have found Duchamp's latest "ready-made"—a coatrack nailed hooks up to the floor—"Droll!" as they did. With the rude, good sense of the practical Pennsylvania Dutch she would probably have pronounced such things "silly" or even "awful." And this was not to speak of what could have ensued had Stevens brought Elsie along on an evening when the Baroness Elsa von Freytag-Loringhoven—who, though the poet did not encourage her, even fleeing her on the street,[42] seemed to have a particular passion for him—was also there, prepared at the drop of a voice, to shed all her clothes and parade herself as the most successful "ready-*made*." The group that celebrated Stevens as one of them—indeed, as one of the greatest among them—could feel sorry that the "Giant" did not have someone at home who could understand him.

Moving to Connecticut was fortunate, then, in many ways. It would be inconvenient or unpleasant for Elsie to while away the time in New York during her husband's business meetings or dinners. At least this is what he would have argued had she expressed a desire to go with him when he did not want her to. With her at home in Hartford, his visits to the Arensbergs' studio or to the apartment of Allen and Louise Norton—acquaintances also connected to the "Others" group—could be more relaxed. He could better appreciate what he saw and heard (Louise Arensberg often played the piano, and Edgard Varèse, who later married Louise Norton, was also a frequent visitor on West Sixty-seventh Street). He could also enjoy himself without the gnawing anxiety that he had excluded Elsie, had immured her in their Chelsea apartment when he was just a short trip uptown. The greater the physical distance between them, the less she would press on his consciousness.

Among the things to be appreciated at the Arensbergs' were some that delighted him and others the poet found "hideous." In the former category he placed the Brancusis he knew. The pieces in his friends' collection included: *The Kiss,* a beautifully subtle work, itself seemingly derived from a pre-Columbian model (from this Brancusi Stevens may have drawn some of the inspiration for his line in "Thirteen Ways of Looking at a Blackbird": "A man and a woman/Are one"); *Young Boy* and *Young Girl,* exquisite abstractions of the essence of the male and female sex; *Princess X.,* a gracefully shaped and polished bronze resembling nothing more than a monumentalized phallus.

Louise Arensberg, in showing this piece to her "puritanical friends," provided a "straight anatomical description, pointing out the head, facial details and shoulders, but intentionally avoiding reference to its obvious phallic shape (in spite of the fact that such a double reading was readily observed by contemporary critics whenever the sculpture was exhibited)."[43] Unfortunately there is no record of how she described it to Stevens. There were also two versions of *Bird in Flight*, one in marble and one in bronze; *Prometheus*, a gnomically ovoid polished marble with ridges faintly suggestive of facial features; and *The Prodigal Son*, which balanced an African torso on the mantel. Though Arensberg may not have owned all these at the time Stevens began frequenting his studio, he acquired most before he and Louise left New York to settle in California. Stevens, then, had a firm base on which to make the judgment he offered to Irish art-historian/poet Thomas McGreevy in a late letter. Contrasting Brancusi to Jean Arp, whom he found "fastidious not forceful," his "forms never constitut[ing] a 'visionary language,'" he observed that Brancusi's things "intimidate one with their possibilities" (*L* 629). This was no small praise from the poet who had, by the time he expressed this in 1949, been attempting to achieve the very same end for more than thirty years.

Another artist whose work Stevens especially liked and had a chance to study closely and long was Jacques Villon, one of the older brothers of Marcel Duchamp (the other was Raymond Duchamp-Villon, the sculptor, whose work was also represented in Arensberg's collection). Villon's dynamically broken planes seem always to be moving up or forward, and his palette—unlike that of the pure cubists who eschewed bright colors to distinguish themselves from the fauves—was gay in tonality. Stevens, who wanted to achieve this gayness in language, must have particularly appreciated this, no less than the use of gentle abstraction to puzzle the viewer. Villon's canvases were as instructive as the strict cubists in uncovering geometrical structures and in connoting the effects of time as the fourth dimension—the category assigned for continuous change. But he instructed with the sweetness of colors and lines conveying that the spirit still aspired, moving upward and outward, as though drawn by a hand still feeling itself moved by the idea of progress. Perhaps this reflected Villon's closer affinity to the futurists than to the cubists. In any case, in view of Stevens's proclivity for the ideal, his search for something that would suffice, it is not surprising that he found Villon's work congenial.

Though he knew Marcel and maintained with him a relationship at a distance into the age when Stevens regretted only Duchamp's "willingness to go about without teeth" (*L* 836), he wavered in his feelings about him and his work. At one point he thought him "an intense neurotic" whose life "was not explicable in any other terms" (*L* 797). Less than a year later he thought him a "good egg" who, in spite of living according to an "old-fashioned" idea of how the "artistic type" should live,[44] had always been intensely modern in the most positive sense (*L* 836). His appreciation of Villon, on the other hand, was unequivocal. It began immediately and was with him all his life. Two years before he died, Stevens described himself as a "great admirer of Villon's work" to Paule Vidal to whom he was writing to ask her to look for and purchase something of Villon's for him (L 795).

One of the Villons in Arensberg's collection would appear to have been signally to Stevens's liking, Sketch for "Puteaux: Smoke and Trees in Bloom," No. 2 (1912) plays on the same ambiguity of surface that Stevens played on in "Sea Surface Full of Clouds." The canvas's dominating gray-green mass could be either the smoke or the trees in bloom. Even careful examination does not clarify. The shadows cast on the ground by what is taken to be the smoke could, looked at in the other way suggested by the title, also be blooming trees or their shadows. In this piece Villon managed to keep viewers totally suspended, unable to resolve the image, uncertain, for as long as they give attention to it, about what is "real." The end result is that they give up the quest to have the canvas represent some portion or aspect of the "real world." Instead, they appreciate the actual "real" canvas, looking at forms as forms, colors as colors, lines as lines. Knowing these elements have been abstracted from an external landscape, they realize that the distinctive arrangement reflects their journey through the consciousness of the artist. In this way the audience comes to understand, feel, the artist's attitude, the evanescent spiritual element of which Kandinsky wrote.

Exposing the individual spirit as openly as Villon did here perfectly illustrated Walter Pach's definition of abstraction in The Masters of Modern Art, a text Stevens knew, Pach having presented him with an inscribed copy on its first publication in 1924. Pach had no doubt refined his perceptions on the subject during discussions with Stevens and others who sat around of an evening in the Arensbergs' studio, looking at what hung on the walls. It is important to note, too, that the kind of expression Villon illustrated and Pach described was the parallel in painting to what Stevens intended in poetry. Seeing each poem as a prayer, a "sacrament of praise," meant that the poem functioned to celebrate each moment of consciousness it instanced, its "occasion," by extending it, keeping it open, its lines and rhythms representing feelings generated in response to the wonders of reality as they were encountered.

In addition to his strong reactions to Brancusi and Villon, Stevens acknowledged the power of Cézanne, Picasso, and Matisse, all of whose genius he came to know intimately from the pieces that hung in Arensberg's studio. Braque, too, was one of his favorites. Stevens liked Matisse's Orientalism of surface, so distinct from the sentimental thematic Orientalism of other nineteenth-century French painters (L 797). He thought each of these figures leaders whom later artists imitated to their disadvantage, preventing themselves in that way from discovering their own paths (L 622). Secondary painters, following these masters—yet another was Paul Klee, whom Stevens also named as a shaper of "modern art"—enjoyed prestige "merely because" what they did was "modern" as well. Late in his life Stevens called the makers of this kind of derivative work "dunces." He saw them, the dealers who carried them, and the consumers who acquired them as "modern art" objects equally as victims of an unexamined commitment to "Free thought, free art, free poetry"—really a commitment not to freedom at all but to a "sort of tyranny" (*L* 574).

Another manifestation of the artistic temperament that Stevens could not bear was pre-Columbian sculpture. When he had grown securely into himself and felt comfortable about making pronouncements like the one about "dunces," he called pre-Columbian art "hideous" (*L* 614). Though Arensberg acquired the greater part of his enormous collection in this area after he had left New York, he had begun buying pieces in 1915.[45] These he interspersed, like his African pieces, among his nineteenth-century and modernist examples. He wanted to suggest through his arrangement the parallels and harmonies he perceived between these early and late expressions of the human spirit in contact with and accepting its animal springs of action. This was, more than anything else, the dominant, common feature of his collection. His unspoken purpose was to create "a radiant and productive atmosphere" (*NA* 57) where the group he gathered could feel free to explore this aspect of personality, held so long in check by inherited Victorian mores.

In this atmosphere Stevens's strong negative reaction to the pre-Columbian pieces was just as valuable in revealing attitudes and thus contributing to the substance of his work as his positive reaction to Villon or to any of the other things he liked. In some ways it was perhaps even more valuable because it precisely circumscribed an area of human experience that he was wholly unwilling to consider. In terms of the overt bestiality and violence that he despised in pre-Columbian art, contrasted with the hidden bestiality and violence in his poetry—and especially evident in *Harmonium*—his harsh judgment and refusal to examine both the pieces and his perception are very instructive.

The personality trait that Stevens had the greatest trouble managing was his violence, his desire to destroy. Whether inverted under the guise of self-sacrifice during his periods of asceticism or externalized as the macabre celebration of death and destruction in many of his poems, the impulse to hurt, punish, chastise, humiliate was with him. If he took on the role of comedian and transformed this impulse into the verbal wit for which he was noted, it was because he knew that the alternative to putting on the comic mask was far too dangerous to risk. Nonetheless, the mask did sometimes fall, as on that famous occasion with Ernest Hemingway after which Stevens ended up with a black eye and broken hand. (This incident will be discussed again in Volume II.) Had Stevens not had words available, this sort of thing could have become a regular feature of his life. It was in a profound yet practical sense that for him poetry was "a health," a "cure." His feelings of hatred, retaliation, frustration became words that killed. The heard and felt impact of their clashed edges, no matter how harsh, was already protectively mediated by reasoned restraint.

It was probably because many of the pre-Columbian artifacts—most notably the Aztec pieces—seemed to reflect the total absence of reasoned restraint that Stevens found them "hideous." It was not simply that in looking at them, he confronted his own deeply controlled and channeled destructive feelings. The creators of these works had not, in making them, imaginatively discharged their carnality. The objects were, rather, ritual aids or evidences of actual violent acts. Stevens felt particularly disturbed about the mythologizing of Indian cultures given to human sacrifice by individuals trying to establish and celebrate an indigenously American ethos. He flatly rejected equating this kind of paganism with that of the Greeks. He did not want the idea of modern America to be allied with these Indian cultures rather than with that of the Europeans simply because of geographical proximity.

Coming to terms with this marked Stevens's transition into his major phase. Having to articulate his feelings for himself and to those around him, like William Carlos Williams, clamoring for a purely native speech, meant Stevens had to expand his notion of native soil without ever having left it—except in imagination. He had to devise a coherent, convincing argument for forging a speech that was, in the broadest and best sense, universal yet still somehow tied to particularity—the thing itself. Bringing these seemingly contradictory elements into solution was in large part what enabled Stevens to evolve what was earlier called his "planetary consciousness" and to create a poetic idiom, an imaginative language, abstracted, "drawn off from," the form of pure reason. "Man's soil" was to be conceived, in Stevens's terms, as not only America but earth itself, the native speech not English but pure reason, expressed as pure music in words—"The Noble Rider and the Sound of Words."

It was because of this intention that near the end of his life Stevens was delighted that Renato Poggioli translated some of his poems into Italian. He wrote him that the project pleased him more than he could express and that he would regard its achievement as a "real trophy" (L 787). He had corresponded with Poggioli over a period of time, being meticulously careful in answering each of his questions and announcing that he wanted to be of every help in ensuring that the Italian would present as close an equivalent as possible. Poggioli's translation satisfied him that this was so. The lines phrased by him were, in Stevens's words, "as simple and exact" (L 787) as his own.

When this intention is fully understood, it becomes brilliantly clear why Stevens moved toward abstraction in his work, naming it as one of the three primary attributes of the "Supreme Fiction." Though his relative inaccessibility and difficulty were frequently blamed on this, often called his cerebral quality, quite ironically, wanting to make himself as universally accessible as possible was Stevens's implicit intellectual rationale for choosing structures of argument and terms of reference drawn from the vocabulary of pure reason. It is not hard to detect Gargantuan ambition lying behind this intention. The desire of the "Giant" to become "man number one" in relationship to poetry translated itself into an ambition as exaggerated as it was hidden. It surpassed even Whitman's epic expectation. Not only did Stevens want all Americans who would ever read him to derive through his lines their intimations of immortality, but he wanted anyone at any future time to have that possibility. Because of this, he knew that the local reality perceived through his particulars could not be limited by temporal references. In this he wanted to outdo even Dante, who obviously had achieved immortality but whose references bound him too closely, in Stevens's terms, to his historical moment. One must become a student of the medieval period in order to appreciate the *Divine Comedy* fully. Stevens was not satisfied to attain the stature and durability of figures like Homer, Dante, and Shakespeare. He wanted to go beyond even them.

Certainly, the more easily his poetry could be translated, the greater the chances for this kind of universality. And the more assiduously specific details of his period were excluded, the greater the applicability to any human being wanting to match his or her relation to the world against another's. It was not so much, then, that Stevens did not care about the wars of his generation, the political machinations of America's leaders, or the everyday pleasures and pains of his time—the sound of cart wheels or trolley bells, the news of corpses rotting in trenches, or the ironically "beautiful" mushroom cloud over Hiroshima[46]—but that he did not want future and faraway audiences to be prevented from perceiving the poems' disclosures by references that would particularize and consequently limit the experience being described.

As noble an intention as this was, it was also an elaborate rationalization. Yet it enabled Stevens to make what he did. He chose for precise and concrete reasons to abstract from reality and be "abstract," examine the subtlest "motions [of] his mythy mind" (*CP* 67) rather than the pithy substance of his days. He was historically prepared to tackle such a task, he had the ambition to attempt it, and looking and listening as carefully as he did to the beauty of innuendos occupied his attention and protected him from having to deal with any situation in which feelings he feared might "bathe him in tears" would be raised.

The grandiosity of the project Stevens envisioned reflected, among other things, the extreme lack of approval he had felt in relationship to his father. Had what he had accomplished at any point in his development been an occasion for Garrett, Sr.'s wholehearted praise, rather than yet another for renewed promptings to do better, it is unlikely that from the very outset of his poetic career Stevens would have planned the "Great Work" his "Grand Poem," a conception he refined along the way to be not even just an American "Great Work," but part of the world's.

One could argue that Stevens's ambition had nothing to do with any sense of emotional deprivation, that what prepared him to follow such a path was simply the kind of recognition and encouragement he received, which reinforced his privileged education and his exposure to a poetic tradition. He had come into contact with some of the best minds of his time as well as with those of his own generation who became the modern period's literary arbiters and patrons of the arts. All these individuals both practically helped and spiritually nourished him through the two major periods when he was "becoming a poet." Later, even after the disappointing reception of *Harmonium,* they continued with their support and pointed out the prejudices of critics and shortsightedness of the public as accounting for the response. Besides the ideal of the poetic "Great Work" being in the air since Mallarmé and the symbolists, and Whitman in America before that, there were Duchamp, Arensberg, Loy and others all talking about the importance of making such a contribution; the time needed a new vulgate of experience that would serve it in the way Dante's *Commedia* once had. (Arensberg himself was at work on the cryptography of Dante during this period.) While each of these elements played its part, none represented the deepest motivating factors; these showed themselves in Stevens's manner and bearing. If any or all of these aspects had been the generating causes of his choosing the project he did, he would have fulfilled the task proudly, "sure//Of the milk within the saltiest spurge" (*CP* 100), as it were. His confidence would have strengthened his speech. His wit would not have been biting. The shyness, which seemed to harden into taciturnity, would not have had to have been softened by alcohol. Had he had a realistic sense of himself, grounded securely in an awareness of self-worth derived from his parents, with his background, his contacts, the encouragement he received, his attachment to the avant-garde, he would have taken on the task as fitting. Instead of the incongruous, almost cowering reticence he felt and displayed—in spite of his desire to hide it in quietness or arrogant poking—there would have been a sense of towering competence much more in keeping with the stature everyone else perceived.

૨♦

Though the move to Hartford had obvious advantages, Stevens found himself missing New York "enormously," as he wrote to his novelist friend Ferdinand Reyher in early June 1916. He added—in a phrase he echoed poetically only a short time later, when he described the female figure in "Le Monocle de Mon Oncle," making believe her starry *connaissance*—that in spite of his nostalgia for that electric town he adored, "Mrs. Stevens, with murderous indifference, pretend[ed] that Hartford [was] sweet to her spirit."[47] It was fortunate for Elsie that she felt this way, especially since in the next three years she would be left to her own devices quite often and for extended periods—on two occasions for more than a month at a time. Even after completing the transfer and working exclusively for the Livestock branch of the Hartford, Stevens continued to travel a great deal, investigating the validity of loss claims and negotiating appropriate settlements. Frequently he was home for only a week or two at a time before going off once more for two or more weeks.

Elsie was used to their long summer separations, which continued after their move to Hartford—whenever and however Stevens could afford it. But these separations were different. Unless her mother or sister came to Hartford, as they sometimes did, she had no company the way she naturally had at the mountain resorts like the one in Woodstock that she came to enjoy and returned to over these next few summers. At home there were no pastimes like the painting, music, or golf lessons that she took advantage of during the summers. In their place, at first, were the demands of settling in a new place, making and hanging curtains, arranging furniture, buying necessary additions. But after these chores had been accomplished—in these years, because of changes in residence within Hartford, she experienced this three times—there was little during this period to call her attention beyond the everyday running of the household and her involvement with the piano. (Eventually Elsie joined the Musical Club of Hartford as well as two study groups, the Bard and Sage Club and the Charter Oak Study Club in which she remained fairly active until the move to Westerly Terrace in 1932; but for the present she did not have these diversions to fill her many empty hours and lonely days.)[48]

Unlike the summer separations, too, which were expected and planned, these others were irregular in every way. Each trip almost invariably lasted longer than first anticipated—at least longer than she anticipated. Stevens's usual habit was to write her and announce when he would return on his arrival at each of the cities from which he would begin to deal with the work at hand. (This often required him to go on to other cities or to visit smaller cities or towns and use the city of arrival as a base.) As the day of promised return approached, he would write or wire to tell her that he would be delayed two, three, five, ten days or more, depending on what he found waiting for him or on the directives from the home office, with which he maintained nightly contact.

Once back at home in Hartford, he never knew when he would have to leave again. Since he was with a new division of the company and was noted for his skill at settling claims, he was depended on a great deal. The nature of this aspect of the business was wholly unpredictable; when loss or damage occurred and a client claimed coverage, it simply had to be taken care of and taken care of well. Some cases involving large sums of money went on over years, requiring Stevens's periodic visits until they were settled. Occasionally he could combine a return visit to one of these sites with a call to a new claims area. In any case, during these years, Stevens's stays at home were more like stays at hotels while his stays at hotels assumed domestic regularity. And since the hotels where he stayed offered all the comforts of home and more, appealing to the American businessman's penchant for luxury, Stevens found that it was when he was away that his manner of life and surroundings more closely matched the imaginings he had begun to conjure years before, while still a law clerk, on some of his first visits to the home of W. C. Peckham, his employer.

In his well-appointed hotel rooms (one he especially liked in Minneapolis had even a working fireplace [WAS 1977, June 2, 1916]) he relaxed with big cigars and books before going down to dine on one of the chef's carefully prepared local specialties. Later he might write a note or letter to Elsie—if, that is, he was not in the middle of one of the poems he was composing or preparing one of the reports he had regularly to send back to the Hartford office. These two commitments demanded full concentration—the closely reasoned reports were models of concision that Henry James would have envied.[49] With his attention split between poems and reports, letters to Elsie became formulaic, in sharp contrast with the letters of their courtship, so full of lyricism and associative power. Elsie must have suffered. She was deprived of both his physical presence and his spirit. She read letters in which all too often identical phrases promised that this was the last trip for a long time, that she would go along next time, or that he had gotten impatient of being away. These sentences reappeared in places she would have wanted to see a spontaneously scribbled, "But I do miss you." She probably did not feel the full extent of her hurt and anger, however, since as he periodically repeated to her, he was doing all this "for her," "for them," "for their future." Under these circumstances it would have been difficult for her to see that she had other, more primary needs that were not being addressed, no less being attended to. Only someone with a great deal of self-assurance and an understanding of genuine equality in the partnership of the sexes could have recognized this. It was no wonder that there were "blow-ups of the nerves." Their causes were constant features of her life.

Since neither she nor her husband could have any way of knowing how long it would be before it was time for him to pack his bag and go off again; their times together during this second phase of their marriage had to have been characterized by pervasive and unspoken uneasiness. Had their personalities been precisely the opposite of what they were—if, that is, they had been relaxed, open, and secure—these periods could have been full of the intensity that uncertain days have (knowing that at any moment separation might come has made even the hell of wartime situations paradise for lovers). But given who they were the intensity inverted itself into tension. It was against this background that Stevens wrote "Le Monocle de Mon Oncle," one of the most direct, though characteristically cryptic, of the poems occasioned by the less than pleasing facts of their marriage. It was against this same background that the rest of the poems of *Harmonium* were written. And leaving this context behind contributed an additional element of pleasure to Stevens's periodic solitary trips to New York when he was back home in Hartford.

Because the letters to Elsie during these years were, with one or two exceptions, so formulaic, it is not particularly rewarding to quote from them. Indeed, and sadly, whatever had in the past gone into his letters to her that now did not find its way into a poem was addressed to those who appreciated him as a poet, as he once thought Elsie had. This category was for the present filled largely by Harriet Monroe and Ferdinand Reyher, who was conveniently traveling in places Stevens had wanted to visit and from which he at least received books and prints through Reyher. In his letters to these literary contacts Stevens displayed the playfulness he used to share with Elsie when he made up stories for her or drew the quick, witty portraits and descriptions that blossomed in his mind as he transformed the days' commonplaces into occasions for imaginings. Poor Elsie, poor Wallace—the more they maintained and strove for the appearances they had been prepared to present, the less possible it became for them to find any of the comfort they each had mistakenly foreseen in the other when it had been their longings rather than coming to terms with themselves in reality that determined their choices.

In the life he had shaped with Elsie, pleasures were increasingly confined to their place in imagination rather than indulged in reality. Poems, plans for the future, memories of what she once was, settings conjured in response to what he read or heard—all these gave pleasure. But in the practical world there was hard work to be done. Before Elsie, he took on more and more the role of responsible, respectable paterfamilias that his father had prepared for him. And even though it did give him satisfaction to do his work for the Hartford, thinking through intricate details and presenting them in an arrangement that had to seem true not only to him but to the various other parties involved in a case, he could not admit it.

It was as though, in some part of himself still tied to his religious background and in spite of his efforts against it, Stevens felt his work to be the Puritan test of election. Being forced to devote the better part of his energy to money-making deals, when what he really wanted was to give the best part of himself to poetry, yet to do the required labor diligently and well was a tribulation as difficult as any saintly test. The strain between these two aspects of his life, the dichotomy it set up, perversely motivated him to give himself fully to each of these diametrically opposed ends. The stronger his yearning to give himself wholly to poetry, the more seriously he proved his passion for it, "whip[ping] from [himself]/A . . . hullabaloo among the spheres" (*CP* 59) late at night, in hotel rooms, in odd moments on trains, on walks to and from the office. This meant that the sacrifice of making a living was all the greater. Being thrifty, sober, and industrious testified to his election. Conversely, the more successfully he applied himself to the work at hand, giving his attention to settling insurance claims, the more pressure he felt to find a day, an hour, when he could see the world arrange itself into a poem. Each extreme fed the other. Up and down between two elements Stevens moved, like the eye of the blackbird in "Thirteen Ways," the first of his poems to illustrate precisely what he meant by "It Must Be Abstract."

"Thirteen Ways" is abstract in its depiction and, because of that, pointed to many particular "facts" which had touched Stevens and from which he had "drawn off" the perceptions he voiced in the poem. "Facts," in Stevens's sense, were closest to William James's understanding of them as makings of the deepest sources of human nature. As critics have noted, one of the strongest "facts" affecting Stevens's composition of this poem seems to have been Hiroshige's ways of looking at Mount Fuji—renderings that contributed as well to "Six Significant Landscapes" (*CP* 73), written months earlier. With this anchorage as reference, it was easy to see both these poems primarily as attempts to describe epistemological problems in pictorial form and to account for their abstraction by saying that it reflected the nature of thought itself. Though these are, of course, accurate observations, they do not reveal enough about the deeper ways in which abstraction worked for Stevens. This cannot be appreciated unless the poem is put back in its temporal context and seen in relationship to other poems written about the same time. Doing this makes clear how Stevens used reality and also provides an understanding of the bases for some of his choices. Seeing this makes him seem more alive.

Before we consider particular poems or passages, it is important to realize the parts played in the composition of his poems by both Stevens's traveling and the kind of work he did for the Hartford. The group of poems written just before "Thirteen Ways" makes apparent some of the effects of his traveling. This group, "Primordia," came out in *Soil* in June 1916. Obviously drawn from changing landscapes he had seen in moving from one part of the country to another, it was composed of five poems under the heading of "In the Northwest," four under the headings of "In the South" and "To the Roaring Wind." Of these, Stevens selected only three for *Harmonium:* the last mentioned here, which closed the volume; "In the Carolinas" (*CP* 4); and "Indian River" (*CP* 112). These last two acquired titles only upon their inclusion in *Harmonium;* the others appear in *Opus Posthumous* (7–9). The first three poems as they were originally grouped in "Primordia" offered ungainly prototypes for three stanzas of the later "Thirteen Ways":

IN THE NORTHWEST

1

All over Minnesota
Cerise sopranos,
Walking in the snow,
Answer, humming,
The male voice of the wind in the dry leaves
Of the lake hollows.
For one,
The syllables of the gulls and of the crows
And of the blue-bird
Meet in the name
Of Jalmar Lillygreen.
There is his motion
In the flowing of black water.

2

The child's hair is of the color of the hay in the haystack,
    around which the four black horses stand.
There is the same color in the bellies of frogs, in clays,
    withered reeds, skins, wood, sunlight.

3

The blunt ice flows down the Mississippi,
At night.

In the morning, the clear river
Is full of reflections,
Beautiful alliterations of shadows and of
    things shadowed.

From the last two lines of the first poem Stevens abstracted two of the hauntingly powerful images of the moving blackbird and the moving river in "Thirteen Ways" (*CP* 92–95):

I
Among twenty snowy mountains,
The only moving thing
Was the eye of the blackbird.

. . . .

XII
The river is moving.
The blackbird must be flying.

From the tenderly observed particular images of child's hair and bellies of frogs, clays, wood, sunlight, in the second he abstracted the later poem's controlling metaphor:

IV
A man and a woman
Are one.
A man and a woman and a blackbird
Are one.

And from the description of ice moving down the Mississippi, from the morning's image full of "reflections," "alliterations of shadows and of things shadowed," he abstracted the central problem posed by "Thirteen Ways":

V
I do not know which to prefer,
The beauty of inflections
Or the beauty of innuendoes,
The blackbird whistling
Or just after.

    Stevens's decision to abstract from the particulars of perception derived from his trips back and forth across the country and to exclude from *Harmonium* the poems closer to those immediate perceptions reflected, at one and the same time, his desire to monumentalize himself as the author of a mythology of his region—in the way Homer mythologized the history and region of the Greeks—and his equally strong desire to turn away from the particularities of his experience. This he did with the distraction offered by meditating on how he could effect this mythologizing; he looked back at the already mediated perceptions that were earlier poems instead of focusing on new perceptions when he was back home in Hartford. If he had looked at Elsie and the details of their common life with the same attention he gave to changing scenes and weather from the windows of railroad cars, the feelings that were prompted would have "bathed him in tears" all too often. It was enough that he recorded them in the poems of his first volume that did result from attention to the domestic scene. "Le Monocle," "Peter Quince," "Domination of Black" are among the poems of this kind. And although they together provided the volume with its core of strength, Stevens knew he could not, without facing certain consequences, continue to examine the "facts" that generated those poems. He chose to look elsewhere, to the effects of wind and weather and to his own past words and perceptions contained in earlier poems and in the journals and letters of his youth. Nearing forty, the "ward of Cupido" (CP 16) chose evasion to celebrate the faith that imagination would save him from the hard, cold facts of his everyday world. It was a world he had fashioned in which he could survive. His opting to abstract was part of his ethical solution to the problem of his life.

Coming to this solution meant he had come to terms with justifying his image as the strong poet he envisioned himself against that provided by earlier strong poets. Stevens had to assert his way as being as viable as Whitman's, Milton's, Shakespeare's, or any of those others whose shades spoke to him of what they had had to conquer and transcend in order to proclaim their potency. So, interspersed in the lines of the poems he wrote now, as he faced what he had to transcend, were responses to those figures, responses that established his difference from them and posited his view against theirs. In Section III of "Six Significant Landscapes" he announced his difference from Whitman. While in "Song of Myself" the American bard identified even with ants, Stevens subtly answered, after announcing that he measured himself and found that he reached "right up to the sun"—certainly higher than the giant Whitman:

> Nevertheless, I dislike
> The way the ants crawl
> In and out of my shadow.
> (CP 74)

Similarly, in "Le Monocle" he held a dialogue with his romantic forefathers, with Villon, Milton, and with those more contemporary figures like Yeats, from whom he separated himself by asserting that he knew "no magic trees, no balmy boughs/No silver-ruddy, gold-vermilion fruits" (CP 16–17).[50] There are many more examples of this kind of definition of self throughout the poems of Harmonium. It is not necessary to indicate each of them, only to realize how preoccupied Stevens was with accomplishing his curious fate, becoming "man number one" at least in words.

In this connection it is important to note again that during this first serious phase of his career as an artist Stevens was as interested in the theater as he was in poetry—perhaps even more so. It was the terrible reaction of audience and critics to the production of *Carlos Among the Candles* that accounted for his turning away from theater, just as a few years later, after the reception of *Harmonium,* he turned away from poetry. Stevens's personality was fragile. In spite of the sustained encouragement he received from those close to him who recognized the significance and power of his work, he could not with equanimity accept rejection or, even worse, derision, from the larger world. His sense of self remained precarious, especially since he had failed so miserably in the primary relationship he once believed would "exceed all Faery." Though he had been awarded a prize for *Three Travelers Watch a Sunrise,* it did not mitigate the embarrassment he felt about *Carlos,* which had been solicited by the Wisconsin Players after *Three Travelers* had appeared.

Stevens had gone to a great deal of trouble to put *Carlos* together. To create the "poetic atmosphere" he wanted to support his central point about how we are created by what is around us, he even enlisted the help of John La Farge's son, Bancel, also a painter. He wanted La Farge to make the models for the backdrops. After reading the play Stevens sent him with his first request, La Farge expressed bewilderment and stated his inability to do the work because of his confusion. Stevens persisted, making a special trip to Mount Carmel, Connecticut, to meet La Farge and his wife, to whom he spoke about the dialogue of sonnets he had once had with Santayana (WAS 2551, October 23, 1917). La Farge finally accepted the commission. An additional element that had to be negotiated was payment. This Stevens managed to his advantage with his best attorney's skills. Unfortunately, however, the effect of the backdrops, once La Farge's sketches had been enlarged to fit them, was less than satisfactory. Worse, on its opening and only performance on October 20, at the Neighborhood Playhouse in New York, the actor forgot the central three of the play's twelve pages.

Luckily this first experience with theater production that had given Stevens "the horrors" (*L* 291) fell amid many successes. In spite of the failure of the production itself, Laura Sherry, the director of the Wisconsin Players, had praised Stevens's work as "by far the most significant of anyone in the country" and put him in the company of John Millington Synge, Anton Chekhov, Emile Verhaeren, George Bernard Shaw, and Hugo von Hoffmannsthal (WAS 2549, August 15, 1917). And even after its giant flop and the hostile, mocking New York press criticisms—clippings of which Stevens sent to Harriet Monroe (WAS 30, November 2, 1917) with a letter blaming himself for the play's failure (*L* 203)—Monroe echoed Laura Sherry's judgment. She still wanted to publish *Carlos* in *Poetry,* and she did in the December 1917 issue. On its appearance, it was, to Monroe's prideful Chicago delight, very favorably reviewed, and Stevens was named a "new champion in the arena of modernism" (WAS 31, December 14, 1917). Nonetheless, Stevens did not again give himself to playwrighting, though he believed, as he expressed in a letter to Reyher encouraging him to try his hand at it, that the theater was "far more important than it looks."

All through the months before and after this mortifying first night there continued to be a demand for his poetry and support from various individuals attached to the Arensberg and "Others" groups. In April Kreymborg had given him unqualified praise as a master, in addition to commending him most for the group of poems ("Valley Candle" [CP 51], "Thirteen Ways" [CP 92], "The Wind Shifts" [CP 83], "Meditation" [not reprinted], "Gray Room" [Palm 23]) that were to appear in a special issue of Others (December 1917), carrying the epigraph "A number for the mind's eye./Not to be read aloud." Kreymborg wrote: "One of the real satisfactions of my life in New York was meeting thee and thy work" (WAS 1514, April 9, 1917). In August 1917 Carl Zigrosser, editor of the Modern School, had written asking for a contribution. Stevens responded that he was at work on a number of things but was about to go away—to Woodstock, New York, to join Elsie for a couple of weeks—and would think of sorting things out after his return (L 203). Though he did not get back to Zigrosser until February 9, 1918 (he noted apologetically that he had had very little time to himself), he sent him what would turn out to be one of his most important poems, "Earthy Anecdote," which opened Harmonium and, later, The Collected Poems. After about ten days he followed up this poem with another, "The Apostrophe to Vincentine" (CP 52), which he thought Zigrosser might prefer since it apparently had less of what the editor thought "symbolism" but Stevens called "theory" in "Earthy Anecdote" (L 204). Zigrosser wisely kept both, publishing the first in the July 1918 issue and the other in December's.

Among the things that occupied Stevens's time, even when he was on holiday in Woodstock, was getting together and sending out another packet of poems to Harriet Monroe. No doubt because of her unflagging support and because she had been the first major editor to publish him, Stevens gave her priority in sending out new work especially since she never failed to ask him for more contributions, even on the rare occasions when she rejected something. From Woodstock, then, on September 1, 1917, he mailed her "Lettres d'un Soldat," together with the book on which they were based and from which he had borrowed sequentially dated epigraphs for each poem of the group. Projecting himself into the persona of a French soldier, substituting France for his motherland, Stevens again explored the theme of death: its connection to the idealism of national pride and sacrifice; the pressure it exerts that inescapably bestows value on surrounding objects; the effect on an individual of knowing he has killed. Comfortable behind this mask, in the thirteen of his poems submitted[51] Stevens played with some of the techniques characteristic of his mature style and set down some of the phrases and comparisons that appeared later attached to other terms. He used abrupt, unexpected contrasts and juggled incongruous concepts and sounds of words and names, like that conjuring "Death" as a "swipling flail" (*OP* 16), where the gayness of the impression created by the sound of the words is contradicted by the opaque impenetrability of even just the word "death." He again evoked the spirit of night as a female (as in "Six Significant Landscapes") but now more specifically and revealingly pointing to his relationship with Elsie: "Like a woman inhibiting passion" (*OP* 12). Death was once more associated with the mother, as in "Sunday Morning," but now even "mightier" (*OP* 14). He disturbed syntax, masterfully using punctuation to create seeming paralogisms that were nonetheless perfectly grammatical and thus doubly and provocatively ambivalent. This is clear in the connection suggested by the colon at the end of the first stanza below:

> Although life seems a goblin mummery
> These images return and are increased,
> As for a child in an oblivion:
>
> Even by mice—these scampered and are still.
> They cock small ears, more glistening and pale
> Than fragile volutes in a rose sea-shell.
>
> (*OP* 13–14)

Equally abrupt transitions characterized particular juxtaposed images, as here these stanzas with their curiously charming mice and beautifully evoked "fragile volutes" counterpointed by the later stanzas' images of death. In the eighth poem (as they appear and are numbered in *OP*), "an atmosphere/Of seeping rose" is followed immediately by a dash, as in his letters when he switched brusquely from something that touched his feelings to an outside, distracting perception; then comes "banal machine," an image that was repeated in various contexts throughout his corpus, as in "Sea Surface Full of Clouds" with its comparison of the ocean to a "machine" (*CP* 98–102).

Yet another poem in the sequence (VII in *OP* 14–15) was composed almost entirely of children's nonsense syllables: "And-a-rum-tum-tum . . ./ And-a-fee-and-a-fee-and-a-fee/And-a-fee-fo-fum. . . ," interrupted by French, "Voilà la vie, la vie, la vie," the "fee" for "la vie" thus subtly suggested as death. These elliptical, punning devices also appeared in later poems, transformations of the wordplay he had first used in his letters to Elsie during the years of their courtship—the same kind of wordplay Garrett, Sr., had used in letters to his son.

Finally, "Death that will never be satisfied" prefigured Stevens's image of the mind that could "never be satisfied . . . never" (*CP* 247). This pointed out a basis of identification between death and the mind, which syllogistically also included "mother" in the identification thereby establishing one of the most important of the poet's mental schemes. His fascination with mind— explored in all facets of his work—brought up feelings he could not escape for his mother and death. And all this came together at the moment when civilization as it had been known came to its death, together with the death of whatever was left of his hopes for a transcendent union with Elsie, the most "mysterious beauté" (OP 12).

All the elements for the continuing "Great Work" were now ready. Though he had not succeeded at the theater—much like Henry James—he incorporated the devices he had conceived for it into what he was writing. This was especially clear in some of the poems in the "Lettres d'un Soldat" sequence, in which at one point there are even parenthesized stage directions at the end of a poetic "Anecdotal Revery" (OP 13). Other incorporations were more subtle, but there was no doubt that dramatic form was becoming integrated into Stevens's conception of what was poetic. If the public was not ready for "Theatre without action or character," in spite of his belief that it "ought to be within the range of human interests" (L 203), he would do the obverse: create a poetic atmosphere informed by action and character, his own, each poem an instance of an ongoing imagined dialogue carried on by the various personae he assumed.

In accounting for Carlos's failure to Laura Sherry, Bancel La Farge observed simply that New York audiences were not able to appreciate "abstraction." "They do not want to think if they can help it," he commented (WAS 2554, February 13, 1918). People who attended theater in New York went largely to be entertained lightly and easily. They had gotten too used to Victor Herbert operettas and other musical comedies. Since Stevens himself delighted in these he could understand that if he wanted to force people to think, he would have to use another form, even though it was true that New York was slowly becoming more sophisticated.

The year 1917 had seen the first exhibition of the Society of Independent Artists at Grand Central Palace. Its opening on April 10 had coincided with Stevens's having had Kreymborg's praise heaped upon him. Since the organization of the Big Show, as it came to be known,[52] was managed largely, again, by Kreymborg's and Stevens's fellow "Others"—Arensberg, its managing director, and Pach, its treasurer, together with William Glackens, Charles Prendergast, and John Covert (Arensberg's cousin)[53]—it must have seemed to Stevens that the work he was doing was understood at least among those in this group to be in the same spirit as what was being represented in this exhibition. The model was the iconoclastic Société des Artistes Indépendants of Paris. The show was to have a wholly liberal platform: "No Jury—No Prizes." To oppose the dogmatic elitism of the National Academy, the intent was to present a display reflecting America's commitment to the struggle for world democracy. Inasmuch as President Wilson had declared war on Germany a few days before, it was easy for both participants and observers to draw the political and cultural implications. This many journalists and critics reviewing the show did, establishing "a direct connection between the democratic policies of the society [whoever paid an entry fee of one dollar and annual dues of five dollars was allowed to submit a work for the annual exhibition] and America's simultaneous struggle for political democracy."[54]

As was the case for the Armory Show, there is no direct evidence that Stevens attended the Big Show; still, it seems impossible that he did not. He was involved with the individuals who were putting it together as well as with many of the artists who would be showing. On the back of a delightful Italian postcard from Walter Pach, dated March 14, 1917, wishing Stevens a Happy Easter ("Buona Pasqua"), and noting that he was sorry to have missed Stevens and Mrs. Stevens when they last called, he commented on the enchanting quality of this kind of humorous Italian family portrait. But he added that this was "nothing compared to what the Society of Independent Artists exhibition [would] have" the following month (WAS 1350, March 14, 1917). Receiving this card at the office in an envelope (Pach observed that he did not want to shock any of the insurance company's officers or workers) must have delighted Stevens, seemingly so staid in his carefully tailored gray three-piece suit. Beneath the polished surface he presented, like the card in the envelope, was a revolutionary member of the avant-garde, a comic iconoclast, following closely in the tradition that another Hartford settler, Mark Twain, had established.

It was during this period that Jean Crotti, a Swiss painter married to Marcel Duchamp's sister, Suzanne, joined the Arensberg circle. He lived and worked for a while with Duchamp in the studio attached to the Arensbergs' apartment. One of the pieces he produced, a portrait of Duchamp made out of wire, which he exhibited at the Big Show, prompted the conservatives' ridicule of the avant-garde in the same way that Duchamp's *Nude Descending a Staircase* had done four years earlier. Crotti's Dada experiment hanging in Section C of the exhibit might even have contributed another associative element to Stevens's "Comedian as the Letter C." Beyond the parallel of Duchamp's consciously worn mask lending one of the bases for comparison, the artificial construction of the portrait itself, made out of wire—violently breaking from any tradition of realism or representation—was similar to Stevens's artificial construction of his poem out of all the possible sounds of the letter *c*.

Indeed, Crotti's portrait was perhaps even more representative of the avant-garde's purpose and effect than Duchamp's famous *Nude* had been. That work, facetiously compared in the press to "an explosion in a shingle factory," had come to stand, since its appearance at the Armory Show, not only as that show's but as the avant-garde's symbol.[55] But though Duchamp's canvas was strikingly unrealistic, it was still an attempt to render three dimensions in two, using traditional materials of paint and canvas. And though the moving figure depicted had recognizably mechanical elements about her, her forms grew out of the past: Duchamp's ties to the cubists and futurists were evident, no less than his indebtedness, following Degas, to the sequential photographs of Jules Marey and the experiments of Eadweard Muybridge.[56] Crotti's wire portrait, on the other hand, was completely alien and provoked not curiosity but outrage and open laughter as the only defenses the public could muster against this invasion into the once-sacred realm of art. It was neither painting nor sculpture; its material was wire, one of the most banal reminders of the technological underpinning that was being used more and more to hold the culture together.

Whether Stevens saw the Crotti portrait at the show or later discussed it with him and others at Arensberg's studio, the idea of it must have captivated him. It was a visual equivalent of the kinds of jokes he had liked to play since his childhood and youth. Though Stevens was not conscious of his own intent to shock the bourgeoisie, being ambivalent about the bohemian posture and not wanting to participate in its sense of "failure to equate its own activities with social ends,"[57] he was still in touch with his own impish impulses to tease and torment, preferably in as simultaneously shocking and hidden a way as possible. He recognized that Crotti—like Duchamp with his *Great Glass* and ready-mades—was waking the public from their all-too-sweet sleep, just as he had awakened his neighbor as a boy, shinnying up the lamppost in the dead of night to scrape off the green paint. They, like him, "Let the lamp affix its beam" on things as they were long enough to see, through their surfaces, the trembling present, the nothing that is not there and the nothing that is.

Though the stated premise of the Big Show and of the participating avant-garde had all to do with an envisioned political role for America and its artists, it was understandably—in light of work like Crotti's or Beatrice Wood's drawing of a nude with a cake of scallop shell-shaped soap in the place of her pudenda—difficult for the general public to apprehend this connection in spite of the many critics and journalists who were explicating how and why these new works expressed this. It is not surprising that Stevens—having everyday contact at the insurance company with individuals who made up this general public—chose to maintain his mild-mannered exterior. Disguised in reality as a well-dressed Connecticut Yankee, he could afford to adventure in imagination, even drawing on business associates, traveling or temporarily settled in different parts of the world, for facts he transformed into poems, fictions. From one such connection—in China during the summer of 1917— he asked for a detailed description of daily life and of the objects, shapes, and colors of his surroundings (WAS 546, June 25, 1917). These elements he combined and transmuted into the "necessary angel of reality," which touched his mind with its "wing of meaning," the knowledge of experience's concrete facts that provided the base for any poetic excursion. More and more over the years Stevens established correspondence with individuals in various parts of the world with whom he had little or no contact except the letters exchanged. From them he garnered the exotic facts he wanted. With them, *on paper,* he could again be himself as he had once been with Elsie.

Toward the end of 1917, after almost two years of continual traveling and periodic promises to Elsie that she would accompany him next time, he announced that he would take her with him to California in late January or February, when he expected to have to attend to some business there. He also wrote this to Harriet Monroe in a letter dated December 3, 1917, advising her that he planned to stop and see her on his way to or from the West. But as it happened, though he finally did find himself in Chicago in the middle of March, it was without Elsie.

One day he was in Indianapolis, where it was hot and close, and the next he was in Chicago, where it was cold and snowy. The sharp contrast to which his traveling exposed him contributed strongly to the kinds of contrasts he set up in his poems. He could not help feeling keenly with all his senses the effects on mood and manner prompted by sudden shifts. Knowing these, he learned to use words and sounds to create similar effects in his lines. But while he was quickly becoming the force of the weather he imagined himself, Elsie was quietly installed in their new residence at 210 Farmington Avenue, where they would live for the next seven years until their daughter had grown to the age that required them to get more space.

On this trip west, no doubt feeling guilty for once more not having brought Elsie along, he wrote her a letter every day. Each one seemed an attempt at convincing her that he was not having a good time (*L* 204–05; WAS 1996, March 15, 1918). Even if he had not had to go to California, there was no apparent reason why she should not have accompanied him to Indianapolis and Chicago, especially since she knew he liked the Windy City enough to imagine living there, as he had expressed to her a year or two earlier, and considering, too, that Harriet Monroe and her circle made so much of him. When he wrote of Monroe to Elsie, he mentioned only going over his "Lettres d'un Soldat" poems and weeding out the bad ones. (One of these, at least, "Lunar Paraphrase" [*CP* 107], he seems to have either thought better of later or reworked to make it so, as it appeared in the 1931 edition of *Harmonium;* the others [now I, VIII, and IX in *OP* 11–16] he simply used as ore from which he mined later ideas and images.) And when he wrote of the work at the office, he could only express how "bored" he was (WAS 1996) and bitter: "People run up their troublesome case until I come along and then expect the word of God to fall from my lips—as if I did not have to study and think, as everyone does." In describing the curious contradiction between what he thought people expected and how he had to work hard like everyone else, Stevens spontaneously and precisely fingered the core of his personality out of which the essential tension of his work was generated, the core against which words were spun, balancing it like the paths of electrons around an atomic nucleus. He wanted to be the God whose words shaped all of what was known. But he felt himself only an "Incapable master of all force," as he described the "creator" in "Negation" (*CP* 97), one of the poems he had just gone over with Monroe.

The reason he could not feel himself capable, never more than the "dilettante . . . half-wish, half-deed," he had feared as a youth he would become—"Half-man, half-star" (*CP* 18)—was made as explicit as it could be in this same poem. The ghost of his father echoing judgments still haunted him. The very word Garrett, Sr., had used to describe his son's poetry when he was still at Harvard, the word that then had the power to make Wallace channel his talent for "painting pictures in words" to the practical end of journalism was still resounding in his mind: "afflatus." Garrett, Sr., could tell, he wrote his son in 1897, from the evidence of the poems he had been sending his mother, that "the afflatus was not serious." In "Negation," by which Stevens may have hoped to negate the judgment of long ago, he drew a self-portrait showing how torn he felt, still "overwhelmed" by that judgment:

> Hi! The creator too is blind,
> Struggling toward his harmonious whole,
> Rejecting intermediate parts,
> Horrors and falsities and wrongs;
> Incapable master of all force,
> Too vague idealist, overwhelmed
> By an afflatus that persists.
> For this, then, we endure brief lives,
> The evanescent symmetries
> From that meticulous potter's thumb.

Even before conceiving the name of "Harmonium," Stevens saw himself struggling, in true Augustinian fashion, toward his "harmonious whole," like the Creator God whom he so delicately evoked and erased at the same time in implicitly comparing himself to Him. This was in keeping with the contradictory ways he felt about himself, as he expressed in his letter to Elsie from Chicago. The same duality was reflected in the Nietzschean mood of the "Lettres" group. (His preoccupation with Nietzsche was particularly obvious in "The Surprises of the Superhuman" [CP 98], in which both the suggestive title and the specific reference to "Übermenschlichkeit" [the idea of the superhuman] made this clear.) Stevens had read the German philosopher as "a young man," as he related (L 409) and not again until the early 1940s.[58] Before this time he had come to feel that Nietzsche had made things not more intelligible but "out of focus . . . as when one has a little bit too much to drink" (L 432). But this judgment was made more than twenty years later than the time he wrote this series of poems, a time when he still seemed to be exploring the viability of Nietzschean concepts. For the moment the philosopher of the superhuman served well as a reference point for Stevens's own ambivalent feelings: wanting to be God-like but knowing the notion of God to be bankrupt; wanting to feel himself free, strong, rid of the shadow of his father but still obviously tied to it. He conceived his voyaging to be an up and down between two elements.

ટ▲

One of the reasons Stevens felt himself so drawn to the avant-garde was that its values were so antithetical to those his father had extolled and represented, values Stevens had taken on and that now held him in their balance, rather than be held and weighed by him. He was one with the world in which he had been bred. He could no more give up his businessman's identity and success, being a pillar of society, than he could will his eyes to change color. The electrons were set securely spinning and hissing in their paths, and only a major disturbance could make them leap to other orbits. Fortunately the pattern of duality had been established early as well, and he counterbalanced his commitment to Calvinist virtues with a desire to escape or to destroy them; hence his intrigue with society's "lunatic fringe."

The visible consequences of this extreme tension were naturally contradictory. On the one hand, belonging to the avant-garde meant eschewing the bourgeois values that had led to the hideous fact of World War I. Consequently, Stevens wrote war poems about the innocent soldier's plight and the inanity of war itself. On the other hand, working for one of the burgeoning branches of the insurance business, which was profiting more and more from increased fears of loss, now exaggerated by almost immediately available news broadcasts of various kinds of disasters around the world, meant sharing national values and attitudes. And so Stevens expressed patriotic enthusiasm and vicarious aggression when he read of or observed evidences of the country's participation in armed conflict. This was more easily understandable before World War I had actually begun, when, for example, he believed that the United States had been too lenient in its recent Mexican involvement and should have used troops to take over. But even after knowing the staggeringly increasing death tolls of the Great War and hearing, through Harriet Monroe, of others, like D. H. Lawrence's firsthand reactions to its horrors, he was still able to muster mightily idealistic calls to action or proprietarily prideful remarks about the strength and ability of troops he saw exercising in different locations on his travels (*L* 206; WAS 2002, May 14, 1918). If he had uttered aloud some of the things he wrote in letters, he could easily have been thought a warmonger. In this aspect of himself it was clear that he had not yet escaped his Victorian heritage, which, among other things, had taught him that shedding one's crimson ribbons of blood for one's mother country was noble.[59]

Anyone stretched as tautly as Stevens between opposing poles was periodically going to experience moments of intense confusion and temporary lack of directed, coherent intention. A prime instance of this occurred during that March 1918 visit to Chicago when, as he wrote to Elsie, he had gone over the "Lettres d'un Soldat" poems with Harriet Monroe. Part of what he had not related to Elsie about what went on in Chicago was something about which he was very embarrassed, though he had also not written of his having met and spoken with Carl Sandburg[60] during an evening arranged by Monroe. Perhaps this was because he wanted to forget this evening, at least temporarily, if it was the same evening about which he later wrote Monroe a note of apology. In that note (*L* 206) Stevens asked Miss Monroe and her family to forgive him for his "gossip about death." He had had "the blooming horrors" thinking about it, he commented, and would have preferred to explain himself to her in person, but because he did not expect to be in Chicago for a good while, he had to write. Stevens had gone on, unconsciously it seemed, at least to him, about death "The subject absorbs me," he added, though he separated himself from the "too many people in the world, vitally involved, to whom it is infinitely more than a thing to think of." Near the end of this profusely contrite missive he penned distantly, "One forgets this," choosing the impersonal third-person pronoun for his subject.

Though he indicated that he was not "vitally involved" but dealt with death only as an idea, an abstraction, even if blooded by thought, what he revealed between the lines of this letter, and no doubt in person that evening, was the point at which the arrow of fear pierced him. This was the point at or around which nothing would suffice, neither the cool cynicism of the avant-gardist nor the proper patriotic zeal of the son of "good Puritans" and Daughters of the American Revolution. It wasn't that this was the first time he had found himself "pierced by a death" (CP 25). Death was, in his case, truly the "mother of beauty." It was the most constant theme of the poems he had written until now, even if he did treat it, as Monroe had put it, with a macabre, Aubrey Beardsley-like manner. But this was apparently the first time he had publicly displayed his obsession, and it continued to haunt him even more since he had done so.

It is important to point out here that this obsession was not, as it might first appear, simply a perverse predilection, the sign of a morbid personality, as might be said of Poe. Stevens was not being defensive or disingenuous when he expressed that he was concerned with death as an object of thought. Since his time at Harvard, when he had already begun to use the thread of imagination to stitch together his feelings and written stories shaded by the presence of death, Stevens had intellectually understood the most devastating effect of the end of the Christian myth. Coming to terms with what he had corroborated about our origins was not debilitating only to Darwin as he grew more neuresthenic with the accumulating facts of his discovery. Anyone who had been reared seriously observing the tenets of Christian dogma and who then had to give up the idea of heaven haunted by hymns and of reunion with loved ones in the hereafter could not help suffering in the face of the most threatening consequence of the loss of faith. Death now meant total and absolute annihilation. There was no hope of "imperishable bliss" and no newly created substitute myth to sustain human beings through the otherwise senseless pain that was an inescapable part of existence—pain that seemed to increase geometrically with each generation, as was glaringly apparent in the years beginning with the First World War. Almost as though to confirm that nature was no less irrational and cruel than its noblest creatures, the influenza epidemic that broke out in 1918 had claimed 22 million by 1920.[61] Even measured against the enormousness of the war's losses—8.5 million dead, 21 million wounded, 7.5 million missing or imprisoned, losses exceeding the combined number of those fallen in all previously recorded wars—this was still greater and seemingly more uncontrollable. In the face of this massive irrationality, suddenly there was nothing that could be counted as even a possible reason or cause. Things simply were as they were. As Stevens expressed in "Gubbinal," a poem he wrote in 1921, when his disillusionment was complete:

> Have it your way.
>
> The world is ugly,
> And the people are sad.
> (*CP* 85)

By this time he not only had had to absorb the idea of the great number of men that were falling, and feel again, through it, the ironic scraping of memories of his parents' deaths, but had had to confront the ultimate experience of death's painful arbitrariness: the loss of his younger sister Mary Katharine (known as Katharine; Stevens referred to her variously as Catharine and Catherine). She had become ill and died in France on May 21, 1919; she had been a Red Cross volunteer.

The year before this tragedy Stevens had explored his obsession with an eye sharply focused through "Le Monocle de Mon Oncle"—after "Sunday Morning" the next major poem to address the consequences of believing in fictions used to protect us from directly facing that "first, foremost law." Through working on this poem, Stevens came to a temporary acceptance of things as they were. He contemplated moving "downward to darkness" with equanimity. The lines describing his descent were as graceful as the pigeons gliding down in casual, unconscious undulations from the building faces of quiet Hartford in late afternoon as he began his walk home. Like one of the "men accomplishing/Their curious fates in war," whom he conjured in the deceptively pedestrian-paced lines of his poem (*CP* 16), he warred. His enemies were those whose myths had once cushioned him from feeling the crude but real fact of death as simple nothingness.[62] Fighting with words that killed relieved him of some of his long-held hostility, so in the poems following "Le Monocle" his attention was freer. Instead of dealing only with his internal world, the battleground where he waged the combat with his studious ghosts, he again turned to the outside world and wrote a number of poems of place or, at least, poems the first stirrings of which were occasioned by visions of real, external landscapes.

These poems, some of which constituted a part of the group published under the title of "Pecksniffiana" in October 1919's *Poetry,* represented responses to what he saw on his extended business trips in 1918 and the first half of 1919—to Tennessee, Florida, the Gulf States, Wisconsin—until he received the news of his sister's death in late May. "Fabliau of Florida" (*CP* 23), "Homunculus et La Belle Étoile" (*CP* 25), "Ploughing on Sunday" (*CP* 20), "Nomad Exquisite" (*CP* 95), and "Life Is Motion" (*CP* 83) belong to this group (only the first three appeared in *Poetry*). Though they each turn around a meditative center evoked by both their repeated images and rhythms, they also clearly belonged to a world outside the poet, the changing locales in which he found himself. Chugging across America in the train's glass coach, he imagined it "ploughing" through the vast distance. Feeling the inescapable rhythm, he began composing "Ploughing on Sunday," later in his hotel room fixing it firmly with a play on one of the meanings of "plough"—the device for making contact with the live rail—he either found in the *Webster's* at the office or simply knew, having picked up the specialized reference from one of the many things he read to satisfy his rapaciously encyclopedic interests. Sitting in his room in cold Milwaukee, working on poems he had brought along (WAS 2009, May 6, 1919)—still incomplete records of visions feeding his memory from earlier trips in warmer climes—he embroidered the pattern of particular sensory details (like the incessant droning of the surf he remembered from Florida) with the magnificently multicolored threads arrayed in his imagination.

These poems were different from those composed before and around the time of "Le Monocle" ("Depression Before Spring" [*CP* 63], "The Death of a Soldier" [*CP* 97], "The Apostrophe to Vincentine" [*CP* 52], "Nuances of a Theme by Williams" [*CP* 18]), all of which had to do with absence, like the particular longing he felt in the Hermitage Hotel in Nashville, Tennessee, in spring 1918 to find a hermitage at the center of his being into which he could retreat. Unable to, he did not speak of having found it until nearly the end of his life, when he wrote the poem indicating precisely how and why the paltriest aspects of the quotidian become transformed by imagination (*CP* 505). Now, in middle age, he was still looking for "the desired" to complete him, fill the absence. He searched in exalted realms, in unspoiled nature, in Florida, and in imagination's pure light—the atmosphere he depicted carefully in "Architecture" (*OP* 16), a poem he also wrote during this period. He sent it as part of his second solicited contribution to the *Little Review*. As "Architecture for the Adoration of Beauty" (a title profaning the sacred subject of the Adoration of the Magi for a particular end), it appeared together with "Nuances of a Theme by Williams" and "Anecdote of Canna" (*CP* 55). At the same time "Le Monocle" appeared in *Others,* and "The Apostrophe to Vincentine" came out in the *Modern School.* This was December 1918—a red-letter month for Stevens. Appearing in three journals simultaneously was not something he would have anticipated. Moreover, the second request from the editor of the *Little Review* meant not only had he stretched himself between the poles represented by *Poetry* and *Others,* but he was now also displaying his muzzy belly in the territory staked out by Pound and Wyndham Lewis, who were on the *Review*'s editorial board.

Composing "Architecture," Stevens addressed himself to defining precisely what made his poems, his style. He named it, as he named each instance touching the quick of his being, his sexuality—as later, in "Sea Surface Full of Clouds"—in French: *chasteté,* his actual chastity enforced by distance when he was away from Elsie and, all too often, by either her or his own reticence when he was with her. Chastity bred his thought, his imaginings, as he cleverly and elliptically indicated by the masterful counterpointing of the sentence of chastity he imposed on himself grammatically in the poem:

. . . .
Let us design a chastel de chasteté.
De pensée. . . .

. . . .

He immured himself in his lines mimicking the way the word "chaste" is captured in the old French spelling of *chastel*. Against this, he juxtaposed the open-ended "De pensée. . . ," incomplete as thought always would be as he attempted to complete his reality, fill his absence with fecund images of "the desired." These images would be, as indeed they proved to be in the later poems of *Harmonium*, "lusty" and "plenteous," like the women he wanted but appeared to enjoy only in his mind. This poem was sent to the journal the issues of which that very same year were burned by the United States Post Office for the installments they contained of Joyce's *Ulysses*. But "Architecture" was so filled with the distracting "poetry of the subject"—arcane words and specialized meanings—that censors could not detect that what Stevens, disguised as comedian, described was far more prurient than the pages they put to flames for inflaming them. Not even the lustiest conceit was too lusty for his broadening, except that he did it as a supremely clever playwright, able to direct the whole play of reality dressed in his mild-mannered barrister's costume. Who would suspect him?

Stevens built the edifice of his "Architecture" very carefully, pointing out his difference from Pound and Lewis and their followers while incorporating Monroe's earlier perception of his "gargoyle grin." He asked, "What niggling forms of gargoyle patter," would distinguish his "speech" amid the "obedient pillars" of a society now facing its collective guilt about the war and its fears of being contaminated by the corrupting influence of increasing numbers of immigrants flooding its shores and displaced children and grandchildren of slaves moving up from the South's soft belly. He would lock his meaning in lawyer's "closes," as he specified in this poem, while playing as well on the architecturally apt reference of "close." Delighting in his ability, after long years of study and practice of both law and letters, he selected his scholarly metaphor precisely. As he well knew, a close is, among other things, "an ideal boundary being there in legal *fiction*" (italics mine). From here he found a name for his poetic idea, his "supreme fiction," its "ideal boundary" marked out by lines drawn long ago, limited only by his aspiration. The aspiration included his desire to be a playwright, which, though frustrated, had never died. Abandoning the project for symbolist drama without character and action—wisely understanding that the public reaction to it, at least in New York, would continue to be like the reactions to the work of Duchamp and his other avant-garde friends—Stevens turned his eye back to a form that included character and action but so arranged that it gave no occasion for direct audience identification. This was central since his severe criticism of the values they held, if he voiced it directly, would mean a fatal blow to his possibility of success. He began, then, investigating the forms of the *commedia dell'arte*. By February 1920 he was immersed in descriptions of its latest manifestation in eighteenth-century Venice, having begun in late 1918 to explore its general forms and beginnings.

Though there was little available in English on the *commedia* before the late 1920s, there had been a number of articles in the journal the *Mask*, beginning in 1910 and 1911, that Stevens could have followed. There was also J. A. Symonds's work on Shakespeare's sources, which touched heavily on the *commedia*, and his 1890 translation of the *Memoirs* of Carlo Gozzi, the eighteenth-century Venetian scenario writer who, with his rival Carlo Goldoni, was responsible for transmitting the tradition of the *commedia* into their time.[63] It is likely that Stevens was familiar with these texts from his Harvard involvement with the work of those actively preserving what they thought most important and beautiful from the classical and Renaissance pasts. In addition, since Stevens read German he also had A. W. Schlegel's general survey of dramatic forms available. He probably consulted these texts before trying to get his own copies of a study of eighteenth-century Italy by Vernon Lee (pseudonym of Violet Paget) and Philippe Monnier's *Venise au XVIIIe siècle* (WAS 1558, November 23, 1920), two of the three available book-length studies in English and French before 1926. The third, Winifred Smith's *The Commedia dell'Arte: A Study in Italian Popular Comedy*, was published by the Columbia University Press in 1912, and it is possible that Stevens found in its bibliography the references to the other two more specialized studies, though he could easily have gotten to Lee from having read one of his articles in the *Mask*.[64] In any case, from the evidence that began to appear in the poems of 1919—his naming of Crispine in "Piano Practice at the Academy of the Holy Angels" (*OP* 21), for example—it is clear that Stevens himself had already started practicing with the elements borrowed from the *commedia* that he managed with masterful virtuosity in 1921 with "The Comedian as the Letter C," the hero of which, Crispin, is—in addition to his other aspects—a development of the *commedia*'s Crispin.

For Stevens, the attraction of the *commedia*'s form in eighteenth-century Venice was dual. On the one hand, following the genius of Gozzi and Goldoni, its forms and characters became secularized, as it were, transformed into more generalized societal types. On the other hand, it became even more stylized and artificial, with marionettes designed to play the traditional roles (the full array is still on display in Venice). In other words, the *commedia*'s forms had become so familiar, so natural a part of the culture by the eighteenth century that in Venice, in Paris and various other locations in Germany, Holland, and the rest of Europe, it could itself be adapted and used as the basis of different new forms (like the Punch and Judy shows in England) and be referred to as the vulgate of comic theater. As such, it was an effective and pleasing artistic instrument for maintaining and modifying social mores—the theoretical realization Meredith and Bergson expanded with eloquence.

Stevens recognized the appropriateness of the form and its history and development because his own relationship to the cast of characters and texts of the past was very much like the relationship of the *commedia* in the eighteenth century to its past, which dated all the way back to the Greeks and Romans, like some of the oldest characters and plot outlines stored in the "old actor's trunk" of Stevens's imagination. It was also similar to the relationship Stevens saw the Bible's having to its past uses. Its formal aspects—images, sounds, rhythms, plots—all were still perfectly viable, just like the *commedia*'s in the eighteenth century, but because of the striking changes in the social order caused by the new world views developing out of science, these aspects had to be made to reappear familiar while carrying the new knowledge and spirit of the age.

Beyond the formal appropriateness of borrowing elements from it, there were more immediate reasons for Stevens's sympathy for the *commedia*. He had in his youth delighted in reciting lines of Paul Verlaine, his favorite symbolist poet, as he noted, who was himself particularly drawn to the *commedia* and the idea of it through the paintings of Watteau.[65] In responding to the *commedia* through Verlaine's *Fêtes Galantes* Stevens was sharing what those gathered in Parisian ateliers looking at Picasso's Harlequin series and listening to and seeing Satie's *Parade* had heard of the Italian comedy's spirit through Verlaine and other French poets of the late nineteenth century who found the characters so appealing. Stevens had early and easily fallen into these roles when he was courting Elsie, addressing her variously as Columbine and Sylvie and himself playing the corresponding Pierrot and Harlequin. There was the poignant recognition of himself, too, in considering the function of the mask in the *commedia*. As Goldoni expressed in his *Memoirs* (which Stevens did read, having ordered a copy on November 23, 1920, which he received sometime before May 13, 1921 [WAS 1558–1561] though he could also have found the description quoted in H. C. Chatfield-Taylor's 1913 biography of the playwright): Though the actor "may gesticulate and change his tone as often as he will, he can never communicate by the expression of his face the passions that rend his soul."[66] But adopting masks could take care of this.

Against a completely fragmented national and world background, it was quite difficult for the super-sensitive poets, painters, and composers to reveal openly the passions rending their souls, especially since they were part of a generation raised to keep face, to maintain appearances in true Victorian fashion. Stevens, who had been experiencing various effects of the accelerating disintegration of the old world view over a long period, suddenly had everything that was painful about his time brought into much sharper focus by the death of his sister. It was as though in confronting this sad fact, as well as in having come into contact, around the same time, with other details of family news, he was once more looking at himself reflected in the glass of his relationship to others and facing the consequences of his attention or inattention to them. Dealing with these matters was shattering; he was shattering just as the culture was, and for many of the same reasons. In the face of this breakup it was even more necessary to wear masks. Acting through them, with them, would allow him to say things, do things, he could not possibly do without them—for fear of being bathed in tears by the pathos of everything.

In his family, he had recently learned after visiting his uncle Harry once more (WAS 2011, May 12, 1919), the progress of the times that now made Stevens feel about Reading the way, as he put it, one would feel "returning from the wars and finding one's best beloved married to a coon" (L 219) also wrought other depressing changes. His other sister, Elizabeth, was so displaced that she had married "a while back" a man twenty-one years her senior; she had recently had a baby. Stevens had had no inkling of either event. Miss Hatch (John Stevens's sister-in-law, who now lived with Uncle Harry in Evanston, Illinois) also related the "usual discouraging news" about Garrett, Jr. He was not doing at all well professionally, and his wife was suffering one illness after another, including "influenza." Only John and his wife seemed to be doing all right—at least on the evidence of a photograph Miss Hatch showed him in which the youngest Mrs. Stevens appeared to be stouter than Stevens remembered her. But, then, John and she had remained in Reading; they had not followed the times. Stevens's response to all this news was to observe to Elsie, with his mask carefully in place: "Well, family affairs are a bore, anyhow, aren't they? It might not be so if we were all millionaires, but not even John, who seems to be so successful, is a millionaire. Uncle Harry is interested in all this sort of thing." The only good part of the visit was Stevens's anticipation of once more having the strawberry shortcake he had had on an earlier visit.

Just two weeks later the news of Katharine's death undid him, as he related in a letter to Elsie (L 212), and he named some of the specific effects of historical changes that had colored the experience of his and his sister's generations: being forced to be away from home to make a living; feeling isolated, often helpless; knowing there was no familial home to which to return. As he wrote of these things, he was away from his home, had been away for more than two months already, and would not return for another week or so. He, too, was serving the cause of progress and belief in the American way, though differently from Katharine. He was even setting money aside, investing it in bonds that Elsie would profit from in the future, as he noted to allay the effect of his present restriction on her (WAS 2010, May 9, 1919). His energies, like those of all who continued in their attempt to make the American dream a reality, were largely diverted from their present sources. The great machine age had begun, and in spite of the explosion of World War I, it could not stop. To ensure that it wouldn't, each of its parts had to work as efficiently as possible for longer and longer days. Only the year before, daylight savings time had been instituted to eke out the last bit of productivity from hot, sticky summer days.

Katharine's death also touched the lingering sting of his mother's death. He put it this way in another letter to Elsie about how terribly he felt about the loss of this wholly "good" young woman with a voice like honey, whom all the soldiers had loved: "In many ways, she was extremely like my mother; so that the loss of her, ends that aspect of life. I am more like my mother than my father. The rest, I think, all resemble my father most" (*L* 213–14). He closed this letter noting paternally—as though to show he was like his father as well, not "extremely like [his] mother," as Katharine was—that with the little money he was enclosing, if Elsie were careful, she should be able to open her savings account with seventy-five dollars on his return (WAS 2014, May 29, 1919). The dreaminess and pure good-heartedness he associated with his mother now remained—as far as he was concerned—only with him and not as completely as it had in his dead sister. These qualities he attached to the values of the age that had passed, a gentle age still able to afford the indulgence of imagination. What his mother and sister had represented was very unlike the progressive age his father had symbolized, devoted to nothing so much as to reason, applying it to everything in the hope that through it, if not through God, the march of human perfectability would continue. Stevens felt himself the product of both these individuals and was still torn between them. It was as natural to be like one and want to do only what was "good"—dream and sing songs of praise phrased as his poems—as it was to be like the other and feel he had to safeguard for the future, work as hard as he could so that he could receive the sign of material prosperity as the mark of his election.

Katharine's death reopened the profound fissure in Stevens's nature, into which the thousands of additional fragments bursting from the current state of affairs in the world tumbled wildly. He was aware of them and watched them fall. He realized that he needed more than one voice to describe all he saw and felt. The imaginative flexibility offered by the various forms and characters of the *commedia dell'arte* over the generations of its existence was something from which he would never cease to profit.

In one of the guises he assumed, he was able—as race riots raged in Chicago—to write "Exposition of the Contents of a Cab" (*OP* 20), a poem that, though he felt he had not learned how to manage in form as yet (*L* 214), revealed his deepest feelings more directly than almost anything else he had as yet composed:

> Victoria Clementina, negress,
> Took seven white dogs
> To ride in a cab.
>
> Bells of the dogs chinked.
> Harness of the horses shuffled
> Like brazen shells.
>
> Oh-hé-hé! Fragrant puppets
> By the green lake pallors,
> She too is flesh,

And a breech-cloth might wear,
Netted of topaz and ruby
And savage blooms;

Thridding the squawkiest jungle
In a golden sedan,
White dogs at bay.

What breech-cloth might you wear—
Except linen, embroidered
By elderly women?

The sharp contradiction between the ambiguity of reference and the intention to expose stated by the poem's title and illustrated by *its* contents reflected the tension of Stevens's being. This, combined with the painfully stressed comparison of the imagined black woman, Victoria Clementina, to the "you" of the last stanza, expressed the poet's sense of the situation in which he, and his culture, found themselves. One of the most important but least addressed effects of the influx to the Northeast of immigrants and southern blacks was the contrast in attitudes toward sexuality. Stevens's figure of the Negress, with a name that carried connotations of both Victoria's prudish reign and the weight of a European past, perfectly embodied this effect. She was dressed in her name, as he in his staid three-piece suit. She took with her—into the nineteenth-century vehicle that would carry her, like the regular forms the poet consistently returned to using—seven white dogs, her sharply defined indulgences, simultaneously sins and virtues. They were, colloquially, the men-about-town, "dogs," to whom she would yield her favors. In the same way Stevens indulged the fantasies that allowed him to continue, to go on, as in the cab. Because they remained in the realm of fantasy, he could remain in reality, following the Victorian morality he could not shed any more easily than the negress could shed her name. Nonetheless, the desires pointed to were sinful.

The stage and character Stevens set here were as savagely comic as any devised by the masters of the *commedia*. Beyond this, imagining the "true," "brazen" reality of the black woman satisfied Stevens's concupiscence, as he conjured elaborately around the "breech-cloth" she might wear. Here was a metaphoric illustration of the kind of completion indulging poetry allowed. The poet devised her in her native environment where she would have her "white dogs at bay," controlling them instead of being threatened by them, as she would have to be with all of them in the cab with her. In the imagined native place the vehicle would become a "golden sedan," like the perfected vehicle of his verse, where he kept his dogs at bay, his fantasies controlled in measured lines.

Exhibiting his mastery and the mark that distinguished his particular trick and talent, Stevens inserted a word borrowed from his "scholar's art" (as he defined poetry [*OP* 167], in prideful contrast with his contemporaries like

Williams and Bynner; even after Stevens's death the latter was still arguing this essential point with his shade).[67] At first reading, "Thridding" seems to have been chosen for the sound it successfully suggests of a sedan threading through jungle undergrowth so thick it snaps back into place after each forward disturbing movement of the cab born by barefoot natives, whose steps fall in dull thuds on the lush tropical floor. As the "poetry of the subject" this is what the word describes. But when the "true subject"—the "squawkiest jungle" made up of the sounds of his words—is explored, "Thridding" reveals something else. It is not just a variant form of "threading," which clever readers have already guessed. As the obsolete form of "third," prevalent down to the sixteenth century, it means an "illustration of forms"—just what Stevens exposed about how poetry functioned for him.

Stevens's reluctance to publish this poem, which Monroe obviously either overcame or ignored—though Stevens again repressed it, not including it in *Harmonium* or in *The Collected Poems*—might have had to do with how successfully he had managed the exposition he intended. Or it might have had to do with an appropriate sensitivity to the possibility of its being misunderstood, either because of the negress with her questionable morality or because of the open sexual content. It is more likely, however, that he felt that the last stanza—precisely because there is no possibility of positively identifying the "you" addressed—might have been misinterpreted by too many, especially those who would read the "you" as himself dressed in another of his many female costumes. Whoever the "you," or as many as it contained, it clearly was the same one whose death he celebrated rather than grieved three years later in "The Emperor of Ice-Cream." By that time he might have believed the reign of Victoria really was dead, as the sinuous sounds of jazz notes and the rising of hemlines almost to reveal "breech-cloths" had begun against all the forces of restraint and even legal Prohibition. (The law was passed earlier in the year Stevens wrote "Exposition," though it was not put into effect until the following year.) It might have seemed in 1922, while Stevens composed the lines for the funeral oration of "The Emperor" that the laws made by the contemporary "good Puritans" could not contain the forces of what they associated with "black magic," any more than kitchen cups could contain the concupiscent curds Stevens whipped.

The music and manner of the blacks, and of those who settled into America well beyond its teeming shores, came to show how dumb to feeling the children of the latter-day saints were. Stevens knew this as well as he knew the locations of the livelier gin mills, which he called—feigning his own genteel feigning—places where the "potato sauterne was both good and inexpensive" (WAS 1557, September 25, 1920). During this time of America's great awakening to the end of its innocence, after World War I, as he gathered his forces to shape the poems that would soon make up his first volume and weighed himself in the scale of middle age only to find himself wanting, Stevens tried for the last time to whip from himself a jovial hullabaloo among the spheres. He tried, in other words—not his own—to break through the restraint he had worn all his life, at least in the way he lived in his imagination, if not in his everyday world.

૨**ી**

At this point in his development Stevens tried to acknowledge feelings more directly and attempted, too, to find an avenue of communication, other than his poems, to express them. With the recognition he now had of the devastating effects of his Puritan background and gentlemanly training, he wanted to act, in some arena at least, in ways that transcended or ignored the forms he had learned from the society of dry men and elderly women. He began this conscious effort almost immediately after his sister's death.

Rather than keep his feelings to himself, as he had about his parents' deaths, he openly expressed to Elsie that he was "completely done up" (L 212) about Katharine and, following this direct admission, went on in the same letter to thank her for reacting with "such good grace" to the ongoing and seemingly endless postponements of his return from this latest stay away. His next breath carried an even more direct description of feeling, perhaps one of the most sincere and spontaneous she had received since their marriage. His words seemed to be shaped around a deep sigh of sadness that could only be relieved by imaginings of peaceful domesticity: "I am as tired of being away from home as it is possible to be . . ." (L 213). "I suppose that when I get home, the window boxes will be in place and that everything will be bright and fresh. I hope so" (WAS 2013).

Four days later he was not reticent to admit he was still overwrought. The Memorial Day parade he saw in Milwaukee "on account of Catharine [sic],"[68] he wrote to Elsie (WAS 2015), "affected [him] deeply. There was a group of women, war-mothers, each of whom carried a gold-star flag, which it was impossible to continue to look at." The next day, a Sunday, writing to her after dinner from the public room of the hotel where in addition to the guests, local women looking for companionship and families on their sabbatical outing gathered, he mentioned one of his most private weaknesses in a touchingly spontaneous manner: "They blow into this room, where one does one's writing, and I swear it is a job for a man, even if he has only one good ear, to think of what he is doing" (WAS 2016). Particularly sensitized now to his having only one good ear probably because of Katharine's having died of mastoiditis, he felt he shared something with her—his hearing loss most likely also the result of childhood mastoiditis. He had never remarked on this impairment before (in the papers as they remain) and never would again. Yet this was an enormously important detail to reveal (as he no doubt knew in his self-consciousness about leaving things behind for posterity). Not knowing this little fact would be like not knowing a painter was color-blind and trying to account for the muted quality of his palette by describing the pigment sources in his place and time or by illustrating how this stylistic element derived from an earlier painter.

Knowing that Stevens had only one good ear is like calling on the "necessary angel of reality" to read the poems. Being deaf or partially deaf in one ear is said to make the head itself seem either a complex percussion instrument like a piano or, by extension, a performing orchestra. One side is like the bass holding and repeating, resounding with the deep whoosh and whir of internal tones as it responds to the tonal waves from outside. The other side, open to all the multitudinous sounds of the outside world, receives, as it were, the countless variations played in the treble.

> The whole of life that still remained in him
> Dwindled to one sound strumming in his ear,
> Ubiquitous concussion, slap and sigh,
> Polyphony beyond his baton's thrust.
>
> *(CP* 28)

The masterful orchestration of Stevens's poetry was not just an intellectualized application of what he had learned from Mallarmé and the symbolists in their adulation of Poe with his gift for musicality or from the connected art for art's sake aesthetic with its desire to have all poetry aspire to the state of music. Stevens's meticulous attention to poetic sound effects also represented his intention to reproduce as closely as he could the way he heard, the way he felt, moving about in constant physical disequilibrium. "Moving up and down between two elements" was as literal in a precise sense as it was a metaphorical description of the way he felt from the time of his childhood about his relationship to others, to ideas, to the strain of being a rational animal torn between imagination and reality. One part of him heard continuous whispering of "heavenly labials" in the "world of gutturals" (*CP* 7) in which he lived.

In now calling his own attention to this physical disability and later choosing to make it public (since the letter containing this bit of information was not one of those destroyed), Stevens focused on another of the distinctive marks of his genius. For the present he was preparing elements to compound in his long epic venture, "The Comedian as the Letter C," which he was to compose within the next two years. There, all the complicate interrelationships of sound and rhythm, playing around the most protean letter of the alphabet—the one letter that would thus best provide the theme for all possible variations—were fully exploited. He had already begun to experiment with the sounds of *c* in "Architecture." He had also begun to include in almost every poem at least one scholarly word to serve as the key unlocking the "true subject" from the "poetry of the subject." Very often the word was one with which he was familiar from his legal training and perusals through old torts and law dictionaries.

In trying to reproduce the way the world sounded to him, Stevens was also doing what composers like Stravinsky and Satie were doing with their innovative orchestrations that re-created the blares of automobile horns, tempos of industry, even the clickety-clack of typewriter keys—as in *Parade.* This attempt to render the present's actual sounds rather than sounds that echoed only internal states, as the pure symbolist composers had done, represented a major change in the way a composer saw himself. It was a change that paralleled some of the aspects of cubism. But more, it prefigured the abstract action painting best known through the work of Jackson Pollock, in which the artist tried to show himself as the moving indicator of what was around him and at the same time the instrument of that indication, the particular rendering. It was this Stevens had attempted to communicate, as he described, in *Carlos Among the Candles:* "The effect was intended to show that we are what is around us."

Though this perception had obvious intellectual roots in the deterministic-mechanistic world view that had been gaining strength as Darwin and, later, Freud became more integrated into the culture, whether celebrated as masters or fearfully scorned as instruments of the devil, it was not so much this that was behind Stevens's intent, even if, as part of the spirit of his age it provided one of the strongest bases for his perception. Stevens was more particularly concerned with the actual physical manifestation of his *being.* The individual was no more than what was around him. He was the receptor of wave vibrations at different frequencies arrayed in changing patterns. These patterns, in turn, were determined by interaction with all other surrounding forces and by the discharging energies of memories and thoughts, which together *seemed* to guide a way through the other forces. It was this concern with the basic physical facts of existence that made Stevens "perceive the essence of the poet" in Giordano Bruno, as the "orator of the Copernican Theory" (*OP* 183); in Gottfried Wilhelm Leibniz, who was able to subordinate his language to the idea of the universe he had derived from the facts of scientific discoveries (*OP* 185–87); and, most recently, in Max Planck, "the patriarch of all modern physics" (*OP* 201). These men were, in Stevens's late mind (the lecture-essay elucidating these preferences and judgments was composed in 1951), more "poets" than Lucretius, Milton, Pope, or Wordsworth, who wrote "philosophic poetry" but were not direct "descendants of Socrates"—not young enough when they composed their poems "to be concerned with the self, not in the sense common to youthful poets, but in the major sense common to the descendants of Socrates" (*OP* 188).

Stevens wanted to see the self as something completely a part of the world. He understood that Socrates gave his attention to language and its function as the indicator of human interactions within the polis when it was clear that for a while at least, there could be no further confirmation of the natural philosophers' speculations about the structure of physical reality. Turning to language and the structure of thought was the only practical thing to do. At least there could be an attempt at agreement on the use of words describing the structures that had already been perceived. What Bruno, Leibniz, and Planck had in common—and the reason Stevens saw them as "descendants of Socrates" and the "truest" poets—was that they all understood the structure of reality as unitary and interactive, with human beings' place in it just another manifestation of the interaction. The shared view of all these men ennobled the idea of man by reducing it. Stevens called this reduction to the "first idea," the "basic slate," the "ultimate hue." The only possibility of experiencing greatness was to perceive oneself as the "merest minuscule in the gales" (*CP* 29) as he described his hero, Crispin. His cipher, "C," was also a metaphor for the speed of light, the invisible element that makes all things visible—the nothing that is not there and the nothing that is.

Stevens had been prepared to come to terms with this way of seeing the relation of a man to his world (which he also admired in Pascal, who voiced it piously) from his long training as a "good Puritan." He had learned well that in order to feel the power of the Almighty, one must become small, "as a little child." This knowledge was reinforced by what he once thought would be the antidote to the inevitable and devastating effects of Calvinism: his involvement, beginning during his "rebellious" years at Harvard, with the art and thought of the East. But it was the pressure of a real fact, Katharine's loss, that was the catalyst at this moment—a moment thickened with determinants into a rich mixture. His reaction to this death transformed his intellectual apprehension of himself as "a small part of the pantomime" (*CP* 93) into an emotional response so deep that it forced him to relinquish the ultimately human quality of pride. He had to come to terms with not being the center of the universe, while contradictorily knowing this to be the only possible perspective from which a human being can view the universe sprawled out all around—like the "slovenly wilderness" in the "Anecdote" he was just now composing about the "jar" he felt in himself about this realization. Before this understanding was canonized as the philosophy of existentialism and neatly categorized in Jean-Paul Sartre's terms and formulas—which, like all conceptualizations, weakened the force of reality generating it—it was much more necessary for an individual himself to resolve this duality in perspective, this absurdity of our relation to the world, which only exists, ultimately, in the language used to describe that relation. Stevens and his contemporaries did not yet have the convenient names that could soothe them into feeling that somehow because others had experienced and rationally classified the absurdity, it was no longer absurd, painful, and constantly threatening.

As noted earlier, Stevens had had the intellectual understanding of this, the ultimate condition of modernism, for a while and had already begun exploring it poetically. One of the primary functions of the figure of "Le Monocle de Mon Oncle" was to raise the central problem of perspectival duality that characterizes perception—vision through a monocle being different from vision through the other eye and from normal binocular vision. Just like the viewing of ourselves as centers of the universe, the monocle, though it helps its user to operate, nonetheless presents a greatly circumscribed area for consideration. Both devices produce a "more than rational distortion" (*CP* 406). Similarly, in other poems, Stevens attempted to consider reality not from his usual monocular perspective but from his planetary perspective, as in "Thirteen Ways." Yet even with these attempts to embody the terms of his abstract apprehension of these things through poetry's completion, he had not then succeeded in breaking through the oldest and strongest walls of his defenses to accept fully how insignificant he was. Still afraid to admit this, he continued to aspire to be "man number one," to disdain others whenever he felt threatened, to control whatever he could control—Elsie, underlings at the office, money (the easiest material to manage, making it seem to every miser that he is a god exercising power)—rather than feel, but not acknowledge, the helpless and frightened child he still knew lived inside him.

However, the impact of Katharine's death broke down Stevens's walls, at least for a while. Before he could repair them, he felt and saw in ways he had never experienced before. It was as though her death were to him what the death of God was to Nietzsche and the death of 8.5 million in the war was to the culture, the event that made it impossible—again at least for a while—to maintain any fiction about the sense of human participation in the world. The only sense came out of the way each moment, as it passed, was managed. The important thing was to regard as many of the myriad aspects of the present as possible, as Walter Pater had realized—though in a time when only very few were willing to see anything beyond the "aesthete's" point—and to enter into a relationship with these aspects. The optimal state was to choreograph these elements into an intricately beautiful and delicate dance of death. For individuals as seriously committed to acting on realizations, as Stevens was, this attention also extended to other people, insofar as they, too, impinged on the present. This meant taking the "other" into consideration, attempting by whatever means to broaden each moment to its fullest by being aware of what was around him. Yet, when he began to do this, he knew that the most important "other" for him was not able to exist beyond the fictions he had created for her.

For the first time in the fifteen years he had known her, Stevens tried to attend to who Elsie was. He tried, as much as he was able without violating her further, to make their relationship work. He sincerely urged her to come along on the next trip he took and equally sincerely wrote to her when she didn't about why and how he wished she had accompanied him. He wanted to include her in his literary life once more, inviting Amy Lowell and Harriet Monroe to Hartford at different times to have dinner with them, rather than limit his meetings with them and the others who formed part of the charmed circle of people enchanted by words to afternoons around impersonal restaurant tables and evenings in salons.

Stevens began to examine and act on the full range of his feelings. As he had done in sharing with Elsie how distraught he was about the loss of Katharine, he continued to be open with her—something he had never done easily, not even with himself, especially not since he had given up keeping a journal years before. When he stopped in Reading on his way back from a short late July 1919 trip to Philadelphia, he related that the "brief survey of the holy city left on [his] mind a most afflicting impression" (WAS 2017). Inflated

diction notwithstanding, simply the ability to tell her he was suffering represented a major change, a change commensurate with that which had come
over Reading. It was more than twenty years since he had left. Then his vision
of it as his *fons Bandusiae* was not incompatible with the way it actually was,
the countryside still pristine enough to serve as the source of an American
Horace's pastoral imaginings. The changes had come slowly, so that even for
years after he could preserve his vision. It remained the standard against which
he measured all other places he visited (*L* 207). But on his seeing it again
now, after seven years (since his mother's funeral in 1912), it could no longer
contain his imaginings or serve as a constant term in his comparisons. Reading's transformation into a dingy, depressed industrial city was complete. To
Stevens's mind it was as unnatural as if a butterfly had turned into a larva, an
ugly grub, imago become ghost. In his "affliction," he appropriately associated it to the "holy city," as distant and inaccessible as the idea of heaven
across the "wide water" in "Sunday Morning." Both were equally unreal,
equally impossible to sustain as wished-for refuges. He was now completely
disinherited. The place where he was born was as divorced from actuality as
the idea of heaven. "Is it a myth that we were ever born?" he had to ask.

His response came in poems. Both "Cortège for Rosenbloom" and "Banal
Sojourn" mourned his own passing insofar as he had identified himself with
the place that had made him feel a "Giant." In the middle of the road of his
life Stevens as the "Comedian" he had made himself abandoned hope that
things as they were could offer him what he required to be happy. He now
recognized the final facts as death and change. Against them he was powerless.
Regardless of his successes—both in the practical world and in the world of
imagination—he did not feel the strength he had been prepared to expect by
the ethic with which he had been reared and which he had dutifully followed,
in spite of himself and his periodic, yet expected and excusable, lapses. These
times of weakness were, after all, according to his tradition, tests of faith.
Each recovery from indulgence or depression, then, was another proof of fortitude, and fortitude evidenced election.

Though none of this was on the surface (Stevens at this point would no
doubt have bitingly derided the notion that he was, in fact, a "good Puritan"), it was at the core of his personality. If it were not, he would have been
able to yield—in reality rather than in imagination alone—to the many se-
ductions tempting his spirit from the time he left Harvard. He would have
been able to take the chances of which he dreamed: going off to Paris,
London, Berlin; leading the purely "literary life" that charmed him; escaping
the rules and regulations of conventional bourgeois marriage and going off
adventurously, as the couple he had so envied whom he described to Elsie in
the last months before their own marriage. But the trap of his Calvinist upbringing held him all the while and still. In spite of giving up the promise of
heaven and accepting the imperfect as his only paradise, he could not escape
the driving force of the work ethic, especially now that he had grown used to

its rewards. As he noted on more than one occasion, he had developed a taste for endives and Rhine wines (*L* 431). Bumming it in some attic where the cupboard was bare simply would not do.

But at this juncture giving up hope meant a healthy acceptance of himself and the choices he had made, though the acceptance did not come without self-mockery and mourning; hence the peculiarly and grotesquely comic tone of "Cortège for Rosenbloom." Who was "Rosenbloom" if not the idealistic "*rose* rabbi" (italics mine) who in the *bloom* of his youth had had hope and considered the future through the proverbial rose-colored glasses? And why was he a Jew if not because the attributes Stevens and his culture associated with the Jew were the very same as those Stevens recognized all too well in himself? From the time of that dinner table argument years before in the boardinghouse about Jews as "gold medal boys," his strong but ambivalent identification with them was clear: He, too, strove to succeed; he, too, was a scholar; he, too, had attended the concerts where he had offhandedly but slurringly commented on their presence; he, too, was given to "feasting" instead of "fasting."

Stevens supplied an additional clue identifying himself with Rosenbloom and the subject of the poem in a letter to Harriet Monroe in December 1920 in which he referred to himself as an "overblown bloom" (*L* 220). More, "bloom" was a word that appeared in some of his most revealing poems, "Le Monocle de Mon Oncle" and "Sea Surface Full of Clouds." Through a play on one of its more arcane meanings—one he would have known from his company of painter friends, if not from one of his adventures amid dictionary columns—he used it to refer to himself hiding behind the opaque surface of his "poetry of the subject." In painters' vocabulary, "bloom" refers to the cloudiness varnish takes on under certain conditions, thus obscuring the carefully drawn lines and tones beneath it. In addition, "finical," the adjective he used in the second line of "Cortège," was the same one he used to describe himself in lightly apologizing to Monroe for being perhaps overly meticulous about the set of proofs he corrected for "Pecksniffiana" (on August 27, 1919). And during the same summer he had compared himself and Elsie to her as "two grave diggers" themselves, in spending the hot months in Hartford, suffering the malady of the quotidian (*L* 215).

"Cortège," then, prefigured "The Emperor," as a mock funeral for his romantic self, the youth who had hoped and dreamed. (The "wizened one/Of the color of horn" of the second stanza of "Cortège" [*CP* 80] reappeared with "horny feet" in "The Emperor.") Appropriately his "carriers," "the infants of misanthropes/And the infants of nothingness," whom he later identified as "sources of the strictest prose" (*L* 464), bore him not to an earthly grave but to "a place in the sky." Done with the pain of earth—"One has a malady, here, a malady. One feels a malady" (*CP* 63)—tired of his "banal sojourn" in the imperfect, as he expressed in the poem of that title (which he explicated as "a poem of exhaustion . . . of any experience that has grown monotonous, as, for example, the experience of life" [*L* 464]), he now moved solidly into the home where he had early felt he belonged: the sky, his "Jovian atelier." From now on he would regard the world from above as one already dead, like a child asleep in its own life.

The months passed, marked by success after success, like the phases of the moon he imagined he had become, showing himself more and more but then again hiding in silence. At the moments he became aware that he had exposed more of his feelings, he quickly withdrew. So, in May 1920, he complained to Elsie in a letter he wrote her from Erie, Pennsylvania, where he was once again away on business, that he had not had a poem in his head for a month (*L* 219). What had been in his head he had sent in fragments to Harriet Monroe in a letter on April 25 (*L* 218). There, in one of the parts of a projected "First Poem for the Meditation of Infants," he described himself in terms of his new planetary avatar, though he generalized it to include all "Earth creatures, two-legged years, suns, winters. . . . " In the same letter to Monroe he also showed his strongly humorous side. This was in marked contrast with the more or less straightforward reportage tinged with tones of tiredness or irony that now filled his letters to Elsie, as he revealed to her the other side of how he was.

But even before the month when he found himself without a poem in his head, he had withdrawn. In New York on February 13, 1920, for example, he did not go to see a production of his *Three Travelers Watch a Sunrise*. While he had already turned away from the theater, this kind of indifference must have been somewhat feigned, though he tried to persuade Monroe that his lack of interest was "truth, not pose" (*L* 216). He observed that this period of withdrawal extended to his poetry. It was perhaps his reading of Carl Sandburg's *Cornhuskers*[69] and rereading some of Eliot's poems (collected in his *Ara Vus Prec* [1919]), that set his simmering mind to hissing and accounted for this temporary halt. He was again measuring himself. In spite of the continuing interest in and encouragement of his work, Stevens remained his own harshest critic. His eye was the microscope of potency, searching out spots of weakness. He felt he had to strengthen himself, cure them, before going on.

This was also another of those periods when business directed Stevens's life and, it seems, did not even allow him enough leisure to compose himself so that he could compose his poems. He had been back and forth to Washington, D.C., several times in the fall of 1919, and now in spring of 1920, beginning with his stay in Erie and moving between there, Youngstown, and Cleveland, Ohio, he would be away and wholly absorbed for more than a month in the most important thing he had ever done for the Hartford. This was the longest trip since that to Tennessee years before. The deal was such a big one— "riding a whale," he described it (WAS 2022, May 30, 1930)—that he was losing sleep (WAS 2021) and, worse, would have to stay away even through Elsie's thirty-seventh birthday. In the same letter in which he told her of this, he sincerely and tenderly expressed his desire that she come out and meet him and spend a few days. He was "distressed" to think of her at home alone. He attempted to soothe her with an aphorism his father might have used: "Be patient . . . for the largest excursion has an end in time." But he added his particular formula: "Nobody would enjoy being at home just now more than I." In the next letter he again described his regret at not being able to be with her on her birthday as well as his disappointment at not having succeeded in convincing her to come out and join him (L 220). This letter had pages excised, so it is impossible to know how direct he was about his feelings. But in a letter written a little more than two weeks earlier (L 219), he had expressed that he was aware of how "abominably" his long absences "upset life at home," and in this one he opened by apologizing that the letters he had written since that one were so distracted, less than she expected. It is more than likely, then, that in the cut portion of this June 5 letter he elaborated as fully as he could both in recompense and in preparation for his return the next week.

The next week came, but he did not return as promised. On June 12 he wrote her again, apologizing profusely and empathizing with how she must have "felt like a widow." But this was, he stressed, the "most difficult situation the Hartford ever had" (WAS 2024). Like a modern-day Ulysses accounting for his delay to a patient Penelope, he went on to strengthen his case by describing how bored he was, how uncomfortable in the now-approaching summer heat in his heavy winter suit, how "blood-curdling" the people with whom he was dealing. Nevertheless, he had met an interesting painter, Ivan Olinsky, who had things in the museum there, so he was not entirely alone. If of nothing else, they could speak of Adolph Alexander Weinman, whom Olinsky knew and who was just now finishing up a bronze bust of Elsie that Stevens had commissioned. If he was not writing more often or more extended, detailed letters, it was because he had to give so much energy to his business letters and reports. One, of only one page, which felt to him like a "death warrant," had taken two hours to get down. He was so worried about what consequences might entail if he made just one mistake. Clever ellipticality and ambiguity were necessary but had to be made to seem solid fact.

To assuage what he imagined as Elsie's frustration, Stevens pointed out, in closing this letter, that she should not be "too put off" since the tremendous effort he was extending now was "worth more than a year of work at [his] desk." It "will help us," he assured her. What he did not indicate was that in addition to this promised material reward, which alone might have been enough to convince himself that his investment of energy was worth it, he was learning a great deal about his craft in exercising his skills in suggestive compression that seemed fixed truth. Consequently, what he began to write after this temporary withdrawal from poetry's sphere was different from what had come before. Though his vision broadened, taking in more from his imagined aerial point of view, his forms became tighter, containing in regularity as controlled as his business reports, references not only to a momentary occasion but to all the associations from the past as evoked by the particular present occasion. The improvisatory movements so close to jazz riffs that had characterized earlier poems now yielded to older classical progressions. "The Man

Whose Pharynx Was Bad" (*CP* 96), "The Doctor of Geneva" (*CP* 24), "The Snow Man" (*CP* 9), "Tea at the Palaz of Hoon" (*CP* 65), "On the Manner of Addressing Clouds" (*CP* 55), "Of Heaven Considered as a Tomb" (*CP* 56), "The Bird with the Coppery, Keen Claws" (*CP* 82) all illustrated this shift and prepared the way for "The Comedian as the Letter C," his most extended classical exercise.

Though Stevens had been trying for a year or so, since his sister's death, to be more attentive to Elsie and though he had included her in at least some aspects of his "literary life," the damage already done to their relationship was too great to permit renewal. It could have been that the last long absence had truly "upset things at home" beyond repair, for by July 12, 1920, about a month after his return, Elsie seems to have withdrawn quite seriously. A note to her mother written on that date shows her handwriting to have become minuscule, rigidly controlled, with her capital *E* etched in a new and fragmented way. She, too, had been touched "as by a death," reduced, but she did not have the compensation her husband found in words.

With her in this state, what Stevens particularly could not share was sexuality, not even in words. His feelings about this he projected in a judgment he made about an article about sex appearing awhile later in *Harper's* magazine (a magazine he did not care for). "You [he was writing to Ferdinand Reyher] know, we have reached a point about sex where we can put it in our pipes and smoke it" (WAS 1561). And as he wrote to him again, apropos of John Rodker's volume *Hymns* (Rodker, a poet who had published in *Poetry,* ran The Ovid Press in England; Stevens purchased many things from him and made Rodker one of his "correspondent friends"), they were so "creative and procreative," so full of "libidos," it was "necessary to keep the book hidden in the piano" (WAS 1557, September 25, 1920). If he was not being humorously hyperbolic here, it meant that even that instrument of pleasure could no longer be played.

Though Stevens found himself intimately wanting in the scale of middle age, he continued to balance himself with regular movements through the phases of his poetic career. In November 1920 he won the Helen Haire Levinson Prize of $200 for "Pecksniffiana." Feeling the weight of this honor compensating for any uncertainty he might have felt on reading Pound's *Hugh Selwyn Mauberley*, which Rodker had sent him from London a few months before (WAS 1583, July 28, 1920), he worked on a "batch of things" in the fall of 1920. But he did not forward these to Monroe before going through another dark phase. "[I] prefer to allow your panegyrics [the Levinson Prize] to fade a little out of mind before I reappear" (*L* 221), he wrote her on December 2. In the quiet of his own withdrawal he studied: the eighteenth century in Venice, Lucien Pissarro's woodcuts, and much more about China and Japan.[70]

As he worked on perfecting his voice, he sharpened his judgments about what was being done around him. Responding to Reyher's request from London to send copies of good, new literary journals, he replied that there weren't any, only *Contact,* which he would forward. He noted that Arensberg was still promising the *summum bonum* to rival the *Atlantic Monthly,* but it was still in a "process of gestation." About the *Dial,* in comparison, he commented that it was mere "foppery." And to Reyher's inquiries about what he thought about establishing a pure American diction, he answered with what he also expressed in weightier words to William Carlos Williams (as recorded in the Introduction to *Kora in Hell*): "The idea of developing a purely American strain is not wunderschön. Ober, lieber Gott ["wonderful. But, dear God"], the result would be, after all, nothing more than a purely American strain" (WAS 1559, January 31, 1921). He added, as though to dismiss the entire subject from consideration, that "literary theorizing [was his] idea of nothing to do"—at least for the time. To keep Reyher abreast of what everyday life was like on this side of the Atlantic, he related that he was seeing lots of Pitts Sanborn in New York. Sanborn was about to publish a volume of sonnets not at all to Stevens's liking. He closed his letter displaying a bit of his old self-effacement, noting that he did not want to write too often in fear that his friend might feel a debt to respond more than he would have liked.

_&_

With the twenties begun, though not yet roaring, the United States still feeling implicit guilt for having lost comparatively few (53,513 battle deaths; 63,195 other deaths) in the war that decimated its European cousins and, more, for becoming increasingly prosperous while the Continent truly had become a wasteland, excitement on the cultural front came from the expatriate travelers and sippers of apéritifs in Parisian cafés. Robert McAlmon, editor of *Contact,* another of those whom Stevens came to know through letters, married Bryher (Winifred Ellerman) on Valentine's Day 1921. In a letter to Harriet Monroe dated March 24, Stevens commented on "how strange it was that Lochinvar McAlmon should have been picked up by the seat of his breeches and carried to her rocky lair by the intense Miss Bryher just after [Monroe] had spoken to [him] of her desire to remain in this country" (L 221–22). Pitts Sanborn also went off to Europe and North Africa for a few months and dutifully kept Stevens posted of news there. On his return in late fall he filled Stevens in with all the details of chats with James Joyce and bicycling in southern France with Wyndham Lewis (WAS 1564). Even Alfred Kreymborg, who had trouble affording lunch in New York, went abroad that late spring (with Harold Loeb), heading for Florence and Rome, where he would publish *Broom.* (Stevens would not be impressed with the result, though he had looked forward to it [L 223].)

All his friends and correspondent-friends were more than attentive to the "Giant" at home, both while on their travels and on their returns. McAlmon, Rodker, and Reyher periodically sent Stevens books or prints he had asked them to scout for. He either sent money or balanced payment with things they wanted from stateside. (Stevens sent Reyher Sinclair Lewis's *Main Street,* for example, in June 1921 as representative of one of the most successful and popular new things.) McAlmon was particularly indulgent of Stevens, even sending him a silk tie from Paris as a gift—an "offering," he called it—in addition to the glazed fruits and honeys he knew the poet liked. He thought the tie would be especially well suited for the friend whom he felt to be like himself: "I realize that emotionally you aren't any more sophisticated than I am, for all our ironic whining, and grand display of cerebration and intellect" (WAS 1150, July 20, 1921).

Stevens was vicariously enjoying the Continental experience through these contacts; he actively pursued this vicariousness, bidding Reyher to search out Rodker, another good friend he knew only "on paper"—"Have a drink on me" (WAS 1561, May 13, 1921), he added playfully. He equally delighted in being able to "command himself" once more in the letters he wrote, communicating openly "there" whatever he felt strongly about: "the emotional purpose of rhythm," his hope to forge an "aesthetic of free verse," or why Matisse and Cézanne (all of whose work he had seen, he noted, and of whom he had read everything he could without having found "a word of common sense on the subject yet") were more interesting than Gauguin (WAS 1561).

Amid the excited flurry of literary exchanges Stevens was hard at work. His travel this summer was limited to a trip in September up the river to Woodstock. He noted in a letter to Monroe that Elsie would not be too pleased about the crowded boat trip, "hobnobbing with so many Jews" (WAS 714, September 2, 1921). Whether or not this was true of Elsie, Stevens's return to this derogatory cultural cliché probably represented some kind of bitterness. This remark might have been the result of his resentment at not being free to expand himself with a trip across the European horizon. Or, it could have been, too, that this attitude belonged to an unspoken code existing among members of a particular group. It was shared, for example, by McAlmon, who described the literary powers in Paris as "a madhouse of Jews talking antiquity—in search of 'form'—they will express the mystic intensely inherent in the race somehow. Cold science and intellect can be reasoned to the ultimate mystery aussi" (WAS 1150). Among the group of literati with whom Stevens felt at ease, this kind of comment was not unacceptable, as though the McAlmons and Stevenses of the country implicitly felt they had to unite against a menace posed by those most astute foreign devils. As McAlmon expressed about the *Dial* group, "They are snobs—confuse art with the conglomeration of Jewish, Russian, sex-obsessed and seriously [?] untrue" (WAS 1158).

Yet Stevens himself, as he had already made apparent, was ambivalent about Jews. He wanted to share in their disposition to "feasting" rather than "fasting"; he admired the secular erudition of rabbis—"When I was a boy I was brought up to think that rabbis were men who spent their time getting wisdom. And I rather think that this is true. One doesn't feel the same way, for instance, about priests or about a Protestant pastor, who are almost exclusively religious figures" (L 751). Nonetheless, he, like so many of his compatriots, was subject to uttering the anti-Semitic slur that unthinkingly

511

bespoke and bespeaks the West's oldest prejudice, which is, perhaps, at bottom, a defense against admitting that the millenial promise offered by Christianity and its concomitant myth of progress and eventual redemption—if, that is, one learns how to live and what to do—was and is just a promise. The characteristic though forced posture of the Jews as outsiders without a deep-rooted commitment to place (until, again, very recently) historically fostered their ability to stand apart, observe, and comment on the culture around them and naturally produced the ironic attitude associated with them, an irony that included an implicit negative judgment on the "others" who, in their terms, foolishly believed the Messiah to have come.

To consider Stevens's anti-Semitic remarks in this light is not to exculpate him from indulging his prejudice any more than any explanation of a prejudice exculpates those who maintain it. Framing his lapses in the broader cultural background, rather, only allows us to see how strong a part the irrational element can play even in the most rational of lives. Later in his life Stevens closely examined this element both in himself and in general terms, and it might not be unrelated that during World War II he was instrumental in helping Jewish emigrés find positions in this country. In any case, by sharing the verbal swipes at the Jews Stevens was, as in almost all aspects of himself, revealing how very "American" he was, while by sharing with the Jews a deep sense of irony about "things as they are," he declared his sympathy for them.

That Stevens viewed irony as a cardinal virtue is clear not only from his own cultivation of it, but also from his comments about Donald Evans, another poet who moved in his circles, but who came to an early end after his wife "ran off with a lounge lizard," as Stevens put it in a letter to Reyher. Quite apart from anything having to do with Jews or anti-Semitism—I believe Evans was not a Jew—he went on to note to Reyher that this poet was "one of the great ironists, one of the pure littérateurs" (WAS 1562, June 1, 1921). Though he might have believed Evans to be an incipient rival when he was alive,[71] he could praise him now that he no longer posed a threat and could even perhaps feel fortunate, for once, about Elsie's all-American proclivity to propriety and wholesomeness—even if she was now wholly immersed in her enjoyment of *Good Housekeeping* fiction (WAS 3984, August 30, 1921)[72] while he hid Rodker's *Hymns* in the piano. Her not being able to share his enthusiasm about the exquisite new aesthetic he practiced and contemplated was small price to pay for the security of knowing he would never be driven to the edge of despair. The life of a Connecticut Yankee had its advantages, though it meant only short vacations to Woodstock from the busy insurance world. There was still imaginary voyaging in strange seas of thought, helped at times perhaps by "potato sauterne" or the "corn liquor" he recommended for a poet whose work he found "suggestive" but far too "attenuated" (L 222). While there were some who found his own most recent things "hideous ghosts of [him]self" (L 223), he would go.

Thus he conceived his voyaging to be an up and down between two elements, the facts of his limitations, the fictions of his desires. If he didn't travel overseas in reality, he did in imagination. And so his hero Crispin was born, fully dressed in the costume Stevens had been preparing for years. Now, doing last-minute alterations, adding embellishments and flourishes, he trumpeted his arrival on the scene:

Hartford, December 21 [1921]

DEAR MISS MONROE:

I return your greetings, most sincerely, and in these Mrs. Stevens joins, although possibly, in her case, rather gingerly, for I have made life a bore for all and several since the announcement of the Blindman prize [a prize for a poem offered through the Poetry Society of South Carolina] in your last issue. To wit: I have been churning and churning [as the roller of big cigars later would churn "concupiscent curds"] producing, however, a very rancid butter, which I intend to submit in that competition, for what it may be worth, which, at the moment, isn't much. But what's the use of offering prizes if people don't make an effort to capture them. My poem is still very incomplete, and most imperfect and I have very little time to give it. But I am determined to have a fling at least and possibly to go through the damndest doldrums of regret later on. But Merry Xmas and a happy New Year to you and to your house.

Always sincerely yours,
WALLACE STEVENS
(*L* 224)

Composing this longest poem was the most formative experience of Stevens's poetic career. He knew it while he was immersed in first doing it and, later, when revising it the summer after it had not won the prize for which he conceived it. Amy Lowell, the only judge, awarded the appropriately named (in this case at least) "Blindman" to Grace Hazard Conkling, in spite of her "lovely" visit with the Stevenses the previous November (1920). Stevens longed for the same kind of immersion again after he had finished:

When I get back from the South I expect to do some short poems and then to start again on a rather longish one, so that sooner or later I shall have something for *Poetry* to which I send what I like most. . . . The desire to write a long poem or two is not obsequiousness to the judgment of people. On the contrary, I find that this prolonged attention to a single subject has the same result that prolonged attention to a señora has according to the authorities. All manner of favors drop from it. Only it requires a skill in the varying of the serenade that occasionally makes one feel like a Guatemalan when one particularly wants to feel like an Italian. (*L* 230)

Stevens had invested his whole being in shaping lines around Crispin and for the first time did not find himself wanting in the scales of perfection. After this it was not the end but the voyaging itself that was important, though he was not yet aware that this was so. As he put it to Monroe apropos of her request to publish the "Crispin poem" in *Poetry* after the loss of the prize, he felt he wanted to continue "to be as obscure as possible until [he had] perfected an authentic and fluent speech for [him]self" (*L* 231).

But that he was more certain of himself than he had ever been was clear from the way he weathered the criticisms and rejections that curiously preceded his losing the "gold medal" to Conkling. In February 1922 he was rejected by Gorham Munson for the *Headsman,* who wrote that the poem he had submitted was "rather bad . . . an unfortunate moment in the life of the author of 'Pecksniffiana.' . . ." He went on to add, "This poem fails to get going into a rhythm of its own. Its first line is frankly bad. Most of the others are merely neutral and labored. The alliterations employed are quite obvious . . ." (WAS 1407, February 28, 1922). And in the same month Gilbert Seldes, editor of the *Dial,* who was accepting a group of poems eventually (in July 1922) published under the title of "Revue" ("Bantams in Pine-Woods" [*CP* 75], "The Ordinary Women" [*CP* 10], "Frogs Eat Butterflies. Snakes Eat Frogs. Hogs Eat Snakes. Men Eat Hogs" [*CP* 78], "A High-Toned Old Christian Woman" [*CP* 59], "O Florida, Venereal Soil" [*CP* 47], "The Emperor of Ice-Cream" [*CP* 64]), had had problems with the "Frogs" poem. Stevens responded to his hesitation, acknowledging that it was not an "amenable" poem but that given its peculiar nature, it perhaps could be published separately rather than as part of the group. Eventually Seldes published it together with the others in spite of his initial equivocation.

Stevens had discovered himself through "The Comedian." This was not a facilely autobiographical poem. He truly had experienced what Crispin did, and it was not in retrospect that he related the adventure. There was a purging and renewal that came through working on its lines that would not be equaled until years later when he composed the long poems of "Owl's Clover" and those of his old age, when he had perfected his "authentic and fluent speech." Yet these mature instances, as beautiful as they are, were not experientially the forges that "The Comedian" was precisely because in this comic epic Stevens was still struggling with language to make it the "crisp salad [he] want[ed]." *Crisp*in's (italics mine) journey was Stevens's battle with everything he had ever learned and wanted to unlearn. Crispin's log recorded the tension attached to the poet's almost overpowering need to be heard above the din of voices that assaulted him from the past. These voices pursued him. They were his Sirens, his Furies, humming and buzzing all around him, as unlocatable as the sounds of his everyday experience of the world, disturbing precisely because he could never, in his semideafness, pinpoint their sources. Everything sang around him like the surge of the sea punctuated by breaking waves in a silently black night, and he wanted to sing beyond the genius of the sea, beyond himself.

During the late months of 1921 and the early months of 1922, feeling the infringing chill of winter banished when he whisked himself away to Florida's venereal soil, he breathed life into the skeleton of the poem, shaping it finally with the flesh and blood of warm earth and sea and the "green freedom of a cockatoo" he sensed as he sipped the scotch magically provided by Judge Powell. But the fruits of this experience would not come until summer, when the long, slow breaths he could again take on his walks in the warm air of Elizabeth Park brought back the feelings of delight and solace he associated with Florida and the South. The first version of the poem had been written in haste and under tremendous pressure. The Blindman Prize had been announced in the December issue of *Poetry,* and the deadline for submissions was January 1, 1922. It was with the rushing stride of vanishing autumn in the park that he had given measure to the first version. Though he had put down the major part of the poem, groups of infelicitous prosaic lines broke the ebb and flow he intended. The last two sections, "A Nice Shady Home" and "And Daughters with Curls," were not yet conceived. And the account was in the present tense, thus limiting the possibilities of expression afforded by the difference in perspective offered by the suggested passage of time.[73] In spite of these imperfections, however, in composing even the first draft, Stevens composed himself, created the glass in which to "search himself." He ground the lines of the poem into a glass where he saw himself reflected. It replaced the glass of others' expectations and perceptions. The poem discoursed "about himself alone/Of what he was, and why, and of his place./And of its fitful pomp and parentage."[74] It was not accidental that his hero was also named for St. Crispin, patron of shoemakers, thus a family patron for Stevens whose maternal grandfather had been a shoemaker.

The whole structure of Stevens's experience shone in this mirror, from his broadest ties to forefathers born across from Europe, like Crispin, in the Atlantic coign, to the most immediate and particular details of current experience, from hearing Erik Satie's *Socrate,* which might even have contributed to the "Socrates of snails" image,[75] to receiving mail from Pitts Sanborn when he was in Bordeaux and later reading his *Vie de Bordeaux,* to staying on Biscayne Bay in Florida. Crispin's nature, like the poet's, had been shaped by his easy identification with what he had come to know and with what he had read. Both were all too easily permeated by others' forces. Their curiosity had, ironically, emptied them of themselves. The long voyage on the sea was necessary purification. Identification with the primary element would, they hoped, drown, flush out all the lesser figures. Identification with the sea would mean finding a voice more powerful and constant than any other.

The exercise worked. Clearly the most concentrated and sustained application of his skills until then, "From the Journal of Crispin" (the title of the first version) in its mocking marked the seriousness of Stevens's commitment to poetry. Though he chose "to regard poetry as a form of retreat" (*L* 230), he meant "retreat" not as mere pastime or escape but in the religious sense: the experience of quiet confrontation with and meditation on oneself and the things of the world. Directing such intense attention to himself—even for the few weeks it took him to write the first version—had the effect he described to Monroe: "All manner of favors drop[ped]. . . ." He found himself, like Crispin, more naked and more strange. Yet he was able to exist in spite of feeling this bareness. He sensed his native strength.

As a comedian himself, appropriately armed with emptiness, Stevens left for Florida in early January 1922. He had never been like this before, though he had been preparing for a while. Before attempting his epic adventure, he had been slowly peeling away the layers of his old self. "The Man Whose Pharynx Was Bad" and "The Snow Man" both were written in the months before Crispin's journal, and they were necessary preparatory exercises. The feelings belonging to these serious reductions of self had to be experienced before he could regard himself from a Jovian perspective and watch himself and the rest of the "planetary pass-pass" as entertainment. The powerlessness—whether expressed as indifference or diffidence, as in "The Man Whose Pharynx Was Bad" (CP 96), or as absolute ambivalence, as in "The Snow Man" (CP 9)—belonged to someone still attached to the things of the world he loved. Each of these things exerted its influence. In "The Man Whose Pharynx Was Bad" it was the romantics who spoke through him: "I am too dumbly in my being pent." In "The Snow Man" it was all he had learned from the "old Chinese" whom he wanted so much to imitate. He metaphorically described the experience they called "the snow man," to be bathed in sweat at the moment of enlightenment, the moment when the shells of self slip away to leave one free to become the "Nothing that is not there and the nothing that is."

But Stevens could not sit titivating by mountain pools as they did. Though the lesson learned from them was invaluable and grounded the ethic he was forging, as part of the intelligence of his soil, he had to find a way through the dense thickets of Calvinism and individualism, the natural growth of the idea of America.

In "The Doctor of Geneva" (CP 24) Stevens addressed the incompatibility of that idea in placing the persona of Calvin—the doctor of Geneva—before the "visible, voluble delugings" of the Pacific, the deceptively named ocean that marked America's natural limit. The doctor's good burgher's background had not prepared him for the powerful elemental fact of the western ocean, any more than the wishes and dreams of the Puritans had prepared them for the harsh winters and brutal conditions that forced them to lie, cheat, steal, and kill while writing to their cousins back home across the sea, that indeed, they had found the New Jerusalem.[76]

And in "Tea at the Palaz of Hoon" (CP 65) Stevens announced the way he would take. It was to be through addressing individualism itself, the sources of this idea of self, but in a comic way, the only way that would allow the social structure to be preserved while being criticized and modified. "Not less because in purple I descended . . ./not less was I myself." Evoking the power of the Greek myths—"ointment sprinkled on my beard . . ./Out of my mind the golden ointment rained"—and the power of Emerson, the first great American mythologizer—"I was the world in which I walked, and what I saw/Or heard or felt came not but from myself;/And there I found myself more truly and more strange"—Stevens propounded what would seem crazy ("Out of my mind . . .") to the leftover Calvinists and progressivists still quailing before nature without admitting it, as they directed their attention, instead, to getting ahead, wanting to believe they were moving ever closer to perfection. The lessons Stevens had learned at Harvard, lessons shaped by the spirits of Henry Adams, William James, George Santayana, were not lost. Having also learned since then how best to stage his comedy, Stevens was fully ready to begin.

The signs of his having taken on the role of the Comedian were not confined to poetry. In the letters he wrote to friends like Reyher during this period, the wry wit that had started to show itself a few months earlier in letters to Harriet Monroe burst into full-scale ironic humor. The first instance (in the correspondence as it remains) of his extending a comic effect through a long letter is also his first typed letter. It seems that without the immediate mirroring of thought, inescapable when writing oneself, he became freer. Dictating to his secretary allowed him to evade the automatic self-reflection that prompts hesitations and censorings and provided him with a captive audience whose no doubt quizzical responding glances must have tickled him to continue the masque:

DEAR REYHER,

Now that the letter writing season has opened again, it might be well for me to drop you a note merely for the sake of getting a reply. During the summer I received the book on Milton. The pages look like Japanese representations of rain. What particularly interested me, however, was that you sent it in a laundry bag. Fancy their having laundry bags just like ours in London! I mean to keep the bag and present it to the Historical Society here. They have all manner of things under glass cases. How nice it would be to put the bag under one, and label it, "Laundry Bag from London presented by Ferdinand Reyher, Esq. after the last time he had his laundry done." I assume that was the last time you had your laundry done, for almost everybody that I have seen this Fall after a trip to Europe seems to have come home without any laundry. I suppose the reason you do not write to me anymore is that you are ashamed to go out of the house, not having anything to wear. Mrs. Stevens and I spent several days in New York last week attending the theatre [*sic*]. The fact that they had nothing to wear had no bearing on the attendance of some of the people at the theatre. But the English are always frightfully prudish. Couldn't you drop a letter from the window? Now I suppose that in reply I shall get a letter from you enclosing a photograph of you in a top hat, taken in Madrid or some such place, just to prove how iil-founded my suspicions are. Anyhow I hope so. Let me know what you are doing, Putnam is advertising your novel quite generously. I meant to get a copy when I was in New York, but overlooked it. There was a very decent little review in the New York Times a month or so ago.

What has become of Rodker? I expected to receive from him some time ago a copy of Bacon's Essays. You know how one pants to read Bacon's Essays. Well, if you are naked, I am all pants, for I have never received the book, and the worst of it is, I suppose, that Rodker has been gobbled up by the Bolsheviki or some other anti-literary coterie.

Sincerely yours,
(WAS 1565, October 28, 1921)

As this letter makes clear, being a comedian allowed Stevens to express his resentments, evasions, guilts, questioning oppositions and personality quirks in an acceptable, even enjoyable manner. Had he instead directly communicated, without humor, feeling neglected because he had not received a letter, feeling opaquely hostile about his friend's book, which he "forgot" to buy, feeling jealous of all those "without clean clothes" in Europe, it is unlikely that he would have continued to have this friend. The comic method he practiced here he perfected over the next eight months in writing and revising Crispin's journal. Moreover, he had revealed in his letter to Reyher how much of an impact Arensberg had made on him. He wanted Bacon's *Essays* so that he could learn more about the figure his friend had taught him to see as another model. And he was about to work on the poem that, he hoped, would be the beginning of his offering to rival the *Divine Comedy,* which Arensberg thought of such major cultural importance, having spent years translating it.

The frankness of the judgments and feelings Stevens could communicate dressed in the cap and bells of the fool he had earlier worn to express himself to Elsie prompted equally direct responses from his correspondents. Reyher answered the above letter in a similar tone, conveying deep affection through it, as well as his own judgments and criticisms. And Robert McAlmon, who had never met Stevens, came to feel, as noted, that they shared the same spirit. He wrote him that he was the only person, besides his mother, with whom he kept in touch. In the letter in which he related this, he also attempted to comfort Stevens by commenting on how difficult the role of poet was in postwar America and yet that there were advantages:

[I] answer your letter the day I get it because I know the god-awful isolation that America inflicts upon it's [sic] intelligent and semi-intelligent souls. We can drink here, get drunk, and enjoy our miseries besotted at least. Djuna Barnes, Mina Loy, Marsden Hartley, and numerous others drift in and out of my scene—and innumerable unhappy, dislocated younger American people shift about me. Whatever is happening in America is quite as modern, unformed, and not half so tiresome with the oughtnesses of art, as what is going on over here. So I can't care much and never did care much about the Little Review since I know how wrongly they have Joyce card ticketed; and I know him as intimately as anyone now. It's a rich new phase that they dwell upon and all Americans aren't new rich to art or to intelligence, in spite of the James generation that was so god-awful respectful towards England and it's [*sic*] stale austerities. Except that in Germany they've blasted through many moral, sentimental and religious prejudices and are about as free— recklessly so—as ever late Greece was.

. . . Write me anytime you're so inclined. You're about the only person but my own family that I keep in touch with, and mother is the only one of the family I write to. Bill Williams and I write spasmodically, but he's upset and churning about in realms of misery, doubt, timid and reckless moments of emotion and ideation, and I don't know how to meet his violent appeal for "faith" of some sort in the value of life, or of literature. He simply should not permit life to keep him a doctor in a small town—but one can't advise. I can't. (WAS 1152, December 2, 1921)

These intimate yet professional glimpses of life on the other side must have made Stevens feel at the same time part of and out of the literary life. On paper he was clearly part of it, keeping company with Joyce, Mina Loy, even Pound and Eliot—in another, later letter McAlmon made a point of comparing Stevens's "hardness" to Eliot's hidden sentimentality (WAS 1157)—but in reality Stevens was more and more isolated. Not only was he not in Europe witnessing the painful excitement of Germany's cultural recovery in the Bauhaus, but he had also given up moving with the New York "artistic crowd," as he put it. He even packed up all the catalogs from galleries and museums he had assiduously attended in the previous ten years in New York and gave them to Hartford's Wadsworth Atheneum (WAS 1567, February 2, 1922).[77] Of course, the old crowd had more or less broken up, with many of them in Europe and Walter Arensberg moved to Los Angeles to escape the heavy social and financial burden he had made into an everyday part of his New York life.[78] Though Stevens now periodically went to New York, both with Elsie—when he treated them to nights at the theater—and alone— when he might have lunch with Marcel Duchamp and share a new aesthetic joke—for the time city life seemed to hold no attractions. In a letter to Reyher he commented on how bleak it seemed now.

Although this attitude probably was in part a defense protecting him from facing the full consequences of what his life with the Hartford meant and what it would have meant to continue in the city with Elsie, it was one that nonetheless allowed him the obscurity he felt he needed, as he had expressed to Monroe, to perfect his craft. There were no distractions in Hartford from the routine he knew: no theaters or restaurants to speak of; no galleries showing new things; no bookstores of note (the owner of the one "serious" bookstore in town did not even recognize Stevens when he periodically stopped in); no unexpected visitors; no calls to meet at such and such a place with so-and-so for a while just to share an idea of an evening. In Hartford his ideas were his private property: "I am a man of fortune greeting heirs." He could collect them, store them, inventory them as he did, making lists of titles in special separate notebooks. Some would grow and prove to be good investments; others would fail, poor speculations. "Money is a kind of poetry," he wrote, disclosing the parallels he recognized in his dark phases when the chill lunar wind of his imagination slowly and persistently worked away at his surface. Each time the surface appeared, it was the same but slightly different. Each revolution brought change. And the changes were always forecast by one of the dear ideas his imagination provided.

In the original version of "The Man Whose Pharynx Was Bad" (which had appeared in the *New Republic,* Vol. xxviii, No. 354 [September 14, 1921], p. 74), Stevens had hypothesized, as a remedy for the "malady of the quotidian," an eternal season:

> . . . .
> Perhaps, if summer ever came to rest
> And lengthened, deepened, comforted, caressed
> Through days like oceans in obsidian
>
> Horizons full of night's midsummer blaze;*
> Perhaps, if winter once could penetrate
> Through all its purples to the final slate,
>
> Persisting bleakly in an icy haze;
> One might in turn become less diffident—
> . . . .
>
> (*CP* 96)

In reality, one could not survive the experience of such a winter, but such a summer. . . . With this consciousness he returned to Florida in January 1922 and returned every winter he could.

The constant and extreme climate of the tropics was the perfect environment for one who was attempting to go beyond the learned conventions, one who could not help experimenting with the notion of a Nietschean *Übermensch.* In Stevens's terms this was a "major-man," who, in the absence of God in heaven, had to shape a new morality. If he seemed "out of his mind," it was to those with "mind[s] of winter"—minds shaped by the inheritance of industrious northern settlers, used to thinking of the future because if they didn't, they could not survive the dead season. They could not afford the lushness of contemplating the present at ease. Southerners were closer to this possibility, closer to the seeming eternity of the tropics.

And Stevens's friend Judge Powell was a true southerner and "christened" the poet properly. Stevens wrote to Elsie from Miami—after having left Atlanta, where she knew he was headed—that he had *had* to go down to Florida, "As it turned out . . . with Judge Powell, although [he] had not honestly supposed it would be necessary when he left home." He hoped she would not be "too envious of such good fortune," he added. "It [was] beautiful, a

---

*These first four lines were later deleted from *Harmonium* and *Collected Poems.*

clear, perfect day of summer weather" (WAS 2027, January 8, 1922). In a letter two days later he provided a fuller explanation of how this bit of fortune had come his way, making it seem that it was purely business-connected and that he was not part of Arthur Powell's "party of friends." He went on to point out that in Long Key, where they ended up and from which they would go fishing for a few days, there were "no ladies." He also stressed that he wished she were there with him in this "paradise" and that they "must [go] together as soon as [they could] and every winter afterwards" (L 224–25).

But in a letter he wrote to Reyher (again typed, as almost all future letters to friends would be) from the office on his return, he painted a different picture, with himself at the center of the "party" from the time it left Atlanta. After making some equivocal remarks about Reyher's novel, which by that time he had read, he went on:

> I have had three or four books sent to me by rowdies that I know during the last few months, as a consequence of which I start at the slightest sound. However, the other books were books of poetry, which probably accounts for my unstrung condition, although there have been a good many contributing causes of unstrungedness. When I was in Miami, I sent you a postcard. Now, that trip to Florida would have unstrung a brass monkey. I went down there with half a dozen other people from Atlanta. I was the only damned Yankee in the bunch. I was christened as a charter member of the Long Key Fishing Club of Atlanta. The christening occupied about three days, and required just two cases of Scotch. When I started home I was not able to tell whether I was traveling on a sound or a smell. As I remember it, it was very much like a cloud full of Cuban senoritas, cocoanut [sic] palms, and waiters carrying ice water. Since my return I have not cared much for literature. The Southerners are a great people. (WAS 1567, February 2, 1922)

After unstringing his instrument as the "Comedian" in his poem, the "lutanist of fleas," as he named himself there, unstrung himself as well. Going beyond the bounds of Prohibition with Judge Powell perfectly suited this moment of his development. Exceeding limits of all kinds in a tropical climate that seemed itself to exceed change felt appropriate.

Florida's Long Key set the tone for Stevens's expansiveness. Knowing that he would return and make the experience of the South an integral part of his life allowed him to accept things as they were in the North with an equanimity he had not had before. Now "The Comedian as the Letter C" could fulfill another of its offered promises. It would be, like the Hundreth Psalm— represented by the letter C = 100—"a joyful noise." As Stevens described it, penciling his comment in his copy, this Psalm was "An exhortation to praise God cheerfully." This he could do now. His poem would provide the model for his secular sacrament of praise. Not God but experience itself would be celebrated and in the master key of C. The last two sections of "The Comedian," added that summer, halfway through the time before his return to Florida the following winter, poetically described the acceptance that made this understanding possible. Stevens was "content" now, like his hero:

> In the presto of the morning, Crispin trod
> Each day, still curious, but in a round
> Less prickly and much more condign than that
> He once thought necessary.
>
> (CP 42)

He had become a realist, and "For realist, what is is what should be." If he had uncertainties, if he felt his "relation" to the idea of the woman he once loved had been "clipped," he now simply accepted these facts, explored them, made out of them "questioners" and "sure answerers." The figure of "daughters with curls" was a cipher for his poems, and each one, from now on, would pose a question, framed by its occasion, which would be answered in the lines he shaped around the associations that up-poured from the ever-deepening reservoir of his being.

The questions were about feeling, the inescapably human irrational element. Knowing in the profoundest part of himself that there could never be a final answer, he knew, too, as he expressed it in Part V of "The Comedian," that silence had to come:

> . . . So deep a sound fell down
> It was as if the solitude concealed
> And covered him and his congenial sleep.
> So deep a sound fell down it grew to be
> A long soothsaying silence down and down.
>
> (CP 42)

It was as though he understood that actual years of silence had to come after *Harmonium*. This, too, was part of the pantomime, practice for death. Resolving the tensions of his middle age meant that part of him—"that monster, the body"—had died. The poem he carefully placed after "The Comedian" in *Harmonium* made it clear:

> FROM THE MISERY OF DON JOOST
> I have finished my combat with the sun;
> And my body, the old animal,
> Knows nothing more.
>
> The powerful seasons bred and killed,
> And were themselves the genii
> Of their own ends.

Oh, but the very self of the storm
Of sun and slaves, breeding and death.
The old animal,

The senses and feeling, the very sound
And sight, and all there was of the storm
Knows nothing more.

(CP 46)

This and "Stars at Tallapoosa," both written after "The Comedian" sometime in 1922, described what he had prefigured years earlier in "Peter Quince," where he noted that "The body dies [but] the body's beauty lives." The beauty he knew lived in his eye, that part shared with the sun, light—the letter *c*—as Plotinus and Emerson had taught him so well:

The body is no body to be seen
But is an eye that studies its black lid.

(CP 71)

Beyond the silence he knew, too, however, that there would be a "return to social nature," *(CP 43)*, as he again had described for Crispin in the last section of the poem. It seemed paradoxical, and it was. But "be" was now "finale of seem," and so he peaceably followed his turns and returns to the sun after each bout with the night, where he "met Berserk/In the moonlight" *(CP 57)*. The volume he next composed, after the long silence following *Harmonium,* would address itself to his "return to social nature."

Having unstrung himself in Florida that winter of 1922, having gone beyond the limits, yet finding himself returning content with what he had chosen, in spite of its imperfections, relieved him. It also allowed him to address these imperfections and dissatisfactions more openly, as he did in "Two Figures in Dense Violet Night" *(CP 85–86)*:

I had as lief be embraced by the porter at the hotel
As to get no more from the moonlight
Than your moist hand.

Be the voice of night and Florida in my ear.
Use dusky words and dusky images.
Darken your speech.

Speak, even, as if I did not hear you speaking,
But spoke for you perfectly in my thoughts,
Conceiving words,

As the night conceives the sea-sounds in silence,
And out of their droning sibilants makes
A serenade.

Say, puerile, that the buzzards crouch on the ridge-pole
And sleep with one eye watching the stars fall
Below Key West.

Say that the palms are clear in a total blue,
Are clear and are obscure; that it is night;
That the moon shines.

Addressing the impossibility of moving beyond his old desires allowed him to use imagination fully, to complete desires with words conceived perfectly in his thoughts. It also allowed the time spent in the North to be the period of hibernation his animal self required. In these periods now, life would have the satisfactions it could have, nourished mostly by the study of beautiful things and occasional contacts with others who in some way shared his spirit.

That spring, for example, back in Hartford, before he felt he could give himself to literature again (he noted to Gilbert Seldes that his "spasms [of poetry] [were] not chronic" [L 226]), he began devoting more time and attention to acquiring books and objects that could feed his need. He expanded his network of correspondents who could send him these delights from faraway places. Among these objects of pleasure were a Renoir print, some Oriental jade figures of lions and a Buddha figure, and fine rare books. The kinds of the things he liked, or "craved," as he put it, though he could not afford them at the moment, were a German-press Latin edition of St. John and a Cranach print (he did not specify whether the Elder or the Younger [WAS 1568, April 6, 1922]). In contrast, his feelings about one thing he did *not* want give a precious glimpse into the nature of his involvement with these "memorabilia of the mystic spouts" (CP 16). Responding to one of Reyher's queries about what he should purchase for him, Stevens observed: "The Hamburg Press Platon may be all that you say it is. But, after all, a book is not only a piece of printing. It has a soul as well as a body, and the idea of Plato in German is something so odious, so vulgar, that I turn from it as quickly as possible . . ." (WAS 1568). Though he loved the sound and shape of German, familiar to him from his childhood days of accompanying his mother while she haggled with farmers' wives in their native speech, though he read German comfortably and did so all his life, though he had even celebrated its echoes in the guttural, slashing plays on *c* in "The Comedian," for the contemplation of the "ultimate Plato" (CP 27), it was vulgar, too familiar perhaps. For his vulgate it was appropriate, but not for Plato, whose thought belonged to the most intricately tuned instrument of the South, the Greek of tenses unimagined in the North, of periods as perfectly balanced as the columns he envisioned by the ructive sea, elegantly poising its pediments of meaning. The "Comedian" had learned that "his soil is man's intelligence."

In this same letter to Reyher in which he expressed his odiousness about the German Plato, he described himself and the way he had been living by using a phrase which he also used on the same day in a letter to Harriet

Monroe, though in the letter to her he did not expand on what the phrase meant, as he did to his friend. He was "like a turtle under a bush," he wrote. He related to Monroe that Carl Sandburg had recently been in Hartford and that Vachel Lindsay was to come the following week, but he left it equivocal whether he had shared in one case, or would share in the other, a comfortable hour or two with his brother poets. In the letter to Reyher he suggested that he remained isolated, adding details about how sharply different his life was when he "got away from town":

> You are . . . one of the treasures of the humble, I being the humble. I don't believe I have seen a soul to whom I have talked about you for a year. I live like a turtle under a bush, and when I get away from town, believe me, I don't stay sober any longer than I must. The amount of talking that I have done about things of this sort during the last year would probably boil down to a few syllables. I pride myself on being a member of the Long Key Fishing Club of Atlanta and of the Brown Derby Club of East Hartford, and I take damned little stock in conversation on philosophy, aesthetics, poetry, art, or blondes. Of course, I hanker for all those things as a fly hankers for fly paper. But experience has taught me that fly paper is one devil of a thing to get mixed up in. You should see some of the letters I get!
>
> Do, Reyher, forgive me for not behaving properly about the [?] . . . but out of the question under the circumstances. Still, I wish I could tell you how much I enjoyed getting your letter. It was like going to the Evangelical Church in Reading and hearing old Dr. Kuendig preach in German on the text "Ich bin der Weg, die Wahrheit und das Leben ["I am the Way, the Truth, and Life"]. Klenhem [?-spelling] Presse Evangelium Sancti Johannes is the sweetest line of poetry I have heard for a long time. Gosh, how I should like to have that book. But I must forswear it.
>
> "One begins to find one's aquarium a bore."

Years earlier, at the moment he thought he had separated himself from his past, he had used a passage from the Song of Solomon in the voice of the turtle to serenade Elsie. He had then proclaimed, in adopting the religious verse for a secular and profane end, his rejection of the values with which he had been bred. Now he became the turtle again since he had just sloughed off, in composing "The Comedian," another withered skin, the uncertain identity improvised out of words learned after his childhood and youth. Whatever might be said of the new self he was discovering—like Crispin, the New World—it was certain of what it was and what it needed. He was who he was and would make whatever adjustments had to be made, without judgment but simply in order to satisfy that being as much as he could. If life at home with Elsie did not allow him the freedom of expression and indulgence he desired, that freedom could be expressed in other situations. If the people with whom he was most often in contact in the insurance world were "bores," it was small price to pay for being able to afford so many of the things he "craved." If he could not travel to Europe as he had once desired, he would have Florida in winter and celebrate its pristine, yet seductive, American localness. This he would integrate with an "idea of the European past," an idea that would no doubt have been deeply disturbed by an actual visit to the devastated battleground. Poetically conceptualizing the constant up and down between two elements that he had experienced all his life was like an experiential version of the lesson Emerson taught in *Compensation* (which Stevens had read at least once as a young man). Rather than question or judge whether one element was good, the other bad, railing sometimes at one or at the other, it was important for one simply to ride them as they came, like waves, using reason as the helm, feeling the fullness of each movement, each tremor of transition between the up and down, each shudder of action like the crest of a breaking wave. It was the attitude of Eastern acceptance that was behind this ability to see whatever was as it was, yet as necessary compensation for something else that couldn't always be seen, though it could be guessed at through the many "possibles" imagination offered: "Let be be finale of seem."

In this spirit Stevens could experience every aspect of his life fully, as it was. But to do so meant that one of the most constant thematic features of his work until now would disappear: desire, yearning. The unresolved free-verse rhythms of the earlier poems of *Harmonium* asked for completion—like the improvisations of jazz to which they were so directly tied. These rhythms mimicked the desire the poet could not then get beyond. But they were replaced after "The Comedian" by long-rolling noble accents of acceptance, like the movement of waves—the way light, the "Letter C," traveled. This acceptance was part of the tradition, the "soil" of which he was a part. Yet even though desire no longer determined the shape or provided the specific occasion of a poem did not mean that Stevens no longer felt it. He did, but he was now able to feel it, know he felt it, accept that he did, and gratify it in whatever ways he could. Sometimes this meant a night of blue grapes and Rhine wine, sometimes the gusty feasting on scotch and southern stories with Arthur Powell and other friends, sometimes the savoring of an image, a line or two describing something beautiful he had just seen or felt.

With this new acceptance of self and things around him, Stevens reacted to whatever came the way his sailor hero Crispin had to in order to survive. Considering the parts of his experience that he could not control as though they were manifestations of the weather, he negotiated his way through them, giving full attention to what had to be done and acting with neither hesitation nor regret. The *New Republic's* most recent rejection of his "New England Verses" in July (WAS 2324, July 14, 1921; the previous year's rejection had brought commendation from Reyher, who stated that he did not think the journal worthy of the work of the "Giant") did not disturb him enough to hesitate too long about Carl Van Vechten's suggestion later that month that he think of putting together the poems he had already written for a first volume.

Three months later he had selected, revised, and arranged the poems, which he protectively dropped off to Van Vechten in New York rather than send them through the mail. Van Vechten presented them to Alfred A. Knopf. A month later a contract with Knopf was signed. Stevens was proud. He wrote to McAlmon about it without delay. He was secure in believing that McAlmon would be delighted, with his earlier praise of the "worldly and sophisticated modern intelligence of Proust"; his disparagement of "Jewish taste" and the "despondent knowingness" of Eliot; and his criticism of the civilization itself "that forced" defenses of "neuroticism and morbidity" (WAS 1157). McAlmon was a most sympathetic supporter and advertiser of what he saw as Stevens's "hard boiled" and "Rabelaisian" (WAS 1158) style. In contrast with what he thought to be Eliot's "egotistically impressionable and broody" despair, he felt that Stevens had the "same despair [but] hardened" and that this attitude was the only one "left anybody with sense, sensibility and intelligence in this industrial, luxurious, bigoted, prohibitionary, censuring, economic organization that some like[d] to call civilization" (WAS 1158).

As Pitts Sanborn was sailing back to America with a contraband copy of *Ulysses* for him, Stevens was "exercis[ing] the most fastidious choice . . . among [his] witherlings," to "pick a crisp salad from the garbage of the past. . . ." (*L* 232). The crossings were many. Both Stevens and Joyce were men made out of words of the past who had tried, with words again, to free themselves from it, the civilization Pound called that "old bitch gone in the teeth." But ironically, while America, the daughter of the "old bitch," accepted the notes of critical despair from foreigners and expatriates and proclaimed the brilliant newness of *Ulysses* and *The Waste Land,* she chastised her most faithful native son, mocking his magnificent measures as marks of a leftover aesthete, a dandy, an imitator of the very forms he mocked himself. America was still too young to have developed a sense of humor about itself so could not recognize its Rabelais.

Luckily, before feeling the bite of these criticisms, the Comedian had renewed himself with other stays in the South—"beautiful and sedately the early and undefiled American thing" (*L* 228–29)—and, most enjoyably, in Florida. He went that winter just after finishing off his crisp salad of poems. Like Crispin, he even crossed to Havana, where he would return with Elsie on a most important cruise the following October and November. Fulfilling himself in his fictionalized hero, Stevens felt protected and comfortable in his difference from what he had been before. He wore his motley costume of "cloak/Of China, cap of Spain" (*CP* 28). He felt particularly close to things Chinese now—with his many objects and books. He expressed to Harriet Monroe his notion that "For a poet to have even a second hand contact with China is a great matter" (*L* 229). The "cap of Spain" he had borrowed from his poet-philosopher friend Santayana, from whom he had learned so much. He was completing the task he had begun at Harvard when he had addressed sonnets to him, voicing his new secularized faith.

With this New World attitude Stevens looked at the South fondly and nostalgically as the place where "religion [was] still . . . active . . . tak[ing] the place of society, art, literature . . ." (L 236). But he was from the North, where "the church was more or less moribund" (L 236). So he saw his work cut out, to create "a final belief" to replace religion's, "a final belief . . . to believe in a fiction which you know to be a fiction, there being nothing else. The exquisite truth . . . to know that it is a fiction and that you believe it willingly" (OP 163). To have others believe in it willingly, it had to give pleasure. This was the project the Comedian set for himself. Knowing this first volume to be only the beginning, he noted to Alfred Knopf on March 12, 1923, his intended title: "The Grand Poem: Preliminary Minutiae" (L 237). Six days later, after communicating with Knopf again, he fell back to "Harmonium" (L 238). But the "grand" intention was never abandoned.

NOTES

INTRODUCTION

1. T. J. Jackson Lears, *No Place of Grace: Antimodernism and the Transformation of American Culture 1880–1920* (New York: Pantheon, 1981), p. 49.

2. Colin McGinn, *The Character of Mind* (New York: Oxford University Press, 1982), p. 12.

3. H. Stuart Hughes, *Consciousness and Society: The Reconstruction of European Social Thought 1890–1930* (New York: Vintage, 1961), pp. 111–12.

4. Katsuki Sekida, tr., *Two Zen Classics: Mumonkan and Hekiganroku* (New York and Tokyo: Weatherhill, 1977), p. 96.

5. R. H. Blyth, *Zen and Zen Classics* (New York: Vintage, 1978), p. 117.

6. Benjamin Lee Whorf, *Language, Thought and Reality,* Selected Writings, ed., John B. Carroll (Cambridge, Mass.: The MIT Press, 1982), p. 25.

7. Ibid., p. 27.

8. Ibid., p. vi.

9. Helen Vendler, "Sizing Up American Poetry," *The New York Review of Books,* Vol. XXXII, No. 17 (November 7, 1985), p. 56.

CHAPTER I. *The Making of a Good Puritan: 1879–1897*

1. In his book *The Revolution of the Saints: A Study of the Origins of Radical Politics* (Cambridge: Harvard University Press, 1965), Michael Walzer develops the theme of the tie between the Puritan virtues and economic growth which will be referred to in passing in this chapter. "The diligent activism of the saints—Genevans, Huguenots, Dutch, Scottish, and Puritan—marked the transformation of politics into work and revealed for the first time the extraordinary conscience that directed the work" (p. 2). Perry Miller has also dealt with this theme abundantly in his many volumes on the Puritans.

2. During this period "An infant was stillborn in 1883 (and possibly two other children, who may have been twins, were born to the couple but did not survive) . . ." (*SP* 7).

3. The farm was taken over by Stevens's brother John, who eventually sold it to "one of the Cornells" (*L* 732), who still lived there in 1951.

4. After Darwin's *Origin of Species* in 1859, discussion about his theory continued in this country well into this century (as we know). Before and around the turn of the century the debate centered at Harvard and involved, among others, William James and Charles Sanders Peirce (who did not agree with Darwin, though he had his own theory of evolution). See Cynthia Eagle Russett, *Darwin in America: The Intellectual Response, 1865–1912* (San Francisco: W. H. Freeman, 1976). See also Gertrude Himmelfarb, *Darwin and the Darwinian Revolution* (New York: Norton, 1968).

5. It is possible, however, that she was self-taught, as was Elsie Moll, Stevens's future wife.

6. Stevens seemed to be somewhat uncertain about his connection with this lineage. See *L* 466.

7. Before this piece of information was uncovered by Stevens, he indicated that John Zeller was very much interested in the German Lutheran Church which was a block away from his house on Walnut Street in Reading (*L* 399).

8. This is remarked on by Thomas De Quincey in his recollection of "William Wordsworth and Robert Southey," *Recollections of the Lakes and Lake Poets,* ed. David Wright (New York: Penguin, 1978), p. 216: "I have heard it said, by the way, that Donne's intolerable defect of ear grew out of his own baptismal name, when harnessed to his surname—*John Donne.* No man, it was said, who had listened to this hideous jingle from childish years, could fail to have his genius for discord, and the abominable in sounds, improved to the utmost."

9. See especially Perry Miller, *Errand into the Wilderness* (New York: Harper Torchbooks, 1956) and *Nature's Nation* (Cambridge: Belknap Press, 1967 and 1974), as well as Sacvan Bercovitch, ed., *The American Puritan Imagination* (New York: Cambridge University Press, 1974), and Sacvan Bercovitch, *The Puritan Origins of the American Self* (New Haven and London: Yale University Press, 1975 and 1976), for extensive discussions and analyses, beginning from sources, of this reality and its consequences in the shaping of the language of American literature as it reflects a specifically American consciousness.

10. See Note 9. And in connection with the cultural rebellion against Puritanism in the first decade of this century—a movement that Stevens could not have ignored and, in fact, participated in spiritually—see Arthur Frank Wertheim, *The New York Little Renaissance: Iconoclasm, Modernism and Nationalism in American Culture, 1908–1917* (New York: New York University Press, 1976), pp.3–17.

11. Quoted by Matthew Arnold, "Literature and Science," *The Portable Matthew Arnold,* ed. Lionel Trilling (New York: Penguin, 1980), p. 428.

12. See *Charles S. Peirce, Selected Writings (Values in a Universe of Chance),* ed. Philip P. Wiener (New York: Dover, 1958); also Russett, op. cit., pp.

62–68, and John E. Smith, *The Spirit of American Philosophy* (New York and London: Oxford University Press, 1963), pp. 3–37 and passim.

13. Smith, op. cit., p. 20.

14. Ibid., p. 28.

15. See Michael O. Stegman, "Wallace Stevens and Music: A Discography of Stevens' Phonograph Record Collection," *The Wallace Stevens Journal*, Vol. 3, Nos. 3 and 4 (Fall, 1979), pp. 79–97, for a valuable listing of what Stevens acquired on these and other buying trips to music stores.

16. The breakdown of particular courses from year to year (there were three terms to each academic year) is as follows: freshman class—Latin, algebra, arithmetic, analytical grammar and composition, English classics, physical geography, and the history of Greece; sophomore class—Greek, Latin (Caesar), algebra, geometry, physics, English (with composition), and the history of Rome; junior class—Greek (Xenophon), Latin (Virgil), geometry, rhetoric, composition, and (optionally) physics; senior year—Greek (two terms on the *Iliad* and one on Herodotus), Latin (two terms on Cicero and one on Livy or Sallust), English literature, American literature, elocution, and something called Mental Philosophy (*SP* 10–12).

17. Holly Stevens notes that it must have been the impact of the elocution course Stevens took during this last year, at the time of the presidential campaign between William Jennings Bryan and President McKinley, that was most responsible for his interest in delivering this speech (*SP* 12).

18. Arnold, op. cit., p. 559.

CHAPTER II. *The Harvard Man: 1897–1900*

1. Most notably, in the context of Stevens's experience, during these years, as a result of the Dawes Commission appointed in 1893, the open lands of the Indian Territory were gradually divided up, against Indian resistance, and made wholly available to white men by 1906 (*Columbia Encyclopedia* [New York: Columbia University Press, 1956], p. 1435). "Earthy Anecdote," the first poem of *Harmonium* and eventually of *The Collected Poems*, seems to evoke the poet's imaginative recollection of this historical moment; the "bucks . . . clattering/Over Oklahoma" could easily be identified with the Indians forced "To the right" and "To the left" before the advancing "firecat" of the railroad, representing the white men's interests.

2. "Benjamin Jowett, the English scholar and theologian, a student of Kant and Hegel, translator of Plato and Thucydides, had died in 1893, after serving for several years as vice-chancellor of Oxford University. At Harvard there was strong interest in his work at this time [during the time of Stevens's attendance]; there was even a 'Jowett Club,' although [Stevens] was not listed as one of its members. But certainly he shared that interest, as evidenced by the fact that he owned Jowett's translation of Plato's *Dialogues* and kept it throughout his life (it was sold by the family in 1959) . . ." (*SP* 19). Stevens

read Jowett's letters in 1898 (*L* 20), as Holly Stevens also notes, and made comments in his journal on certain passages he copied: "On page 153 Vol. II are some thoughts on poetry which I must put down here: 'True poetry is the remembrance of youth, of love, of the noblest thoughts of man, of the greatest deeds of the past.—The reconciliation of poetry, as of religion, with truth, may still be possible. Neither is the element of pleasure to be excluded. For when we substitute a higher pleasure for a lower we raise men in the scale of existence.'" As Holly Stevens comments, these thoughts had an obvious influence on Stevens's later developments of the ideas that went into "Notes Toward a Supreme Fiction." I add that they were also specifically elaborated in his "Three Academic Pieces," delivered first as a lecture at Harvard in 1947, then published in the *Partisan Review* before being collected in *The Necessary Angel* (discussion of these pieces will be taken up in Chapter XI of Volume II of this biography). Stevens went on in his journal in 1898 to record the following:

> Of poetry which falls short of this high vocation he [Jowett] speaks with strong condemnation:—"It is, in Plato's language, a flattery, a sophistry, a strain, in which, without any serious purpose, the poet lends wings to his fancy and exhibits his gifts of language and metre—Such an [*sic*] one ministers to the weaker side of human nature; he idealizes the sensual; he sings the strain of love in the latest fashion; instead of raising men above themselves he brings them back to the 'tyranny of the many masters' from which all his life long he has been praying to be delivered." (*SP* 19–20)

3. Ernest F. Fenollosa, *Epochs of Chinese and Japanese Art: An Outline History of East Asiatic Design* (New York: Dover, 1963), Vol. I, pp. xviii–xx.

4. Stevens's sonnet, to which Santayana wrote a sonnet in response, appeared in the *Harvard Monthly* for May 1899 (it was written on March 12, 1899 [*L* 482 n]); it follows:

> Cathedrals are not built along the sea;
> The tender bells would jangle on the hoar
> And iron winds; the graceful turrets roar
> With bitter storms the long night angrily;
> And through the precious organ pipes would be
> A low and constant murmur of the shore
> That down those golden shafts would rudely pour
> A mighty and a lasting melody.
>
> And those who knelt within the gilded stalls
> Would have vast outlook for their weary eyes;
> There, they would see high shadows on the walls

From passing vessels in their fall and rise.
Through gaudy windows there would come too soon
The low and splendid rising of the moon.

(*SP* 32–33)

Santayana must "have spent the evening writing his reply because the next morning in [Stevens's] mail there was a sonnet from him entitled ['Cathedrals by the Sea,' Reply] to a Sonnet Commencing 'Cathedrals Are Not Built, etc.'" The sonnet was eventually published in *A Hermit of Carmel and Other Poems* (New York: Scribner's, 1901), p. 122:

> For aeons had the self-responsive tide
> Risen to ebb, and tempests blown to clear,
> And the belated moon refilled her sphere
> To wane anew—for, aeons since, she died—
> When to the deeps that called her earth replied
> (Lest year should cancel unavailing year)
> And took from her dead heart the stones to rear
> A cross-shaped temple to the Crucified.
> Then the wild winds through organ-pipes descended
> To utter what they meant eternally,
> And not in vain the moon devoutly mended
> Her wasted taper, lighting Calvary,
> While with a psalmody of angels blended
> The sullen diapason of the sea.

5. When William Carlos Williams won the Russell Loines Poetry Award in 1948, Stevens wrote him:

> Loines was not a man who wanted to be, but was not. He was carried along into other things, but never forgot poetry. So that whatever others might see in the award, I wanted you to see the man back of it and to realize how happy he would have been in seeing this honor done to you in his name. He was not an outsider with money; he was an insider, and sincerely devoted, as you yourself are,—and Marianne Moore herself could not say more. (*L* 591)

Three days before, to make Williams "see the man back of" the award, Stevens had written:

> When I went to Cambridge Russell Loines was living in the attic of the house in which I was to live. This house was an old-fashioned dwelling. It was owned by three old maid daughters of Theophilus Parsons who in his day was a professor at the Law School. Loines had come to Harvard after

leaving Columbia principally in order to become a member of Charles Eliot Norton's class in Dante. In those days Loines was very much of a poet, not that he wrote a great deal of poetry—but he was intensely interested in it and thought about it constantly. His room was lighted by a long slanting trap window in the roof. There was only one other window. It was heated by a little Franklin stove. It required about all the time of an old colored man to keep that and the other stoves and numerous grates in the house going. That room meant everything to Loines. I am not sure whether he remained in Cambridge to go to the Law School. In any event, the following spring he gave up his room and I took it. I kept it only a single year. Then I took a room below it on the second floor because there was more space and because it was more convenient.

Loines spent three or four years in London studying admiralty law. His father was a partner in Johnson & Higgins. On his return to New York he went into the office of Johnson & Higgins handling admiralty losses. Occasionally, he would find some way of showing his extraordinarily friendly spirit. I remember being invited to dinner once and getting there an hour too early. As it happened I saw him shortly before his death when we were both on a train on the way from Washington to New York. At that time he was living on Staten Island. As a boy he had lived on Columbia Heights, where Marianne Moore lives now.

It all comes to this: that when you receive the Loines Award you are receiving something that comes to you in the name of a sincere lover of poetry. It is just my luck to have known Loines. I thought you might be interested. . just happened to think of it: I was a good walker in those days; but Loines was long and thin and when he let himself out it was impossible to keep up with him. He used to raise his head a little as he walked as if he got something out of moving so rapidly. (L 588–89)

6. As Holly Stevens notes (*SP* 13), adding that she still has a watercolor by Pope which used to hang in the front hall of the Stevens house on Westerly Terrace in Hartford.

7. Holly Stevens notes that this last word might have been "alone" and been misset by the typesetter, who could easily have misread Stevens's handwriting (*SP* 16).

8. Bynner left on his first trip just after the period of about two years when, with his old friend Arthur Ficke, he successfully carried off the noted *Spectra* hoax:

The story of the hoax is told by William Jay Smith in his introduction to *The Works of Witter Bynner: Light Verse and Satires* (1978). Very simply, it was WB's exasperation with the Imagists that prompted him to start a new school of poetry, which he called Spectra. Using the name Emanuel Morgan, WB urged Ficke to write for the school under the name of Anne Knish. The

Spectra school, said to be located in romantic and poetic Pittsburgh, sought the spectra of the eye and of life, that point just out of the direct vision. The nonsense was evident, but it was not a time when people were easily certain what was and what wasn't serious in the world of poetry. The result was that for two years Morgan and Knish published Spectra poems in all the best magazines and later published the volume *Spectra.* WB's letters show the delight he took in the hoax and the energy he gave to it. WB wrote some of his best poetry as Emanuel Morgan and always, after that, had another self to release, doing so in his last book, *New Poems 1960,* in which he went back to the role of Morgan, but Morgan as an older man. (*Witter Bynner: Selected Letters,* ed. James Kraft [New York: Farrar, Straus, Giroux, 1981], p. 47)

Stevens had early recognized Bynner's talent, inviting him—the first in his class—to join the *Harvard Advocate* board in 1900. Perhaps both Stevens's playing with various pseudonyms during his college years, the many named personae he used in his later poetry, and Bynner's similar playing had to do with readings in Buddhism as part of their undergraduate involvement with the Orient. In Volume III of the Harvard Oriental Series, *Buddhism in Translations* by Henry Clarke Warren, first published in 1896 (reprinted, New York: Atheneum, 1982), we find the following, which seems to provide a philosophical underpinning for transcending notions of individual identity: "When we come to examine the elements of being one by one, we discover that in the absolute sense there is no living entity there to form a basis for such figments as 'I am I' or 'I'; in other words, that in the absolute sense, there is only name and form. The insight of him who perceives this is called the knowledge of the truth" (p. 134). More particularly, in terms of Stevens's preoccupation with "things as they are" is this passage, which is Buddha's answer to the question "And how, O priests, do the intelligent know the truth?":

We may have, O priests, a priest who knows things as they really are, and knowing things as they really are, he is on the road to aversion for things, to absence of passion for them, and to cessation from them.

Thus, O priests, do the intelligent know the truth. (p. 135)

9. On this basis Müller suggested connections between Buddhist doctrine and early Greek philosophy, language bearing the same relation to thought as the notion of the "I," or ego, to "things as they are":

. . . when we come to examine the growth of mythology in the narrower sense of the word . . . we shall then see how all that has been called either animism, or anthropomorphism or personification has its common root in a much deeper stratum of thought, namely in the psychological necessity of our conceiving all objects as subjects like ourselves. . . . By means of this intellectual process which enabled the earliest speakers to use the sounds expressive of subjective acts and states with reference to all that had become

objective to them in outward nature, we are enabled to understand the gradual formation of four classes of objective roots. . . . (*Science of Thought* [New
York: Scribner's, 1889], p. 325)

Stevens explored this perception exhaustively late in his career, from the mid-
forties on, as he focused more and more specifically on the connections
between sounds and subjective states in both his poetry and his theoretical
writing. This area will be discussed in Chapters XI and XII of Volume II.

10. Though the date of this note is not known, it is possible that Stevens
read Johnson as part of his English 7 course, the second semester of the
1898–99 academic year.

11. Spreading his intellectual wings, Stevens critically observed:

Barrett Wendell says in his "Principles" [probably *English Composition: Eight
Lectures* etc., New York: Scribner's, 1892 (*L* 25 n)] that we cannot but
admire the skill with which a thing be done whether it be worth doing or
not. His opinion is probably just if he limits the pronoun "we" to mean
rhetoricians and the like. (*L* 25)

12. As Holly Stevens notes, *L* 25 n.
13. Wendell, op. cit., p. 273.
14. Ibid., p. 279.
15. Ibid.
16. Ibid., p. 280.
17. Many critics have written on this aspect of Stevens's work, notably
and specifically Robert Buttel, *Wallace Stevens: The Making of Harmonium*
(Princeton: Princeton University Press, 1967), and Michel Benamou, *Wallace
Stevens and the Symbolist Imagination* (Princeton: Princeton University Press,
1972). See also my dissertation, "By Their Fruits: Wallace Stevens, His Poetry, His Critics" (CUNY, 1977, under Joan Richardson-Picciotto), pp.
111–76.
18. This notion began to crystallize early in Stevens's development. It had
obvious connections with Oriental thought and was also no doubt reinforced
by the young man's reading of Schopenhauer's "psychological observations"
(*L* 88), which he came to sometime between 1897 and 1906. In
Schopenhauer, "On Aesthetics," *Essays and Aphorisms,* ed. and tr. R. J. Hol-
lingdale, (London and New York: Penguin, 1981), p. 156, we find the following, which bears on Stevens's understanding of the imagination and of its
ties to the all-important "abstract":

If, however, the individual will sets its associated power of the imagination
free for a while, and for once releases it entirely from the service for which it
was made and exists, so that it abandons the tending of the will or of the
individual person which alone is its natural theme and thus its regular occupation, and yet does not cease to be energetically active or to extend to

their fullest extent its powers of perceptivity then it will forthwith become completely *objective,* i.e. it will become a faithful mirror of objects, or more precisely the medium of the objectivization of the will appearing in this or that object, the inmost nature of which will now come forth through it the more completely the longer the perception lasts, until it has been entirely exhausted. It is only thus, with the pure subject, that there arises the pure object, i.e. the complete manifestation of the will appearing in the object perceived, which is precisely the (Platonic) *Idea* of it. The perception of this, however, demands that, when contemplating an object, I really abstract its position in space and time, and thus abstract its individuality. For it is this *position,* always determined by the law of causality, which places this object in any kind of relationship to me as an individual; so that only when this position is done away with will the object become an *Idea* and I therewith a pure subject of knowledge.

Schopenhauer, also influenced by Oriental texts, was building the thought bridges between East and West that Max Müller, for example, would cross, followed by at least two generations of Harvard students. In 1946, when Stevens wrote "Human Arrangement," he seemed to acknowledge his debt to Schopenhauer, particularly as he had expressed himself above:

> Place-bound and time-bound in evening rain
> And bound by a sound which does not change,
>
> Except that it begins and ends,
> Begins again and ends again—
>
> Rain without change within or from
> Without. In this place and in this time
>
> And in this sound, which do not change,
> In which the rain is all one thing,
>
> In the sky, an imagined, wooden chair
> Is the clear point of an edifice,
>
> Forced up from nothing, evening's chair,
> Blue-strutted curule, true—unreal,
>
> The centre of transformations that
> Transform for transformation's self,
>
> In a glitter that is a life, a gold
> That is a being, a will, a fate.

(CP 363)

Other readers of Stevens have also pointed out connections to Schopenhauer, though not in this particular way. Harold Bloom, most recently, in *Wallace*

Stevens: The Poems of Our Climate (Ithaca and London: Cornell University Press, 1977) has linked Stevens's understanding of "order" to Schopenhauer's thought.

19. Wendell, op. cit., pp. 288–89.

20. Wendell's description of these two aspects seems to have begun from his late-Victorian reformulation of Alexander Pope's eighteenth-century sensibility, following his quoting from the poet: "True wit is Nature to advantage dress'd,/What oft was thought, but ne'er so well express'd" (*An Essay on Criticism*); see Wendell, op. cit., p. 276.

21. Ibid., pp. 282–83.

22. One of these, Dante, Wendell praised as being the most successful artist in words, the first who "spoke to him" (Ibid., pp. 18; 286–87).

23. On this occasion Stevens had gone back to the Williamsburg section of Brooklyn to visit the school he had attended for a year; his uncle had since then died—apparently a suicide—so it is possible that the young man did not want to let on that he was from Pennsylvania, where it was known that his uncle had family connections. This incident will be dealt with more fully in the next chapter.

24. There were, including this one, six short stories published before 1900; this one appeared in the *Advocate* on March 6, 1899 (Vol. LXVI, No. 9, pp. 135–36); the others came out as follows:

"Her First Escapade," *Harvard Advocate,* Vol. LXVI, No. 7 (January 16, 1899), pp. 104–08;

"Part of His Education," *Harvard Advocate,* Vol. LXVII, No. 3 (April 24, 1899), pp. 35–37;

"The Higher Life," *Harvard Advocate,* Vol. LXVII, No. 8 (June 12, 1899), pp. 123–24;

"Pursuit," *Harvard Advocate,* Vol. LXVIII, No. 2 (October 18, 1899), pp. 19–20;

"The Nymph," *Harvard Advocate,* Vol. LXVIII, No. 6 (December 6, 1899), pp. 86–87; signed "John Fiske Towne."

In 1900 the last three stories appeared:

"Hawkins of Cold Cape," *Harvard Advocate,* Vol. LXIX, No. 1 (March 10, 1900), pp. 8–12; signed "Carrol Moore";

"In the Dead of Night," *Harvard Advocate,* Vol. LXIX, No. 6 (May 23, 1900), pp. 83–86;

"Four Characters," *Harvard Advocate,* Vol. LXIX, No. 8 (June 16, 1900), pp. 119–20.

See J. M. Edelstein, *Wallace Stevens: A Descriptive Bibliography* (Pittsburgh: University of Pittsburgh Press, 1973), for a complete listing of Stevens's early publications, including editorials for the *Advocate,* etc. Edelstein's bibliography lists not only all of Stevens's work but all the critical work on Stevens until 1973, including dissertations, books partially about Stevens, book reviews, musical settings, and more. It is an invaluable scholarly tool.

25. "Self-Respect," for example, was completely erased, though it was still legible to Holly Stevens, who reproduces it in *SP* (23):

> Sun in the heaven,
> Thou are the cause of my mirth,
> Star in the evening
> Thine is my province since birth;
> Depths of the sky
> Yours are the depths of my worth.

26. As Holly Stevens notes, Harold Bloom has called the sixth sonnet quoted below in this text ("If we are leaves that fall upon the ground . . .") "pure Shelley" (*SP* 31).

27. On the connections between Whitman and Stevens in general, many critics have written. Buttel, op. cit.; James Baird, *The Dome and the Rock: Structure in the Poetry of Wallace Stevens* (Baltimore: Johns Hopkins Press, 1968); and Joseph N. Riddel, *The Clairvoyant Eye: The Poetry and Poetics of Wallace Stevens* (Baton Rouge: Louisiana State University Press, 1965), are among those who have pointed out significant affinities. More extensively and recently, however, Diane Wood Middlebrook, *Walt Whitman and Wallace Stevens* (Ithaca and London: Cornell University Press, 1974), and Harold Bloom, op. cit., have developed the ties between the two poets. John Hollander, too, *The Figure of Echo: A Mode of Allusion in Milton and After* (Berkeley, Los Angeles and London: University of California Press, 1981), indicates how Stevens uses the "of" of Whitman's titling in many of his ambiguous genitive constructions.

28. Stevens's omission of the apostrophe after "ladies" here was a characteristic error, as Holly Stevens has somewhere noted and as is apparent from going through Stevens's manuscript letters, poems, and journals at the Huntington Library.

29. It is possible that Stevens had accompanied Sally Wily on earlier occasions when she named flowers in the countryside around Reading, for one of the poems he seems to have composed during the spring of 1899 is addressed to a "You" who could easily be her:

> You say this is the iris?
> And that faery blue
> Is the forget-me-not?
> And that golden hue
> Is but a heavy rose?
> And these four long-stemmed blooms
> Are purple tulips that enclose

So and so many leaves?
Their names are tender mumbling
For you who know
Naught else; through my own soul
Their wonders nameless go.

(SP 36)

30. I am indebted to John Hollander for this observation.

31. There was the volume of Emerson at his aunt Mariah's, though we can't know which titles it contained. But at Christmas 1898 Kate Stevens presented her son with a twelve-volume set of his *Works* (Boston: Houghton, 1896–98). Stevens heavily marked many of the essays (the volumes are now at the Huntington Library), including "Nature" (First Series), 1836, the fourth paragraph of which is the one quoted here.

32. The pigeons, for example, as Holly Stevens and Robert Buttel note in this context.

33. In his "Adagia" Stevens later defined surrealism in these terms: "The essential fault of surrealism is that it invents without discovering. To make the clam play an accordion is to invent not to discover. The observation of the unconscious, so far as it can be observed, should reveal things of which we have previously been unconscious, not the familiar things of which we have been conscious plus imagination" *(OP* 177).

34. The various pseudonyms he used were: John Morris 2nd, John Fiske Towne, Hillary Harness, Carrol Moore and Carrol More, R. Jerries, Kenneth Malone, and Henry Marshall. The possible significance of some of these will be discussed at the end of this chapter.

35. The complex of associations surrounding Stevens's choice of the harmonium as a controlling figure will be slowly unfolded through following chapters. In this context, however, apropos of Stevens's dealing with pain, what he called "pathos," it is useful to note the following passage from Schopenhauer "On Suffering in the World," *Essays and Aphorisms* (loc. cit., p. 46): "That spiritual pain is conditional upon knowledge goes without saying, and it is easy to see that it will increase with the degree of knowledge. We can thus express the whole relationship figuratively by saying that the will is the string, its frustration or impediment the vibration of the string, knowledge of the sounding-board, and pain the sound."

For a detailed discussion, including earlier critical perceptions, of the formal elements contributing to the poet's intention to compose "The Whole of Harmonium: The Grand Poem," connecting it to the symbolist aesthetic, exemplified by Mallarmé's desire for the *grand Oeuvre* as well as to Whitman's *Leaves of Grass* and to roots in the Chinese tradition of poetry anthologies, see my dissertation, loc. cit., pp. 93–106 and accompanying notes. Non-technical and relevant aspects of this encompassing intention will be taken up here in the last chapters of Volume II.

36. On more than one occasion Stevens expressed his feeling that "gaud-

iness" was one of the most desirable aspects of poetry. In 1933 he selected "The Emperor of Ice-Cream" as his favorite poem because, as he noted to William Rose Benét, it wore "a deliberately commonplace costume, and yet seem[ed] to contain something of the essential gaudiness of poetry . . ." (*L* 263). I think Stevens chose this particular word because of its derivation from the Latin *gaudeo*, "to take pleasure in, rejoice." It would thus be connected to one of the three necessary features of the "Supreme Fiction": "It Must Give Pleasure."

In this context, see also Eleanor Cook, "Riddles, Charms and Fictions in Wallace Stevens," *Centre and Labyrinth: Essays in Honor of Northrop Frye,* eds., Eleanor Cook, Chaviva Hošek, Jay MacPherson, Patricia Parker, and Julian Patrick (Toronto: University of Toronto Press, 1983), pp. 227–44.

37. The Philippines were invaded in February 1899 as part of the escalation of the Spanish-American War.

38. Richard E. Welch, Jr., reviewing Stuart Miller, *The American Conquest of the Philippines, 1899–1903* (New Haven: Yale University Press, 1982), *New York Times Book Review,* November 21, 1982, p. 11.

39. In choosing to incorporate the name of John Fiske in this pseudonym, Stevens may have been naïvely pointing to the fact that he was beginning to confront one of the essential problems of his age's crisis of belief. John Fiske, born in 1842 in Connecticut, "turned away in his teens from the Calvinism of his ancestors to the fairer prospect of English and French positivism." He attended Harvard; his hero became Herbert Spencer. His life's work—beyond a failed law practice—was to attempt "taming the idea of evolution and then leashing it to an optimistic theism." On this theme he wrote free-lance articles for the *North American Review, Atlantic Monthly,* and *Nation;* he taught at Harvard for two years, but did not receive—even after publishing his *Outlines of Cosmic Philosophy, Based on the Doctrine of Evolution*—as he had hoped, the position in history vacated by Henry Adams in 1877. In his *Outlines* Fiske thought he had worked out the "proper relationship between science and religion. 'Though science must destroy mythology,' he asserted, 'it can never destroy religion; and to the astronomers of the future, as well as to the Psalmist of old, the heavens will declare the glory of God.'" (Russett, op. cit., pp. 48–50; 79).

Grappling with the same ethical issues as Fiske, the young Stevens must have been at least minorly preoccupied with this, in the end, failed figure.

40. See Alfred Kreymborg, *Troubadour: An Autobiography* (New York: Boni & Liveright, 1925), p. 239.

CHAPTER III. *New York: 1900*

1. *Appleton's Dictionary of New York and Its Vicinity* (New York: D. Appleton & Co., 1900). The caution under "Apartment Houses and Flats" about such inexpensive residences reads: "Before locating in a moderate priced house [that is, up to seven rooms for as low as $600 per year], careful inquiry as to

the character of the inmates is advisable." (p. 4). For "Tenements," the warning was that much stonger; the entry notes that half of New York's population at the time lived in tenements.

2. Holly Stevens has, I think correctly, observed (*SP* 73) a connection between the figure of the peacock woven into the bathroom rug and "Anecdote of the Prince of Peacocks" (*CP* 57). I would like to add that the same figure could have been flitting about, slightly changed when Stevens composed these lines for "Sunday Morning" (*CP* 66):

> Complacencies of the peignoir, and late
> Coffee and oranges in a sunny chair,
> And the green freedom of a cockatoo
> Upon a rug mingle to dissipate
> The holy hush of ancient sacrifice.

In this poem, too, an "Elysium of Elysiums" is evoked.

3. It should be noted that Stevens reported that he had picked up the expression "a high-toned old Christian woman" from his friend Judge Arthur Powell.

4. "Facts" in the context of Stevens's use of the word should, I think, be understood in connection with William James's important use in *The Varieties of Religious Experience* (New York: Doubleday, Image Books, 1978) a text with which Stevens was undoubtedly familiar: "Individuality is founded in feeling; and the recesses of feeling, the darker, blinder strata of character, are the only places in the world in which we catch real fact in the making, and directly perceive how events happen, and how work is actually done." (p. 483)

5. George Santayana, *The Middle Span,* Vol. II, *People and Places* (New York: Scribner's, 1945), p. 152.

6. This contributed, I think, to Stevens's later focus on "The Irrational Element in Poetry" (*OP* 216–28).

7. See Note 4 above.

8. *Essai sur les données immédiates de la conscience* appeared in 1889; *Matière et mémoire* in 1896; *Le Rire* in 1900. The significance of this last work will be discussed in Chapter VII.

9. T. S. Eliot, "The Love Song of J. Alfred Prufrock," *The Complete Poems and Plays* (New York: Harcourt, Brace & World, 1962), p. 3.

10. For a detailed discussion, see Richard Jenkyns, *The Victorians and Ancient Greece* (Cambridge: Harvard University Press, 1981).

11. The "Harlem Rag" became popular first in 1897; the "Maple Leaf Rag," in 1899. Roger Shields (in an essay printed on the record jacket of *Americana,* Vol. IV, *The Age of Ragtime* [VOX, Turnabout, October 1974]) describes the general impact of this form:

> A lilting and stimulating music once swept across America with an unprecedented intensity and universality of appeal. Ragtime, THE popular craze

from around 1897–1917, is special because it is the first distinctive American music. New and shocking, yet thoroughly enchanting to the general public, ragtime was also quickly embraced and respected abroad: Debussy, Stravinsky, Satie, Milhaud, Hindemith, and other European figures happily worked with ragtime elements. The serious musical establishment at home, however, embroiled itself in great controversy over this music—some groups even banned playing it! Naturally Charles Ives, the great exception, early vamped and stylized ragtime in many works. [This is interesting in connection with the affinity between Ives's and Stevens's work and life. In this context, see Lawrence Cramer, "'A Completely New Set of Objects': Wallace Stevens and Charles Ives," *The Wallace Stevens Journal,* Vol. 2, Nos. 3 and 4 (Fall 1978) pp. 3–14.] After World War I, and given the European stamp of approval, other American composers (such as Antheil, Copland, Barber, and Virgil Thompson) were strongly influenced by ragtime and jazz styles. It would of course be impossible to conceive of the development of 20th Century popular and jazz music without the background and pervasive influence of ragtime.

I think it is equally important to recognize the influence of ragtime and jazz on the free-verse rhythms of modern poetry, in Stevens's case particularly evident in *Harmonium.* This will be dealt with in a later chapter here.

12. This phrase comes from the description of "Concert Saloons" in *Appleton's Dictionary:*

> . . . a class of resorts such as respectable people do not visit. Formerly Broadway, in the neighborhood of Bleecker st., was full of them; but of late years they have come to confine themselves almost entirely to the Bowery. In them women are employed as attendants, and a lavish display of gas-jets and paint and tinsel outside serves to give the passer-by an impression of splendor within which the reality by no means warrants. The women are seldom good-looking, vulgar as a rule, and ignorant always. The music is furnished from a badly thumped piano, the liquors sold are vile, and the women insist on being treated constantly to a concoction which they dignify with the name of brandy, and for which they charge accordingly. The frequenters of these places are chiefly foolish young clerks and mechanics, who labor under the delusion that this is "seeing life." Strangers should be very careful about going into them, for the police make spasmodic and irregular raids on them. . . . (p. 64)

13. Roger Shields notes that many rags incorporated the waltz themes of Stephen Foster, Daniel Emmett, and Louis Gottschalk. Stevens knew at least the Gottschalk waltzes from Kate Wily's playing, as he recorded in an early journal entry quoted in the previous chapter.

14. This is as Roger Shields describes on the same record jacket. For a more extensive discussion, see Marshall W. Stearns, *The Story of Jazz* (London and New York: Oxford University Press, 1977).

15. John Crowe Ransom, for example, in "Poets Without Laurels," which first appeared in 1938, speaking of Stevens's "Sea Surface Full of Clouds," noted: "That it has not been studied by a multitude of persons is due to a simple consideration which strikes us at once: the poem has no moral, political, religious, or sociological values. It is not about 'res publica,' the public thing. The subject matter is trifling" (*The World's Body* [Baton Rouge: Louisiana State University Press, 1968], p. 59). A completely different reading of this poem, indicating how profoundly concerned it was with morality, is offered in my dissertation, loc. cit., pp. 111–98, and in shortened form in my "A Reading of 'Sea Surface Full of Clouds,'" *The Wallace Stevens Journal,* Vol. 6, Nos. 3 and 4 (Fall 1982), pp. 60–68.

16. Allan Chankin, "Wallace Stevens' Romantic Landscape Notes on Meditation: 'No Possum, No Sop, No Taters,'" *The Wallace Stevens Journal,* Vol. 5, Nos. 3 and 4 (Fall 1981), p. 43, notes that this poem is directed in part to depicting the South during such a period, though the image is romanticized in a Keatsian meditative mode. He notes, too, that the expression is a southern colloquial one. Though this might be the case, the rhythmic echoes of the poem tie it to the "Possum and Taters" rag as well.

17. Shields, op. cit.

18. Ibid.

19. This punning is put to full use in "The Comedian as the Letter C" as well: "Crispin/The lutanist of fleas, the knave, the thane,/The ribboned stick, the bellowing breeches . . ." (*CP* 28) is obviously a juggler-entertainer. And throughout the poem images of cutting appear, reinforced by metric clippings, until finally the poem ends with "So may the relation of each man be clipped." In his desire to "stem verboseness in the sea" (*CP* 28), "to drive away/The shadow of his fellows from the skies" (*CP* 37)—that is, to proclaim with his own voice over the echoes of the "man-poets" who had come before him—the poet was involved in a desire for symbolic castrations, "clippings," that were, more neutrally, surgical trimmings, modifications, parodies, of others' styles.

20. "Culture and Anarchy," *The Portable Matthew Arnold,* loc. cit., pp. 472–73.

21. See *SP* and Buttel, op. cit.

22. As quoted by Buttel, op. cit., p.5n from Horace Gregory and Maria Zaturenska, *A History of American Poetry, 1900–1940* (New York: Harcourt, Brace & World, 1946), p. 10.

23. Buttel, op. cit., p. 5.

24. Ibid.

25. It is interesting to note, through Holly Stevens's connecting the "Crispine, the blade," of this poem with her father's memory of the "knife-presenting misses," the plays on cutting and "Crispin" indicated above in Note 19 and earlier in the text.

26. *Appleton's Dictionary,* loc. cit., p. 98.

27. Ibid., p. 100.

28. Ibid., p. 158.

29. *Old New York in Early Photographs, 1853–1901,* selected by Mary Black (New York: Dover, 1976), p. 146.

30. This seems suggestively linked as well to T. S. Eliot's Madame Sosostris in "The Waste Land," loc. cit., p. 38.

31. "Holidays in Reality," *Wallace Stevens: A Celebration,* eds. Frank Doggett, Robert Buttel (Princeton: Princeton University Press, 1980), p. 105.

32. *A Child's Garden of Verses* (Boulder: Shambhala, 1979), p. 62.

33. *From Scotland to Silverado,* ed. James D. Hart (Cambridge: Belknap Press, 1966), p. 231. This edition contains *The Silverado Squatters* complete.

34. See Jenni Calder, "Introduction," *The Strange Case of Dr. Jekyll and Mr. Hyde* (New York: Penguin, 1979), pp. 8–14.

35. *Scotland to Silverado,* loc. cit., p. 195.

36. Ibid., pp. 266, 260.

37. Ibid., pp. 229–30.

38. Ibid., p. 271.

39. In this connection it is interesting to note another piece of Stevenson's work that Stevens could have known, "The Philosophy of Nomenclature" (*The Works of Robert Louis Stevenson,* eds. Charles Curtis Bigelow and Temple Scott, Vol. IX [New York, Philadelphia, and Chicago: Nottingham Society, 1908], pp. 358–61). This wonderful essay, built around the perception that "the influence of our names makes itself felt from the very cradle," also contains an observation about the bond that automatically forms between two individuals who discover themselves to have the same or similar-sounding names. Stevens, not being named for a family member, could, because of this, have unconsciously sought identification with Stevenson, called Mr. Stevens in *The Silverado Squatters.*

40. *Scotland to Silverado,* loc. cit., p. 213.

41. *Child's Garden,* loc. cit., p. 28.

42. *Scotland to Silverado,* loc. cit., p. 191.

43. Ibid., p. 212.

44. Lafcadio Hearn, "Fuji-no-Yama," *Exotics and Retrospectives* (Rutland, Vermont, and Tokyo, Japan: Charles E. Tuttle, 1977), pp. 3–36. This volume was first published in 1898 by Little, Brown & Co. in Boston; Stevens read Hearn and in at least two instances referred to what he had read to Elsie Moll during the years of their courtship. In addition, Hearn's pieces appeared regularly in *Harper's* magazine, which Stevens occasionally read. It is not unlikely that he knew this essay.

45. *Scotland to Silverado,* loc. cit., p. 228.

46. *The Figure of Echo,* referred to in Note 27, Chapter II.

47. *Scotland to Silverado,* loc. cit., p. 277.

48. Ibid., p. 254.

49. Ibid., p. 255.

50. I am indebted to John Hollander for hearing the echo of Milton's "Ode on the Morning of Christ's Nativity" in Section X of "The Man with the Blue Guitar," where this image appears.

51. *Works of Robert Louis Stevenson,* loc. cit., pp. 267–84.

52. Ibid., p. 267.

53. However, the connections between Stevens and Whitman have been explored by critics. See Note 27, Chapter II.

54. W. Jackson Bate, *John Keats* (Cambridge: Belknap Press, 1982), p. 73.

55. In his Introduction to *The Portable Steven Crane* (New York: Penguin, 1982), pp. vii–xxvi, Joseph Katz gives the details surrounding the death and funeral of the young writer. One critic of Stevens—I think it was R. P. Blackmur—connected Stevens's attendance at the funeral with his description of the funeral in "The Emperor of Ice-Cream."

56. Bate, op. cit., p. 77 and passim.

57. In a letter written in 1946 to John Gould Fletcher, Witter Bynner noted that Santayana had been particularly interested in Stevens as an undergraduate and that he probably still was interested at the time (*Selected Letters,* loc. cit., p. 189).

58. Introduction, *Portable Crane,* loc. cit. The map of Manhattan reproduced in *Appleton's Dictionary* (loc. cit., pp. 82–83) shows how in 1900 Avenues A and B, extending into the slum areas of the "East End" (now Sutton Place), bordered the shore opposite Blackwell's Island.

59. Holly Stevens notes this as well in connection with Stevens's first impressions of Chelsea Square, where he later chose to live with Elsie Moll just after their marriage (*SP* 81).

60. This he did in his Introduction to *A Victorian Anthology* (Boston: Houghton Mifflin, 1900); Stedman was the first to coin the term "Victorian."

61. Like that at the Astor House, where, according to *Appleton's Dictionary* (loc. cit., p. 53), ". . . a good chop . . . baked potato, a bit of water-cress, plenty of good bread and English pickles" could be had for between thirty and forty cents.

62. The details of Stevens's testing a word out on an employee at the Hartford will be given in Chapter XI, Volume II.

63. By R. M. Milnes in David Gray, *Poems* (Boston: Roberts, 1864).

64. Ibid., p. 159.

65. Ibid., p. 22.

66. Gray composed his own epitaph. It begins, "Below lies one whose name was traced/in sand—"—a certain echo of Keats. Ibid., p. 54.

67. Ibid., p. 156.

68. As observed by Milnes in his Preface and as indicated clearly in Gray, op. cit., Sonnet XV, p. 170.

69. Ibid., p. 157.

70. Ibid., p. 164.

71. Ibid., p. 161.

72. Ibid., p. 174.

73. From a poem of Ou Yang Hsiu, Sung dynasty, translated here by Kenneth Rexroth, *One Hundred Poems from the Chinese* (New York: New Directions, 1971), p. 60. It is impossible to know which translation Stevens might have read.

74. Gray, op. cit., p. 170.

75. Bate, op. cit., p. 86.

76. Ibid., p. 85.

77. Ibid.

78. For a full discussion of the connections between *Paradise Lost* and "Le Monocle de Mon Oncle," see my dissertation, loc. cit., pp. 494–532.

79. One of the things he heard was Tchaikovsky's Piano Concerto No. 1 in B-flat Minor (Opus 23). As evidenced by his "Discography," Stevens had a very strong liking for piano music.

80. See especially Benamou, op. cit.

81. André Lagarde and Laurent Michard, *XX Siècle: Les Grands Auteurs Français* (Paris: Bordas, 1966), p. 53.

82. Ibid., p. 55.

83. As Holly Stevens also notes (*SP* 94), quoting the appropriate passage from *NA* 56–57.

CHAPTER IV. *The Opposing Law: 1901–1904*

1. See Russett, op. cit., and Lears, op. cit., for comprehensive discussions of this.

2. Edward S. Ellis and Charles F. Horne, *The World's Famous Events*, 4 Vols. (New York: Francis Niglutsch, 1919), Vol. 4, pp. 1683–85; *Columbia Encyclopedia*, loc. cit., p. 1702.

3. *The Timetables of History*, compiled by Bernard Grun (New York: Simon & Schuster, 1982), p. 457.

4. *Columbia Enclyclopedia*, loc. cit., p. 1702.

5. Ibid.

6. As Heinz R. Pagels maps in *The Cosmic Code: Quantum Physics as the Language of Nature* (New York: Bantam, 1983), Planck's paper of 1900 ushered in the physics of the twentieth century. It was followed in 1905 by Einstein's paper on the special theory of relativity. After these, physics was transformed though there was resistance to giving up the Old World view:

> Planck's idea of the quantum, further developed by Einstein as a photon, the particle of light, implied that the continuous view of nature could not be maintained. Matter was shown to be composed of discrete atoms. The ideas of space and time held since the age of Newton were overthrown. Yet in spite of these advances, the idea of determinism—that every detail of the universe was subject to physical law—remained entrenched in Einstein and his entire generation of physicists. (p. 23)

By the 1920s the quantum theory of atomic phenomena was created; Werner Heisenberg and Niels Bohr, part of the new generation of physicists, formulated laws of quantum mechanics for atoms. Nuclear physics began. Einstein moved to the sidelines after 1926 (Pagels, pp. 42–43). The materialist world view was dead.

7. *Columbia Encyclopedia,* loc. cit., p. 1702.

8. Ibid., p. 1435. See also Chapter II, Note 1.

9. Peter Brazeau, *Parts of a World: Wallace Stevens Remembered* (New York: Random House, 1983), pp. 257, 262–63, 280.

10. These include: *The Naval War of 1812* (1882), biographies of Thomas H. Benton (1887) and Gouverneur Morris (1888), *The Winning of the West* (4 Vols., 1889–96), *African Game Trails* (1910), *The New Nationalism* (1910), *Progressive Principles* (1913), *Through the Brazilian Wilderness* (1914), and his autobiography (1913); *Columbia Encyclopedia,* loc. cit., p. 1435.

11. One of the key Emersonian concepts concerning man's relationship to nature comes from his essay "Nature," *Essays by Ralph Waldo Emerson,* Second Series (New York: Thomas Y. Crowell, 1926), in which an individual's health and vigor are indicated by how he or she may become "erect" like nature:

> Man is fallen; nature is erect, and serves as a differential thermometer, detecting the presence or absence of the divine sentiment in man. By fault of our dullness and selfishness, we are looking up to nature, but when we are convalescent, nature will look up to us. We see the foaming brooks with compunction; if our own life flowed with the right energy, we should shame the brook. The stream of zeal sparkles with real fire, and not with the reflex rays of sun and moon. (p. 387)

Popularly understood, of course, in order to determine one's health, one had to measure oneself by proving oneself in nature; hence, the importance of hunting, fishing, etc.

12. The incident of Stevens's fistfight with Hemingway will be taken up in a later chapter, as will his various expressions of artistic admiration for him, the latter being the reason for the qualifier *"personal* hostility."

13. Witter Bynner recalled Stevens this way during his early New York years: "I saw something of him in New York where he read me amazingly fine passages from a diary he kept.

"He used to take lengthy walks along the Hudson and I remember especially liking the diary jottings he made on those excursions. It was at that time, I believe, that he was wearing a young but heavy beard" (Bynner, *Selected Letters,* loc. cit., p. 189).

14. As quoted by Holly Stevens (*SP* 96):

> There is also the story of the down and out Stevens sitting on a park bench at the Battery watching the out tide and thinking to join it, as a corpse, on its way out to the sea (he had been a failure as a reporter). As he sat there

watching the debris floating past him he began to write—noting the various articles as they passed. He became excited as he wrote and ended by taking back to the *Tribune* (?) office an editorial or a "story" that has become famous—in a small way among the newspaper offices.

But that finished him as a newspaper man. It may very well be that that moment was his beginning as a poet.

This "story" has not been located.

15. I found this coinage of "*dis*ease" in Lears, op. cit., where it is used throughout the text.

16. "Such eminent cultural figures as William James, Charles Eliot Norton, and Henry Adams suffered from neurasthenic symptoms. . . . The anxious desire to flee 'morbid self-consciousness' often fed on itself and generated further immobilizing introspection. By the early twentieth century, the problem seemed general; references to 'our neurasthenic epidemic' proliferated in the established press. 'On every street, at every corner, we meet the neurasthenics,' a *North American Review* writer observed in 1908" (Ibid., p. 50). See also pp. 49–57 passim and 243–47.

17. Ibid., pp. 4–58.

18. I have adopted this term from critical discussions of nineteenth-century Russian novelists who depicted characters—perhaps best exemplified by Ivan Goncharov's *Oblomov*—no longer having a place in the social order that was collapsing. As a result, these figures, bred as gentlemen, often found themselves on the brink of despair. They were fictional prototypes of the "existential man," but without the courage to act or an arena in which to act; their only recourse was either endless rationalization bordering on madness or extreme neurasthenia.

19. Lears, op. cit., pp. 225–41.

20. Among those Lears describes, in addition to those already mentioned in the text and in Note 16 here, are G. Stanley Hall and Van Wyck Brooks; see pp. 218–97 for details on all.

21. Lears's observations concerning fascism are useful to note in this connection:

"[The] tradition of antimodern dissent has survived most conspicuously in avant-garde art and literature—the cultural 'modernism' that has so often protested the effects of modernization. To be sure, the avant-garde quest for authenticity has often merged with twentieth-century hegemonic cultures, not only in consumer capitalism in America but fascism in Europe: the Italian Futurist Filippo Marinetti became an enthusiastic Fascist, urging his followers to 'sing the love of danger, the habit of energy and boldness.' But alongside the fascination with energy for its own sake, there has been an insistent desire to locate a transcendant Being in the midst of frenetic becoming" (Ibid., p. 309).

22. Ibid., pp. 243–60.

23. Holly Stevens also notes this in the context of her father's thoughts about changing his career (*SP* 101).

24. Or Sylvia, as Holly records in "Holidays in Reality," loc. cit., p. 106.

25. Lears, op. cit., pp. xiii, xiv, xv, 32, 41–47, 143, 167, 195, 202–03, 303–04.

26. Ibid., pp. 100, 102, 108, 109, 117, 118, 143, 222.

27. Ibid., pp. 10–11.

28. Henry James in *The American Scene,* first published in 1907, "genteely" translates this fear into critical aversions for various groups such as the Italians and Jews:

> The Italians, who, over the whole land, strike us, I am afraid, as, after the Negro and the Chinaman, the human value most easily produced, the Italians meet us, at every turn, only to make us ask what has become of that element of the agreeable address in *them* which has, from far back, so enhanced for the stranger the interest and pleasure of a visit to their beautiful country. They shed it utterly, I couldn't but observe, on their advent. . . . (From the edition of the same title, with an Introduction and notes by Leon Edel [Bloomington and London: Indiana University Press, 1968], p. 128)

> There is no swarming like that of Israel when once Israel has got a start, and the scene here bristled, at every step, with the signs and sounds, immitigable, unmistakable, of a Jewry that had burst all bounds. That it has burst all bounds in New York, almost any combination of figures or of objects taken at hazard sufficiently proclaims; but I remember how the rising waters, on this summer night, rose, to the imagination, even above the housetops and seemed to sound their murmur to the pale distant stars. It was as if we had been thus, in the crowded hustled roadway, where multiplication of everything was the dominant note, at the bottom of some vast sallow aquarium in which innumerable fish, of over-developed proboscis, were to bump together, for ever, amid heaped spoils of the sea. (Ibid., p. 131)

As will be noted, at certain "critical" points of his own, Stevens shared this aversion.

29. Milton J. Bates, *Wallace Stevens: A Mythology of Self* (Berkeley, Los Angeles and London: University of California Press, 1985), pp. 49–82; and *SP* 247.

30. As reported in a telephone interview with Mrs. Richard Bissell, December 13, 1982.

31. *The Essays or Counsels Civill & Morall of Francis Bacon Lord Verulam* (New York: E. P. Dutton, 1910), p. 80.

32. Reported in an interview with Herbert P. Schoen, December 17, 1982. This perception of Stevens's needing his martinis "so he could have a

good time" is reinforced by the recollections of his niece by marriage, Anna May Stevens (Brazeau, op. cit., p. 279).

33.

> In America the delayed reaction to naturalism was perhaps the result of neglecting the vast forces for social change, and the moral and social problems, that arose in American society at its high point of industrialization; but with Frank Norris, Stephen Crane, and Hamlin Garland in the 1890's a tradition developed which has been remarkably persistent. By this date naturalism in Europe was giving way to a new aestheticism and symbolism . . . and the impressionistic element was pushing through to create the uncertain surface of much modernist writing and painting. Naturalism was the transition point at the end of an era in Europe; in some countries and in some writers it has persisted significantly into the new century. (*The Fontana Dictionary of Modern Thought,* eds. Alan Bullock and Oliver Stallybrass [London: Fontana/Collins, 1977], p. 411)

Seen in this light, Stevens's proclivity for what early critics and reviewers chidingly called his "symbolist" and "impressionistic" imagination was not at all an atavism attached to an affected longing for a recently past European sensitivity, but a mark of his connection to the avant-garde.

34. Anthony Sigmans, whom Stevens was to hire for the Hartford, first met Stevens at the Commodore Hotel in New York where the poet-insurance executive was staying. Sigmans remembered the poet's telling him, just after asking Sigmans if he had had dinner, that he had just eaten "several pounds of Pennsylvania Dutch sausage, one of his favorites." Apparently Sigmans had eaten, so they "did the town," drinking ceaselessly from one night spot to another. Sigmans also noted the charming detail that Stevens "never failed, upon entering a club, to tip the orchestra leader and have the orchestra play 'Have You Ever Seen a Dream Girl [*sic*] Walking,' which was popular at the time and one of his favorites." This was in 1934 (Brazeau, op. cit., p. 76).

35. In addition to its appearance in the translation of Buddhist texts and in Matthew Arnold, as noted in Chapter II, the phrase was also used by John Ruskin, F. H. Bradley, and T. E. Hulme. It seems to have belonged to the vocabulary of the spirit of the age. Stevens could have come across it in any one of the above-mentioned sources and, quite likely, too, in reviews that were part of the many journals he read.

36. Jerome Bump, "Stevens and Lawrence: The Poetry of Nature and the Spirit of the Age," *Southern Review,* Vol. 18, No. 1 (Winter 1982), pp. 44–61, has most recently dealt with Stevens's use of the pathetic fallacy.

37. John Hollander has observed that in this way Stevens's experience paralleled that of Milton, who, in his *Areopagitica,* named Edmund Spenser a better teacher than Thomas Aquinas.

38. See Note 15, Chapter III.

39. Lears, op. cit., p. 202.

40. Ibid.

41. The incomplete state of this entry is accounted for by the fact that its reverse contained entries from July and August 1904 that were later excised, either by Stevens or by Elsie (*SP* 114). It should be noted that it was in late July or very early August 1904 that Stevens met his future wife and that these entries were probably clipped because of the details they revealed about the budding relationship.

42. Lears, op. cit., pp. 13–14.

43. There are other suggestive echoes in these lines as well. One comes from Gustave Flaubert, *The Temptation of St. Anthony*, tr. Kitty Mrosovsky (New York: Penguin, 1980), p. 71, which I imagine Stevens to have read in French. As St. Anthony begins to hallucinate around a scent that recalls woman, he exclaims: "It's a long time now since I saw any! Maybe some will come? Why not? What if I suddenly . . . hear mule bells tinkling up the mountain. I almost think. . . ." Another, noted by John Hollander, comes from Goethe's *"Kennst du das Land, wo die Zitronen blühn. . . ."*

44. Heinrich Heine, *Poetry and Prose*, eds. Jost Hermand and Robert C. Holub (New York: Continuum, 1982), p. 5. This text also contains the original German versions of the poems I quote. I do not know whether Peckham read in German or in translation.

45. Heine, "Ideas—Book Le Grand," loc. cit., p. 181.

46. Heine, "The Harz Journey," loc. cit., p. 125.

47. Ibid., pp. 47 and 49; also important in this context is the following passage from the beginning of Chapter 11 of "Ideas—Book Le Grand":

> *Du sublime au ridicule il n'y a qu'un pas, madame!* [From the sublime to the ridiculous there is only one step, madame!] But life is basically so fatally serious that it would be unbearable without such a connection between the pathetic and the comic. Our poets know that. The most horrible images of human madness are shown to us by Aristophanes only in the laughing mirror of wit. Only in the doggerel of a puppet show does Goethe dare to utter the great pain of the thinker who comprehends his own nothingness, and Shakespeare puts the gravest indictment about the misery of the world into the mouth of a fool who is anxiously rattling his cap and bells. (p. 204)

48. Ibid., p. 140.

49. Lears, op. cit., pp. 27–32 passim.

50. Ibid., p. 28.

51. Ibid., p. 54.

52. Bynner, op. cit., p. 189. It is interesting here to look at the entries Bynner made in his journal apropos of the evening Stevens also described in the journal entry of April 9, which is quoted in the next sentence and farther on in the same paragraph in the text. Here, then, are Bynner's entries:

April 8: In the evening at the Francis drank with Wallace Stevens till we were drunk. We slept hard in his room.

April 9: Stevens is not only likable but a wholesome friend—particularly as antidote to chatter-brains with tenderer manners. Through being much alone, he has gone daffy a little. His egotism is monumental. My intrusion with an egotism of my own confused him by not wholly displeasing him. It was the same in Cambridge. (James Kraft's Biographical Introduction, *Witter Bynner: Selected Poems*, ed. Richard Wilbur [New York: Farrar, Straus, Giroux, 1978], p. xl)

It should be noted that Barrett Wendell was a friend of Bynner's uncle (p. xxviii), and that in addition to spending time with Stevens in New York, Bynner "often visited Mark Twain late at night at 21 Fifth Avenue" and "saw a good deal of Henry James" during 1905 (pp. xxxviii–xxxix). He also admired John Dewey, "with whom he marched up Fifth Avenue for women's rights," and had many contacts with painters of the ashcan school (p. xxxviii). One wonders whether Bynner ever invited his friend, whom he perceived to have gone "daffy" from "being much alone," to join him with one or a group of these other acquaintances. If he did, there is no evidence.

CHAPTER V. *It Will Exceed All Faery: 1904–1907*

1. *Timetables,* loc. cit., p. 457.
2. Quoted from Arthur Davison Ficke by Harriet Monroe, *A Poet's Life* (New York: Macmillan, 1938), p. 390.
3. Ibid.
4. See Note 35, Chapter II, and Stegman, op. cit.
5. Holly Stevens connects this image, properly I think, to the play her father later wrote, *Carlos Among the Candles* (*SP* 140).
6. Stevens's rephrasing of Tennyson's observation—just preceding his puppets' play as Stevens's observation precedes his "dolls"—that "nature is one with rapine" (Part I, IV, iv) seems to be picked up again in one of Stevens's later poems. Tennyson goes on after his observation to illustrate it with "The Mayfly is torn by the swallow, the sparrow spear'd by the shrike." Stevens's updating of this for a twentieth-century audience that named man, too, as an actor in this "rapine" is suggested by the title of his 1922 "Frogs Eat Butterflies. Snakes Eat Frogs. Hogs Eat Snakes. Men Eat Hogs" (*CP* 78).
7. It is possible, too, that Stevens remembered Tennyson's raven when he composed his lines around the "blackbird" that similarly reminded him of his natural state.
8. This "memorandum" introducing Elsie's excerpts from her husband's letters to her is, indeed, puzzling. Did she mean to illustrate through what she chose to record that in spite of Stevens's seeking to find sources for his commitment to good, "say in Nature," he nonetheless shared her proper

"Christian spirit"? Was she composing her own "missal" to read from in the service of her husband's memory? These and many other questions present themselves.

9. Thomas Hardy, *The Trumpet-Major* (London: Macmillan, 1974), p. 91.

10. Thomas Hardy, *Under the Greenwood Tree; or, The Mellstock Quire* (New York: Penguin, 1978), p. 33.

11. From the flyleaf of Stevens's volume at the Huntington Library, part of the Wallace Stevens Collection.

12. Henrik Ibsen, *Pillars of Society and Other Plays,* ed. Havelock Ellis (London: W. Scott, 1901 [?]), p. xxx, the same copy referred to in previous note.

13. Ibid., p. xxv.

14. Ibid., p. 44.

15. Ibid., p. 55.

16. Milton Bates, "Stevens in Love, The Woman Won, The Woman Lost," *English Literary History,* Vol. 48 (1981), p. 254; and letter from Elsie to her sister dated August 30, 1921 (Huntington Library).

17. Brazeau, op. cit., p. 256; and evidenced by correspondence between Stevens and his father that will be referred to in the following chapter.

18. Stevens first refers to this essay in his journal entry of April 5, 1906 (*SP* 163). The first four letters were published serially in the *Saturday Review;* all eight are collected in the volume of the same title first published in London by J. M. Dent in 1901. References to page numbers in the following notes are from the second edition published by the same company in 1907 as G. Lowes Dickinson, *Letters From John Chinaman.*

19. Ibid., pp. 32–33.

20. Ibid., pp. 23–26 and 42–50.

21. Ibid., pp. 6–7.

22. Ibid., pp. 8–9.

23. This clipping was laid inside the back cover of Stevens's copy of the Psalms.

24. Paul Elmer More, *Shelburne Essays,* First Series, (New York and London: G. P. Putnam, 1904), p. 200.

25. Ibid., p. 195.

26. Ibid., p. 197.

27. Ibid., p. 198.

28. See Note 15, Chapter III. The metaphor of the sea surface changing in aspect as clouds move across the sky also appears frequently in Vedantic texts, many of which More clearly knew and which Stevens also could have known. William James connects the image of the moving sea with music, which gives us an "ontological message" in *The Varieties of Religious Experience,* (loc. cit., pp. 410–11). James, too, was obviously familiar with the Vedas.

29. More, op. cit., pp. 200–02.

30. Ibid., p. 203.

31. Ibid., p. 204.

32. More pointed out that this "instinct" in its deepest sense was the religious impulse (p. 216) and indicated, too, that Buddha embodied it.

33. Ibid., p. 219.

34. John Davidson, *Holiday and Other Poems* (New York: Dutton, 1906), is part of Stevens's library at the Huntington. In his recent biography of T. S. Eliot, *T. S. Eliot: A Life* (New York: Simon & Schuster, 1984), Peter Ackroyd notes Davidson as an early influence on this poet as well (p. 23).

35. Davidson, op. cit., p. 38.

36. Ibid., p. 53.

37. Ibid., p. 88.

38. Ibid., p. 32.

39. Ibid., p. 137.

40. This suggests that Stevens also read Kakuzo Okakura's *The Book of Tea* (New York: Fox, Duffield & Co., 1906). Okakura detailed the connections between tea brewing and Chinese ceramics ([New York: Dover, 1964], p. 13). Elsewhere Okakura cited Charles Lamb, who "wrote that the greatest pleasure he knew was to do a good action by stealth, and to have it found out by accident" (p. 7 of Dover edition); Stevens had copied this motto—without quotation marks or reference to a source—into one of his notebooks and also sent it in a letter to Elsie Moll. He could have read it either here or in the essay of Charles Lamb referred to by Okakura, which he had, on another occasion, recommended to Elsie. In any case Okakura continued in his text to paraphrase from Lamb and to add his own gloss: "For Teaism is the art of concealing beauty that you may discover it, of suggesting what you dare not reveal. It is the noble secret of laughing at yourself, calmly yet thoroughly, and is thus humor itself,—the smile of philosophy" (p. 7). Stevens obviously took these words deeply to heart. They reinforced the perception that opened Okakura's volume, a perception that also seems to have had its influence on Stevens, who wrote of the "imperfect" as "our paradise": "Teaism is a cult founded on the adoration of the beautiful among the sordid facts of everyday existence. It inculcates purity and harmony, the mystery of mutual charity, the romanticism of the social order. It is essentially a worship of the Imperfect, as it is a tender attempt to accomplish something possible in this impossible thing we know as life" (p. 1 of Dover edition).

41. Brazeau, op. cit., p. 20.

42. Many anecdotes revealing this quality pepper the recollections of those who worked with Stevens at the Hartford. See Ibid., pp. 12–93.

43. As reported the following day to Herbert Schoen, who related it to me during an interview, December 17, 1982.

44. Ibid.

CHAPTER VI. *The Book of Doubts and Fears: 1907–1909*

1. Milton W. Brown, *American Painting: From the Armory Show to the Depression* (Princeton: Princeton University Press, 1972), p. 39.

2. This paragraph is my translation from the original French from Charles Louandre's Preface to "Discours de Nicholas Machiavel Sur la Première Décade de Tite-Live," which Stevens transcribed into his journal (*SP* 182).

3. The 1906 publication of *The Jungle,* which contained descriptions of conditions in the Chicago stockyards, contributed to the passing of the U.S. Pure Food and Drug Act later that same year.

4. *Timetables,* loc. cit., p. 460.

5. Bliss Carman and Richard Hovey, *Songs from Vagabondia* (Boston: Copeland & Day, 1895). This volume was inscribed "To Elsie, Xmas, 1907" (*SP* 186).

6. Ibid., p. 6.

7. Ibid., p. 11.

8. Ibid., pp. 14–15.

9. Ibid., pp. 19–20.

10. Ibid., p. 31.

11. Bliss Carman and Richard Hovey, *More Songs from Vagabondia* (Boston: Copeland & Day, 1896), p. 2.

12. Ibid.

13. Ibid., p. 75.

14. See Notes 27 and 35, Chapter II, and Edelstein, op. cit., as well as the Annual Bibliographies of the Modern Language Association, after 1971 for references to critics who have dealt with these ties.

15. In *Songs from Vagabondia,* (loc. cit.) "Laura Dee" follows (pp. 44–46) a poem entitled "The Kavanagh" in which the figure of "McMurrough" and later an imaginary "emperor" appear. Echoes of these could perhaps have contributed to Stevens's figure of "MacCullough" and his "Emperor of Ice-Cream."

16. Carman & Hovey, *More Songs,* loc. cit., p. 7.

17. This subject is fully discussed in J. C. B. Gosling and C. C. W. Taylor, *The Greeks on Pleasure* (Oxford: Clarendon Press, 1982).

18. Ibid., pp. 13–25 and passim.

19. Ibid., pp. 45–46 and passim.

20. In a footnote added in 1915 to "The Sexual Aberrations"—the first of his "Three Essays on the Theory of Sexuality" of 1905—Freud glossed his earlier use of the term "sublimated." The passage from the 1905 text plus the note are particularly interesting to consider in connection with Stevens's exquisite attention to seeing—looking not *at* facts but *through* them—and his concern with what he called in "Peter Quince" the "body's beauty." Here, then, are the passage and note from Freud:

> The same holds true of seeing [that a great deal of pleasure is derived from it, as from touching]—an activity that is ultimately derived from touching. Visual impressions remain the most frequent pathway along which libidinal excitation is aroused; indeed, natural selection counts upon the accessibility of this pathway—if such a teleological form of statement is permissible—

when it encourages the development of beauty in the sexual object. The progressive concealment of the body which goes along with civilization keeps sexual curiosity awake. This curiosity seeks to complete the sexual object by revealing its hidden parts. It can, however, be diverted ("sublimated") in the direction of art, if its interest can be shifted away from the genitals on to the shape of the body as a whole.*

*There is to my mind no doubt that the concept of "beautiful" has its roots in sexual excitation and that its original meaning was "sexually stimulating." (Sigmund Freud, *On Sexuality: Three Essays on the Theory of Sexuality and Other Works*, tr. James Strachey, ed. Angela Richards, Vol. 7 of The Pelican Freud Library [Middlesex, England: Penguin Books, 1977], p. 69)

21. As noted by Malcolm Cowley, *Exile's Return* (New York: Penguin, 1979), p. 123, without mention of Stevens. The lines he quotes are from "Salutation the Second," in "Lustra" collected in Ezra Pound, *Personae* (New York: New Directions, 1951), pp. 85–86.

22. Only a few of these have been available until now, appearing in *L* 79–81, 85–86, 93–94, 106–109. "Elsie's Book" is cataloged as "WAS 1772" in the Huntington Library's Wallace Stevens Collection. A number of the excerpts are from letters appearing in *L* or in the collection that were not destroyed, indicating that Elsie meant to preserve in her notebook a particular sense of her husband for herself. They are presented here, then, to communicate this sense, even though repetitions will occur because of the earlier and elsewhere printed excerpts or letters. Some notes appear through the listing here; they point either to additions or comments made by Holly Stevens or to associations that shed light on other aspects of Stevens or his work.

23. As Holly Stevens observes (*SP* 187), it is uncertain whether her father wrote this poem.

24. This invocation could hint at another association for "The Emperor of Ice-Cream." Reading through *The Meditations of Marcus Aurelius* (tr. Jeremy Collier [London: Walter Scott, date-?]) makes it appear certain that Stevens knew the *Meditations* and learned from them, carefully following the "Good Emperor"'s advice, such as ". . .—make for yourself a particular description and definition of every object that presents itself to your mind, that you may thoroughly contemplate it in its own nature, bare and naked, wholly and separately" (p. 41); or this observation: "Things are not carelessly thrown on a heap, and joined more by number than nature, but, as it were, rationally connected with each other. And as things that exist are harmoniously connected, so those that become exhibit no mere succession, but an harmonious relationship" (p. 60); or this: "Let your soul work in harmony with the universal intelligence, as your breath does with the air" (p. 137), or this, in connection with the image of the "two golden gourds" in "Le Monocle de Mon Oncle" (*CP* 16):

A wise man, therefore, must neither run giddily nor impatiently and contemptuously into his grave. He must look upon death as nature's business, and wait her leisure as he does for the progress and maturity of other things; for as you wait for a child to come into the world when it is ready, so you should stay in the other case till things are ripe, and your soul drops out of the husk of her own accord [pp. 145–46];

or, in connection with the "abstract," "Penetrate the quality of forms, and take a view of them, abstracted from their matter; and when you have done this, compute the common period of their duration" (pp. 150–51); or, finally, in connection with Stevens's "Course of a Particular": ". . . the soul of the universe . . . pursues its course towards each particular . . ." (p. 151).

The "aureole" (in Mallarmé's sense of the halo of associations around a poet's use of a word) of allusions circling "The Emperor" for Stevens seems to radiate endlessly. Perhaps this is why it was his favorite poem, at least until 1933, its "gaudiness" being, in large part, the density of suggested links. Many have already been offered as possibilities, both in the text and in the notes. Though it is not germane to the discussion at this point, I should also like to add that Stevens's "Emperor" in his "Ice-Cream" seems to point back, too, to Dante's Satan as depicted in Canto XXXIV of the *Inferno,*

> The Emperor of the sorrowful realm was there,
>   Out of the girding ice he stood breast high,
>   And to his arm alone the giants were
>
> Less comparable than to a giant I. . . .

For still more allusions, I refer the reader to my dissertation, loc. cit., pp. 602–27.

25. Odors figured importantly for Stevens, especially in connection with the women closest to him. He remembered his mother's smell, "so fresh and clean" as she lay dying, Elsie's "sachet [as] wonderful," and even imagined in an early poem the "odor of a star." These instances will be referred to more particularly at various points in the text.

26. The individual poems appear in *SP* 190–96.

27. From the dated inscriptions on the flyleaves, it appears that among the other things Stevens read during this period were a volume of *Poems* by Alice Meynell, 9th ed. (London: J. Lane, 1904)—he marked many lines, some that seem to be echoed later in "Peter Quince"—and T. Sturge Moore's *Correggio* (London: Duckworth; New York: Scribner's, 1906), various passages marked. Stevens perhaps read this second volume to find out more about the painter of *La Zingarella,* a canvas that particularly moved him; its significance will be discussed later in this chapter.

28. *Letters by Matthew Arnold, 1848–88,* ed. George W. E. Russell, 2 Vols. in 1 (New York: Macmillan, 1900).

29. Ibid., p. ix.

30. Ibid., p. 208.

31. Ibid., pp. 225–26.
32. Ibid., p. 250.
33. Ibid., p. 265.
34. Ibid., p. 267.
35. Ibid., p. 288.
36. Ibid., p. 368.
37. Herbert W. Paul, *Matthew Arnold* (New York: Macmillan, 1903).
38. Ibid., p. 2.
39. Ibid., p. 15.
40. Ibid., p. 174.
41. Ibid., p. 56.
42. Ibid., pp. 94–95.
43. In this letter Stevens observed: "In Martinique, the wind breaks down iron doors. Here [in New York] it blows your hat into an ash-barrel" (*SP* 198). He could have been remembering reports of the 1902 volcano eruption in Martinique that destroyed the town of St. Pierre.
44. Herbert Schoen referred to Stevens this way during the interview of December 17, 1982.
45. Soren Kierkegaard, *Repetition*, eds. Howard V. Hong and Edna H. Hong (Princeton: Princeton University Press, 1983), p. 138.
46. Kenneth Grahame, *The Wind in the Willows* (New York: New American Library/Signet, 1969), p. 124.
47. This he had not heard since Cambridge, when, as he noted, he remembered Professor Norton's twirling his forefinger around his thumb by way of expressing his pleasure (WAS 1802).
48. William Carlos Williams, *Autobiography* (New York: New Directions, 1967), p. 108.
49. "[H]onest John in his stove-pipe," for example, led to a comparison of the world in the gray January weather to a "solemn Doctor of Philosophy" (WAS 1803), who emerged fully dressed as "The Doctor of Geneva."
50.

—Well, about that dance. I think I probably said "Oh my!" and sighed. But that was in New York. It made no impression at all in Reading [he seems to mean the New York man versus the Reading man]. The grief-stricken dancer at the Academy was worse, comparatively, when she walked—you saw the physical peacock at every step.—Let the lady dance for the gallery.—The dance itself: imagine Anna Rigg [apparently a Reading acquaintance] doing it—leaning back or swinging by the neck. What a sweet, pastoral way of spending the time! It is simply an exhibition.—But it makes all the difference who is doing it. The same thing in a cake-walk would be dull—the dancing of the day is not a fireside matter. The dance was part of the general rage. It is the only one I saw.—I saw none of the Salome, or the rest. It may be that I am an old prune, but there you are. A propos. (WAS 1805, January 13 and 14, 1909)

In spite of feeling like "an old prune" on the sidelines now, later in life Stevens let down his own hair on more than one occasion during his "business" weekends in New York, spinning into mad polkas and mean rumbas (Brazeau, op. cit., pp. 17, 90).

51. Sadly testifying to how difficult this must have been for her, this was one of the portions Elsie later copied into her stenographer's notebook.

52. During this period Stevens was reading Thackeray; *The History of Henry Esmond* seems to have offered him food for thought, providing, perhaps, a loose pattern for Crispin's later voyage to the New World and, more particularly, a phrased perception about the course of love that echoes in the "It comes, it blooms, it bears its fruit and dies" of "Le Monocle" (*CP* 16): "It has its course, like all mortal things—its beginnings, progress and decay. It buds and it blooms out into sunshine, and it withers and ends" (New York: Penguin, 1980, p. 153). He also read Elizabeth Gaskell's *Cousin Phyllis,* the theme of which echoed his own yearning to "go back to the peace of old days" (London: Dent; New York: Dutton, 1970 [p. 89]) as industrialization obliterated more and more of the pastoral world. During this period, too, Stevens read Stevenson's *A Child's Garden of Verses* and recommended it to Elsie (*L* 129).

53. These were Ethelbert Nevin's *Sketchbook,* which, besides the popular "Narcissus," probably contained his musical setting for "Wynken, Blinken and Nod"; Edward MacDowell's "Marionettes"; Arthur Whiting's "Album of Short Pieces"; and Adolf von Henselt's "If I were a bird . . ." ("Si j'etais oiseau . . ."), which, Stevens noted to Elsie, the "very well-known [Ossip] Gabrilowitsch, the Russian pianist, played at his last concert" (WAS 1810). Gabrilowitsch, a student of Anton Rubinstein's at the St. Petersburg Conservatory, later married the concert singer Clara Clemens, daughter of Mark Twain, after his emigration to this country, where he became the conductor of the Detroit Symphony Orchestra.

54. This enthusiasm seems to have been part of a broader cultural interest in European authors, especially French and German, at the time, as America attempted to see beyond its own horizon. See Wertheim, op. cit., p. 13.

55.

> Date al vento le chiome, isfavillanti
> Gli occhi glauchi, del sen nuda il candore,
> Salti su 'l cocchio; e l'impeto e il terrore
> Van con fremito anelo a te d'avanti.
>
> L'ombra del tuo cimier l'aure tremanti
> Come di ferrugino astro il bagnore,
> Trasvola; e de le tue ruote al fragore
> Segue la polve de gl'imperi infranti.
>
> Tale, o Roma, vedean le genti dome
> La imagin tua ne'lor terrori antichi:

Oggi una mitra a le regali chiome,

Oggi un rosario che la man t'implichi
Darti vorrien per sempre. Oh ancor del nome
Spauri il mondo e i secoli afflatichi!

(Give to the wind thy locks; all glittering
Thy sea-blue eyes, and thy white bosom bared,
Mount to thy chariots, while in speechless roaring
Terror and Force before thee clear the way!

The shadow of thy helmet like the flashing
Of brazen stars strikes through the trembling air.
The dust of broken empires, cloud-like rising,
Follows the awful rumbling of thy wheels.

So once, O Rome, beheld the conquered nations
Thy image, object of their ancient dread:
To-day a mitre they would place upon

Thy head, and fold a rosary between
Thy hands. O name! Again to terrors old
Awake the tired ages and the world!)

"Thy image, object of their ancient dread:" in the third stanza is an allusion to the figure of "Roma" as seen on ancient coins. *Poesie di Giosuè Carducci, 1850–1900* (Bologna: Nicola Zanichelli, 1909), p. 363; translation by Frank Sewall, *Carducci's Poems* (New York: Dodd, Mead & Co., 1892), p. 57.

56. In *The Complete Tales of Henry James*, ed. Leon Edel, Vol. 3, 1873–75 (Philadelphia and New York: Lippincott, 1962), p. 25.

57. Stevens marked various passages in his volume of Campion (*Songs and Masques, with Observations in the Art of English Poesy*, ed. A. H. Bullen [London: A. H. Bullen; New York: Scribner's, 1903]). One line that made a deep impression—as Stevens had marked it elsewhere, in an anthology containing the same poem of Campion's (VII from the *Fourth Book of Airs*)—was "There is a garden in her face . . ." (p. 114). Stevens also noted details of the clothing of the Gardener and the Gardener's son from the description of an entertainment given by Lord Knowles (pp. 185–86). The last could have contributed to Crispin's costume in "The Comedian."

58. Goldsmith's comic plays. Stevens was especially fond of the comic theater because resolution always occurs.

59. See Wertheim, op. cit., pp. 79–96.

60. Ernest Jones, *The Life and Work of Sigmund Freud*, edited and abridged in one volume by Lionel Trilling and Stephen Marcus, (New York: Basic Books, 1961), pp. 267–68.

61. Bynner, *Selected Letters*, loc. cit., pp. 26–27.

62. Ibid., pp. 24–25.

63. Ibid., p. xxii.

64. Holly Stevens mistakenly dates this letter May 3, but it was a Sunday, which fell on May 2 that year; the Huntington also dates this May 2.

65. Brazeau, op. cit., p. 119.

66. This perception, connected with all the associations to the up and down movement traced from the first chapter on, will be taken up in relationship to Stevens's own application of it as form in Chapter X of Volume II.

67. From Keats's Preface to *Endymion*.

68. Brazeau, op. cit., pp. 15, 27, 30.

69. See Notes 16, 17, 19, 20, 21, Chapter IV.

70. Interestingly, six centuries earlier the *Pearl*-poet in *Pearl* created one of the most highly structured poems in English on an equally important, but opposite, occasion: the death of his young daughter.

71. Brazeau, op. cit., pp. 276, 247, in which the wife of Ralph Mullen, one of Stevens's assistants at the Hartford, remembers that Stevens complained to her husband about Elsie: "She prepares such enormous meals. It's all I can do. She expects me to eat these tremendous meals every day." This is ironic in light of Stevens's having been so interested in "grub" and her complaining about it before they married.

CHAPTER VII. *The Great Glass: 1909–1915*

1. Stephen Kern, *The Culture of Time and Space* (Cambridge: Harvard University Press, 1983), p. 13.

2. F. T. Marinetti, "The Foundation and Manifesto of Futurism" (1908), *Theories of Modern Art: A Source Book,* ed. Herschel Chipp (Berkeley, Los Angeles, and London: University of California Press, 1968), pp. 284–89.

3. Kern, op. cit., p. 72.

4. Brazeau, op. cit., pp. 263–64.

5. Ibid., p. 264.

6. As Holly Stevens notes in *SP* (247), where she also describes how the landlord, Adolph Alexander Weinman, who lived below, knew when Elsie was angry by the way she would pace loudly around the apartment, slamming doors.

7. The process by which "323" became "322" is enticingly perplexing; the one certain feature, that it was somehow reductive, is clear. But what inner considerations or preoccupations could have come together to make Stevens misremember his first and only address of eighteen years might even have challenged the Viennese master from whom we learned about parapraxis. Though only Stevens himself could truly uncover the intricate harmony of associations that led to this slip, it is interesting to speculate about some of the more obvious slides into error because the linking process operating here discloses something about the movement between images and symbols in his poetry as well.

The most obvious reason for the substitution, of course, is that Stevens had just written "Mrs. Wallace Stevens." Because he was preoccupied with his mother, the other Mrs. Stevens, now at home alone and still grieving, he started to write her address. Another, or concomitant, possibility is that he was wishing that Elsie would have been able to be with his mother, comforting her. This would have meant that he would have repaired the situation which had resulted in his feeling guilty about not having resolved his relationship with his father before he died. It also would have meant that he would not have to fear that his mother still blamed Elsie and, by extension, him, for any of the emotional pain Garrett and she had suffered over his rejection of them. Yet another possibility is that after writing his name, he temporarily forgot the "Mrs.," who had been the spark igniting the slowly smoldering situation he had had with his family. In other words, he was transported back to a time before even Harvard had made its "enormous difference in everything" and had simply begun writing his own address beneath his name.

8. I am indebted to Lisa Steinman at Reed College for enriching my appreciation of this aspect of Stevens's relationship to his moment. She is at work on a manuscript dealing with the attitudes of different modernist poets to technology and science.

9. In *Speech and Reason,* containing D. Wilfred Abse, "Language Disorder in Mental Disease," and a translation of *The Life of Speech* by Philipp Wegener (Charlottesville: University Press of Virginia, 1971), Abse notes that "One of Wegener's major findings is that the logical predicate (that segment of the sentence which carries more emotional tone, the accentuated part, often but not necessarily coinciding with the grammatical predicate) is the key element of the sentence" (p. 6). Wegener was a late-nineteenth-century scholar of comparative philology who shared some important sources with Freud.

10. It seems there was another visit on the weekend of July 13 and 14 (two days before his mother's death on the sixteenth), but there is no record of Stevens's memories of this occasion. The evidence for his being in Reading on this weekend is a note he sent to Elsie on the fifteenth, promising to send her lotion and referring to the "boresome" train ride he had back to the city (WAS 1928). Since on July 30 Elsie sent him a postcard of Park Mansion and indicated that her room was "around on the other side of the main building" (WAS 2050), it is unlikely that this weekend trip of Stevens's had been to Vinemont (where Park Mansion was located). Vinemont was only a short distance from Reading, but Stevens seems not to have stopped to see Elsie.

11. As Buttel, op. cit., also notes, p. 82.

12. William Carlos Williams, for example, did not attend; according to his wife, what he remembered as the show was its rehanging for its fiftieth anniversary in 1963.

13. Other critics have also noted the importance of these contacts; among them: Buttel, generally on these and on the significance of the works displayed at the show and in Arensberg's studio; Brazeau, op. cit., p. 9; and generally, A. Walton Litz, *Introspective Voyager: The Poetic Development of Wallace*

Stevens (New York: Oxford University Press, 1972). Glen McLeod, *Wallace Stevens and Company: The "Harmonium" Years* (Ann Arbor: UMI Research Press, 1983), also elaborates on these and other possible influences.

14. Milton W. Brown, *The Story of the Armory Show* (New York: Joseph H. Hirshhorn Foundation, distributed by the New York Graphic Society, 1963), p. 49.

15. Ibid., p. 29.

16. Ibid., p. 49 for the rest of the quotations and facts in this paragraph.

17. For a fuller discussion of this, see the work of E. H. Gombrich, especially his recent, *The Image and the Eye: Further Studies in the Psychology of Pictorial Representation* (Ithaca: Cornell University Press, 1982).

18. Walter Pach, *The Masters of Modern Art* (New York: Viking, 1929), p. 47.

19. The strength of the Stein collection was in Renoir, Cézanne, Matisse, and Picasso. In addition, Eugène Delacroix, Paul Gauguin, Maurice Denis, and Félix Vallotton were represented, and there were the Japanese prints that had been among the first things Leo Stein acquired. By 1911, however, Leo began turning away from cubism as Picasso was exploring it, while Gertrude bought more and more of his work independently. This interest was directly connected to her own creative pursuits. As noted by Leon Katz ("Matisse, Picasso and Gertrude Stein," *Four Americans in Paris* [New York: Museum of Modern Art, 1970], p. 51), her involvement with painting and painters served to clarify her own work with "revolutionary aesthetic reorientations" in writing.

20. Robert Hughes, *The Shock of the New* (New York: Knopf, 1980), p. 55, draws and expands on this parallel. It should be noted, too, that a Rube Goldberg drawing appeared in the one and only issue of *New York Dada* in April 1921, the same month as the "Big Show," a follow-up of the Armory Show, opened. The magazine was edited by Marcel Duchamp and Man Ray. The "Big Show" was the First Exhibition of the Society of Independent Artists; it will be discussed in the following chapter.

21. See Marshall Brown, "Mozart and After: The Revolution in Musical Consciousness," *Critical Inquiry,* Vol. 7, No. 4 (Summer 1981), pp. 689–706.

22. Sekida, op. cit., pp. 84 and 392; D. T. Suzuki, *Zen Buddhism: Selected Writings,* ed. William Barrett (Garden City, New York: Doubleday, 1956), pp. 105–06 and passim.

23. For original programmatic essays, manifestos, theoretical descriptions, see *Theories of Modern Art,* loc. cit.; for observations by Bynner, see his *Selected Letters,* loc. cit., and *Prose Pieces,* ed. James Kraft (New York: Farrar, Straus & Giroux, 1979); for Williams's, see *Autobiography,* loc. cit., and *Imaginations* (New York: New Directions, 1970); see also Walter Pach *An Hour of Art* (Philadelphia and London: Lippincott, 1930); and Kreymborg, op. cit. For scholarly discussions, see McLeod, op. cit.; Bram Dijkstra, *The Hieroglyphics of a New Speech: Cubism, Steiglitz and the Early Poetry of William Carlos Williams*

(Princeton: Princeton University Press, 1969); Fiske Kimball, "Cubism and the Arensbergs," *Art News Annual,* Vol. XXIV (1954), pp. 117–22; Francis Naumann, "Cryptography and the Arensberg Circle," *Arts Magazine,* Vol. 51, No. 9 (May 1977), pp. 127–33; also his "The New York Dada Movement: Better Late Than Never," *Arts Magazine* (February 1980), pp. 143–49; also his "Walter Conrad Arensberg: Poet, Patron, and Participant in the New York Avant-Garde, 1914–20," *Philadelphia Museum of Art Bulletin,* Vol. 76, No. 328 (spring 1980), pp. 1–32.

24. He even made a trip to his grave, following up on his belief (common at the turn of the century) that Bacon was Shakespeare. Arensberg later published six books on the subject: *The Baconian Keys* (Pittsburgh: Privately Published, 1928); *The Burial of Francis Bacon and His Mother in the Lichfield Chapter House* (Pittsburgh: Privately Published, 1924); *The Cryptography of Shakespeare* (Los Angeles: Howard Bowen, 1922); *The Magic Ring of Francis Bacon* (Pittsburgh: Privately Published, 1930); *The Secret Grave of Francis Bacon at Lichfield* (San Francisco: John Howell, 1925); *The Shakespearean Mystery* (Pittsburgh: Privately Published, 1928).

25. Pach, *Masters,* loc. cit., p. 22.

26. Ibid., p. 23.

27. Ibid., p. 78.

28. Ibid., p. 79.

29. Ibid., p. 84.

30. "As for me, all I know is that I know nothing" (Socrates in Plato's *Phaedrus*); "Nothing can come out of nothing any more than a thing can go back to nothing" (Marcus Aurelius, *Meditations,* IV, iv, p. 50); and Lear's "Nothing can come of nothing" (I, i) and "Nothing can be made out of nothing" (I, iv).

31. Pach, *Masters,* loc. cit., p. 84.

32. This is an inference drawn from what Stevens communicated to Robert Pack and from the fact that his copy of Meredith (long in the attic when he wrote to his inquiring critic in 1954) dated from 1897 (*An Essay on Comedy, and the Uses of the Comic Spirit* [New York: Scribner's, 1897]), suggesting that it was one of the texts he came to know during his Cambridge years.

33. Robert Pack later published *Wallace Stevens: An Approach to His Poetry and Thought* (New Brunswick: Rutgers University Press, 1958).

34. Daniel Fuchs, *The Comic Spirit of Wallace Stevens* (Durham, N.C.: Duke University Press, 1963), also develops this point.

35. This was both an abstraction and an expansion of earlier theories of the comic, Baudelaire's, for example, which drew instances from Molière and Shakespeare.

36. Bergson made this point repeatedly. See, for example, pp. 146–50 in "Laughter" ("Le Rire"), *Comedy* (Garden City, N.Y.: Doubleday/Anchor, 1956). The book also contains Meredith's essay.

37. Fuchs also notes this point. It should be noted as well in connection with Meredith's essay that Stevens seems to have gotten two of the terms

associated with his "Comedian as the Letter C" from this essay: Meredith calls comedy a "jade" ("jades" affect the "sequestered bride" in Stevens's poem); Meredith's comedian presents his audience with what he sees through a "spyglass," one of Crispin's necessary accoutrements.

38. *Dictionary of the History of Ideas: Studies of Selected Pivotal Ideas,* ed. Philip P. Wiener, 4 Vols. (New York: Scribner's, 1973), Vol. 1, p. 467.

39. Edward Ballard, "Sense of the Comic," *Dictionary of the History of Ideas,* loc. cit., Vol. 1, p. 470.

40. There are throughout Bergson's piece images used significantly by Stevens, images already resonating with other possible influences. Bergson describes an "idea," for example, as "something that grows, buds, blossoms and ripens" (p. 81); we think of "It comes, it blooms, it bears its fruit and dies." Bergson compares the mind to a "sheet of subterranean water, the flow of images which pass from one to another" (p. 87); we think of "Sea Surface Full of Clouds." Bergson also uses the images of "dolls" or "marionettes" like Stevens, again in "Le Monocle." In terms of Stevens's overall musical metaphor, Bergson observes, "A comic effect is always obtainable by transposing the natural expression of an idea into another key" (p. 140). Again, in connection with "Sea Surface," Bergson describes laughter, the effect of the comic: "Such is also the truceless warfare of the waves on the surface of the sea, whilst profound peace reigns in the depths below" (p. 189). There are also other parallels to be explored such as Bergson's connection of the use of the comic and "abstraction" (p. 170) and the focus on just the sound of words, ignoring their meaning (p. 182).

41. The association between being a comedian and being itinerant is also contained in the original linked etymologies of barber and comedian in Greek (see p. 114 here). As the barber went from town to town, he told stories he had collected along the way, thus making himself welcome for more than his professional skill.

42. Brown, *Story of Armory Show,* loc. cit., pp. 118–19.

43. An observation made by Alfred Kazin in his course on "God and Man in American Literature" during the fall 1983 term at the Graduate School of the City of New York.

44. Elsie was described in these terms by Herbert Schoen during the interview of December 17, 1982. His impression is abundantly supported by the recollections of others interviewed by Brazeau.

45. See Note 53, Chapter VI for some examples.

46. As described by Leo Marx in his review, *New York Review of Books* (March 15, 1984), p. 29, of John R. Stilgo, *Metropolitan Corridor: The Railroad and The American Scene* (New Haven: Yale University Press, 1983).

47. The original cost of the piano was $1,200. It must have cost Stevens at least half that amount.

48. See Edelstein, op. cit.

49. R. W. Emerson, *Nature, the Conduct of Life* (London: Dent; New York: Dutton, 1963), p. 4.

50. Emerson, "Nature," (Second Series) *Essays,* loc. cit., p. 387.

51. As noted earlier, Arthur Ficke's description from Monroe, op. cit., p. 390.

52.

Poets have made more wars than kings, and war will not cease until they remove its glamour from the imaginations of men.

What is the fundamental, the essential and psychological cause of war? The feeling in men's hearts that it is beautiful. And who have created this feeling? Partly, it is true, kings and the "armies with banners"; but, far more, poets with their war-songs and epics, sculptors with their statues,— the assembled arts which have taken their orders from kings, their inspiration from battles. Kings and artists have united to give war its glamour, to transmute into sounds and colors and forms of beauty its savagery and horror, to give heroic appeal to its unreason, a heroic excuse to its rage and lust.

All this is of the past. The race is beginning to suspect those old ideals, to give valor a wider range than war affords, to seek danger not at the cannon's mouth but in less noisy labors and adventures. (Reprinted in Monroe, op. cit., pp. 341–42)

As will become clear from future discussion, Stevens shared Monroe's feeling about the relationship between poetry, art, and war.

For a detailed analysis and description of what this change in attitude meant for the culture generally as well as in relationship to particular poets, see Paul Fussell, *The Great War and Modern Memory* (New York: Oxford University Press, 1975).

For a psychological reading, see Sigmund Freud, "Thoughts for the Times on War and Death," *On Creativity and the Unconscious: Papers on the Psychology of Art, Literature, Love, Religion* (New York: Harper & Row/Torchbooks, 1958).

53. From the closing sentence of Albert Camus, *The Stranger,* translated by Stuart Gilbert, (New York: Vintage, 1954), p. 154.

54. Jean-Paul Sartre, "Man As Self-Creator," *Existentialism and Humanism* (New York: Philosophical Library, 1949), pp. 108–17.

55. Monroe, op. cit., p. 428.

CHAPTER VIII. *The Iconoclast in the Glass Shattering: 1916–1923*

1. Brazeau, op. cit., pp. 30, 67, 77.

2. Stevens used the *Oxford Concise Dictionary* at home (*L* 674) as well as Lewis and Short's *A Latin Dictionary* (*L* 275). At the office he used an "old-fashioned Webster's" (*L* 674)—the first edition of the *International.* He also frequently went—or more often sent underlings from the office—to the State Library in Hartford to search out meanings in the complete *Oxford English Dictionary.* At least one such employee commented that Stevens's later use of

the words carried eleventh and twelfth meanings (see Brazeau, op. cit., pp. 25, 40, 48, 68).

3. It was published in Philadelphia by Nicholas L. Brown. The dedication reads:

TO

Wallace Stevens
in gratitude
Donald Evans
in reverence
Walter Conrad Arensberg
an idol
The Reverend Albert Parker Fitch
an image
Carl Van Vechten
why not?
Emily Latimer
her book

AND

Rose of the World
FOR YOU

4. Kreymborg, op. cit., p. 220.
5. See Witter Bynner, *Selected Letters,* loc. cit.
6. Monroe, op. cit., pp. 342–43. In connection with Bynner's perhaps recommending Stevens to Monroe, James Kraft in his biographical Introduction to Bynner's *Selected Poems,* (loc. cit., pp. xlii–iii), suggests that the two poets regarded each other uneasily as rivals and that Bynner advised Knopf not to publish Stevens's poems a few years later. But Kraft also notes that the two poets maintained contact and correspondence over the years in the interest of preserving the early friendship. Since Arthur Ficke, perhaps the one closest to Bynner, and his partner in the Spectra hoax, praised Stevens's poetry as the best example of Spectrism (in the unpublished draft of the "preface" to *Spectra* [Morse, op. cit., pp. 73–74]), I think it not unlikely that Bynner would have recommended Stevens's poems to Harriet Monroe in an attempt to infiltrate *Poetry* with Spectrist work to counter that of the imagists.
7. Bynner, *Selected Letters,* loc. cit., p. 48.
8. Endleaf of Witter Bynner, *The New World* (New York: Knopf, 1922).
9. This was first published in English under the title of *The Art of Spiritual Harmony* (London: Constable & Co., 1914); it has been reissued as *Concerning the Spiritual in Art* (New York: Dover, 1977). If Stevens did not read this text, there are nonetheless—in spite of his turn away from the imagists' formal program for poetry—many reverberations between his spirit and Kandinsky's. One will serve to illustrate here. Speaking of how associations of images,

lines, etc., are formed, Kandinsky notes: "Colour is the keyboard, the eyes are the hammers, the soul is the piano with many strings. The artist is the hand which plays, touching one key or another, to cause vibrations in the soul" (p. 25).

10. Natan Zach, "Imagism and Vorticism," *Modernism,* eds. Malcolm Bradbury and James McFarlane (Middlesex, England and New York: Penguin, 1981), p. 238.

11. Among the passages where the closeness is striking are: "The unseen shall become the seen" (p. 10), which seems to echo in "Let be be finale of seem"; "Above the shadowy passes . . ." (p. 25), which seems to echo in the mountainous shadowy passes of "Le Monocle"; "A little hill among New Hampshire hills/Touches more stars than any height I know" (p. 59), which seems to have touched Stevens's mind when he imagined the tree to which all birds go in their time in "Thirteen Ways."

12. Collected in *The Poetry Anthology,* eds. Daryl Hine and Joseph Parisi (Boston: Houghton Mifflin, 1978), p. 6.

13. Ibid., p. xlii.

14. Ibid.

15. Eliot, "The Love Song of J. Alfred Prufrock," loc. cit., p. 3. The description of the sky reddened by shells is borrowed from Fussell, op. cit., p. 68; for its significance to poets and writers, see pp. 51–69 passim.

16. Arensberg's volume was highly praised to Stevens in a letter from Pitts Sanborn.

17. Ezra Pound, V from *Hugh Selwyn Mauberley, Personae,* loc. cit., p. 191.

18. In his Introduction to Mina Loy, *The Last Lunar Baedeker* (Highlands, N.C.: The Jargon Society, 1982), Roger Conover describes the birth of *Others* and how central Stevens was:

> In February, 1915, the contact that led to *Others* was made. The evening began like many others at Allan and Louise [now Mme. Edgard Varèse] Norton's Greenwich Village apartment. Donald Evans, Wallace Stevens, Carl Van Vechten, Walter Conrad Arensberg, and other *Rogue* contributors were gathered at the editors' home to discuss the future of *Rogue.* Alfred Kreymborg was also present. He had recently folded his magazine, *Glebe,* and was interested in Arensberg's idea of a new magazine, succeeding *Rogue,* dedicated to experiment throughout. "More imagistic than the Imagists" was his notion of how it must start out. A few days later Kreymborg was invited to Arensberg's studio to continue their initial discussion. They talked all night, and when the two men shook hands after breakfast, it was to seal their agreement on the new magazine that would make its debut in June. *Others* would exert itself on behalf of poets who were leading the revolt against *Poetry;* it would feature the work of men and women who were testing themselves in new forms. Who [*sic*] did they have in mind? One poet

. . . was Mina Loy. . . . Wallace Stevens was the other poet they agreed to approach that night. "They alone," Kreymborg asserted, "would create the magazine we have in mind." (pp. xxxv–vi)

19. Naumann, "Walter Conrad Arensberg: Poet, Patron," loc. cit., p. 17.
20. In the closing passage of Walter Pater's conclusion to *The Renaissance* (New York: Modern Library, ?), pp. 198–99:

> For our one chance lies in expanding that interval [of life], in getting as many pulsations as possible into the given time. Great passions may give us this quickened sense of life, ecstasy and sorrow of love, the various forms of enthusiastic activity, disinterested or otherwise, which come naturally to many of us. Only be sure it is passion—that it does yield you this form of a quickened, multiplied consciousness. Of such wisdom, the poetic passion, the desire of beauty, the love of art for its own sake, has most. For art comes to you proposing frankly to give nothing but the highest quality to your moments as they pass, and simply for those moments' sake.

21. This is especially clear in his essay on "Hamlet," for example, but it is also apparent in "Tradition and the Individual Talent," both collected in *The Sacred Wood* (London: Methuen, 1966 [reprint of original 1920 edition]). I am indebted to Denis Donoghue for reminding me of this about Eliot. Christopher Ricks has also made the same observation, as reported in a review of his *The Force of Poetry, The New York Times Book Review*, March 17, 1985, p. 11.
22. See Arturo Schwarz, "The Alchemist Stripped Bare in the Bachelor, Even," *Marcel Duchamp*, eds. Anne d'Harnoncourt and Kynaston McShine (New York and Philadelphia: The Museum of Modern Art and Philadelphia Museum, 1973), pp. 81–98.
23. Aristotle, *Niomachean Ethics*, trans. H. Rackham (London: Heinemann and Cambridge, Mass.: Harvard University Press, 1962), p. 66; Stevens in "The Emperor of Ice-Cream." There was a copy of the *Ethics*, an edition of 1893, marked, in Stevens's library. My feeling is that this was a text Stevens returned to many times; it should be remembered, in this context, that Book X of the *Ethics* is devoted to "pleasure" in all its aspects, culminating in how it allows one to live a "harmonious" life and contributes to the harmonious operation of the state, through the careful management of the "irrational principle."
24. As the century has progressed, expectedly, work has been done on precisely this connection between admitting animality—that is, truly feeling the reality of Darwin's evidence—and sexuality. Freud was obviously one of the first to begin working in this area. Others like George Groddeck (*The Book of the It* [New York: International Universities Press, 1976]—it was from Groddeck's formulation of the "it" (*es* in German) that Freud derived his "id" much in the same way William James derived his term "pragmatism" from C.

S. Peirce—and *The Meaning of Illness* [New York: International Universities Press, 1977]) and, later, Ernest Becker, *The Denial of Death* (New York: Free Press/Macmillan, 1973), made this connection explicit. Becker calls this animal nature our "creatureliness" and draws clear lines between an unwillingness to accept it and our unwillingness to accept death as simply part of a larger natural cycle.

25. In *Stanza My Stone: Wallace Stevens and the Hermetic Tradition* (West Lafayette: Purdue University Press, 1983), Leonora Woodman explores the poet's connection to this tradition and carefully links major images to it. She does not, however, place Stevens's familiarity with it in the Arensberg circle.

26. For readers interested in this particular aspect, Arensberg's papers are at the Francis Bacon Library in California; this archive also contains a great deal of unpublished material by and about Duchamp.

27. See Stephen Toulmin and Jane Goodfield, *The Architecture of Matter* (Chicago and London: University of Chicago Press/Phoenix, 1982), pp. 123–35.

28. See *Marcel Duchamp,* loc. cit., generally. A visit to the Arensberg Collection at the Philadelphia Museum also brings this point home quite clearly, as many of Duchamp's described intentions on the plates accompanying his works there expand on the importance of playing with language and titles.

29. Naumann, "Walter Conrad Arensberg: Poet, Patron," loc. cit., p. 10. A catalog of the pre-Columbian pieces in Arensberg's collection was published in 1954 by the Philadelphia Museum of Art.

30. Loy, op. cit., p. xvi.

31. Stevens is not mentioned in the Introduction to the above as one of those who knew her.

32. Loy, op. cit., p. xv.

33. Ibid., p. xvii.

34. Ibid., p. xviii.

35. Ibid., p. xxiv.

36. Ibid., p. xxvi.

37. See Note 18 above.

38. Loy, op. cit., p. 325.

39. Eliot, "The Love Song," loc. cit., p. 5.

40. Loy, op. cit., p. xlvii: the others were Duchamp, Beatrice Wood, Arlene Dresser, and Charles Demuth.

41. Carl Van Vechten, "Rogue Elephant in Porcelain," *Yale University Library Gazette* (October 1963), p. 49; Brazeau, op. cit., p. 10.

42. Paul Mariani, *William Carlos Williams: A New World Naked* (New York: McGraw-Hill, 1981), p. 161. Williams, op. cit., pp. 168–69, reports that—it seems after this incident—Stevens was afraid to go below Fourteenth Street when he was in the city because of her.

43. Naumann, "Walter Conrad Arensberg: Poet, Patron," loc. cit., p. 19.

44. This was consistent with Duchamp's commitment to simplicity in

life, the asceticism in material terms to be compensated for by endless exfoliations of mind.

45. Naumann, "Walter Conrad Arensberg: Poet, Patron," loc. cit., p. 10.

46. Charles Berger in *Forms of Farewell: The Late Poetry of Wallace Stevens* (Madison: University of Wisconsin Press, 1985), has recently presented a brilliant reading of "The Auroras of Autumn" as Stevens's response to the explosion; this will be taken up in Chapter XI of Volume II.

47. Letter of June 3, 1916, no WAS catalogue number; in Box 71, Folder 6 (1-A), Huntington, Wallace Stevens Collection.

48. Brazeau, op. cit., p. 234.

49. Concision is a quality Henry James highly extolled in his *Notebooks*.

50. For an exposition of the terms of this dialogue, see my dissertation, loc. cit., pp. 476–534; see also Barbara Fisher, "Ambiguous Birds and Quizzical Messengers: Parody as Stevens's Double Agent," *The Wallace Stevens Journal*, Vol. 9, No. 1 (Spring 1985), pp. 3–14.

51. There had originally been seventeen poems in the sequence, but the other four have not been found in Stevens's manuscript folders (*OP* xix).

52. Rockwell Kent described it this way, as related by Francis Naumann, "The Big Show. . . ," *Artforum* (February 1979), p. 35.

53. Ibid., p. 34.

54. Ibid.

55. Brown, *American Painting*, loc. cit., p. 49.

56. Theodore Reff, *Degas: The Artist's Mind* (New York: Metropolitan Museum/Harper & Row, 1976), pp. 293–94; see also Paul Souriau, *The Aesthetics of Movement* (Amherst: University of Massachusetts Press, 1983).

57. Brown, *American Painting*, loc. cit., p. 7.

58. He became interested again in 1942, following Henry Church's curiosity; for connections between Stevens and Nietzsche, see Milton J. Bates, "Major Man and Overman: Wallace Stevens's Use of Nietzsche," *Southern Review*, Vol. 15, No. 4 (October 1979), pp. 811–39 and his *Mythology of Self,* loc. cit., pp. 247–65.

59. See Fussell, op. cit., pp. 18–29.

60. After the publication of his volume *Cornhuskers* (New York: Henry Holt, 1918), for which he won the 1919 Pulitzer Prize for poetry, Sandburg sent Stevens an autographed copy with a note: "Here is one of thirteen ways of looking from a skyscraper," written on the typescript of a poem (laid in), "Hats" (*L* 215 n).

61. *Timetables of History,* op. cit., p. 473.

62. For a fuller analysis of Stevens's attacks on these figures, see the discussion of "Le Monocle de Mon Oncle" in my dissertation, loc. cit.

63. Pierre Louis Duchartre, *The Italian Comedy,* tr. Randolph T. Weaver (reedition of 1929 text published by George C. Harrap & Co.; New York: Dover, 1966), p. 21.

64. Vol. III (1900–11).

65. Duchartre, op. cit., pp. 23, 36–37.

66. Ibid., pp. 46–48.

67. Contained in an article which appeared in the *Ezra Pound Newsletter*, April 10, 1956, reprinted in Bynner, *Prose Pieces,* loc. cit., p. 141.

68. That Stevens spelled her name with a C is especially interesting in light of his fascination with the letter as evidenced by "The Comedian as the Letter C."

69. Stevens found the volume to be like "So much fresh air, fresh feeling, simple thinking, delightful expression, delight*ed* expressions," though, he added, the longer pieces did not "stir" him (*L* 216).

70. He had obtained long before the desired catalog of the exhibition of Japanese prints at the Fine Art Society's Galleries held in spring 1909 (*SP* 235); his dating on the flyleaf indicates that he had received it in August 1909, but he went through it again now; he looked over the marginal notes he had made in his copy of Reverend Samuel Beal, *Buddhism in China* (London: Society for Promoting Christian Knowledge; New York: E. & J. B. Young, 1884); he also wanted a copy of a book he had once gone through and now remembered, Herbert A. Giles, translation of Sung-ling P'u, *Strange Stories from a Chinese Studio* (Shanghai: Kelly and Walsh, 1916), and referred to the manual on Japanese prints put out by the Victoria and Albert Museum years before, of which he had a copy (WAS 1558, November 20, 1920).

71. See Buttel, op. cit., and especially McLeod, op. cit., on connections between the poetry of Evans and Stevens.

72. See also Bates, "Stevens in Love," loc. cit.

73. See Louis L. Martz, "'From the Journal of Crispin': An Early Version of 'The Comedian as the Letter C,'" in *Wallace Stevens: A Celebration,* loc. cit., pp. 3–45.

74. Ibid., p. 45.

75. Sidney Feshbach, "Wallace Stevens and Erik Satie: A Source for 'The Comedian as the Letter C.'" *Texas Studies in Literature and Language,* XI (Spring 1969), pp. 811–18.

76. See Perry Miller volumes referred to in Note 9, Chapter 1.

77. John Teahan of the Wadsworth Atheneum reported in a telephone conversation on December 4, 1984, that these had not been gathered together in the library there but were scattered throughout the collection.

78. Before this Stevens had had a falling-out with Arensberg that resulted in his not visiting the studio when he was in New York; the reason for the falling-out was related by Stevens in a letter to Weldon Kees in November 1954 (*L* 850); this is also noted by Brazeau, op. cit.

Index

575

INDEX

STACKS PS3537.T4753Z758 1986   AUG
Wallace Stevens

3 2304 00001484 3